LANGUAGE AND LEARNING

The philosophers and scholars of the Hellenistic world laid the foundations upon which the Western tradition based analytical grammar,
linguistics, philosophy of language, and other disciplines probing the
nature and origin of human communication. Building on the pioneering work of Plato and Aristotle, these thinkers developed a wide range
of theories about the nature and origin of language which reflected
broader philosophical commitments. In this collection of ten essays a
team of distinguished scholars examines the philosophies of language
developed by, among others, Plato, Aristotle, Epicurus, the Stoics and
Lucretius. They probe the early thinkers' philosophical adequacy and
their impact on later theorists. With discussions ranging from the
Stoics on the origin of language to the theories of language in the
twelfth and thirteenth centuries, the collection will be of interest to
students of philosophy and of language in the classical period and
beyond.

DOROTHEA FREDE is Professor of Philosophy at the University of
Hamburg. She has written numerous articles on Greek philosophy
and her previous publications include *Philebos* (1992) and (with André
Laks) *Traditions of Theology, Studies in Hellenistic Theology* (2002).

BRAD INWOOD holds the Canada Research Chair in Ancient Philo-
sophy at the University of Toronto. His recent publications include
The Poem of Empedocles (Second edition, 2001) and *The Cambridge
Companion to the Stoics* (2003).

LANGUAGE AND LEARNING

Philosophy of Language in the Hellenistic Age
Proceedings of the Ninth Symposium Hellenisticum

EDITED BY

DOROTHEA FREDE AND BRAD INWOOD

CAMBRIDGE
UNIVERSITY PRESS

CAMBRIDGE UNIVERSITY PRESS
Cambridge, New York, Melbourne, Madrid, Cape Town, Singapore, São Paulo

Cambridge University Press
The Edinburgh Building, Cambridge CB2 2RU, UK

Published in the United States of America by Cambridge University Press, New York

www.cambridge.org
Information on this title: www.cambridge.org/9780521841818

© Cambridge University Press 2005

First published 2005

Printed in the United Kingdom at the University Press, Cambridge

A catalogue record for this book is available from the British Library

Library of Congress Cataloguing in Publication data
Symposium Hellenisticum (9th : 2001 : Hamburg, Ger.)
Language and learning : philosophy of language in the Hellenistic Age
edited by Dorothea Frede and Brad Inwood.
p. cm.
Includes bibliographical references and index.
ISBN 0 521 84181 X (hardback)
1. Language and languages – Philosophy – Congresses.   2. Philosophy, Greek – Congresses.
I. Frede, Dorothea, 1941–   II. Inwood, Brad.   III. Title
P107.S96   2001
401 – dc22   2004057027

ISBN 0 521 84181 X hardback

Contents

v

Contributors

JAMES ALLEN Professor of Philosophy, University of Pittsburgh

CATHERINE ATHERTON Professor of Philosophy and Classics,
University of California, Los Angeles

JONATHAN BARNES Professor of Philosophy, Sorbonne, Paris

DAVID BLANK Professor of Classics, University of California, Los
Angeles

SUSANNE BOBZIEN Professor of Philosophy, Yale University

CHARLES BRITTAIN Associate Professor of Classics, Cornell University

STEN EBBESEN Professor at the Institute of Greek and Latin, University
of Copenhagen

A. A. LONG Professor of Classics, University of California, Berkeley

INEKE SLUITER Professor of Classics, University of Leiden

ALEXANDER VERLINSKY Professor of Classics, University of
St Petersburg and researcher at the Bibliotheca Classica Petropolitana

Preface

The ninth Symposium Hellenisticum was held in Haus Rissen at Hamburg, 23–28 July 2001 under the sponsorship of Hamburg University. Nine of the ten papers presented here are revised versions of drafts distributed to the participants in advance and discussed at the meetings; Bobzien's paper could not be presented at the conference and the editors are pleased to be able to include it. The final versions of all the papers bear the mark of much discussion, reflection and revision over the months following the conference.

The participants at the Symposium (and their affiliations at the time) were: Keimpe Algra (University of Utrecht), James Allen (University of Pittsburgh), Julia Annas (University of Arizona), Catherine Atherton (Oxford University), Jonathan Barnes (University of Geneva), Gábor Betegh (Central European University, Budapest), David Blank (University of Reading), Susanne Bobzien (Oxford University), Tad Brennan (Yale University), Charles Brittain (Cornell University), Myles Burnyeat (Oxford University), Walter Cavini (University of Bologna), Sten Ebbesen (University of Copenhagen), Theodor Ebert (Erlangen University), Dorothea Frede (Hamburg University), Nikolai Grintser (Moscow State University), Christoph Horn (Bonn University), Frédérique Ildefonse (University of Paris), Anna Maria Ippolo (University of Rome), Brad Inwood (University of Toronto), André Laks (University of Lille), Anthony Long (University of California), Gretchen Reydam-Schils (Notre Dame University), David Sedley (Cambridge University), Ineke Sluiter (University of Leiden), Gisela Striker (Harvard University), Alexander Verlinsky (University of St Petersburg), Hermann Weidemann (Münster University). Thanks are due to all participants for their engagement in discussion and to the readers for their helpful suggestions that are reflected in the revisions of the contributions. We are especially grateful to our editor, Michael Sharp, and the production editor, Mary Leighton, for their support and patience, and to the two anonymous readers for their careful and helpful criticism, in particular to the reader who undertook the arduous task of reviewing the revised versions of the articles at short notice.

Financial support came from a generous grant by the Deutsche Forschungsgemeinschaft and from the home Universities of some of the participants. The organisers of the Symposium wish to acknowledge the generous assistance without which this conference could not have been held.

One of our tasks was to impose, as best we could, some measure of standardisation on the varieties of conventions used by the contributors in the joint bibliography at the end of the volume. The titles of the works of ancient authors have been given in accordance with the editions used by the authors. Modern authors are listed by name and year. Quotations in Latin are not italicised, apart from single words or words deserving special emphasis. Quotations from Greek and Latin in the main text are accompanied by translations. The indices do not aim at completeness but pick out the major terms and the more sustained discussion of passages. Most welcome help was given by the copy-editor, Linda Woodward, and in the compilation of the indices by Euree Song MA.

Dorothea Frede and Brad Inwood

Abbreviations

In addition to more familiar abbreviations, the following will be found in this volume:

CAG = *Commentaria in Aristotelem Graeca.*

CIMAGL = *Cahiers de l'Institut du Moyen Age Grec et Latin.* Copenhagen.

CPhD = *Corpus Philosophorum Danicorum Medii Aevi.* Copenhagen.

FDS = Hülser, K.-H. (ed.) (1987–8) *Die Fragmente zur Dialektik der Stoiker.* Stuttgart–Bad Cannstatt.

LS = Long, A. A. and D. N. Sedley (eds.) (1987) *The Hellenistic Philosophers,* with trans. and comm. (2 vols.). Cambridge.

PL = Migne, J.-P. (ed.) (1844–65) *Patrologia Latina.* Paris.

SSR = *Socratis et Socraticorum Reliquiae,* vol. IV. coll. disp. apparatibus notisque instruxit Gabriele Giannantoni (1990). Naples.

SVF = von Arnim, H. (1903–5, 1964²) *Stoicorum Veterum Fragmenta,* vols. I–III. Stuttgart.

Introduction

Dorothea Frede and Brad Inwood

Despite the fact that Greek culture (and consequently Roman as well) was intensely language conscious, the systematic investigation of language, its origin, its structure, and its varieties was a relative late bloomer in the ancient world. This is bound to surprise us. To be sure, there were reflections on the relation between speech and its objects from early on among the poets, the Presocratic philosophers, and especially among the sophists, the first professional rhetoricians and teachers of 'how to do things with words'. That such concern did not immediately lead to the development of language as a field of research seems to be due to several factors. Though the Greeks were aware of the existence of different languages, the acquisition of a foreign language was not part of even an elite education in the Greek world, but was left, rather, to professional interpreters. Furthermore, despite a great wealth of speculation on the origin of culture, language was not a major topic in those considerations. Though there is a host of stories of divine gifts of craftsmanship to human beings, including the civic virtues as a means of survival and the Promethean clandestine handing down of fire, there is no parallel depiction of a miraculous distribution of language to a miserable horde of speechless primitive men. The lack of a mythological account of the origin of language is certainly no accident in a religious culture that presupposes that there is a language common to gods and men: such a mythical background quite unreflectively presupposes that language has 'always' been around, even before the creation of humankind (if such a creation was part of the common lore).

These conditions changed when the gods no longer stood in the limelight of the interpretation of the world, its origin and its order. Once philosophy had replaced the mythical explanation of the world, the existence and nature of language was no longer taken for granted. It is therefore no accident that Plato and Aristotle recognised the importance of the use of language as the decisive distinguishing feature between man and beast, and raised questions concerning the meaning and the proper use of words, as well as their combinations to form sentences. Plato, famously, in his dialogue *Cratylus* for the first time addresses the problem of the status of language as such, i.e. whether it exists by nature or by convention, and what constitutes the 'correctness of names'. Aristotle in his logical investigations not only analyses the structure of propositions and the types of oppositions between them, but also includes quantifiers and modal terms. But since in the main the interest of the great philosophers of the classical age (and their followers) focused on questions of proper definition, on the avoidance of ambiguities, and on the structure of basic affirmations and negations, their investigations of linguistic phenomena remained within narrow limits.

If the interest in language as a whole increased significantly in the schools of the Hellenistic age this is due to several distinct factors. First of all, both the Stoics and the Epicureans, albeit in a quite different sense, were not only physicalists but also 'creationists', in a way that naturally led to the question of the origin of humankind, its culture and its language. The Stoic theory of the development of an eternally recurrent world order under the guidance of divine reason included an account of the emergence of human beings and their command of language in each emergence of the world order. The Epicureans, by contrast, believed in the formation of an infinite sequence of world orders on the basis of purely mechanical interactions of the atoms and their conglomerates. This mechanical world view had to provide a rather different account for the development of higher faculties of humankind and for the status of language, quite generally. A second important factor that contributed to the concern with language was the increased antagonism and fierce competitiveness between the schools in the Hellenistic age, especially once the Academic sceptics had made it their mission to defeat any kind of 'dogmatism', i.e. the teaching of positive doctrine, about the nature of the world. Their criticism not only focused on the content of the dogmatists' creed, but also on their epistemological and methodological justifications. This challenge led to an increase in vigilance and care on the dogmatists' side concerning the linguistic precision and formal accuracy of their arguments, as well as concerning the criteria of truth which they proposed.

Though the concern with the origin of language and the defence against attacks from outside provided something like a common background for the concern with language, it would be misleading to speak of a 'philosophy of language' *tout court* as an autonomous discipline within the schools of the Hellenistic age. Questions of language were regarded as important by the schools, but their motivations were often quite different, as was the context within which they addressed linguistic problems. Each school not only dealt with these problems on the basis of its own philosophical presuppositions, but also with different ends in view. Moreover, linguistic phenomena were treated differently in connection with questions of logic, epistemology, ethics, physics and/or theology. The closeness of the ties between the study of language and the different parts of philosophy also explains why the development of grammar as a systematic discipline was taken up rather late by the philosophers. Its systematisation and maturation owes a lot to the work of a quite different set of scholars: if the study of language and grammar finally came of age this is largely due to the great philologists and literary critics in the Alexandrian library whose results gradually began to exert an influence on the philosophers. Only after the study of the grammatical structure of the Greek and Latin languages and their peculiarities had reached a certain level of sophistication did questions of grammar and syntax become a matter of philosophical reflection and a supplement to the analysis of the logical structure of propositions.

The different background of the philosophical treatment of language, its direction and its growth is mirrored in the topics discussed at the ninth Symposium Hellenisticum in Hamburg from July 23 to 28, 2001. Some of the papers assembled in this volume are dedicated to the treatment of particular problems of language within one of the schools of the Hellenistic age, while others address a problem that spans several centuries, and still others range across several schools. Given the diversity of the interest in questions of language (and, where applicable, grammar) during Hellenistic times, the deplorable scarcity of sources makes it particularly hard to reconstruct an overall picture. For we are not dealing with the remains of *one* ancient road whose course might easily be discerned from a bird's eye view. Instead, we are confronted with a host of scattered pieces that belonged to quite different roads, that lead in confusingly different directions, and whose intersections are far from secure. Despite these discrepancies the different contributions address a set of basic concerns among the major schools of philosophy during the Hellenistic period, which not only supplement each other but also point to interesting congruencies. It is these congruencies that explain the emergence of a general interest in linguistic problems that finally led to more or less standardised views on the structure of language and grammar in late antiquity. This gradual consensus became the tradition that was revived in the Middle Ages. The collection of papers helps explain the emergence of such a tradition and at the same time illuminate the connections between the philosophical and the linguistico-grammatical problems which are all too often treated in isolation from each other, to the detriment of both disciplines.

There are three main centres of interest that received special attention from all schools in the Hellenistic age and its aftermath. (1) There is the question of the origin of language or languages. Though the notion of a 'wise inventor' of language was generally treated with disfavour, the problem of the etymology of linguistic expressions and their reference to reality posed a challenge to all philosophical schools. (2) Special attention was also given to the question of the interdependence between language and thought in general, particularly in view of the importance attributed to rhetoric and other forms of self-expression. (3) Last, but not least, is the concern with the question in what sense 'language' can be treated as a technical subject with rules of its own, so that grammar is not merely a matter of empirical research and linguistic observation. This problematic also extends to the question of the precision of language and the avoidance of fallacies as well as to the relation between the grammatical and the logical functions of key terms in a language. Needless to say, each of these three topics would have deserved a conference of its own. The present volume does not pretend that the contributions do more than address some of the most pertinent aspects of each of these fields.

(1) The questions of the origin of language, the possibility of exploiting etymology as a means of interpretation, and the justification of the 'correctness of speech' was a particular challenge to the Stoics and Epicureans because both schools are concerned with a 'naturalistic' account of the rise of human culture. The articles of James Allen and Anthony Long deal with the Stoic theory of language and both take Plato's *Cratylus* as their point of departure. The *Cratylus* is not only the first known work that highlights the alternative views that language is either based on nature or on convention (in a stricter or wider sense), but also explores the claim that there is a 'correctness' of language. The Stoics seem to have known that work and made it the reference point in their 'naturalistic' account of language. Though very little is known about the Stoic views on the early stage of culture in each cosmic cycle, it is clear that they did not hold an evolutionary view to the effect that human beings developed from a primitive level akin to that of animals; instead they assumed that there was an early natural stage in the history of humankind that was superior to their own day, and used it as an incentive to recapture its insights.

James Allen ('The Stoics on the origin of language and the foundations of etymology') shows that this assumption explains the Stoics' preoccupation with etymology as part of their concern with a time 'when language was still young' and the product of a primordial wisdom. Since they held a naturalist rather than a conventionalist view the Stoics assumed that there had been a primary stock of words that somehow 'imitate' the nature of the objects in question and could therefore be used as a natural standard of correctness. Since they assumed that there had been a high level of rationality among humans at a primordial stage, the Stoics saw nothing unnatural in proposing the notion of an original 'name-giver' as a hypothetical construct. Such a construct escapes the sceptic's ridicule because it merely assumes that the human need and the ability to converse rationally with each other, which manifests itself in every individual at a certain age, must also have been part of the nature of the (assumed) first generation of human beings. The 'naturalness' of names consists, then, in their suitability for communication with others; though it presupposes a mimetic relation between words and certain kinds of objects, it is not confined to onomatopoetics; instead it makes use of other means to augment language by associations and rational derivations of further expressions that are gradually added to the original stock of words. This explanation, as Allen points out, may make the etymologies less interesting and relevant in our eyes; but though the Stoics did not assume mechanical laws of derivation that would allow them to recover the 'cradle of words', attempts at rational reconstructions of the relation between different expressions provided them with a means to discover and to correct later corruptions of thought and so to play a crucial role in philosophical progress. Despite certain similarities of concern with the naturalist position in the *Cratylus*, the Stoic position therefore differs in more significant ways from the Platonic position than is usually acknowledged.

Anthony Long ('Stoic linguistics, Plato's *Cratylus*, and Augustine's *De dialectica*') also elaborates on the influence of Plato's *Cratylus* on Stoic theory. But he goes much further than Allen with his hypothesis that the Stoics not only made use of Plato's dialogue, but did so in a way that justifies the presentation of many central features of their linguistic theory as being the result of a revisionary reading of the *Cratylus*. It is a reading that makes Socrates' suggestions about the 'natural' relation of names to things much more coherent than they are in the dialogue itself. This also applies to their etymological explanation of the names of the gods that they suggested as a revision of a corrupted tradition and a return to the original name-givers' comprehension of the true nature of the universe. Given their 'synaesthetic' reconstruction of the relation between phonetics and semantics, the Stoics could avoid the *Cratylus*' more absurd features of onomatopoetics, as Long shows by analysing different forms of 'naturalism', including 'formal and phonetic naturalism', and their application by the Stoics that not only includes names but also the famous *lekta* or 'sayables'. Long contends that the Stoics not only found a better balance between the phonetic and the formal constituents of meaningful discourse than emerges from Plato's dialogue itself, but restricted their use of etymology as a back-up to their theology, i.e. the naturalistic reconstruction of the names of the gods. As an additional witness to the sophistication of the Stoic linguistic theory Long adds an appendix on the four-fold semantic distinction (between *dicibile, res, verbum*, and *dictio*) in St Augustine's *De dialectica*, which he takes to be largely of Stoic origin.

The Epicureans also held that language is part of the natural emergence of human culture. But here the similarity between the Stoic and the Epicurean theory of language ends. For instead of an early stage of rationality and inspired 'name-givers', the Epicureans proposed a quite different account of the evolution of language as part of their mechanical reconstruction of the order in nature, which includes an animal-like primitive stage of human beings. Unfortunately the information on this early stage in the development of humans as cultural beings in Epicurean theory is extremely meagre; attempts to reconstruct it have to rely on a few lines in Epicurus' *Letter to Herodotus* and in Lucretius' poem.

Alexander Verlinsky ('Epicurus and his predecessors on the origin of language') valiantly attempts a reconstruction of the different stages of Epicurus' evolutionary picture by a confrontation with some of his predecessors' views that had been inspired by Democritus. The picture that emerges is intriguing and suggestive. While some of the predecessors assumed that human language was derived from animal sounds that were gradually articulated and assigned to objects, Democritus seems to have regarded gestures as the initial way of signification; he therefore explained the development of sounds from being merely expressive to their function as signifiers by pointing out specific situations that first suggested to early human beings the means of such communication. For Epicurus by contrast, two different stages have to be distinguished. Though Epicurus agrees with his predecessors that the first utterances of human beings were emotional expressions like those of the animals, they not only displayed a greater variety because of a much richer natural endowment for such articulation, but the sounds also received their functions as signifiers through a kind of social covenant. Verlinsky derives the existence of a second stage in Epicurus' theory of a linguistic development from the evidence of a treatise by Ptolemy that indicates that language became greatly enriched not only by the composition of new words derived from the first, natural ones, but also by a selection among the variants that had arisen from the various spontaneous designations of the same things. The separation of these two stages allows Epicurus to give a more sophisticated explanation for the diversity of languages that developed because of the different external conditions of life in different societies.

While Verlinsky is concerned with a reconstruction of the evolution of Epicurus' theory of language against the background of earlier developments, *Catherine Atherton* takes a frankly evaluative approach. Her paper is concerned with the limitations of the Epicurean account of the nature and origin of language ('Lucretius on what language is not'). She subjects the Epicurean theory of the emergence of language to a sharp critical scrutiny and challenges its justification and its success on a variety of crucial points. She does so by drawing attention to some important differences between Lucretius' account and the Epicurean original that is known to us only from his short summary in the *Letter to Herodotus*. As Atherton points out, these differences show that Epicurus quite explicitly assumed that humans are natural users of signs, an ability that is due on the one side to a rich natural endowment to vocalisation that far outstrips that of other animals, and on the other side to social pressure for cooperation that resulted in the emergence of names. Despite the seeming attractiveness of this explanation of the emergence of language, Atherton points to grave philosophical problems within the Epicurean theory. There seems to be an unbridgeable gap between the natural vocalisations caused by the impact of the situation and properly intentional communication. For the latter presupposes a system of communication that is based on a conscious and free use of signs and the conceptualisation of sounds as names. As Atherton points out with reference to contemporary theories of communication, the Epicurean emergentist view of the development of human nature and the limits his mechanistic laws of nature impose is incompatible with the inventiveness that leaves room for the free play that is necessary for the intentionality presupposed by the use of names as signifiers. This difficulty is not restricted to the Epicurean theory; it applies to all naturalistic and emergentist theories of language and therefore presents a challenge to contemporary naturalist explanations of language as well.

(2) While the origin of language remained a topic that fascinated philosophers to the end of antiquity, continued attention was also given to questions of the appropriate use and function of language as a means of social intercourse. Not all ancient philosophers made language a matter of explicit reflection. But all of them used it in a more or less conscious manner. Most eccentric was no doubt the way of communication chosen by the Cynics, in particular by their founder and model, Diogenes of Sinope, also called 'the Dog'. As a critic once remarked, when the violinist Nigel Kennedy stands

in front of a symphony orchestra he appears like a parrot surrounded by a herd of penguins. *Ineke Sluiter*'s contribution ('Communicating Cynicism: Diogenes' gangsta rap') promises a similarly colourful contrast to the more conventional investigations in this volume. But the addition of colour is not the main intention of this paper. Like Atherton's paper, it shines a philosophical spotlight on the question of what would count as 'communication' and agrees that some kind of intention is required along with a form of behaviour that serves to indicate something. Sluiter aims to show that the Cynics, while not concerned with a theory of language in the conventional sense (unremarkably, since their concern with theory was minimal) were quite conscious of the importance of the modes of communication, both verbal and non-verbal, that anticipate modern notions of self-representation as a philosophical message. Thus Diogenes intentionally used shocking transgressive forms of non-verbal communication that puts the body and its processes to philosophical use. Though this non-verbal communication was meant to shock in a new way, it had certain precedents in features of ancient comedy and satire. These forms of art display the same kind of precarious balance between momentary outrage and a lasting message. It is important to remember that this exploitation of audience reaction is a feature of all aspects of Cynic 'philosophy' – here as with the other schools philosophy of language reveals its intimate links to the rest of their message. If it is fair to say that the Cynics lived their philosophy quite generally, then in Sluiter's essay we see how it is that they *performed* their philosophy of language.

Yet if the Cynic's communication is to achieve an effect beyond the momentary outrage it must be transformed into anecdote and accepted in the literary tradition, a transformation that robs it of its bite and ultimately makes it harmless. That there is a form of communication that lives on the ambiguity between the outrageous and the traditional not only represents Cynicism's self-undermining message, but also establishes a tie to modern forms of self-expression like gangsta rap – a fact that accounts for the essay's provocative title.

Sluiter is not alone in focusing on the practical effect of the philosophical interest in language. *Charles Brittain* ('Common sense: concepts, definition and meaning in and out of the Stoa') also focuses on an important aspect of the philosophical analysis of language: its relation to reality and to the conceptual apparatus in the human mind, which on most theories connects reality to language. To the naïve mind, a concept like 'common sense' would not seem to be in need of development since it must have been in place since the dawn of human reasoning. Nor is that the issue of Brittain's paper. Instead, he focuses on the development of a *theory* of common sense that is based on the connection between a stock of rational conceptions that is the common possession of all humans and the words which map naturally onto those conceptions and so give expression to them. The Stoics themselves did not maintain that everyone can acquire conceptions that successfully capture the essence of things; such success presupposes the uncorrupted mind of the wise; so these normative concepts do not seem to be an obvious source for a theory of common conceptions that are open to all. As Brittain contends, it would nevertheless be wrong to attribute such a theory to the later Platonists despite the fact that they advocated the existence of universally acceptable word-meanings that are open to every human being's grasp. For Platonists regarded these meanings as mere accidental features of the thing in question. What was needed to establish a theory of common sense was a combination of the two theories: the 'preliminary definition' of a term with universal acceptance that lays claim to at least a partial grasp of the thing's essence. En route to this solution Brittain offers, *inter alia*, a reconstruction of the mechanism at work in the formation of common concepts with abstract and general contents and seeks to solve the conundrum of how definitions of the words corresponding to the concepts are formed. He does so by carefully sifting through different sources that employ Stoic vocabulary (such as 'preconceptions' or 'common conceptions') but that differ significantly from the Stoic view that all humans have at least a partial grasp of a thing's essential properties, rather than mere accidental properties. This assumption paves the way towards a theory of 'common sense' that establishes a direct connection between the concepts and the objects of the world and explains how ordinary language-speakers have at least an outline understanding of the world. Such a theory, so Brittain argues, is the upshot of Cicero's treatment of preconceptions as the basis of definitions. The rendering of 'preconception' (*prolepsis*) as shared by all – by *communis mens* and finally by *communis sensus* – justifies the attribution to Cicero of at least 'a fragment of a theory of common sense' in civic and political matters that everyone in principle can understand. This was a theory that deeply influenced the later rhetorical tradition and thereby became a lasting asset in cultural history.

(3) The more technical issues concerning the function of language, its structure, properties and anomalies, and its relation to the world are taken up from three quite distinct perspectives in this volume. *David Blank* ('Varro's anti-analogist') investigates the concern with grammar as a philosophical discipline by a reconstruction of the controversy between analogist and anomalist theories of language as witnessed in Varro's *De lingua Latina*,

a major ancient source on ancient linguistic theory, even though it has survived only in part. The 'accepted view' on this issue so far has been that the
protagonists in the controversy were Crates of Mallos who argued for the
anomalist faction and contended that there are no rules of grammar and
that *de facto* usage alone was the criterion of correctness, and Aristarchus
of Samothrace, the proponent of the view that grammatical phenomena
follow analogical patterns. Blank purports to show that no such debate
between these alleged two schools of grammar can have existed; for Crates
was an exponent of technical grammar who put great emphasis on philological methods. If there was disagreement between him and Aristarchus
it must have concerned the explanation of particular grammatical phenomena, in which Crates proposed the use of analogically correct forms of
speech, which Aristarchus rejected in favour of the customary forms. The
real debate between analogists and anti-analogists, so Blank contends, was
between philosophical *as opposed to* grammatical empiricists (or sceptics)
and rationalist grammarians who advocated the adherence to rules, while
the empiricists held that observation of common usage is all that is necessary
to assure the correctness of speech.

Grammatical correctness was not the only issue that occupied the
Hellenistic philosopher's concern with language. The question of 'semantical correctness' has a much older pedigree because the sophists as well as
the paradox-mongers in the Megarian tradition had made the treatment of
fallacies and the exploitation of ambiguities part of their stock-in-trade. The
avoidance of such pitfalls was therefore a major issue among the philosophers, as witnessed by the attention paid to such problems by Plato and
Aristotle. That the Stoics still regarded them as a major challenge may at first
blush seem strange, since one would expect that the shop-worn exploitation
of blatant ambiguities must have appeared both ludicrous and tiresome.
As *Susanne Bobzien* ('The Stoics on fallacies of equivocation') shows, the
Stoics had philosophical reasons for the development of strategies to handle
'lexical' ambiguities, because they regarded fallacies of ambiguity as complexes of propositions and sentences that straddle the realm of linguistic
expression (the domain of language) and the realm of meaning (the domain
of logic); moreover, there is also a pragmatic component because being
deceived is a psychological disposition that can be reduced neither to
language nor to meaning. Not all arguments are, after all, as transparently
fallacious as is the example that exploits the ambiguity of 'for men/manly'
and concludes that a 'garment for men' must be courageous because manliness is courage. Bobzien provides a detailed analysis of the relevant passages,
lays bare textual and interpretative difficulties, and explores what the Stoic

view on the matter implies for their theory of language. She points up that the Stoics believe that the premisses of the fallacies, when uttered, have only one meaning and are true, and thus should be conceded; hence no mental process of disambiguation is needed, while Aristotle, by contrast, assumes that the premisses contain several meanings, and recommends that the listeners explicitly disambiguate them. Bobzien proffers two readings of the Stoic advice that we 'be silent' when confronted with fallacies of ambiguity, and explicates how each leads to an overall consistent interpretation of the textual evidence. Finally, she demonstrates that the method advocated by the Stoics works for all fallacies of lexical ambiguity.

That the Stoics were the instigators of the emphasis put on linguistic observations in ancient philosophy is uncontested. To what degree they are rightly accused of paying more attention to expressions rather than to things is quite another matter, despite the fact that this reproach was voiced repeatedly in antiquity by authorities such as Galen and Alexander of Aphrodisias and has lasted through the nineteenth century AD. If the Stoics have enjoyed a better press since the twentieth century it is because they were taken to be logicians for logic's sake, committed formalists who stopped just short of inventing the appropriate type of artificial language. That this picture needs revision is argued by *Jonathan Barnes* ('What is a disjunction?') in a painstaking investigation of the treatment of connectives in Apollonius Dyscolus' essay with that title and Galen's *Institutio logica*. Barnes shows that Apollonius' text is coherent and thereby undermines a long-standing prejudice about the Stoic impact on the development of traditional grammar: contrary to what has been assumed (*via* an unwarranted textual emendation in a crucial passage of Apollonius Dyscolus) Apollonius does not criticise the Stoics' meddling with grammar, but rather their insufficient interest in some of its finer points. Far from adopting a purely formalistic stance, the Stoics distinguished between natural and non-natural disjunctions and colligations. They used these considerations not only to distinguish between natural and occasional disjunctions, but also between grammatical and semantical nonsense. Since no other text besides Apollonius' attributes the conception of 'natural disjunctions' to the Stoics it is a question whether it actually is of Stoic origin rather than derived from the Peripatetics or an invention by certain grammarians. As Barnes shows, the interconnections and boundaries between natural language and formal logic did not only play a crucial role in the treatment of disjunctions by Apollonius Dyscolus. They are also the basis of Galen's criticism of Stoic logic on the differentiation between complete and incomplete conflict and implication, whose intent was to show what is and what is not a legitimate use of conjunctions. If that distinction is at stake, then Galen's view on disjunctions and conjunctions turns out to be coherent, despite initial appearances to the contrary. The differing parties accused each other of not having paid sufficient attention to the *pragmata*; however, their complaint is not that the facts in the world have been ignored, but rather that the meaning of the terms has not received sufficient attention.

It is a generally accepted view that 'philosophy of language' as well as 'grammar' as a philosophical discipline were invented in antiquity by the Stoics or by grammarians inspired by them. It is also the accepted view that these achievements were passed on to the Latin West in the Middle Ages through authors like Priscian and Boethius, to be augmented and refined by the schoolmen from the beginning of the twelfth century on. But though the general route of the tradition that indirectly relates to the beginning of linguistic philosophy in Hellenistic times is uncontested, there is little knowledge about any direct influence of the Hellenistic philosophers on that period. *Sten Ebbesen* ('Theories of language in the Hellenistic age and in the twelfth and thirteenth centuries') takes his readers into the relatively uncharted waters of the influence of Hellenistic philosophy on the Middle Ages by tracing Stoic influence on certain issues. Ebbesen focuses on three points. First he points out how the question of 'imposition', i.e. the assignment of phonemes to natural things was taken up by the members of the Porretan school in order to show how moral and rational vocabulary arose through a transformation of the natural vocabulary, so as to allow discussion of non-natural phenomena in the sphere of culture, reason, and even theology. Second he shows that Boethius of Dacia and other members of the 'modist school' in the late thirteenth century developed a theory of formal grammar and logic, a theory that showed how the 'modes' of signifying, supplemented by a theory of representing logical relationships, is based on modes of understanding and ultimately related to the modes of being. Though among the modists the conviction prevailed that language is based on convention they did not hold that expressions are introduced at random; hence etymology, as first adumbrated in Plato's *Cratylus*, has its role to play in linguistic theory. Finally Ebbesen shows that the static conception of the modists that assumed invariable rules of language was changed into a dynamic theory of language by Roger Bacon, whose theory allowed for changing rules of language without loss of intelligibility.

Thus we find in the Middle Ages ghost-like replicas of the controversies among the ancient philosophers of language, whether it concerns the 'imposition of words' inspired by Plato's *Cratylus*, the quest to account for the relation between language and the objects in the world that was a main concern of the Stoics, and the controversy between analogist and anomalist accounts of language. Ebbesen does not claim that those medieval discussions were based on any direct knowledge of the Hellenistic philosophers or on that of Plato's *Cratylus*. He holds, however, that these medieval positions could not have been developed had there not been the rich tradition of the Hellenistic age, passed on to them in the reflections of Boethius and Priscian.

Despite their variety and the enormous period of time covered (from the Presocratics to the thirteenth century), all these papers are united by their authors' determination to consider the study of language as a whole and as such. They do not force onto our ancient forebears the distinction between linguistics and philosophy of language which we have come to take for granted (often without sufficient critical challenge). The ancients, perhaps wisely and perhaps not, regarded the systematic study of language, our most distinctive human faculty, as being an activity that conditions and influences our views on all kinds of philosophical problems. In an age of scholarly specialisation and overspecialisation the authors' contributions provide inspiring reminders of the loss incurred by our acceptance of such narrow confinements.

The sophistication and diversity of Hellenistic traditions addressing problems of language will make the study of those linguistic theories an intriguing subject to all students of the history of language theory in general. A novice in Hellenistic philosophy will also find that the study of the different schools' concern with language and linguistic phenomena provides an excellent introduction to the doctrines of the various schools, since it sheds light on their epistemology as well as on their logical, ethical and physical presuppositions.

CHAPTER I

The Stoics on the origin of language and the foundations of etymology

James Allen

I

The Stoics were notorious for their addiction to etymology.[1] Chrysippus very likely invented the term, which is first attested in book titles of his (D.L. 7.200).[2] And many Stoic etymologies have come down to us.[3] So, for instance, Chrysippus derived λαός (*laos*, people) from λαλῶ (*lalō*, speak), and maintained that people are so called because speech is what sets human beings apart from other animals; ἄνθρωπος (*anthrōpos*, human being) yields a similar message by alluding to the possession of articulate voice (διωρθρωμένη ὄψ, *diōrthrōmenē ops*) (Herodianus, *Reliquiae GG* 3.1.108, 9–16 Lentz = *FDS* 671). Fate (ἡ πεπρωμένη, *peprōmenē*, or ἡ εἱμαρμένη, *heimarmenē*) is the perfected (πεπερασμένη, *peperasmenē*) administration of the world and, so to speak, something strung together (εἱρομένη, *eiromenē*) by the will of god (Diogenianus *apud* Eusebium, *PE* 6.8.1–10 = *SVF* 2.914). It would be easy to add more examples, but these should be enough to give the flavour of Stoic etymology. The belief that words encode descriptive content that can be recovered by finding the words

---

[1] Hostile witnesses include Cotta, the Academic spokesman in Cicero's *De natura deorum* (3.63); Augustine (*De dialectica* 6); Galen, *PHP* 104, 17–26; 206, 6–12 De Lacy; Quintilian thinks that etymology is very well in its place (1.6.28 ff.), but that its most devoted practitioners are guilty of many absurdities (32). Sextus Empiricus maintains that etymology is useless as a standard of correctness (*M.* 1.241–7). Plutarch unsurprisingly finds Stoic etymology silly (*Quomodo adolescens poetas audire debeat* 31E), but even a Stoic like Seneca can question its value (*De beneficiis* 1.3.6–10 = *SVF* 2.1082).

[2] The titles are in the section of the catalogue of his books concerned with the articulation of ethical concepts, one of the areas where the Stoics appealed to etymological evidence. But where did the discipline itself belong? There is a cryptic reference to the correctness of names at the end of Diogenes Laertius' treatment of Stoic dialectic (7.83). Long and Sedley 1987: vol. II, 187–8, take the passage to dismiss the study of names as of no importance to the dialectician. For a contrasting view, see Mansfeld 2000: 592–7. If Augustine's *De dialectica* is ultimately modelled on a Stoic source, it is evidence that etymology figured in at least some Stoic handbooks of dialectic. Indirect evidence is found in authors who may have been influenced by the Stoics on this point (Cicero, *Acad. post.* 1.32; Sextus Empiricus, *M.* 7.9; Alcinous *Intr.* 6).

[3] See the examples of Stoic etymology collected by Hülser *FDS* frs. 650–80.

14

from which they are derived is the basis for Stoic etymology as it was for the etymologies proposed by Socrates in the *Cratylus*.[4] And as these examples show, the information that the Stoics believed that they were able to recover in this way may be important and illuminating. On their view, the opinions reflected in the words that were formed at the beginning of human history, when language was young, were in important points superior to those of their own day, and their motive for practising etymology was the recovery of this primitive wisdom.[5]

In common with many of their ancient contemporaries and predecessors, the Stoics believed that the first generation of human beings had no parents and sprang like other living things from the earth.[6] But the Stoics also believed that, because the cosmos passes through cycles of destruction and rebirth, human kind and human culture arise over and over again. There must, then, be first speakers in each cycle of human history. And though the first speakers may have formed some words out of others, if they did, they first required a stock of words that had been endowed with meaning without being derived from other words. If pushed back far enough, then, etymology's search for origins must come to a stop with these primitive words.

Thus the Stoics faced a historical question about how words first came to be used and what the first words were. If it was from these historically first words that later words were derived, they will also have been primary in another sense, by being the elements operations upon which yielded other words, which could serve in their turn as the basis for further developments. I believe that the Stoics did hold a view along these lines, but it is important to realise that this is not the only way of conceiving the elements of a vocabulary. For example, if names are somehow supposed to depict the items they name – the view that is examined in Plato's *Cratylus* – the elements might be sounds with intrinsic mimetic characteristics and words compositions out of them – good to the extent that they put the elements together so as to depict the items they name accurately and bad to the extent that they fall short of this mark. Such a view is not concerned in the first instance to answer questions about how languages began and developed over time, and it is compatible with a range of views about how they did. For example, though it could be that the historically first words stood in the closest relation to the elements, it might also be that, like painting

---

[4] See esp. Sedley 1998b.
[5] On the dark subject of Stoic views about the first humans see Frede 1989: 2088–9, and now Boys-Stones 2001.
[6] On Zeno, see *SVF* 1.124; cf. 2.739; Cornutus, *ND* 23, 3; 39, 15 ff. Lang; S.E. *M.* 9.28.

on a certain view of its history, languages have advanced over time as an increasingly firm grasp of the elements permitted the composition of words that were truer to life than their predecessors.

The Stoics' first words should, I suggest, be viewed as the elements of an essentially historical process that unfolds through a series of ordered stages over time. An interpretation of this kind does not by itself require any particular view about how primitive, underived words were invested with meaning. The meanings of the primitive words might, for instance, have been fixed arbitrarily by convention so that it was a matter of chance which meaning was assigned to which primitive word, while the composition of derived words was governed by rules of some kind. Nonetheless such evidence as we have suggests that, in the famous if not always clearly defined ancient debate about whether names are by nature or convention, the Stoics took the side of nature. Of course, the term 'name' (ὄνομα, *onoma*) as it figures in this controversy applies broadly to verbs and adjectives as well as proper and common names. The traditional title for the controversy seems to have stuck despite the progressive distinction of ever more parts of speech in antiquity.

Our most important piece of evidence about the Stoics is a passage in Origen, the Christian apologist active in the third century AD. In the course of adverting to the 'profound and obscure question regarding the nature of names', he says that the Stoics believe names are by nature, as the first verbal sounds (πρῶται φωναί, *prōtai phōnai*) imitate the things of which they are names, on the basis of which fact they introduce elements (στοιχεῖα, *stoicheia*) of etymology (*Cels.* 1.24 = *SVF* 2.146, *FDS* 643).

Chapter 6 of Augustine's *De dialectica* offers what was probably a fuller version of the same Stoic account.[7] I say 'probably' because, for all we know, the material in Augustine that is not in Origen could belong to a Stoic account which went beyond that on which Origen's report is based. The state of the evidence leaves us little choice but to speak without distinction of the Stoics and their views, even though it is a plausible assumption that those views changed over time and, in particular, that the account preserved by Augustine is the product of a fairly late effort at tidying-up, which may have gone beyond anything to be found in the old Stoa. In any case, Augustine too makes imitation the point of departure for word formation (10.1–3). The first words are formed on a simple onomatopoetic principle. They name the sounds that they are like. So '*tinnitus*', '*hinnitus*',

---

[7] Cited from Jackson and Pinborg 1975, who retain the page and line numbers of W. Crecilius' nineteenth-century edition.

and '*balatus*' are the names for the clash of bronze, the whinnying of horses, and the bleating of sheep respectively. Obviously this principle will yield only a very limited supply of words, but it is augmented considerably by a second quasi-imitative principle, which permits words to name qualities, or objects with qualities, that affect other senses in a way like that in which the word affects the sense of hearing (10.3–9). Thus '*mel*', honey, is said to affect hearing sweetly and '*crux*', cross, is said to affect it painfully. Words belonging to these two classes Augustine calls the cradle (*cunabula*) or alternatively the root (*stirps*) or seed (*sementum*) of words (10.9–11; 11.13–14).

The next principle allows a word to be transferred – either with or without phonetic alteration – to an item that resembles the item to which it was first applied (10.10–13). Let us call it similarity *in re* to distinguish it from the two forms of similarity *in sono* just mentioned. So '*crura*' (singular '*crus*'), legs, are allegedly so called because their length and hardness by comparison with other parts of the body resemble these qualities of the *crux* (cross). This example shows how a word formed directly without being derived from other words can serve in its turn as a basis for the formation of new words. Other permitted forms of word formation by transference are collected under the head of *vicinitas* (proximity, association) (10.13–21; 10.23–11.9). A word may be transferred from container to thing contained or vice versa, from whole to part or vice versa, from effect to cause or vice versa. Last comes the most notorious principle of ancient etymology, namely the transfer of a word from one item to another that is somehow contrary to it. Thus a grove (*lucus*) is said to be so called because of the fact that it is not light in it (*lucus a non lucendo*) and war (*bellum*) because it is no pretty thing (*bellum quod res bella non sit*) (10.21–3).

Though Augustine's first exposition of the principles follows this order, it is plain that, after the original, imitative words are in place, similarity *in re* and the different forms of *vicinitas* can be applied to them and words formed from them in any order you like (11.18 ff.). Thus the word '*vis*' (force) means what it does because of the forceful character it owes to the letter V. Bonds and binding (*vincula*, *vincio*) are so called by a form of *vicinitas* because they exert force. Vines (*vites*) are so called because their effect is to bind the stakes around which they grow. A road is called a '*via*', however, from its similarity *in re* to vines; like them it is winding. Alternatively '*via*' can be derived straight from '*vis*' by *vicinitas*, since a road is the effect of the force of the feet that tread on it.

The evidence preserved by these two authors is the basis of the assumption that has guided efforts to understand the Stoic position ever since.

According to it, the Stoics were committed to a view about a natural standard of correctness for names akin to those discussed in Plato's *Cratylus*.
In particular, they assigned a crucial part in their account to the imitation
by names of the things they name. To be sure, this assumption is not as
well founded as it might be. It is not entirely clear that Origen is giving the
Stoics' grounds for asserting that names are by nature rather than his own
reason for taking them to hold this view, namely that, according to them,
the first words are imitations. Nonetheless, in what follows I shall be chiefly
concerned to understand what the Stoics meant by claiming that names are
by nature, if they did, or in what sense theirs was a view that names are by
nature even if they did not put it in so many words themselves. According
to the interpretation that I will defend, the Stoic view differs in important
respects from the forms of naturalism explored in the *Cratylus*, and I shall
conclude by comparing the two to bring out the distinctive features of the
Stoic position as I understand it.[8]

II

The Stoics were not the only philosophers interested in the origin of language and the correctness of names in antiquity, and we would do well
to sort out the issues in contention, especially since the sources from later
antiquity on whom we must rely sometimes proceed as if a single question
were in dispute, viz. whether names are by φύσις (*physis*, nature) or by θέσις
(*thesis*).[9] The term '*thesis*' came to mean convention and may sometimes be
so translated. That it need not mean this is clear from the *Cratylus*, where
it means imposition. This meaning lives on in the expressions θέσις τῶν
ὀνομάτων (*thesis tōn onomatōn*, the imposition of names), which Chrysippus seems to have used,[10] and πρώτη θέσις (*prōtē thesis*, first imposition).[11]

---

[8] For a contrasting view, which sees a closer relation between Stoic views and the *Cratylus*, see in this
volume Long.

[9] S.E. *M.* 1.143–4, cf. 37, *M.* 11.241–2, *P.H.* 3.267–8; Aulus Gellius 10.4, Simplicius, *in Cat.* 40.6 ff.,
187.7 ff. Kalbfleisch; Origen, *Exh. Mart.* 46. Sometimes, but not always. Origen is careful to distinguish different things that can be meant by the claim that names are by nature (*Cels.* 1.24). Proclus
does the same (*in Cra.* 7.18 ff. Pasquali). Ammonius distinguishes different senses of both *physis*
and *thesis*, and explains how in one sense of *physis* and one of *thesis* names can be by both (*in Int.*
34.20 ff. Busse; cf. Stephanus, *in Int.* 9.7–10, 13 Hayduck).

[10] According to Diogenianus, in the fragment on fate cited above, Chrysippus argued for his views
about fate from the *thesis* of the names for it (*apud* Eusebium, *PE* 6.8.1–10 = *SVF* 2.914). References
to the *thesis* of names in Diogenianus' criticisms suggest that this was Chrysippus' own phrase (*PE*
6.8, 11–24, not in von Arnim). Cf. Philo, *De opif. mundi* 148; *Quaest. in Gen.* 1.20; Varro *LL* 5.3; 6.3;
7.1–2; 8.5; 10.51, 60.

[11] Dionysius Thrax, ch. 12; Porphyry *in Cat.* 57.20–58, 7 Busse; Ammonius *in Cat.* 11.8–12.1; 13.7;
Simplicius *in Cat.* 15.6–13 Kalbfleisch. N.B., however, that, especially in the commentators, the

Far from being opposed to nature, something like *thesis* in this sense turns out to be a precondition for both conventionalist and naturalist views of correctness. It is acts of *thesis* or imposition by legislators or makers of names that are to be judged by how well they conform to the natural standard of correctness if there is one, and those same acts which give rise to a conventional standard of correctness if there is not (cf. 425b). The terms employed for convention in the dialogue are συνθήκη (*sunthēkē*, compact) and ὁμολογία (*homologia*, agreement), never *thesis*. Aristotle too speaks of *sunthēkē* (*Int.* 16a19; 17a2).

Later Platonists and others give us a clue about the relation between the two senses of '*thesis*' when they insist that names are not the product of any chance *thesis* or of *thesis* without qualification, but rather one that is fitted by nature to the things being named (Alcinous, *Intr.* ch. 6; Proclus, *in Cra.* 16.18; 18.14 Pasquali; Stephanus, *in Int.* 9.19–22; 10.7 Hayduck; Aulus Gellius, 10.4; cf. *Crat.* 390a).[12] The view that words owe their meaning to nothing more than imposition unconstrained by a prior standard of correctness amounts to conventionalism.

To find a way for names to be by nature that excludes their being by *thesis*, where this means imposition, we can turn to Epicurus, who maintains that names did not at first come to be by *thesis* but by nature. Something comes to be by nature according to his distinction when it is not the work of an agent acting as an agent, but is the outcome of causal processes set in train without deliberation, choice, intention or the like. And according to Epicurus, the first words were the result of spontaneous episodes of vocalisation. In the spirit of their master, Epicurus' later followers, Lucretius and Diogenes of Oenoanda, ridicule the idea that names were originally imposed by Gods or exceptional human beings, who then taught them to the masses (Lucr. 5.1041 ff.; Diog. Oen. fr. 10, cols. 3–5).[13]

There were, then, two distinct questions to which nature and *thesis* were alternative answers, one about which parts to assign to nature as opposed to deliberate imposition in the origin of language, the other about the standard of correctness governing the formation and use of words. A purely natural account of the origin of language in the style of Epicurus deprives the second question of a point – at least as applied to the first words. Talk

---

idea of a first or original imposition becomes something of an 'analytical device', used to distinguish the simple assignment of meaning to terms, allegedly the subject of the *Categories*, from the differentiation of nouns and verbs, which on this view is the concern of the *De interpretatione* (cf. Philoponus, *in Cat.* 11, 6 ff. Busse).

[12] Cf. Fehling 1965.

[13] Cf. Dahlmann 1928: 41–4; Schrijvers 1974; Blank 1998: 176 (*ad* S.E. *M.* 1.142).

of a standard of correctness makes the most sense in connection with the kind of practices that can live up to or fall short of such a standard. Causal interactions between human beings and their environment in the course of which they are induced to emit sounds are not among these, at least at this level of description. But as we have seen, those who believe that language begins with the deliberate imposition of names are permitted to ask whether there is a natural standard of correctness to which the name givers were, and we perhaps still are, answerable. And in this case, the two questions may be connected, for the kind of natural correctness it is necessary to recognise may well depend on the part it is to play in an account of the origin of language by the *thesis* or imposition of words. The answers the Stoics gave to these questions were, I shall suggest, related in just this way.

III

Let us turn to the *Cratylus* for illumination about what a natural standard of correctness might be. We should then be in a better position to understand what part such a standard might have played in Stoic accounts of the origin of language. My suggestions about those views will be developed in part through a comparison with better attested Epicurean views. Then as promised, I shall conclude by comparing the Stoic view with the positions explored in the *Cratylus*.

Up to this point, our idea of a natural standard of correctness has been that of a standard applying to the imposition of words, against which the efforts of makers or legislators of names may be judged (cf. 390a). To maintain that there is a natural standard is to say that it is not for the legislators to impose names arbitrarily or just as they see fit. In the dialogue this view is put forward by Socrates on behalf of Cratylus in opposition to Hermogenes, who believes that word-meaning is purely and simply a matter of convention. But though this view of the relation between the imposition of names and a natural standard of correctness seems for the most part to meet with the approval of Cratylus, he sometimes seems to have a more radical independence from human agency in mind.

There is a running joke in the dialogue about the name, 'Hermogenes', not being the correct name for Hermogenes the man (384c, 429b, 438c). The consequence, which is both comical and puzzling, is that I could take myself to be saying something about Hermogenes as I pronounce the name 'Hermogenes' and the other words with which it combines to form a sentence, and be taken by others to be doing so, while in fact I was saying something else entirely about someone or something else or saying nothing at all because the terms that I was using were not the naturally correct names for Hermogenes and the features or activities that I am attempting to ascribe to him. It sometimes seems that, according to Cratylus, it is not so much that a name ought to depict what it names as accurately as possible, as that it names, or really names, precisely what it depicts, so that it can lose its power to name a certain item as the result of the smallest change, even though those who use it do not have the least difficulty making themselves understood by means of it (431de, 433c, 436c).

All parties to the dialogue agree on the importance of names for teaching, a point which will later also be emphasised in a different way by the Stoics. But though Cratylus does not demur when Socrates characterises names as instruments by which *we* teach one another and *we* distinguish things (388b), he does not really regard names as instruments used by teachers to convey their knowledge to students or by dialecticians to elicit from their interlocutors a deeper understanding of the matter under discussion. Rather, he takes names themselves to be our teachers and believes that studying them offers us our best and only chance to learn the true nature of things (435d; cf. 438a–b). This is of a piece with the extreme naturalism which is behind the joke about 'Hermogenes' and which threatens to put the relation between a name and the thing whose name it is entirely beyond the reach of human intervention. On this view, it is as if the naturally correct name N for thing X means X prior to and independently of being used by anyone to mean X. It is a natural fact, not made by human beings or alterable by them. As a result, the use of N by people to mean X is in a way only accidentally connected with its really or naturally meaning X.

Cratylus has recourse to a more than human power that imposes names to evade another difficulty, viz., how it was that those who imposed the first names acquire the knowledge necessary to impose them correctly if it is through names and only through names that we can gain knowledge (438c; cf. 425d). But his appeal to a divine guarantor also ensures that, at least some of the time, people use names to mean what they – the names – really mean by nature. The result is to reduce the function of *thesis* to that of a rubber stamp.

By contrast, Socrates assigns a place of crucial importance to the use of names by speakers to make their thoughts understood to their auditors (434e). And he assembles a host of considerations to show that a name can discharge this function without conforming perfectly to the natural standard of correctness, or perhaps even without conforming to it at all.[14] So, for instance, according to the account of the mimetic value of the phonemes out of which names are made that is proposed by Socrates and accepted by Cratylus, the *rhō* in σκληρότης (*sklērotēs*, hardness) indicates hardness because of its likeness to hardness, while the *lambda* indicates softness (435b–d). How is it, then, that we take the word to mean hardness rather than softness? Cratylus is quick to acknowledge that it is because we rely on custom (434e). But custom, as Socrates immediately goes on to observe, either is or depends upon a convention of some kind (434e–435d).

Socrates' deceptively modest interim conclusion that custom and convention also have a contribution to make and that what a name is used to mean and what it purports to depict can diverge (435ab) is a step on the way to the dialogue's main conclusion, viz. that names – viewed as likenesses – are only as good as their makers and can and should be assessed from the perspective afforded by an independent knowledge of the realities whose names they are (438d ff.). For if Socrates' etymologies are correct, many if not most Greek words encode false Heraclitean assumptions about the nature of reality, without preventing those who use them from achieving a true understanding of reality through their own inquiries or conveying it to others. But it also has the effect of calling into question at least the more radical forms of naturalism.

How much of what has gone before is undone by Socrates' interim conclusion is hard to say.[15] The question is pressing in the dialogue because Socrates' investigation of naming was originally undertaken to discover if there is something right in Cratylus' thesis that names are by nature (390de), yet Cratylus' own understanding of this thesis has not withstood examination. Something like Socrates' mimetic account of names was essential to Cratylus' radical naturalism, but it may be that it can be put to other uses as well. How seriously we should take Socrates' insistence that he continues to be pleased by the idea that names should be as like to things as possible and where, if anywhere, Plato stood on the question are, of course, questions outside the scope of this inquiry (cf. 435c).[16]

---

[14] See esp. Williams 1982, who puts the point in this way: a name need not be a correct name to be a name at all or, alternatively, there are two kinds of correctness only one of which is necessary for a name to serve as a name.

[15] Cf. Barney 2001: 136.

[16] The question how seriously to take Socrates arises because, if he is right, the considerations that make *thesis* necessary if names are to be used by speakers to mean things to each other suggest that it may be sufficient as well. Cf. Schofield 1982.

For our present purpose, it is most important that we are now in a position to distinguish between two ways of understanding the claim that names are by nature.

(i) The name N means X by nature prior to its use by human beings to mean X.

(ii) The name N is naturally suited to be used by human beings to mean X.

The possibility of a view of the first type was demolished together with Cratylus' position. But the possibility that a view of the second type can be successfully defended remains open. On such a view, there is something about a name which makes it naturally suited to serve human beings as an instrument by which to make their thoughts about an item intelligible to each other: N is so to speak a natural choice when it comes to *meaning* X. But before N can serve a community of speakers as a name for X, it must become common knowledge that it is to be so used. *Thesis*, then, cannot be confined to the role of a rubber stamp, and this means that there is and must be an element of convention, even in the imposition of naturally correct names (cf. 435b).

The view that names are imposed, but that their imposition is answerable to a natural standard of correctness, continued to have its supporters. Unsurprisingly, most of its adherents followed Plato's lead, and took conformity to the standard of natural correctness to be a matter of imitation. To vindicate a mimetic account of natural correctness within the framework of the *Cratylus*, it would presumably be necessary to discover how depicting their *nominata* makes names able, or better able, to fulfil their didactic function. On the suggestion that we are considering, however, though they belonged to the broad consensus, the Stoics believed the first and most important function for which words should be naturally suited was the creation and gradual extension of a vocabulary, and the natural standard of correctness for words, including an imitative component, will be the one by satisfying which words are able, or best able, to discharge this function. The two functions do not exclude each other, but, according to this suggestion, the difference in emphasis affected both the nature and extent of the part played by imitation in the Stoic account.

IV

Let us then bring the Stoics' views into connection with what we know or can guess about their views concerning the origin of language. As announced above, I shall use the better attested Epicurean account as a foil.[17] The first and most important lesson to be drawn from the comparison is that the choice between nature and imposition cannot do justice to Stoic views about the beginnings of language as long as this contrast is understood as it was by the Epicureans.

In a famous passage, Lucretius inveighs against the mistake of supposing that the organs with which we are endowed by nature are *for* the use to which we put them, the eyes for seeing, the limbs for walking, the tongue for speaking and so on (4.824 ff.). Rather, he insists, we happened to find a use for them. On this Epicurean view, only intentional actions performed by agents such as ourselves can be correctly described as for the sake of an outcome. The formation of the cosmos, the emergence of the different species of living things, the stages through which members of these species pass on their way to maturity, the organs of which they make use are, none of them, for the sake of anything or the result of anything that was for their sake. Hence the two stage account of the emergence of human abilities favoured by the Epicureans. First comes a natural phase, in which something – a bodily organ or its activity, a part of the environment or its behaviour – produces and is seen to produce a beneficial result without deliberate effort by an agent. There follows a second phase, which begins with deliberate attempts to reproduce the result and goes on to embrace efforts to systematise and improve the means of so doing. Epicurus' account of the origin and development of language is merely one instance of this wider pattern (*Ep. Hdt.* 75).

We are accustomed to oppose this kind of view to Aristotelian natural teleology. Because the Stoics conceive the natural world as a whole governed by divine reason, their discussions of nature are full of references to divine reason and its artistic activity of a kind which have no place in Aristotle's. Nonetheless, even though the Stoics believed that everything that occurs by nature is ultimately subsumed in the government of the universe by divine providence, they leave room for a contrast between things that come about by nature and those whose source is human agency.

In particular, on this view, a great many things must come about by nature if reason itself is to develop in a human being. The Stoics agree with Epicurus and Aristotle in calling these developments natural. They part ways with Epicurus but not Aristotle by supposing that they take place in order that reason may develop. The fact that they eventually also part ways with Aristotle by supposing that the natural development of human reason takes place owing to divine agency is less important for our present purpose.

---

[17] For detailed treatments of Epicurean views, see in this volume, Atherton, Verlinsky.

What matters is that human reason develops through a sequence of stages that occur as and when they do for its sake. This is part of what teleologists of any stripe mean when they assert that human beings are rational by nature. It is very different from what Epicureans mean by saying that an ability arises naturally. Indeed the sense of nature at issue is unavailable to the Epicureans. In Aristotelian terms, the origin of language according to Epicurus, for example, is not so much natural as spontaneous or automatic.

The view that language is the outward expression of reason, which is reflected in some of the sample etymologies with which we began, was especially dear to the Stoics. If they had a story about the origin and development of language, it will belong in their account of the natural growth of reason.[18] To the Epicureans' way of thinking, the chief merit of their own account is its gradualism. According to it, the power of articulate speech emerges by degrees out of forms of behaviour that we share with the lower animals (cf. Lucr. 5.1056–90). The alternative, as they present it, requires someone who is already a past master of language, a god or a wise man, to teach a multitude without a tincture of language to speak. As we noted, Lucretius and Diogenes of Oenoanda especially dwell on the absurdities of this view. But if Diogenes' remarks were aimed at the Stoics, as is sometimes supposed, they were directed against a caricature, for there is no reason to believe that the Stoics were committed to such a view.

Because the power of articulate speech, like the reason to which it gives expression, is part of our nature according to the Stoics, it can be the outcome of a gradual natural development. If we are to be able to express our thoughts in articulate speech when reason is sufficiently developed for us to have thoughts, we must have suitable speech organs and we must be practised enough in their use to make them answer to our purpose.[19] The Stoics were not, for example, obliged to deny the relevance of infant babbling to the development of speech, either in a child born into a community already speaking a language or, perhaps, even in the first development of language.[20]

---

[18] Cf. Dahlmann 1932: 7, 14, who, however, seems to think that this means that, unlike the Epicureans, the Stoics will not have felt obliged to describe the process in detail. Perhaps, but I think that a different kind of explanation was required, viz. not how a sequence of fortuitous occurrences could give rise to the power to speak, but how the events necessary to its development are the opposite of fortuitous.

[19] We are furnished with speech organs by nature for the sake of articulate speech. So Balbus on behalf of the Stoics (N.B. 'nostri', i.e. 'our people') (Cicero, *ND* 2.149; cf. *Leg.* 27).

[20] Chrysippus maintained that when children first begin to utter words, they are not speaking in the strictest sense, but 'as it were speaking' (Varro *LL* 6.56), but presumably this is an important step on

What is more, if acts of *thesis* have a part to play in the formation of language, nothing prevents them from doing so at a relatively advanced stage in a development that is through and through natural, but whose first stages are natural in the narrower sense that is opposed to deliberate exercises of the will. And if, as is often supposed, exceptional individuals played a prominent part in the process, it will not be because they introduced the use of words to a mute population unversed in linguistic activity of any kind.[21] Rather they will have taken the lead in an enterprise for which all human beings are suited by nature and towards which they are all naturally impelled.

To be sure, the Stoics were no more able than we are to observe the growth of the complementary faculties of reason and speech anywhere except in long established communities, where children learn a language together with much else from their elders. And if they ever supplied a detailed account of the first beginnings of language, it has not come down to us. But the same human nature must assert itself in the less common and less easily imagined conditions obtaining at the beginning of a cycle of human history, and there is a fair amount of testimony that bears in different ways on the natural growth of human reason and the place of speech in human nature, to which we can turn for clues about how it might have been that speech and language were supposed to emerge in these exceptional conditions.[22]

A number of passages tell us about the process of concept formation which gives rise to reason (Aëtius 4.11 = *SVF* 2.83; D.L. 7.52; S.E. *M.* 8.56; Augustine, *De civ. dei* 8.7).[23] For our present purpose, it is important that this development is at first natural; then comes a later stage at which we can choose to add further concepts to the original stock by investigating

the way to speech properly so called. Quintilian cites Chrysippus on the importance of good nurses because of the influence they exert on growing children, and if von Arnim was right to continue the extract as far as he does, Chrysippus laid special emphasis on the fact that children imitate the speech of their nurses (1.1.15–16 = *SVF* 3.733).

[21] Evidence bearing on Stoic views about the primitive condition of mankind is sparse. Seneca, *Ep.* 90 takes partial exception to Posidonius, according to whom mankind was originally ruled by wise kings who were responsible for advances of almost every kind. No mention is made of speech and language, however. Stoic influences have been suspected behind Philo of Alexandria's talk of Adam as the earth-born king entrusted with the imposition of names (*De opif. mundi* 148; *Quaest. in Gen.* 1.20).

[22] Sextus Empiricus tells us that according to certain of the later Stoics the first earth-born humans so surpassed those of the present day that their sharpness of mind amounted to an extra organ of sense (*M.* 9.28). The form of the attribution suggests that the claims the Stoics were willing to make on behalf of the first humans grew over time. Even so, these were gifted human beings who realised their human nature better than people nowadays, not beings with another nature.

[23] On Stoic views about concept formation, see in this volume, Brittain.

a question for ourselves or seeking tuition from another. Nothing is said about the effect on this process of the presence or absence of cultural and social conditions nor about whether it, or part of it, takes place in advance of or together with the development of the ability to speak.

To this evidence we can add passages about ethical development that describe how a human being's natural attachments, whose first object is his or her own constitution, expand by degrees to embrace other humans and ultimately the community of all rational beings. Like the passages about concept formation, these are highly idealised. Their point is to inform us about human nature, not to take account of the influence different conditions might have on its development. And some of them pass with remarkable briskness from natural developments that are bound to occur unless violently impeded to further developments that would take place were we to continue down the path on which nature has started us – a condition which is rarely if ever realised – instead of succumbing to corrupting influences as we almost invariably do. Nonetheless a point of crucial importance emerges clearly enough. According to the Stoics, nature sees to it that human beings do what there are reasons for them to do before they are in a position to appreciate or be moved by those reasons (cf. Cicero, *Fin.* 3.66).

Two natural attachments especially important to the present inquiry stand out among the details of the Stoic account. We are naturally impelled to knowledge, which we value for its own sake. Even as children we delight in making discoveries regardless of whether they have any obviously beneficial consequences for us (Cicero, *Fin.* 3.17; cf. 2.46; *Off.* 1.12–13). And we have a natural impulse towards the society of other rational beings, which is the origin of justice. Often speech figures in this context as the bond fashioned by nature to unite human beings in society (Cicero, *Off.* 1.12, 50; *Fin.* 2.45; *Rep.* 3.3). But we have a natural impulse to speech not only because of the contribution it makes to social order. Speech serves the natural impulse we have to learn from others and to teach them (*Fin.* 3.65–6; *Off.* 1.50; *ND* 2.148). We are, then, fitted by nature for a life of sociable rationality or rational sociability, and the society of rational beings towards which we are impelled by nature does more than provide for needs for sustenance and safety; it is a community of teachers and learners.

These themes come together in a passage in Cicero's *De natura deorum*, whose broader context is the Stoic doctrine that human beings are the object of the gods' providential care (2.133 ff.). In support of this, the dialogue's Stoic spokesman, Balbus, describes in considerable detail the organs of the human body and the faculties belonging to human nature

before concluding that the form and arrangement of the body's parts and
the power of the mind cannot be the product of chance (153). In the course
of developing this theme, Balbus turns to the mind and reason and extols
the incredible power by means of which we grasp truths and what follows
from them, produce definitions and so attain knowledge, than which there
is nothing better even among the gods. Next comes the power of speech,
which enables us to learn what we do not know and teach others what we
do know, as well as calm the frightened, exhort, persuade and tame the
passions. This power, we are told, bound us together in the society of cities,
laws and justice by freeing us from a savage and uncivilised life. Finally
Balbus celebrates the incredible skill displayed by nature in devising the
vocal organs that enable us to exercise this power (149).

On the Stoic view, the first speakers of a language will have been human
beings with a human nature like this, so formed as to want to make their
thoughts known to each other and equipped at the same time by nature with
the organs necessary to do so by means of articulate speech. My suggestion
is that any naturalness that the Stoics may have claimed for names should
be understood in relation to the human nature whose realisation it assists
in these special conditions.

According to the proposal under consideration, then, the first purpose
of the principles of word formation described by Augustine will have been
to guide the earliest humans in their first attempts at communication.[24]
What makes a word N a natural name for an item X, then, would not be a
tendency to mean X prior to its use to mean X, but rather the possession of
a feature that lends itself to the purposes of a rational being who wishes to
let it be known that he is thinking about X and bring others to do the same.
The Stoics' idea would have been that their principles of word formation
represent the best, in the sense of the most rational, way for a community
of rational beings disposed by nature to share their lives and thoughts

---

[24] One can believe as the Stoics do that human beings are so constituted by nature as to form communities knit together by speech, without thinking that certain words or sounds are naturally suited
to the expression of thoughts about certain things. So for instance, Ammonius, a neo-Platonic
philosopher and Aristotelian commentator active in the fifth and sixth centuries AD, setting out
from a conception of human nature and human origins like the Stoics', assigns a crucial part to the
purely conventional imposition of names.

Nature, seeing that this animal was destined to become social, gave it voice (*phōnē*), so that by means
of it they could signify their thoughts to each other; and having come together, human beings made
compacts (συνεθέντο, *sunethento*) with each other to name this perchance 'wood', that 'stone', and
to make the sound (*phōnē*) 'Socrates' significant of this particular substance and the sound 'walk
about' significant of this particular activity (*in Cat.* 11, 8–14 Busse; cf. Porphyry, *in Cat.* 57, 20–58,
7 Busse).

with each other to go about building a vocabulary of mutually intelligible words.²⁵ This does not require that there be a single best name for each thing. Language can begin, and once begun develop, in different ways in conformity to the Stoics' principles. Indeed in his exposition of them, Augustine speaks of the freedom (*licentia nominandi*) they permit (10, 11).

If this is right, it is not surprising that the first words are imitative. If there is an obvious way for rational beings to begin to direct each others' attention to what they are thinking about and at the same time to make it plain that this is what they are doing, it is by imitation. It is also not surprising to find the Epicureans, with their very different assumptions, making involuntary exclamations the beginning of speech. According to Proclus, the fifth-century AD neo-Platonic philosopher, Epicurus compared the beginnings of speech to coughing, sneezing, crying out and the like (*in Cra.* 8.4–7 Pasquali). Happening to observe that natural unplanned vocal utterances make known our condition and state of mind to others and theirs to us, we discover how to use our voices to this end.

Nothing hinders the Stoics from assigning a similar part to the observation of potentially useful occurrences and deliberate efforts to reproduce them. Indeed there is some evidence that they did (Cornutus *ND* 34, 3–6 Lang; Seneca *Ep.* 90, 22–4). But I suspect that from the Stoic point of view what is missing from accounts of the emergence of human abilities like the Epicureans' is attention to the rational powers that make us able to profit from experience and improve upon what we have observed. Without our rational nature, which on their view can only have been devised for us by providence, all the potentially fruitful experiences from which we might learn would leave us none the wiser. Thus Cornutus, the first-century AD Stoic, who takes Prometheus to symbolise forethought, interprets the myth of the theft of fire as an allusion to the intelligence and foresight which enables us to understand the use of fire, and takes the belief that Prometheus was the discoverer of the arts to be a reflection of the fact that we require intelligence and foresight to discover them (*ND* 32.8–11; 33.6–8

²⁵ Dionysius of Halicarnassus, the late first-century BC rhetorician, is sometimes cited in this connection.

Nature makes us imitative (*mimētikoi*) and able to impose (*thetikoi*) names by which matters are indicated in accordance with certain similarities that are reasonable and capable of moving the intellect (*Comp.* 16).

Though the Stoics are not mentioned, I believe that this is the kind of view they held. There follows a list of onomatopoetic words like those cited by Augustine, which were said to be taught by nature, but Dionysius goes on to cite words that are likenesses of a much broader range of features in the manner of the *Cratylus*, which is the only authority he cites.

Lang).[26] What is more, the Stoics will have held that, without the intellectual curiosity which is a part of this nature, our intellectual abilities would not have developed in the directions and to the extent that they have.

V

But if it is not surprising to find the Stoics emphasising deliberate efforts to imitate the things meant by words in their account of the origin of language (as opposed to the efforts to imitate spontaneous episodes of vocalisation to which the Epicurean account appeals), I should also like to suggest that it is not surprising that this sort of imitation is assigned a smaller and more limited part by the Stoics than it is in the *Cratylus*. If the proposal advocated here is correct, one of their aims was to explain how people first came to use the words they did to mean the things they meant by them. Though the *Cratylus* is full of references to the imposition of names by name-givers in an earlier period of history, it is not chiefly concerned with the historical origins of speech and language. As has often been observed, like the myth in the great speech of the *Protagoras*, such talk can be interpreted as a device, in this case one intended to throw light on the nature of names.[27] Whether and how the account of natural correctness that emerges should be brought into connection with a historical invention of language is left vague. The dialogue is instead concerned to explain how names might be naturally suited to their *nominata* in a way that could accommodate Cratylus' position among others, and it has been taken by many to describe an ideal that has never been realised and perhaps never will be.

Socrates maintains that to have a chance of succeeding an account must satisfy two requirements (422cd):

(a) There must be a single standard of correctness for all words, both the primary words and those whose meaning is explained by the words from which they are derived.

(b) This standard must be such that, by conforming to it, names indicate or reveal the things whose names they are.

To this end, though not without hesitation, Socrates puts forward his mimetic account of word composition. This account differs in two especially important respects from the Stoic theory we have been considering. It is mimetic through and through, and it takes names to be correct to

---

[26] Cf. [Aeschylus] *Pr.* 447, where Prometheus observes that before his gift of art, human beings looked but looked in vain, listened but listened without hearing.
[27] Cf. Kretzmann 1971.

the extent that they imitate the essence of their *nominata*. Beginning with letters and syllables and proceeding through the words formed out of them to the words formed out of other words, it explains how words function as mimetic compositions (cf. 422d). As in other arts like music and especially painting, the elements contribute their mimetic content to that of the whole composition (cf. 423d, 424bc, 429a, 430b, 431d). This is why there was a problem with *sklērotēs*.

The imitation of essence sets name-making apart from the other mimetic arts. In the course of making this point, Socrates touches on strictly onomatopoetic words of *something* like the kind employed by the Stoics in their theory (cf. 423e). His attitude toward them is revealing. He insists that people who imitate the sounds that sheep or roosters make are not naming them, and he maintains that this form of imitation belongs instead to music because it imitates the sounds a thing makes rather than its essence. To be sure, the Stoics' onomatopoetic words are not names of the things whose sounds they imitate but of the sounds themselves. Sounds have essences (423e). Could not onomatopoetic words, then, imitate these essences? Perhaps, but Socrates does not pause even for a moment to identify a special, strictly onomatopoetic principle of word formation for the names of sounds.[28] Instead he proceeds to sketch a vastly more ambitious account of imitation by names based on the idea that the state of the vocal organs as a name is pronounced imitates the item it names. This account does not make a special place for the imitation of sounds, but is somehow supposed to permit names to imitate all the things of which there are names.

The Stoic principles of word formation look like a hodgepodge by comparison. What gives them unity, I have been arguing, is the ways in which they serve the needs of the early speakers of a language. The strictly onomatopoetic words that come first recommend themselves because of their obviousness. The very first words are likenesses, but it is not because they depict, let alone capture the essence of, things that they name them. Rather it is because likeness is an especially perspicuous way of drawing attention to what one wishes others to attend to that they were the first names to be imposed. Though the principle of likeness on which they depend is already quite different, the quasi-imitative words that follow are, on this view, a natural and easily grasped extension of this idea.

Words based on similarity *in re* no longer need to imitate the items they name. As we follow the chain of associations which lead from one word to

---

[28] Cf. Barwick 1957a: 76.

another, the basis of the new formation can change over and over again. The words that result are not mimetic compositions in the way in which those of the *Cratylus* were supposed to be. The sound of a name imposed because it somehow resembles its nominatum (similarity *in sono*) need not retain its mimetic value when that name, or a version of it, is imposed on a new nominatum similar to the first nominatum (similarity *in re*) because the point of resemblance between the original and the new nominatum need have nothing to do with the feature of the first that the sound was somehow like. Consider '*crux*' (cross) and '*crura*' (legs), and recall that while the *crux* was supposed to be so called because the painful impression made on the ears by the word resembles the pain caused by the thing, *crura* were supposed to be so called because the length and hardness of the legs resemble these features of a cross. The meaning of words earlier in the chain, though relevant to the explanation of how a derived word came to mean what it does, need not itself be a part of the later word's meaning. The same is true of the various principles which permit a name to be imposed by *vicinitas*. Though obviously inferior as imitations, the words formed after the first, imitative words are, once imposed, not inferior as names.

If the Stoics did hold that there was a natural standard of correctness by conforming to which some words are the naturally right ones, then, it cannot have been mimetic accuracy.[29] On the suggestion that I am defending, it is possible for words to be naturally correct according to the Stoics, because language is a product of reason in the sense that its immediate authors are rational beings exercising their rational powers and there is a rational way to proceed in the imposition of names.[30]

But if this was the Stoic view, their account of natural correctness seems to make etymology a far less interesting affair than the account in the *Cratylus* promised to do. According to that account, though not everything for which there is a name will be important, by depicting the essence of the things they name, the names of a language conforming to the dialogue's mimetic principles will make available the most important and interesting truths about things, including the most important things there are. By contrast, on the Stoic account, it appears that the information recovered by etymology may not only fail to be about something interesting, but even when it is about matters of the utmost importance, may fail to tell us anything of interest about them.

---

[29] Cf. Long 2002: 408: 'the meaning of the word . . . is not delivered or explained by the sound; rather, the word's sound is appropriate to but not constitutive of its significance'.

[30] Just as there is in the construction of systems of inflection and derivation (cf. Varro *LL* 8.5, 7). Cf. Frede 1978: 68–70.

As we have seen, the examples given by Augustine are, so far as their broader import goes, studiously dull. To judge by the instances that he gives of words formed on the basis of similarity *in re*, for example, the point of similarity on which the transfer of a word, or a phonetically altered version of it, depends can be incidental in the extreme. Consider once again the case of '*crux*' and '*crura*'. The same is true of words formed by the different varieties of *vicinitas* and by sequential applications of them and similarity *in re*. Almost any point of similarity or any association will do.

Yet the examples of etymology with which we began are full of interest, and the Stoics' motive for pursuing etymology was, as we noted, to recover the primitive wisdom that is preserved in them. The problem is only apparent, however. As we saw, the Stoics' interest was not and could not be indulged in isolation from questions about the historical origin and growth of language, and their account of how words are formed obviously could not simply be tailored to the needs of etymology. Rather its first task was to explain how the practice of using words to express thoughts arose and developed in the special conditions that prevail at the beginning of each cycle of human history among beings disposed by nature to a life of sociable rationality. Because the imposition of names follows a rational pattern, however, it is in principle possible to retrace the steps by which a word came to be. To be sure, in many cases, as the Stoics acknowledge, it will not be possible in actual fact (*De dialectica* 9.18–20; 11.11–12; cf. Varro *LL* 7.2). And as we have seen, even when it is, not all the information that can be recovered by etymology will be of significance. But the Stoics think that many words will preserve information about their makers' understanding of the nature of things that is valuable enough to make etymology worthy of the energies that they devoted to it.

The clearest examples are furnished by words formed on a principle that does not figure in Augustine's system, namely compressed descriptions.[31] Thus Chrysippus derived the word καρδία (*kardia*, heart) from κράτησις (*kratēsis*, dominion) and κυρεία (*kureia*, authority) because the heart contains the dominant and ruling part of the soul (Galen, *PHP* 206, 13 ff. De Lacy). I suspect that the relation between the words formed on this principle and those formed in the ways described by Augustine is simple, and that the absence of this principle from Augustine's list is not an especially serious problem. The business of describing, and therefore of composing compressed descriptions, could hardly advance very far with a supply of words limited to the imitative words that constitute the cradle of words.

---

[31] Emphasised by Barwick 1957a: 32.

Thus apart from explaining with various degrees of plausibility how many
words which could hardly be viewed as descriptions were formed and came
into use, the principles that come into effect after the cradle of words is
in place explain how a stock of words adequate to the task of description
arose.

But even though the straightest route to etymologies of the richly informative kind that were most highly prized by the Stoics is *via* words formed
in this way out of compressed descriptions, those formed in accordance with
the other principles may also contain insights worth recovering. Augustine
describes the task of etymology as explaining the origin of words (*originem
explicare*) (9.3; 9.19; cf. Quintilian, 1.6.28). According to Varro, it inquires
why and whence (*cur et unde*) words arise (*LL* 5.2). But as we have seen,
the kind of explanations that are offered by Stoic etymology do not rely
on quasi-mechanical principles operating independently of the conscious
thoughts of those who are responsible for imposing new words. Rather the
explanation of why a word that had its origin in another word came to be
imposed in its new meaning crucially relies on their thoughts about relations of similarity, association or opposition between the item named by
the new word and that named by the word from which it is derived. That
is, etymological explanation affords a glimpse of what the early makers of
names thought about the items on which they imposed names.[32]

This is why the Stoics believed that they were able by means of etymology
to penetrate through the errors and confusions that had grown up over time
to recover the precious insights of the earliest and least corrupted human
beings.[33] Thus Cicero proposes to derive '*fides*' (trust) in the Stoic spirit
from '*fiat*' (let it be), because what is said or promised comes about (*Off.*
1.23). And the Stoics themselves embrace the etymologies, already found in
the *Cratylus*, for the oblique forms of 'Zeus', Δία (*Dia*) and Ζῆνα (*Zēna*),
which explain them with reference to the facts that Zeus is responsible for
living (ζῆν, *zēn*) and that it is through (δία, *dia*) him that all things come
about (*Cra.* 396a; D.L. 7.147).

VI

On the interpretation that I have been defending, then, the views preserved
for us by Augustine and Origen belong to a Stoic attempt to explain how
languages capable of serving the needs of essentially rational and sociable,

---

[32] N.B. Varro *LL* 8.1–2, who speaks of recovering the *voluntas impositoris*.
[33] On the Stoics' belief that they are able to read through poetry to recover the insights inadvertently
preserved by the poets, see Frede 1989: 2087; Long 1992; cf. Most 1989.

i.e. human beings arose and developed through the exercise of those beings' rational powers. These powers could not be applied to this end unless certain conditions were satisfied before the appearance of reason, but human nature has been so formed that they will be satisfied. Even though what takes place in this way unassisted by human reason can be called natural by contrast with what takes place owing to human reason, both the natural and the rational elements are embedded in the development of humanity's rational nature and can be fully understood only in relation to it. In this sense they both deserve to be called natural. And since there is a right way for reason to prescribe which names are to be imposed, there is a sense in which acts of imposition can be held to a natural standard of correctness.

It is a plausible conjecture that the Stoic account reconstructed on the basis of Origen and Augustine's evidence is a relatively late attempt to answer questions about the beginnings of language that are raised by Stoic views about human origins in such a way as to provide secure foundations for long-standing but perhaps not yet systematised Stoic etymological practice. On this account, the recovery of the insights of the earliest speakers that etymology makes possible is, to be sure, a by-product of the rational character of a language's development. But from the Stoic perspective, it is not a mere by-product, but yet another consequence of Providence's design to ensure that the world, both natural and manmade, is full of signs.[34]

[34] I am grateful to other participants in the Symposium Hellenisticum and an audience at Cornell for their many helpful comments and criticisms, to Tad Brennan for taking the trouble to write up his reactions to the first version of this paper and, especially, to Julia Annas for her written comments on later versions.

CHAPTER 2

Stoic linguistics, Plato's Cratylus, *and Augustine's* De dialectica

A. A. Long

Stoic philosophers, probably at least from the time of Chrysippus, were interested in Plato's *Cratylus* and were influenced by the dialogue. This is not directly attested in so many words, but its correctness is frequently and rightly assumed. Two points of similarity are self-evident.[1] First and most significant is the Stoics' recourse to etymologising. We have copious evidence of Stoic etymologies, especially for the names of gods. Some of these etymologies are identical to ones advanced by Socrates in the *Cratylus*, and the principles involved are also identical: interpreting the name under investigation by aligning it with one or more words whose meaning is known, on the basis of phonetic similarity between the two sets of words. Thus the Stoics, like Plato's Socrates, explain the name Zeus and its inflection Dia by reference to *zēn*, 'to live', and *dia* meaning 'because of': the name Zeus signifies 'the cause of life'.[2]

The second point of immediate similarity is the concept of elementary or primary sounds that signify things mimetically. Socrates advances this proposal as an analytical device for discovering whence names, that are compounded out of letters and syllables, derive their capacity for representing things correctly, i.e. as they really are (421c–425c). He then develops the hypothesis that the ancients took elementary sounds or letters to imitate things or properties of things, especially motion.

According to Origen, the Stoics took the basis of names to be nature as distinct from convention (*thesis*), with the 'primary sounds (*tōn prōtōn onomatōn*) imitating the things of which they are the names, and hence

---

The *Cratylus* parts of this paper, an earlier draft of which was greatly improved by comments from David Sedley, was originally written for a colloquium at Berkeley on the *Cratylus*, which took place in April 1997. A shorter version of it has already appeared in M. Canto-Sperber and P. Pellegrin, eds., *Le Style de la Pensée. Recueil de textes en hommage à Jacques Brunschwig* (Paris, 2002), 395–411.
[1] See Barwick 1957a: 70–9.   [2] Cf. *Cra.* 396a–b and D.L. 7.147 (*SVF* 2.1021).

36

they adduced [them as] elements of etymology' (*Cels.* 1.24 = *SVF* 2.146, Hülser *FDS* 643).[3]

Origen's brief report can be supplemented by material attributed to the Stoics by Augustine in his work *De dialectica* 6.[4] There we are told that they traced the origin of all words to one of three relations between sounds and things – onomatopoetic similarity (*similitudo*), affinity or prox-imity (*vicinitas*, a looser degree of similarity), and opposition (*contrarium*, exemplified by the notorious *lucus a non lucendo*). Augustine probably derived his material from lost parts of Varro's voluminous works on gram-mar. Even if his report is contaminated by non-Stoic theory or by the-ory developed only by some later Stoics, we can probably accept the gist of it as applicable to orthodox members of the school from Chrysippus onward. That is to say, Stoics looked to nature as distinct from convention in accounting for primary words, though not perhaps in ways precisely adumbrated in Plato's dialogue.[5]

So much for the state of the question. In this paper I shall suggest that the Stoics' reflections on the *Cratylus* were not confined to the work's etymologies and analysis of primary names. I shall propose that they also gave serious thought to a number of further ideas that Socrates canvasses. In addition, I shall argue that parts of their linguistic theory can be interpreted as a revisionary reading of the *Cratylus*, a reading that makes Socrates' various proposals much more coherent than they are presented as being in the dialogue itself.

This hypothesis is obviously speculative, but speculation is unavoidable when we attempt to track down the texts and antecedent ideas that may have shaped the foundations of Stoicism. Recent scholarship has had consider-able success in looking to Plato's dialogues and the early Platonic tradition as especially promising material for exercising such formative influence. So

---

[3] In the last sentence I understand *ta prōta onomata* as the direct object of *eisagousin*. Origen continues by contrasting the Stoic sense of the objective naturalness of names with the Epicurean theory that what makes names natural is their being the utterances of the earliest human beings. For comparison between the two theories, see Allen (this volume), who notes that referring names to *thesis* need not imply a conventionalist contrast with nature; see also Barney 2001. That it does so here, however, is guaranteed because Origen's *thesis* contrasts Aristotle's conventionalism with the Stoics' naturalism.
[4] Not included in *SVF*, but largely excerpted by Schmidt 1839: 23–5. The work is sometimes called *De principiis dialecticae*. I cite it here from the edition by Jackson and Pinborg 1975.
[5] What the Stoics meant by claiming that names are by nature is the main point of Allen's paper in this volume and his discussions of Plato's *Cratylus* and Augustine. While his paper and mine overlap in some of the material they discuss, they differ in their scope and emphasis. Allen is chiefly concerned with the question of what etymology contributed to Stoic theory on the *origins* of language, whereas I look to the *Cratylus* and to Augustine for illumination on Stoic linguistics more generally.

far as Stoic linguistics is concerned, the *Cratylus* will doubtless have been only one seminal work to ponder. But even if I don't succeed in proving that it played a dominant role, a comparison between the dialogue and Stoicism should be instructive.

THE RATIONALE OF STOIC ETYMOLOGIES

Why did the Stoics go in for etymological analysis of the gods' names? The answer, clearly given in Cicero's *De natura deorum* book 2 and in Cornutus' *Compendium of the Tradition of Greek Theology*, rests on two anthropological assumptions.[6] First, the Stoics assumed that the gods were given their names by early people who had an intelligent understanding of the general structure of the world. Second, they assumed that these people, in naming the gods, wished to signify the segment of the natural world that the gods, in the view of these wise persons, control or symbolise. Hence, for instance, the name Hera signifying 'air' (*aēr*, an etymology from the *Cratylus*, 404c) or the Homeric epithet of Zeus, *ana Dōdōnaie* ('O Lord of Dodona'), derived by Cleanthes from *anadidōmi*, meaning 'send up' and related to the Stoic doctrine of air vaporising from the earth.[7] The Stoics recognised that such etymologies had little or nothing to do with activities of the gods according to mythology. They explained this discrepancy by supposing, as Cicero puts it on their behalf (*ND* 2.63–4), that an absurd story, such as the tale of Cronos' castration of Ouranos, is a fictional perversion of a correct understanding of nature, namely: that the celestial fire is a procreative power without need for genitals.

Greek mythology, on this view, is a corrupted and childish narrative of the role of the gods, as signified by their correctly assigned original names when deciphered by etymology. Thus Cornutus writes: 'The ancients were not nobodies but competent students of the world, and well equipped to philosophise about it via symbols and riddles' (76.2–5 Lang). The task of the Stoic etymologist is to try to recover the true beliefs about the world encoded in the gods' names and epithets – beliefs which have been overlaid by subsequent superstition. This Stoic practice is often called allegorisation, but that is very misleading.[8] They did not seek to elicit the true but covert messages of Homer or Hesiod themselves; rather, they sought to recover

[6] For the evidence and detailed discussion of it, see Most 1989 and Long 1996b: 69–75.
[7] Plutarch, *De aud.* 31D (*SVF* 1.535); cf. Long 1992: 80 n. 48, 81.
[8] My main purpose in Long 1996b is to distinguish the Stoics' etymological ventures from the allegorical interpretation of literature characteristic of Philo of Alexandria, for instance.

the linguistic rationale of those much earlier persons who originally gave the gods the names and epithets they have in the work of these poets.

Plato's Socrates in the *Cratylus* gave the Stoics many precedents for their anthropological assumptions. First, his recourse to Homer and Hesiod as evidence for a 'natural' fit between the significance of divine names and their bearers (cf. *Cra.* 397e, 402b, 406c). Second, his focus on the linguistic rationale of the 'earliest' Hellenes.[9] Third, his claim, paraphrased long afterwards by Cornutus (see above) that: 'the original givers of names were probably no ordinary people but students of astronomy (*meteōrologoi*, 401b) and subtle talkers'. Fourth, and most important, his repeated assumption that the original name-givers had definite opinions about the structure of the world, opinions that they designedly encoded in the names they invented (cf. *Cra.* 397d, 399d, 402b, 411b). This last point – the encoding of the name-givers' beliefs in the names chosen – is Socrates' principal reason for advancing the thesis that the names he has been explaining were intended to exhibit the nature of things (422d).

The beliefs, of course, that are given pride of place in the *Cratylus* are radical Heracliteanism. Socrates, at the end of the dialogue, argues that phonetic analysis of names does not unequivocally support the Heraclitean thesis (436b–437c) and further, that if the early name-givers had such beliefs they were certainly not grounded on knowledge, including knowledge derived from names (438a–439b). What Socrates never challenges, as far as I can see, is the thesis that early people's beliefs, whether true or false, are encoded, at least to some extent, in the names they gave to things.[10] How would the Stoics have reacted to the dialogue's focus on Heracliteanism?

Strangely enough, this question appears never to have been previously asked, but its import is obvious when we reflect that the Stoics looked back to Heraclitus as a major authority for their cosmology and theology.[11] Should their faith as Heracliteans in etymologising not be severely shaken by Socrates' final results? Not at all, I respond, for several independent reasons.

First, the Heracliteanism that Socrates invokes is a Platonic interpretation or travesty, mediated doubtless by the real Cratylus, who took himself to be improving on Heraclitus by denying that one can step into the same river even once (Aristotle, *Metaph.* 4.1010a13). There is no reason to attribute to Heraclitus himself flux so radical that nothing can persist unchanged for

---

[9] 397c. But Plato, unlike the Stoics apparently, displays considerable interest in the possibility of many Greek names having a foreign origin (*Cra.* 409d).

[10] See Sedley 2003, esp. ch. 2, where the author powerfully argues that Plato considers the etymologies advanced in the *Cratylus* and in other dialogues to be exegetically sound.

[11] See my treatment of Heraclitus and Stoicism in Long 1996b: 58–84.

even a micro-second, and no reason to think that the Stoics took Heraclitus to be saying so. They would not be impressed by Plato's epistemic worries about radical Heracliteanism.

Second, Stoic etymologies are not Heraclitean in any sense that is distinctive of that philosopher, least of all as represented by Plato. Stoic etymologies signify stable features of the world, features that they probably supposed were compatible with their interpretation of Heraclitus. They were presumably familiar with his striking antithesis between the 'name' of the bow and its 'function', which trades on the fact that *bios* signifies life with one accentuation and the bow, a death-dealing instrument, with another (DK22 B48). This Heraclitean 'etymology' will have supported their recourse to 'opposition' as a principle of name-making.

Third, the Stoics could, and if Varro is evidence for their views did, agree with Plato that many of the names in contemporary usage have undergone change and deformation since they were first in circulation.[12] Hence the difficulty of matching the phonetic properties of some names to nameable features of the world is no decisive argument against the practices of the earliest name-users.

The Stoics, then, could respond that *their* etymologising is entirely consistent with *their* Heracliteanism. I suggest that they read the *Cratylus* as an encouragement to their own enterprise – of looking for meanings that could be plausibly attributed to those who first named the gods, and who had broadly correct beliefs, Stoically interpreted, about the world, which they encoded in the names they gave to divine beings.

LETTERS AND SYLLABLES

Stoic and Cratylean etymologies are a sort of phonetic dictionary. That is, they seek to explain the unknown meaning of a word by reference to the known meaning of another word that shares in some of the first word's phonetic properties. The question of primary names comes up in the dialogue when discussion turns to the alphabet (424b). Socrates proposes that if names are naturally significant, and their natural significance is conveyed by their alphabetic properties, letters themselves, the elements of names, had better be intrinsically revealing about the nature of things. Thence the suggestions that the letters *iōta, rhō* etc. are imitative of motion and are significant accordingly.

---

[12] See the passages of Varro's *De lingua latina* excerpted by Barwick 1957a: 65–9.

The Stoics saw nothing of value, I think, in this last proposal. What they hypothesised instead, according to Augustine *De dialectica* 6, is that certain words (not individual letters or syllables) affect our hearing in ways that manifest precise similarity between sound and referent.[13] In the case of *hinnitus* (whinnying), *balatus* (bleating), *clangor* (blaring) and *stridor* (grating), word-sound corresponds directly to sounds made by horses, sheep, trumpets and chains respectively: 'You clearly see that these words sound just like the actual things signified by these words.'[14] In the case of words for non-sounding things, the formative 'similarity' is 'tactile, generating names in which the smoothness or roughness of the component letters affects the hearing in ways that correspond to the smooth or harsh sensations produced for touch by the actual things' (*Sed quia sunt res quae non sonant, in his similitudinem tactus valere, ut si leniter vel aspere sensum tangunt, lenitas vel asperitas litterarum ut tangit auditum, sic eis nomina pepererit).*[15] These two kinds of 'similarity', by which we are sensuously affected as we would be by the actual things, are 'the virtual cradle of words' (*quasi cunabula verborum*).

The Stoic proposal, as characterised by Augustine, does not imply that the sound of these onomatopoetic words simply *is* its meaning.[16] You cannot tell, from hearing *clangor*, that a speaker of this word is referring to the blare of trumpets specifically; still less can you tell, simply from hearing *crux* (an example of 'similarity'), that the word signifies cross. What you can tell, according to the theory, is some salient feature of the word's referent – that it is a rough thing as distinct from something sweet, like the referent of *mel* (honey). This latter word, supposedly, affects our hearing as sweetly as honey itself affects our taste.

This theory of word formation is synaesthetic. The sound of some words affects us sensuously (agreeably or harshly etc.) in ways that supposedly

---

[13] Augustine notes that Cicero ridicules Stoic theory on the origin of words, perhaps referring to *ND* 3,61–3 where etymologies of the gods' names are mocked. On his own authority he says that the Stoics claim every word's definite origin to be explicable, to which he advances the objection of an infinite regress of explanation. Later in the chapter, however, he says that the Stoics take the origin of some words to be hidden.

[14] *Perspicis enim haec verba ita sonare ut ipsae res quae his verbis significantur.* If Augustine's examples here are Stoic, as he explicitly leads us to presume, it is worth noting that the main stream grammatical tradition cited *hinnitus, balatus* etc. as 'inarticulate sounds, not capable of being written', and hence refused to admit them as words: see the excerpts from Marius Victorinus and other grammarians in Hülser *FDS* 500–6.

[15] Varro classifed *crux* (cross) and *trux* (savage) as harsh sounds and *lana* (wool) and *luna* (moon) as smooth ones; cf. Varro fr. 113 Goetz–Schoell, cited by Sluiter 1990: 35.

[16] Hence I hesitate either to charge Augustine with misunderstanding the Stoics, or to charge the Stoics themselves with conflating meaning and referent in these cases, as Sluiter 1990: 34–6, is inclined to do.

correspond to the ways we would be actually affected by a property of the word's referent. The word *mel*, in its sweetness, sounds like the sweetness of the thing it signifies. In addition, the letter 'v' helps to form syllables containing a 'dense and powerful sound', as in such words as *vis* (force), *violens* (violent), *vincula* (chains) etc. I suggest that this theory may be plausibly interpreted as a Stoic adaptation of Socrates' proposal that letters and syllables are semantically correlated with the properties of things. That theory runs into trouble in the *Cratylus* when Socrates picks a word signifying hardness, *sklērotēs,* and containing two letters, *lambda* and *rhō,* which supposedly resemble opposite properties – softness and hardness respectively. Socrates then infers that *sklērotēs* cannot simply derive its correctness as a name from nature because its *lambda* represents the opposite of hardness (434c–e). In the *Cratylus* this wrecks the proposal that *all* the elements of a correct name must mirror the properties of the items named by them. By allowing proximity and opposition, in addition to similarity, as factors in word formation, the Stoics gave themselves the room to avoid the problems Socrates presents to Cratylus.[17] We need not say that mere convention is at work when explaining words that have a sensuous effect partly different from or even opposite to that of their significates. Some kind of affinity or proximity or even direct contrariety are principles, natural principles, in the formation or usage of certain words: e.g. *piscina* signifying a bath that actually contains no fish (*pisces*) or *bellum* (war) in contrariety to *bellus* (beautiful).

By looking to synaesthetic relationships between word and significate, rather than the direct mirroring of properties, the Stoics offer a looser but a less problematic explanation of the connection between primary word-sounds and significance. They could defend the looseness of the rationale by saying that it was never their intention to propose that meaning in general, let alone a speaker's meaning, could be reduced to the synaesthetic properties of words. Yet, there must be something about the phonetic properties of words that equips them to be expressive of meaning. Hence it is reasonable to assume that, in order to satisfy this condition, words are formed on the basis of certain rules as distinct from mere cultural conventions. The *Cratylus*, I think, stimulated the Stoics to come up with a better set of these rules than anything Socrates advances there. More importantly, however, it may have stimulated them to arrive at the most sophisticated account of meaning proposed in classical antiquity.

---

[17] Barwick 1957a: 77, suggests that Stoics after Chrysippus (he hypothesises Diogenes of Babylon) were prompted to introduce the second and third methods of word formation (proximity and opposition) as a defensive move against criticism, probably from the Academics.

SOCRATIC AND STOIC PHONETICS AND SEMANTICS

Someone reflecting on the *Cratylus* might plausibly take the dialogue to be suggesting five different positions about a name's successful, or at least intended, designation of its referent.[18]

1. *Moderate conventionalism*: speakers use the conventional names to signify their referent. According to this theory, meaning is a relation that holds between things and an agreed usage of purely conventional names. You find out what a name means by seeing what the social group who uses it are referring to. (Hermogenes I, referring to *Cra.* 384c–d)

2. *Radical conventionalism*: speakers use any name they individually like to signify their referent. According to this theory, meaning is a relation that holds between things and a non-agreed usage of arbitrary names. To know what a name means, you need to know what the individual speaker, who may be using a purely private language, is referring to. (Hermogenes II, referring to *Cra.* 385d–e)

3. *Formal naturalism*: a speaker uses names that pick out and communicate the form of the thing named. No rules are given for the phonetic requirements that such names must meet, but they will be correct 'in whatever syllables' they are expressed 'as long as they render the form of the name appropriate to each thing'. (Socrates I, referring to *Cra.* 388b–390a; 393d)[19]

4. *Etymological naturalism*: the intended correspondence of at least some names in current usage to features of the world can be ascertained by etymological analysis. Such names are phonetically derived from other words of known meaning. (Socrates II, referring to 397a ff.)

5. *Phonetic naturalism*: a speaker uses names whose constituent letters and syllables represent the properties of the thing named. (Socrates III, referring to 421d–426b)

Setting the two conventionalist theses on one side, I want to focus on their three successors. The chief interpretive problem about *formal*

---

[18] I do not mean to imply that each of these five positions could or should be read as mutually exclusive or as alternatives to each one of the others. Some take what I call Hermogenes II to be simply an extension of Hermogenes I, although I find that hard to square with the absence of any reference to agreement or social convention when Hermogenes states it at 385d 7–9. As for what I call Socrates I–III, the question of their consistency with one another is not my concern, but rather the fact that they each focus upon a distinct claim about what makes a name naturally correct.

[19] For my purpose here, I trust it is not necessary to discuss the notorious difficulties of these passages. What chiefly matters for my topic is the fact that, as Kretzmann 1971: 129, puts it, the 'model correct names' are each 'a translinguistic entity which cannot be identified with any sound or marks'. There is much to be said for the suggestions of Silverman 1992: 37–41, that a proper understanding of the meaning of such names presupposes or is a definition of the Forms that they name.

naturalism – rendering in the name the form of the name naturally appropriate to each thing (390a) – is that no rules are given for how actual words are to be constructed accordingly, i.e. what letters and syllables to use. The theory is strong in its suggestion that meaning transcends its phonetic representation: the same meaning or form can be expressed in different languages or perhaps in different words of the same language. But the theory gives us no clue about how to construct actual names that will meet its semantic requirements of separating and communicating things and doing so in ways that take account of such problems as homonymy and ambiguity. Socrates' formal naturalism has nothing specific to say about phonetics.

Etymological naturalism uses phonetics to align one or more words of known meaning with the word whose original significance is under investigation. Phonetics is here a recognitional guide to semantics, but meaning is not treated as a function of alphabetic properties. It is simply assumed that some words are self-evidently meaningful – e.g. *zēn* = to live – and that these words will explain the meaning of phonetically similar words. We are not told why or how *zēn* signifies to live.

Phonetic naturalism seeks to repair this gap by its account of the naturally representative features of individual letters. It seeks, unsuccessfully of course, to achieve a one to one correspondence between a verbal sound and its significate.

Socrates in the *Cratylus*, then, makes three contributions to language theory that leave unresolved the relation between semantics and phonetics. In particular, formal naturalism is cavalier about phonetics, while phonetic naturalism is cavalier about semantics. Hence the dialogue's aporetic conclusion: nature and convention are both admitted their role, but the relation between them is left unclear (435a–c). The problem about phonetic naturalism points in the direction of conventionalism. Yet radical conventionalism (to which Socrates had driven Hermogenes from his more moderate starting-point, *Cra.* 385d–386a) seems to make meaning and truth arbitrary, just the problem that formal naturalism seeks to overcome.

Is it reasonable to suppose that the Stoics have directly reacted to these theories and difficulties of the *Cratylus*? I see good reason to think so. For the sake of brevity and clarity, I will restrict my observations about Stoic linguistics to three crucial distinctions that they drew, between (1) signs (*sēmainonta*) and significations (*sēmainomena*), or words and meanings; (2) expressions (*lexeis*) and sentences (*logoi*); (3) word-meaning and speaker's meaning. After exemplifying these points, we shall see how they bear on the *Cratylus*.

Let us take the English locution, 'It is light', and use Stoic theory to elucidate its linguistic and semantic components.[20] The sounds or written symbols have an alphabetic structure, which means that they could be linguistic signs; their structure, moreover, is not arbitrary because they correspond to the way speakers of English utter sounds in conversation or symbolise these articulated sounds in writing. So we have an instance of a particular language use – in Stoic terminology, a *lexis* which is also a *dialektos*, i.e. a form of discourse pertaining to a specific ethnic group (D.L. 7.56). Not only does the sound or writing of 'It is light' conform to English, in its articulation of letters and syllables, it is also made up of English words – i.e. sounds or written symbols that are standardly used when English speakers or writers want to say something; and these words are syntactically related, as can be ascertained from their order and inflections. Given the fact that we have a string of sounds or written symbols that is identifiable as a grammatical structure of actual words, we have what could be a fully fledged sentence (*logos*). Can we, then, determine, whether this is so, and if so, what this structure of words is a sign of? Can we identify it as a meaningful set of sounds or written symbols and identify its meaning?

By recourse to a dictionary and a grammar book, we can determine that English speakers might utter 'It is light' when they wish to express one of at least two different thoughts they might have – either a thought about the time of day or a thought about something's weight. This combination of words, taken by itself, is significant in the sense that, irrespective of context or a particular speech act, its phonetic properties and grammatical configuration are signs of a meaning that users of English are competent to express and understand. But it is not these properties and syntax as such that confer meaning on the expression; what does so is the fact that English speakers express their thoughts to one another by using such signs and syntax as these. Independently of context, moreover, 'It is light', is completely ambiguous. In order to disambiguate these words, we need to identify the speaker's meaning.[21] Let's say that he or she wishes to express the thought that it is time to get up. They can do so by saying, 'It is light', but they could also express this thought by saying, 'Il est matin' etc.

Speakers use their words as signs for what the Stoics called *lekta* – sayables or meanings or above all statements – which they could in principle express

---

[20] For a fuller analysis of what immediately follows, see Long 1996c: 120–7. The evidence I draw on is entirely found in D.L. 7.55–9.

[21] I have no direct evidence to support this claim. However, I think it must be what the Stoic theory implies. For although a speaker's words may be ambiguous, the Stoics never seem to suggest that ambiguity pertains to the semantic content or *lekton* a speaker intends to express; see next note.

in any one of numerous languages. What they mean is what they say; and these sayables, though expressible in this or that set of words and identifiable accordingly, are not reducible to or simply identifiable with the linguistic signs that they use. And, as we have seen, their words might be ambiguous, a topic closely studied by the Stoics.[22] Word-meaning can never, then, be more than an approximate guide to speaker's meaning.

According to the Stoics, meaning is primarily a relation between a speaker or hearer and a *lekton*. The *lekton* is the meaning or fact or truth or falsehood that we express or understand by means of spoken or written language. Stoic *lekta* are neither words nor things nor thoughts in the sense of particular mental states: they are semantic and logical structures, thinkable and expressible, but objective in their availability to anyone to think and express and understand in any language.[23]

Consider the *lekton* now in relation to Socrates' formal naturalism where he invokes the Form of name as the basis for correct name-giving and name-using (390a). There we are told that a name will be well constructed if it meets the general conditions of naming (to discriminate between beings and give instruction about how they really are) and represents the form of the name *natural* to each being in 'whatever' syllables. Socrates' position here is that the semantic value of well constructed names, though they have to be formed out of appropriate material (just as a shuttle has to be), is not primarily a function of their phonetic configuration. Of first concern to the expert name-maker is the names' formal properties – their capacity to discriminate and communicate the nature of the thing that they name.

---

[22] See Atherton 1993, especially 136–9. She is clearly right to emphasise the fact that what is ambiguous, according to the Stoics, is *lexis* (in the Stoics' terminology), i.e. a linguistic utterance as understood by an audience irrespective of the speaker's intentions. If, however, when she writes: 'Signifying is something utterances do, not speakers' (162), she intends to withhold speaker's meaning from the Stoics, I disagree. (She seems to allow it on p. 467.) From D.L. 7.56 it is clear that a *logos*, an utterance which is necessarily meaningful, derives part of its semantic status from 'the thought of the one who issues it'. The position of the Stoics, with respect to word-meaning and speaker's meaning, is well stated by Frede 1994a:111, where he writes: 'A *lekton* not only is what gets said, but is also (i) what is signified by the expression used to say something, and (ii) what the speaker has in mind, what he thinks, when he utters the expression.' See Varro, *De lingua latina* 6.56 (probably reporting Chrysippus, but omitted from *SVF* 2.143): *Igitur is loquitur, qui suo loco quodque verbum sciens ponit, et is tum prolocutus, quom in animo quod habuit extulit loquendo*. See further, pp. 52–3 below.

[23] The bibliography on *lekta* is now extensive. For the basic evidence, see Long and Sedley 1987 ch. 33, and for recent discussion, Brunschwig 1994 ch. 6 and Frede 1994a. Frede makes a very persuasive case for the proposal that the primary notion of the *lekton* was 'metaphysical', having to do neither 'with the meaning of expressions, or the intentional object or content of thoughts, but with facts', and that 'on the standard notion of a *lekton* facts, true propositions, remain paradigms' (115–16). I agree, and I think that this strengthens the likelihood that, in developing the notion, they were influenced by Socrates' formal naturalism. For, however we interpret the idea that the purpose of names is to render the forms of the things named, the upshot is a thesis connecting the correctness of any name to its signification of facts. See my brief remarks in Brunschwig and Lloyd 1996: 559.

Two or more phonetically distinct names can satisfy this condition. Ergo: the truth-value of a name cannot be simply read off from its phonetic configuration. Socrates' formal naturalism is vague and embryonic, but it incorporates two crucial insights: first, that a theory of meaning cannot be given without taking account of truth; and second, that what speakers mean, including the truths that they seek to express, is not simply reducible to the phonetic features of the particular language they happen to use.

This theory surely points in the direction of Stoic *lekta* and their distinctness as semantic and logical items from the alphabetic constituents of language.[24] *Lekta*, to be sure, are not names, but Socrates' 'names', at this part of the dialogue, resemble *lekta* in being capable of being said 'truly or falsely' (385c).[25] The 'forms' that confer meaning, truth and falsehood on these names (whatever may be their relation to the so-called Theory of Forms) resemble *lekta* in being objective as distinct from psychological states of affairs (unlike Aristotle's 'mental experiences' (*pathēmata tēs psychēs, Int.* 16a6)); and if we may think of them as 'incorporeal' (which seems reasonable) their nature as such could have influenced the incorporeality assigned to Stoic *lekta*.

The suggestion that the Stoics have reflected on Socrates' formal naturalism seems to me to gain plausibility when we connect it with the fact that Socrates' other two proposals in the *Cratylus*, etymological naturalism and phonetic naturalism, were undoubtedly influential on the Stoa in the ways we have already seen. In particular, the Stoics give an account of primary word formation which echoes Socrates in its use of onomatopoeia, but also resolves the ensuing difficulty of accounting for vocalised sounds that are only proximately congruent with, or are even antithetical to, their *nominata*. If I was right in my interpretation of Augustine's evidence, the Stoics, unlike Socrates, distinguish word-meaning from word formation: the meaning of the word *crux* (cross) is not delivered or explained simply by its sound; rather, the word's sound is appropriate to but not fully constitutive of its significance.

In their logic the Stoics exhaustively studied the truth conditions and formal properties of *lekta*. In their linguistic theory, they studied the structure of words and sentences. Did they succeed, where the *Cratylus* fails,

---

[24] I am not suggesting that the Stoics' use of the term *lekton* owes anything to the *Cratylus*. In that dialogue, as distinct from the *Sophist*, Plato tends to use *onoma* as his term for any word or phrase, even though Socrates can treat *onomazein* as only a part of *legein* (387c; cf. 431b). The absence of any strict use of *onoma* for name or noun as distinct from verb is indicated by the fact that at 421e Socrates proposes to try to discover the *rhēmata* 'through which a name is said'.

[25] This important claim will be immediately prior to the 'shuttle' passage if we follow Schofield 1972 in positioning 385b2–d1 immediately after 387c5.

in finding a good balance between the formal or semantic constituents of meaningful discourse, on the one hand, and the phonetic constituents on the other hand? That is too large a question for me to answer properly here. But my summary answer is yes, for the most part.

They recognised first, that languages are rule-governed systems, and not merely conventional signs; and second, that every language incorporates a lexicon (*lexeis*) – a set of phonetically and graphically articulated signs or expressions of what we can call word-meanings.[26] Third, they recognised that every speech act involves an intentionality, with respect to its meaning, that can never be simply read off from its constituent words and *their* meanings. But words, according to the Stoics, are not arbitrarily chosen or merely conventional signs. There is a system to the formation of words, which has its roots, albeit only its roots, in the onomatopoetic capacity of speech.[27] In addition, and much more important, there is grammar. What enables words to express *lekta*, according to the Stoics, has much less to do with affinity between sound and sense than with grammatical configuration. Plato's findings in later dialogues, especially the *Sophist*, were doubtless very useful to the Stoics here, but in the *Cratylus*, by focusing only on names (albeit loosely construed), he could hardly come up with anything resembling an adequate account of sentence meaning.[28]

At the end of the *Cratylus* (438d–439d) Socrates argues that study of names is not the right route to knowledge of reality: we should try to study things in themselves rather than names, whose inventors may well have had erroneous conceptions that are reflected in their coinages of names. How would the Stoics have reacted to this observation? Notwithstanding their etymological practices, I think they would have agreed with what, very likely, is Plato's own point. Their dialectician treats studying what something is as a question quite distinct from studying what it is called (D.L. 7.83), and on one possible interpretation of that difficult text the wise man will not bother himself about investigating the correctness of the names customs have assigned to things.[29] The Stoics do not seem to make

---

[26] Both of these points, especially the second, may be read as a direct retort to Diodorus Cronus, who had identified all meaning with speaker's meaning, and thus denied the possibility of ambiguity (see Long and Sedley 1987: vol. I, 227–30). However, if my general thesis about the Stoics' close reading of the *Cratylus* is right, the two points may also be treated as a rejection of Hermogenes I and II.

[27] For convincing arguments concerning the limited role the Stoics assigned to onomatopoetics as a principle of etymology, see Allen this volume.

[28] The imprint of the *Sophist* on the Stoics' treatment of *lekta* as the meanings of declarative sentences is excellently sketched by Sedley 1996: 97–8. Notice, however, that this dialogue, unlike the *Cratylus*, has nothing to say about meaning transcending its linguistic expression.

[29] See Long and Sedley 1987: vol. II, note on 31C.

any extensive use of etymology in establishing the foundations of their system, and, very strikingly, the topic is not even mentioned by Diogenes Laertius in his treatment of their dialectic (7.43–83), which is our most comprehensive treatment of this part of their philosophy. They operate, rather, by invoking criteria of truth and by means of arguments, with a view to establishing a coherent set of true *lekta* concerning the nature of things. The Stoics were primarily interested in etymology as a back-up to their theology, believing that their own scientific views about the gods were adumbrated in the ancient names assigned to these beings.

For the sake of simplicity, I have spoken of the Stoics in this paper as though they were a monolithic group. That, of course, was far from the case. I do not think that the earliest Stoics sat down with the *Cratylus*, and appropriated and modified it *in toto*. What happened, I suggest, was much more piecemeal. They were initially attracted to it by its etymologising and perhaps because of its focus on Heraclitus. They were also stimulated, at an early stage, by Socrates' formal naturalism, and its potentiality for connecting meaning, in whatever language it is expressed, with the signification of fact. Much later probably, as their grammatical interests developed, they turned to the dialogue for its proposals about word formation. Stoic evidence on that topic, as I have mentioned, is meagre, and nothing again is said about it by Diogenes Laertius in his doxography of their theories. Under the influence of Hellenistic grammarians, and possibly challenged by the revival of interest in Plato's doctrines, some Stoic or Stoics, I conjecture, studied the dialogue as a whole, interpreting it without irony as a serious pioneering venture in linguistics. The outcome, if this is right, could explain the set of responses I have attempted to chart in this paper.

AUGUSTINE *DE DIALECTICA* 5

The *Cratylus* was a fruitful resource on language for Stoic philosophers to think with, following, as they so often did, lines of inquiry pursued by Plato's Socrates. Augustine's *De dialectica* offers us precious insights into the afterlife of Stoic linguistics. In the final part of this paper I offer a brief commentary on the fifth chapter of Augustine's treatise where the author presents a four-fold classification of the semantic items involved in discourse.[30]

---

[30] My comments are based on the edition of the text made by J. Pinborg with translation, introduction and notes by B. D. Jackson (Jackson and Pinborg 1975).

Scholars differ widely in their analysis of this material, but whatever they do with it they tend to agree on its partial novelty and sophistication.[31] I too find the passage fascinating, but I also find it, with one possible exception, thoroughly Stoic or at least largely Stoic in ultimate inspiration. Apart from wishing to show that, I also want to propose that Augustine helps to consolidate the Stoic distinction I have drawn above (pp. 45–6) between word-meaning and speaker's meaning.

Not being an Augustine specialist, I can say nothing about how this chapter bears on Augustine's epistemology and linguistics in his other writings. Some of these writings, especially *De magistro*, are relevant, but my presumption here is that the four-fold classification can be adequately discussed from within the confines of the chapter where it appears.[32]

The context

The *De dialectica* is an incomplete treatise on basic grammatical and logical features of discourse. If the work is an authentic composition by Augustine, as modern scholars have convincingly argued it to be, it will have been one of his earliest essays.[33] It begins in a school-book manner that has close affinities with the similarly entitled work of Martianus Capella.[34] In his first three chapters, which take up only a page and a half, Augustine first distinguishes simple and combined terms; then, combined terms that make statements and those not subject to truth or falsehood; and third, simple and combined statements, exemplifed by 'Every man is walking' and 'If he is walking, he is moving'. It is this third group, the simple and combined statements, that forms his main topic in *De dialectica*. The work so far already has strongly Stoic antecedents but the diffused influence of Aristotle's *Categories* and *De interpretatione* is also evident.[35]

A fourth short chapter follows, which presumably determined the plan of the largely unfinished parts of the book. Augustine sets out a two-part division of his subject-matter:

1 *De loquendo*: on speaking simple terms.
2 The part dealing with combined terms that form sentences, which he divides into three sub-divisions:

---

[31] Selections of the voluminous bibliography may conveniently be found in Jackson and Pinborg 1975, O'Daly 1987 and Stock 1996. For monographs on the text see Pépin 1976 and Ruef 1981.
[32] For Augustine's reflections of Stoicism in *De magistro*, see the outstanding article by Burnyeat 1977.
[33] See Jackson and Pinborg 1975: 1–75, and Pépin 1976: 21–60.
[34] See Jackson and Pinborg 1975: 122.   [35] See Jackson and Pinborg 1975: 121–5.

(a) *De eloquendo*: on sentences that do not express propositions.
(b) *De proloquendo*: on simple sentences that express propositions.
(c) *De proloquiorum summa*: on compound sentences that express complete conditionals.

Assuming that Augustine intended to treat all four of these divisions, his work breaks off at its tenth chapter where he discusses the ambiguity of single terms. He did not complete even that part of *De dialectica*. Chapter five, then, to which I now come, is his introduction to the first division of dialectic concerned with simple terms. We shall find, however, that although the semantic theory he sets out there is exemplified by simple terms the concepts he deploys are also pertinent to a general theory of meaning.

Outline of chapter 5

1 Definitions of *verbum* (word), *res* (thing), *signum* (sign), *loqui* (to speak) and *articulata vox* (articulate utterance).
2 Every *verbum* is a sound. Therefore, written letters are not *verba* but *signa verborum* (signs of words).
3 *Verba* concern dialectic not as sounds but as the discussible signs of things when they refer to things.
4 (a) The status of *verba* as *signa rerum* (signs of things) is not affected by the fact that *verba* themselves are *res;* for the mind recognises and distinguishes their dual status.
  (b) If a *verbum* is uttered *propter se*, i.e. with a view to some question being asked about the *verbum* itself, it is the *res* subject to investigation; but we call the *res* in this case a *verbum*.
5 Whatever is perceived by the mind as distinct from the ears and is held enclosed (*inclusum*) in the mind itself is called *dicibile* (sayable).
6 A *verbum* that is uttered not *propter se* but *propter aliud aliquid significandum* (for the sake of signifying something else) is called *dictio*.
7 The thing itself, as distinct from the *verbum* or the *verbi in mente conceptio* (the conception of a word in the mind), is called *res* in the strict sense.
8 The items designated by 4–7 need to be kept distinct.
9 (a) *Verbum* is both a *verbum* and signifies a *verbum*.
  (b) *Dicibile* is a *verbum*, yet it does not signify a *verbum* but what is understood in the *verbum* and contained in the mind.
  (c) *Dictio* is a *verbum* but it signifies both (a) and (b), meaning that which takes place in the mind through the *verbum*.
  (d) *Res* is a *verbum* which signifies whatever is left over from the significance signified by 9 (a)–(c).

10 Examples of 9 by means of *arma* (arms or weapons):

  (a) In asking 'What part of speech is *arma* ?' the italicised *verbum* and it alone is spoken for its own sake=4(b), whereas 'What part of speech is' is spoken for the sake of that *verbum*.

  (b) *Verba* that are perceived in the mind prior to utterance are *dicibilia* = 5/9(b).

  (c) When uttered these *dicibilia* become *dictiones*. Thus, when uttered by Virgil, as distinct from the grammarian, *arma* was a *dictio*; it was not said *propter se* but to signify the wars waged by Aeneas or the hero's weapons.

  (d) These wars or weapons, which could be ostensively indicated or touched, if they were now actual (irrespective of their being thought about), are *res* in the strict sense.

Analysis and Stoic antecedents

1 Dicibile *(sayable)*

Unlike some commentators, I find *dicibile* the least problematic term in Augustine's four-fold classification. The word is not attested before him and only a couple of times in neo-Latin;[36] but I see no reason to doubt that it refers to the Stoic *lekton*, and does so with a more accurate translation than all the more familiar Latin renderings of that term, including Seneca's string of versions: *enuntiativum, effatum, enuntiatum* and *edictum* (*Ep.* 117.13). All of these renderings are appropriate to designate a complete *lekton,* or an *axiōma* which has been expressed; but they are ill suited to render the modality of *lekton,* as meaning 'sayable' or 'what can be said', or to encompass 'deficient *lekta'* (predicates without a subject) or the significance of expressions in general.[37]

Augustine does not define *dicibile* by reference to its 'subsistence in accordance with a rational impression', nor does he characterise it as incorporeal.[38] But the way he does define it, as 'that which is perceived by and contained in the mind and understood in the *verbum*' (5/9(b)), corresponds very closely with the Stoic testimony given by Sextus Empiricus: 'the actual thing revealed by the vocal sound and which we apprehend as

---

[36] *Dicibilis* is not found in Lewis and Short or the *Oxford Latin Dictionary*. It is used to translate *lekton* by William of Moerbeke according to Kretzmann 1970: 773 n. 7, and see Jackson and Pinborg 1975: 126–7.

[37] In offering *arma* as an example of a *dicibile*, Augustine (like S.E. *M.* 8.12), ignores what I take to be the strict Stoic doctrine, according to which the meaning of a single noun is not a *lekton* but a *ptōsis*: see Long 1971a: 104–6.

[38] For this apparently standard definition, see D.L. 7.63 (LS 33F) and S.E. *M.* 8.70 (LS 33C).

it subsists in association with our thought' (*M.* 8.12(LS 33B)). Augustine's language, it is true, may suggest that he takes the *dicibile* to be something psychological rather than purely logical or semantic, but *animo tenetur inclusum/continetur* (5/9(b)) is too vague to warrant a very precise interpretation of his claim.[39] Perhaps, like some moderns, he viewed the *dicibile/ lekton* as a mind-dependent entity, but what his language emphasises, in my view, is the idea that the *dicibile* as distinct from the *verbum* is something purely mental in its content and apprehension, irrespective of its metaphysical status. I am inclined to interpret his description of the *dicibile* as 'being held in the mind enclosed' (*inclusum*) (5) as a mark of its privacy as distinct from the publicly audible *verbum*.

2 Res

Augustine's scheme is structured throughout by his distinction between the shared status that all his four terms have as verbal sounds, and their distinctive status as signifiers. We may, as some have done, see an anticipation here of the modern distinction between the 'mention' and the 'use' of words; but what I take us to have historically is an application of the Stoic distinction between the utterance of words (*propheresthai* or *loqui*) and the use of words to signify something (*legein* or *proloqui*).[40]

Of particular interest in this regard is Augustine's treatment of *res*. As 'the thing itself', i.e. the extra-linguistic referent, his *res* corresponds exactly to the Stoic *tunchanon* (S.E. *M.* 8.11–12 (LS 33B)). However, Augustine (9(d)) also assigns *res* the intriguing status of a *verbal* signifier that does not signify verbally (i.e. via the mind's understanding of a meaning) but by its capacity literally to point or touch. Here (following his examples in 10(d)) we seem to have something very close to the celebrated passage in the *Confessions* (1.8) with which Wittgenstein begins his *Philosophical Investigations*. Augustine explains there that he first learnt the meaning of words by observing the bodily movements and facial expressions of people when they uttered sounds that indicated their intention to point to things. I take it, then, that a *res verbum* could be exemplified by Wittgenstein's 'slab' accompanied by, or at least implying, direct touch of the slab or a gesture of pointing at it.

Our evidence for the Stoics' interest in deictic reference is confined to their analysis of the truth-value of 'definite' or 'demonstrative' propositions

---

[39] See Atherton 1993: 294 n. 68, who says that 'the claim that the *dicibile* is contained in the mind gives it a different, psychological, status from that of the *lekton*, which supervenes on certain sorts of impressions'.

[40] See D.L. 7.57 and my n. 23 above.

in sentences introduced by a pronoun such as 'this one' (*houtos*).[41] They would hardly have counted *houtos* as a *res* in Augustine's sense, and we would expect them to say that a word like 'slab' signifies verbally, in the way that appellatives (*prosēgoriai*) in general do. However, I suspect that his *res verbum* is not about deictic reference as such; it concerns, as he says, the significance 'left over from the significance signified by *verbum, dicibile*, and *dictio*' (9(d)). After all, the *res* is strictly 'the thing itself'. Presumably, then, what the *res* as a word signifies ostensively or by touch is the external thing in all its particularity and actual texture – something that language can never completely signify or the mind take in.

The Stoics may lie behind this interesting thought, but the closest I can find to their saying something like it is Zeno's observation that even a *kataleptic* impression does not grasp all of an object's properties (Cicero, *Acad.* 1.42).

3 Verbum

Augustine's *verbum* taken generally is a word, i.e. an articulated sound that is 'the sign of a thing' (4(a)). Assuming a Stoic background, how should we identify his *verbum* when it appears within the four-fold distinctions of my sections 9–10 above? Should we opt for *lexis* or for *logos*? The answer surely is *lexis*, defined in Stoicism as 'articulate sound, such as *hēmera*' (day) (D.L. 7.56).[42] It is true, of course, that the scope of Stoic *lexis* extends over any articulate expression, including the paradigmatic meaningless sound *blituri* (D.L. 7.57), and hence is not *necessarily* a verbal sign, as is Augustine's *verbum*. But a meaningless word is still a word. It is quite wrong to say that 'Stoic *lexis* is an articulate but non-significant sound';[43] rather, *blituri* registers the exceptional case. The Stoics plainly thought that *lexeis* in general are the meaningful words that form the lexicon of any language. However, *lexeis*, taken by themselves, do not express someone's particular thought. In order to do that, they need to be made into a *logos*, defined as: 'a signifying sound issuing from thought, such as "It is day"' (D.L. 7.56).

In this paper I previously (p. 48) characterised *lexis* as the Stoics' term to pick out words when we ask what a word, as distinct from a speaker, means. We can also, of course, ask phonetic or grammatical questions about a *lexis*, as Augustine does in his example of speaking a word 'for its own sake' (10(a)). But I see no reason why 'speaking a word for its own sake' should not include such questions as 'What does *feline* mean?' or 'What is

[41] S.E. *M.* 8.98 (LS 34H), D.L. 7.70 (LS 34K). [42] As proposed by Haller 1962: 93.
[43] So Jackson and Pinborg 1975: 125.

the French word for *cat*?' Augustine says that a *verbum* signifies a *verbum* (9(a)), and an illustration of that claim (given his general definition of the *verbum* as a sign of things, where things can include words) would be that *feline* means '*cat*'. I don't think this suggestion breaches his distinction between *verbum* and *dictio* (6) because, in my example, *feline* is not being uttered in order to signify something else (i.e. something non-linguistic), but 'for its own sake'.

4 Dictio

If *verbum* in the four-fold scheme most closely corresponds to Stoic *lexis*, the obvious Stoic candidate for Augustine's *dictio* is *logos*. We have just noted the Stoic definition of *logos* as a meaningful speech act. I conjecture that Augustine or his Roman source chose *dictio* because, as a *nomen actionis*, it excellently conveys the import of speaking what is in one's mind.

Augustine says that a *dictio* (9(c)) is a *verbum* that signifies both a *verbum* (in the sense of 9(a)) and a *dicibile* (9(b)).[44] Given my previous translations into Stoic terms, I interpret him to be saying that a speech act or *logos* signifies both (or better, signifies the conjunction of) a *lexis* in the sense of a semantically charged expression(s) and the specific *lekton* which the speaker has in mind and means to say. That, I submit, is precisely what the Stoic terms and theory, or for that matter any good semantic theory, should involve. The words that we use in order to converse and think have meanings independently of our immediate thoughts and intentions; otherwise they would not be available to us as our lexicon. But we use them to express *lekta* that are not themselves reducible to words even though words are the signs by which we express what we think.

I conclude, then, by admiring Augustine for a highly intelligent (albeit compressed) rendition of Stoic semantics. Given the paucity of our Stoic sources, I would favour including *De dialectica* chapter 5 as well as chapter 6 (on the origin of words) in a future collection of Stoic material on language.

---

[44] Hence I don't quite agree with Burnyeat 1977: 11, that Augustine uses *dictio* for 'the word considered along with its meaning . . . in contrast to *verbum* or the word as sound'. For while the *verbum* (and the *dictio* too) are sounds, Augustine is explicitly not concerned with words as sounds at the point (9(a)–(c)) where he distinguishes *verbum* from *dictio*.

CHAPTER 3

Epicurus and his predecessors on the origin of language*

Alexander Verlinsky

Epicurus' theory of the origin of language has been investigated many times, both in the context of his general theory of the origin of culture and in its own right. Among the various aspects of his theory that have attracted attention, the epistemological has played the most important role. What I try to provide here is not a complete account of the successes and limitations of previous studies, but an outline of Epicurus' theory about the development of language as it can be reconstructed from his own writings and from other relevant texts. In trying to elucidate the details, I will concentrate on some which are controversial and others which have gone altogether unnoticed by scholars. It is, of course, possible that some of the texts I shall use to throw light on the less clear aspects of Epicurus' theory may reflect nothing more direct than the *influence* of Epicurean ideas. I hope I shall manage to use such evidence with suitable caution. As the title of this chapter suggests, my subject includes the relation of Epicurus to his predecessors. I will discuss this mainly from the point of view just mentioned, by asking what is known of the stages of development of human language discerned by thinkers before Epicurus.

I EVIDENCE

Our main evidence for Epicurus' theory of the origin of language is the passage of his *Letter to Herodotus* 75–6, which represents a concise version

* This is a revised and expanded version of the paper presented at the Ninth Symposium Hellenisticum. I am grateful to participants for their helpful comments in discussion and afterwards. Versions of one or another parts of this paper were read on various occasions in St Petersburg, and the comments of my colleagues there have been helpful in refining my argument on a number of specific points. I am grateful to Stephen Wheeler for his assistance with my English expression in the first draft, and to Alastair Blanshard who helped to overcome some linguistic difficulties in the final stage. I owe a special debt to David Sedley, both for his valuable comments and for correcting of my English in the revised version. It goes without saying that all remaining mistakes are mine. The Alexander von Humboldt foundation generously supported my stay in Berlin in Summer 2001, when I worked on this paper. It was completed in the extremely congenial environment of the Center for Hellenic Studies (Washington, D.C.).

of the relevant section of book 12 of his *On Nature*;[1] this text discusses the natural origin of names in relation to a two-stage theory of the development of civilisation, their further development at the rational stage, and the origin and development of the words for 'things not [previously] taken into consideration' (οὐ συνορώμενα πράγματα). Lucretius' account of the natural origin of names (*De rerum natura* 5.1028–90), which, like Epicurus' own, forms a part of the history of civilisation, does not include the second, rational stage of the development of language and does not mention 'things not previously taken into consideration'. Nevertheless, this passage of Lucretius, which like the philosophical contents of *De rerum natura* generally, has roots in Epicurus' *On Nature*,[2] supplies confirmation for the idea of the natural connection between words and objects, which is only implicit in the *Letter to Herodotus*. I shall try to show that Lucretius 5.1028–9 refers to the development of human sounds from their spontaneous utterance into conscious use for the designation of things, and that another passage (5.1019–23) confirms this interpretation and also hints at the historical development of the articulation of sounds; the latter passage has no analogue in the mainstream Epicurean tradition, but finds a striking parallel in the treatise of Agatharchides, who presumably used an Epicurean source. A short account in Diogenes of Oenoanda's epitome of Epicurean physics (fr. 12 Smith 1993) also omits the second stage, but contains some arguments against the hypothesis of the invention of language which are missing in Lucretius. Special attention is due to the account of the two-stage development of language in Ptolemy's *On the Criterion* (4.2–6), which in spite of some reservations can be used as evidence for the Epicurean theory, and is especially important for the second stage, neglected by other sources.

2 THE EVOLUTIONIST PREDECESSORS OF EPICURUS

At least one element of the theory of the spontaneous origin of language was well known long before Epicurus. From the middle of the fifth century BC,

[1] On the composition of Epicurus' *magnum opus* and its relation to the two epitomes of this treatise, the *Letter to Herodotus* and *The Letter to Pythocles*, see Sedley 1984: 381–7, at 387, and his recent book, cited in the next note; cf. the table of content of the *On Nature* in Erler 1994: 96; 98.

[2] This was argued persuasively by David Sedley in Sedley 1998a. More specifically, it is plausible that Lucretius' and Diogenes of Oenoanda's polemics against the theory of the invention of language, as well as very similar arguments against the theories of the invention of religion used by Sextus Empiricus in *M*. 9.30–3, go back to book 12 of *On Nature*, in which Epicurus argued, in connection with his theory of the origin of culture, both against the idea that language arose due to *thesis* (*Ep. Hdt.* 75) and against the idea of Critias that the gods were invented (Philod. *De piet* 1.8.225–31; 19.519–41 Obbink 1996 = [27.1, 2] Arrighetti 1973), see Kleve 1963: 104–7, and Verlinsky 1998.

or perhaps somewhat earlier, an idea began to prevail that the first stage of
the human language was characterised by animal-like sounds, which were
gradually articulated and assigned to things. This idea is represented in
explicit form in the Protagorean theory of Plato's *Protagoras* (322a). Man
'quickly articulated voice and names with skill' (φωνὴν καὶ ὀνόματα ταχὺ
διηρθρώσατο τῇ τέχνῃ).[3]

The emergence of human language is mentioned in Sophocles' *Antigone*
(staged in the 440s): '[man] has taught himself speech, thought swift as
the wind and practices designed to protect the state' (καὶ φθέγμα καὶ
ἀνεμόεν/φρόνημα καὶ ἀστυνόμους/ὀργὰς ἐδιδάξατο, 354–6). It is probable that φθέγμα means specifically the phonetic aspect of developed
human language, thus implying evolution from unarticulated to articulated sounds.[4]

To turn to theistically coloured theories, Theseus in Euripides' *Suppliant
Women* (420s) while attributing to an unnamed god various gifts which
helped human beings to rise from their animal-like state also mentions the
predisposition to articulated speech (201–4):

αἰνῶ δ' ὃς ἡμῖν βίοτον ἐκ πεφυρμένου
καὶ θηριώδους θεῶν διεσταθμήσατο,
πρῶτον μὲν ἐνθεὶς σύνεσιν, εἶτα δ' ἄγγελον
γλῶσσαν λόγων δούς, ὥστε γιγνώσκειν ὄπα.

I praise the god who created an ordered life out of a chaotic and brutish one, by
endowing us, first, with reason, and by giving us, then, a tongue, a messenger of
words, so that we are able to distinguish sounds.

Euripides, on the one hand, considers the primitive stage to be chaotic
and brutal; on the other hand, it is evident that the tongue as the
physiological instrument of speech could only be given simultaneously

---

[3] I suppose that διαρθρόω normally going with φωνήν here forms some sort of *zeugma* with ὀνόματα.
The sense is that man articulated sounds and thus created words, rather than that two different kinds
of articulation are implied (it may be, as André Laks suggested to me, that ὀνόματα διηρθρώσατο
means specifically the process assigning words to things, but I see it rather as implied than as
expressed explicitly). The authenticity of Plato's representation of Protagoras' doctrine has been
often questioned (e.g. by Cherniss 1977: 269; Friedländer 1964: 1, 378 n. 7; Dodds 1973: 9), but for a
defence of the Protagorean character of the ideas and even of the form of the fable see: Müller 1967
(1999): 253–77 (esp. 254–8); B. Manuwald 1996: 102–31. For my present purpose it is sufficient that
the idea of the evolution of human sounds was known in Plato's time, but one can see an indication of
Protagorean authorship in the evident lack of interest in this idea in Plato's writings (it is significantly
absent from the *Cratylus*).

[4] φθέγμα is an unusual designation of the human language, but Euripides refers to animal nature as
ἄφθογγον (E. *Tr.* 671), implying unarticulated sounds (cf. the analogous usage of *mutum* in Latin).
Probably, it was the same contrast between unarticulated sounds of animals and articulated words of
human beings that made Sophocles use this expression.

with man's creation.[5] Hence, it can be inferred that the inborn ability to articulate sounds, which was granted to human beings as a part of providential care, only later developed into speech. The ability to distinguish spoken sounds (and, hence, to understand others) turns out, according to Euripides, to be a consequence of the fortunate construction of man's speech organs (in this theory man's inborn intelligence might also be considered as a feature helping man to distinguish sounds, i.e. to hold in memory multiple variations of sounds and their meaning).

These concise narratives make it clear that the difference between animal sounds and human language, and, analogously, between the primitive and the developed stages of human speech, was understood on the one hand in terms of articulation, that is distinctness of sounds, and on the other in terms of semantic value: the unarticulated sounds of animals and primitive human beings were not related to objects, whereas in developed human language articulated sounds are assigned to things and refer to them. Only Aristotle specifically emphasises the difference between the emotive character of animal sounds and the conceptual character of human language (*Pol.* 1253a9–15). It is, however, probable that this difference, perhaps in a vaguer form, had been recognised already in earlier speculations, for unarticulated sounds can evidently have only an emotional value. (Of course, the unarticulated sounds of primitive man could be considered to have not only an expressive, but also a communicative character, for it is easy to imagine that animals can communicate with each other. Such was for example the opinion of Aristotle at *Pol.* 1253a12–14, who opposed the emotive sounds of animals to the conceptual language of humans, but at the same time recognised that there is communication among animals on an emotional level, that is about pleasure and pain.)

It is not easy to decide exactly how the development of language in these theories was viewed. We know of no suggestions about what motivated the first people to articulate sounds and then to attach them to objects. This process might be simply understood as the fulfilment of a social need that emerged from the growing complexity of human relations. But the condensed versions of the theories available to us stress only the starting and finishing points of the development.

---

[5] Another possibility is that man possessed developed speech from the beginning, and that due to this divine gift he could attain the other goods of civilisation. This is possible, but the description of primitive human life as θηριώδης suggests rather the absence of articulated speech. γλῶσσα evidently means tongue and not language, as the majority of scholars rightly assume: it has the latter meaning only when it designates a specific language, not linguistic ability as such. Hence, it seems that Euripides means a predisposition to articulate sounds, for which process the tongue was usually considered the main instrument, and not their actual articulation.

We also possess three later narratives depicting the origin of human culture (from Diodorus Siculus, Vitruvius and Lactantius), for which some scholars, notably T. Cole,[6] suggested a Democritean provenance. Lactantius' passage differs from Diodorus and Vitruvius in that he represents an immediate beginning of both society and linguistic communication, whereas Diodorus and Vitruvius presuppose the existence of (at least rudimentary) social bonds. Lactantius' narrative, which comes from a source inimical to utilitarian explanations of the origin of language and society, looks like a schematic condensation of the original doctrine.[7] What, however, unites all three narratives, is that they represent a non-teleological and non-theological vein of explanation of language. At the same time they describe the origin of language by the imposition of names, and in Diodorus and Vitruvius the relationship between words and objects is stated explicitly to be accidental. In this they differ importantly from Epicurus' theory, the most notable representative of non-teleological and non-theological explanations of culture in the Hellenistic period. This general consideration is, for me, an important argument in favour of the Reinhardt–Cole hypothesis of the Democritean provenance of the doctrines in Diodorus and Vitruvius (Lactantius is more problematic), however modified they might be due to the intermediate sources.[8] But it is important for present purposes only that these narratives follow the pattern known from the evidence of fifth-century theories: human language develops from unarticulated sounds, through articulation, into words assigned to things.

τῆς φωνῆς δ' ἀσήμου καὶ συγκεχυμένης οὔσης ἐκ τοῦ κατ' ὀλίγον διαρθροῦν τὰς λέξεις, καὶ πρὸς ἀλλήλους τιθέντας σύμβολα περὶ ἑκάστου τῶν ὑποκειμένων γνώριμον σφίσιν αὐτοῖς ποιῆσαι τὴν περὶ ἁπάντων ἑρμηνείαν. τοιούτων δὲ συστημάτων γινομένων καθ' ἅπασαν τὴν οἰκουμένην, οὐχ ὁμόφωνον πάντας ἔχειν τὴν διάλεκτον, ἑκάστων ὡς ἔτυχε συνταξάντων τὰς λέξεις· διὸ καὶ

---

[6] Cole 1990: 60–9. His main predecessor was Reinhardt 1912, whose arguments Cole tries to maintain and expand against the criticism of Spoerri 1959; the main predecessor of Spoerri in this criticism was Dahlmann 1928.

[7] According to Brandt 1890 ad loc. and Brandt 1891: 243–4, Lactantius borrowed this utilitarian theory from Lucretius, whose poem was certainly known to him, and modified it freely; see also Heck 1966: 92. But the differences between the two theories are significant, and as far as concerns the origin of language it is improbable that development from gestures to signifying sounds, only implicit in Lucretius, could have impelled Lactantius to invent the whole explanatory episode. That Lactantius followed a theory close to the one used by Diodorus was already, before Cole, claimed by Westphalen 1957: 36–48 (who argues in favour of the Democritean provenance of these ideas) and by Spoerri 1959: 156–8 (who argues against this provenance).

[8] It is perhaps better to speak about one tradition according to which language arose gradually due to cooperation of people in their everyday activities rather than to try to restore the doctrine as it was represented in the original source of this view.

παντοίους τε ὑπάρξαι χαρακτῆρας διαλέκτων καὶ τὰ πρῶτα γενόμενα συστήματα τῶν ἁπάντων ἐθνῶν ἀρχέγονα γενέσθαι. (D.S. 1.8.3–4)

While the sounds [of the first people] were indistinct and confused, they began gradually to make, by the way of articulation, words, and by imposing for each other designations for each object before them, they thus discovered expressions for everything. And, since such tribes were dispersed over all the inhabited world and each of them imposed the words at random, they had not one and the same language. This is the origin of the various kinds of articulated languages, the groupings which emerged originally having become ancestors of all nations.

in eo hominum congressu cum profundebantur aliter[9] spiritu voces, cotidiana consuetudine vocabula ut obtigerant constituerunt, deinde significando res saepius in usu ex eventu fari fortuito coeperunt et ita sermones inter se procreaverunt. (Vitr. *De arch.* 2.1.1.)

When in this band of [primitive] men meaningless sounds were uttered through grunts, they began to impose words at random in their everyday associations, and then, by signifying things [by words] more and more frequently, they due to chance event began to speak and thus created conversation amongst themselves.

Vitruvius thus represents the initial stage of unarticulated sounds, the subsequent arbitrary (cf. Diodorus) assignment of them to things (with their articulation implied), and the unusual progression from signifying single objects to continuous speech.[10] When describing the discovery of fire just before the passage cited, Vitruvius also mentions the use of gestures before the stage of articulated semantic sounds: *cum animadvertissent commoditatem esse magnam corporibus, ad ignis teporem . . . alios adducebant et nutu monstrantes ostendebant quas haberent ex eo utilitates* ('When they perceived that the advantage was great from the heat of the fire . . . they brought others and pointing it out by signs they showed what advantages they had from it').[11]

---

[9] The reading *aliter* is doubtful and has been variously emended, see Spoerri 1959: 141 n. 31; Cole 1990: 33 n. 10. It may, however, reflect ἄλλως of the Greek original (*'without purpose'*, *'in vain'*), as was suggested to me by Alexander Gavrilov, and, if so, mean the purely emotive using of sounds, without any intention to designate things, cf. the single *aliter* in Goetz and Gundermann 1888: ii, 394.9: *aliter video* = παραβλέπω (see *TLL* i, 1654.4–5); Tryph. *Dig.* 41.1.63.3: *nihil agens, sed aliter ambulans* (it is supposed that *aliter* in this passage translates the Greek ἄλλως, *TLL* i, 1653.78). For *voces profundere* as an expression for uttering of inarticulate sounds cf. Cic. *ND* 2.149, cited by Cole: *lingua . . . vocem immoderate profusam fingit et terminat.*

[10] I disagree with the attempt of Cole 1990: 60 n. 1 to harmonise the last stage of evolution represented in Vitruvius with Diodorus.

[11] Gestures are not mentioned in the episode, which is narrated by Diodorus (1.3.3) in the Egyptian part of his book closely resembling Vitruvius (see Cole 1990: 183f.), for the surrounding context is modified (by Diodorus himself rather than by his source, as Cole assumes), and the Egyptian Hephaestus is represented as an inventor of fire, instead of an anonymous member of the speechless human herd as in Vitruvius.

alii eos homines, qui sint ex terra primitus nati, cum per silvas et campos erraticam degerent vitam nec ullo inter se sermonis aut iuris vinculo cohaererent, sed ... bestiis et fortioribus animalibus praedae fuisse commemorant, tum eos, qui aut laniati effugerant, aut laniari proximos viderant, admonitos periculi sui ad alios homines decucurrisse, praesidium implorasse et primo nutibus voluntatem suam signifi- casse, deinde sermonis initia temptasse ac singulis quibusque rebus nomina impri- mendo paulatim loquendi perfecisse rationem. (Lact. *Inst. Div.* 6.10.13–14)

The supporters of one doctrine of the origin of human society assume that the humans, who in the beginning were born from the soil, led a wandering life, and were not connected by bonds either of language or of justice, but . . . served as food for the wild animals, who overpowered them. [These writers suppose] that further some humans, who either, wounded themselves, managed to escape [from the beasts], or who saw the beasts lacerate their relatives, having become apprised of their danger, ran to some other people and asked for help. At first, they signified their wish by gestures, but then tried to begin speaking and by imposing names on each particular thing they gradually created the art of speech.

One important element, not attested before Plato's *Cratylus* (385d–e), is the explanation in Diodorus of the multiplicity of languages by referring to the arbitrary character of the imposition of names in primitive commu- nities. It must be noted, however, that the arbitrary relation of words to objects is attested for Democritus, although not directly in the context of the origin of language (Procl. *In Crat.* 16. p. 6.20–7.16 Pasquali = DK68 B26 = fr. 563 Luria).

It is interesting, further, that two of the narratives, namely those of Vitruvius and Lactantius, accept gestures as a primitive kind of commu- nication, implying evidently that sounds, which were not yet articulated and not assigned to objects, had a primarily or even exclusively expressive function. As mentioned earlier, such a strict distinction is not attested for the earliest speculation on the subject. Perhaps, the greater attention to ges- tures as a specifically human means of communication suggested a contrast between the emotive function of primitive unarticulated sounds and the designating function of articulated words.[12]

---

[12] As far as I know the earliest passage describing the language of gestures as a natural way of com- munication, that might have been used if people had not had spoken language, is *Cra.* 422e–423b. Plato does not have in view the evolution from gesture to sound, but stresses that gesture is the only way to communicate for those whose organs of speech are damaged. It is easy to see that the use of gestures by the dumb could (a) suggest the role of gestures in an evolutionary account, for those who think that the speech organs of the first humans were not adequately developed, as in the Epicurean theory (see below), and (b) minimise their importance for those theories which take for granted that the organ of articulation of the first human beings was sufficiently developed from the beginning. It is also worth noting – bearing in mind the Epicurean theory – that gestures for Plato are mimetic (= descriptive) designations of unseen objects, while Lucretius means that gestures naturally refer to observed objects without being descriptions of them.

Another remarkable feature of these later narratives is the attempt to represent the gradual development of language and to explain it by specific accidental situations which first suggested to people a new means of communication.[13] Lactantius depicts the situation when humans began for the first time to use sounds to designate objects instead of relying only on gestures. Vitruvius, further, seems to explain the development from previously posited, isolated designations of things to connected speech. The dependence of these rather unusual evolutionary elements on theories that existed before the time of Epicurus cannot be proved, although some details of his own theory look like an accommodation to or reaction against these explanations of language evolution (see below). If we take into account how little we know about theories of the development of culture in the fifth and fourth centuries BC, the possibility that Epicurus was acquainted with some earlier attempts to investigate the causes of the development of language cannot be neglected.

3 THE MOTIVATION OF EPICURUS' NATURALISTIC THEORY OF THE ORIGIN OF LANGUAGE

Two main reasons for assuming the spontaneous origin of words have usually been suggested. First, that it was important for Epicurus to maintain the non-subjective, constant relation of words to objects, thereby making the word an immediate tool of research, without searching for definitions as a prerequisite of an investigation.[14] Second, that the thesis of the natural origin of language, as well as of other aspects of civilisation, excluded divine intervention in the development of civilisation and thus helped us to attain *ataraxia*.[15] Both explanations are plausible, and do not exclude each other. It must, however, be considered in addition that, although the absurdity of the idea of the divine inventor is mentioned by Diogenes of Oenoanda, the argumentation used by both him and Lucretius is directed against the hypothesis of a *human* inventor. The main epistemological foundation of this polemic is that nothing can be invented as such without an analogy in our experience. Invention as a rational act can thus only be possible as an improvement on something that previously existed.[16] The development of

---

[13] Cole 1990: 62; 67 rightly emphasises this tendency of the discussed theories, as far as it concerns the factors of development, and contrasts it with the naturalistic automatism of the development according to Epicurus' theory. He does, however, underestimate the gradualist character of the development of language in the latter theory; see below.

[14] Long and Sedley 1987: I, 101.   [15] B. Manuwald 1980: 5–6; Hossenfelder 1996: 218.

[16] This epistemological aspect becomes especially clear if one compares the polemics in Lucretius against the invention of language, and Sextus' polemics against the invention of religion (*M.* 9.30–3), probably going back to Epicurus' *On Nature*, see above n. 2.

language was regarded by Epicurus (*Ep. Hdt.* 75) as a paradigm case for the general evolution of culture. Hence, it is possible that one of the reasons for his naturalism in the theory of language was his attempt to explain, evidently for the first time, all peculiar human features which could not be explained as imitation of animal behaviour and of natural processes, as the development and combination of inborn abilities, not controlled by the activities of the intellect.

4 EPICURUS, *EPISTULA AD HERODOTUM* 75–6 (= LS 19A)

Ἀλλὰ μὴν ὑποληπτέον καὶ τὴν φύσιν πολλὰ καὶ παντοῖα ὑπὸ αὐτῶν πραγμάτων διδαχθῆναί τε καὶ ἀναγκασθῆναι· τὸν δὲ λογισμὸν τὰ ὑπὸ ταύτης παρεγγυηθέντα ὕστερον ἐπακριβοῦν καὶ προσεξευρίσκειν ἐν μέν τισι θᾶττον, ἐν δέ τισι βραδύτερον καὶ ἐν μέν τισι περιόδοις καὶ χρόνοις [ἀπὸ τῶν ἀπὸ τοῦ ἀπείρου] <κατὰ μείζους ἐπιδόσεις>, ἐν δέ τισι κατ' ἐλάττους. ὅθεν καὶ τὰ ὀνόματα ἐξ ἀρχῆς μὴ θέσει γενέσθαι, ἀλλ' αὐτὰς τὰς φύσεις τῶν ἀνθρώπων καθ' ἕκαστα ἔθνη ἴδια πασχούσας πάθη καὶ ἴδια λαμβανούσας φαντάσματα ἰδίως τὸν ἀέρα ἐκπέμπειν στελλόμενον ὑφ' ἑκάστων τῶν παθῶν καὶ τῶν φαντασμάτων, ὡς ἄν ποτε καὶ ἡ παρὰ τοὺς τόπους τῶν ἐθνῶν διαφορὰ ᾖ· ὕστερον δὲ κοινῶς καθ' ἕκαστα ἔθνη τὰ ἴδια τεθῆναι πρὸς τὸ τὰς δηλώσεις ἧττον ἀμφιβόλους γενέσθαι ἀλλήλαις καὶ συντομωτέρως δηλουμένας· τινὰ δὲ καὶ οὐ συνορώμενα πράγματα εἰσφέροντας τοὺς συνειδότας παρεγγυῆσαί τινας φθόγγους τοὺς ἀναγκασθέντας ἀναφωνῆσαι, τοὺς δὲ τῷ λογισμῷ ἑλομένους κατὰ τὴν πλείστην αἰτίαν οὕτως ἑρμηνεῦσαι.[17]

(75) We must take it that even nature was educated and constrained in many different ways by actual states of affairs, and that its lessons were made later more accurate, and augmented with new discoveries by reason faster among some people, slower among others, and in some ages and eras <by greater leaps>, in others by smaller leaps. Thus names too did not originally come into being by imposition, but men's own natures underwent feelings and received impressions which varied peculiarly from tribe to tribe, and each of the individual feelings and impressions caused them to exhale breath peculiarly, in accordance with the different location of each tribe. (76) Later, particular coinings were imposed within the individual races, so as to make the designations less ambiguous and more concisely expressed. And those people who comprehended the things which previously were not taken into consideration, introduced words which they were constrained to utter, while other people, having chosen among these words with the help of reason, thus created usage that corresponded to the main cause of the uttering of such words. (tr. Long and Sedley with considerable changes)

---

[17] On the whole I follow the version of the text in Von der Mühll 1922. I retain, however, ἀλλήλαις of **BP** and **F** (corr.; ἀλλήλους **F**) after ἀμφιβόλους γενέσθαι, following in this Long and Sedley 1987: II, 98 (most editors including Von der Mühll accept Meibom's emendation ἀλλήλοις).

This passage is the only remnant of Epicurus' theory of the origin of culture, otherwise known to us through extracts from his successor Hermarchus in Porphyry's *On Abstinence*, some passages in the treatises of Philodemus, and above all the detailed narrative in Lucretius, which may be treated as a reliable representation of Epicurus' ideas on this subject (see above n. 2). Epicurus starts by formulating the general principle of the two-stage development of culture, and exemplifies it further with the help of his doctrine of the origin of language. According to this two-stage pattern, which also dominates other Epicurean discussions concerning the beginning of culture,[18] all attainments represent at first the simple reactions of human nature to external influences, or the imitation of what humans find in their environment. In the later stage these acquisitions are supplemented by rational refinement and additional discoveries (Epicurus obviously avoids calling the achievements of the earlier stage 'discoveries'). I shall assume in what follows that Epicurus treated the natural and rational stages as two successive chronological phases,[19] and not that he simply assumed two phases for any human achievement no matter when it takes place. I suppose, in other words, that the Epicureans postulated some sort of development of human rationality in the course of cultural progress, which can be compared with the development of an individual from birth to maturity.

5 THE NATURAL STAGE

Presumably Epicurus adduces the two-stage development of language as the most striking example of the development of culture. It is beyond doubt that certain combinations of sound are necessitated in the natural stage by certain emotions and certain visual representations. What is, on the contrary, controversial is the relation of these vocal combinations to objects themselves. Some scholars have suggested that the first natural utterances were influenced by certain emotions, but were not related directly to objects, and that it was only at the later, rational stage that the connection between words and objects was established in purely conventional form.[20] The main arguments in favour of such an interpretation have been (1) Lucretius' formulation at 5.1028–9 ('It was nature that compelled the utterance of the various noises, and usefulness forced the pronunciation of the names of

---

[18] For Lucretius see B. Manuwald 1980.   [19] See B. Manuwald 1980: 18–21.
[20] Giussani 1896: I, 280–2; De Lacy 1939: 87–8; E. and Ph. De Lacy 1941: 140 (this view is not reflected in E. and Ph. De Lacy 1978; Wigodsky 1995: 62 n. 22 reports that De Lacy did not hold this opinion later); Bailey 1947: III, 1487; 1490; Schrijvers 1974: 338–9.

things': *at varios linguae sonitus natura subegit | mittere et utilitas expressit nomina rerum*), which taken in isolation from its immediate context seems to imply this understanding of two stages; (2) the alleged similarity of the theory at Diodorus Siculus 1.8.3, which has for a long time been taken as Epicurean;[21] (3) the ambiguity of the initial sounds.[22]

None of these arguments is persuasive. (1) Lucretius' words surely have nothing to do with the two-stage development described by Epicurus, and they can be plausibly interpreted as pointing to another aspect of evolution not mentioned in *Ep. Hdt.* 75–6 (see below). (2) Diodorus' theory cannot be taken as evidence for Epicurean views;[23] more specifically, the account of the development of language here is inconsistent with *Ep. Hdt.* 75–6. (The cause of the differences between languages in Diodorus is the accidental character of the imposition of words, which were artificially articulated during this process; Epicurus, on the contrary, explains these differences by the influence of local peculiarities upon the initial utterances, which otherwise would have had to be the same for the same objects.) (3) Although the ambiguity of the natural utterances does suggest that the relation of words to objects in Epicurean theory must not be conceived in the terms of strong one-to-one connection, the attempt in the second stage to *eliminate* ambiguities presupposes that words were related to objects already at the previous stage.

Various scholars have argued in favour of the view that Epicurus regarded the first natural sounds as closely corresponding not only to emotions that provoked the specific sounds, but also to the objects that were in each case the cause of these emotions.[24] This interpretation certainly prevails today, and I summarise the main arguments, partially adduced already in previous studies. (1) As is mentioned in *Ep. Hdt.* 75, the first sounds were provoked not only by πάθη, 'affections', but also by φαντάσματα, 'representations', and that implies the relevance of the objects themselves to the utterance of specific combinations of sounds.[25] (2) Epicurus explains the differences

---

[21] In Diodorus the first sounds are represented as unarticulated and meaningless, and the further stage as their articulation and assignment to things. Bailey 1947: III, 1488 did not address the arguments in Reinhardt 1912 against the Epicurean provenance of Diodorus' theory and for Democritean influence upon it; Dahlmann's dissertation (1928), which was directed against both these claims, probably remained unknown to Bailey.

[22] Schrijvers 1974: 338.

[23] It was stressed by Reinhardt and Cole, who defended its dependence from Democritus, as well as by Dahlmann 1928 and Spoerri 1959, who rejected this idea (see above n. 7).

[24] Dahlmann 1928: 16–17; Vlastos 1946: 52–4; Cole 1990: 62 n. 5; Sedley 1973: 18 n. 91; Konstan 1973: 46–8; Wigodsky 1995: 61–2.

[25] Lucretius describes (5.1056–8) the utterance of spontaneous sounds, analogous to those that are uttered by animals, as *pro vario sensu varia res voce notare*.

between languages by the variability of spontaneous utterances from one territory to another, suggesting thus that at least the initial stock of word forms and their references in each language goes back to this primitive stage. (3) Epicurus does not mention the assignment of words to things as a process separate from emotive utterance, and the second stage in *Ep. Hdt.* 76 is characterised as an improvement in the means of communication, which suggests that words were already related to objects at a previous stage.[26] (4) Demetrius of Laconia (*PHerc.* 1012, LXIV Puglia 1988) says 'the first utterances of names came about by nature': φύσει δὲ τὰς πρώτας τῶν ὀνομάτων ἀναφωνήσεις γεγονέναι. (5) Diogenes of Oenoanda (fr. 12 II–IV Smith 1993) characterises the first sounds of the earth-born men as αἱ πρῶται ἀναφθέγξεις . . . τῶν τε ὀνομάτων καὶ τῶν ῥημάτων.[27]

The two last testimonies do not preclude a further improvement of natural sounds,[28] but imply that there were initial differences between these utterances relative to the *objects* which provoked them, and, moreover, some sort of rudimentary morphological differences, which made it possible to develop from them a real vocabulary. Further, the polemics of Lucretius and Diogenes against the idea of an inventor of language imply that their alternative explanation – that words emerged naturally – involves the origin of words which were sufficiently articulated and related to objects: otherwise, if they had in view only the spontaneous origin of combinations of sounds which needed further articulation and assignment to objects, it could not serve as the refutation of the idea of the name-giver or *onomatothetēs*, whose primary task had to be the accomplishment of these processes. As for the idea of the spontaneous origin of *unarticulated* sounds, it was already by the time of Epicurus relatively trivial in this evolutionary context, and could not have earned his theory the special place it attained among ancient accounts.

If natural sounds were related from the beginning to specific objects, it means that Epicurus regarded these emotionally reactive utterances as

[26] This consideration cannot, however, be regarded as a conclusive argument in favour of the *initial* relation of words to things, for Epicurus could have omitted the intermediate stage of such assignments. It will be argued below that Epicurus omits, whereas Lucretius mentions, the beginning stage of the use of words for communication. The initial connection of words and things must be assumed in the other arguments just mentioned.

[27] In view of this Epicurean evidence it is reasonable to give credence to such extra-school testimonies, as Sextus (*M.* 1.143), who presumably here uses an Epicurean argument, and Proclus' doxographical note (*In Crat.* 17. p. 7.22 Pasquali = fr. 335 Us.), *pace* Fehling 1965: 227–8, who argues for the deformation of Epicurus' idea in the later tradition. Both passages represent in a more definite form the idea of the spontaneous origin of *onomata*, which were reactions to objects and hence related closely to them. It must be noted that Sextus stresses specifically the spontaneous origin of the phonetic *form* of the word.

[28] See Konstan 1973: 47 n. 30.

having been spontaneously articulated at least to some degree to correspond to objects considered generally. Epicurean theory, as far as I can see, keeps silent about the process of original articulation,[29] but the evidence cited above, especially the passages from Demetrius of Laconia and Diogenes of Oenoanda, implies that the first sound combinations were definite and constant enough to be regarded as the foundation of a primitive vocabulary, and even that at least crude differences between the grammatical forms go back to this spontaneous stage.

It is also significant that Lucretius compares the prolific variability of human language with spontaneous sounds of animals, varying in accordance with various emotions (5.1056–61, cf. 1087–90 = LS 19B):

> Postremo quid in hac mirabile tantoperest re,
> si genus humanum, cui vox et lingua vigeret,
> pro vario sensu varia[30] res voce notaret?
> cum pecudes mutae, cum denique saecla ferarum
> dissimilis soleant voces variaeque ciere,
> cum metus aut dolor est et cum iam gaudia gliscunt.

Lastly, why is it so surprising that the human race, with its powers of voice and tongue, should have indicated each thing with a different sound to correspond to a different sensation? After all, dumb animals, tame and wild alike, regularly emit different sounds when afraid, when in pain, and when happiness comes over them. (tr. Long and Sedley)

The evident meaning of this comparison is that the variability of human vocabulary differs only in degree from the variability among the sounds of animals of the same species.[31] The superiority of humans consists in the higher quality of their organ of voice and tongue (*vox et lingua*),[32] and

---

[29] There are some interesting polemical passages on articulation in Philodemus, *On Poems*, but as far as I can see they do not imply a definite understanding of how the articulation developed historically.

[30] I accept, as most scholars do, Bentley's correction of the manuscript *varias*, relying on the similar verse 5.1090, *pace* Brunschwig 1977: 164 n. 15, who follows A. Ernout in retaining the manuscript reading.

[31] It is difficult to decide whether Lucretius, by saying not only *variae* but also *dissimilis*, implies an explanation of the differences between human languages, namely an analogy between differences of the physiology of the speech organs of animal kinds, and the comparable differences of human races (see below).

[32] I understand these words as the explanation of humans' superiority over animals at the starting point of the evolution of mankind. It is evident both from the expression Lucretius uses and from the comparison with the sounds of animals, that he has in view the unconscious utterance of sounds as reaction to an object, and not the intentional designation of it (see below *contra* scholars' attempts to conflate these two processes). Things are thus automatically 'marked' by the prolific human sounds, but it does not follow that the humans at this earliest stage realise that relation and deliberately use it (cf. below n. 78). The alternative interpretation of the phrase *cui vox et lingua vigeret*, which was suggested to me by André Laks, is that Lucretius means the more advanced

we may infer, first, that articulation plays an important role even in the process of spontaneous formation of words, and, second, that the ability of animals and human beings to articulate differs only in degree.[33] The third inference might be that the crucial difference between animal and human sounds consists in the fact that the former express only emotions by their sounds, while the latter from the very beginning also 'mark' certain things in accordance with specific emotions. If one takes this comparison literally, it would mean that the cause of human superiority in verbalisation is not intellect, but simply a stronger predisposition to form phonetic compounds.[34]

Hence, these words about the superiority of the human organs of speech seem to suggest that Lucretius does not have in view man's stronger predisposition to articulate in a conscious and deliberate way that is realised later in the course of his gradual cultural development. Rather he is assuming that already in the spontaneous phase human beings have an immediate superiority of articulation.[35]

In comparison with previous attempts to explain the emergence of human language and its distinctive features, Epicurean theory at first sight looks simplistic. It tries to avoid the gap between unarticulated sounds and the words of a developed language, by assuming that the emotive sounds of the first men are reasonably articulated and already related to certain

stage, when the articulating abilities of humans have already been developed. In the latter case it is possible to understand *notare* in the sense of 'designate'. I see no decisive argument against such an understanding (it corresponds better to the fact that Lucretius uses the similar phraseology *cuncta notare vocibus*, 5.1043–4 when characterising the activity of a hypothetical *onomatothetēs*). However, the human ability, which is called *notare res*, is compared with purely emotive sounds of animals, not with, e.g. their signals to each other, and this spontaneous character of animal sounds is stressed by Lucretius at 5.1087–90. So I prefer to understand *notare res* as the spontaneous emotive reaction of the first human beings to objects rather than their later attempts to designate things, on which see sections 8 and 9.

33 Both the picturesque representation of the animal sounds and the character of Lucretius' argument prove that the designation of animals as *pecudes mutae* can be taken as conventional and as having only relative force.

34 Whether it was really Lucretius' idea is difficult to decide. He stresses only the emotive side of animal sounds, and we do not know whether the Epicureans thought that it might be useful also for animals to designate specific objects and situations. We may suppose that Lucretius took for granted the higher complication of the human mental processes in comparison with that of animals, such as man's ability to form *prolēpseis*, cf. Polystratus, *De contemptu*, i–iv Indelli 1978, who probably has in view this superiority of humans. It is important that the intellect seems to play no role, according to this theory, in the formation of the crucial difference between the emotive animal language and the human one which designates objects (contrary to the view of Aristotle, *Pol.* 1253a9–15, see above section 2).

35 This does not preclude the idea of the further development of articulation, but as I try to prove below (see section 8), even these improvements were represented by the Epicurean theory as the consequence of the physical and emotional evolution of mankind, not as the result of deliberate efforts.

objects. The theory thus abolishes the process of artificial articulation and the initial stage of positing names, for that process implies that the relation of words to objects depends on the competence of the name-givers. At least one aspect of this simplification could be explained by the fact that by the time of Epicurus it had been recognised that the sounds of animals could not be regarded as simply unarticulated, but that the degrees of articulation varied greatly from species to species (considerations of this kind are known from the treatises of Aristotle[36]). It is probable that Epicurus, who evidently did not admit the possibility that animals could learn the articulation of sounds, as Aristotle accepted for some cases (*HA* 536b11–20), found the inference unavoidable that the high level of articulation, e.g. in birds, is achieved spontaneously, as an automatic emotive reaction, due to the more complicated structure of the organs of sound.

As regards the causes of language differentiation, it seems that the main emphasis is placed upon specific visual representations and emotions. Hence I suppose that Epicurus meant specific features of objects which acted upon men, and perhaps additional environmental factors which influenced the utterances. The physiological differences between the races could also play a role in the differentiation of languages, as some scholars have suggested, but the concise text of Epicurus' letter contains, in my view, no reference to this factor.[37] Epicurean narratives concerning the origin of civilisation contain no evidence about the role of racial or ethnic differences of physiology.

Sedley has suggested that Epicurus' explanation of language differences could be a polemical answer to Aristotle's argument in favour of the convention theory (*Int.* 16a3–8). According to Aristotle, the identity of πράγματα among various peoples and the fact that different names correspond to these πράγματα can serve as a proof that the relation of words to objects relies on a conventional agreement. Epicurus on the contrary, starting from the premise of the spontaneous origin of words, argued that varieties of designations of the same objects in various races imply differences between the objects (πράγματα) influencing different peoples, which could be

---

[36] See Ax 1978: 245–71(= Ax 2000: 19–39).

[37] *Pace* Apelt 1955: 257; Bailey 1947: III, 1487; Brunschwig 1977: 166. Like some other scholars (including Long and Sedley 1987: I, 98), I understand ὡς in the phrase ὡς ἄν ποτε καὶ ἡ παρὰ τοὺς τόπους τῶν ἐθνῶν διαφορὰ ᾖ (Usener; εἴη MSS) as having relative, not consecutive, value and take καὶ as emphatic, not as introducing some additional cause. Although παρὰ implies the causal relation between locality and the sounds uttered in it, it does not follow necessarily that Epicurus has in view physiological differences between people influenced by locality. He could assume the direct influence of climatic and other environmental factors upon language, as e.g. the author of the Hippocratic *On Airs* does, cf. also n. 31.

explained by peculiarities of environment.[38] If this is right, Epicurus had to assume that minimal differences between similar objects caused considerable variations in their naming. But it is also possible that Epicurus could take into account some further differentiation of words in the course of their usage. After all – or so I suspect – his primary concern was the constancy of the *relation* of word to object, and not the preservation of the initial form of the word.

6 THE RATIONAL STAGE (*EP. HDT.* 75) AND THE EVIDENCE OF PTOLEMY

ὕστερον δὲ κοινῶς καθ' ἕκαστα ἔθνη τὰ ἴδια τεθῆναι πρὸς τὸ τὰς δηλώσεις ἧττον ἀμφιβόλους γενέσθαι ἀλλήλαις καὶ συντομωτέρως δηλουμένας.

Later, particular coinings were imposed within the individual races, so as to make the designations less ambiguous and more concisely expressed.

As was said earlier, it is improbable that Epicurus regarded the rational stage as the initial assigning of words, previously associated only with emotions, to objects by an arbitrary agreement. It is, however, still unclear what sort of imposition of words Epicurus has in mind, when he says that its purpose was to make references less ambiguous and more concise. Sedley originally suggested that τὰ ἴδια are generic names, such as 'tree', introduced additionally to the names of species, such as 'oak', 'fir' and 'alder' which arose spontaneously as reactions to the respective objects.[39] But generic names were of particular interest to Epicurus, and if the spontaneous origin of words was important for his epistemology, as seems plausible, he certainly would have regarded generic names as having arisen naturally, not at this second stage. After all, if the names of species could arise as natural utterances, why could not the names of genera? Later Long and Sedley interpreted the second stage as a less important reform of language, namely as the introduction of inflections, linking words and prepositions.[40] This is plausible in itself, but the subject of Epicurus' theory was *onomata* and not language as a whole. Some scholars, relying on the correct observation that the rational stage played a secondary role in the Epicurean theory, have supposed that Epicurus means not the introduction of new elements of language, but the improvement of those which arose naturally and their fixing in a corrected

---

[38] Sedley 1973: 18; Hossenfelder 1996: 221–2 wrongly represents Sedley's thought, taking it as if according to Epicurus πράγματα themselves are different in various lands.
[39] Sedley 1973: 19.   [40] Long and Sedley 1987: 1, 100.

form.[41] But the expression τὰ ἴδια τεθῆναι implies rather the introduction of some new names. This is powerful evidence in itself, but there is one important piece of indirect evidence in favour of this interpretation which has not been appreciated by scholars hitherto.

The rational stage of Epicurus' theory can be compared with the second stage of the doctrine related in Περὶ κριτηρίου καὶ ἡγεμονικοῦ (4.2–6) by Ptolemy, who probably was influenced by the Epicureans, as the participants of the Liverpool–Manchester seminar on this treatise noticed:[42]

(2) πρῶτον δ᾽ ἐπειδὴ καὶ τοῦτο αὐτὸ διαλεγόμενοί πως ποιοῦμεν, προσπαραμυθητέον ὅτι τοῖς μηδέπω διηρθρωκόσιν τὴν τῶν πραγμάτων φύσιν, ἀλλ᾽ ἔτι ζητοῦσιν, ἀπαραποδιστότερον ἂν γένοιτο τὸ τὰς συνηθείας καὶ τοῖς πλείστοις καθωμιλημένας κατηγορίας ἐπιφέρειν ἑκάστῳ τῶν ὑποτιθεμένων· ὕστερον δ᾽ ἂν εἴη τὸ οἰκειότερον αὐτῶν ἐπισκοπεῖν. (3) τῶν γὰρ διὰ τοῦ λόγου σημασιῶν τὰς μὲν πρώτας εἰκὸς ὑπὸ τῶν μηδέπω παραδόσεώς τινος ἐπιτυχόντων φυσικῶς ἀναπεφωνῆσθαι, πεποιημένας ἀπό τε τῆς τῶν προσπιπτόντων παθῶν καὶ ἀπὸ τῆς τῶν φωνῶν ἰδιοτροπίας, τὰς δ᾽ ἐφεξῆς ἀπ᾽ ἐκείνων ἤδη κατὰ τὴν πρὸς τὸ οἰκεῖον ἐφαρμογὴν συνθέσεώς τινος καὶ ἤδη προσηγορίας τυχεῖν, (4) τῶν ἀνθρώπων διὰ τὸ κοινωνικὸν τῆς φύσεως πειρωμένων ἀεὶ διασημαίνειν ἀλλήλοις τὰ προσπίπτοντα, μὴ παρόντα μόνον ἀλλὰ καὶ ἀπόντα, καὶ μὴ αὐτὰ μόνον, ἀλλὰ καὶ τὰς ἑαυτῶν πρὸς ἕκαστα διαθέσεις. (5) ἐκείνοις μὲν οὖν κατὰ τὸ φυσικώτερον τέλος ἦν τῆς χρήσεως τῶν ὀνομάτων τὸ καὶ διὰ τῆς φωνῆς δύνασθαι σημαίνειν καὶ ἐπ᾽ ὄψιν ἄγειν τὰ πράγματα τοῖς πλησίον, εἴτε δι᾽ ἑνὸς ἢ πλειόνων εἴθ᾽ ὁπωσδήποτε ἄλλως τὸ τοιοῦτον αὐτοῖς ἠδύνατο προχωρεῖν· (6) ἤδη δὲ τοῖς ἐφεξῆς ἐπὶ πλεῖστον ἐπιμεληθεῖσι τῆς τῶν ὀνομάτων πολυχωρίας ἐπῆλθεν ἐκ περιουσίας καὶ περὶ τούτων αὐτῶν ὥσπερ νομοθετεῖν, καὶ τοῦτο ἡγεῖσθαι τὸ μέγιστον φιλοσοφίας, ὡς μηδενὶ ἂν συγχωρῆσαι μηδαμῶς ἑτέρως διασημαίνειν τὰ πράγματα, κἂν εὐθὺς ὦσιν αὐτοῖς τοῖς δηλουμένοις παρηκολουθηκότες, ὅπερ ἐστὶ μόνον ἴδιον τέλος τοῦ προφορικοῦ λόγου.

(2) But we are doing all this by spoken discourse, so we must first add a further word of advice. Those who have not yet clearly articulated the structure of reality but are still enquiring will find it presents fewer obstacles if they apply customary usages and the most widely accepted terminology to all the subjects they discuss: examination

---

[41] Cf., e.g.: Dahlmann 1928: 100; A. Manuwald 1972: 91–2; Brunschwig 1977: 169–70. I previously held the same opinion in my Russian papers on Epicurus' theory.

[42] Long 1988: 195 n. 47 and Liverpool–Manchester seminar 1989: 221 on 4.1.1–6. For other probable borrowings from and the reflections of the Epicurean theory see Liverpool–Manchester seminar 1989: 223 on 7.3.5 and Long 1988: 195 n. 47; 197 with n. 54. Ptolemy's view of language has not undergone detailed scrutiny since Lammert 1920–1. But Lammert seriously misunderstands the theory, does not take into account its resemblance to Epicurus' views, and fails to find support for his claim of a Stoic source for Ptolemy's theory of the origin of language: neither the spontaneous origin of words, nor the two-stage development of language is attested as Stoic doctrine. There is a note on the language section in the Italian translation of Ptolemy's treatise by Manuli 1981: 77–8 n. 80.

of more appropriate nomenclature may take place later. (3) It is reasonable to assume that the earliest verbal expressions were uttered naturally by people with no previous traditional usage to follow: they must have been the product of the particular features (a) of the experiences they had and (b) of the expressions themselves. The next generation of verbal expressions probably was made from the previous ones by the way of composition and the conscious naming, in accordance with features of named things. (4) Because of their natural sociability human beings are always trying to inform each other of the things that happen to them, not just the things present to their experience but also things not present, and not just the occurrences themselves but their own reactions to different kinds of situation. (5) Thus, to the earlier people the purpose of the use of words was, as is most natural, to be able to point things out to other people by means of speech and to bring them before their sight. It didn't matter whether they were able to achieve this purpose by one word or several or by other means whatever. (6) But their successors after they have worked hard to enrich linguistic usage, were led by the superfluity of names to lay down, as it were, laws about the words themselves. They considered this the chief task of philosophy. The result was that they would not permit anyone to describe things in any other than the way they prescribed, even if they immediately understood perfectly the meaning of what was being stated, which is the only proper purpose of uttered *logos*. (text and translation according to Liverpool–Manchester seminar 1989; changes to the latter are discussed below)

As far as the first stage is concerned, this account implies that natural utterances are caused by the emotions, which evoke variable phonetic compounds, as is stated by the Epicurean theory.[43] Ptolemy's account implies also that these sounds are related from the beginning to certain objects (they are called σημασίαι, 4.3).

The change introduced by the second stage of the development of language, described in 2.3–5, is that words are now created purposefully. The words coined at this stage are surely not the product of an arbitrary agreement.[44] On the contrary, it is assumed that they are created in accordance with named objects, probably by establishing the relation between the etymology of the word and the features of the *nominatum* (τὰς δ᾽ ἐφεξῆς ἀπ᾽ ἐκείνων ἤδη κατὰ τὴν πρὸς τὸ οἰκεῖον ἐφαρμογὴν συνθέσεώς τινος καὶ ἤδη προσηγορίας τυχεῖν[45]).

---

[43] Cf. Ptol. 4.3: πεποιημένας ἀπό τε τῆς τῶν προσπιπτόντων παθῶν καὶ ἀπὸ τῆς τῶν φωνῶν ἰδιοτροπίας and Lucr. 5.1058: *pro vario sensu varia res voce notaret*. The parallel suggests that Ptolemy has in mind the correlation of emotions and sounds rather than two independent factors of the variability of language, as is implied by the Liverpool–Manchester translation.

[44] *Pace* Lammert 1920–1: 36f., who wrongly represents the second stage as an arbitrary imposition of names.

[45] I cannot agree with the understanding of this sentence in Liverpool–Manchester seminar 1989: 191 ('the next generation of verbal expressions probably arose out of the first through a general consensus based on their suitability for their particular functions, and at this stage communication became

The difference between these stages is explained further (4.5–6) in terms of the univocity of linguistic expressions.[46] In the first stage, people tried only to indicate things and their attitudes to them, and it didn't matter whether they designated the same thing with one word or several. In the second stage, on the contrary, restrictions concerning word usage were introduced so as to exclude the naming of things otherwise than was prescribed, i.e. to avoid the ambiguity of the previously existing usage. The second stage is represented thus as the creation of new words, on the one hand, which was presumably necessary to designate new concepts,[47] and as the establishing, on the other, of a univocal nomenclature in view of the diversity of natural names used for the same things.

The second stage is in Ptolemy's view a not altogether justified restriction of the means of communication (4.6). The reason is that language at the previous stage was clear enough in spite of the variability of designations for the same things (4.5), and the following linguistic legislation, apparently unsuccessful as it could not suppress customary usage, initiated a dogmatic insistence on a single mode of expression and, consequently, fruitless discussions concerning the meaning of words as a preliminary to scientific research.

This scheme of the development of language serves in Ptolemy as the foundation for the difference between the usage of customary words and more technical vocabulary in scientific discourse. He states that customary usage suits those who are still in the process of research and have not achieved knowledge. The words which are more appropriate to objects

---

possible'). Although σύνθεσις sometimes means 'agreement', the expression συνθέσεώς τινος καὶ ἤδη προσηγορίας τυχεῖν with σημασίας as subject can hardly have the meaning that words have been constituted in accordance with agreement and began to be used in communication. The translation of Manuli 1981 is not correct either. I suspect that συνθέσεως τυχεῖν means that words were made by artificial composition, probably from more simple ones produced previously as natural utterances (compare for σύνθεσις as formation of words from more elementary ones, Simpl. *Cat.* p. 186.37 Kalbfleisch, *CAG* VIII). As for the awkward expression (σημασίας) προσηγορίας τυχεῖν (normally it is persons and things that can serve as a subject in this construction), its possible sense here is that the words were formed by the voluntary act of naming (προσηγορία), by contrast with previously spontaneous utterance.

[46] It seems preferable to understand ἐκείνοις at 4.5 as pointing to the first stage mentioned above in 4.3, and ἤδη δὲ τοῖς ἐφεξῆς in 4.6 as corresponding to the second stage in 4.3 (τὰς δ' ἐφεξῆς ἀπ' ἐκείνων). Another possibility is that ἐκείνοις refers both to these two stages, and that ἤδη δὲ τοῖς ἐφεξῆς introduces the third, previously unmentioned stage (both the Liverpool–Manchester seminar 1989: 191 and Manuli 1981 are not clear on this point). From the linguistic point of view both variants are possible, but the first harmonises better with Ptolemy's general distinction between common usage and technical vocabulary.

[47] I take the words ἐπιμεληθεῖσι τῆς τῶν ὀνομάτων πολυχωρίας as pointing at the further attempts to enrich the vocabulary, rather than uneasiness concerning the multiplicity of words, as in the Liverpool–Manchester translation. The latter is surely meant by the words ἐπῆλθεν ἐκ περιουσίας καὶ περὶ τούτων αὐτῶν ὥσπερ νομοθετεῖν with περὶ τούτων αὐτῶν implying that people had to lay restrictions upon the vocabulary which they themselves previously were at pains to enrich.

must be examined later (4.2). At the beginning of his treatise Ptolemy (2.6) characterises these two cognitive states of internal *logos* (λόγος ἐνδιάθετος) as 'opinion and supposition' (δόξα καὶ οἴησις) and 'knowledge and understanding' (ἐπιστήμη καὶ γνῶσις) respectively. So customary usage corresponds historically to the first, natural stage of word formation, while exact terminology, which must be achieved at the end of an investigation, corresponds to the more advanced stage.[48] In reality Ptolemy is at pains to prove the applicability of common usage to scientific purposes.[49] As follows from his reasoning in ch. 6 and from the example in 7.1–2, Ptolemy purports to exclude debates concerning the meaning of words at the preliminary stage of scientific investigation. It seems that the theory of the origin of language which Ptolemy adopted attracted him primarily because it attributes a natural character and hence unmediated comprehensibility to customary usages (6.2). Although he proclaims the desirability of exact terminology, he shows no interest in it. In other places he speaks as a conventionalist, who is interested only in things (5.4), and is ready to accept any change to their designations (7.2). Ptolemy treats the differences between languages as a conventionalist, seeing in them a proof that *nomina* have no objective connections with their *nominata* (5.6), in contrast with his doctrine of the origin of words.

This latter account has a remarkable resemblance to the Epicurean theory. Ptolemy assumes the emotive origin of (presumably articulated) words and their initial correspondence to certain objects (4.3). His narrative shares with Epicurus the requirement to follow customary usage.[50] Ptolemy's negative attitude to technical definitions and his insistence on the clarity of the meaning of words also resembles Epicurus' position (cf. *Ep. Hdt.* 38; D.L. 10.31 = fr. 257 Us.; D.L. 10.33; fr. 92; 258 Us.).[51] In this respect Ptolemy's account can serve as welcome confirmation of the hypothesis that the immediate clarity of a word's meaning was related to the natural origin of words in Epicurus' theory.

As far as I know Ptolemy is the only source for the second stage of the development of language besides the *Letter to Herodotus*, 76. It is

---

[48] Compare the development from τὰς συνηθείας καὶ τοῖς πλείστοις καθωμιλημένας κατηγορίας to τὸ οἰκειότερον in scientific research (4.2) with the historical evolution from emotive utterances to the creation of words κατὰ τὴν πρὸς τὸ οἰκεῖον ἐφαρμογὴν (4.3).

[49] The evaluation of spontaneous utterances, namely that they were understood immediately and served successfully for communication, in spite of synonymies and other linguistic inexactness (4.5–6), is the same as applied to contemporary ordinary usage (6.1–2). In the latter case Ptolemy admits that in cases of homonymy an additional elucidation regarding the nominatum can be helpful (6.1), but for the most part meaning can be grasped properly with the help of context (6.2).

[50] See the evidence in Sedley 1973: 20–1.   [51] Cf. Sedley 1973: 21.

reasonable to ask whether it throws light on Epicurus' opinion concerning the character of this stage. Both Ptolemy and Epicurus assume that the purpose was to make linguistic expressions less ambiguous (compare Epicurus' ὕστερον δὲ κοινῶς καθ' ἕκαστα ἔθνη τὰ ἴδια τεθῆναι πρὸς τὸ τὰς δηλώσεις ἧττον ἀμφιβόλους γενέσθαι ἀλλήλαις καὶ συντομωτέρως δηλουμένας). We may even suggest that Epicurus' words πρὸς τὸ τὰς δηλώσεις . . . γενέσθαι . . . συντομωτέρως δηλουμένας imply the same contrast as we see in Ptolemy between the first stage, when no attention was paid to how things should be designated, by one word or many (4.5), and the second stage, when a single and presumably more economical mode of expression was established (4.6).

It can be seen from Ptolemy's account that this improvement was partly the composition of new words with an etymology relating to the features of the object, and partly the selection of one single variant among previous designations of the same word. Epicurus mentions only one process, namely the establishing of designations specific to every tribe, which was meant to make communication more univocal and concise. It is possible, however, that the second process, the selection of one single word among those which existed previously, is alluded to by Epicurus in the ensuing part of the *Letter to Herodotus* (ch. 76), when he describes the second, rational stage of the development of designations for οὐ συνορώμενα πράγματα (see below). The purpose of this improvement surely had to be also that of avoiding the ambiguities of the previous stage.

If the theory of Ptolemy can be regarded as evidence for Epicurus' theory, it is tempting to understand the words τὰ ἴδια τεθῆναι in the latter as the introduction of the new words coined from already existing natural ones in accordance with etymological correctness. In that case, Epicurus took into account secondary word formation, which is in itself quite probable.[52]

It is interesting that Ptolemy represents the advanced stage of the development of language not only as introducing exact terminology, but also as initiating empty quarrels about the meanings of words and as insisting on a single mode of expression. It doesn't follow from the *Letter to Herodotus* that Epicurus treated the second stage in a negative manner. There is, however, evidence that Epicurus on the whole regarded the rational phase of the development of culture with ambivalence,[53] and, more

---

[52] On the etymological implications of Epicurus' theory see Long and Sedley 1987: I, 101, who refer to fr. 271 Us. = LS 5D, and S.E. *M.* 9.47 = LS 23F.

[53] See discussion in B. Manuwald 1980: 51–61; the best known example are the errors concerning the nature of gods, which arose at the second stage of development (Lucr. 5.1183–1203); the ambiguity of reason as being able to discover also τὰ χείριστα is mentioned in relation to the origin of culture by Philodemus (*On Music* 4.22, xxxiv 32–3 Neubecker 1986).

specifically, Ptolemy's evaluation of the second stage of the development
of language may reflect Epicurus' negative attitude to theoretical grammar
with its attempts to prescribe the normative rules.[54]

It must be added that Ptolemy assumes that, in spite of the attempt
to introduce unequivocal designations, language still preserves ambiguous expressions. It follows that this rationalisation of language did not
remove the more primitive vocabulary and that on the whole common language preserves its natural origin. This view would also be appropriate for
Epicurus.

7 THE WORDS FOR οὐ συνορώμενα πράγματα (*EP. HDT.* 76)

τινὰ δὲ καὶ οὐ συνορώμενα πράγματα εἰσφέροντας τοὺς συνειδότας παρεγγυῆσαι τινὰς φθόγγους τοὺς ἀναγκασθέντας ἀναφωνῆσαι, τοὺς δὲ τῷ λογισμῷ ἑλομένους κατὰ τὴν πλείστην αἰτίαν οὕτως ἑρμηνεῦσαι.

Giussani's understanding of this passage has been influential. He con-
jectured that Epicurus was referring to the introduction by some people of
things which were previously unknown, and their creation by these people
of designations for them: some of these names, those for things coming
from abroad, were created instinctively; the other ones, for concepts which
were unattainable by most people, were selected rationally.[55] Thus, Giussani
and all those who followed him imply that Epicurus speaks about two independent modes of word formation for 'things not [previously] taken into
consideration' (οὐ συνορώμενα πράγματα), instinctive and rational.

The implausibility of this interpretation consists in making Epicurus
mention foreign objects, the origin of whose names could scarcely be a
difficulty, and this in such a condensed account as our section of the *Letter
to Herodotus*.[56] But the main argument against it is the close resemblance of

---

[54] This attitude can be supposed if one compares Epicurus' acceptance of the lower grammar attested
by Sextus (*M.* 1.49 = fr. 22 Us.) with Epicurus' well-known denial of the utility of liberal arts for the
wise (fr. 117, 167, 227 Us.). Blank 1995: 178–88, esp. 184–5, adduces possible reasons for Epicurus to
attack the higher, more technical art of grammar (Blank, 180f. also plausibly connects the negative
attitude of the Epicureans to the more specialised level of *technai* in general with their evaluation of
the advanced stage of cultural development).

[55] Giussani 1896: I, 273; 276. Giussani added μὲν before ἀναγκασθέντας: τοὺς <μὲν> and τοὺς δὲ are
according to him two kinds of φθόγγοι, while ἀναγκασθέντας ἀναφωνῆσαι and ἑλομένους are
related to one and the same category of people, τοὺς συνειδότας. This variant of emendation and the
concomitant interpretation was accepted by Bailey 1926: 48–9; 1928: 268; 1947: III, 1487–8; Arrighetti
1973: 66–7; Hossenfelder 1996: 223–4, and other scholars, see on the history of interpretation of this
passage Verlinsky 1994/5.

[56] Giussani's interpretation entails also a syntactical difficulty: it leaves the infinitive ἑρμηνεῦσαι hang-
ing. Giussani translated it as 'e cosi riuscivano a far li (scil. soni) capire', but there is no καὶ
before ἑρμηνεῦσαι. The attempt of some scholars, e.g. Hicks 1925, Arrighetti 1973: 66 and Conche

this passage to the formulation of universal principles of cultural development at the beginning of *Ep. Hdt.* 75, as was noticed long ago by Dahlmann.[57] This parallelism indicates that as well as in his general formulation Epicurus has in view two categories of people: (1) those personifying nature, who are taught by objects and are compelled by them, this time to utter sounds designating them; and (2) others, personifying reason, who later accept rationally this experience of these objects and modify the previous, natural designations of them. In accordance with this parallelism, the manuscript text should be retained,[58] with the consequence that τοὺς δὲ in the second half of the sentence should be understood[59] as indicating the other category of people, not as the other category of sounds.[60] The meaning of the whole passage, as I understand it, is as follows: 'as for the things that were not grasped (by all), some people who were conscious of them taught the others, while introducing these things, those designations of them which they were constrained to utter; while other people later, who grasped these things with the help of reason, have chosen among natural designations more exact ones in accordance with main reason which evoked previously their utterance'.[61]

According to such an interpretation the words for the things which Epicurus characterises as 'not [previously] taken into consideration' (οὐ συνορώμενα) were created, according to him, in the same two-stage process of natural, compulsory utterances and subsequent rational modification, as was manifested in the emergence of all other words; they do not represent a separate, later process.

Two major linguistic objections have been either explicitly made or tacitly assumed against this interpretation: that the characterisation of the persons

---

1987: 120–1 to construct ἑρμηνεῦσαι after αἰτίαν is hardly tenable, for the infinitive of purpose is construed for the most part after nouns with adverbial meaning, such as ἀνάγκη (Kühner–Gerth 1898/1904: II, 13–14); Bailey 1926: 249, having noticed that 'this is doubtful Greek', suggests accepting the construction in spite of it, in view of 'Epicurus' laxness in these matters', but Epicurus normally in such cases uses the infinitive with the genitive of the article (Widmann 1935: 167–8).

[57] Dahlmann 1928: 12. This correct observation was neglected by most scholars, but see Cole 1990: 62; A. Manuwald 1972: 92 with n. 2.

[58] Either retained with minimal emendation, suggested by Usener 1887: 27, who deleted τοὺς before ἀναγκασθέντας (it can be treated as a result of quasi-dittography), or retained exactly as transmitted, as Von der Mühl 1922 did (τοὺς ἀναγκασθέντας can be understood as standing in the attributive position in relation to τοὺς συνειδότας notwithstanding a hyperbaton which is unusual but not unparalleled in Attic prose).

[59] See Usener 1977: 22.

[60] This must be stressed against Hicks 1925, who follows Usener 1887 in deleting τοὺς, and Conche 1987, who retains the manuscript text, but supposes that τοὺς δέ relates to the other category of sounds as Giussani did. On the difficulty of constructing ἑρμηνεῦσαι after αἰτίαν in this case see n. 56.

[61] I take ἑλομένους in the sense of 'choose', not 'accept', and suppose that its object is 'words'.

who introduced unknown things as the people who comprehended things (οἱ συνειδότες) and of the things themselves as 'not [previously] taken into consideration' imply a level of intellectual development incompatible with the natural stage.[62] Against these doubts it is necessary to recall that Epicurean authors assign to the earlier, spontaneous phase of cultural development not only the invention of fire, clothes and housing, but also the first social contract (Lucr. 5.1019–27), and an empirical recognition by 'finer natures' (χαριέστατοι) of the utility of mutual non-violence, a recognition which is characterised as 'non-rational memory' (ἄλογος μνήμη), and is thus contrasted to the further understanding (ἐπιλογισμός) of this utility (Porph. *De abstin.* 1.10.2 = Hermarch. fr. 34 Longo Auricchio 1988 = LS 22N2).[63] Moreover, the expression 'the people who comprehended' (οἱ συνειδότες) itself does not suggest that any specific knowledge is involved in the comprehension. The verb σύνοιδα usually has no theoretical implications, but designates (apart from its use in a moral context as the consciousness of one's own actions (more often bad than good), for the first time attested in Democr. DK 68 B297) either understanding in a broad, ordinary sense, or knowledge based on direct acquaintance with the event in question.[64] As the data supplied by the *TLG* show (I checked all cases where

---

[62] Hence Sedley 1973: 17–19 suggested placing a full stop after φθόγγους, and adding μὲν οὖν between τοὺς and ἀναγκασθέντας (cf. Long and Sedley 1987: I, 97; II, 98). Sedley supposes that Epicurus points to the third stage in the development of language, namely the introduction of words for rational concepts, especially for philosophical ones, by some experts (presumably not by the invention of new words but by the reapplication in a metaphorical sense of those which previously existed), and then sums up the whole process of creating the language: 'hence some men gave utterance under compulsion and others chose words rationally, and it is thus, as far as the principal cause is concerned, that they came to use language'. This emendation entails some minor difficulties (the lack of a subject for ἑρμηνεῦσαι and of an object both for this verb and for ἀναφωνῆσαι and ἑλομένους makes the sentence somewhat abrupt), but my major objection is that for reasons adduced further in the text, the passage does not need any emendation.

[63] It is true that the phrase οὐ μόνον ζημίας ἔταξαν οἱ πρῶτοι τοῦτο συνειδότες in Porph. *De abstin.* 1.9.4 = Hermarch. fr. 34 Longo Auricchio 1988 = LS 22M8) refers to the rational stage of development (see Long and Sedley 1987: II, 137), and points to the more complicated recognition than is available at the earlier stage. However, it does not follow necessarily that συνειδέναι in Hermarchus designates the specific ability which appears only at this advanced stage and is summarised more definitely as ἐπιλογισμὸν ἔλαβον τοῦ συμφέροντος (Porph. *De abst.* 1.10.4 = LS 22N3, cf. 1.8.2 = LS 22M3); see the next note. I agree on this point with B. Manuwald 1980: 21 n. 82. Unlike him, I see no difficulty in supposing that the first phase of the formation of words for the οὐ συνορώμενα πράγματα is completed already at the first stage of the development of culture.

[64] E.g. Th. 1.73.2; Aristoph. *Eq.* 595; Isocr. 6.83; 8.4; Demosth. *Exord.* 5.3; Pl. *Theaet.* 206a2 with acc. (about something previously directly seen); cf. Pl. *Phaedo.* 92d3 (with the dative of the participle, an understanding probably presupposing an experience). As far as I can see the verb is not used in Epicurean texts in any technical philosophical sense. It does not occur in Epicurus, and in the examples from the Epicurean authors known to me it is used in a manner not differing from its usual semantics: (1) the general meaning 'to be conscious of one's own', usually with the dative and the accusative, as 'to be conscious of one's own (bad) deeds', Philod. *De piet.* 1.71.2035 Obbink 1996 or 'to be conscious of one's own achievements', Polystr. *De contempt.* XVII 6 Indelli; cf. Philod.

a plural form of the participle is used), οἱ συνειδότες may be used absolutely, without a specification, only in the legal sense of 'witnesses'. Hence, in our passage this word must be connected closely with πράγματα: οἱ συνειδότες are the men who have noticed or comprehended these things and are not to be understood as special group of 'experts' or 'sages' in a generic sense, as has been suggested by some scholars.

It is necessary, further, to take into account that the usual meaning of συνοράω is 'to notice', 'to consider' or 'to comprehend',[65] not 'to look at' or 'to see' in a literal sense. Epicurus consequently has in view neither things which were not seen previously,[66] nor things which are in principle imperceptible,[67] but rather those which could not be comprehended by all members of the tribe as easily as ordinary physical objects could.[68] The persons who introduced them should have possessed some specific experience unavailable for their comrades (they could also possess some specific abilities of memorising it as Hermarchus' story about pre-rational 'fine natures' presupposes).

There are things which, on Epicurus' view, are comprehended by the senses, but which at the same time can only be grasped with difficulty. Examples of such things are 'motion', 'rest' and 'time' on the one hand and 'liberty' and 'slavery' on the other. Epicurus and his followers treated entities of this kind as τὰ συμπτώματα, accidental properties of physical bodies.[69] Epicurus warns his pupils against treating these qualities as

---

Rhet. vol. I. p. 141.15 Sudhaus (1892) = *Rhet.* lib. II, *PHerc.* 1672, XXXV 15 p. 263 Longo Auricchio 1977 (συνοίδασιν ἑαυτοῖς μεθόδους); (2) the technical sense 'to be a witness' (Philod. *Rhet.* vol. I. p. 260.6 Sudhaus 1892); (3) it occurs in Hermarchus [see previous note], where it probably implies direct acquaintance with the things in question, as in Plato's passages cited above in this note.

[65] E.g. Pl. *Phaedr.* 254d; *Lg.* 965b etc. Epicurus uses the present in the sense 'to consider' *Ep. Hdt.* 38. p. 5.12 ; 63. p. 19.15 Us.; the aorist has the meaning 'to comprehend' or to 'understand', *Ep. Pyth.* 99. p. 44.2 Us.; *Nat.* XXVIII 8 v Sedley 1973; sometimes the present can also have the latter meaning (*Ep. Pyth.* 116. p. 55.7 Us.; *Nat.* XXVIII 13 III inf.; XI sup. Sedley 1973).

[66] Giussani 1896: I, 276 rightly translates 'cose ignote, almeno da principio, alla generalità dei parlanti quella lingua', but then wrongly identifies them with imported things (these hardly could be called in Greek οὐ συνορώμενα πράγματα).

[67] It was the opinion of Apelt 1955: 258 ('manche nicht durch das Auge wahrgenommene Dinge'), Dahlmann 1928: 11 ('*res quae non videntur*, . . . *abstracta*'); Cole 1990: 62; A. Manuwald 1972: 92 A. 2; Sedley 1973: 18. Philippson 1929: 666–7, after having pointed out rightly that συνοράω usually denotes intellectual activity, then returns strangely to understanding these things as those which are not perceived by senses, but can be comprehended only by reason, such as atoms and space. However, the things which cannot be seen in principle are called ἀόρατα, *Ep. Hdt.* 59. p. 17.20 Us. et al.

[68] The only example I was able to find for the expression οὐ συνορώμενος is Plut. *Pyrrh.* 28.4; its meaning here is 'being not noticed (at the given moment)'.

[69] Accidental properties are discussed in *Ep. Hdt.* 70–1. Epicurus himself adduces only 'time' as an example, which is a property of specific kind (ibid. 73). The other ones are known from Demetrius of Laconia: 'motion', 'rest', 'day', and 'night' (S.E. *M.* 10.219–24), and Lucretius, 1.456: *libertas, bellum, concordia*; on this doctrine see Sedley 1988.

unseen and incorporeal (*Ep. Hdt.* 70), and, according to him, they are comprehended primarily through the senses (ibid. 71. p. 24.10–11 Us.); presumably, however, inductive reasoning had to play some role at the stage in which the concepts of these qualities were formed. It is possible that Epicureans regarded 'justice' as one such entity: it was not apprehended from the beginning, but a rudimentary understanding of it appeared already at the natural stage of human development, and the concept of justice achieved its final formation in the following rational stage.[70] Epicurus could suppose that the natural utterance for 'justice' appeared already at the pre-rational stage and then was modified after the rational comprehension of this concept.[71]

It is significant that just for grasping accidental properties Epicurus stresses the relevance of the linguistic aspect: he recommends that one follow common usage in order to understand the essence of them (*Ep. Hdt.* 70). More specifically, in the case of 'time', which is obviously the most complicated among them,[72] he states (*Ep. Hdt.* 72–3 = LS 7B6), that this concept cannot be inquired into by referring it to mentally observed *prolēpseis* (προλήψεις) like other concepts (namely by concentrating on the 'first meaning' of the relevant word, as is explained in *Ep. Hdt.* 37–8). Epicurus warns against attempts to find another, allegedly more appropriate word for it, or to define it through some seemingly similar essence. It follows that linguistic usage cannot be as helpful this time as it is in the cases when the current word has, according to Epicurus, obvious reference. However, once again Epicurus states that common usage is important, although in a somewhat different way. Epicurus recommends analogical consideration of the evident occurrences in accordance with which such expressions as

---

[70] According to Hermarchus, the utility of mutual non-violence, which corresponds to the philosophical concept of justice (Epicurus, *Sent.* 31–8), was noticed by οἱ χαριέστατοι as the result of the primitive experience called αἴσθησις (Porph. *De abst.* 1.10.4 = LS 22N4) and was preserved by 'irrational memory', ἄλογος μνήμη (1.10.4 = LS 22N3). At the second stage outstanding people comprehend justice rationally, and create laws, following the same principle of justice (Porph. ibid.). Long 1971: 120, relying on the fact that justice is according to Epicurus a *prolēpsis* (*Sent.* 38) and as such must have a sensory origin, suggests plausibly that it is comprehended 'by repeated sense-experience of certain kinds of acts', which corresponds to the process as it is represented by Hermarchus.

[71] This suggestion concerning the linguistic aspect of justice is no more than hypothesis. I can only point out that the first compacts between primitive humans are accompanied by attempts to express the concept of justice by gesture and emotive sounds (Lucr. 5.1019–23, see below section 8). Cole 1990: 73 n. 7 suggested that in Epicurus' *Sent.* 31 σύμβολον must be taken as 'word', not as 'covenant', which could imply that τὸ τῆς φύσεως δίκαιον is the rationally created designation for a concept which has a natural origin, but his interpretation is far from certain.

[72] 'Time' is called by Epicurus (*Ep. Hdt.* 73) ἴδιόν τι σύμπτωμα differing from such accidents as 'day' and 'night', and according to Demetrius of Laconia (S.E. *M.* 10.224–6), it is an accidental property of accidental properties (such as 'day' and 'night') of physical bodies (such as 'air'), σύμπτωμα συμπτωμάτων (ibid. 10.219).

'short time', 'long time' are pronounced[73] and grasping by some sort of induction (ἐπιλογισμός) what is referred to by the word 'time' itself:

ἀλλὰ μόνον ᾧ συμπλέκομεν τὸ ἴδιον τοῦτο καὶ παραμετροῦμεν, μάλιστα ἐπιλογιστέον. καὶ γὰρ τοῦτο οὐκ ἀποδείξεως προσδεῖται ἀλλ᾽ ἐπιλογισμοῦ, ὅτι ταῖς ἡμέραις καὶ ταῖς νυξὶ συμπλέκομεν καὶ τοῖς τούτων μέρεσιν, ὡσαύτως δὲ καὶ τοῖς πάθεσι καὶ ταῖς ἀπαθείαις, καὶ κινήσεσι καὶ στάσεσιν, ἴδιόν τι σύμπτωμα περὶ ταῦτα πάλιν αὐτὸ τοῦτο ἐννοοῦντες, καθ᾽ ὃ χρόνον ὀνομάζομεν.

. . . But we must merely work out empirically what we associate this peculiarity with and tend to measure it again. After all, it requires no additional proof but merely empirical reasoning, to see that with days, nights, and fractions thereof, and likewise with the presence and absence of feelings, and with motions and rests, we associate a certain peculiar accident, and that it is, conversely, as belonging to these things that we conceive that entity itself, in virtue of which we use the word 'time'. (tr. Long and Sedley)

It means that all people have a clear understanding of what the words 'long time' etc. refer to, but that the reference of the word 'time' can be grasped only by some sort of induction and abstraction of some identical content from various processes in which the entity 'time' is involved. Language is an unerring guide in discovering such processes. This, I believe, is a clue to what Epicurus means when describing the origin of words for the entities called things not taken into consideration (οὐ συνορώμενα πράγματα) and also to the reasons for including them in the epitomised version of his teaching. The designations for such entities were formed spontaneously as the people had experience of the processes such as change of day and night in the case of time. Later on, the rational cognition of these things was achieved by focusing on the constant content of related impressions and by choosing the constant phonetic variants that accompanied these impressions (cf. Ptolemy on choosing a single and more concise expression at the rational stage, instead of the more chaotic way of designating typical of the natural one, above section 6). It is easy to see what the motives were for the discussion of the origin of such a word: the absence of a clear *prolēpsis* of such an entity as time could provoke suspicion that its designation is a conventional token which has no universally valid concept underlying it.

[73] αὐτὸ τὸ ἐνάργημα, καθ᾽ ὃ τὸν πολὺν ἢ τὸν ὀλίγον χρόνον ἀναφωνοῦμεν, συγγενικῶς τοῦτο περιφέροντες, ἀναλογιστέον . . . My interpretation differs from one proposed in Long and Sedley 1987: 1, 34; 37 in taking αὐτὸ τὸ ἐνάργημα . . . ἀναλογιστέον as referring to accidents such as days, nights and their parts on one hand, and to motions and rest on the other, which are named in the following part of the passage, not to time itself (cf. Asmis 1984: 33 with n. 35).

If this interpretation can be accepted, it means that Epicurus had in view only two stages in the development of language, not three, as some scholars have supposed (the third one being for the words, which designate οὐ συνορώμενα πράγματα). It means also that Epicurus in accordance with his general principle of cultural development assumed a natural, spontaneous origin for those words which have usually been regarded as having purely rational notions as their reference, and consequently as having to be situated as far as possible from emotive sounds.

8 BEGINNING OF VOCAL COMMUNICATION: LUCRETIUS AND AGATHARCHIDES

In this section I shall try to show that the Epicurean theory of the origin of language implies a more complicated process of evolution than most scholars usually allow. As mentioned above (section 1, Evidence), Lucretius devotes the majority of his discussion of the origin of language to the refutation of the doctrine that it originated from a wise inventor (5.1041–90), and concentrates consequently on the natural origin of words. He mentions explicitly neither the deliberate improvement of language, which is known to us from the *Letter to Herodotus* 76, nor the special category of names for the οὐ συνορώμενα πράγματα, and at first sight seems to completely ignore the evolution of language. However, in a passage, which precedes the polemics just mentioned, Lucretius names two factors in the origin of language, *natura* and *utilitas*, in a manner that could imply an idea of its historical development (5.1028–33 = LS 19B1):

At varios linguae sonitus natura subegit
mittere et utilitas expressit nomina rerum
non alia longe ratione atque ipsa videtur
protrahere ad gestum pueros infantia linguae,
cum facit ut digito quae sint praesentia monstrent.
sentit enim vis quisque suas quod possit abuti.

It was nature that compelled the utterance of the various noises of tongue, and usefulness forced the pronunciation of the names of things. It was rather in the way that children's inarticulacy itself seems to impel them to use gestures, when it causes them to point out with a finger what things are present. For everyone can feel the extent to which he can use his powers. (tr. Long and Sedley with modifications)

It is *prima facie* tempting to identify the words *varios linguae sonitus natura subegit mittere* with the first spontaneous stage of origin of words, and *utilitas expressit nomina rerum* with the second, rational stage from the *Letter to Herodotus*. This interpretation was attempted by Giussani. As has been mentioned above, Giussani understood this second stage as the assignment to objects, by way of conventional agreement, of sounds which were previously related only to emotions. This interpretation of the rational stage as conventional is wrong, but it is more important in the present context that on this interpretation Giussani could refer the analogy to the gestures of children only to the first part of the mysterious formulation, *varios linguae sonitus natura subegit mittere.*[74]

This interpretation entails at least two difficulties: first, why did Lucretius illustrate the spontaneous sounds of the first people by children's gestures, not by their sounds? Giussani recognised this contradiction and tried to explain it by another hypothesis: that Epicurus did not distinguish clearly between the spontaneous emission of sounds and an instinctive intention to signify. This might be true so far as concerns the theory of Epicurus, but it does not explain why Lucretius chose gestures and did not mention sounds, if the sounds had from the beginning not only emotive, but also semantic value. The second difficulty of Giussani's interpretation is that there is nothing in Lucretius' text which could be understood as related to the second stage: neither the instinctive gestures of the child, nor the sounds of animals (5.1056–90) can be taken as the explanation of the rational stage, no matter how one interprets this latter.

Giussani's attempt to find in Lucretius the rational stage of Epicurus' theory was refuted by Dahlmann, who at the same time argued convincingly against the interpretation of this stage itself as a conventional imposition of names (see above).[75] Dahlmann related both parts of Lucretius' formulation to the natural stage: the spontaneous sounds of the earth-born men served from the beginning not only as expression of emotions, but also as designations of objects. He rightly pointed out that the child's gestures are not an appropriate analogue for the natural origin of sounds, and inferred that the analogy is related not to 5.1028, but to both verses 1028–9.[76] Thus, under the influence of both *natura* and *utilitas* the first, earth-born humans began to use sounds for signifying things. This interpretation seems to be plausible, if we take into account Lucr. 5.1028–40 only. It is easy to imagine that,

---

[74] Giussani 1896: I, 280–2.
[75] Dahlmann 1928: 16–17. Dahlmann's dissertation apparently remained unknown to Bailey (see above n. 21).
[76] Dahlmann 1928: 17: '*pueri gestu res praesentes significant utilitate ducti, sicut primi homines, quibus facultas varios linguae sonitus emittendi data erat, res pro vario sensu varia voce notare impellebantur*'. Dahlmann's interpretation was accepted by Spoerri 1959: 135–6; Offermann 1972: 153–4; R. Müller 1974: 99 n. 228.

according to Lucretius, the emotive sounds of every individual, improving together with the development of his speech organ, take on naturally the signifying function which was first performed by the human hand. It would mean that Lucretius distinguishes, at least in individual development, the emotive and signifying functions of sounds.

It must, however, be noted that the passage 5.1028–40, even taken by itself, suggests a more definite distinction between two functions of human sounds, expression and signifying, than Dahlmann admits.[77] Even if we accept the simultaneous origin of both functions, Lucretius' formulation still implies that there were two processes at work – spontaneous reaction to objects, which cannot be called useful by itself, and the at least partially intentional signifying of objects, which certainly fulfils human need, and cannot be uncontrolled in the way that emotive sounds are.[78]

It seems further that Lucretius' formulation and the following analogies concern primarily not the development of sounds (e.g. their semantic value or the level of their articulation), but rather the development of the signifying function. For the human child is depicted not as screaming, but as using gestures, in contrast to the young of animals in the ensuing examples adduced by Lucretius, who use the same organs as the adults of each species. In other words, Lucretius may imply a semantic and/or articulatory difference between *sonitus linguae* and *nomina rerum*, but what concerns him is the change from gesture to sound as means of signifying, and he obviously admits that the sounds of a newborn child do not have this signifying function.

These considerations could be harmonised with Dahlmann's suggestion, in the form that Lucretius drew the distinction between emotive and signifying functions of human sounds, and assumed ontogenetic development from spontaneous utterances into the conscious use of sounds for designating objects. In this case, the first generation of humans to appear on the earth already went through the same development, which is typical for contemporary individuals too.

---

[77] It is not clear from Dahlmann's argument against Giussani whether he admitted at least the onto-genetic development from emotive to signifying sounds.

[78] It can be seen both from the words of Dahlmann cited in n. 76, which paraphrase Lucr. 5.1058, and from his preceding comments on this verse (p. 16), that he was misled by Lucretius' expression *pro vario sensu varia res voce notarent* (cf. 5.1090), which he understood as implying both the influence of objects, causing emotions, and the simultaneous signifying of them. But nothing in the series of analogies of animal cries implies that their sounds were provoked by *utilitas*, and, accordingly, Lucretius means that the emotive sounds of humans were uttered without any sense of utility, in the same way as Epicurus represents the first stage in *Ep. Hdt.* 75. Hence, *notare* means here not 'to signify', or 'to designate' things, but rather 'to mark' them, i.e. 'to utter a certain combination of sounds as a reaction to a certain object', a process, which must be distinguished from the conscious signifying of the same objects (cf. above n. 32).

There are, however, important reasons to hold that both Giussani's and Dahlmann's interpretations are wrong: Lucretius' formulation does involve an evolution of language, but a different aspect of this evolution in comparison with the two stages, natural and rational, mentioned by Epicurus. Thus, according to Bailey, Lucretius refers in his words *utilitas expressit nomina rerum* not to the rational stage of *Ep. Hdt.* 76, when according to Bailey purely emotive sounds were deliberately assigned to things, but to some intermediate stage, not mentioned in Epicurus' letter. Bailey represented this intermediate stage as 'the forming and assigning of names to things'. It was still a natural process, as the first reactions of voices were, 'but accompanied by a sense of the advantage (*utilitas*) of such distinctions'.[79] This interpretation was developed in the right direction by Cole, Sedley and Schrijvers, who used the analogy of the child's gestures as pointing to the beginning of vocal communication, thus rightly supposing that the main difference between the *sonitus linguae* and *nomina rerum* lies not in their relation to objects, but in their functioning.[80]

The difficulties of interpreting how vocal communication was achieved will be discussed later. It must first be stressed that another passage of Lucretius supports the hypothesis that in 5.1028–9 the historical evolution of the functions of human sounds is meant. It is the passage in which the establishment of compacts between primitive people is represented (5.1019–23 = LS 22κ2):

tunc et amicitiem coeperunt iungere aventes
finitimi inter se nec laedere nec violari,
et pueros commendarunt muliebreque saeclum,
vocibus et gestu cum balbe significarent
imbecillorum esse aequum misererier omnis.

Then too neighbours began to form friendships, eager not to harm one another and not to be harmed; and they gained protection for children and for the female sex, when with babyish noises and gestures they indicated that it is right for everyone to pity the weak. (tr. Long and Sedley)

---

[79] Bailey 1947: III, 1490, cf. 1491 *ad* 1028–9. I shall return later to Bailey's explanation of how this intermediate stage began. Bailey thought that Lucretius illustrates the spontaneous sounds of the first humans by 'the elementary cries of the baby' (not mentioned by Lucretius), and the latter by the attempts of animal young to use their limbs before they are completely developed; the intermediate assignment of words to things is illustrated, in Bailey's view, by the cries of animals (5.1056–90). It was a residuum of Giussani's interpretation, as well as his own understanding of the intermediate stage as '*forming* of names' (under the influence of Diodorus' theory, which Bailey regarded as Epicurean) that prevented Bailey from seeing that the analogies must work exactly the other way round.

[80] Cole 1990: 61 and n. 3; Sedley 1973: 18 with n. 91; Schrijvers 1974: esp. 340–6 and 353–62.

As this passage proves, while early men were establishing compacts about 'amicities' and non-violation of each other's wives and children[81] they still used unarticulated sounds (*balbe*) and gestures. Attempts to suppress the literal meaning of *balbe* or to make children the subject of unarticulated speaking by some scholars have been unsatisfactory:[82] the passage certainly demonstrates that the Epicurean theory acknowledges a stage at which sounds were not sufficiently articulated, and gestures were used if not as the sole, then as at least the most important means of communication.[83]

It is less clear what the immediate cause of the following development was. But, quite unexpectedly, we possess an interesting narrative of the Alexandrian ethnographic writer Agatharchides (second century BC), preserved in two versions (D.S. 3.18.6; Phot. *Bibl.* Cod. 250.450a41–b11 Henry), which shows a remarkable similarity to Lucr. 5.1019–23. Agatharchides describes the primitive people *Ichthuophagoi*, an example of extreme insensibility, who unlike the first men described by Lucretius stay calm when their wives and children are killed. Agatharchides emphasises in the same context that due to their lack of passions, the *Ichthuophagoi* possess only unarticulated sounds and gestures:

(Phot.)
ὅθεν . . . ἐγὼ νομίζω μηδὲ χαρακτῆρα εὔγνωστον ἔχειν αὐτούς, ἐθισμῷ δὲ [καὶ]⁸⁴ νεύματι, ἤχοις τε καὶ μιμητικῇ δηλώσει διοικεῖν πάντα πρὸς τὸν βίον.

---

[81] The doctrinal implications of the causes of the first compacts as represented by Lucretius, who has often been regarded by scholars as unorthodox in this passage, were discussed recently by Algra 1997.

[82] I mean the strange idea of Giussani and Bailey in their commentaries ad loc. that the subject of *significarent* is not *finitimi*, but *pueri*, as well as the proposal of G. Müller 1975: 279 n. 2 to change (following Sauppe) *pueros* to *pueri* and thus to transform *pueri muliebreque saeclum* into the subject of *commendarunt* and *significarent*. But the transmitted text is in good order. For *commendare* in the sense 'to commend to the care of somebody' see Lucr. 5.860–1. The doubts concerning the picture of ordinary men using gestures and unarticulated sounds, which probably stimulated these artificial interpretations of the passage, are unfounded; cf. also Konstan 1973: 44–5, who rightly rejects the attempts of Spoerri 1959: 136f., 218 ('Zusätze zu S. 137 Anm. 11') to deny that the Epicurean theory assumed the stage of unarticulated (or, more correctly, of insufficiently articulated) sounds.

[83] Philippson 1929: 675 probably had in view Lucr. 5.1022, when he assumed that the initial combinations of sounds were according to the Epicurean theory unarticulated and meaningless (as in D.S. 1.8.3), and that at the later stage 'they became sound-gestures (Lautgeberde), pointing together with body-gestures (Körpergeberde) to objects'. The Lucretius passage means, however, only that insufficiently articulated sounds, which were, as I argued before, from the start related to objects, accompanied the signifying gestures at the first stage. It is not clear, whether these sounds were used already at this stage to signify objects together with gestures or were only an emotive concomitant of them. I prefer the latter interpretation (see below).

[84] It seems that καὶ must be deleted.

I suppose that it is for this reason [i.e. due to their insensibility] they do not have easily understandable speech, but in accordance with acquired habit they furnish to themselves everything that is needful with the help of gestures of the head, unarticulated sounds and imitative representation.

(Diod.)

διὸ καί φασιν αὐτοὺς διαλέκτῳ μὲν μὴ χρῆσθαι, μιμητικῇ δὲ δηλώσει διὰ τῶν χειρῶν διασημαίνειν ἕκαστα τῶν πρὸς τὴν χρείαν ἀνηκόντων.

They say that it is for this reason that they do not have articulated speech, but point out each of the things they need by means of imitative representation with the help of hands.

Agatharchides, as other passages of his testify, was well acquainted with Epicurean doctrines,[85] although he surely cannot be considered an Epicurean. The close resemblance of the passage to Lucr. 5.1019–23, which as far as I know has not been noticed, suggests a common Epicurean provenance for both pieces. The Agatharchides passage confirms, (a) that in Lucr. 5.1022 *balbe* characterises ordinary men, not children; (b) that this word implies poorly articulated sounds.

Hence, according to the doctrine which was known both to Lucretius and to Agatharchides and was probably the doctrine of Epicurus himself, the sounds of primitive men were not sufficiently articulated.[86] This means, that, although the Epicurean theory assumes that from the beginning the sounds corresponded to certain objects, and, hence, were partially articulated (see section 5 above), they were nevertheless not articulated sufficiently, and for this reason gestures were used for communication at that stage.

The unarticulated sounds mentioned by Lucretius and Agatharchides can be interpreted either as an emotive concomitant of 'gesture speech', which has no communicative function, or as a rudimentary means of communication, needing the help of gestures due to their insufficient articulation. The first possibility implies that at some stage in the development of mankind

---

[85] Compare the statement (D.S. 3.18.2) that the *Ichthuophagoi* like their severe mode of life, for they regard the removal of pain as itself happiness, with Epicurus, *Sent.* 3. Also the formulation of the wonderful compacts between another tribe of *Ichthuophagoi* and seals (Phot. *Bibl.* Cod. 250, 450b12–15), is close to *Sent.* 31, 33 and Lucr. 5.1020, but in contrast to Epicurus' thought these compacts are opposed to normal human relations. In this tribe the people and seals defend each other's wives and children (D.S. 3.18.7). According to Epicurus, such relations are limited to human beings, and only to those who are able to maintain them (*Sent.* 32); on this debatable point see Verlinsky 1996: esp. 134–5. I suppose that Agatharchides is parodying Epicurean ideas, presumably pointing to occurrences which contradict the generalities of cultural development assumed by Epicurus, rather than that we may call him an Epicurean with Leopoldi 1892: 58.

[86] The unarticulated sounds of another tribe of *Ichthuophagoi* are mentioned by Agatharchides in D.S. 3.17.1, 3.

human sounds took over the signifying function accomplished previously by gestures. The latter variant would mean that in the Epicurean theory there was no sharp contrast between the emotive and signifying functions of sounds, but that rather it was assumed that speech developed gradually from the use of both sounds and gestures into the use of sounds as the main means of communication. The former variant seems to be more plausible in view of Lucretius 5.1028–9, where children's gestures imply that the initial sounds are not signifying (see above).

The Lucretius and Agatharchides passages may further imply that the Epicureans did not represent the first humans as crying out constantly by reacting to any object they saw. Rather, as can be inferred also from the account of animals' sounds in Lucr. 5.1056–90, it was specific situations involving strong emotions that could stimulate the utterance of sounds destined to enter the language.[87] We have no evidence whether the Epicureans took into account the difference between purely spontaneous utterance and partially intentional sounds used, for example, to attract attention. At least, none of the animal sounds adduced by Lucretius implies a signal to members of the same species. Rather, the traditional contrast between emotive sounds and sounds referring to things played the fundamental role. The meaning of Lucr. 5.1019–23 could thus be that those emotive sounds (related all along to objects, but still not used for signifying them) which were insufficiently articulated, were used to accompany gestures, as is typical of the deaf, and that this, due to the initial correspondence of specific sounds to specific objects, suggested to them the further use of sounds in the same role as was already being served by gesture.

But – and this is especially important – the comparison of the passages of Lucretius and Agatharchides suggests an answer to the question, of what was according to Epicurus the main cause for the transformation of sounds into the primary tool of signification. The contrast between the primitive people of Lucretius and the *Ichthuophagoi* of Agatharchides shows that it was emotional development that influenced the linguistic development of the former and the linguistic backwardness of the latter. Hence, according to the Epicureans it is the growth in the variability of emotions that is the primary cause of the development of human language. Taking into account Epicurus' idea that there is a close relation between emotion and sound, it is plausible to suppose that according to him the development of emotions automatically causes the improvement of vocal articulation.

[87] Otherwise it would be difficult for the Epicureans to explain why we do not observe humans at every moment creating their vocabulary spontaneously, thanks to external influences, but instead they have to learn the local language.

It is also evident that the same lack of emotional development makes the *Ichthuophagoi* indifferent to the fortunes of their wives and children.

On the other side, as we know from Lucretius, the softening of men due to the growth of civilisation (Lucr. 5.1014) made them more emotional and led to compacts protecting their wives and children. At the same time Lucretius represents primitive people as still using both gestures and sounds comparable to the *Ichthuophagoi*. We may suppose that in some moment of subsequent development sounds, which had already become finely articulated, were transformed into a means of reference to objects, thus replacing gestures, which had previously been used for this purpose. This development had to take place according to the Epicureans at the stage following the compacts between the softened humans. Agatharchides may in his usual manner be answering the Epicurean theory, with his paradoxical depiction of people whose arrested emotional development prevented them from attaining normal speech.

9 THE MOVING FORCES OF ACQUIRING SPEECH: INSTINCT OR EXPERIENCE?

It is time to return to Lucr. 5.1028–40. We have seen that Dahlmann's suggestion, that the first humans from the beginning possessed the developed ability both to utter emotive sounds and to use them as names for signifying things, is wrong.[88] It is necessary to assume that, contrary to its *prima facie* significance, the child's gesture somehow explains not the ontogenetic development of human functions, but the transformation from signifying gesture to signifying sound in the course of mankind's historical development. It can be explicated (in combination with Lucr. 5.1019–23 and Agatharchides' passage) as follows: when the sounds of humans became, due to the softening of their nature, articulated enough, it was the inborn ability to signify things which made it possible to use sounds instead of gestures for signifying.[89] It is also clear now that the *sonitus linguae* and the

---

[88] Of course, even in this case one could suspect that the analogy to children points only to the inborn ability of humans to signify in general, both by gesture and sounds, and not to the evolution of language, implied in Lucr. 5.1019–23. But in this case the analogy leaves unexplained how the decisive point in the development took place, namely how the *sonitus* became *nomina rerum*, although the manner of expression Lucretius uses (*utilitas expressit nomina*) implies such an explanation.

[89] There has been discussion among scholars as to whether the analogy to children's gestures refers to 5.1028, or to 5.1029, or to both. It is evident that it does not elucidate the spontaneous origin of sounds, but it can be taken as explaining how the designation of things could begin if these spontaneous sounds are developed enough (the variability of the sounds of animals represented at 5.1056–90 illustrates directly the higher degree of variability of human sounds, which makes them appropriate to designate objects, see above). In the programme of book 5 the beginning of language

nomina rerum differ not only in respect of their functions, but also in respect of their degree of articulation, although the development of articulation is not the aspect Lucretius tries to explain by the analogies.

Now let us return to a difficulty already mentioned above: how is it possible to harmonise the idea of the evolution, in which the factor of *utilitas* played the decisive role, with the instinctive gestures of the child, which are used as an analogue of this development? Scholars have assumed that the expression *utilitas expressit* implies some sort of experience, more precisely an observation that sounds possess features which could be useful, and the ensuing conscious use of sounds for communication.[90] Such an interpretation, however, contradicts the analogy with the gestures of the child, which implies that the emergence of the signifying function of sounds can be explained not by observation and experience, even of the most primitive kind, but rather by instinct and external compulsion. Both expressions **protrahere** *ad gestum* and **facit** *ut digito monstrent* with *infantia linguae* as subject are in favour of such an understanding. Moreover, in view of these reasons the sentence *utilitas expressit nomina rerum* can be interpreted also as characterising a process of compulsion:[91] it is the instinctive feeling of utility, or, in other words, the need to communicate that compelled them to use sounds for designating things, as it compels the child to designate things with his gestures.[92]

is described in a formulation close to 5.1028–9 as follows (5.71–2): *quove modo genus humanum variante loquella | coeperit inter se vesci per nomina rerum.* The subject is thus the explanation of how verbal communication started, which is the same as the beginning of designating things explained at 5.1028–9.

90 Bailey 1947: III, 1491, *ad* 5.1029: 'people noticed the similarity of involuntary utterances in similar situations, and having realised the utility of this constant relation began to assign definite sounds to definite objects'. Cole 1990: 61 with n. 3: 'whereas nature compelled men to associate certain sounds with certain objects, the idea of using these sounds for communication came only when men perceived that their sounds were understood by others, i.e. useful'. Sedley 1973: 18 with n. 91: 'Men utter sounds instinctively in reaction to objects and feelings, and, noticing that they have one sound to correspond with each object or feeling, they find it useful to employ the sounds as labels.'

91 Contrary to the neutral understanding of *exprimo* in this passage in the sense 'express', 'create', typical of Giussani, Bailey and many other scholars, it is preferable to understand the verb here nearer to its literal sense 'to squeeze out' (H. Oellacher so cites this passage in *TLL*, s.v. *exprimo*, col. 1786; for 'compulsory' meaning of *exprimo* in Lucretius cf. 5.487, 1098). In Lucr. 4.549–50 *voces . . . exprimimus* is the physiological process of 'pressing out' the sounds (cf. other examples of *exprimo* for forcible uttering *TLL*, s.v. *exprimo*, col. 1785), cf. Schrijvers 1974: 354, who rightly stresses the coercive connotations of *protrahere* and *exprimere*, but attempts to accommodate these notions to the trial-and-error process of acquiring language which he supposes (see below).

92 Schrijvers 1974: 342–4 argues that *utilitas* usually does not mean 'need', but only 'usefulness', which is right, and infers that it must point to some sort of empirical process, which he tries to harmonise with the notion of instinctiveness implied by *exprimere*. I suspect that the inference is incorrect. It seems rather that *utilitas* as subject implies no definite cognitive process of recognising what is useful, but only the utilitarian character of action itself (cf. Cic. *Fam.* 1.8.2: *ut me pietas utilitasque cogit*).

As far as I can see there is no evidence that the mentioning of *utilitas* implies necessarily for Epicureans *recognition* of the usefulness of something. Thus Bailey, arguing that '*utilitas* in Lucretius always has the sense of a recognised adaptation to an end, not however, in a teleological sense',[93] refers to two passages, 4.853 and 5.1047. It is convenient to start from the latter. The passage is a part of the argument against the thesis that there was an inventor of language (5.1046–9 = LS 19B4):

praeterea si non alii quoque vocibus usi
inter se fuerant, unde insita notities est
utilitatis et unde data est huic prima potestas,
quid vellet facere ut sciret animoque videret?

Besides, if others had not already used sounds to each other, how did he get the preconception of their usefulness implanted in him? How did he get the initial capacity to know and see with his mind what he wanted to do? (tr. Long and Sedley)

It was thus impossible according to Lucretius to foresee this usefulness before verbal communication existed. It follows that either this communication existed from the beginning, or it appeared at some stage of development without an empirical recognition of its usefulness. It has been argued above that the Epicureans did not accept the former possibility, and it is reasonable to assume that they preferred the latter. But, in any case, the argument concerns only *notities utilitatis*, and the passage does not prove that *utilitas* itself points necessarily to the recognising of something as useful *a posteriori*.

The second passage comes from Lucretius' polemic against the idea that limbs and organs were created (by an alleged creator of the world) for the sake of the functions they perform. He argues from the non-existence of the function before the organ existed, and from the standard Epicurean argument of the impossibility of foreseeing the usefulness of something which does not yet exist (4.853–5 = LS 13E4):

illa quidem seorsum sunt omnia quae prius ipsa
nata dedere suae post notitiam utilitatis.
quo genere in primis sensus et membra videmus.

Quite different from these [i.e. from the artefacts that were devised for the sake of their use] are all the things which were first actually engendered and gave rise to the preconception of their usefulness subsequently. Primary in this class are, as we can see, the senses and the limbs. (tr. Long and Sedley)

---

[93] Bailey 1947: III, 1491.

Lucretius certainly means that the appearance of function precedes the recognition of its usefulness. But again it is *notities utilitatis*, not *utilitas* itself, that is involved in the polemic. It is an argument against the possibility of creating an organ before it has been used, parallel to the argument against an inventor of language. It does not explain what the phrase *utilitas expressit nomina rerum* could properly mean, and does not preclude coercion by this force, as implied by the analogies I have adduced.

But even the scholars who accept the compulsory character of the action of *utilitas* in this passage and who assume at the same time the interpretation of 5.1029 as referring to the second stage of the evolution of language try to weaken this coercive sense in their interpretation of the process implied by the phrase *utilitas expressit nomina rerum*. Thus, G. Pfligersdorffer suggested that the compulsory action of utility influences the process of naming in a general sense, and that naming itself is an empirical 'sorting' of appropriate and inappropriate words.[94] This is easily refuted by the fact that neither the gestures of the human child, nor the activities of young animals compared with gestures, can serve as even a remote analogue to this hypothetical process, not to mention that selection itself is hardly compatible with the Epicurean principle of the natural relation of words to objects.

More interesting is the attempt of Schrijvers, who examines in detail the analogies Lucretius uses, and warns especially against their possible teleological interpretation. Agreeing with him in some points,[95] I disagree, however, as far as it concerns his interpretation of Lucretius' analogies as pointing to an empirical process of acquiring abilities. Schrijvers supposes that Lucretius has in view an *empirical* realisation by the first humans of the utility of their vocal organs, and a resulting development from involuntary vocal reflexes to the conscious use of the organs of speech for signifying objects.[96] One of the crucial problems is the meaning of *sentit*. Schrijvers argues that the only possibility for saving the doctrine which underlies Lucretius' reasoning from the taint of teleology is to take it not as the immediate feeling of how organs and limbs function, but as the gradual recognition of this by trial and error. It must be conceded that the word *sensus* is ambiguous, and that it can designate not only instinctive feeling

[94] Pfligersdorffer 1988: 140–3.
[95] Schrijvers 1974: 343–6: it is plausible to interpret with him the action of *utilitas* as referring to the previous episode of the formation of compact (it was the useful purpose of communicating with each other that impelled humans to develop their speech faculty), not as a hint at some observation of correlation between sounds and things, which is not mentioned in Lucretius. It is right, furthermore, that the development of young animals, as represented by Lucretius, implies the acquisition of *useful* reactions, presumably under the influence of some challenge, and thus throws light both on the action of *utilitas* on the gesture of a human child in its ontogenetic development and on the attempts of humans to communicate by sounds in the course of historical evolution.
[96] Schrijvers 1974: 347; 354–9.

but also consciousness of empirical fact – for example, in Hermarchus, consciousness of the usefulness of mutual violence at the primitive, 'natural' stage of the development of culture (see above). It is doubtful, however, whether *sentit* is an appropriate verb for the *gradual* process of recognition. Further, it must be stressed again that neither the gestures of a child nor the activities of young animals imply the use of trial and error in the acquisition of these abilities, as Schrijvers suggested. Lucretius on the contrary insists that understanding of how to use the organ appropriate for a specific function arises without any cognitive process, even before the organ itself has been developed completely.

We possess a very close parallel to Lucretius' reasoning in the passage from Galen's *De usu partium* (1.3, III. 6 K. = I. p. 4.13–5.5 Helmreich), in the context of a teleological argument for the doctrine that the soul determines the functioning of the parts of the body, not *vice versa*. Galen adduces examples of the development of functions in animal kids, almost identical to Lucretius', and even his phraseology coincides sometimes with that of Lucretius. He concludes this section with a formulation virtually identical to the verse of Lucretius, *sentit enim vis quisque suas quod possit abuti* (5.1033).[97] Galen apparently has in view the inborn ability to use the organs. It is reasonable to suggest that Galen is adapting the Epicurean doctrine to the needs of the teleological camp. It does not follow, however, as Schrijvers assumes, that Lucretius uses *sensus* otherwise than Galen uses αἴσθησις, implying gradual recognition by trial and error of how to use these organs.[98] The development of abilities in animals was both before and

[97] αἴσθησιν γὰρ πᾶν ζῷον ἀδίδακτον ἔχει τῶν τε τῆς ἑαυτοῦ ψυχῆς δυνάμεων καὶ τῶν ἐν τοῖς μορίοις ὑπεροχῶν (p. 4.23–5 Helmreich). The parallel supports the reading *vis* (QO *vim* AB) . . . *suas* (L. Müller; *suam* MSS) and the dependence of *vis* on *sentit*, as Bailey holds, not on *abuti*. In accordance with the restrictive meaning of *quoad* (Hofmann, Szantyr 1965: 654, cf. Lucr. 5.1213), accepted after Lambinus by many scholars, as well as its contracted form *quod*, retained by Diels and J. Martin (cf. Lucr. 2.248; 850), it is possible to understand this verse as follows: 'every being feels how far its powers can be used', i.e. how far they have been developed. If this is right, the formulation can throw light on the development of language: the animal young feel that they can already use the organs and limbs they have, the human child feels that he can use his hand for gestures (but not his tongue for signifying things), and, last of all, the early humans felt that they could use sounds for designating objects, as soon as owing to their emotional development their speech organ became appropriate for this function.

[98] Schrijvers 1974: 361. Even if it is true that Galen's words πῶς οὖν ἐστι δυνατὸν φάναι τὰ ζῷα πρὸς τῶν μορίων διδαχθῆναι τὰς χρήσεις αὐτῶν, ὅταν καὶ πρὶν ἐκεῖνα σχεῖν, φαίνηται γιγνώσκοντα; (p. 5.2–5 Helmreich) imply a polemic against the Epicureans, it would be rash to infer that he found in the Epicurean texts a direct statement that animals learn their functions from trial-and-error attempts to use their organs. The Epicurean doctrine of the pre-existence of organs in relation to their function (see below) would be enough to provoke his objection. It must be noted that X. *Cyr.* 2.3.9, which is adduced as the *locus classicus* for the idea of acquisition by both humans and animals of their proper functions without any teacher, was not *teleological* reasoning. *Pace* Schrijvers I see no difference in emphasis between Lucretius and Galen as regards the development of organs in animal young. Both point out that they are only beginning to develop.

after Lucretius the standard example of inborn behaviour, and if Lucretius thought otherwise we would expect him to say so. I suppose rather that the teleological implications of the immediate recognition by human and animal young of their functions were not clear for Epicurus, whose doctrine Lucretius is presumably following.

In the anti-teleological polemics of Lucretius already mentioned (4.823–42) there are no traces of the idea of the function of organs being *gradually* recognised. It is stated there that the functioning of organs and limbs must pre-exist the grasping of their usefulness, *notities utilitatis*, by the alleged creator of the human body, which makes his existence impossible (*quae prius ipsa | nata dedere suae post notitiam utilitatis*, 853–4). It does not, however, follow, from the sentence just adduced, as Schrijvers admits,[99] that the realisation of the usefulness of the organ must also precede its use. It is extremely unlikely that the Epicureans assumed a period in which living beings gradually adapted their organs to their uses. The extinction of those species whose organs were not appropriate to secure survival (Lucr. 5.837–56, 871–7) suggests rather that those beings which were felicitously constituted were able to use their organs immediately: otherwise they could not have survived.[100]

But whereas the evidence for trial-and-error acquisition of functions in the Epicurean doctrine is weak, we find there instead an indication of reactions which are acquired without experience and at the same time are immediately useful, this being the appropriate answer to external challenges to the Epicurean doctrine. In the same section (4.822–57), Lucretius, while refuting the idea that the organs and functions of the human body were created for the purpose of their usefulness, implicitly rejects the analogy

---

[99] Schrijvers 1974: 355; 361.

[100] Long and Sedley 1987: 1, 64–5 suggest that the instinctive awareness of their functions by animals and children in Lucr. 5.1033–40 can be made compatible with the idea of the pre-existence of the organ to its function in Lucr. 4.823–57, if we suppose that according to Epicurus 'the original members of each species . . . had to learn to use their bodily equipment from scratch, but that what they learnt was inherited by their descendants, thus becoming part of each species' nature'. I suggest instead that Epicurus tacitly assumes that the awareness of the usefulness of an organ follows immediately upon the appearance of the animal (after many unfortunate creations) with the organ that is crucial for surviving: the story about the survival of the fittest animals in Lucr. 5.837–54 might suggest that Epicurus was not explicit on *how* exactly the first members of each species have learnt their functions. The significantly later beginning of language and hearing in comparison with the existence of tongue and ears, 5.838–40 (Lucretius presumably means specifically the hearing and understanding of language, cf. for a similar idea 5.1055) is presumably a specific case (the verses imply that vocal communication is a relatively late process). It is admittedly not a statement of the significant temporal space between the origin of an organ and its functioning in principle, but a way of arguing, in favour of the pre-existence of the organ in comparison with its function, from the more obvious case (when the temporal distance between the appearance of the organ and the start of its functioning is large) to the more problematic, such as seeing and other functions (when this distance is unnoticeable).

with technical tools which supporters of teleology could use: namely, that the organs of the body like instruments produced by craftsmen are created with a view to their usefulness. Lucretius here draws a distinction between the functions of organs, which cannot exist before the organs are created, and thus cannot have been foreseen by their hypothetical creator, and the functions of tools, which existed long before tools are invented. The important thing here is that Lucretius admits the existence of many skills which appear without experience and recognition of their usefulness: only the corresponding products of art can be considered to have been created for the sake of their use, just because the relevant functions appeared earlier than these artefacts (4.843–52 = LS 13E3):

At contra conferre manu certamina pugnae
et lacerare artus foedareque membra cruore
ante fuit multo quam lucida tela volarent,
et volnus vitare *prius natura coegit*
quam daret obiectum parmai laeva per artem.
Scilicet et fessum corpus mandare quieti
multo antiquius est quam lecti mollia strata
et sedare sitim prius est quam pocula natum.
Haec igitur possunt utendi cognita causa
credier, ex usu quae sunt vitaque reperta.

By contrast, fighting our battles with bare hands, mutilating limbs, and staining bodies with blood, existed long before shining weapons began to fly. Nature compelled men to avoid wounds before the time when, thanks to craftsmanship, the left arm held up the obstructing shield. Presumably too the practice of resting the tired body is much more ancient than the spreading of soft beds; and the quenching of thirst came into being before cups. Hence it is credible that these were devised for the sake of their use, for they were invented as a result of life's experiences. (tr. Long and Sedley)

It is remarkable, and probably no accident, that many of the habits and skills mentioned here reappear in book 5 of Lucretius, in the description of the natural condition of humans which is close to the animal state.[101] Hence I suppose that the action of *utilitas* in Lucr. 5.1029 does not differ greatly from the action of *natura* in 4.843–52. It is, however, clear that

---

[101] Cf. *lacerare artus foederaque membra cruore* (4.844) with *arma antiqua manus ungues dentesque fuerunt* (5.1283, cf. 5.966–9); *fessum corpus mandare quieti* (4.848) with *saetigerisque pares subus silvestria membra | nuda dabant terrae nocturno tempore capti, | circum se foliis ac frondibus involventes* (4.970–2); *sedare sitim prius est quam pocula natum* (4.850) with *at sedare sitim fluvii fontesque vocabant, | ut nunc montibus e magnis decurrus aquai | claricitat late sitientia saecla ferarum* (5.945–7). Contrary to the famous motif of animals as teachers of the first humans (Democr. DK 68 B154 = fr. 559 Luria), which is also known to Lucretius (5.1379–81), here instinctive reactions are implied, emerging independently in man and animal.

both processes are different from the action of nature when it compels the utterance of emotive sounds in 5.1028 (*varios linguae sonitus natura subegit mittere*). If we take the gesture of a child as an analogue for the development of mankind from signifying gesture to signifying sound, this process can be understood as the obtaining of a new skill prepared by the previous improvement of articulation, but needing no experience or observation, as these are not necessary for the pre-technical skills represented in the anti-teleological passage of Lucretius (4.843–52). It is possible that Epicurus in his formulation of the principles of cultural evolution (ἀλλὰ ὑποληπτέον καὶ τὴν φύσιν πολλὰ καὶ παντοῖα ὑπὸ αὐτῶν πραγμάτων διδαχθῆναί τε καὶ ἀναγκασθῆναι, *Ep. Hdt.* 75) means not only simple compulsory reactions, such as spontaneous utterances, but also the faculties acquired due to functions proper to the human physical constitution as responses to external challenges. These might include the primitive skills mentioned in the passage just cited, and also the origin of the later and more complicated ability to signify by sounds.

Consequently, combining Lucr. 5.1028–40 with 5.1019–23, we can understand the evolution of language in Epicurean theory as (1) development of articulation due to softening of men in the course of cultural growth, and (2) the transition from gestures to sounds as the means of designating objects, of which the latter took place at a later stage, but instinctively, as a realisation of the inborn faculty to signify objects.

It is probable, although not certain, in view of the passages of Agatharchides and Lucretius, that it was exactly in the forming of compacts for the security of the weaker that sounds began to be used to signify objects. In the Lactantius passage (cited in section 2), which represents another direction of thought according to which the relation of words to objects had been established only through the act of positing names, a critical situation is depicted, in which humans, having previously used gestures to express their thoughts, suddenly found in sounds a new means to fulfil their needs. If the Epicurean tradition also acknowledged the decisive situation in which the change took place, it is possible that the further constant use of sounds for reference was viewed as some sort of social invention. But it is equally probable that the Epicureans limited themselves to pointing out the general conditions, namely the emotional 'softening' of early humans and development in articulation as its consequence, and regarded the change of the main means of communication as their necessary and universal consequence.

I mentioned at the beginning those theories that assume the development of the functions of human sounds, and the role of gestures as predecessors of sounds in their signifying function. As Cole rightly emphasised, the typical explanation of changes in the theories of Diodorus, Vitruvius and Lactantius was a representation of the situation in which an unusual coincidence of circumstances suggests to people a new skill.[102] It is, however, important, that only in Lucretius do we find an attempt to reflect upon gesture as an inborn faculty of man, anticipating the special function of sounds for referring to objects, thus stressing more the general preconditions of development rather than occasional situations which help to realise latent abilities.

It may be asked what made Epicurus propose such a complicated development of vocal communication. I guess that he wanted to avoid, on the one hand, assuming that primitive man, solitary as he was,[103] already possessed linguistic communication, and, on the other hand, assigning this ability to divine or human inventiveness. His decision, as he spells it out, seems to be in accordance with the general tendency of his theory of cultural development to represent the initial phase of development as consisting from as simple achievements as possible and, consequently, to multiply constitutive parts of these achievements so as to make the whole process plausible.

10 CONCLUSION

Epicurus' theory has sometimes been treated as initiating speculation about the origin of language. According to these scholars, earlier speculation concerned the relation of names to things, not the origin of words. But in fact Epicurus develops and elaborates an evolutionist approach to the origin of language which arose long before him, at least from the middle of the fifth century BC. Of course, there was also another tradition of speculating about the origins of language which began before Epicurus: starting from the earliest etymological analysis of words, this other approach culminates in Socrates' attempt in the *Cratylus* to represent the development of language from the sounds which imitate the physical features of the world into the simplest words, the *etyma* of all the other ones, and to the additional words which could be etymologised. It was often said that the *Cratylus* is not about the origin of language. In reality Socrates derives a very specific theory of its origin from the simplest elements, starting from the premiss of

---

[102] Cole 1990: 60–9.

[103] I assume that the primitive phase which precedes cultural development in Lucretius (5.925–1010) goes back to Epicurus himself. It is the sole stage of stagnation in ancient evolutionary theories, as far as I know: man is represented as lacking all needs except those which are satisfied by instinctive, animal-kind reactions, and, consequently, as lacking any need of cultural advantages.

the existence of extraordinary, philosophically wise name-givers, who have created language from the beginning with a penetrating view about the nature of things.[104] Understandably, this theory pays no attention to such questions as what predisposition for language man had or how the ability of articulation and communication developed. This approach, analytical with respect to the structure of language and intellectualist with respect to the moving forces of development, was taken over in the Hellenistic age by the Stoics.[105]

It is evident that Epicurus, inimical to the acceptance of any non-natural rational agency, human or divine, as a moving force in the development of civilisation attempted to develop a theory which would have relied more on inborn abilities and allegedly primitive discoveries.[106] Consequently, his theory of the origin of language abandons the analytical approach: language develops not from its simplest phonetic elements, but immediately from pre-words, which are further improved as far as concerns their articulation, exactness of reference, and so on.

It is more difficult to interpret Epicurus' relation to previous evolutionist doctrines. T. Cole, to whose penetrating observations I owe much, regards Epicurus' theory as an attempt to modify a Democritean conception of the partially accidental development of culture through trial and error, in which specific situations which caused inventions played an important role.[107] According to Cole, Epicurus transforms the teaching of his predecessor into a theory of progress necessitated mainly by the features of human nature itself and by its environment. Epicurus' theory of the origin of language, as an important part of his general theory of cultural evolution, turns out also, according to Cole, to be more mechanistic and less gradualist than the theory of his predecessor.

It is right that Epicurus assigns more importance than his predecessors to the general factors in the development of language, such as human nature and environment. Moreover, it is probable that he was the first to elaborate them thoroughly. I may add that Epicurus' account of the first,

---

[104] It is irrelevant in this context how seriously this picture is meant as a historical account. See in favour of Plato's personal commitment to this hypothesis Sedley 2003 and *contra* Verlinsky 2003.

[105] See Long and Allen in this volume.

[106] The fact that Epicurus was more concerned to confront doctrines about wise culture-bringers than teleological doctrines asserting that man has a fortunate but natural predisposition for cultural development, would explain, in my view, why his theory contains a latent internal danger – there is little to prevent someone (as can be seen from the case of Galen) from re-interpreting the inborn abilities postulated by his doctrine in a teleological vein.

[107] Cole 1990: chs. 4 and 5. Cole relies partially on the fragments of Democritus, but more significantly on such evidence as doctrines adduced by Diodorus, Vitruvius and Lactantius, which only plausibly reflect the Democritean tradition.

natural stage of development only includes successful human reactions and discoveries, the ones which go on to form the foundations of culture. This stage lacks any unsuccessful attempts and mistakes, as represented in Diodorus. This too (see note 106) gives Epicurus' theory of human nature a hint of teleology; one could interpret it more teleologically than Epicurus ever intended. But the analysis in this paper proves that in working out the different functions of language, in following stages of their development and in explaining the contemporary level of communication Epicurus' theory certainly surpasses, from the point of view of gradualism, the entire preceding evolutionist tradition. There was a general tendency in Epicurus' theory of the origin of culture to rework the previous tradition about inventions with a tendency to reduce them to minimal discoveries and to trace them back to such elementary factors as instinctive reactions and the simplest possible observations. The origin of language, being the most difficult case to be accounted for by this theory occupied a place of honour in Epicurus' representation of his doctrine.

CHAPTER 4

Lucretius on what language is not

Catherine Atherton

In his *Letter to Herodotus* (75f.),[1] Epicurus offers a strikingly non-teleological theory of the origin of (spoken) names, the first phase of which (75) is emphatically and explicitly naturalistic:

In consequence [one must suppose] that names too did not come into being at the start by imposition, but that the very natures of men, people by people, undergoing particular experiences and getting particular impressions, expelled in a particular way the air which was moulded by each experience and impression, according too to the variation between the peoples produced by the places [they lived in].[2]

The details are much contested, but the general picture seems to be the following: in early humans, involuntary vocal responses were produced indirectly by the external environment, directly by internal psychophysical states themselves caused by external objects. These vocalisations were shaped both by the different objects which came to be named by these vocalisations, and by the physiological and psychophysical idiosyncrasies of the populations of different regions.[3] The notion that people may be differently constituted not only physiologically, but also psychologically, according to their physical environment, was, of course, a fairly common

---

[1] The modern literature on this passage is vast, and, as this paper will be concerned rather with Lucretius' (version of the) theory than with the (version of the) theory in the *Letter* or with the relation between the two, reference will be made as needed to the discussions which have done most to shape the interpretation offered here, without the usual preliminary summary of the scholarship as a whole. The summary of Epicurus' theory in the main text is particularly indebted to Sedley 1973: 18, and to Brunschwig's 'Epicurus and the problem of private language' (Brunschwig 1994: 21–38), esp. 26–31; (all references are to this paper); cf. also Giussani 1896: I, 277.

[2] ὅθεν καὶ τὰ ὀνόματα ἐξ ἀρχῆς μὴ θέσει γενέσθαι [ὑποληπτέον, supplied from start of 75; see n. 8], ἀλλ' αὐτὰς τὰς φύσεις τῶν ἀνθρώπων καθ' ἕκαστα ἔθνη ἴδια πασχούσας πάθη καὶ ἴδια λαμβανούσας φαντάσματα ἰδίως τὸν ἀέρα ἐκπέμπειν στελλόμενον ὑφ' ἑκάστων τῶν παθῶν καὶ τῶν φαντασμάτων, ὡς ἄν ποτε καὶ ἡ παρὰ τοὺς τόπους τῶν ἐθνῶν διαφορὰ εἴη.

[3] That environmental differences are in play is clear from the – much-disputed – clause beginning 'according too to . . .', the 'too (καί)' being the real bone of contention. It may have genuine supplementary force; I have assumed it does, following Brunschwig 1994: 27–9, 32, Long and Sedley 1987: II, 98 ad loc., on the grounds that differentiation of intentional states according to differentiation of their objects, and not just of their owners' ethnicity, should find a place in the theory. It may, however, be redundant (as at *Ep. Hdt.* 72; so Usener 1977: s.v.).

one in antiquity, and not at all a 'curious idea', as Bailey describes it (1926: 248, *ad Ep. Hdt.* 75.8).[4] In brief, that different things have different names within languages, and that the same things have different names in different languages, are alike explained by differences in both the constitutions and the environments of different peoples, who come to make up different language communities.

Epicurus does not say so, but the failure of his account – and of all other extant Epicurean sources, Lucretius included – to make provision for any other linguistic features and properties, suggests that what was intended by the Epicurean theory was an explanation of the origins of language in general, not of names alone, even though it is names alone which the evidence explicitly concerns. Only Diogenes of Oenoanda's report tells us (probably) that nouns and verbs are included in its scope (10.3.1f. Smith), and even he does not mention other sorts of word, or even other sorts of referring expression, and does not explain how syntactic or grammatical differences, whether formal or functional, came into being. In what follows I shall accordingly speak indifferently of 'the origins of names' or 'the origins of language'.[5]

Lucretius' account of the origin of names in Book 5 of the *De rerum natura* (1028–90) ought to conform to some Greek original, and David Sedley has indeed argued (1998a) that, although it is not a model Lucretius follows slavishly, the structure and the contents of the *DRN* do to a considerable extent reproduce those of the first fifteen books of Epicurus' *On Nature*, this being the 'precedent' for 'such a combination of cosmology and anthropology

---

[4] The *locus classicus* is of course the Hippocratic *Airs, Waters, Places* (περὶ ἀέρων ὑδάτων τόπων) (*CMG* I.I, ed. Diller 1934: e.g. c. 4, people who live in cities exposed to cold northerly winds will have 'characters more savage than gentle' (τά τε ἤθεα ἀγριώτερα ἢ ἡμερώτερα), while inhabitants of cities exposed to easterlies will 'be better in both temperament and intelligence' (ὀργήν τε καὶ σύνεσιν βελτίους) (c. 5); c. 24, wherever the land is soft and well watered, in summer the water hot and in winter cold, there the inhabitants will be 'slow to take up crafts, and not subtle or sharp' (ἔς τε τὰς τέχνας παχέες καὶ οὐ λεπτοὶ οὐδ' ὀξέες). See also [Aristotle] *Problems* 14.1, 14.7ff., 909b1ff., esp. 15, 910a26ff. (people who live in hot climates are cleverer (σοφώτεροι)); Polybius 4.20f., and 21.2 for the general principle that climate is the chief cause of ethnic differences in character as well as in body shape and pigmentation.

[5] The interpretation of Diogenes' *onomata* and *rhēmata* has been disputed, as has the force of the expressions 'sounds' (φθόγγοι) and 'soundings out' (ἀναφθέγξεις) used of them by Diogenes. In the first pair, some (e.g. Spoerri 1959: 137; Brunschwig 1994: 34) see 'articulated sounds' and 'nouns and verbs'; others (e.g. Smith 1993: 373) see 'words and phrases'. In the second, some see (vocal) sounds (e.g. Chilton 1962: 161, Smith 1993: 373); others (e.g. Casanova 1984) see words ('parole'). Interestingly, a later argument in this same passage – that there could not have been kings (?) or written letters (γράμματα) when there were not even 'sounds' (12.4.6–14) – also apparently puts spoken sounds centre-stage. The parallel passage at 40.1.2 Smith, which Milanese cites (1996: 275), actually puts a *phthongos* on the very cusp between a mere cry of pain and a word, for this particular 'sound' is the conventional exclamation οἴμοι, 'alas'. Such 'interjections' are notoriously difficult to categorise in grammatical and semantic terms: see n. 111. These passages, and their implications for the limits of Epicurean glossogenesis, will be discussed in Atherton (forthcoming).

on such a scale' that Kenney suspects Lucretius never had (1977: 20). Unfortunately, all that survives of Epicurus' account of the origins of names is the summary thereof in the *Letter*, where Epicurus also discusses other worlds – known from fr. 82 Usener (= scholiast *ad Ep. Hdt.* 74) to have been another topic in book 12. If it did appear in Epicurus' *magnum opus*, as is plausible, nothing of it is known to survive (cf. Sedley 1998a: 121–2, Morford 2002: 122).

Scholarly debate about the extent of Lucretius' 'orthodoxy', in this as in so many other areas, has long been more lively than conclusive; and as this paper will not be greatly concerned with identifying either Lucretius' sources, or his opponents, it will not much worry us if all that can safely be said is that Lucretius' account has as its context, as does the *Letter*, the story of the emergence of civilisation; and that – again as in Epicurus – its emphasis is on the naturalness of names to humans, with marked opposition to the notion of divine or heroic name-givers devising names for language-less humans in the original stages of linguistic development. The gift of naming, or of language in general, has to be seen as something at once unique to us – and ultimately as what makes possible the expression and transmission of Epicurus' divine wisdom (e.g. 3.12)[6] – while nonetheless failing to constitute a mark of our special status in the overall scheme, or rather non-scheme, of things.

Whatever book 12 of *On Nature* may have looked like – and perhaps greater similarities would have been visible between it and our text – in comparison with the *Letter* Lucretius' account is a very odd fish indeed. On the one hand, it does not contain a general programmatic statement of the principle of development which opens Epicurus' anthropology, subsequently applied to the emergence of language (cf. Garbo 1936: 248; Bollack et al. 1971: 236, Brunschwig 1994: 22):

One must, moreover, suppose that nature[7] too was both instructed and constrained in many different ways by circumstances/things themselves; and that reason later elaborated, and added further discoveries/inventions to, what had been passed on

---

[6] Perhaps the repeated allusions to words as the medium for Epicurus' message are also significant: 5.50, 53, 54 (Epicurus' sayings/writings; cf. 6.24); 57, 99, 272 (Lucretius' task); 113 (Lucretius' 'oracles': 110f., 121). As Taylor 1947: 185 observes, Epicurus' 'great truths' could not have been discovered without the 'rise from savagery' of which the invention of language is so prominent a part. The puzzle is that Lucretius nowhere *says* as much.

[7] The personification of *natura* at *DRN* 5.1028, which continues with *utilitas* in 1029 and *infantia linguae* in 1031 (cf. Offermann 1972: 153, 155, who also observes the shift to personal subjects in 5.1041ff.), is a feature shared with the *Letter*. Lucretius' preference for the personified *natura* more usually contrasts strikingly with Epicurus' standard choice of less vivid locutions such as 'by nature' (φύσει) and 'it is naturally (the case)' (πέφυκε); cf. Sallmann 1962: 281, 232, Manuwald 1980: 29. Note also Lucretius' characterisation of nature as 'maker of things' (*rerum . . . creatrix*) (5.1362), itself of methodological importance: see n. 16 of this chapter.

to it by [nature], more quickly in some cases [*or:* amongst some peoples], in others
more slowly, and in some periods and times . . .[8]

Nor does it mention – at least explicitly and beyond reasonable doubt –
the later stages of linguistic development, which Epicurus clearly goes on
to describe: a phase when names 'were imposed communally, people by
people, with a view to their indicatings becoming less ambiguous for each
other, and indicated more concisely';[9] and a phase when, it seems (this
portion of the text is uncertain), new terms were introduced for items not
apparent to sense.[10] Neither stage appears in Lucretius' version (cf. e.g.
Bailey 1947: 1488, *ad* 5.1028–90: Lucretius 'entirely neglects the later stages
in which words were invented θέσει, unless, indeed, we can see a trace of
this idea, as Giussani does (= 1896: 1, 280), in the use of the word *utilitas*
("usefulness") in 5.1029 and 1048').[11]

Again, it is true that Lucretius repeatedly uses words connoting variation
(cf. Pigeaud 1984: 131–2), thus applying the familiar Epicurean model of
variation within fixed parameters; similarly, the impossibility of human
name-givers is not (*pace* Bailey 1947: 111, 1489, *ad* 5.1028–90) a mere appeal
to 'common-sense', but rests implicitly on the principle that no atomic
complex can be unique (2.1070–91).[12] Yet Lucretius does not expressly
distinguish variation *between* human languages from variety *within* them

---

[8] Ἀλλὰ μὴν ὑποληπτέον καὶ τὴν φύσιν πολλὰ καὶ παντοῖα ὑπὸ αὐτῶν τῶν πραγμάτων
διδαχθῆναί τε καὶ ἀναγκασθῆναι· τὸν δὲ λογισμὸν τὰ ὑπὸ ταύτης παρεγγυηθέντα ὕστερον
ἐξακριβοῦν καὶ προσεξευρίσκειν ἐν μὲν τισὶ θᾶττον, ἐν δὲ τισὶ βραδύτερον καὶ ἐν τισὶ περιόδοις
καὶ χρόνοις . . . The text then becomes uncertain, but it does not affect our discussion.

[9] ὕστερον δὲ κοινῶς καθ᾽ ἕκαστα ἔθνη τὰ ἴδια τεθῆναι πρὸς τὸ τὰς δηλώσεις ἧττον ἀμφιβόλους
γενέσθαι ἀλλήλοις καὶ συντομοτέρως δηλουμένας . . . I read Meibom's ἀλλήλοις (referring to
users) for the ἀλλήλαις (referring to the indications) of most MSS. Some wish to retain ἀλλήλαις:
pro, Bollack et al. 1971: ad loc., p. 150, cf. p. 237 (arguing that each of the original systems of names
would be ambiguous only for users of the other systems), Pigeaud 1984: 124; *con*, Brunschwig 1994:
30 n. 16. See also n. 16 this chapter.

[10] The Greek text runs: . . . τινὰ δὲ καὶ οὐ συνορώμενα πράγματα εἰσφερόντας τοὺς συνειδότας
παρεγγυῆσαι τινὰς φθόγγους τοὺς ἀναγκασθέντας ἀναφωνῆσαι, τοὺς δε τῷ λογισμῷ ἑλομένας
κατὰ τὴν πλείστην αἰτίαν οὕτως ἑρμηνεῦσαι. The interpretation of the last clause is fraught with
controversy. Various texts and interpretations can be found in e.g. Usener 1887: 27; Giussani 1896:
1, 276–7; Bailey 1926: 48, 248–9; Dahlmann 1928: 10–11; 183; Bollack et al., 1971: 150–1, 238; Long
and Sedley 1987: 1, 97, *ad* 19A4–5, 100; 11, 98; Cole 1990: 62; Verlinsky, this volume, pp. 000–000.
But again, fortunately, this does not bear much on our topic.

[11] Also Dahlmann 1928: 15; Bailey 1926: 247; Spoerri 1959: 136; Chilton 1962: 161–2; Boyancé 1963: 247;
Nichols 1976: 132. Total neglect is rejected by Offermann 1972: 155, 156 (who stresses *inter alia* 'began'
(*coeperit*) in 5.72), and by Manuwald 1980: 41. I will address Giussani's caveat below (pp. 135–7).

[12] The number of kinds of vocalisations, being themselves atomic (4.536ff.), must be restricted
(cf. e.g. De Lacy 1957, Vlastos 1965). Presumably we humans are sufficiently alike in our cognitive and psychological endowment to make it impossible for any one of us alone to form the
preconception of names without experience thereof (cf. 5.1043–45). See further, pp. 129–37, on this
aspect of Lucretius' argumentation.

(cf. Dahlmann 1928: 15, 21; Bailey 1947: III, 1488, *ad* 5.1028–90; Pigeaud 1984: 132), although the allusion in the programmatic statement at 5.71 to 'differing talk' (*uariante loquella*) may hint at the former. Certainly there is no sign of recognition that the *kinds* of differentiation within and between languages are radically different (although this is not to be expected in an ancient text).

Variety and richness within a single language are conveyed by Lucretius' vivid representation *cum* description of vocalisations in dogs, horses and birds, a passage which takes up over a third of the whole treatment of language (24 lines (5.1063–86) out of 63 (1028–90)). This, it has often been observed (e.g. Bailey 1947: III, 1494, *ad* 1063–72), is a *tour de force* of observation and *mimēsis*; it also, as we shall see, plays an important role in the argumentation of the whole. This sort of variety is probably illustrated by the use of Greek words[13] in 5.1036 (cf. Sedley 1998a: 56). But as for the principle that local variation is partially responsible for the variety of tongues, it is nowhere visible: Lucretius does perhaps allow a restricted medical application of the theory of environmental influences on different human constitutions at 6.1119f. and 1136f., while 3.741ff. emphasises the shared birth of soul and body; but book 5 does not allude to this point of theory, nor, *a fortiori*, does it raise the possibility that soul, body, and vocalisation alike may all be affected by an organism's environment. That the vocalising birds of 5.1078 are called 'various' (*variaeque*) may well bring out both the variety and the stability of their differentiation by species (cf. 2.146) in respect of vocal display and physical appearance alike (1.590): but humans, of course, belong to a single species, and speak a multitude of tongues no less for that. In short, there is no sign of Epicurus' attempt to transfer natural variation amongst human populations to their languages.

Even so crucial a step in Lucretius' story of the rise of civilisation as the reason for the 'usefulness' (*utilitas*)[14] of having phonetic labels for things is left unstated: instead, the merest hint is given, at 5.71f. ('. . . how the human race began to use different talk amongst themselves by way of names for things') and at 5.1046f. ('. . . if others too had not used vocalisations amongst themselves . . .'), that it enables, or facilitates, communication

---

[13] *Scymni* is actually a *hapax* in Latin literature. The translation of the Greek epithet πτεροφόρος 'wing-bearing' as *pinnigerus* (5.1075, with Robin ad loc., 1962: III.147) is perhaps a similar, albeit significantly different, example: calques show the power of different languages to capture the same semantic content in different phonologies. Alternatively, shared forms may link meanings across languages: see Friedländer 1941: 20–1 on 6.93 (*callida Musa | Calliope*, 'cunning Muse, | Calliope').

[14] That *utilitas* does not mean 'need, necessity', as had often been assumed by interpreters (e.g. Boyancé 1963: 244, Salem 1990: 192), but 'usefulness', and that *usus* here means 'use, experience', not 'need', has been amply demonstrated by Schrijvers 1974: 342–3, 1999: 60–1.

between individuals within human populations. Epicurus' account too does not specifically state that names were used for purposes of communication. This point has to be inferred from the fact that at the second stage of language development, as we saw, efforts are made to make acts of indicating more effective both semantically and pragmatically (*Ep. Hdt.* 76). Names thus seem to be a way of meeting the need for the sort of reciprocal comprehension which is required for anything but the most basic mutual cooperation, which in turn has to be present if stable human societies are to thrive (cf. Schrijvers 1999: 41, 103). But – supposing this to be on the right track – it still remains to show why communication should itself be useful. Of course, a plausible story can be told on the matter (see e.g. Cole 1990: 67, 70; Brunschwig 1994: 24; Schrijvers 1999: 41, 61–2, 103). The point to be noted here is that Lucretius, like his master, does seem to be leaving us, his readers, very much to our own devices.

For one omission Lucretius' account can perhaps be excused: it does not so much as hint at the methodological importance of Epicurus' linguistic naturalism.[15] For this aspect of Epicurean theory is treated separately in the *Letter* (37f.), and its absence from the *DRN* is entirely consistent with Lucretius' general tendency to neglect methodology, at least explicitly.[16]

Another, much larger, lacuna in Lucretius' account cannot be overlooked, however: its failure to spell out the causal mechanism[17] by which the same, as well as different, external objects could have different impacts on different human subjects (cf. Schrijvers 1974: 338). Indeed, given that the whole thesis that different sensations and emotions caused by different objects naturally and reliably give rise to different vocalisations is in effect compressed into a single line – 5.1058 – it is very much to be doubted whether Lucretius' explanation of the origin of language would be intelligible without prior knowledge of Epicurus' account of the causal mechanisms underpinning the varied vocalisations on the description of which Lucretius lavishes so much care. It is an important structural feature of the passage that illustrations of the variety of non-human vocalisation, both across species, and by members of the same species when exposed to different states of affairs, or in different emotional states, or both, are sandwiched between what

[15] The nature, and the source, of the primacy which privileges certain meanings of words (D.L. 10.33, *Ep. Hdt.* 37) have been much debated, and I do not propose to pursue it much further here; but see nn. 39, 54.
[16] Explicit methodology is not entirely absent (5.526–33, 6.703–11), of course, but there is no exact parallel to the opening paragraphs of the *Letter*. It is impossible to analyse Lucretius' methods of argument in this paper, a topic also reserved for Atherton (forthcoming); but see main text, below, pp. 111–14.
[17] On the causal story, see esp. Sedley 1973: 18; Long and Sedley 1987: 1, 100–1; Brunschwig 1994: 22–9.

amount to two assertions of the general claim that humans are naturally much better vocalisers than the other animals (1057; 1090, with 1088), a theme also touched on in the opening argument against a single human name-giver (1044). (On the relation between the arguments, see further below, pp. 108–9.) It is from these main components that the core of the Epicurean theory has to be put together, and its construction makes considerable demands on Lucretius' readers.

First, the description just alluded to, of the various noises that non-human animals make in response to the feelings they undergo in the course of exposure to a variety of emotionally or physiologically charged situations, must be combined with Lucretius' earlier observation (1031f.) of pre-linguistic gesturing in children. This yields a scenario in which externals – and here external *particulars* must be prominent amongst the items in view – give rise in humans to 'varying sensation' (*uario sensu*) (1058) which 'correspond to' (*pro*) (ibid.) the wide 'variety of vocal noises' (*uaria... uoce*) (ibid.) uttered by humans, much as they are by non-humans. The translation 'sensation' is intended to cover both sense perceptions and feelings (especially ones of pleasure and pain), which I take to be the extension of the Latin term here, and to correspond to the 'impressions' and 'experiences' of *Ep. Hdt.* 75.[18]

At some point, however, there was a new development, apparently not observed in any other animal species: human vocalisations became ways of marking or labelling (cf. *notaret*, 5.1058; *notare*, 1043, 1090) different 'objects' (*res*), a novelty possible only because of the innate, untaught, human semiotic disposition for which Lucretius adduces evidence in 1031f. The outcome was the creation of the *nomina rerum* of 1029, although the role of *utilitas* still stands in need of clarification.[19] What is more, the vocalisations became signs, not for the sensations which are the proximate causes of those vocalisations, nor for the complexes, or *Gestalten*, of objects

---

[18] Lucretius' own usage runs the gamut from 'organs of sense' (3.550, 5.570, possibly 1.303, 3.661), *via* 'sense perception' (e.g. 1.422, 693, 750; 2.432; 3.238, 361), a combination of this with 'sensation' more generally, especially feelings of pleasure and pain (e.g. 2.435, 652, 880; 3.238, 685, 768; 5.125; at 2.403 and 422 the senses are capable of pleasurable sensation), and hence 'awareness' of any kind, the *uitalis sensus* (e.g. 2.890, 916; 3.527, 615), to the special case of 'mental awareness' (1.460, of past, present and future; cf. *sensus animi*, 3.98, 216, 578). Solmsen 1961 does not, I think, take into account the fact that for Epicureans the sensations of pleasure and pain have an aitiology like that of sense perceptions (cf. D.L. 10.32), so that there is nothing odd in *sensus* (like αἴσθησις) applying to both. However, Lucretius does not distinguish between intentional and non-intentional states (as might be the case with Epicurus' distinction between impressions and feelings), and so *a fortiori* does not single out those states which are associated with reference to features of the environment, still less those associated with deliberate reference. See further, pp. 130–5.

[19] I deal with this briefly below (pp. 135–7) and at length in Atherton (forthcoming).

and events in which subjects found themselves, but for individual items, whether or not assigned to a type, or as tokens of the type of object which causes those internal states, or for the types themselves. The text does not distinguish between these possibilities, nor does it make allowance explicitly for the fact that some vocalisations did in fact become signs for subjects' internal states.

This process of (re)construction is, surely, a fairly tall order for a non-philosophical reader; and it would still only yield the bare bones of the theory. Crucially, Lucretius does not even say in so many words that the use of vocal noises as labels for objects is the outcome of combining these two natural human capacities-*cum*-dispositions, the tendency to vocalise and the tendency to use signs. In fact nature is linked explicitly only with the former, at 1028.

On the other hand, and much to its credit, Lucretius' account makes explicit, or at least comes close to making explicit, as Epicurus in the *Letter* certainly does not, the two natural endowments – for vocalisation of unparalleled variety and richness, and for the use of signs or labels for things in communication with others of our kind – which combined to make language itself an unremarkable development. In contrast, Epicurus implies merely that 'indicatings' of things are being made at the first stage of development, without explaining what is being indicated, or how it was that humans were able to produce them.[20]

Further, like Diogenes of Oenoanda, but unlike the Epicurus of the *Letter* (cf. Kleve 1978: 67), Lucretius engages in polemic both entertaining and persuasive against the sustainers (unnamed)[21] of the theory that there was a single name-giver (for each language?). Four arguments are on offer (1041–90), in what is in effect a series of concessions – reminiscent of Gorgias' *On what is not*, as observed by Giussani (1896: 1, 283) – to his opponent: no one person could have been privileged as the sole labeller and vocaliser; but (supposing that he could) where would the idea of phonetic markers (names)

---

[20] A comparable appeal to the use of 'symbols' for objects is made in Diodorus Siculus' narrative of early human prehistory (1.8.3), but his terminology may well argue against a naturalistic approach, even if Diodorus was influenced by Epicurean ideas in this area – as claimed by Bailey 1947: III, 1490f., who puts Diodorus in Democritus' (*via* Hecateus of Abdera) and Epicurus' camp. (More plausible is a parting of the ways between the two atomists: cf. e.g. Dahlmann 1928: 40–1; Vlastos 1946: 53–5; Spoerri 1959: 134–41, esp. 135 and n. 1; Cole 1990: 67.) Further, Diodorus does not attempt to justify his introduction of such signs by appeal to the natural behaviour of human infants. On this aspect of Lucretius' argument, see pp. 132, 134, 136.

[21] The identity of this putative name-giver is disputed: the usual suspects (cf. e.g. Robin 1962: III, 144, *ad* 5.1041; Bailey 1947: III, 1489, *ad* 5.1028–90; 1493, *ad* 5.1041–3) are the νομοθέτης 'rule-giver' of Plato's *Cratylus*, Democritus, sundry rhetoricians, and Pythagoras (suggested by Boyancé 1963: 245). One point in this debate has relevance for us: see n. 42, and pp. 124–5 below.

have come from?; and (supposing that it did come from somewhere) how could one person have forced others to follow and listen to him? (For a similar concessional strategy, cf. 2.541ff., 4.473ff.; also 1.603ff., 897ff.) The third of these moves is found in Diogenes' text as well (12.4.3ff.).²² The first two (5.1043–5, 1045–9) appeal, implicitly, to Epicurean metaphysics (see p. 104 above) and epistemology (pp. 133–7 below) respectively. The last (1056–90), when combined with the thesis of an innate human propensity for using signs (1030–2; cf. 1043), turns out actually to be positive and explanatory (cf. Boyancé 1963: 246): name-givers are not only impossible, they are also, fortunately, unnecessary, because between them nature and utility can do all the work. Ordinary humans came to language unaided except by the examples set by nature herself (1372) and by the promptings of *utilitas*, just as was the case with all the other discoveries which made civilisation possible (cf. Frédouille 1972: 14; Boyancé 1963: 242).

The overall impression given by Lucretius' account is thus a curious combination of striking insight, remarkably vivid description, and tantalising obscurity. Perhaps the difference in purpose between the *Letter* and *On the Nature of Things* – one a workman-like *aide mémoire* for adepts (*Ep. Hdt.* 36f.), the other a work of persuasion aimed, ostensibly at least, at the uninitiated (4.18f.) – are at the heart of their differences in their treatment of *glossogenesis* (so Dahlmann 1928: 15). But we must not go too far, and expect nothing of real philosophical sophistication from Lucretius – a misprision long since exploded. In what follows I propose to treat Lucretius' account of the origins of language as a serious contribution to the tradition of speculation on this thorny topic, one worthy of detailed analysis and judicious appraisal. Its defects, as much as its merits, will, I believe, prove illuminating: and that is because many of them point precisely to the difficulties faced by today's versions of the kind of naturalistic *glossogenesis* which Epicurus and Lucretius championed so brilliantly.

It is the coupling of our capacities for vocalisation and for using signs for objects in such a way as to yield a viable Epicurean theory of the origins of language that poses the first of the two objections I shall be raising to Lucretius' account, objections which I take to be the most serious of

---

²² I assume Chilton 1962: 164f. is right in taking 12.11.9f. as referring, like *DRN* 5.1050f., to the amassing of people, not of words. Bailey (1947: III, 1489, *ad* 5.1028–90) thinks it highly probable that Lucretius' arguments must go back to Epicurus' attack on the *Cratylus*, given their similarity to Diogenes'. But Diogenes has nothing corresponding to Lucretius' first two considerations, at least in the extant text; and 'ideas' (ἐπίνοιαι) (not 'preconceptions' (προλήψεις, *notities*)) are mentioned at 10.2.1, but in the context of technical, not linguistic, innovation.

the numerous difficulties it poses. My second objection, which will be set out more briefly, takes its start, as noted, from the principles of Epicurean psychology and epistemology, and indeed suggests that those principles themselves pose one of the gravest threats to the whole Epicurean case for a natural origin for language.

CAUSES AND COMMUNICATIONS

If all that Lucretius had on offer were samples of the expressiveness of non-human vocalisations, with the implicit message that human *voces* are yet more varied and expressive, all might be well logically. This sort of interpretation of his argument has often found favour (see already Whitney 1875: 236, 244). The unwelcome consequence would be, however, that this part of his account would have nothing to say about the emergence of *names*. Lucretius would be presenting us with a class of phenomena into which human vocalisations evidently fall, albeit at the alpha-plus end of a spectrum of distinctness and variety. The argument, typically[23] characterised in the literature as analogical[24] or as *a fortiori*,[25] would run as follows: since non-humans express, or communicate, each of their feelings and sensations so well, even though they are inarticulate, then it is all 'the more fair/reasonable' (*magis . . . aequumst*) (5.1089) that humans, who are capable of articulate utterance, should be able to express, or communicate, each of their feelings and sensations by means of a variety of vocalisations. The channel of communication would be the same (i.e. auditory) for both human and non-human animals, while the means of production of the sound, and perhaps too its mode of reception,[26] will be merely similar, not identical, since the human tongue introduces a new creative factor.

As we ponder this difference, several other hidden assumptions come to light.

[23] An exception is Annas 1993: 69 with n. 57, who claims that in *DRN* 5.1056–90 'human language use is seen as a development of the ways that animals make different sounds in different circumstances'. Yet neither Epicurus nor Lucretius makes an *explicit* case that our primitive ancestors first vocalised as animals, and later began to vocalise, articulately, as humans. Annas' suggestion also raises the problem of how crucial features of human language (intentionality *imprimis*) could have come into being. Both of these difficulties will be explored in Atherton (forthcoming).
[24] Thus Bailey 1947: III, 1490, *ad* 5.1028–90; cf. 1926: 248, *ad Ep. Hdt.* 75.7ff.; Giussani 1896: 1, 274, 284; Boyancé 1963: 246; Janson 1979: 152; Schrijvers 1974: 363; Costa 1984: 118, *ad* 1028–90; Schiesaro 1990: 158.
[25] Cf. Brunschwig 1994: 34; Sluiter 1990: 205. A parallel to the form of Lucretius' argument, thus interpreted, can be found in Cicero *Acad.* 2.121.
[26] I will not enter into the related problems of whether non-human animals are capable of categorical perception, and whether such perception is always associated with speech. For a helpful discussion, see Hauser 1996: 534ff.

(1) Our ancestors vocalised. The grounds for this assumption are presumably that we moderns do so too – which opens the way to the potentially devastating objection that, since our spontaneous cries of pain, delight or surprise show no sign of developing into language(s), and in fact pose a categorisation problem for the language specialist (see Sluiter 1990: 173ff.), there is no reason to believe theirs did either.

(2) Non-human animals' 'sensations' or psychophysical states, such as fear, pain or joy (5.1061), which are of necessity hidden from perception, can be inferred from, or otherwise identified on the basis of, their (vocal) behaviour, and hence can safely be appealed to in theory construction – in this case, in an account of the origin of names.

(3) Such states and such vocal behaviours are sufficiently like ours for some sufficiently broad description of the causal mechanism which binds them to apply and have applied to humans too. The similarity between human and non-human emotion is close enough for Lucretius to assume both here and elsewhere that non-humans may be subject to the same emotions as ourselves, ones with at least comparable physiological and psychological components: cf. 3.296f. with 288f., 294f., on anger and 'hotness' of temperament (emotional states being conceived of as at once physiological and psychological); 4.1192ff., 986ff., on sexual desire and dreaming (with Annas 1993: 69). Lucretius may be assigning to primitive human and contemporary non-human cries either the same or similar causes. If the former, then this passage will in effect be a comparison between two kinds of vocalisation distinguished, most likely, by the presence or absence of articulacy. If the latter, it would constitute an analogy, with non-human vocalisations standing to non-human inner states as human ones do to human inner states.

(4) Articulacy of vocalisation makes expression of a given emotion or sensation easier, richer, or in some other way more successful; or makes possible expression of an otherwise inexpressible emotion or sensation; or both of these.

What is needed here is to test the fit of the theory to the general pattern of Lucretian (and of Epicurean) methods. In particular, it needs to be established what the exact relation is between the four comparanda (past human vocalisation and its causes; present-day non-human vocalisation and its causes), and what cognitive status is to be assigned to the presumption that some of these causes (sc. non-human psychological states) are accessible to us on the basis of animal behaviour. The first of these points is what is going to occupy us in the main part of this chapter. I will say a little here about the second question: how we get access to non-human psychological states (I am assuming Epicureans were not troubled by the problem of other *human* minds). This difficulty could, clearly, be resolved only (if then) on the basis of a complete study of what Epicurean epistemology and methodology has to say about the nature and scope of 'evidence'; so I offer just a couple of observations, reserving fuller investigation for another occasion.

First, Lucretius probably alludes to a process of inference from behaviour to inner states at 5.1062: we can 'come to know' (*cognoscere*) from 'things which are evident' (*rebus . . . apertis*) the variation in non-human cries associated with different emotions; since non-humans' emotions and sensations can hardly count as 'evident' to the senses,[27] they must be inferred from vocalisations (and perhaps from other behaviour too). Thus, even if the relevant non-human behaviour is itself self-evident, the causal mechanism governing it involves reference to psychophysical states the epistemological status of which is itself obscure. (A helpful contrast can be had from what I take to be an argument for the existence of a psychological capacity, that for volition, in non-humans, at 2.257ff. See further, pp. 127–8 below.) Further, if non-humans' inner states are hidden from us, or are assigned only by analogy with our own, it is hard to see how they could be legitimately appealed to in turn in order to explain human behaviour. The comparison with modern-day children's instinctive signalling behaviour at 5.1030–2 (manual gestures are to them as articulate utterances were to their primitive ancestors) may escape this objection – assuming, of course, the constancy of human nature.

Second, another opening for methodological analysis of Lucretius' argumentation is afforded by his offering, on the one hand, a positive causal account of glossogenesis, and, on the other, cumulative negative arguments that to maintain a rival thesis 'is madness' (*desiperest*) (5.1043). One possibility here is to begin by assuming that Lucretius' explanation of the origin of language is on a par with his explanations of meteorological and seismic phenomena. The fundamental questions will therefore be: whether the inaccessibility of the distant past is sufficiently like that of current phenomena whose causes are inaccessible to us for Epicurean methodological constraints appropriate to explanations of the latter to apply to the former – that is, whether the origins of language could even at the time have counted as something 'evident'; and whether Lucretius' explanation itself even counts as a 'theory', given that it purports to account for a single

---

[27] Lucretius typically uses *apertus* to mean 'visible' or generally 'perceptible': see 1.297, 915; 4.54, 596; and cf. *aperte*, 2.141. At 4.467 'evident matters' (*res apertae*) are contrasted with the 'unclear matters' (*dubiae res*) the mind adds thereto, and presumably also means 'things (clearly) perceived'.

historical event or type of event, not for recurring natural phenomena such as volcanic eruptions or the phases of the moon.

The first question has already been touched on (above, pp. 111–12). To answer the second would (again) require a far fuller investigation of Lucretius' historiographical method. But if Lucretius proceeds along the lines laid down by Epicurean methodology for theoretical explanations, then the minimum to be expected is an argument that the explanation's theoretical rival(s) is/are incompatible with certain relevant phenomena, the implication being that the Epicurean story, free of such damaging consequences, is not incompatible with them,[28] and some positive argument or evidence that the explanation offered is in fact explanatory – whatever that might mean. One problem will therefore be that Lucretius' arguments may be resistant to final analysis: for example, the proof that the sun is roughly as large as it appears (5.564ff.) may be forged from positive evidence (that of analogy with terrestrial fires) or from negative evidence against its rivals, all other theories conflicting with the phenomena (viz., that of terrestrial fires). Epicurean methodology appears to require the latter; but Lucretius' fourth, positive, argument against the name-giver perhaps falls within the range of what might be called 'probative analogies', identified by Allen 1998: 308–16 as essential to Epicurus' own scientific method; and we have seen that that analogy threatens to collapse in on itself (p. 112 above).

Lucretius' practice, in any case, does not match this hypothetical programme. He considers only one possible rival to the Epicurean theory, that of the single name-giver (or more likely one for each natural language). His first move is to demonstrate the rival theory's incompatibility with Epicurean psychology and epistemology (1043–9), a consideration which will occupy us below (pp. 133–4). Only then is incompatibility with phenomena, in the counterfactual scenario occupying 1050–5, brought into play: but that scenario does its job by analogy, rather than by bearing the burden of proof directly. Lucretius' chief consideration – implicit, but fairly plain to see nonetheless – is that the theory to be discredited implies a proposition about present-day phenomena which is incompatible with a crucial presupposition made by his opponents and temporarily granted by Lucretius: viz., that all *other* humans besides the name-giver lacked language at that time. The only rival theory to which Lucretius gives house-room can thus be safely dismissed as internally incoherent. If Lucretius' theory does

---

[28] On compatibility with the phenomena as a condition for theoretical truth, see esp. Epicurus *Ep. Hdt.* 79f., *Ep. Pyth.* 86f.; Diogenes of Oenoanda 8.3; *DRN* 5.526–33, 703–11, 6.703–11; S.E. *M.* 7.211–16; D.L. 10.34; and cf. Asmis 1984: 321–30; Long and Sedley 1987: I, 94–6; Schiesaro 1990: 66ff. See also nn. 27, 29.

not make such an assumption, to that extent it will be internally coherent, and will not be incompatible with this evidence. Whether it does, in
fact, escape the trap it lays for its rival remains to be seen (see further,
pp. 134–7).

What of the explanatory power of Lucretius' theory? This is its capacity
to account for the origins of human naming practices in terms of the crucial
concepts invoked at 1028f.: 'nature' and 'usefulness'. Here a main role is
played by the long comparison at 5.1056ff. between human and non-human
vocalisations. It is not clear how far utility plays a role in this analogy or
comparison. Given that what we do with our vocalisations is name things,
then presumably the usefulness of having names for things played some
part in the emergence of names. I will touch on this aspect of the argument
later (pp. 135–6). The importance of nature to Lucretius' theory is nearer to
hand: it would not be *aequum* for us to have as a gift of nature such vigorous
tongues (1057) and yet to keep silent, when animals bark, whimper, growl,
neigh, crow, shriek, and so on to their hearts' content.

The difficulty I wish to stress here is not that human speech is semantically loaded, and internally structured, in radically different ways from
non-human vocalisation.[29] Rather, it is this: its not being surprising that
humans use a variety of vocalisations as labels or names for a variety of
things, because non-humans too make all sorts of vocalisations in response
to their sensations, even though they are not even capable of articulate
vocalisation, is, as it stands, a *non sequitur* of the first order. Articulacy
does not afford a more efficient way of doing what non-humans are already
doing. Lucretius is evidently aware of some such difference, since he never
uses terms which credit non-humans with naming, or even with communication. But what has labelling things with *uoces* to do with whimpering,
howling and cawing?

Now it is common in the literature on this passage[30] for non-human cries
to be described as 'emotional' or as 'expressive' of inner states, and fairly
common too not to see difficulties in a theory that makes vocal responses
to sensations or emotions the origin of names. It is indeed reasonable to
suppose that such vocalisations are expressive of some inner state, and hence
significant in *some* sense: the difficulty rather stems from the fact that they

---

[29] These points will be fully investigated in Atherton (forthcoming). See also pp. 133–4.
[30] Cf. Giussani 1896: I, 271–8, 281; Dahlmann 1928: 8; De Lacy 1939: 87–8; De Lacy and De Lacy 1978:
140; Bailey 1947: III, 1490, *ad* 5.1028; Robin 1962: III, 146, *ad* 5.1056ff.; Boyancé 1963: 247; Pellicer
1966: 273, 285–7; Arrighetti 1973: 183, *ad Ep. Hdt.* 75; Müller 1970: 308–9, 1972: 44, 95 with n. 217;
Long 1971b: 122; Konstan 1973: 45; Sedley 1973: 18; Schrijvers 1974: 340–1, 341 n. II, 347, 363, 1999:
58; Kleve 1978: 57; Bertoli 1980: 22; Costa 1984: 118, *ad* 1028–90; Pigeaud 1984: 126; Long and Sedley
1987: I, 100 (more circumspectly); Salem 1990: 214–15; Sluiter 1990: 20.

are described by Lucretius, as by Epicurus, in terms which threaten to make these vocalisations *uncontrollable*. Further, no explicit distinction is drawn by Lucretius, or by Epicurus, between non-humans' *expression* of their feelings, on the one hand, and their *communication* thereof to their fellows, on the other. For example, the horse's whinnying may serve to call the mares' attention to his physiological readiness to mate, but this does not imply that he is communicating his state to the mares, if by 'communicating' is meant something like the deliberate passing on of information (more on this point shortly); still less does it constitute an indication to the mares of amorous intentions. Likewise, the bullock's aggressive behaviour may inform us about his angry state (cf. Pigeaud 1984: 130), but in itself this gives us no reason to believe that the animal is trying to tell us something about itself. (A helpful contrast here is Lactantius' description of animals greeting one another (*De ira* 7.7f.).) Giussani, for one, glosses over this distinction when he remarks that 'gli animali e quegli uomini per naturale necessità esprimono, comunicano agli altri que' loro sentimenti e pensieri' – a fact which, it is assumed, makes their vocalisations into a language (1896: 275.)[31] It is not that a distinction between expression and communication of feelings or other inner states cannot be read into Lucretius' examples (or into Epicurus' historical sequence): the difficulty is that neither author draws our attention to it as an important feature of the theory, so that it cannot be assumed without more ado that it is at work there.

The question, then, is whether sufficient provision is made in Epicurean glossogenesis for the need that language users have of controlled, voluntary or intentional vocalisation. For the unwelcome consequence of the sort of interpretation summarised above will be (as I hope to show) that, whatever Epicurus says on the matter, names must have appeared *after* the first stage, when all that humans could make were automatic responses to stimuli, but *before* the second stage, that of improvement by consensus, in an intermediate stage that is never even mentioned.[32] The critique I shall use is based on the work of Lyons (1977: 4, 33–4), who in turn uses and adapts some of the basic concepts of modern information or communication theory (as described in e.g. Cherry (1978: 169ff.; a summary in Lyons 1977: 41–50) and some older work in semantics (e.g. Gardiner 1932, Morris 1946,

---

[31] Giussani comments ironically on 5.1085-8 'Come se tutto stesse nella *varietà* di suoni che si possono emettere!' (1896: I, 138; emphasis in original). This seems, however (cf. 1896: I, 282), to be meant as a criticism of what Giussani takes to be Lucretius' almost total neglect of the second stage of language creation, that of *thesis* (1892: 280) – which is supposedly compressed into one line (5.1029) – rather than of Lucretius' failure to explain how involuntary expressive vocalisations could become names. On *thesis*, see p. 104 above, p. 122 below.

[32] Cf. Brunschwig's doubts about when nouns appeared, on Epicurus' account (1994: 25 n. 9).

Stevenson 1944) which asserts the fundamental importance to meaning and communication of the psychological states of the users of a language.

In 'information theory' the fundamental concept, 'information', is defined formally, with regard to signals, in terms of the statistical probability of a signal's occurrence within a system. In this technical sense of 'information', the more probable the occurrence of a signal in a system, the less information it carries. Lyons, however, distinguishes between the meaningfulness of a signal to its sender, what he calls its 'communicativeness', and its meaningfulness to a recipient of a signal, its 'informativeness', along the following lines: in any system of 'communication', in this sense, signals (or, more loosely, the messages which they encode) must be free, that is, not determined by context or generally by factors beyond the sender's control. In particular, if the sender has no choice but to send a signal, that signal cannot be communicative, only informative, to the extent that 'it makes him [i.e., the recipient] aware of something of which he was not previously aware'.

Acts of communication, in the sense expounded by Lyons (and there are, of course, many other senses besides this one), are thus impossible where the informant has no choice about passing on the information (of course, the meaning of 'choice' here will stand some refinement). If the sender of a signal cannot help but pass on the information that p, then an audience can find out that p from the signal's source, but cannot find out that the signaller intended to pass on the information that p, even if the signaller did so intend, but her intention to do so was not what determined the emission of the signal. This nice distinction may explain why yawning is considered so impolite in Western societies: it is on the awkward cusp between the informative and the communicative. Ironically, yawning is of course one of the most 'catching' of behaviours: see Provine 1983, 1989.

Lyons observes of his principle that it 'is frequently expressed in terms of the slogan: meaning, or meaningfulness, implies choice'. We might add that if the recipient of a message or signal has no choice but to respond in a certain way (that is, cannot select amongst responsive behaviours), then that response signal itself cannot be communicative. The analysis yields the insight that linguistic signs are typically informative, but that typically they are far more than that besides, because speakers typically are in control of their utterances, and recipients of utterances typically in control of their responses, even if both the probability, and the expectation, of the issuing of a given signal in a given context are very high. (A very simple example: your saying 'Good morning' on first meeting a colleague early in the day, and then her saying 'Good morning' back.)

So here, briefly, are three very simple scenarios. They are simplistic, too, in a number of ways, but they will help make clear the principles needed in order to see what is wrong with the Epicurean account, and the analysis can be made less schematic, and more sensitive to the realities of communicative situations, as required.

First, a breeding queen cat can be said to 'call' when in oestrus. (Anyone who has heard this noise can only agree on the suitability of the word.) The cat's cries are superbly informative about her readiness to mate – informative, that is, given the sensory equipment and behavioural responses which all normal mature toms possess, and informative to us too, with our more theoretical understanding of feline sexual behaviour. The toms now possess the information, which they did not have before, and perhaps could not have acquired in any other way, that Puss is ready and willing to mate, or at least is approachable on the subject. Thus Puss's cries, her 'calling', will evoke a response, if there are toms in the neighbourhood, and a further response if they can get to her and she is agreeable. This sort of 'calling' is clearly not something controllable, the female having no say over whether she 'calls' or not: her hormones compel her to it.

The second scenario is a typical episode of human/non-human inter-action mediated by vocalisation, where the animal has acquired a learned stimulus-response pattern of the kind basic to animal training. When its trainer 'calls' a dog by its name ('Spot!'), she calls it voluntarily; when she issues a command ('Sit!'), she has the intention that the dog should hear and obey. If it is well trained, it does obey – better, it will have no choice in the matter, its response being now (at least in behaviouralist theory) as automatic as its unlearned reflexes.

The third and final scenario is a case of human/human interaction medi-ated by vocalisation. Let us suppose the trainer proudly calls the owner's attention to the dog's well-drilled response ('Look at Spot!').

Certainly, effects are or can be elicited by vocalisation in all these cases, under appropriate conditions, but in only two of these scenarios is it abso-lutely clear that something more is going on than the passing on of informa-tion – that communication is being achieved; and on a somewhat stronger, more controversial sense of 'communication', only one, in fact, will pass muster. In the first scenario, the cat cannot control the issuing of the signal that she is ready to mate. However informative it is to toms or to us, the signal cannot be reckoned meaningful from the sender's point of view, since the issuing of the signal has not been selected by the cat from amongst possible behaviours. In simple terms, her vocal activity is caused by a physiological state over which she has no control. That production of

the vocalisations is not, however, causally independent of internal physiological (or psychological) states at the time signals are issued will prove
important later (pp. 128–9).

In the second and third scenarios, in contrast, Spot's trainer does in some
intuitively obvious sense control the issuing of the linguistic signals that
she uses in dealing with both Spot and Spot's owner. We would not hesitate
to say that she has chosen to issue the signals from a range open to her in
that situation. Further, we would also be willing to say that she intends the
dog to pay attention to her, and the owner to pay attention to Spot. In
the second scenario, the trainer's saying the dog's name is informative to
the animal that he is the object of her attention. (In fact, it might be claimed
that the dog cannot in principle distinguish when someone is talking *about*
him, from when she is talking *to* him.) But the dog's response is, though
learned, more comparable to the cat's response to its hormonal surge than
it is to the dog owner's response to the trainer's utterance: the dog cannot
(at least in theory) but respond, unlike the owner, who has the option of
taking no notice of the call on his attention. If we impose the additional
requirement that for communication to take place an audience's response
to an utterance must be controlled by the audience, then only the third
scenario will clearly qualify as a case of communication. There is the same
result if we prefer the even stronger condition that the response be in part
motivated by recognition that that utterance was itself communicative,
it being debatable whether the dog can recognise intentions to pass on
information.

These descriptions are, as noted, simplistic; but they are enough to sketch
the outline of a serious difficulty for the naturalistic account of the origins
of language which Lucretius has on offer. For Lucretius claims that 'nature
forced/constrained' (*subegit*) primitive humans to emit cries (5.1028), while
the later assertion that animals' sensations 'compel' (*cogunt*) (1087) them
to vocalise is undoubtedly parallel to the claim about humans (cf. Konstan
1973: 48, with n. 46). But the examples just given of deliberate action
and coerced behaviour, natural or learned, show that what is needed is a
precise weighing of the contribution made by each factor in the process of
glossogenesis.

Unfortunately, Lucretius' choice of vocabulary does not help us as much
as we might like. There are two clear syntactic parallels for Lucretius' use
of *subigere* here (= *OLD* s.v. 6a). At 6.787, it connotes external physical necessity (the sun's rays 'force' snow to melt). 3.1077 is closer to our
text: a psychological force, lust for life, 'drives' people 'to tremble amid
doubtful dangers' (1076). Obviously, such a force can, at least in principle

and in some individuals, be overcome by other psychological factors (cf. 3.319–22).

As for 'compel' (*cogere*) (5.1086), Lucretius' use can be assigned to two principal categories:

(1) In the first, that of straightforward physical processes, belong cases of external forces or objects acting on (other) objects, (one or other of) the peculiar properties of which may, however, be said or implied to contribute to the effect produced. For example, the lightness of poppy seeds contributes to their mobility (3.197), although the lightness of fire or clouds is not mentioned at 6.464, 734.[33]

(2) *Cogere* is also applied to psychophysical and physiological processes of the kind in play in 5.1086, i.e. where the states or movements of organisms are involved.[34] The extent to which an effect is inevitable once the 'compelling' cause is active appears to vary from example to example, and can only be worked out case-by-case; it is clear only that some, undetermined, degree of necessity or constraint must be in play.

A similar vagueness of meaning and breadth of application characterises Lucretius' use of the verb 'draw, drive' (*protrahere*) to describe human infants whose very inarticulacy 'draws them on' to make gestures (5.1030f.). Lucretius employs forms of this verb in a sense appropriate to this context – where the abstraction *utilitas*[35] shows that something other than a mechanical process is underway – at 1.409, 4.189, and 5.1450 (cf. 1159); only 6.564 refers to the result of a simple physical action. His meaning is consistently one of a force of some kind applied externally to a resisting, or at least uncooperative, object, but one whose contribution to the process is either non-existent, or left implicit (cf. Schrijvers 1974: 354; 1999: 70).

What Lucretius is *claiming*, therefore, is that humans' superior vocalising abilities made the exploitation of those abilities in naming unremarkable: what he is *assuming* is that animal vocalising occurs under the constraint or force exercised by psychological and/or physiological states themselves

---

[33] A single feature of the affected object may be emphasised (e.g. 4.322; cf. 6.995). At 2.284–93 (esp. 291), what protects (some) complexes from being 'forced to endure and undergo' things by their own 'internal necessity' (*necessum | intestinum*) is the swerve – which must, therefore, be an event internal to the object. At 1.323, the work of 'time and nature' is surely in fact the work of the different natures of different things. 1.1010 presents an especially complex case, involving the necessary properties of body, void and the cosmos.

[34] There are four broad subcategories: (a) rational or inferential, including responses to evidence (e.g. 1.976, 2.869, 6.55; cf. 1.371, 499; 2.887); (b) emotional (3.60, 68; 5.1167; 6.16); (c) general psychophysical (at 2.282 the body is 'forced' to move by the soul; 3.523); (d) specific psychophysical (2.420; 3.487; 4.686, 762; 5.957).

[35] See n. 7 on these abstract expressions.

the natural effects of external objects or their properties. More fully, and
more precisely, if we follow the animal model of constrained vocalisation,
then our own peculiar human natures must have formed alliances with (the
perceived properties of) external objects to produce causal sequences each
of which is constructed out of (a perceived property of) an external object,
a corresponding sensation, and a corresponding vocalisation. At the atomic
level, the sequence is indeed describable in purely physical or 'mechanical'
terms: the atoms constituting or shed by objects, or in the visual 'films'
(εἴδωλα, *simulacra*) which objects emit, impinge on the sense organs, the
movements of which are transmitted to the soul, which in turn sets the
vocal chords, tongue and other relevant parts in motion.

There is evidently no guarantee built into this type of causal chain that
interventions in them by (other internal states or processes of) individual
humans would be sufficient to ensure clear, deliberate and regular emission
of vocalisations at appropriate times and places, as opposed to random and
idiosyncratic ones (in which case not only communication, but the bare
passing on of information, by the exploiting of shared natural associations
of vocalisations with objects, would be spotty at best and impossible at
worst). To apply a simple dichotomy: if certain human vocalisations were
names from the start, Lucretius' grouping of them with non-human vocalisations as no more than what nature has given us, is simplistic at best
and obfuscatory at worst; if, on the other hand, they became names, then a
process of appropriate intentional control must have begun at some point –
but how? Lucretius does not say.

If, then, early humans were indeed 'forced' or 'compelled' to utter such-
and-such noises in response to such-and-such sensations themselves caused
by such-and-such stimuli, those noises would have to have been brought
under appropriate control by the vocalisers: for if they could not, they could
never have become communicative. If humans subject to some physiological or psychological state could not help but produce a given vocalisation,
then the vocalisation could be informative to others of the utterer's being in
that state, but it could not serve to communicate this to an audience. That
is, if humans in face of some object or state of affairs could not help but
produce a given vocalisation, then the vocalisation could be informative to
others of the presence of that object or realisation of that state of affairs, but
it could not be employed to communicate to an audience that that object is
present or that that state of affairs was realised. Further, if communication
requires the intention to pass on information, it might be further argued
that at least some cases of communication require recognition on the part
of the recipient that the communicator has that intention; that natural

language is just such a case;[36] and that the Epicurean theory cannot explain this fact.

In brief: whatever the role of *utilitas* in the emergence of names turns out to be (see pp. 135–6 below), it could not have got so much as a toe-hold on our capacity to vocalise were we unable to control that capacity, or unable to control it in the relevant way(s).[37] Dahlmann may well be right to attribute to Lucretius the belief that '*homines natura, quidquid sentirent atque vellent, secum communicare cupiverunt*' (1928: 9), but without such appropriate control communication, as defined, is simply out of the picture.

Given the radical character of this objection to Lucretius' account, it would be reasonable to expect Epicurus' own (version of the) theory to share the defect I have identified. And the *Letter* does not in fact offer an explanation of how involuntary cries – instances of how 'nature too was both instructed *and constrained*' (*Ep. Hdt.* 75)[38] – came to be voluntary, and in such a way that they could be intentionally used and interpreted as signs. Indeed, the very fact that the second stage is that at which 'indicatings' (δηλώσεις) were improved (76) of itself shows that 'indicating', or signifying, of some kind was going on at the first stage; while the fact that the improvements were limited to cutting back on ambiguity and longwindedness show, that the later signifying was fundamentally of the same kind as the earlier. At the first stage, then, humans were *already* engaged in deliberate indicating of objects or states of affairs as part of communicational interactions with others of their kind. The point was first made by Brunschwig: 'the two comparatives . . . convey that what is being attempted is just slightly to improve the univocity and economy of language. The transformation that the linguistic conventions produce on the natural language is merely one of degree: it is not a transformation in kind' (1994: 32).

It is striking how Epicurus' account emphasises both the naturalness, and the passivity, of our initial cognitive and vocal adventures – a little as though reeds had feelings, and expressed them in whistles and pipings when the wind blows through them (cf. 5.1382f.); but it also assigns to nature – or rather, to men's natures – an active role in the second stage

---

[36] This has been the line taken by intention-based semantics (e.g. Grice 1989b, 1989c, 1989d, 1989e; cf. Schiffer 1972, 1981, Avramides 1989: 39ff., 1997), and a fruitful comparison can be drawn between Epicurean and modern intention-based thinking about the origin of language: see Atherton (forthcoming).

[37] This point has not, I think, been sufficiently appreciated in the literature: see e.g. Glidden 1994: 140; Cole 1990: 61 and n. 3; Bertoli 1980: 25.

[38] Later on in the process (*Ep. Hdt.* 76), necessity might have worked too on some of the (inventors of) names for non-sensible objects, on one interpretation of this much-debated text: see n. 10.

(cf. Brunschwig 1994: 23, modifying Bollack et al. 1971: 22, 236).[39] Here individual humans are the vessels in which the external world meets the internal – two faces of one nature, which both undergoes compulsion, and learns from experience – and which put the results on display in the shape of vocal sound. The crucial point for us is that primitive vocal sound is said to have been 'shaped by each experience and impression' (ὑφ' ἑκάστων τῶν παθῶν καὶ τῶν φαντασμάτων), *not* by any personal subject; and this is so even though the interaction of the humans' atoms with those of the perceived object must give the utterers in a given community some influence – albeit not a conscious one – on the sound that comes out (this is clear from the fact, crucial to Epicurus' version of naturalism (see pp. 101–2 above), that the process happens 'people by people').

Now the second stage involved (and, if it is continuing, still involves) the use of 'reasoning' (λογισμός), which makes its advances at different rates, and thus presumably imports some degree of contingency; and of course communal imposition of names and improvement thereof will require deliberate choice amongst alternatives. Yet whatever variations the differences amongst 'men's natures' might have introduced at the first stage too, those differences or variations surely cannot have ruled out appropriate control over vocalisation in some groups: for those groups would then never have developed language. Boyancé criticises Lucretius for failing to explain in detail 'comment on est passé de cette expression spontanée et émotive à un langage organisé, capable d'être échangé et compris' (1963: 247). The problem, I should say, is a different one – that vocal expression looks to have been causally determined, not spontaneous; and the suspicion now is that it was *Epicurus*, not Lucretius, who failed to spot that difficulty.

The other main sources – Proclus and Sextus Empiricus – which report Epicurus' theory are also, unfortunately, of a much later date, far less likely to be (wholly) reliable, and their value far harder to judge; but on the whole they do suggest that the processes at work in the invention of names were to some unspecified degree a matter of physiological necessity.

According to Proclus (*Comm. in Plat. Crat.* 17.13–16), Epicurus said that the earliest language-users 'did not impose names knowledgeably (ἐπιστημόνως) but as being moved naturally, like those who are coughing

---

[39] 'Preconceptions' (προλήψεις) may have been, in part at least, what Epicurus had in mind here, since they are passively formed from sense perceptions, but have an active role in understanding and inquiry: cf. e.g. Goldschmidt 1978: 157, 160. Brunschwig 1994: 24 suggests 'experience, concepts, language', especially the last, as the bridge between man's primitive condition and his adult/civilised state.

and sneezing and bellowing and howling and groaning'. This report comes in the context of a distinction (17.1ff.) between four different applications of the term 'by nature' or 'naturally' (φύσει), which together constitute the framework of a classification of naturalistic theories of the origins of language. These are: (i) as organisms and their parts are (17.1f.); (ii) as the activities and potentialities of items in group (i) are (17.2–4; the examples show that group (i) includes natural substances such as the elements); (iii) as shadows and reflections are (17.4); (iv) as artificial likenesses of natural objects are (17.5).

Proclus tells us that Epicurus' names fall into his group (i), but the examples suggest that group (ii) is more appropriate: Epicurus was talking (primarily) about the naturalness of the activity of imposing names on things, which is like seeing and hearing – something that is both an activity belonging to our human nature, and one set in motion in a more or less automatic way, in relation to appropriate objects, just as seeing is a naturally given power which is automatically exercised on appropriate objects under the right conditions. The derivative 'naturalness' of names will lie in their causal history, as the creations of this sort of natural movement in their creators. (This is why Usener's emendation of the text ('second' (δεύτερον) for 'first' (πρῶτον) at 17.5) makes good sense.) Naming will have taken place independently of what the namers may have believed about the vocalisation or the object named. The character of these processes can accordingly be compared to the causal purity which elevates perceptions and preconceptions to the level of absolute cognitive reliability (cf. Taylor 1980).

But there are differences. Coughing, and the like, do not, at least normally, in waking subjects, lie below the threshold of awareness, as perception and concept-formation do.[40] More important, however, is the *passivity* of those processes, which is what puts them beyond the reach of opinion and all its ills, but is not obviously matched in the responsive behaviours referred to by Epicurus. Are they indeed beyond the control of the subjects? (Other interactions with the environment, prior or continuing, could also be in play.) The first pair in Proclus' list can certainly be automatic: both can be expulsions of matter interfering with a process essential for life, breathing; both are samples of the functioning of the body's homeostatic systems. Yet we would surely agree intuitively that to some, ill-defined or even undefinable, extent, both can be controlled, or at any rate – and this is no small

---

[40] This point relates to perception *qua* alteration in the sense organs caused by contact with external atomic structures (e.g. reception of the *simulacra* in the case of vision), not to perception *qua* psychological or subjective experience. I refer to Brunschwig 1994: 35 for this distinction.

complication – interfered with by other causal processes. As for the last three items in Proclus' list, these look to be expressions of psychological distress, perhaps evoked by physical trauma, and tokens of them may or may not be controllable or otherwise preventable, according to circumstances.

Further, the closeness of the examples to simple animal behaviours is plain. Indeed, much as Lucretius' account places human vocalisation in the same broad category as non-human cries, so Epicurus' examples look to be assuming a continuum of human and non-human behaviours, in order to demonstrate, or emphasise, the naturalness of the former, although a progression may be implied from more or less involuntary coughing and sneezing (present in both humans and some non-humans) to the more vol- untary lowing and barking (present in animals and imitated by humans), to groaning or moaning, which may be involuntary or voluntary (e.g. when in great pain or in mourning). If authentic, the examples suggest that the vocalisations which were (made into?) names were (originally?) unlearned responses – ones not acquired by teaching, habituation, training or imita- tion – to changes in the utterer's internal states, whether physiological or psychological or both.

'Naturalness', too, is itself a concept much in need of clarification. The concepts structuring Proclus' classification (17.1ff.) are those of 'expertise' (τέχνη) and 'knowledge' (ἐπιστήμη) and their opposites (cf. Schrijvers 1974: 352). Hence (pace Dahlmann 1928: 8) the 'natural' is here to be interpreted not (necessarily) as what is beyond an agent's control, although it might be affected by other factors, or as what is causally determined, but rather as marked out by the absence of rational, systematic understanding of whatever is being done – in this case, naming.[41] Admittedly, the conceptual scheme applied by Proclus might not have been Epicurus' too. One reason for thinking that it was is that it makes good sense for Epicurus to have been presenting here his own ideas precisely with a view to counteracting the thesis of an authoritative name-giver skilled in the science or expertise of naming.[42] This would be especially appropriate were Epicurus' target the name-giver of the *Cratylus*, where Socrates introduces the crucial notion of the correctness of an action, including the action of naming, and assigns

---

[41] A useful parallel, which may well be Epicurean, can be found at Cicero *ND* 2.81f. It is also instructive to compare Galen's twinning of the concept of the 'expert' or 'technical mode' (τεχνικῶς) with that of the 'goal-directed' (τινος ἕνεκα), and, conversely, of the concept of the 'wholly non-technical' (οὔθ' ὅλως κατὰ τέχνην) with that of the 'non-goal-directed' (οὔθ' ἕνεκά του) in his account of the controversy over biological teleology at *UP* 17.6–12 K. Note also the distinction – with a clear Epicurean pedigree – reported by Eusebius (*Praep. evang.* 4.3.6.1ff.), between the products, not of nature, but of 'chance' (τύχη), and those of knowledge.

[42] This is where the identity of Epicurus' opponents (n. 21) becomes relevant to our discussion.

knowledge of such correctness uniquely to the technical expert in each field (387e6ff.). In contrast, it is hard to see what expertise there could be of coughing or groaning. Such a context – a critique of the *Cratylus* which traces its lineage in part back to Epicurus' own criticisms of that dialogue's expert name-givers – would also explain the odd structure of the passage, in which no example of the first and third senses (the Aristotelian and Platonic antecedents of which are plain to see) is offered, but in which Epicurus' opinion is given, then Cratylus', then Epicurus' again, then Socrates'.[43]

If this interpretation is correct, Proclus' report may show us Epicurus taking on the opposition with some of his customary polemical swagger. It is this tendency of Epicurus to (over-)simplification in certain contexts which may explain why Giussani found in the Proclus passage no more than an absurd exaggeration of the doctrine (1896: I, 279). Brunschwig offers the more balanced view that the 'polemical irony' of this testimony suggests some simplification of the issues, but that 'the indispensable rectification' must not be carried 'beyond the point at which this doxographical tradition would become unintelligible' (1994: 38). The distinction which interests us – that between controlled and uncontrolled vocalisation – would then be dimly visible in the background behind the figures of the knowledgeable and of the compulsive, internally coerced name-giver.

The picture that emerges from Sextus Empiricus' résumé of what is clearly Epicurean theory, at *M.* 1.143,[44] is subtly different from what we learn from Proclus: 'the first people who uttered (ἀναφθεγξάμενοι)[45] names produced their natural vocalisation (ἀναφώνησιν), like the cry on feeling pain and the shout on feeling joy or surprise (ὡς καὶ τὴν ἐπὶ τῷ ἀλγεῖν κραυγὴν καὶ τὴν ἐπὶ τῷ ἥδεσθαι ἢ θαυμάζειν ἐκβόησιν), and that is the way in which they mean that some names are of such a kind, others of such another, by nature'. The first vocalisations here are explicitly linked to emotional-*cum*-physiological states (and pain and joy are two of the emotions mentioned by Lucretius as evoking animals' cries, *DRN* 5.1061), but the relationship between cry and state, while natural, is not explicitly described in causal terms: the cry occurs 'on the occasion of' (ἐπί) the feeling. It remains open to us humans, usually, to control our groans of pain or whoops of joy. But if naturalness does not always connote inevitability, some degree of it must have been present in the originary correlations

---

[43] I am grateful to David Blank for making this final point, and for sharpening various other distinctions applied in this section.

[44] On the passage in its context, see Blank 1998: 178, ad loc.

[45] This verb and its cognate noun have a distinctive Epicurean flavour: cf. e.g. Diogenes of Oenoanda 12.3.2.

between objects and vocalisations: for if vocalisers could have changed
their cries at will, or on a whim, communal systems of communication
exploiting those correlations could never have grown up.

The theories offered by Diodorus Siculus (1.8.3f.), Vitruvius (*Arch.* 2.1.1),
and Lactantius (*Inst. div.* 6.10.10–13) have also been claimed to betray
Epicurean influence, and something should be said about their bearing
on this objection to the Epicurean theory.

In none of them does an explicit transition from uncontrolled to controlled vocalisation play any role. In fact, Diodorus simply posits a move
from meaninglessness and inarticulacy to articulate symbols (and cf. 1.16.1,
on Hermes' work in articulating human speech).[46] Vitruvius may perhaps
allude to initial random vocalisation,[47] but says nothing about how or when
deliberate signifying came into being. Lactantius thinks that nods whereby
each man could 'signify his desire' (*uoluntatem suam significasse*) preceded
the 'beginnings of speech' (*sermonis initia*) and the imposition of names, as
if controlling vocalisation were not even an issue. The same difficulty besets
the theory set out by Ptolemy (*Crit.* 7.18ff.) whose account, as Verlinsky
plausibly argues (this volume, p. 92), is also at least partly Epicurean in
origin: 'it is likely that the first significations by means of discourse, formed
both from the psychological states which affected <people>, and from
the peculiar character of the vocal sounds, were sounded out naturally by
people who had not yet had benefit of any instruction' (7.19–22).[48]

Given this sizeable lacuna at the heart of the Epicurean account, how are
we to view Lucretius' howling, whimpering, whinnying, neighing and cawing beasts and birds? Perhaps they, or some of them, are in the sort of entirely
uncontrollable physiological state assigned to Puss earlier (scenario 1).
Perhaps their cries, or some of them, are – to use a modern jargon again –
'stimulus-bound' and subject to 'releaser mechanisms', the variety they
display being the result of variety in the external objects and in the resulting psychological-*cum*-physiological states, which in turn cause the cries;
and Lucretius, as we have just seen, does indeed say that 'various sensations
force' (*cogunt*) the animals 'to utter various vocalisations' (5.1087–8).

It may well be that the need to introduce some appropriate psychophysical source(s) for relevant control of vocalisation did not strike Epicurus, or

---

[46] On Diodorus' sources, see n. 20. It is precisely on the grounds that he does include an opening phase
of inarticulacy that Spoerri 1959: 135–6 and Brunschwig 1994: 34 denied his account an Epicurean
pedigree.

[47] The text is unclear, however: see Cole 1990: 33 n. 10.

[48] τῶν γὰρ διὰ τοῦ λόγου σημασιῶν τὰς μὲν πρώτας εἰκὸς ὑπὸ τῶν μηδέπω παραδόσεώς τινος
ἐπιτυχόντων φυσικῶς ἀναπεφωνῆσθαι πεποιημένας ἀπό τε τῆς τῶν προσπιπτόντων παθῶν,
καὶ ἀπὸ τῆς τῶν φωνῶν ἰδιοτροπίας.

Lucretius, as problematic. There is some evidence that Epicurus recognised a distinction between animals that are, and animals that are not, subject to something like moral assessment, some animals not being straightforwardly identical with their atomic 'constitutions' (συστασεις) (e.g. *Nat.* 25, 1056 5.1.11, Laursen 1995: 16). Given the criterion by which it is defined, such animals must be able not merely to learn, and to modify their behaviour – including, presumably, their signalling and vocalising behaviour – but to do so in response to experiences based on reward and punishment directed toward the acquisition of very particular dispositions: otherwise it is hard to see why we should think of them as liable to 'the mode of admonition and correction' (τῶι νουθε[τ]ητ[ι]κῶι τρόπωι καὶ ἐπανορθωτικῶι) (25, 1191 7.2.5.2–4, Laursen 1995: 31). But the origin of such modifications remains notoriously mysterious.[49] Other evidence about the Epicurean school points to disagreement about the status of animals, and gives little or no guidance on the issue of intentionality.[50]

As for Lucretius, Bailey raises the broad objection to his account of 'volition' (*uoluntas*) (4.877–906) that, because it requires acceptance by the soul of 'atomic films' (*simulacra*) of the intended action (e.g. walking), no such images could exist before agents had engaged in the relevant behaviour (1947: III, 1490, *ad* 5.1028–90). It might be argued instead that such images could never by themselves go to create a concept of *deliberate* activity of any sort, for this is beyond the power of mere perception to capture and convey, at least if it is as bare and stripped a thing as Lucretius' refutation of scepticism requires (4.379–85; cf. D.L. 10.31). His account thus exhibits, at best, the circumstances under which volition is exercised, not how it is itself created or constituted, much as one argument for the swerve at 2.215ff. (a text at least as controversial as *On Nature* 25) assumes that there is such a thing as *uoluntas*, of which we are aware in our own actions, which we know to be absent from our own involuntary movements (*DRN* 2.258, 272–6,

---

49 Text of this book from Laursen 1987, 1995, 1997. On the interpretation of the phrase 'the things produced' or 'the developments' (τὰ ἀπογεγεννήμενα), see also e.g. Long and Sedley 1987: I, 109–10, Purinton 1996.

50 Thus, for example, contracts between ourselves and other animals are in principle, and by implication, permitted by Epicurus in *RS* 32 (cf. Long and Sedley 1987: II, 113, *ad* 20J; 130, *ad* 22A2), but ruled out explicitly, and in principle, by Hermarchus, who seems to reserve to humans the capacity for 'empirical reasoning' (ἐπιλογισμός) (Porphyry *Abst.* 1.12.7). (I assume it is right to assign this account to Hermarchus – see Bouffartigue and Patillon 1977: 118; Longo Auricchio 1988: 137–41; Cole 1990: 72 – with reservations, perhaps, about some passages.) Cf. Annas 1993: 67–8, 70 with n. 60, who thinks the lack of clarity in the sources on this issue is to be explained by the lack of clarity on the topic of non-human rationality. The whole issue of where the Epicurean line of demarcation runs between human and animal behaviour, especially vocal behaviour, will be further discussed in Atherton (forthcoming).

279), the effects of which we can observe even in other non-human, animals (263–71),[51] and which is somehow accounted for only by the swerve. Such volition is implied by the willingness of some non-human animals to find refuge with humans (5.868–70), since such behaviour speaks of a capacity to pursue perceived, long-term advantage – something far removed from an automatic response to immediate dangers or enticements. Again, in our passage Lucretius uses the example of the noises dogs make as they 'pretend' (*imitantur*) to bite the pups they are playing with (1067–9). But pretending to do something requires appropriate selection of and control over, and perhaps awareness of, the relevant behaviour – even the expectation of being understood as faking by the fakee.[52]

This last requirement would clearly take us fully into the realm of communication, in the sense outlined earlier (p. 116). It does not, however, obviously entail rationality (cf. 3.753); more argument and inquiry would be required to determine exactly what it *does* entail. True, horses are said by Lucretius to have a 'mind' (*mens, animus*) (2.265, 268, 270; cf. Annas 1993: 67), and animals are said to dream, as we do, about the important events in their lives (4.984–1010; cf. Sorabji 1993: 28–9). But (*pace* Annas 1993: 67) at 3.299 there is nothing necessarily rational about the stag's 'mind', for this, being governed by cold air currents, is more like its 'natural temperament' ('intellect' (*animus*), 288, and 'nature' (*natura*), 302, are clearly synonyms for *mens* here). Similarly, the horse's *mens* may be (the physiological basis of) its consciousness or subjectivity, not (that of) its rationality. Again, whatever precisely the role of the swerve in volition, such behaviour does not entail that some sort of 'free will' faculty, floating free of all causation, is either necessary or sufficient to account for such controlled, goal-directed behaviour as is involved in communication; and is just as far from meaning that Epicureans thought that it was. My point is that Lucretius does not draw our attention to the requirements for communication which I have argued for here.

Somehow the distinction has to be explained between an organism's overall causal responsibility for a bit of behaviour – say, emission of a vocalisation – and its being responsible for it in such a way that it can be said to have chosen or to have intended to emit that vocalisation as a means of communication. It is obscure just what is required, in terms of an organism's psychological

---

[51] I read 'of the horses' (*equorum*) for the MSS 'of whom' (*quorum*) in 2.264, on the grounds that it makes best sense of the reference to 'living things' (*animantibus*) in 256, and is consonant with the other evidence in Lucretius for animal volition (see main text).

[52] Intentional deception may have a role to play in naturalistic glossogenesis. See Atherton (forthcoming).

or physiological equipment, for it to be capable of communicative intent, and obscure too when that intent is present (so that what counts as a case of communication remains moot even if we agree on what constitutes 'communication'). Further, what explanations of non-human behaviour we accept as legitimate or possible will be guided by theoretical as much as empirical considerations. Thus to interpret as intentional a plover's apotropaic behaviour, whereby it feigns injury to a wing in such a way as to lure a predator away from its nest, would entail that the plover has beliefs about other animals' beliefs, then rule-following may seem a far more economical and plausible alternative (see Hauser 1996: 569ff. for a discussion) – always provided, of course, we can find some way of getting the animal to follow the rules without intentionality. Generally speaking, non-human signalling behaviour might well be open to more complex explanations than are compatible with the crude behaviourist scenarios I sketched earlier, but ones which are still non-intentional in character; and today such explanations would be preferred on the general grounds that *ceteribus paribus* more parsimonious theories are better than less parsimonious ones.

Investigation of what Epicureans made of these larger background issues cannot be properly undertaken in this paper. So I shall simply assume that Epicureans believed either that they had an answer to the question, how random atomic movements have yielded controlled behaviour and intentional action, or that they did not need to give one, and turn briefly instead to the *kind* of control which is required, and how it fits into Lucretius' scheme for explaining the origins of language.

POINTING AND PRECONCEPTIONS

It is vital, first of all, not to lose sight of the facts that the vocalisers' own internal states constitute the causal sequences which lead from external objects to vocalisations, and that in consequence these sequences may be open to alteration from within the organism itself. Lucretius' descriptions of the process at least do not imply, as we saw, that these sequences, once set in motion, cannot be broken, and thus issue in a different outcome (a different vocalisation, or no vocalisation at all) from the one it would have had, had it not been interfered with. But one special sort of intervention must be in play: that which is somehow connected to the (perceived) usefulness of the behaviour. This is explicit in Lucretius' account (5.1029), although not in Epicurus'; it has come up for us already in the behaviour of animals sensible enough to trade protection for domestic service (868–70); and it is fundamental to the Epicurean explanation of the origins of justice and law, with which in Lucretius' prehistory of man the rise of language is intimately, if obscurely, connected (1021–7).[53]

Remember that what Lucretius is claiming is this:

So, if different sensations compel animals, dumb as they are, to issue different vocalisations, it is so much more reasonable (*aequum*) for humans to have then been able to mark out different things with different vocalisations. (5.1087–90)

Lucretius' argument must run as follows: many animals, including humans, vocalise naturally, in a variety of ways (stated at 1059–61, illustrated at 1062–86). The variety is due, in part, to differences in sensations received (1061f., 1087); such differences might be species specific, but Lucretius rather appealed to differences between types of emotion assumed to be common to the higher animals, such as parental affection, sexual desire, fear and anger (see already p. III above on this point). It is also due to differences in vocalising ability; humans surpassing other animals in this regard (1057f.). Early humans were forced to vocalise by their own internal states, much as non-humans were and are (1028, 1087), but they introduced a use for these already differentiated cries, that of naming objects (1089f.). The upshot is that this development is not surprising, since the resource put to this new use was both naturally and widely available.

For the transformation of instinctive, automatic cries into names to get under way, there must at some point in time have been a state of affairs in which the presence of some object – let us call it A – was not needed to produce in some vocaliser(s) the vocalisation which (*ceteribus paribus*) was causally associated with As in this proto-community – vocal noise *a*. What happens next? Cole thinks that 'the first person to form and utter the "natural" word for something is immediately understood by his companions' (1990: 72).[54] The difficulty with this claim becomes clear when we try to say what the 'understanding' would be of in such a case. We grant that the noise-makers will have noticed that a token of a given noise has been made by one of their number. (Perhaps there was then an exchange of *a*-type noises, in which case the 'freeing up' of the noise, its detachment from the {object –> internal state –> vocalisation} causal sequence, must already have begun, with people already having some control over the production of *a*-type noises.) But *ex hypothesi* no one could yet be in

---

[53] This important topic cannot be broached here; full discussion in Atherton (forthcoming).
[54] *Pace* Cole, however, Cicero *Fin.* 1.30 does not constitute a parallel to *Ep. Hdt.* 38 in the field of ethics: the former describes the principle that the natural goodness of pleasure is immediately grasped in much the same way as are secondary properties of physical objects; the latter prescribes finding the 'first concept' associated with each vocalisation.

a position to utter *a* as *a sign for As*. For it looks as though, if a vocaliser
had already hatched the idea of using the noise in this way, that he will
thereby qualify as the name-giver Lucretius is at pains to dismiss as absurd
and impossible (1048f., '. . . whence was given to this man to know and
to see in his mind's eye what he wanted to do?', where what is out of the
question is 'marking everything out | with vocalisations', 1043–4).

So let us suppose that someone present at the random uttering of noise *a*
goes off and fetches an A. What would be new about this association would
be that it was the vocalisation that, so to say, 'produced' the object, not the
other way round. Now the noise-makers notice that (a token of) the noise
had been associated by one of their kind with (a token of) the object(-type)
the presence of (other tokens of) which in the past had made them produce
(other tokens of) the noise. Notice that in this scenario the noisemaker who
goes off to fetch an A must already have acquired the ability to associate the
noise with the object in its absence, so that a different sort of link is in play
between noise and object than that which manifests itself in the {object –>
sensation –> vocalization} chain. Presumably this *a*- and A- related
behaviour is what will ultimately allow for a community-wide association
of a noise-type and an object-type. What is the link, then, and how has it
come into being?

That some sort of physiological or psychological response to the vocalisation which was not caused by the presence of an A – call it a^* – is implicated
in the account is plain, since without it noise a^* will be just that, a noise:
it has to be associated by a hearer with As, and association of this sort is
a psychophysical process. Further, it has to be associated with the same
kind of thing by all hearers, since otherwise the process by which the noise
becomes a community's name for the same type of thing cannot get started.
The most plausible psychological link must be memory. Noise a^* reminds
the hearer of As, and his thinking of them makes him go off and look for
one. (It helps to think of As as especially tasty tit-bits, so that someone
might well have had wistful memories of absent As in the past.) Up until
now he has not – and this would be crucial – been made to think of them
by noise *a* alone, since *ex hypothesi* this vocalisation had previously always
been causally produced by the object. (As Hammerstaedt 1996: 228 points
out, a word 'può indicare una certa realtà anche nei momenti in cui quest'
ultima non si percepisce più o non ancora', and somehow or other this
fact has to be accommodated in any semantic theory; pointing at objects
in one's presence (5.1030–2) is not an adequate parallel for word-use.)

We can also suppose that the noise-making behaviour, the subsequent
fetching behaviour, and finally the exhibition of the A, are remembered by

members of the group.[55] We have also gathered from Lucretius' example of the pointing infant (1030–2) that humans are natural sign-makers. So we may surmise that (tokens of) the noise began to be used when members of the tribe wished to direct the attention of others to those objects, instead of, say, pointing at one, or going to fetch one and then exhibiting it. The necessary ingredient of *intentional* use of the noise in order to bring to mind the object would thus be secured, and provided other users understood the intention (as they already understood, we assume, the intentions behind pointing gestures), the materials are in place for a convention regarding use of the noise as a sign.

The problem now, I would suggest, is that the account assumes what it is supposed to be explaining: intentional use of vocalisations as signs for objects.

What is evoked in the noise-making community by a^* cannot be, as it is in the case of externally caused vocalisations, a sensation of an A, e.g. that of a tiger, since it does not have the right causal history. Epicurus seems to think that in contemporary users the response to a name is the coming to mind of an 'outline' (τύπos) of the object in accordance with a preconception (D.L. 10.33), and, implausible as that claim may be on empirical grounds, it is surely right that names cannot and do not have the same effect on users as do objects themselves (someone's uttering the word 'tiger' in my living room, for example, will not have the same effect on me as my finding a tiger there). So the psychological bridge must rather be a memory of a sensation caused by an A and automatically classified by type; perhaps it is a preconception of As.[56] Noises, therefore, must already be capable of evoking memories or preconceptions of objects; they are to that extent freed from the {object –> sensation –> vocalisation} chain, and the sensations which originally produced the vocalisations have no direct role in the naming relation. We would consequently expect the noise *not* to end up as the name for the sensation of an object. But nor does it end up as the name for the preconception associated with it: it

---

[55] Here one might compare the role of 'non-rational memory' (ἄλογos μνήμη) in Hermarchus' account of the evolution of laws against homicide, before 'empirical reasoning' (ἐπιλογισμόs) came to be required to turn people away from violence – at any rate, those capable of rational thought. Manuwald 1980: 21f. suggests that Hermarchus' 'non-rational memory' stage in the development of law is a special application of Epicurus' first, pre-rational, stage in human prehistory as a whole.

[56] The main texts in this difficult area are: D.L. 10.31, 33; *Ep. Hdt.* 37f., 82. It seems highly unlikely, as suggested by Robin, that a preconception could be acquired by a species, rather than by an individual, so that 'un individu, même dépourvu du toute expérience personnelle du langage, doit ressentir le besoin fonctionnel de s'exprimer par des gestes (1031 sq.) ou par des sons articulés (1057 sq.)' (1962: III, 144, *ad* 5.1046–9). Leaving aside its failure to keep apart language proper from sign language, this analysis overlooks the fact that preconceptions can be acquired only as a result of experience. (Cic. *ND* 1.43 (Velleius) is not a counter-example.)

becomes instead the name for its external cause(-type). (This is to ignore the question of vocalisations that do in fact become names for psychophysical states.)

At this juncture the objection can be raised that for the noise to be a name someone has to utter the noise *with the intention of referring to As*. Names, the objection runs, do not merely remind people of things (I am assuming here, for the sake of the argument, that they are indeed reminders of some sort).[57] Nor is it just that they can be regarded, as a class, as items meant to remind people of things (which is why, on this approach, we can use names in the way we do: to communicate). The crucial points which can be levelled against Lucretius are that we use names to *refer* to things, and that we do so with the expectation of being *understood as referring* to them. How, then, did Lucretius' primitive community get in the way of using, and of understanding, vocalisations in this way?

The issue at stake is thus, in part, that before anyone could get the idea – the preconception – of the usefulness of vocalisation for communication, people had already to be using such noises, and to be doing so in order to communicate with each other, this being the most plausible interpretation of what Lucretius means by 'had used the vocalisations amongst themselves', 5.1046f.[58] (and this is indeed activity experience of which can be interpreted as a necessary condition for someone else's engaging in it). Admittedly, someone might have formed a general concept of the factual or causally grounded associations they had observed in their community of noise(-type) *a* with object(-type) A, noise(-type) *b* with object(-type) B, and so on. But if that is all that Lucretius means – the mere association by the noise-makers of noise with thing – then members of the community could not (yet) have come into possession of the general concept of vocalisation used *in order* to make others think of a certain object, and thus of its usefulness for that purpose.[59]

---

[57] A link with the theory of commemorative signs, reported by Sextus Empiricus (*P.H.* 2.97–9, *M.* 8.141–51, cf. 316–19), is possible; full discussion in Atherton (forthcoming).

[58] Bollack 1978: 156 claims that '. . . l'idée de l'avantage de la langue découle de son existence'. But, if names could be recognised as useful only from and after being used, how did they come to be used in the first place? Dahlmann asserts that men '*sensimque sonis linguae inter se utentes summae eos esse utilitatis intellexerunt*', 1928: 9; which is to assume that these *uoces* were of the same kind, and were performing the same function, as names, since otherwise they could not have given rise to a preconception of the usefulness *of names*.

[59] Thus Schrijvers 1999: 71–2 is right that what gave us the concept of the usefulness of the organs of speech was not their potential for use, but their actual use 'et ainsi la volonté de s'en servir'. But he also claims (1999: 71) that from a series of perceptions of the acts of signifying 'l'utilité saute aux yeux'. For Epicureans, however, usefulness is not the sort of thing, strictly speaking, that can be perceived at all: cf. p. 127 and n. 40, above, with Brunschwig 1994: 35, whose distinction between perception as the 'abstract limit of analysis', and perception as what is subjectively experienced, will still not get us to perception of such properties as usefulness.

There is even more at stake, however. A distinction will indeed have to be made between a noise's making a hearer think of A, and its being used in order to do so; and it is true that it is the latter notion, in general terms, which is needed here. But the precise problem is different: it is that to get the idea of the usefulness of noises as names, it would not be enough even for one's fellows to be making *a*-noises deliberately and thereby reminding people of As, if they do so (and this is the crux) without the intention of doing so by referring to As.

It is quite impossible, in fact (*pace* Janson 1979: 154), for humans to have had the ability to talk a long time before they used it (4.837–40). If the usefulness of names for communication is the only thing which can produce the preconception thereof, then it seems reasonable to infer that, similarly, the preconception of names can only come from experience of names; but if use of names requires a preconception of names, then we are caught in (to use a modern phrase) a Catch 22. There can be no *first* use of names. How to break out of this vicious circle? A possible answer is: by having primitive humans put their disposition to vocalise at the service of their disposition to use signs, in such a way that a new use of existing vocalisations becomes possible.

The idea is this: a vocaliser, having already observed the chance, unintended, but fairly regular, association between noise and object made by himself and his fellows, sees that vocalisations can be used as a novel kind of way of doing what had previously been done (and continues to be done, instinctively, by human infants: 5.1030–2) in an *ad hoc* and rather inefficient way, viz., referring to things, much as had been done by using gestures – only now with such advantages as freeing hands for other tasks, being able to refer to things not present, or to communicate in the dark, and, above all, considerably increased precision and constancy of reference. Yet if a vocaliser can do that, he will already have invented names. And (the twist in the tale) *so will everyone else*: for we humans all have these gifts equally, as Lucretius' first argument has reminded us (1043–5). The Epicurean account thus works, ironically, only if space is found, alongside our other remarkable talents, for what the school's methodology and psychology is in danger of ruling out: imagining what we have never perceived, without aid of prior preconceptions.

This is, indeed, the solution suggested by Lucretius' own account: in it he stresses how very unremarkable it is for humans to put their unparalleled vocalisation capacity to use in 'marking all things out' (cf. 5.1043f.), as if, crucially, the disposition to 'mark things out' were already present, and were simply finding a new outlet – one which is entirely 'reasonable' (*aequum*) in the circumstances. At no point does Lucretius claim that the signalling of external objects is itself emergent in the primitive human community.

Cole has indeed suggested that there was an 'analogical extension' by reason, of the principle involved in natural signing (1990: 74), although the psychology of this process remains unclear.[60] And a Lucretian expression of this result can be extracted from the crucial lines 5.1028–9:

At uarios linguae sonitus natura subegit
Mittere, et utilitas expressit nomina rerum.

But nature forced [men] to emit the tongue's various
sounds, and usefulness moulded names for things.

It can fairly be said that in the correct interpretation of the verb I translate 'moulded' (*expressit*) lies the solution to the problem of the role of necessity in the whole affair, since, on one reading, it connotes a (quasi-)mechanical forceful process, a kind of expulsion; on another,[61] it refers to a shaping or forming process, possibly one performed by (something like) an intelligence pursuing a goal.[62] The latter option looks, as a whole, more consonant with the context: one would expect an appeal to utility to be conceived in terms of an agent's doing something that has a certain result or effect, although the agent need not be aware of its activity as purposeful, as long as it is equipped with some sort of 'feedback' which allows it to pursue, on the whole, what is as a matter of fact beneficial and avoid, on the whole, what is harmful. (Indeed, the extent to which the process is conscious remains moot.) If there is a physical process of ejection of matter involved in such cases, it must be mediated and directed by a physically realised faculty geared to the organism's survival and capable of responding appropriately to the environment and its incursions.[63] On the other hand, Lucretius' own usage of the verb elsewhere is against this reading,[64] which in any case would

---

60   Analogy is one of the routes to the formation of 'thoughts' or 'ideas' (ἐπίνοιαι) at D.L. 10.32, which may include preconceptions, mentioned in the next sentence (33); but, as Long suggests (1971b: 119; cf. Goldschmidt 1978: 161), preconceptions may be the sorts of ideas formed by direct 'incidence' (περίπτωσις) of external stimuli on the senses, with analogy, resemblance or combination being responsible for the other kinds of ideas. The similarity between this list and the Stoic classification at D.L. 7.52 (cf. Cicero *Fin.* 3.33f.) is remarkable, although the latter is more systematic (cf. Goldschmidt 1978: 159–60).
61   Cf. Bailey 1947: III, 1491, ad loc., cf. III, 1490, with Schrijvers's comments (1974: 34).
62   See *TLL* s.v. part I, II A2a, b; *OLD* s.v. 2a, 4c, vs. *TLL* s.v. part II, *OLD* s.v. 6. It is helpful to contrast Cicero's appeal to a coining metaphor at *Rep.* 3.3.
63   Such a process seems to be envisaged by Lucretius at 5.945ff.
64   There are fifteen examples of simple causal processes to which forms of *exprimere* are applied (e.g. 5.453, 487; 6.181f., 212, 275, 478). There is a single exception: 4.299, a highly unusual case in which, in order to explain the left-to-right reversal of reflections, a still flexible plaster mask gets turned

founder on the difficulty we have already encountered as a consequence of Epicurean epistemology itself.

But the thought cannot be that the usefulness of having names acted to give articulateness and/or semantic determinacy to names, much as the metal worker or sculptor imposes a definite geometrical or iconic shape on relatively amorphous metal or stone. For without some measure of precisely those properties (determinacy of shape, and of reference or content), it is hard to see how the primitive vocalisations could be called 'names' at all.[65] They would amount to no more than all-purpose attention sharing gestures, like the infant's pointing activity, when what is needed is an explanation of the emergence of names peculiar to objects.

Nor can Lucretius mean, however, that the usefulness of having vocalisations as names for things 'forced' certain vocalisations, themselves the products of nature, into names: for names, obviously, must already exist to give rise to the conception of their usefulness. This interpretation would, in effect, make the benefit conferred by the having of names itself produce those names in the first place (as if a coin, and not just the metal, pre-existed the coining process).[66] A sequence of this kind is indeed possible for artefacts (4.843–52) which perform (better, more efficiently, more conveniently) an already known function: but names are supposed not to be 'pure' artefacts – just how pure they are is, in a sense, just what is now at issue, and indeed makes this whole inquiry a contribution to the general question of where (if anywhere) Epicureans drew the boundary between the natural and the artificial. (Interestingly, there seems to be no Epicurean correlate of the Stoic distinction (D.L. 7.54) between naturally formed 'ideas' (ἔννοιαι), which are preconceptions, and other kinds.)[67]

So if primitive humans could not have got the idea of 'marking things out', and of doing so 'with vocalisations', from conversation with others, since *ex hypothesi* no such thing as 'conversation' existed, nor from nature,

---

inside-out when hurled against a hard surface, so that what was the left side of the 'face' is now the right, and *vice versa*. This usage seems to combine the 'moulding' or 'shaping' and the 'forcing' meanings of the verb, although the presence of the participle 'pushed out (*elisam*)' does tend to emphasise the former.

[65] This point is finessed by Dahlmann: '*ex quibus* [sc. vocal sounds] *paulatim utilitate rei cognita nomen firmum cuiusque rei statuerint*' (1928: 16) – as if names were *already* in existence when the *sonitus linguae* were being forced out.

[66] This is the mistake that Janson seems to commit, 1979: 152; cf. 153, when he has Lucretius saying, in effect, that 'Man started to talk because he was naturally endowed with the means to do it, *and because it was at that time useful*' (my emphasis).

[67] According to Nichols, who is discussing precisely the first coming into being of language, for the Epicureans '[t]here is a natural origin and cause of everything that men do, discover, invent', 1976: 136. True: but what *else* is involved, and at what stage?

which knows only, through its creatures, of the regular, causally mediated, association of features of the world with vocalisations, the neatest response is that this is something instinctive: indicating objects in a communicative context is something humans do spontaneously and untaught. Lucretius shows us a prelinguistic child engaged in trying to create shared focus of attention on an object or feature of the environment: he does not (though he has often been assumed to) describe a child's first attempts to learn to *talk*. This approach not only tactfully draws attention away from the enormous differences between the situations facing today's learners and our prelinguistic ancestors, it draws it toward our unlearned bent to engage in communication.

CONCLUSIONS

So natural signs – natural in their causal origin – of internal states produced by external objects have become, thanks to their usefulness, non-natural signs of external objects – 'non-natural' not in having no natural relation with the objects they signify, but in that relation's being irrelevant to their function: to their being used as intentional signs by a linguistic community. The birds Lucretius refers to at 5.1078–86, the ones popularly said to call up the winds, if they were indeed making a genuine invocation, must be *addressing* something or someone, and this implies at least the availability of a way of referring to the addressees; reference in general is always to something, and linguistic reference must always be freely chosen. But we have seen that this is just what is missing from Lucretius' account as it stands: it is not possible to pass from animals' vocal responses to their feelings, *via* birds' supposed summoning of the winds, to designative or naming activity, as if involuntary cries, summonses and names could all be lumped together as vocalisations. Further, the use of vocalisations as stable vehicles of intentional reference to fixed features of the world can be explained only on the assumption that humans are more imaginative – for want of a better word – than Lucretius' account seems to admit. Every human being, not some lonely privileged individual, divine or divinely inspired, is capable of crossing from a prelinguistic state to possession of a natural language over the bridge formed by his or her own dispositions to vocalise and to use signs for objects in contexts of communication. If the assumption that such dispositions are merely the luck of the atomic draw is felt as unsatisfactory, Lucretius would no doubt challenge us to find fault with the principles and methods of Epicureanism from and by which this account has been constructed; and we cannot console ourselves that the means we moderns have won to see into the remote past have made us into authorities on the origins of language. I hope that this exploration of the question from one particular set of empirical starting points has clarified the problems the naturalistic tradition still faces.[68]

[68] I would like to thank David Blank, Brad Inwood and all the participants at the Symposium for their helpful and insightful comments on earlier drafts of this paper. Its title is a tribute to Wardy's superb study (1988), from which I have learned so much about the right way(s) of reading Lucretius.

CHAPTER 5

Communicating Cynicism: Diogenes' gangsta rap[*]

Ineke Sluiter

I INTRODUCTION

In recent years, there has been an upsurge of interest in ancient Cynicism, which has benefited in particular from renewed attention to the notion of rhetorical practice. It was recognised that even though the Cynics never formulated an explicit body of philosophical theories, their life-style could be analysed as the exercise of a philosophical rhetoric, intended to convey a particular set of ethical messages.

In this contribution, I will focus on Cynic strategies of communication, and on problems of the interpretation of Cynicism resulting from their communicative choices. First, I will look at the Cynics' use of transgressive non-verbal communication with the help of modern socio-linguistic theories of non-verbal communication and impression management. The Cynics scandalise their audience by their conscious use of the body and its processes for philosophical purposes; anthropological ideas about transgression will be helpful here (section 2).

In section 3, I will turn to verbal communication, and investigate the Cynics' characteristic use of language and literature, regarded as an aspect of their self-fashioning. Here, I argue that Cynic ideas on language correspond to a specific type of folk-linguistics, represented for us by a well-delineated literary tradition of *iambos* and comedy. I claim that the literary representations of Cynicism that have come down to us cannot be fully understood, unless their intertextual relations with other ancient transgressive genres are explored.[1] The literary representations of the Cynics acquire a fuller

---

[*] I would like to thank the participants of the Symposium Hellenisticum 2001, particularly Julia Annas, for discussion, and the members of the Amsterdam Hellenist Club and the colleagues of the Department of Classical Studies at the University of Pennsylvania, for valuable comments.
[1] Note that I do not use 'intertextuality' in the restricted sense of *Quellenforschung*, but in the wider sense of the term, i.e. to refer in general to the place of a text, regarded as a locus of absorption and transformation, in a network of other texts and genres, and more specifically to the relationship of that text and other specific texts, a relationship of which the partners in the literary communication are aware. Cf. Pfister 1985 and Broich 1985: 31.

meaning when they are seen to resonate within a web of comparable texts, notably the tradition of *iambos* and ancient comedy (section 3).

Finally (section 4), I will raise the question of the effectiveness of the consciously self-undermining aspects of Cynic communication, again by comparing them to other transgressive genres like satire and gangsta rap. Throughout, my main focus of attention will be Diogenes, supplemented with some Antisthenes and later Cynics.

My paper rests on the assumption that, since so much of what we know of the Cynics' performance is through the literary shaping of their lives in the form of telling anecdotes and narratives, we should be paying special attention to the essentially literary nature of the representation of Cynicism and particularly of its fountainhead, Diogenes; we must not deny the uncompromisingly literary and artistically contrived nature of our sources. This will be particularly relevant when we consider the impact of Cynicism on its audience: the experience of the primary, original audience, often represented as the internal audience in the narrative, differed considerably from that of the reading or listening external audience of the (semi-) literary versions of Cynicism. The embrace of the Cynics by the literary tradition must have had a thoroughly domesticating effect. The question whether and how far Diogenes himself actually lived his life as if he was 'writing' it as a text (see below, section 4), immediately endangers the value of the ensuing interpretation, because of the circularity it entails. While emphasising the socio-cultural *Sitz im Leben* of the representations of Diogenes, my interpretation does not intend to deny the real impact that Cynicism had especially on other philosophers. The Stoics in particular derived considerable inspiration for their ethics from Diogenes' life, regarded as an authentic attempt to embody a philosophy and distinguishable from fake imitators of its external aspect.

2 NON-VERBAL COMMUNICATION AND THE ACTION-*CHREIA*

In this section, we will study some of the most salient points of Cynic communication: its theatricality, its use of non-verbal communication, its preference for transgressive forms of communication, and its preferred literary form, the *chreia*.

A naïve view of Cynic communication could have it that any conclusions drawn by the general public from observing the Cynic life-style and Cynic behaviour are just an unintended by-product of the Cynic way of life. This would entail that the Cynic has no programme and no didactic intentions, but that their natural life-style is indeed just that, natural, and uncultivated;[2] if this is elevating to anyone, it is an epiphenomenon of the rule of nature. The didactic effect achieved by the Cynic performance is that of a role-model, who embodies a way of life without explaining it, but offers his or herself for imitation. Even a superficial reading of the sources on Cynicism reveals how untrue such a view would be to the representations we have. In spite of the Cynics' self-production as human beings who simply embody certain ideas and convictions without making any conscious attempt at propagating those ideas, their interaction with their environment is more often than not carefully stylised to invite observation and reflection, and to provoke quite specific reactions.[3] There is an unmistakable didactic stance (cf. βουλόμενος νουθετῆσαι 'wanting to admonish/rebuke').[4] The very theatricality and artificiality of this procedure – the combination of apparent artlessness and simplicity with a sly appeal to public attention – was a source of irritation to Plato,[5] who objected to Diogenes' studied naïveté and the puffed-up arrogance which he perceived underneath.[6] A Cynic needs an audience.[7] Plato's comparison of Diogenes to an 'out-of-control Socrates' (or a 'Socrates gone mad')[8] may suggest some similarity in the public interaction between both philosophers (i.e. Socrates and Diogenes) and the Athenian audience, while at the same time emphasising the totally different *modus operandi*. Socrates, Plato and their followers are happy to have one partner in dialogue – or not even that, since the consummate Platonist would be self-sufficient to achieve 'dialectical upward mobility' all by him or herself, in a dialogue with his or her own soul. The Cynic performance would be meaningless, however, without an audience, and consequently, the Cynic consciously chooses to be in the public arena; indeed, it would be hard to imagine a Cynic hermit.[9] It seems worthwhile to analyse this theatrical, self-dramatising didactic stance of the Cynics further.

---

[2] On their ideal of living according to nature, cf. Höistad 1948: 39.

[3] For economy's sake, I will not always repeat 'the representation' (of their interaction, etc.) – *sapienti sat*.

[4] *SSR* v b 188 = D.L. 6.35; see below, at note 38; cf. on the Cynic's missionary intentions, Moles 2000: 422; on Cynic pedagogy, Höistad 1948: 15.

[5] For the competition between Plato and Diogenes, see e.g. *SSR* v b 55–67, e.g. 59; Branham 1996: 88–9, 98–9. The very emphasis put by Diogenes and the Cynics on the body and its processes seems a provocation to Platonism.

[6] Cf. D.L. 6.26 (*SSR* v b 55): πατῶν αὐτοῦ [= of Plato] ποτε στρώματα κεκληκότος φίλους παρὰ Διονυσίου, ἔφη, 'πατῶ τὴν Πλάτωνος κενοσπουδίαν'. πρὸς ὃν ὁ Πλάτων, 'ὅσον, ὦ Διόγενες, τοῦ τύφου διαφαίνεις, δοκῶν μὴ τετυφῶσθαι' (etc.); *SSR* v b 57 (= D.L. 6.41); *SSR* v b 60 (Plato's remark ὡς χαρίεν ἂν ἦν σου τὸ ἄπλαστον εἰ μὴ ἦν πλαστόν'.

[7] Döring 1993: 340.   [8] *SSR* v b 59 (D.L. 6.54 et al.).

[9] Moles 2000: 429 points out that while we hear of occasional Cynics in the country, most of them lived in the context of a polis.

Classicists have become more aware of the various strategies that are available in the production of self (Goffman 1959: 248–51; cf. Branham 1996: 87), the way we constantly present a 'front' to an audience (Goffman 1959: 24),[10] the different roles we play in different contexts (on stage, backstage), and to different audiences (Goffman 1959: 49), and how we deal in impression management, developed as a form of game theory by Goffman (1970). The initial theory of self-production (Goffman 1959) was based to a large extent on the comparison with the theatre: the dominating metaphor is to see life as a theatrical performance. Now, as I said, the theatricality of the Cynics' public behaviour leaps to the eye,[11] not only because they force themselves on their spectators, but also by their careful self-presentation, e.g. through the use of certain fixed 'props'.[12] Therefore it should be possible to apply some of these insights of socio-linguistics to the analysis of Cynicism as a rhetorical (and didactic) practice.

Since I intend to concentrate on non-verbal elements in Cynic communication, I will also be using modern theories of non-verbal communication.[13] Of course, a well-articulated theory of non-verbal communication was available even in antiquity itself, in the form of the theory of *actio/pronuntiatio/*ὑπόκρισις, which dealt with the presentation of rhetorical speeches.[14] In modern times, ideas on non-verbal communication go back to the groundbreaking study of Hall,[15] who was one of the first to systematically regard culture as a form of communication,[16] and they have been applied to classical texts by e.g. Donald Lateiner.[17] Concepts that will be particularly useful here are, among the so-called 'Primary message systems' distinguished by Hall (1959: 62–81), e.g. the use of food and eating

---

[10] In the context of the Cynics, it is also important to distinguish (with Goffman 1959: 24, 27) between the 'personal front' developed by Diogenes, which turns into an 'established front' with the (yet) more stylised Cynics of e.g. the second century BC; see also Krueger 1996: 225.

[11] See also Branham 1996: 91.

[12] For these *Cynicae familiae insignia*, the knapsack and walking-stick, see *SSR* v b 152–71, Apul. *Apol.* 22. Other 'props' (used in a non-technical sense) include Diogenes' barrel, or the beards that are one of the hallmarks of the second-century BC Cynics. Cf. Malherbe 1982: 49 on the use of dress and conduct in Cynic self-definition.

[13] For the terminology, cf. Lateiner 1995: 15 'the widest descriptor, *nonverbal behaviors*, has the virtue of including both intended nonverbal *communication* and the many unintentional acts or sounds, often out-of-awareness, that reveal so much of us. The term further comprehends tactemics, proxemics, and chronemics (the symbolic use of touch, distance, and time), strepistics (nonvocal body sounds like clapping and knee slapping), and paralanguage (vocal but nonverbal factors beyond lexemes)'.

[14] See in particular Cic. *De or.* 3.213–25 (222 *est enim actio quasi sermo corporis*); Quint. *Inst. Or.* 11.3 (esp. on *gestus*, 11.3, 65–71). Of course, ancient theory is mainly prescriptive and deals with the delivery of speeches. Modern theory has been used here because of its wider scope.

[15] Hall 1959; 1966; see also Ekman and Friesen 1969; less important: Ruesch and Weldon 1972.

[16] Hall 1959: 51. The most influential representative of this view is now, of course, Geertz 1973.

[17] Lateiner 1987; 1995; see also Boegehold 1999, and Bremmer and Roodenburg 1991: chs. 1 and 2.

(Hall 1959: 62, 64), clothing and physical attributes to mark e.g. status, and the use of space (territoriality) (Hall 1959: 68, 187–209). In the latter context, it is important to analyse the so-called proxemics of a communicative situation, i.e. the social manipulation of space,[18] and to distinguish between intimate, social and public space. In intimate space, one is very close to the person one is communicating with (a lover, a child, a very close friend), in social space one keeps a certain, moderate distance as from e.g. acquaintances or colleagues;[19] in public space one is 'on stage', and has to raise one's voice to reach a larger group of people. The distance one keeps from other people, or inversely, an invasion of someone's personal space, may be a strategy of submissiveness or domination. It is more normal for a subject to approach a king – and then to keep a respectful distance – than for a king to approach a subject. Yet, the latter is what we constantly see emphasised in the anecdotes about Diogenes and Alexander.[20] It is Alexander who approaches Diogenes, who usually never even gets up from his sitting position.[21] The proxemics of other such stories are given a slightly different twist: when Diogenes was taken prisoner and led before Philippus (the direction of movement more in line with what one would expect from their respective status), he claimed to be there to check out what Philippus was doing, thereby reversing 'agency' (D.L. 6.43; *SSR* v b 27). And both Perdiccas and Craterus are said to have threatened to kill Diogenes, if he did not come to them (D.L. 6.44; *SSR* v b 50): again, the proxemics of the situation are abnormal. In other stories, it becomes clear that Diogenes refuses to distinguish between the territory reserved for public performance (the market-place) and the private space where one performs intimate tasks like eating or taking care of other biological needs (see below). And what is more, in ignoring this distinction, he forces the people he is interacting with to be 'on stage' with him. Nor does he recognise such a thing as 'sacred space'.[22] In Diogenes' view, one can use any space for any purpose (D.L. 6.22). On the other hand, his posing as a cosmopolite, while

---

[18] See Hall 1959: 187–209; Lateiner 1995: 14–15. [19] Cf. Lateiner 1995: 49.

[20] On these anecdotes, see Branham 1996: 88 n. 23.

[21] See *SSR* v b 32 and 33. In Plut. *Vit. Alex.* 14.2–5, 671D–E, Alexander approaches Diogenes, who is lying in the sun and proceeds to sit up. Alexander is standing and is ordered to step out of Diogenes' sun; in Plut. *De exil.* 15, 605D–E, Diogenes is sitting in the sun, and Alexander approaches him (ἐπιστάς). In Arrian *Anab.* 7.2, 1–2, Diogenes is lying in the sun (κατακειμένῳ) and Alexander approaches him (ἐπιστάς), cf. D.L. 6.38 (ἡλιουμένῳ . . . ἐπιστάς); cf. also *SSR* v b 34 (D.L. 6.60) Ἀλεξάνδρου ποτὲ ἐπιστάντος αὐτῷ; *SSR* v b 39 (Epict. *Diss.* 3.22, 92) πάλιν Ἀλεξάνδρῳ ἐπιστάντι αὐτῷ κοιμωμένῳ. For ἐπιστάς and conjugated forms, see also D.L. 6.68 (*SSR* v b 40).

[22] Cf. Moles 2000: 429 on Diogenes' claim (D.L. 6.73) that there was nothing wrong in taking something out of a temple. Note, incidentally, that these anecdotes involving the provocative use of space seem to make it perfectly clear that Diogenes is aware of the distinctions between different kinds of space – or rather, of the mistaken societal conventions involving space.

suggesting that he should be 'at home' everywhere, in fact gives him an opportunity to operate as an 'outsider' everywhere.

Theatricality and conscious self-fashioning can work in any number of stylistic registers, and involve both verbal and non-verbal forms of communication.[23] Although the Cynics use both, I will be concentrating on the latter. Now, there is nothing particularly remarkable about non-verbal communication and symbolic action as such. We do it all the time. Among the many instances where action takes the place of words, we will just refer to the symbolic advice imparted by Thrasybulus, the tyrant of Miletus, to his young colleague Periander of Corinth, as described by Herodotus (*Hist.* 5.92f–g). In reaction to the (verbalised) question by a messenger, how Periander could govern his city best and most safely, Thrasybulus took the man for a walk out of town, and while he constantly kept asking why the messenger had come to him, he kept cutting off all the tallest ears of wheat that he could see and throwing them away, until he had destroyed the best and richest part of the crop. The messenger never understood what was going on, but Periander could read this advice perfectly well, and realised that he would have to destroy all potential competition. In fact, without realising it, the messenger is involved in a dialogue, a turn-taking situation like a game, and interestingly the messenger's bafflement is due to the fact that he believes Thrasybulus never takes his turn. As he says to Periander on his return: the man never gave him any advice at all (5.92f3 ὁ δὲ οὐδὲν οἱ ἔφη Θρασύβουλον ὑποθέσθαι). In fact, of course, at every renewal of the messenger's question, there is a symbolic answer – it is the messenger, rather than Thrasybulus, who never fulfils the next turn of confirming his understanding of his interlocutor's response. These forms of symbolic interaction are common, as are the concomitant risks of misreading what is communicated or even, as here, a failure to see that there is any attempt at communication at all (the messenger does not ask for clarification, he just does not see at all that this is a communicative situation). What is different in Cynicism, as in other forms of transgressive communication, is the conscious attempt to put bodily functions that are usually considered improper in company, to communicative use.

The Cynics' preferred mode of communication is a transgressive one, in that they defy commonly held cultural codes, values and norms,[24] but at

---

[23] On Cynic self-fashioning and impression-management, cf. Branham 1996: 86; on self-fashioning, Greenblatt 1980 (e.g. 9, and *passim*).
[24] I use Babcock's (1978: 14) definition of 'symbolic inversion', which may be taken as a synonym of 'transgression': '. . . any act of expressive behaviour which inverts, contradicts, abrogates, or in some fashion presents an alternative to commonly held cultural codes, values and norms be they linguistic, literary or artistic, religious, social and political'. See further Stallybrass and White 1986: ch. 1.

the same time they lay claim, implicitly or explicitly, to moral superiority
for their behaviour, which can be construed as a return to a state of natural
simplicity. In this context belongs the emphasis on bodily processes. It has
been pointed out before that the Cynic uses his body as a trope.[25] Instead
of being symptoms of a natural and uninhibited *laissez-faire*, bodily functions are turned into forms of symbolic action, a language either entirely
unsupported by words, or, more frequently, a non-verbal medium used to
strengthen the effect of language (while at the same time the linguistic utterance serves to reinforce and help interpret the non-verbal sign). Cynic non-
verbal communication is incorporated into dialogues with non-Cynics: the
non-verbal action often constitutes a regular 'turn' in the turn-taking of
dialogue, and out of the whole scala of non-verbal communication available to any language user, there is a clear predilection for the transgressive
forms.[26] Stories about Cynics often feature elements like eating,[27] spitting,
farting, urinating or defecating, and masturbation or sexual intercourse,[28]
and in fact the context of these stories never once allows for an interpretation of the transgressive action as the result of the coincidental and therefore
meaningless call of nature. The Cynic clearly exercises his choice to either
urinate or not urinate, for instance, as when at a banquet some guests had
been treating Diogenes like a real 'Dog' by throwing bones at him, and
he proceeded to urinate against them just before he left (D.L. 6.46). This
is a clear instance where seemingly 'natural', yet transgressive behaviour is
used in a well-considered non-verbal argumentative move. Diogenes himself exploits his nickname not only in a literal (and therefore non-verbal)
way, as in the example just discussed, but also metaphorically (i.e. expressed
verbally) as when he explained that he wagged his tail at those who gave him
things, barked at the ones who didn't, and bit whoever was bad (D.L. 6.60,
SSR v b 143).[29]

---

[25] Branham 1996: 100, who points out that the use of the body becomes a visible expression of Diogenes'
exemption from social control.

[26] See Krueger 1996: 225–7. An example of non-transgressive non-verbal behaviour, a compelling silence
illustrating the moral superiority and authority of the Cynic comes from Lucian's *Life of Demonax* 64:
there was civil discord in Athens (and apparently people were having it out in the *ecclesia*). Demonax
entered, and by his very appearance made the Athenians fall silent. He saw that they were remorseful
already, and left 'without having said a word himself either' (ὁ δὲ ἰδὼν ἤδη μετεγνωκότας οὐδὲν
εἰπὼν καὶ αὐτὸς ἀπηλλάγη); cf. note 51.

[27] Eating is, of course, strongly regulated by societal convention in any period or place. For transgressive
eating, see e.g. *SSR* v b 60, 147, 186–7 (eating in the wrong place, namely the market), 93–5 (eating
of the wrong (uncooked) food).

[28] E.g. D.L. 6.46 (*SRR* v b 146), 69 (*SSR* v b 147).

[29] Cf. *SSR* v b 149. The anecdote about Diogenes' death being the result of his eating raw meat may
also be a reference to his dog-like behaviour (*SSR* v b 93–5), as is, of course, the version that he
was bitten by a dog (*SSR* v b 96). Tail-wagging and biting are also metaphorically connected with a
description of Cynic style by Demetrius (*On Style* 261).

The conscious use of transgressive non-verbal behaviour rewards further analysis. Take the anecdote about Crates (D.L. 6.94; *SSR* v l 1), who comforted Metrocles after an embarrassing incident in the middle of a philosophical training session with Theophrastus: Metrocles had broken wind and was so mortified that he proceeded to lock himself into his house ὑπ᾿ ἀθυμίας ('totally despondently') with every intention of starving himself to death. Note that the farting was unintentional and meaningless, and led to a traditional and socially conditioned (if slightly excessive) response.[30] No message was involved in the bodily process.[31] Of course, to a Cynic, the embarrassed reaction is misplaced and shows a lack of philosophical sophistication. So when Crates was asked to help, he took it upon himself to comfort Metrocles. To that end he *purposely* ate lupins (θέρμους ἐπίτηδες βεβρωκώς), which are known to produce gas. D.L. continues the anecdote as follows (= *SSR* v l 1):

ἔπειθε μὲν αὐτὸν καὶ διὰ τῶν λόγων μηδὲν φαῦλον πεποιηκέναι· τέρας γὰρ ἂν γεγονέναι εἰ μὴ καὶ τὰ πνεύματα κατὰ φύσιν ἀπέκρινετο. τέλος δὲ καὶ ἀποπαρδὼν αὐτὸν ἀνέρρωσεν, ἀφ᾿ ὁμοιότητος τῶν ἔργων παραμυθησάμενος. τοὐντεῦθεν ἤκουεν αὐτοῦ, καὶ ἐγένετο ἀνὴρ ἱκανὸς ἐν φιλοσοφίᾳ.

He tried to persuade him first by verbal argument that he had done nothing base. For it would have been an abnormal phenomenon if gas was not passed the natural way. Finally, he also broke wind. And that comforted him, a consolation derived from the similarity of their actions. From that time onwards he was his student, and became a competent philosopher.

Crates' breaking wind mirrors that of Metrocles, but it is an entirely contrived action intended to reach a certain effect. The non-verbal communication does not stand by itself but follows on verbal attempts, which were not effective (the imperfect suggests that no result has been reached as yet, or better, that the narrative sequence has not been completed, but that another, and more important step in the narrative is yet to be expected (ἀνέρρωσεν)). Crates must have anticipated that words alone would not do the trick – hence the lupins taken well in advance. If he intended to produce a situation mirroring the original and embarrassing one, this also

---

[30] Cf. Goffman 1959: 52 on the problems created when meaningless elements in non-verbal communication are interpreted as meaningful ones.

[31] Although in this case, too, there was always the risk of the fart being construed as meaningful, e.g. as a sign of disrespect, or (only marginally less bad) a lack of self-control and a sign of having indulged in the wrong kinds of food before a lecture. According to Radermacher 1953: 235 this was one of the reasons the Pythagoreans abstained from beans. To the Stoics, farting was theoretically acceptable, but they did not go so far as to make it a part of their philosophical repertoire as the Cynics did (Radermacher 1953: 237). Among non-philosophical Greeks, farting could be construed as a sign of being startled, feeling joyful or to convey disrespect (Radermacher 1953: 237).

necessitated the combination of words and then the farting in the middle of it, cf. the description of what had happened to Metrocles as . . . ποτὲ μελετῶν καὶ μεταξύ πως ἀποπαρδών. But the non-verbal action also confirms by example what had already been communicated verbally, and it produces not just a consolatory, but also a protreptic effect:[32] Metrocles gives up his self-imposed house arrest and takes up philosophy again. Note how there is a clear element of competition between the various philosophical schools: Crates succeeded where Theophrastus failed.[33] There is no indication of whether or not Metrocles realised that Crates' action was planned – and one wonders whether it would have made a difference? In any case, what we have here is protreptic,[34] although maybe the non-Socratic, or the crazed Socratic way.

Yet, there is a gap between farting to show someone that it is all right to do so, and farting to get across a message of disrespect or independence or similar sentiments.[35] In the latter case, this particular form of body language is a choice of stylistic register, in the former, it is almost self-referential in nature: the farting refers to farting, and it is the unruffled demeanour of the agent that is the vehicle of the lesson that the process is a natural one.[36] We have already seen an example of the use of non-verbal communication as a conscious choice of a transgressive stylistic register in Diogenes' urinating on his attackers, although it was hard for them to argue with this behaviour in someone they had been treating like a dog – they had, as it were, forced a transgression of human behaviour on him. A more shocking version is reported in D.L. 6.32 (*SSR* v b 236):

εἰσαγαγόντος τινὸς αὐτὸν [sc. Diogenem] εἰς οἶκον πολυτελῆ καὶ κωλύοντος πτύσαι, ἐπειδὴ ἐχρέμψατο, εἰς τὴν ὄψιν αὐτοῦ ἔπτυσεν, εἰπὼν χείρονα τόπον μὴ εὑρηκέναι.

---

[32] Although consolation and protreptic may be considered separate philosophical genres, the two are fairly close together here: παραμυθέομαι seems to refer to the kind of comforting encouragement also present in Pl. *R.* 450d–451b. The kind of consolation offered here is that of similarity, the *consolatio* ἀφ' ὁμοιότητος.

[33] Cf. the anecdotes about Plato and Diogenes, *SSR* v b 55, and the one involving Aristotle discussed below.

[34] Cf. Döring 1993 on the need for an audience and the effect of advertising and promoting the Cynic lifestyle.

[35] This is also a form of behaviour attributed to Crates, this time capped wittily by Stilpo (D.L. 2.117 = *SSR* II o 6, in an argument to prove that Stilpo was unaffected and good with ordinary people): Κράτητος γοῦν ποτε τοῦ κυνικοῦ πρὸς μὲν τὸ ἐρωτηθὲν οὐκ ἀποκριναμένου, ἀποπαρδόντος δέ, 'ἤδειν', ἔφη [sc. Stilpo], 'ὡς πάντα μᾶλλον φθέγξῃ ἢ ἃ δεῖ'. Note that Stilpo takes Crates' non-verbal behaviour as an act of communication. On Diogenes' view of farting as a social comment, equal to outspokenness, see Krueger 1996: 233.

[36] Note, incidentally, that the fact that Crates remains undisturbed by his own bodily processes is not commented on in the anecdote.

Someone had invited Diogenes into his luxurious house. This man tried to prevent him from spitting when he had cleared his throat. Diogenes then spat into the man's face, stating that he couldn't find a worse place.

This is clearly transgressive behaviour, something that may have begun as a natural urge to clear one's throat, but that was quickly turned into an action *chreia* (see below) accompanied by a verbal explanation: Diogenes' host took better care of his surroundings than of himself. Even here, though, one cannot help but feel suspicion of how natural the action was even at the beginning. Diogenes' behaviour is a punitive insult, with the verbal *chreia* thrown in as an exegetical move.

Other examples of Diogenes' non-verbal communication confirm his consistent use of transgressive behaviour in a self-conscious and theatrical bid for attention,[37] as when he was walking around in the Stoa backwards, inviting the mockery of the bystanders, to whom he could then point out that they were living their lives the wrong way around (Stob. 3.4, 83, *SSR* v b 267). Walking backwards in public may not look as offensive as spitting or farting, but it is clearly an inversion of the social code. Sometimes transgressive behaviour is explicitly associated with a didactic intention as in D.L. 6.35 (*SSR* v b 188), where Diogenes is dragging around a wine-jar through the Kerameikos by a piece of string tied around its neck, because he wants to admonish (βουλόμενος νουθετῆσαι) someone who had dropped a piece of bread and was ashamed to pick it up again.[38] Diogenes' refusal to distinguish between the accepted social usage of the index and middle finger is a last example of self-consciously transgressive behaviour used to provoke someone to show their true colour: Diogenes pointed out a sophist using his middle finger, and when the man threw a fit, he said: 'There you have him! I showed him to you!' Epictetus, who tells the anecdote, explains that you can't point out a man the way you would a stone or a piece of

---

[37] Cf. Branham 1989: 52, 'The portrait of Diogenes preserved by tradition is of a self-dramatizing iconoclast who lived in the streets and taught anyone who would listen by paradox, subversive wit, and hyperbole.'

[38] The exact point of the admonishment is not altogether clear, although some points can be made. The text runs (D.L. 6.35, *SSR* v b 188) ἐκβαλόντος δ' ἄρτον <τινὸς> καὶ αἰσχυνομένου ἀνελέσθαι, βουλόμενος [sc. Diogenes] αὐτὸν νουθετῆσαι, κεράμου τράχηλον δήσας ἔσυρε διὰ τοῦ Κεραμεικοῦ. The story is reminiscent of the several props used by Diogenes to test whether his would-be followers had sufficiently managed to put aside their sense of misguided shame: he would ask them to follow him while carrying a fish or a piece of cheese (these anecdotes follow immediately on the one discussed here, D.L. 6.36, *SSR* v b 367). Clearly, Diogenes is demonstrating a form of 'correct' *anaideia* as a lesson, by doing something potentially equally or even more embarrassing. There is certainly a sense of climax: quickly 'picking something up' could count as a quick solution to the problem and is not nearly as bad as 'dragging something behind you' – which takes longer and is more conspicuous. Of course, the Kerameikos must have been littered with pieces of pottery like the *keramos*, which must have made the action seem more absurd: at least for the piece of bread there may have been some true need.

wood. You have only 'pointed out' a man as a real man, when you have shown his ideas – and the sophist's reaction showed him up for what he was (*SSR* v b 276).[39]

Branham (1996: 102–3) offers a good analysis of the physical peroration Diogenes adds to his praise of Heracles, as represented in the eighth oration of Dio Chrysostomus: after having ended his speech by referring to Heracles' cleaning of the stables of Augias, Diogenes sat down and defecated (8.36 καθεζόμενος ἐποίει τι τῶν ἀδόξων, note the euphemism). This is a very clear example of his refusal to acknowledge a separate 'backstage' area, where biological needs are supposed to be taken care of.[40] For Diogenes, public and private space are collapsed into each other. This action *chreia* serves as a signature under the speech; it is an allusion to the stable of Augias, a transgressive move mirroring the outrageous comparison between Heracles and the Cynic philosopher, a dramatic enactment of the Cynics' beliefs and thereby a validation of Diogenes' role as a Cynic preacher, and an empowering form of self-mockery all at once (thus Branham 1996: 102–3).

The anecdotes, whether involving sayings or actions, that we have studied so far, belong to the most typical form in which the Cynics' interaction with their environment was stylised in the literary tradition: the *chreia*, a pithy saying or telling action attributed to some definite person, as the definition in the rhetorical tradition has it.[41] There are several issues that should be mentioned in this connection. First of all, the *chreia* is a *literary* form, the written reflection of a philosophy that was primarily supposed to be communicated orally.[42] The form of the *chreia* is stylised, but it is supposed to capture the essence of the Cynic life-style in particularly telling moments. This suggests that the *chreia* should lend itself to 'thick description', i.e. 'an account of the intentions, expectations, circumstances, settings and purposes that give actions their meanings'.[43] And, in fact, that is what I have been trying to do with them.

---

[39] Cf. D.L. 6.34 (*SSR* v b 502).
[40] Cf. Goffman 1959: 121, 128; Krueger 1996: 227 (no separation between public and private space).
[41] Cf. Hermog. *Prog.* 3–4, p. 6–8 R.; Theon, *Prog.* 5–6, p. 96–100 Spengel; Aphth. *Prog.* 3–4, p. 3–10 R. See further Kindstrand 1986; Hock 1997: 764–9, 772; Branham 1989: 54, 58; 1996: 86.
[42] Cf. Branham 1996: 83, 'Cynicism remained the most orally oriented of all the ancient philosophical traditions.' This is not to say that the Cynics did not produce written work: they did, extensively so, see the list of titles in D.L. On the *chreiai*, see Kindstrand 1986. Collections of *chreiai* centred around the Spartans, 'wits', kings and rulers, and philosophers, esp. Socrates and the Socratics (Kindstrand 1986: 231).
[43] The term is derived from Geertz 1973, the quotation comes from Greenblatt 1997: 16, who emphasised that the 'thickness' is not a characteristic inherent in the object, but rather one that belongs to the interpretation. New Historicism as embodied by Greenblatt, focuses precisely on the 'petit récit', it uses anecdotes, not as a simplistic miniature version of the cultural phenomenon that is being interpreted, but as a 'scene' – the analysis of different scenes highlights a culture's internal diversity.

However, not only is the *chreia* the literary stylisation of a way of life, there is also some evidence that the way of life itself is stylised: not everyone believes that these sayings, i.e. the material itself out of which the *chreiai* were formed, were always the happy result of Diogenes' wit combined with the accidents of life. D.L. 5.18 (*SSR* V B 68) shows a carefully controlled and monitored interaction between Aristotle and Diogenes (incidentally, another illustration of competition between philosophical schools).[44]

Διογένους ἰσχάδ' αὐτῷ [sc. Ἀριστοτέλι] διδόντος νοήσας ὅτι, εἰ μὴ λάβοι, χρείαν εἴη μεμελετηκώς, λαβὼν ἔφη Διογένην μετὰ τῆς χρείας καὶ τὴν ἰσχάδα ἀπολωλεκέναι.

When Diogenes offered him [sc. Aristotle] a fig, it occurred to Aristotle that if he didn't take it, Diogenes would have a *chreia* ready. So he took it and said that on top of the *chreia* Diogenes had lost the fig.

The anecdote is framed in the traditional way: Diogenes creates a dramatic setting (he offers a fig to Aristotle), which can serve as a context for the *chreia* which is to follow. In this particular little story, Aristotle suspects this, i.e. he reads Diogenes' offer as a first move in a turn-taking event. This is an almost perfect demonstration of Goffman's ideas on impression management in terms of game theory (1970): there is a contest of assessment between the participants, and the moves are calculating ones.[45] Like a chess-player, Aristotle anticipates Diogenes' ultimate intention (to express a certain pre-conceived and well-practised witty thought (μεμελετηκώς)), and also second-guesses what move of his own this *chreia* could be meant to be a reaction to. He suspects he is meant to decline the offer.[46] Instead, he accepts, and thereby robs Diogenes both of the fig and his chance of proffering his *chreia*. In fact, not only does Diogenes lose the opportunity of stating this particular *chreia* of his, he also loses the whole '*chreia*-slot' in the turn-taking event. For it is Aristotle who accompanies his non-verbal move (acceptance of the fig) with verbal wit. If anything, this anecdote reveals the ritual aspects of the *chreia*-scenes, rituals which can be perceived and consciously manipulated by the participants. This also undermines the notion that the Cynic reacts spontaneously and naturally to whatever

[44] Cf. above on Plato and Diogenes, and Theophrastus and Diogenes. The anecdote featuring Aristotle is one of the few in which Diogenes 'loses', cf. also *SSR* V B 62 (against Plato). Crates 'loses' in a similar incident involving figs against Stilpo, D.L. 2.118 (= *SSR* II O 6).
[45] Goffman 1970: 14, 85; cf. Goffman 1959: 6.
[46] Why does Aristotle think he is supposed to reject the fig? Because that would be a civilised person's instinctive reaction to the approach of Diogenes? Because of the sexual connotations of figs?

events cross his path: in this case, it is suggested, the scene is laid quite carefully, and a script had been prepared.[47] Self-dramatisation is therefore part of the literary representation of Diogenes.

It is interesting to note that even in ancient theory there was room for the possibility that a *chreia* would take the form of an action. The standard example, very suitable for the classroom, was Diogenes' (or Crates') spotting a poorly behaved boy, and proceeding to strike the boy's pedagogue.[48] Characteristic for the action *chreia* is that there has to be a context, which would reasonably give rise to an opinion and can be construed as the stimulus. The action can always be replaced by a statement of opinion: as Theon puts it, action *chreiai* indicate a certain meaning without using speech (αἱ χωρὶς λόγου ἐμφαίνουσαί τινα νοῦν). The equivalence of the action to a speech act is made clear in Hermogenes' example of a mixed *chreia*: On seeing a poorly behaved boy, Diogenes struck the pedagogue (action *chreia*), saying (verbal *chreia*): 'τί γὰρ τοιαῦτα ἐπαίδευες;' The γάρ-sentence motivates the prior action of striking, treating the action as a piece of text; and indeed it could well have been replaced by a statement like: 'you deserve to be struck', or 'I should strike you for this'. A similar phenomenon can be observed in the anecdote which has it that when Diogenes saw a clumsy archer, he sat down right beside the target saying 'so that I won't be hit' (ἵνα μὴ πληγῶ, D.L. 6.67, *SSR* v в 455). The ἵνα-clause modifies the 'main clause' expressed in the action.

Non-verbal communication as a replacement of speech acts is also in evidence in the cases where in the turn-taking of philosophical debate an action fills the slot of one 'turn' (D.L. 6.39, about Diogenes):[49]

ὁμοίως καὶ πρὸς τὸν εἰπόντα ὅτι κίνησις οὐκ ἔστιν, ἀναστὰς περιεπάτει.

Similarly, in reaction to the man who claimed that there is no movement, he got up and walked around for a while.

Here, the effect derives in part from the relative cultural value of verbal argument and mute 'natural' acting. This is not simply a case where empirical

[47] Kindstrand 1986: 224, notes the implication of this anecdote that Diogenes was not averse to the 'conscious fabrication of a cutting reply'.
[48] See Quint. 1.9, 5 *Etiam in ipsorum factis esse chrian putant ut: Crates, cum indoctum puerum vidisset, paedagogum eius percussit*; Hermog. *Prog.* 6, 10 'πρακτικαὶ δέ, ἐν αἷς πρᾶξις μόνον, οἷον Διογένης ἰδὼν μειράκιον ἀτακτοῦν τὸν παιδαγωγὸν ἐτύπτησε;' Theon, *Prog.* 98, 29–99, 2 πρακτικαὶ δέ εἰσιν αἱ χωρὶς λόγου ἐμφαίνουσαί τινα νοῦν e.q.s. *SSR* v в 386, 388.
[49] Cf. *SSR* v в 481 (Simplic. *in Ar. Ph.* 1012, 22–6): τέτταρας εἶναί φησι τοὺς περὶ κινήσεως τοῦ Ζήνωνος λόγους, δι' ὧν γυμνάζων τοὺς ἀκροωμένους ἀναιρεῖν ἐδόκει τὸ ἐναργέστατον ἐν τοῖς οὖσι, τὴν κίνησιν. ὥστε καὶ Διογένη τὸν κύνα τῶν ἀποριῶν ποτε τούτων ἀκούσαντα μηδὲν μὲν εἰπεῖν πρὸς αὐτάς, ἀναστάντα δὲ βαδίσαι καὶ διὰ τῆς ἐναργείας αὐτῆς λῦσαι τὰ ἐν τοῖς λόγοις σοφίσματα.

evidence is used to invalidate a logical argumentation: in highbrow culture, that should still have taken the form of a (verbal) debate between the empiricist and the rationalist. In this case, though, the sophistication of the counter-intuitive position defended in debate ('there is no movement') is unmasked as philosophical pretentiousness by the down-to-earth everyday action of walking around.[50] In the version of the anecdote reported by Simplicius, the fact that Diogenes' communication is non-verbal is underlined by the explicit addition of the fact that 'he did not say anything'.[51]

The force of physical ἐνάργεια is exploited in combination with a verbal utterance in Diogenes' riposte to Plato's proposed definition of 'a human being' as a 'featherless biped creature'. When the proposal met with applause, Diogenes plucked a chicken, brought it with him to the lecture and said: 'here you have Plato's human being'. The turn-taking effect is underlined by the third move, Plato's emendation of the definition by the addition of 'with flat nails' (*SSR* V B 63 = D.L. 6.40).[52] These examples indicate that there are more philosophical genres that can be covered non-verbally: not just consolation and protreptic, but also elenchus.

3 THE CYNICS ON LANGUAGE AND LITERATURE?

Although in the preceding sections I concentrated on the non-verbal aspects of Cynic communication, it is clear that the majority of stories about the Cynics involve their use of language. Cynic rhetoric has been studied and analysed very well by Branham (1989, 1996): it is a 'rhetoric of laughter' (Branham 1989), although it is laughter with a sting; a rhetoric of 'paradox, subversive wit and hyperbole' (Branham 1989: 52), and one, as we have seen, that teaches by example (Branham 1989: 58). It is characterised by improvisation and humour (Hock 1997: 763). The one-liners which we find in the literary version of Cynicism probably did form a preferred mode of communicating a philosophical life-style.[53] Similarly, the choice of genre fits

---

[50] For the use of the body in rhetorical exempla/enthymemes, see Branham 1996: 98. For the relative value of words and deeds, see section 3.

[51] *SSR* V B 481 (see note 49); cf. Lateiner 1995: 13 on the use of silence.

[52] Oddly, Navia 1998: 56 interprets this as, 'A concrete featherless chicken was, therefore, *all* that Plato would have needed to define the human species' (*sic!*).

[53] For the anecdote (the literary version of the one-liners delivered in real life) as a vehicle for the propagation of philosophy, see Branham 1996: 86 n. 17. Long 1996a: 31 submits that 'in the case of . . . Diogenes . . . anecdote and aphorism should be construed as the essential vehicles of his thought', although at the same time it remains necessary to complicate this picture by insisting that it primarily conveys the literary *representation* of that thought. On Long's attempt to anticipate this problem by depicting the Cynic lifestyle as a 'studied attempt to construct a life that would breed just the kind of anecdotal tradition D.L. records' (ibid.), see below, section 4.

the contents of Cynicism perfectly.[54] Interestingly, Cynic use of language was felt to be characteristic enough to deserve the label κυνικὸς τρόπος (Dem. *On Style* 259–61), and Demetrius links it in one breath with the style of comedy (ibid. 259). Throughout, the apparent unconventionality of the Cynics' beliefs also characterises their forms of expression, in accordance with their attempts to 'deface the currency'.[55]

Beside the fact that the Cynics *used* language in a certain way, did they also theorise about it? Can we distinguish a Cynic philosophy of language? Antisthenes was obviously interested in questions of language and logic, although his status as a logician is a matter of some dispute – however that may be, his work is fairly technical in nature, belongs in the sophistic tradition, and as far as we can tell has no direct link to the main concerns of Cynicism, so I am leaving him out of account here.[56] Both Antisthenes and Diogenes did take an interest in the literary use of language, and produced literature, but again no theory has come down to us, if there was any. Typically, they appear to have been mostly interested in the parodic genres.[57] With good justification, there is no chapter on the Cynics in the section on Logic and Language of the *Cambridge History of Hellenistic Philosophy*.

However, three points about Diogenes' views on language deserve special mention (for the relationship between Diogenes and literature, see below). First of all, as illustrated by some of the action *chreiai* discussed above, there is a clear preference for deeds over words. This attitude is documented e.g. in *SSR* v b 283 (Stob. 2.15, 43), where it is related how Diogenes was praised by the Athenians for a speech he had made about self-control. His reaction was 'May you perish miserably, since you are contradicting me by your deeds.'[58]

---

[54] Branham 1996: 85 speaks of the 'expansion of the . . . domain of literature through the transformation of oral, quotidian, and utilitarian forms of discourse'.
[55] On 'Defacing the currency', see Branham 1996: 90 n. 30.
[56] Some of his works which must have been relevant in this respect are, e.g. (D.L. 6.17), *On Names* l. v, *On the Use of Names: a Controversial Work, On Questioning and Answering*. Antisthenes' main contention on the impossibility of contradiction is transmitted through Aristotle, *Top.* 104b20; *Met.* 1024b32–4 is the main source for his view that for any A there is only one *oikeios logos*. On Antisthenes' views on language, see *SSR* iv, 240–1, 248–9; Decleva Caizzi 1966, e.g. nos. 36, 38, 44–9; p. 78, 81; Brancacci 1990. Epictetus' remark (1.17, 12) ἀρχὴ παιδεύσεως ἡ τῶν ὀνομάτων ἐπίσκεψις is in the Antisthenic tradition, Höistad 1948: 157; this is opposed to the anti-intellectualist stance which Höistad 1948: 158 also detects in the Cynic tradition, see D.L. 6.103.
[57] Cf. Adrados 1999: 542 'in their [= the Cynics'] hands, the epic became parody, the Socratic dialogue diatribe, they developed the *chreia* and created all kinds of jokes, anecdotes, romances; they obtained new shades from the ancient iamb and choliamb, wrote biographies of their heroes, into which they introduced all these elements, used in the way that interested them'.
[58] *SSR* v b 283 (Stob. 2.15, 43): Διογένης λόγον τινὰ διεξῄει περὶ σωφροσύνης καὶ ἐγκρατείας καὶ ὡς ἐπῄνουν αὐτὸν οἱ Ἀθηναῖοι, ὁ δὲ 'κάκιστα ἀπόλοισθε' εἶπε, 'τοῖς ἔργοις μοι ἀντιλέγοντες.'

Of course, this was a widespread idea,[59] but one that gained pregnancy by
Diogenes' life-style, which could be seen as an illustration of the principle.

The second point is that the value cherished most by the Cynics was
freedom of speech, παρρησία.[60] According to Diogenes, it is the best thing
there is;[61] for the Cynic Demonax it equals freedom and truth (Lucian, *Life
of Demonax* 3, 11). As we will see, Cynic promotion of παρρησία puts
the Cynics in the tradition of ancient comedy. It looks as if their *licentia*
included a claim to the right to express themselves non-verbally in the
scandalous stylistic register discussed above.[62]

A final point was made by Tony Long (1996 and 1999) and illustrated
by among other things D.L. 6.27 (*SSR* v b 280) 'Asked where one might
see good men in Greece, he said: "Men nowhere, but boys in Sparta"':
in apophthegms such as this one, Diogenes shows that he accepts the
normal connotation of Greek words (in this case 'man'), but has original
insights into their correct denotations. His demands on the relationship
between connotation and denotation are stricter than the conventional
ones. There is nothing and nobody in Greece to which the label 'good
man' might be said to refer appropriately, but if a boy is taken to be a
budding man, the grown men of Sparta (as we would normally call them)
can be said to be on their way to becoming 'real' men even in Cynic eyes. In
a similar way, the Athenians are really 'women' to Diogenes.[63] Of course,
the theoretical notions remain completely implicit, but the concerns about
evaluative language expressed by Diogenes in apophthegms like this one,
can be paralleled in serious intellectuals like Thucydides and Plato.[64]

On the other hand, it should be pointed out that such play on the gap
between connotations and conventional denotations of words is also at the
basis of much humour in comic genres. To give but one example: when the
women in Aristophanes' *Ecclesiazusae* are rehearsing to be men because they
want to attend the *ecclesia*, one of them accidentally addresses her men-
impersonating colleagues as 'women'. 'Are you calling these men "women",
you fool?!', says Praxagora. And the woman explains apologetically, 'It's

---

[59] The distinction between words and deeds can be found already in Homer, cf. Buchholz 1884: 120–2;
Heinimann 1965: 43–6. Heinimann points out the original complementarity of the two, without
either one being valued above the other. Later, the notions became polar opposites (esp. in the dative
'ονόματι vs ἔργῳ), and deeds came to be valued higher than (mere, empty) words (Heinimann
1965: 53).
[60] Cf. Sluiter 2000.   [61] D.L. 6.69, *SSR* v b 473.   [62] Cf. Krueger 1996: 233.
[63] E.g. D.L. 6.59, *SSR* v b 282.
[64] Cf. Plato *R.* 474d3–475a2; 493b3–c6 (esp. c); *R.* 560e–561a; Thuc. 3.82.4 (see on all these passages,
Sluiter and Rosen 2003). In all cases, we are dealing with words that express a certain evaluation
(ἀξίωσις). Mostly, they are words that are in general use, but whose specific application serves a
particular evaluative purpose.

because of Epigonus over there [in the audience]: I happened to look in his direction and thought I was addressing women . . .' (Ar. *Eccl.* 165–9). The passage is hilarious for its utter confusion about the applicability of the labels 'men' and 'women'.[65]

The conclusion must be that the Cynics live a certain rhetoric, but that whatever linguistic ideas are at the basis of that rhetoric (notions about the hierarchy between words and deeds, the ideal of παρρησία, ideas about the match between meanings and referents) can be readily paralleled in 'popular linguistics', the folk-linguistic counterpart to 'popular morality'; they are especially prominent in comedy. And that in turn has consequences for the evaluation of the Cynic enterprise as a whole.

4 DOES SHOCK THERAPY WORK?

There is an inherent problem with transgressive artistic genres that rely for their effect on a sense of scandalised shock in their audiences. As Ralph Rosen has shown (with Donald Marks), biting satire shares with e.g. gangsta rap a combination of cultural sophistication and the suggestion of raw power. The latter is mainly the product of the scandal of transgression, trademark of the genre. The sophistication consists in the conscious allusion and intertextual connectedness to cultural traditions: the self-fashioning of the Aristophanic comic poet evokes a tradition of long-suffering critics of society, who adopt a didactic or quasi-didactic tone, but whose project is inherently self-defeating. They need to be lone rangers, comically isolated in their outraged sense of what needs to be done, without any serious hope of convincing anyone.[66] Similarly, the gangsta rapper shocks and scandalises completely only those members of his audience who miss or refuse to appreciate the embeddedness of the genre in African-American traditions of doing the dozens (a game of verbal virtuosity and one-upmanship) or the 'signifyin' monkey' (a trickster figure, again singled out by his verbal wit and agility), while those who focus on those tamer (?) aspects of the genre, fail to connect with the raw message that is also contained in it. Although it is still possible to relate to both these aspects, one somehow always fails

---

[65] No doubt compounded by the fact that male actors were playing women who were trying to look like men, but whose 'true' gender kept intruding – while according to the joke, not even the gender of the audience was reliable and stable.

[66] This reading of ancient comedy presupposes (as I believe is the case) that the comic poet does not have a serious programme which he tries to sell to his audience – and this in spite of the phenomenon of the parabasis. The comic poet is reconciled to the effect of his persona, in much the same way that at least many representatives of the gangsta rap genre must also be, highly aware as they are of the artificial and indeed artistic nature of their creations.

to do so *simultaneously*: gangsta rap is like one of those drawings that can be interpreted as two different three-dimensional objects, but never at the same time. The mental image one construes keeps flipping back and forth between the different options. The self-defeating nature of the satirical genre, doomed to a success that can never be more than partial, looks like an interesting parallel for the Cynic enterprise. So the question arises: is Cynicism an art form? And if so, does that preclude it from being a serious philosophical enterprise? And did it ever work?

From the aspects we have studied so far, it would certainly look as if the Cynic owes a major debt to the comic buffoon, the persona of the comic poet, and the iambic tradition. Transgressive verbal and non-verbal behaviour is, of course, the stuff of farce and high comedy. Remember the opening of Aristophanes' *Frogs*, where the slave Xanthias is complaining bitterly to his master Dionysus that he is carrying heavy luggage without being permitted any of the usual jokes: he can't say that he needs to take a shit, or that he will start farting if someone doesn't take his load off him (vs. 8–10). In the same comedy, Dionysus himself cannot control his bowel movements, when he is scared to death by the doorman of the Underworld (v. 479 ἐγκέχοδα). In the *Ecclesiazusae*, the heroine's husband Blepyrus comes out of bed, looking for a quiet place to relieve himself, and thinks that, since it's night, any place will do: 'οὐ γάρ με νῦν χέζοντά γ' οὐδεὶς ὄψεται' ('for now nobody will see me when I take a shit', v. 322) – of course, this is never really true when one is on stage. The comic effect depends in part on the double-edged use of space. The very public sexual discomfort to which the men in *Lysistrata* and *Ecclesiazusae* are reduced again shows us the use of the same stylistic register for (comic) effect. Obviously, the list of examples can easily be expanded.

Of course, although in all these cases bodily processes are deployed to entertain the spectators, one cannot maintain that they are used to convey any ulterior messages. But there is more comic material that goes into the making of a Cynic. The typical persona projected by the poets in the iambographic tradition and in Old Comedy is one of a boastful, self-righteous, socially minded, but also grumpy and dyspeptic figure with a fundamentally didactic presence.[67] The Cynic's self-fashioning is definitely in this tradition, and reinforces the idea that the Cynic's stylistic means stem from this same tradition – remember that Demetrius connects the style of comedy and the Cynic style (κυνικὸς τρόπος, *On Style* 259). Note, incidentally, that the didacticism of the comic poet ('I'm doing this all

---

[67] Rosen 1988: 18–21; Sluiter and Rosen 2003.

for the common good and in your best interest, even if nobody seems to appreciate it . . .') ultimately remains powerless and ineffective, and in fact, this is in part why the texts are comic to begin with (see below). Moreover, apart from the choice of stylistic register and the comparable process of self-fashioning, resulting in the projection of the persona of an isolated, buffoon-like, unheeded teacher, the ideal of παρρησία is also one that is shared by the Cynics with the iambographic and comic traditions.[68] All of this suggests that there is some form of intertextual connection between representations of the Cynics' performance and that of the iambographic tradition and the comic theatre.[69]

However, Cynicism's intertextual background is more complicated than that. Diogenes had relatively well-documented literary interests and felt that his life could be described in the terms of high tragedy.[70] The fact that Diogenes thinks of himself in tragic terms (and turns those labels into claims to pride and happiness) again demonstrates the theatrical aspect of his self-fashioning. He can see himself as a dramatic character, and may have modelled his life partly on examples derived from literature. This was certainly a feature that became part of the Cynic tradition. Later Cynics also appropriated certain literary predecessors, with Odysseus, Thersites, Heracles and Telephus especially prominent in the Cynic imagination.[71] Theoretically, this could be said to add epic and tragic elements to the creation of the Cynic persona, although never in a straightforward way.

In the second sophistic, Thersites, the one buffoon-like figure in the *Iliad*, was praised for his παρρησία and made into a Cynic demagogue

---

[68] There are several sources detailing cases in which comic licence was restricted. Mostly, these sources are unreliable reflections of Hellenistic ideas about the genre. The one certain case is a measure taken between 440 and 437, whose extent and range is unclear. In addition, Aristophanes was sued by Kleon, and there is a fragment by Eupolis (99, 29) which indicates some juridical restriction. It is probable that legal action was only undertaken when it was felt that due democratic process was threatened by poetic παρρησία (as was felt to be the case when Kleon was mocked in the presence of non-Athenians). On these political considerations, see Wallace 1994: esp. 123. For a careful weighing of the sources, see Halliwell 1991: esp. 63–6; Csapo and Slater 1995: 165–85; Sommerstein forthcoming.

[69] Cf. Adrados 1999: 605: 'The Cynics consciously placed themselves within the tradition represented by the ancient iambic poets, scathing paupers; by the Aesop of legend, witty and persecuted; by Socrates, poor and acting against the values of "normal" society' – Adrados does not distinguish here between the Cynics themselves and literary representations of Cynicism.

[70] D.L. 6.38 (*SSR* v в 263) 'εἰώθει [sc. Diogenes] δὲ λέγειν τὰς τραγικὰς ἀρὰς αὐτῷ συνηντηκέναι· εἶναι γοῦν "ἄπολις, ἄοικος, πατρίδος ἐστερημένος, | πτωχός, πλανήτης, βίον ἔχων τοὐφ᾽ ἡμέραν".' This is an adaptation of E. *Hipp*. 1029. The term πτωχός does not occur in Euripides, only in Aeschylus and Sophocles *OR* and *OC*; the only tragic occurrence of πλανήτης is in Sophocles *OC*. The suggestion of possible identification with the dethroned vagrant king who fully knows his destiny is interesting.

[71] On Heracles and Odysseus, see Höistad 1948: 22–73, 94–102. On impression management on the basis of literary examples (literary stereotyping), Branham 1989: 14.

(Κυνικόν τινα δημηγόρον, Lucian *Life of Demonax* 61). Diogenes wrote a work called *Heracles*, and Herculean πόνος remained a Cynic ideal. The wanderings and patience of Odysseus, who returned to his own palace dressed as a beggar, equally struck a chord. Again, the figure of Telephus gave ample scope for Cynic theatricality and self-dramatisation. Euripides' *Telephus* told the story of the king in rags, who had been wounded by Achilles' spear, suffered from a festering wound, and had been told that what had wounded him, would eventually also heal him. The tragedy was parodied endlessly by Aristophanes, who focused on the miserable way the king-beggar looked,[72] and apparently that was one of the most striking aspects of the play. Crates from Thebes in particular was so inspired by seeing the tragedy *Telephus* performed that he sold all his possessions and devoted the rest of his life to philosophy (D.L. 6.87–8; *SSR* v H 4).

One important thing to note about all these tragic and epic heroes, however, is that without exception they lend themselves quite readily and regularly to comic distortions. Heracles can be a figure in comedy as well as in tragedy, Odysseus features in satyr-plays, Telephus is parodied in the comic theatre, and the presence of Thersites in Homer's *Iliad* was a reason in antiquity to consider Homer the father of comedy as well as tragedy. The intertextuality and literary imitation that goes into the self-fashioning of the Cynics has a streak of buffoonery *throughout*. The conscious play with and resonances of the literary tradition make Cynicism definitely at least partly into an art form.[73]

Before dealing with the question of whether this precludes (literary) Cynicism from being a real 'philosophy', and considering its effectiveness, this is probably the place to take issue with a very seductive looking proposition by Tony Long, who considers the Cynic lifestyle as a 'studied attempt to construct a life that would breed just the kind of anecdotal tradition Diogenes Laertius records' (1996: 31). The question is whether we can ever penetrate the merciless literarity of the tradition to get to the unmediated Diogenes and his projects, without resorting to propositions which

---

[72] Cf. the list of Aristophanic references in Rau 1967: 217, e.g. Ar. *Nub.* 921–4; *Ach.* 440–4 (Dicaeopolis models himself on Telephus extensively); *SSR* v B 166, v B 564. Apart from his beggarly appearance, it was mostly Telephus' stratagem of holding baby Orestes hostage in order to get a hearing that was much parodied.

[73] For reasons of space, I do not go into the intertextual relationships with other philosophers, although they are undoubtedly there. The figure of Socrates must have influenced Diogenes both in person and perhaps also through his literary representation as a character in Plato: however that may be, in Socrates' case, too, there is clearly a potential for caricature – in fact, Socrates is also a good example of philosophical theatricality (cf. his alleged satyr-like qualities). That Plato is somehow considered a foil as well is clear from the provocative insistence on the body, and from the anecdotes showing overt competition (see above, at notes 33 and 34).

must remain caught up in circularity. In the virtual absence of independent sources,[74] it seems preferable to me to reconcile ourselves to the fact that we basically have nothing but literary sediments of Cynicism, the literary representation of a tradition, which rewards literary analysis.[75] The literary shape of philosophy may be quite far removed from the lived experience of the Cynics, and it can teach us nothing about how close a match there is between Diogenes' intentions and the actual tradition we have. In fact, in view of the use to which some of these literary representations of Cynicism were put, it is likely that we are dealing with a highly stylised and domesticated version of Diogenes' performances.

Is it possible for a 'life-style', and an artistically and intertextually stylised one like Cynicism at that, to constitute a 'real philosophy'? This was a question raised already in antiquity, and I do not think it is a very productive one.[76] However, the question of whether this particular way of life would be the result of, lead to or equal a philosophically consistent programme, does seem a legitimate one. Could Cynicism in its literary representation ever be taken seriously? Could it work?

As I said in my introduction, there is no denying that (historical) Cynicism had some effect on the philosophical tradition: later philosophers acknowledged Cynic formative influences and students of the philosophical tradition recognised and incorporated a Cynical contribution without trouble. The Stoics in particular bear witness to this fact.[77] It is possible, therefore, to study the philosophical contents of Cynicism through its

---

[74] See below on the Stoa as heirs to the Cynical tradition.

[75] On the literary shaping of philosophical subject-matter, cf. Döring 1993: 337–8, 341; Branham 1996: 82–3.

[76] Moles 2000: 420–2 argues, not unconvincingly, that it is a way of life with philosophical claims and that the opposition between the two is false. The way of life shows that the philosophical programme, based on the desirability of a 'life according to nature', can in fact be executed. The way of life becomes both the test for the philosophical programme and a way to teach it to others.

[77] There is an acknowledged Cynic streak within Stoicism, which is responsible e.g. for the Stoics' predilection for blunt directness in their speech, cf. *FDS* 243–6, e.g. *FDS* 244 = Cic. *Off.* 1.35, 128 *nec vero audiendi sunt Cynici, aut si qui fuerunt Stoici paene Cynici*. The Stoic school tradition traces its lineage from Socrates over Antisthenes, Diogenes the Dog and Crates to Zeno, Cleanthes and Chrysippus (*FDS* 118–29), although there are also groups within Stoicism trying to distantiate themselves from the Cynics. The Cynics also share their philosophical *telos* with the Stoics, and according to some, the similarity between the schools makes Cynicism into a kind of short-cut to virtue (*FDS* 138 = D.L. 6.104–5: Ἀρέσκει δ' αὐτοῖς [sc. the Cynics] καὶ τέλος εἶναι τὸ κατ' ἀρετὴν ζῆν, ὡς Ἀντισθένης φησὶν ἐν τῷ Ἡρακλεῖ, ὁμοίως τοῖς Στωικοῖς· ἐπεὶ καὶ κοινωνία τις ταῖς δύο ταύταις αἱρέσεσίν ἐστιν. ὅθεν καὶ τὸν Κυνισμὸν εἰρήκασι σύντομον ἐπ' ἀρετὴν ὁδόν). Cynic influence on Stoic political theory is also clear (LS 67 A–H). But although Chrysippus may have praised Diogenes for publicly masturbating and then commenting that he wished he could satisfy his hunger just as easily by simply rubbing his stomach (*SVF* 3.706 = Plut. *De Stoic.repugn.* ch. 21, 1044B), Chrysippus never went as far as to engage in this kind of behaviour himself or to recommend it to would-be Stoics.

effects on other philosophers. The effects of historical Cynicism are also visible in the distinction made in the (Stoic) tradition between 'authentic', and clearly much appreciated Cynicism, and perverted forms, in which all that remained was the transgressive self-production without there being any 'genuine' content.[78] What I am *not* arguing, therefore, is that literary analysis is the only valid approach to the whole phenomenon of Cynicism, and that philosophy plays a minor part, if any, in our study of it. However, the philosophical arguments have to be made in a fairly indirect way, precisely because of the form the literary tradition on Diogenes takes. And whereas the Stoic reactions to Cynicism may confirm that the literary tradition was based on some historical reality, this does not mean that the literary tradition should not constitute an object of research in its own right. In fact, the approach advocated here, where the stories about Diogenes are considered to form part of a web of texts and references, shows how unlikely it is that we can use them as straightforward historical evidence.

So, although there are some indications that historical Cynicism influenced the philosophical tradition, this does not settle the question about the status or reliability of our literary tradition. And in fact, if we look at the societal effects, i.e. the reception of Cynicism, there are several indications that the performance of the Cynics was viewed in much the same light as that of the comic poets or the satirists. And it is worth noting explicitly that the transgressive aspects of *those* genres had been so encapsulated in a 'safe' and confined space – e.g. the performance in the theatre – that they had effectively been turned into 'appropriate' behaviour, since it was expected and even required from the genre and the occasion. In the case of the Cynics, we see that the *chreia* was rapidly turned into one of the subject-matters of choice for primary education – which would be certain to remove any serious stinging effect it might have had. Choice bits of Diogenes were incorporated in the curriculum of the grammarian and were rehearsed to death in all the various commutations of grammatical form, cases and syntactical embedding that the school teachers could think of. The content of the *chreia* was felt to be both entertaining and moralising

---

[78] Cf. in particular Epictetus' diatribe 3.22 *On Cynicism*. Cynicism 'without god' will easily turn into nothing but public displays of indecency (3.22.2); being a true Cynic is not just a matter of getting the right props (3.22.10). An authentic Cynic must have *aidōs* (3.22.15), in fact, the true Cynic turns out to be something of a super-Stoic (cf. e.g. 3.22.19 on the quality required of the Cynic ἡγεμονικόν). The true Cynic is a man with a divine mission (3.22.23) etc. – this is the ideal, but reality often falls far short of it (3.22.50). Notice that there is some tension between the notion of authenticity and the artificiality of some of the communicative strategies attributed to Diogenes by the literary tradition.

enough to help shape the minds of future citizens – surely not future Cynics.[79] As Krueger remarks (1996: 238): 'The meaning of the stories of Cynic shamelessness was not the same as the acts they described.' And while several anecdotes featuring Diogenes registered the scandalised shock of the audience,[80] we should remember that the reaction of the internal audience of the narrative does not necessarily constitute an accurate reflection or prediction of that of its external audience, i.e. of the people who would hear or read the anecdote in question. Indeed, the external audience's relish at the story may well have been considerably increased by their sense of superiority to those actually or allegedly present at Diogenes' performance. In this sense, the supposedly transgressive Cynics were used to preserve and strengthen the establishment by their incorporation into educational practice. Their transgression is bridled and in a sense robbed of its effect by being turned into a 'licensed release' of carnivalesque expressions.[81] We should also take into consideration that the actual presence of the Cynic philosophers must at best have been minor and marginal most of the time, in most of the places of the Greco-Roman world. However, in this case as in so many others, 'what is socially peripheral is often symbolically central'.[82] The symbolic role of the transgressive Cynic in the public imagination is far greater than any actual social importance they may have had,[83] while the nature of that role seems to be the domesticated reinforcement of a fairly moderate, not to say trivial, public morality.

In fact, there is at least one story in Diogenes Laertius which suggests that the Athenians had managed to integrate the eccentric Diogenes into their image of their society to such an extent, that no serious sense of scandal could still attach to him; rather, they were apparently fondly regarding him

---

[79] Cf. Morgan 1998: 185–8. She notes how the student is supposed to identify with Diogenes as a typical powerful Greek male (ibid. 188). It is true that Diogenes has a certain rugged maleness and self-sufficiency to offer for imitation, and therefore *selective* identification is possible and in order – in that sense he definitely has more school-appeal than the run-of-the-mill comic hero. His moral seriousness must have been recognised. However, Morgan does not comment on the fact that the school version of Diogenes also constitutes a denial and inversion of important aspects of his self-constructed persona. For Diogenes in school, see also Krueger 1996: 224.

[80] E.g. *SSR* v B 236 (Gal. *Protrept.* 8) (somebody whose face Diogenes had spat in) ἀγανακτοῦντος δ' αὐτοῦ; *SSR* v B 279 (Theodoret. *Graec. affect. cur.* 12.48–9) . . . μεμψαμένου τινὸς τὸ γινόμενον; *SSR* v B 269 (D.L. 6.63) πρὸς τὸν ὀνειδίζοντα ὅτι κτλ. *SSR* v B 186 (D.L. 6.58) ὀνειδιζόμενος (sc. Diogenes). Diogenes being laughed at by the bystanders: *SSR* v B 267 (Stob. 3.4, 83). On the role of the internal audience, see also Krueger 1996: 237–8.

[81] Cf. Stallybrass and White 1986: 13.   [82] Babcock 1978: 32; cf. Stallybrass and White 1986: 20.

[83] Cf. Babcock 1978: 32 'The carnival, the circus, the gypsy, the lumpenproletariat, play a symbolic role in bourgeois culture out of all proportion to their actual social importance.' However ahistorical this may sound, it is an insightful illustration of the role of the 'other' as a foil for one's own sense of identity. For 'imaginative sustenance', cf. Stallybrass and White 1986: 21.

as their pet eccentric. For when some boys had harrassed Diogenes and damaged his barrel, the Athenians punished the boys, and gave Diogenes a new barrel. A new barrel. They did not offer him a house, or any other kind of 'normal' shelter, but simply accepted the fact that Diogenes would need a new barrel, without coming to the conclusion that they should all abandon their houses and follow Diogenes' example. In that sense, they showed themselves quicker students than Plato, who, according to several anecdotes, on more than one occasion sent to Diogenes as a gift much more than he needed or had requested.[84]

5 CONCLUSION

So what, on balance, is the effect of Diogenes' apparently consciously self-undermining rhetorical and performative strategies?[85] In the literary representations we have, he seems to be happy to align himself with the 'warners' whose fate it is that they are not listened to seriously, who, in fact, cannot be listened to seriously without losing their status. He contented himself with the status of a marginal figure, who needs a society with a clearly recognisable nucleus, or he would lose his footing and orientation. Cynic behaviour is essentially parasitic on a society with rules and norms. The preferred stylistic register is a transgressive one, both when communication is verbal and non-verbal. In the latter case, it fully exploits the communicative possibility of the philosopher's body. The Cynic's role goes with a strongly self-fashioning attitude, with conscious role-playing and constant performance, with turning life itself into an intertextually readable form of art. The Cynic belongs in the literary tradition of *iambos* and comedy, he embodies the didactic but ever unheeded voice of the comic poet, while the polis is the theatre in which he performs. The Cynic engages in a form of impression management that turns what for anyone else would be the calm and relaxation of 'back-stage' into the spot-lit stage itself, by refusing to separate the private and public realms. The undeniable theatricality of the Cynics' performance is reinforced by their literary representation as

---

[84] Cf. *SSR* v B 55 (D.L. 6.26 etc.). Diogenes' reaction that Plato is sending him too much stuff, just as he never replies to the actual question asked, may be a criticism of Plato's long-windedness (apophthegms are a lot shorter than dialogues), but it also replicates the reproach constantly made by Socrates to his sophistic interlocutors.

[85] Philosophers may 'not succeed' (i.e. not persuade, not convert) for any number of reasons: the audience may be unwilling to receive the message (perhaps the norm) and any message may be coopted by the dominant culture and be trivialised. The question raised here is whether the Cynic strategy is inherently self-defeating (even though there may be success stories even here: cf. the anecdote about Metrocles). I owe these observations to James Allen and Julia Annas.

self-fashioning and quasi-literary figures, who consciously play with literary and mythical examples, and evoke epic and tragedy, but always with an undermining and satirical twist.

The scandal of the philosophical use of the body is made harmless by Diogenes' domestication (a fate he shares with most dogs) and his incorporation into the pedagogical practice of the Greeks. A systematically self-undermining and artistically allusive philosophy, conveyed in a scandalous stylistic register, goes the way of all satire: it can never be more than partially successful. Either the sting is removed, or the artistry.

CHAPTER 6

Common sense: concepts, definition and meaning in and out of the Stoa[1]

Charles Brittain*

The prevalence of philosophical appeals to universal agreement in ancient thought indicates that a limited notion of 'common sense' was around, at least implicitly, from the fourth century BC. But, despite the partial justification Aristotle gave for such appeals, a developed *theory* of common sense was not possible until the Socratic insight that rationality is in some sense constitutive of all adult human beings was adapted and elaborated by the Stoics.[2] In this paper, I argue that the earliest theory of common sense in the ancient world was not this Stoic doctrine – the theory of the 'common conceptions' – but a transformation of it found in Cicero's later rhetorical works.[3]

This transformation is part of a broader series of developments, from the Stoic understanding of common conceptions, and in the direction of 'common sense', in a variety of later philosophical and rhetorical traditions ranging from Carneades in the second century BC to Simplicius in the sixth century AD. Some of the earlier stages of this process seem relatively clear. Carneades initiated a sceptical attack on Chrysippus' theory of common conceptions, by reducing them to common-sense beliefs, and showing how

* I am very grateful for the considerable help I have received from Tad Brennan, Henry Dyson, Stephen Menn and Zoltan Szabo, and from the participants in the Symposium Hellenisticum, especially Jonathan Barnes, Brad Inwood and Dorothea Frede.
[1] In this paper, 'concept' is used for the genus of which 'preconception' (*prolēpsis*) and 'conception' (*ennoia*) are species. A 'conception' is something in an individual's mind; and its intentional object, at least in some Stoic theories, is a 'conceptual object' (*ennoēma*).
[2] On Aristotle's use of consensus arguments, see e.g. Owen 1961 and Schian 1993: 91–133. The clearest arguments Aristotle gives to justify any such appeal are in his defence of the principle of non-contradiction in *Met.* 4.
[3] One might think that Epicurean and medical empiricism present rival or at least promising candidates for this role; I ignore them here owing to constraints of space and the difficulty of reconstructing their views in any detail. See e.g. Asmis 1984 Part I: 19–80 (with further references) and Chandler 1996, on the Epicureans; and Frede 1990 and Allen 2001: 87–146 on the Empiricists.

the Stoics' doctrines conflict with those beliefs.[4] And in the hands of his more dogmatic Academic successors (Philo, Cicero, Plutarch), this form of argument acquired a more positive role, parallel to that of the various traditional arguments from *consensus omnium* of the Hellenistic schools, with the result that, rather than merely showing the inconsistency of the Stoics, it was taken to show the falsity of their basic doctrines.[5] But the later stages of the process are obscure. By the late second century AD, Alexander of Aphrodisias systematised Aristotle's hints at fundamental 'common-sense' constraints on philosophical inquiry in a way that seems to reflect a reinterpretation of the Stoic common conceptions; and Galen already seems to offer a theory of definition identifying a limited use for 'common sense', which was later disseminated by Porphyry, and may derive in part from the Stoic theory, though its nature and purpose is significantly different from Cicero's.

My aim here, however, is not to trace these more general developments but to identify a possible mechanism of translation from a Stoic theory about rationality to a different kind of theory, one that posits a general and immediate relation between *ordinary* thought or concepts and the essential nature of the world: a theory of 'common sense'. The basic idea is that we can discern a change from a Stoic to a common-sense theory of the relations between ordinary thought and its expression in language, 'preconceptions' or common conceptions, and definitions. A full study of this change would involve understanding five difficult topics: (a) the Stoic theory of common conceptions; (b) the Stoic theories of definition; (c) Cicero's reception of the Stoic theory of common conceptions; (d) Cicero's rhetorical theory of definition; and (e) at least some later rhetorical and philosophical theories of definition and common conceptions. Since the evidence for these topics is either too sparse (a and b) or too great (d and e) and the subjects are confusing, this paper offers only some fragments of such a study. Part 1 investigates some puzzles concerning the Stoic theory of common conceptions (a); Part 2 tries to reconstruct a Stoic theory of preliminary definition capturing the content of common conceptions (b), partly on the basis of some later evidence (my gesture at (e)); and Part 3 suggests that Cicero's rhetorical works may provide one route by which the common conceptions ended up as common sense (d).

---

[4] This is a principal point of Plutarch's *De communibus notitiis*. It is also more or less evident in some of the sceptical speeches in Cicero's philosophical works, and in some of the arguments Sextus borrowed from the Academics – e.g. in *De finibus* 4.21, 55, 67–8, and *M.* 9.137–66, esp. 138 (cf. *De natura deorum* 29–39).

[5] I attempted to trace Philo's contribution to this change in Brittain 2001 ch. 2.iv and ch. 3.iv.

166 C. BRITTAIN

PART I THE STOIC THEORY OF COMMON CONCEPTIONS

Section one: Meaning and signification

The Stoics believed that the mental or psychological experience of adult human beings is entirely constituted by 'rational thoughts' (Diogenes Laertius, 7.51). One consequence of this which our sources point out is that every adult 'impression' or occurrent psychological episode has a corresponding incorporeal 'sayable' (*lekton*, D.L. 7.63), i.e. some kind of 'rational' content. Another consequence – less explicit in the sources, and hence less universally recognised – is that all adult impressions, including perceptual impressions, are at least partly conceptualised. (This is more obvious if we recall that the Stoics thought that the faculty of 'reason' is constituted by a set of concepts, and hence that 'rational thoughts' are episodes that occur in a part of the soul that is 'conceptual' in a literal sense; see Galen, *PHP* 5.3 cited below.) So one function of a Stoic theory of concepts will be to determine, and at least partly, to constitute (through their own content), the 'rational' content of our thoughts or impressions.[6]

The Stoics also believed that the meaning of a sentence someone is uttering at least typically has something to do with the thought they are thinking concurrently. Our sources in this case, however, are much less forthcoming about the details of this relation. It is fairly clear that the Stoics tried to distinguish 'significant speech' from other vocal productions by identifying part of its cause as the activation of the speaker's concepts in the concurrent thought (which would then 'imprint, as it were' the air in the vocal cords; see Galen, *PHP* 2.5, cited below). But it is less clear whether this implies a theory of meaning (or fragment of one) that identifies the content or 'sense' of the utterance with the content of the activated concepts in such a way that the sense is *constituted* by the thought, or merely claims that the content of those concepts plays some role in determining which sense the utterance will have. In the latter case, we can say that the 'speaker's meaning' is typically determined by the thought and hence by the concepts the speaker has, but it will not follow that they determine, let alone constitute, the meaning of the sentence. On either account, however, it is clear that a second, unsurprising, function of a Stoic theory of concepts will be to determine, to some extent, at least the speaker's (and hearer's) meaning of the sentences we utter.[7]

If we consider what the Stoics say about such things as god or the good, however, we can see, I think, that there is often a considerable gap between

[6] See Frede 1987: 151–76. [7] See Barnes 1993.

what ordinary people take themselves to be expressing in their thoughts or utterances, and what, according to the Stoics, their thoughts and utterances actually 'signify'.[8] For ordinary people often say or think things like 'I don't know why god is harming me' or 'That's the right thing to do, but not the most beneficial,' without thinking that they are enunciating contradictions. But the Stoics think that 'god' signifies a blessed and imperishable animal that is beneficent to men, and that 'good' signifies benefit or not other than benefit, and hence that ordinary people are radically confused about the nature of god and the good, and that the 'ordinary' or 'linguistic' meaning of these words requires radical revision.[9] (These examples are examined in more detail below.)

These cases are particularly interesting, I will argue, because the concepts involved belong to the privileged set of concepts that the Stoics called 'the common conceptions'. If this is right, it follows that the Stoic theory of the common conceptions cannot be a 'common-sense theory', when the latter is characterised as one that posits a general and immediate relation between *ordinary* thought or concepts and the essential nature of the world, since in these cases ordinary thought and concepts clearly fail to pick out the essential features of their objects.

But in order to establish this claim, it is necessary to examine the exiguous and controversial evidence for the Stoic theory of common conceptions in some detail. In the remainder of this part, I will argue that the Stoics took the common conceptions to be constitutive of reason and the basis from which philosophical inquiry, and hence ultimately wisdom or perfected reason, sprang.[10] But since this is, I think, the standard view, I will focus on some of the more puzzling features of the Stoic theory of common conceptions, and in particular, their relation to ordinary thought.[11] Further, since much of the apparent evidence is commonly taken to have been contaminated either by incipient Platonism (Cicero, Epictetus) or by the development towards the 'common sense' we are trying to examine (Cicero, Plutarch, Alexander, Sextus), I will use – where possible – only texts that most of us

[8] I rely here on the force of Diogenes of Babylon's claim that nouns in general signify 'common qualities' (D.L. 7.58) – though this is not unproblematic, as Barnes 1999: 207–9 notes, and on the identifications of the relevant 'qualities' at e.g. Plutarch, *St. rep.* ch. 38, 1051F (*SVF* 3.A.33), on god, and Sextus, *M.* 11.22 (*SVF* 3.75), on goodness. See sections three and four below.

[9] The Stoics' disagreement with 'ordinary' language and thought about the good is explicit in e.g. Plutarch, *St. rep.* 17, 1041E, id. 30, 1047E–1048A, and Cicero, *Paradoxa* 7, and the passages in n. 4 above; cf. Atherton 1993: 94 n. 60.

[10] Cf. Schofield 1980, Frede 1994b.

[11] Cf. Sandbach 1996, Pohlenz 1940 and 1970, and e.g. Long and Sedley 1987: I. 239–41, 249–53. By 'the Stoic theory', I mean the theory probably invented by Chrysippus, and applied by Diogenes and Antipater. Finer discriminations between Stoic views don't seem possible.

168

can be reasonably confident about.[12] An unfortunate result of this method is that, although the use of common conceptions by the Stoics, and by Chrysippus in particular, seems guaranteed by Plutarch's polemic in *De communibus notitiis*,[13] they appear to be mentioned explicitly in only four secure Greek fragments.[14] For this reason, I start with a general review of the secure evidence about Stoic concepts (section two), before turning to the nature of the common conceptions (section three), and their theoretical uses and the problems these uses suggest (section four).[15]

Section two: Stoic concepts

The most expansive piece of evidence we possess about Stoic concepts is the report in 'Aëtius', *Placita* 4.11. I cite this in full, since it serves as a useful anchor for the puzzles that follow.

When human beings are born, the governing part of their souls is like a piece of paper ready to be written on, and each one of its conceptions is written into it. The first method of 'writing' is via the senses. For when they perceive something white, for example, they retain a memory of it once it has gone. When there are many memories similar in form, we say that they have experience (experience is a plurality of impressions similar in form). Some conceptions come about in the ways mentioned, without skill; others already require teaching and attention. The latter are just called 'conceptions' (*ennoiai*); the former are also called 'preconceptions' (*prolēpseis*). Reason, in virtue of which we are called 'rational' <animals>, is said to be constituted by preconceptions at around the age of seven. Conceptual objects (*ennoēmata*) are phantasms of the thought of a rational animal – i.e. when a

---

[12] Cf. Pohlenz 1970: 1, 244–6, Todd 1973: 61–3, or Obbink 1992: 224–31. I avoid uses of the relevant terms that are not clearly tied to something a Stoic is supposed to have said.

[13] Plutarch's dialogue begins with an unnamed 'friend' soliciting help from 'Diadumenus' in response to what turns out to be a Stoic accusation that the former 'philosophises contrary to the common conceptions' (*Com. not.* ch. 1, 1058F). But it is notable that there are no direct quotations from Chrysippus or other Stoics using the phrase 'common conception'. (The closest Plutarch comes to this are apparent paraphrases at 1059B, 1082E, and 1083B, which use 'preconception and conception', but presumably mean by the latter 'common conception'.) The phrase thus *could* be a later one projected back onto the Stoics by our sources, as Susanne Bobzien suggested to me. But Plutarch's title, the use of this phrase in similar Stoic contexts by all our sources (see next note), Alexander's general preference for 'preconception' in other contexts, and the Stoics' theoretical need for something like 'common conceptions' (see section three), make this very unlikely.

[14] The relatively secure examples of common conceptions are from Alexander, *De mixtione* 154. 28–30, (*SVF* 2.473, cited in n. 44 below); S.E., *M.* 11.22 on the good (*SVF* 3.75, cited in n. 46); *M.* 9.123 on holiness (*SVF* 2.1017, cited in n. 71); and, though this is not explicitly Stoic, *M.* 9.196 on God (*SVF* 2.337, cited in n. 71). Origen yields two further possible cases, both on moral topics (*SVF* 3.218 and 2.964). Simplicius provides further possible cases (*in Ench.* pp. 68–9 Dübner, 319–21 Hadot), which are discussed in Part 2 (see n. 111).

[15] A full treatment of topics (a)–(d) on page 165 would show, I think, that Cicero in fact supplies the most detailed and plausible presentation of the Chrysippian theory (topic (c) above). He discusses the Stoic theory of concept formation in *Ac.* 1.42, 2.21–2 and 30–1 and *Fin.* 3.33; he employs common conceptions in *ND* 2.13, 45, *Fin.* 3.21 and *Tusc.* 4.53–4; and, arguably, he does both in *Leg.* 1.22–34.

phantasm occurs to a rational soul it is called a 'conceptual object' (its name derives from 'intellect' (*nous*)). So the ones that occur to non-rational animals are just phantasms; but the ones that occur to us and to the gods are generically phantasms and specifically conceptual objects. (*SVF* 2.83=*FDS* 277)[16]

The problem that will most concern us is to identify the distinction between preconception (*prolēpsis*) and conception (*ennoia*). This text asserts that preconceptions are the species of concepts that arises in us 'without skill' or without requiring 'teaching and attention', i.e. it seems, *naturally*. There are three reasons to ascribe this doctrine to Chrysippus. First, he distinguishes preconception and conception in two fragments.[17] Secondly, in one book at least, he claimed that the criteria of truth were perception and preconception (D.L. 7.54, *SVF* 2.105), and Diogenes glosses the latter as a '*natural* conception of the general characteristics <of a thing>' (in Sandbach's translation).[18] And thirdly, we have further evidence for a category of 'natural' conceptions that were in some sense criterial.[19] Hence I take it that <u>preconceptions are natural conceptions</u>.

---

[16] Aëtius, 4.11 (*SVF* 2.83): ὅταν γεννηθῇ ὁ ἄνθρωπος, ἔχει τὸ ἡγεμονικὸν μέρος τῆς ψυχῆς ὥσπερ χάρτην εὔεργον εἰς ἀπογραφήν· εἰς τοῦτο μίαν ἑκάστην τῶν ἐννοιῶν ἐναπογράφεται. Πρῶτος δὲ [ὁ] τῆς ἀναγραφῆς τρόπος ὁ διὰ τῶν αἰσθήσεων. αἰσθανόμενοι γάρ τινος οἷον λευκοῦ, ἀπελθόντος αὐτοῦ μνήμην ἔχουσιν· ὅταν δὲ ὁμοειδεῖς πολλαὶ μνῆμαι γένωνται, τότε φαμὲν ἔχειν ἐμπειρίαν· ἐμπειρία γάρ ἐστι τὸ τῶν ὁμοειδῶν φαντασιῶν πλῆθος. Τῶν δὲ ἐννοιῶν αἱ μὲν φυσικῶς γίνονται κατὰ τοὺς εἰρημένους τρόπους καὶ ἀνεπιτεχνήτως, αἱ δὲ ἤδη δι' ἡμετέρας διδασκαλίας καὶ ἐπιμελείας· αὗται μὲν οὖν ἔννοιαι καλοῦνται μόνον, ἐκεῖναι δὲ καὶ προλήψεις. Ὁ δὲ λόγος, καθ' ὃν προσαγορευόμεθα λογικοὶ ἐκ τῶν προλήψεων συμπληροῦσθαι λέγεται κατὰ τὴν πρώτην ἑβδομάδα, ἔστι δὲ ἐννόημα φάντασμα διανοίας λογικοῦ ζῴου· τὸ γὰρ φάντασμα ἐπειδὰν λογικῇ προσπίπτῃ ψυχῇ, τότε ἐννόημα καλεῖται, εἰληφὸς τοὔνομα παρὰ τοῦ νοῦ. Διόπερ τοῖς ἀλόγοις ζῴοις ὅσα προσπίπτει, φαντάσματα μόνον ἐστίν. ὅσα δὲ ἡμῖν καὶ τοῖς θεοῖς, ταῦτα καὶ φαντάσματα κατὰ γένος καὶ ἐννοήματα κατ' εἶδος.

[17] Galen, *PHP* 5.3 (*SVF* 2.841, cited in n. 25 below): reason is constituted by a collection of certain conceptions (*ennoiai*) and preconceptions (*prolēpseis*); Plutarch, *Com. not.* 1, 1059B (*SVF* 2.33): Chrysippus removed the confusion about preconceptions and conceptions caused by the sceptics by setting each right and in its proper place.

[18] D.L. 7.54 (*SVF* 2.105): ὁ δὲ Χρύσιππος διαφερόμενος πρὸς αὐτὸν ἐν τῷ πρώτῳ περὶ λόγου κριτήριά φησιν εἶναι αἴσθησιν καὶ πρόληψιν. ἔστι δ' ἡ πρόληψις ἔννοια φυσικὴ τῶν καθόλου. Von Arnim doesn't recognise this gloss as a 'fragment' of Chrysippus, perhaps because its source is probably Posidonius (see 7.54 fin.). But if so, the gloss is as authentic as the ascription of the criteria to Chrysippus. Kidd 1989 argued that the next element in Posidonius' report is unreliable; but if we should distrust anything in his summary of Chrysippus' views, it is presumably the claim that the scholarch 'contradicted himself' by saying in one book that the criterion was the cataleptic impression and in another that it was perception and preconception – both criteria are or derive immediately (or naturally) from cataleptic impressions.

[19] Chrysippus mentions '*connate preconceptions*' (*emphutos*) in Plutarch, *St. rep.* 17, 1041E (*SVF* 3.69): Τὸν περὶ ἀγαθῶν καὶ κακῶν λόγον ὃν αὐτὸς εἰσάγει καὶ δοκιμάζει συμφωνότατον εἶναί φησι τῷ βίῳ καὶ μάλιστα τῶν ἐμφύτων ἅπτεσθαι προλήψεων'– cf. *sumphutos* at *Com. not.* 24, 1070C. Alexander claims that Chrysippus took '*common conceptions*' to be criteria we get from nature (*SVF* 2.473, cited in n. 44 below); Plutarch claims that the Stoics responded to the *Meno* by reference to *natural conceptions* (Sandbach fr. 215f. *SVF* 2.104, cited in n. 61 below); and Origen, for what it's worth, mentions a *natural conception* of God (*SVF* 2.1052). See also n. 47 below.

To understand this distinction, it is useful to consider first what we learn about the *nature* and *contents* of concepts as such. Aëtius reports that we get the preconception of whiteness after a process involving perceptual impressions, memories and experience – i.e. a set of remembered perceptual impressions.[20] But it is unclear whether the concept is constituted by that experience under certain conditions – e.g. if the experience is the ground of a disposition in an adult that amounts to the possession of a concept – or by a further and distinct item in the soul.[21] However, Plutarch (*Com. not.* 47, *SVF* 2.841) informs us that a concept is 'a kind of impression' (*phantasia tis*), and hence characterised by the physical properties of impressions as such, and that concepts are defined by the Stoics as 'stored thoughts' (*enapokeimenas noēseis*).[22] In *De sollertia animalium* 961c, this definition is supplemented with the information that thoughts 'are called "conceptions" (*ennoiai*) when they are stored, but "rational thoughts" (*dianoēseis*) when they are activated'.[23] Hence, since any rational impression is technically a 'rational thought' (*dianoēsis*, D.L. 7.51), it is likely that the Stoics tried to identify <u>concepts as a particular kind of rational thought</u>, presumably ones that were general and abstract in a sense yet to be determined.[24]

The suggestion that concepts are distinct things in the soul, beyond sets of prior impressions, seems to be confirmed by Chrysippus' claims in Galen, *PHP* 5.2–3 that reason is constituted by 'a collection of certain (*tinōn*) conceptions and preconceptions', and that these are both *parts* of reason and *parts* of the soul (*SVF* 2.841 and 3.471a; cf. Aëtius, 4.11, cited above).[25] Chrysippus thought that the 'governing part' (*hēgemonikon*) of

---

[20] Aëtius' phrasing suggests that 'experience' is entirely constituted by a set of memories, and hence that it is not a further item in the soul beyond those memories or remembered impressions. This account clearly does not cover rational 'experience' of the kind Chrysippus appeals to in his *telos* formula (*SVF* 3.4, 12–15), though the Stoic definitions of 'art' suggest that we need not posit an additional mental item for the rational kind either – see *SVF* 2.93–7.

[21] Gould 1970: 59–66 seems to be alone in taking the first alternative; Sandbach 1996: 25, by his translation of the gloss on preconception, and e.g. Frede 1994b: 52–4 favour the second.

[22] Plutarch, *Com. not.* ch. 47, 1084F (*SVF* 2.847): φαντασία γάρ τις ἡ ἔννοιά ἐστι, φαντασία δὲ τύπωσις ἐν ψυχῇ . . . 1085a. ἀλλ᾽ οὕτω παρακούουσιν ἑαυτῶν, ὥστε τὰς ἐννοίας ἀποκειμένας τινὰς ὁριζόμενοι νοήσεις, μνήμας δὲ μονίμους καὶ σχετικὰς τυπώσεις, τὰς δ᾽ ἐπιστήμας καὶ παντάπασι πηγνύντες ὡς τὸ ἀμετάπτωτον καὶ βέβαιον ἐχούσας, εἶτα τούτοις ὑποτίθεσθαι βάσιν οὐσίας φερομένης ἀεὶ καὶ ῥεούσης. Concepts appear to differ in kind from 'memories', which are defined next (1085B) as stable and fixed imprintings (*tupōseis*), although, since a concept is itself an imprinting which is presumably stable and fixed, it is possible that the different definitions consider the same things under different descriptions.

[23] Plutarch, *Soll.* 961C: ὥσπερ ἀμέλει καὶ τὰ περὶ τὰς νοήσεις, ἃς ἐναποκειμένας μὲν ἐννοίας καλοῦσι κινουμένας δὲ διανοήσεις.

[24] D.L. 7.51 = *SVF* 2.61; cf. [Galen] *Def. med.* 126, *SVF* 2.89.

[25] Galen, *PHP* 5.3 (*SVF* 2.841): ἀναμιμνήσκων ἴσως ἡμᾶς τῶν ἐν τοῖς περὶ τοῦ λόγου γεγραμμένων, ὧν σὺ διῆλθες, ὡς ἔστιν ἐννοιῶν τέ τινων καὶ προλήψεων ἄθροισμα.' ἀλλ᾽ εἴπερ ἑκάστην τῶν

the soul did not become rational, and hence that the rational part of the soul – i.e. reason, the relevant set of concepts – did not exist, until the age of seven (or possibly fourteen). Although the details of the process by which this radical transformation comes about are obscure, the generation of reason (*to logistikon/dianoia*) seems to amount to precisely the formation of concepts, i.e. a change from the prior state of the animal's 'governing part'.[26] And once reason is established, it is defined as the *part* in which subsequent thoughts or impressions occur (D.L. 7.159, *SVF* 2.837 – cf. 839). This suggestion seems to be confirmed by an argument from Diogenes of Babylon that the rational faculty (*dianoia*) is in the chest because:

it is plausible that speech is made significant by the conceptions in the rational faculty and sent out thence, i.e. once as it were imprinted, and that the activities of thinking and speaking are temporally coextensive. (*PHP* 2.5, *SVF* 3.D. 29)[27]

Irrespective of the precise relation between thought and meaningful speech presupposed by this argument, it seems plausible that an individual sentence should be 'as it were imprinted' by a limited number of individual concepts combined in a determinate thought, rather than by sets of prior impressions.[28] So much for the *nature* of concepts.

One way to think about the kinds of *content* Stoic concepts may have is to consider the preconceptions we are fairly securely informed about – that is, the concepts we know of that arose naturally, or without teaching or attention. These concern holiness, the gods, white, and growth, as well as – probably – goods and bads, and mixtures.[29] The simplest example is the one used by Aëtius: we see white things, remember lots of white things, and then, presumably, end up with a concept of white. It seems plausible to construe Diogenes Laertius' gloss on the latter with Sandbach as an example of 'a natural conception of the general characteristics <of a thing>' (*tōn katholou*) (D.L. 7.54), where the thing is *whiteness*, and its general

---

[26] ἐννοιῶν καὶ προλήψεων εἶναι μόριον νομίζεις τῆς ψυχῆς, ἁμαρτάνεις διττά. πρῶτον μὲν γὰρ οὐ ψυχῆς ἐχρῆν. ἀλλὰ λόγου ταῦτ᾽ εἶναι μόρια φάσκειν, ὥσπερ οὖν καὶ γράφεις ἐν τῇ περὶ λόγου πραγματείᾳ.

[26] See nn. 55–7 below.

[27] Galen, *PHP* 2.5.12–13 (*SVF* 3.D.29): καὶ ἄλλως δὲ πιθανὸν ὑπὸ τῶν ἐννοιῶν ἐνσεσημασμένον τῶν ἐν τῇ διανοίᾳ καὶ οἷον ἐκτετυπωμένον ἐκπέμπεσθαι τὸν λόγον καὶ παρεκτείνεσθαι τῷ χρόνῳ κατά τε τὸ διανενοῆσθαι καὶ τὴν κατὰ τὸ λέγειν ἐνέργειαν. καὶ ἡ διάνοια ἄρα οὐκ ἔστιν ἐν τῇ κεφαλῇ, ἀλλ᾽ ἐν τοῖς κατωτέρω τόποις, μάλιστά πως περὶ τὴν καρδίαν.

[28] See Frede 1987: 152–7, Barnes 1993: 57–61 and section one above.

[29] **Preconceptions**: holiness (S.E., *M.* 9.123, *SVF* 2.197); Gods (*Com. not.* 32, *SVF* 2.126; *St. rep.* 38, *SVF* 3.A.34); white (Aëtius, 4.11, *SVF* 2.83); growth (*Com. not.* 44, *SVF* 2.762). **Natural conceptions**: goods and bad – though Chrysippus only says that his doctrine of goods and bads depends on <some, unspecified> *connate* conceptions (*St. rep.* 17, *SVF* 3.69, cited in n. 19); God (Origen, *SVF* 2.1052). **Common conceptions**: mixtures, the good, the fine and just, holiness, gods – see n. 14 above.

characteristics include being a colour or configuration of bodies.[30] At any rate, the content of the other examples of preconceptions, although they are more complex and perhaps involve a degree of reasoning (see section three below), is something like this. Our preconception of a god, for instance, is of 'a blessed and imperishable animal that is beneficent to men' (*St. rep.* 1051F). This, like the other cases, looks like *an abstract and general content*.

A problem for this view is Sandbach's suggestion that Aëtius' account of the formation of preconceptions contains a lacuna, which should be supplemented directly by the various lists of ways in which the Stoics think things are 'conceived' (*nooumena... enoēthē*, D.L. 7.52–3, *SVF* 2.86).[31] These ways include by 'direct encounter' or perception, and by similarity, analogy and composition of or with things conceived in the first way.[32] The problem is that the examples used in these lists suggest that these are primarily ways of actively *imagining* non-existent, or non-present, but *particular* things. This difficulty can be resolved, however, by distinguishing two senses of 'conceive' (*noein*): the sense here is simply 'think of' or 'imagine', as opposed to 'perceive'; the sense we are interested in is 'have a conception of'.[33] The former is no doubt an element in the process that produces the latter, but it cannot amount to the whole story for the Stoics.[34] For it seems clear

---

[30] S.E., *M*. 11.8–11 suggests that the Stoics used the term '*katholikon*' to designate the indefinite universal conditionals which Chrysippus thought were equivalent to definitions; see Bett 1997: 54–5 and Bobzien 1999: 112–13. If so, given the relation between preconceptions and definitions (see Part 2), Sandbach's construal seems plausible.

[31] Sandbach 1996: 25–6, followed by e.g. Pohlenz 1940: 82. Aëtius appears to give only the first of what he summarises as several 'ways mentioned' in which preconceptions come about. For doubts about this supplement, cf. Long and Sedley 1987: II. 241.

[32] D.L. 7.52. (*SVF* 2.87): τῶν νοουμένων τὰ μὲν κατὰ περίπτωσιν ἐνοήθη, τὰ δὲ καθ' ὁμοιότητα, τὰ δὲ κατ' ἀναλογίαν, τὰ δὲ κατὰ μετάθεσιν, τὰ δὲ κατὰ σύνθεσιν, τὰ δὲ κατ' ἐναντίωσιν.... νοεῖται δὲ καὶ κατὰ μετάβασίν τινα, ὡς τὰ λεκτὰ καὶ ὁ τόπος. φυσικῶς δὲ νοεῖται δίκαιόν τι καὶ ἀγαθόν· καὶ κατὰ στέρησιν, οἷον ἄχειρ. Diogenes lists: (a) direct encounter (e.g. perceptible things); (b) similarity (e.g. Socrates from his picture); (c) analogy: (i) increase (Cyclops) and (ii) decrease (Pygmy); (also by analogy, the centre of the earth); (d) transposition (eyes on chest); (e) composition (centaur) ; (f) opposition (death). To this primary list he adds: (g) *a kind of transition* (*lekta* and space); (h) *naturally* (something just and good); and (i) privation (a handless person). In *De finibus* 3.33–4 (*SVF* 3.72), Cicero lists (a), (e), (b) and *collatione rationis*, which produces (h). In 3.34 the latter is distinguished from the two sub-categories of (c): (ci) and (cii). In *M*. 8.56–60, Sextus lists (a), (b), (ci), (cii) and (e); in *M*. 9.393–5 (a), (b), (e), (c), (ci) and (cii); and in *M*. 3.40–2 (a), (b), (e) and (ci) and (cii). In the latter two passages, Sextus groups all his categories except (a) into a genus, 'by transition'. (Sextus' lists aren't ascribed to the Stoics.)

[33] Cf. Brunschwig 1994: 99–103. The two senses seem to overlap in some cases, for instance in the report that Chrysippus thought that 'generic pleasure is *noetic*, while the specific pleasure that we encounter is perceptible' (Aëtius, 4.9.13, *SVF* 2.81).

[34] The latter two of Sextus' three lists of ways in which we achieve 'thoughts' (*noēseis*) of things – cited in n. 32 above – suggest as much since they are given in the course of arguments that we cannot 'conceive' of a line without breadth. That is, Sextus is arguing that there cannot be fully abstract general 'concepts' because we cannot have determinate representations ('thoughts') that are

that one can *imagine* a five-footed monster without having a concept of it in the requisite Stoic sense, just as one can *see* a rhododendron without having a Stoic concept of that class of shrub.[35] (This is not to claim that we only have preconceptions of general classes, like whites, goods, gods, etc. We may be able to form abstract natural concepts of particulars, for instance, of particular people. But if we can, they aren't relevant here, since they are unlikely to be constitutive of reason or criterial for progress in philosophy.[36])

The only hint of a Stoic mechanism that could generate *abstract* preconceptions 'naturally' from sets of particular perceptions or memories is supplied by one of the supplementary categories in D.L. 7.53: 'by some kind of transition, like our thoughts of *lekta* and of space'. This notion of 'transition' seems quite distinct from the other imaginative procedures given in Diogenes, including the sub-class of 'analogy' in his exposition. It is perhaps the kind of 'transition' alluded to by Sextus in *M.* 8.275–6 (*SVF* 2.223), where he distinguishes rational from non-rational animals by the former's possession of 'transitional and synthetic impression', which explains their grasp of the concept of 'logical consequence' (*akolouthia*).[37] Unfortunately, it is not at all clear how it does so.[38]

Two final questions concern the 'logical' *form* of the content of Stoic concepts. Assuming that concepts are distinct things in the soul, and that their contents are abstract, and general, we still need to know whether each of them has a unique 'sayable' (*lekton*) for its content, and, ideally, whether those *lekta* are 'predicates' (*katēgorēmata*) or 'propositions'

---

not particular. It is not clear to me what the Stoics thought about the representational content of the impressions or thoughts that express abstract propositions; but they clearly did think that we can 'conceive' of abstract objects in some sense. See also n. 38 below.

[35] The Stoic conditions for concept possession are more stringent than those of most modern philosophical accounts – see Frede 1999: 319–20 and Brittain 2002: 258–66.

[36] See e.g. Barnes 1999: 207–8, and, *contra*, Brunschwig 1994: 45, 54–5. I think that this is related to the issue of the existence of Stoic metaphysical 'cases' of the kind Frede 1994c argues for.

[37] S.E., *M.* 8.275 (*SVF* 2.223): <οἱ δὲ δογματικοὶ> ... φασιν ὅτι ἄνθρωπος οὐχὶ τῷ προφορικῷ λόγῳ διαφέρει τῶν ἀλόγων ζῴων (καὶ γὰρ κόρακες καὶ ψιττακοὶ καὶ κίτται ἐνάρθρους προφέρονται φωνάς) ἀλλὰ τῷ ἐνδιαθέτῳ, οὐδὲ τῇ ἁπλῇ μόνον φαντασίᾳ (ἐφαντασιοῦτο γὰρ κἀκεῖνα) ἀλλὰ τῇ μεταβατικῇ καὶ συνθετικῇ· διόπερ ἀκολουθίας ἔννοιαν ἔχων εὐθὺς καὶ σημείου νόησιν λαμβάνει διὰ τὴν ἀκολουθίαν. The translation of this passage is controversial; see Long and Sedley 1987: II. 319.

[38] A related question concerns Aëtius' report that '*ennoēmata* are phantasms of the thought of a rational animal – i.e. when a phantasm occurs to a rational soul it is called an *ennoēma*' (*SVF* 2.83, cited in n.16). Aëtius is probably wrong to identify any 'phantasm' as an *ennoēma*; see Long and Sedley 1987: II. 185. But he may have meant that abstract 'thoughts' (*noēseis*) in general, and specifically the concepts (*ennoiai*) he has been explaining, supervene on representational 'images' of some kind, whose 'objects' are phantasms. I imagine the latter to be something like Lockean 'general ideas', but concepts are, I think, always treated as though they had purely abstract contents.

(*axiōmata*). Although the second question is controversial, three bits of evidence strongly favour the view that the contents of concepts are 'propositions'.[39] One is Plutarch's definition of concepts as 'thoughts' and 'impressions' (*Com. not.* 47, *Soll. an.* 961C, cited above), which can only be complete *lekta*. Another is the conclusion of Cicero's report of the formation of concepts in *Ac.* 2.21–2, which apparently offers 'If something is a man, it is a mortal animal capable of participating in reason' as an example of the content of a concept.[40] The third is the fact that preconceptions are considered to be true, and amount to knowledge (cf. *Ac.* 2.22 and e.g. *St. rep.* 38).[41] Thus I take it that the content of a preconception is probably one or more 'propositions'.

The first question, however, is the more relevant one here. Given the roles of concepts as constituents of ordinary rational thoughts and determinants of speaker's meaning, it seems necessary that the proper content of each concept should be a unique *lekton*. For if it were not, it is hard to see how rational impressions could express determinate thoughts in the absence of a mechanism for determining which part of a given concept's content was relevant to each thought.[42] This also seems right in view of the criterial function of preconceptions (see *Ac.* 2.22), although it introduces some difficulties, since some of the roles the Stoics ascribe to our preconceptions require them to be more complex than this result appears to allow (see section four below).

At any rate, there is, I hope, some reason to think that preconceptions are natural conceptions, and that conceptions are a distinct kind of rational impression, whose content is abstract and general, and probably takes the form of a unique *lekton*, and perhaps of a unique 'proposition'.

[39] Frede 1987: 156 argues for the predicate view, partly on the basis of S.E., *M.* 7.246 (*SVF* 2.65), which is itself a highly controversial text – see Heintz 1972: 116–18.

[40] Cicero, *Ac.* 2.21: *cetera series deinde sequitur maiora nectens, ut haec quae quasi expletam rerum conprehensionem amplectuntur: 'si homo est, animal est mortale rationis particeps'. Quo e genere nobis notitiae rerum inprimuntur, sine quibus nec intellegi quicquam nec quaeri disputarive potest.* ('Next follows the remaining series linking more important terms, which contain, as it were, a full apprehension of the things, e.g.: "If something is a man, it is a mortal animal capable of participating in reason." From this class our concepts of things are impressed, without which one cannot understand, investigate, or argue anything.') I say 'apparently', since the claim in the next sentence (the last above) makes it a bit unclear whether the definition of man just given is itself a concept; see Reid 1885: 200 ad loc.

[41] But both of these points are surmountable: the Stoics apply 'true' to impressions etc. in a derivative sense, and talk indiscriminately about cataleptic impressions and *catalēpseis*. The main problem for the propositional view is to account for the manner in which conceptual contents 'conjoin' as constituents of a *simple* proposition in thoughts such as 'This is red'.

[42] See Frede 1987: 152–5. Perhaps this consideration is undermined once we allow for the possibility that the conceptual content is a complex *lekton*. Some evidence suggests that it may be a conditional; but it seems that there may be a number of conjuncts contained in its consequent (as in the case of god), and it isn't clear that this number must be small.

Section three: Stoic common conceptions

The identity of the class of 'common conceptions' in Stoic epistemology, and even the correct construal of the phrase itself, is controversial. Nevertheless, some points are clear. First, the common conceptions are general or *universal concepts* in the sense reviewed briefly above, rather than merely local 'empirical generalisations'.[43] If the latter were a correct description of the common conceptions, the Stoics' conceptual terminology would be remarkably inconsistent. That it wasn't is clear from the secure examples we have. One is from Alexander:

He [Chrysippus] tries to confirm that there are these different kinds of mixture through the common conceptions, which, he says, we get from nature as our paramount (*malista*) criteria of truth. At any rate, he says that we have one impression of things composed by juxtaposition, and another of things mixed together when the elements perish, and another of things mixed and interpenetrating each other in such a way that each element preserves its own nature. But we wouldn't have this difference in our impressions if absolutely every element in every mixture were composed by juxtaposition. (*De mixtione* p. 217.2–4, *SVF* 2.473)[44]

It is clear from the remainder of this work that Alexander thinks that the Stoics' notion of total interpenetrative mixture – one of the three impressions he mentions – is falsely supposed by them to be a common conception (cf. 218.11–19). That this is the right *kind* of candidate for a common conception in Alexander's view is shown by his own candidate, 'the conception that the full is no longer able to receive anything in itself' (ibid.) – i.e. an abstract and fully general conception.[45] Sextus provides another fairly clear example in *M.* 11.22 (*SVF* 3.75; see Part 2 below):

43 The latter is the view advocated by Todd 1973, followed by Obbink 1992: 202–7. Todd (ibid. 48 and 53–4) argues that we should identify (i) in the following citation from Alexander as a common conception, and (a) as a preconception: ' ...[i] the fact that many bodies preserve their own qualities both in lesser and greater visible masses ([a] as can be seen in the case of incense, which, though attenuated in burning, preserves its own quality to a large extent) (*Mixt.* 217.14–1).' Obbink seems to conflate Todd's view with Schofield's, but Schofield 1980 takes the common conceptions to be preconceptions, and does not think that the latter are 'empirical generalisations' of the kind Todd argues for.

44 Τὸ δὲ ταύτας τὰς διαφορὰς εἶναι τῆς μίξεως, πειρᾶται πιστοῦσθαι διὰ τῶν κοινῶν ἐννοιῶν, μάλιστα δὲ κριτήρια τῆς ἀληθείας φησὶν ἡμᾶς παρὰ τῆς φύσεως λαβεῖν ταύτας. ἄλλην γοῦν φαντασίαν ἔχειν ἡμᾶς τῶν καθ' ἁρμὴν συγκειμένων καὶ ἄλλην τῶν συγκεχυμένων τε καὶ συνεφθαρμένων καὶ ἄλλην τῶν κεκραμένων τε καὶ ἀλλήλοις δι' ὅλων ἀντιπαρεκτεινομένων οὕτως ὡς σῴζειν ἕκαστον αὐτῶν τὴν οἰκείαν φύσιν· ἣν διαφορὰν φαντασιῶν οὐκ ἂν εἴχομεν, εἰ πάντα τὰ ὁπωσοῦν μιγνύμενα παρέκειτο ἀλλήλοις καθ' ἁρμήν.

45 Cf. Plutarch's similar candidate in the same context at *Com. not.* ch. 37 1077E (*SVF* 2.465). Todd's identifications of Stoic preconceptions are thus incompatible with the next page of Alexander's *De mixtione*, as well as with the remaining evidence on Stoic concepts. The motivation for Todd's view is Alexander's remark at pp. 227.10–228.4, after he has said that the view that body passes through

The Stoics define the good in the following way, relying on the common conceptions: 'The good is benefit or not other than benefit.'[46]

These common conceptions are presumably identical with the 'connate preconceptions' Chrysippus claimed to be relying on for his doctrine of the good (*St. rep.* 17, *SVF* 3.69); and preconceptions, section two has argued, are Stoic concepts.[47]

Secondly, Alexander's claim that the common conceptions were supposed by Chrysippus to be *criteria of truth* is supported, I think, by all the evidence that we have.[48] An obvious way to understand this is to identify them as preconceptions or as a subset of preconceptions, since they are the only non-perceptual criteria Chrysippus is known to have named elsewhere (D.L. 7.54). In support of this identification is the fact that several sources appear to use 'common conception' interchangeably or in tandem with 'common preconception'.[49] Further, since preconceptions are natural conceptions, this would explain both why the common

body is contrary to the common conceptions, that the Stoics confirm this with the alleged evidence of heated iron. Todd thinks that this shows that we should take p. 217, which has the same example, to show that the Stoic *theory* of mixture is confirmed *by a common conception* about heated iron. This is a possible interpretation of p. 227, though one that ignores Alexander's use of the terms 'conception' and 'preconception'.

[46] οἱ μὲν οὖν Στωϊκοὶ τῶν κοινῶν ὡς εἰπεῖν ἐννοιῶν ἐχόμενοι ὁρίζονται τἀγαθὸν τρόπῳ τῷδε 'ἀγαθόν ἐστιν ὠφέλεια ἢ οὐχ ἕτερον ὠφελείας.'

[47] The use of two terms meaning something like 'connate' (*emphutos* and *sumphutos*) at *St. rep.* 17, 1041E, and *Com. not.* 24, 1070C, to qualify our ethical concepts is problematic. Plutarch suggests in the latter passage that Chrysippus isolated these concepts as in some sense dependent on impressions 'internal' to our nature, in contradistinction to 'perceptions' from the outside world. (Unfortunately the text is corrupt at the vital point at the end of 1070C, where Plutarch gave Chrysippus' own terminology – see Cherniss' app. crit. and note 'c', ad loc. p. 744.) Presumably the internality of such impressions has something to do with the process of '*oikeiōsis*', as Pohlenz 1940: 85–96 suggests. It seems likely that such impressions are connected to the equally obscure doctrine of indestructible 'starting points' (*aphormai*) to virtue – on which see n. 59 below.

[48] See Alexander, *Mixt.* 218.11–12: the Stoics say we should use common conceptions for proofs, since they are *natural* criteria of truth. The bulk of our evidence either shows the common conceptions being used criterially, or claims that they – or some of them – are preconceptions (e.g. Alexander, *Mixt.* 281.11–20), and hence criterial on Chrysippus' view, or argues that the Stoics are wrong because their views conflict with the common conceptions.

[49] In tandem: S.E., *M.* 9.123 (*SVF* 2.1017), Plutarch, *Com. not.* 1060A. In general, Plutarch, Alexander and Sextus all seem to move from one word to the other without an obvious motive beyond variation. For instance, when discussing the gods in *Com. not.* chs. 31–4, Plutarch criticises the Stoics for contravening the common conceptions, while all the Stoic evidence he cites talks of our *preconception* of god. But Plutarch sometimes seems to be distinguishing them as two kinds *common* concept, e.g. at 1059E, which connects the conception of demonstration (*apodeixis*) with the preconception of confirmation (*pistis*). And Alexander sometimes seems to use 'common conception' as if it were a translation of more familiar terminology – whether Aristotle's at *in Top.* 18.20 (*archai* are called 'physical and common conceptions'), or both Aristotle's (the general 'supposition') and his own ('the common preconception') at *in Met.* 982ab, pp. 8–10.

conceptions are called '*conceptions*', and why Alexander says that they come from nature and sometimes calls them '*natural*' conceptions or preconceptions.[50]

A third point concerns the sense in which these conceptions are 'common' (*koinos*). The obvious meaning of this adjective is 'shared'.[51] The most obvious groups that might share the conceptions in question are the Stoic doctrines, the Stoics, the wise and all rational human beings. Since our sources often say that the common conceptions belong to all men, and since we expect *natural* Stoic criteria of truth to be available in principle to all rational adults, it is likely that the relevant sense of 'common' is roughly 'shared by all human beings *qua* rational'.[52] (I note that this is only roughly correct in order to leave room for disassociating the common conceptions from common sense or the *consensus omnium* in section four.) Further, if this is correct, it is easy to see why the common conceptions are shared by the Stoics and the wise, and why their contents are common to Stoic doctrines.

Thus, I take it to be clear that the Stoic common conceptions are concepts, criteria of truth, and, in principle at least, common to all men *qua* rational. The more difficult questions are whether they are identical with preconceptions, or with a sub-set of them, or also include some conceptions. (Section four deals with their criterial functions and how common they are in fact.)

---

[50] See Alexander, *Mixt*. 218.15, 17, 20. Origen calls what looks like the preconception of god a 'natural conception' at *SVF* 2.1052.

[51] See the definitions of '*koinos*' by the commentators on Aristotle's *Categories* 1 a1, e.g. Porphyry *in Cat.* 62.16–29. *Pace* Obbink 1992: 225–7, principles are 'fundamental' or 'basic' (Obbink's favoured translations of '*koinos*') just when they are *shared by* or common to more than one science. (Proclus explains Euclid's 'common conceptions' – i.e. the 'axioms' in Proclus' terminology – at the beginning of the *Elements* as the set demarcated by two criteria: they are indemonstrable and self-evident principles accepted by all (and so what Proclus calls 'common conceptions/preconceptions' in his own terminology), and they are common to several genera (*in Eucl.* 193–6).)

[52] Common conceptions or preconceptions are said to belong to all men in e.g. S.E., *M*. 9.123 and 196, Plutarch, *St. rep.* ch. 38, 1051F (implicitly), and Alexander, *Mixt.* 213.10, though the relevant conception is only later identified as common.
  There is also some evidence that the Stoics had a doctrine of 'common reason' (*koinos logos*) in the sense of 'reason belonging to all men' – see D.L. 7.201–2 (*SVF* 2.16, line 20), a header in the catalogue of Chrysippus' books, Cicero, *Leg.* 1.23 and Marcus Aurelius, 4.4. (cf. 6.35 and Epictetus, *Diss.* 1.3.5). But this is problematic for two reasons: first, 'common reason' more standardly refers to the universal reason that pervades the world, i.e. God (see Cleanthes' *Hymn to Zeus* 1.12, or e.g. *SVF* 2.599 and 937); and secondly, in Cicero and Marcus, 'common reason' grounds our obedience to the Law or 'right reason' in a way that is unclear, and possibly non-Chrysippian, whilst the Chrysippian header seems to identify 'common reason' with 'right reason' (since it avers that the virtues and sciences are constituted from it).

If common conceptions are, in principle, common to all, it is unlikely that they are identical with the set of preconceptions, since, as Sandbach pointed out, it would be unnecessary to talk of 'common' preconceptions or conceptions if none were non-common or 'private' to some smaller group.[53] This point can be strengthened by considering the genesis of preconceptions from perception: it seems clear that some groups of people will naturally arrive at some preconceptions on the basis of quotidian experience that is inaccessible to other groups, given the nature of their terrain – e.g. experience of llamas and alpacas.[54] Although one might object that this view is incompatible with Chrysippus' claim that preconceptions are criteria, there is no reason to think that relatively 'private' preconceptions are any more subjective than 'common' ones – in either case, what makes them criterial, or gives them epistemological warrant, is the natural process by which they arise, not public agreement on their contents.[55] Similarly, while Chrysippus is said by Galen to claim that each conception and preconception constitutes a part of reason (*PHP* 5.3, *SVF* 2.841), we do not need to infer that each person's reason is entirely constituted by exactly the same concepts even at the first onset of rationality. For Chrysippus' vague characterisation of reason as 'a collection of certain conceptions and preconceptions' (*ennoiōn te tinōn kai prolēpseōn athroisma*, ibid.) probably means 'some conceptions *and* some preconceptions'; and if the common conceptions are or include a sub-set of preconceptions, that may suffice to avoid any threat of homonymy of 'reason'.[56]

Perhaps more interesting is the idea that some of the 'common conceptions' might be conceptions strictly speaking, since this would imply that there are some conceptions that it is *natural* for humans to acquire by their own deliberate attention or their social training. But, although some evidence favours this possibility, it is hard to see how we can hold both that some common conceptions are in fact specifically conceptions – following

[53] Sandbach 1996: 23–5. Sandbach also notes that Epictetus' claim at *Diss.* 1.22.1 that 'preconceptions are common to all men' must be restricted to moral preconceptions, since Epictetus himself talks of the preconceptions of a builder and musician and of all the other craftsmen (4.8.10) and of Cynicism (3.22.1).

[54] If these examples seem too culture specific, cows and horses are presumably also ruled out as potential objects of preconceptions. But if so, our preconceptions begin to look too general to do their job. Further, if one can have a preconception of whiteness, one can presumably have one of turquoiseness, but there have probably been cultures without regular access to that colour.

[55] *Contra* Doty 1976: 146. Frede 1994b: 55–6; and 1999: 319–20 and Scott 1988: 146–7 argue that the natural mechanism that generates them from cataleptic impressions warrants the content of preconceptions.

[56] The use of '*te . . . kai*' as opposed to simple '*kai*' makes it likely that '*tinōn*' applies to both nouns.

the suggestive wording of Chrysippus' definition of reason – and that they are non-derivative criteria – as preconceptions are on his view at D.L. 7.54.[57] So, while it is possible that they extend to a limited number of conceptions, *the common conceptions are probably a sub-set of preconceptions.*

Section four: Problems in the Stoic theory

Chrysippus thought that reason was constituted by certain conceptions and preconceptions, some of which, I have argued, are the common conceptions. A vital implication of this claim is that we start off our rational lives with a stock of preliminary, but secure, knowledge about the world.[58] The point of starting out with this set of concepts is to enable us to gain further knowledge about the world by a process of inquiry, and hence arrive at the state of wisdom or perfected reason.[59] Unfortunately the general process of development implied by this theory is set out most perspicuously in controversial sources like Cicero (e.g. *Ac.* 2.21–3 and 30–1) and Epictetus (e.g. *Diss.* 2.11 and 17). But this complex of ideas is also attested widely in other sources.[60] The most significant of these is Plutarch, fr. 215F (Sandbach):

[57] See Frede 1994b: 55. Something like this is suggested e.g. by the apparently contradictory reports that the concept of the good arises 'naturally' (or at least, the 'thought' (*noēseis*) of *something* just and good, D.L. 7.52, *SVF* 2.87), and that we acquire it by a process of reasoning (*collatione rationis*, Cicero *Fin.* 3.33–4). One might try to resolve this by distinguishing between the onset and development of 'reason' in youths – which would also explain the discrepancy between Aëtius, 4.11 (*SVF* 2.83, cited in n. 16 above) and D.L. 7.55 (*SVF* 3.D.17), Iamblichus ap. Stobaeus 1.48.8 and a scholion (both in *SVF* 1.149), concerning the age at which we become rational.

[58] See Frede 1994b: 53–6. That preconceptions amount to or immediately yield knowledge is clear from their criterial status, and also from Antipater's explicit statement that the preconception of God is a case of 'clarity' (*enargeia, St. rep.* ch. 38, 1051F (*SVF* 3.A.38) – cf. *Ac.* 2.17).

[59] Something like this is implied by the doctrine of *natural* 'starting points' (*aphormai*) for virtue – and hence wisdom – possessed by all human beings; see D.L. 7.89 (*SVF* 3.228 – cf. 229); Stobaeus 2.60 (*SVF* 3.264.1–2); id. 2.60 (*SVF* 1.566); and Origen (*SVF* 2.988.10–11). It is unclear to me, however, what form the *aphormai* take in our souls, e.g. whether they are tendencies or dispositions to form certain conceptions or beliefs, or those conceptions or beliefs themselves. In Origen's account (the most detailed we have), the *aphormai* appear to precede and point to the formation of the (common) conceptions of the fine and the shameful, and yet they already constitute part of 'the nature of reason'. This suggests that they may be (or be derived from) a basic sub-set of our common preconceptions that is concerned with 'moral facts' but does *not* yet include the central concepts involved in ethics. On this view the doctrine amounts to the belief that minimally successful functioning as a human being inevitably requires concepts or beliefs that imply the correct concepts of ethics (cf. *SVF* 3.225 and 229–30).

[60] On inquiry and discovery, see – in addition to the passages from Cicero and Epictetus noted above – Clement, *Strom.* 6.14 (*SVF* 2.102; cf. 103), and S.E., *P.H.* 2.1–11. On the link between perception, concepts, definitions and 'the whole art of' dialectic, see Augustine, *CD* 8.7 (*SVF* 2.106), cited below, and D.L. 7.42. *Ac.* 1.42 explicitly ascribes a similar general view to Zeno, but this is still an Antiochian report (despite its anti-Antiochian reporter).

That it is unclear whether it is possible to inquire and make discoveries, as the *Meno* problem suggests. <For we can't inquire about or discover> either what we know – since that is pointless – or what we don't know – since even if we encounter the latter, we won't recognise it any more than things we encounter accidentally . . . . The Stoics explain this by the natural conceptions. But if they mean that these are potential, our reply will be as before [viz. that the problem concerns actualised knowledge]. And if they mean that they are actualised, why do we inquire about things that we know? (*SVF* 2.104)[61]

So preconceptions – and hence common conceptions – are supposed to enable us to acquire further knowledge, and, given sufficient tenacity, wisdom.

The way this is ideally meant to work seems to be that the inquirer begins with the content of his preconception of the thing he is inquiring about, and eventually ends up with a formal definition expressing his knowledge of it. This overall process is summarised by Augustine:

<The Stoics> thought that <dialectic> should be derived from the bodily senses, claiming that from this source the mind conceived its concepts (which they call '*ennoiai*') – that is, concepts of the things which they articulate by definition . . . (*CD* 8.7, *SVF* 2.106, cf. S.E. *P.H.* 2.1–12, D.L. 7.42)[62]

We can see roughly, and briefly, how this might work in practice by considering an example. The content of our preconception of god is set out by Antipater in the first book of his *On the Gods*, like this (*St. rep.* 1051F, *SVF* 3.A.33):

Prior to our whole inquiry, we can briefly call to mind (*epilogioumetha*) the clear evidence [von Arnim: conception] that we have about god. Well, we conceive of god as a blessed and imperishable animal that is beneficent to men.[63]

The final definition Antipater came up with was presumably something like:

---

[61] Plutarch fr. 215f (Sandbach): Ὅτι ἄπορον ὄντως εἰ οἷόν τε ζητεῖν καὶ εὑρίσκειν, ὡς ἐν Μένωνι προβέβληται· οὔτε γὰρ ἃ ἴσμεν· μάταιον γάρ· οὔτε ἃ μὴ ἴσμεν· κἂν γὰρ περιπέσωμεν αὐτοῖς, ἀγνοοῦμεν, ὡς τοῖς τυχοῦσιν. . . . οἱ δὲ ἀπὸ τῆς Στοᾶς τὰς φυσικὰς ἐννοίας αἰτιῶνται· εἰ μὲν δὴ δυνάμει, τὸ αὐτὸ ἐροῦμεν· εἰ δὲ ἐνεργείᾳ, διὰ τί ζητοῦμεν ἃ ἴσμεν; εἰ δὲ ἀπὸ τούτων ἄλλα ἀγνοούμενα, πῶς ἅπερ οὐκ ἴσμεν.

[62] *ipsi Stoici . . . a corporis sensibus eam [dialecticam] ducendam putarunt, hinc asseverantes animum concipere notiones, quas appellant* ἐννοίας, *earum rerum scilicet quas definiendo explicant; hinc propagari atque conecti totam discendi docendi rationem.*

[63] Plutarch, *St. rep.* 1051F (*SVF* 3.A.38): ὧν ἵνα τοὺς ἄλλους ἀφῶ πάντας, Ἀντίπατρος ὁ Ταρσεὺς ἐν τῷ περὶ Θεῶν γράφει ταῦτα κατὰ λέξιν· 'πρὸ δὲ τοῦ σύμπαντος λόγου τὴν ἐνάργειαν [von Arnim: ἔννοιαν], ἣν ἔχομεν περὶ θεοῦ, διὰ βραχέων ἐπιλογιούμεθα. θεὸν τοίνυν νοοῦμεν ζῷον μακάριον καὶ ἄφθαρτον καὶ εὐποιητικὸν ἀνθρώπων·'

God is an immortal rational animal, perfect or noetic in happiness, un-receptive of any evil, and providential of both the cosmos and the things within it. (D.L. 7.147, *SVF* 2.1021)

(The example may be misleading in its details, but it should serve as a rough guide.[64])

One problem with this process concerns the nature of the result. Imagine that things go well: we have no difficulty in drawing on or expressing briefly the content of the relevant preconception, e.g. of god; we do the research appropriate to this subject, and a lot of conceptual thinking. The result is presumably that we have acquired quite a few further beliefs about the subject and a technical understanding of it. Hence, it seems, we now have a different concept from the one we started out with, perhaps a 'technical thought' (*technikē noēsis*, D.L. 7.51), but at any rate a conception rather than a preconception, since our concept now comes from teaching and attention (cf. Aëtius, 4.11). The problem is that we are supposed to hold onto our preconception, in order to use it not merely as a foundation for detailed knowledge, but also as a criterion or canon for confirming our developed understanding.[65] This difficulty is more serious in the case of foolish inquirers, who fail to use their common conception as a criterion for their further beliefs, and thus end up as e.g. anti-providentialists. Such inquirers have clearly modified – i.e. *subtracted* an element from – their original concept, and hence, it seems, no longer have the preconception.

Perhaps this is not much of a problem: good inquirers can remember the content of their preconception, and bad inquirers have perverted their reason, and are no longer of much interest.[66] But it points to a second problem concerning how we draw on the content of the preconception in the first place. For unless they start researching on this topic as soon as they become rational, it seems likely that ordinary people will already have a range of true and false beliefs about the object of inquiry. Hence either they won't have the preconception any more, or, if they do, its content may be confused and no longer stand out as the obvious starting point for inquiry.

---

[64] D.L. 7.147: Θεὸν δὲ εἶναι ζῷον ἀθάνατον λογικὸν τέλειον ἢ νοερὸν ἐν εὐδαιμονίᾳ, κακοῦ παντὸς ἀνεπίδεκτον, προνοητικὸν κόσμου τε καὶ τῶν ἐν κόσμῳ· The example is Sandbach's, 1996: 25. Whether this is actually a formal definition or not is unclear, since there are various other ways in which orthodox Stoics might have tried to define god – for instance, by following Zeno in *SVF* 1.102 and 171–2. (I am unsure how to understand 'perfect or noetic in happiness'; the text is perhaps corrupt – see Marcovich's Teubner ad loc. Pohlenz's emendation ('rational or noetic, and perfect in happiness') is clearly superior to Marcovich's ('rational, perfect and noetic in happiness'), since 'noetic' is a quality standardly ascribed to the Stoic gods in contexts where one might expect 'rational' – see e.g. *SVF* 1.120, 2.310 or 652.)

[65] On this function of the common conceptions, see below and Striker 1996: 62–8.

[66] On the perversion of reason, see the texts collected at *SVF* 3.228–36.

The Stoics can resolve this problem by distinguishing the ideal pattern of rational development from the one familiar to the rest of us. But this seems superficial, since it is clear that they want to claim not just that all of us have incorruptible low-level 'starting points' (*aphormai*) for knowledge, but also that we are somehow able to recognise the 'common conceptual' truths contained in e.g. their ethical 'paradoxes', *despite* the perversion of our reason. And this points to a more general problem about concepts, suggested by the second arm of Plutarch's dilemma in fr. 215F (above): it doesn't ever seem to be the case that we have an interesting pre-reflective concept that is properly expressible in a single formula.[67] If so, we can't start to inquire just on the basis of the preliminary knowledge contained in the 'clear evidence' of our preconception, let alone from evidence that we can identify as 'clear' (as Antipater recommends at *St. rep.* ch. 38, 1051F).

The Stoics have at least something of an answer to this problem for ordinary inquirers, but before considering this, it is worth looking at their response to the first arm of Plutarch's dilemma. In Augustine's account of the process, the Stoics are said to 'articulate' the things they have concepts of by defining them (*CD* 8.7, above). This metaphor of 'articulation' is one that is found repeatedly in Cicero, and also appears in the catalogue of Chrysippus' books in Diogenes (7.199).[68] It seems to capture an important feature of the Stoic account, in that the theory ideally involves filling out rather than revising the initial knowledge contained in one's preconception. So, for example, we start off conceiving of god as blessed and beneficent to man, and, ideally, end up understanding that his blessedness consists in being perfect, i.e. exercising virtue continually, his beneficence in universal providence, and so on. A large part of this process seems to depend on discerning the relations between our preconceptions, though part also consists in acquiring new factual beliefs – for instance, that the world is in fact god. But in either case, there doesn't seem to be any problem with solving Meno's dilemma by denying the first arm. For inquirers discover new information either by structuring their antecedent knowledge ('articulation') or by applying it to the world. In the first case, however, it is notable that there

---

[67] The mutually conflicting Stoic accounts of our preconception of god may be one indication of this. At any rate, Antipater's version in *St. rep.* 1051F differs slightly from the one in *Com. not.* 1075E, which replaces 'imperishable' with 'immortal' and 'beneficent to men' with 'philanthropic and caring and beneficial'; and considerably from the one in Cicero's *ND* 3.45–6, which has god as 'an animate thing', 'than which nothing in all of nature is more excellent'.

[68] At D.L. 7.199 (*SVF* 2.16), the catalogue has a new heading 'Ethics: concerning the articulation of ethical conceptions', Ἠθικοῦ λόγου τοῦ περὶ τὴν Διάρθρωσιν τῶν ἠθικῶν Ἐννοιῶν. (Von Arnim also supplies a similar addition for the Logic heading at 7.189 (his 2.13).) This has been doubted as a late interpolation or a sign of the lateness of the formation of the catalogue, but the reasons adduced for scepticism about early Stoic use of this term are feeble; see Tieleman 1996: 201.

is a sense in which the inquirer already knows the conclusion: as Plutarch suggested, it is potentially there in the inquirer's set of preconceptions.[69]

The common conceptions have a second criterial function, which is well attested in our sources: they serve as negative criteria, or as standards of knowledge which can be used to rule out some false beliefs and theories. The most common examples of this use concern the Epicurean conception of god. The argument, at least in its paradigm form, is straightforward: if your conception of god is incompatible with an element of the content of my preconception, e.g. with providence, you have an erroneous conception of god.[70] Sextus, however, offers a variant of this, when he argues that the preconceptions of god or of holiness – these are the two cases explicitly mentioning the common conceptions – prove the *existence* of the gods and of something holy (*M.* 9.196 and 123, *SVF* 2.337 and 1017).[71] There is nothing surprising in this as such: a preconception is precisely a conception formed by nature on the basis of repeated experience of a kind, and hence it is legitimate to infer from its existence to the existence of the kind (particularly if the kind is immortal). But it rather invites a demand for proof that these are in fact preconceptions, and thus returns us to the Stoic response to the problem of the apparent incapacity of ordinary inquirers to identify the content of their preconceptions.

The general form that response must take is pretty clear, I think: the Stoics need to argue that there is evidence supporting the identification of some particular concept as a preconception. Given their theory on the nature of preconceptions, such evidence ought to show either that the concept has an appropriate causal history or that it is deeply embedded in human nature – i.e. that it arises naturally. At least two texts show that this is what

---

[69] Hence I don't agree with Malcolm Schofield that the Stoics face any particular difficulties in proving something that is already clear (1980: 289–91). Schofield resolves the problem in Stoic theology by distinguishing the knowledge generated by the preconception that god exists from the proofs that the world is god (ibid. 302–4). But the preconception Balbus appeals to in *ND* 2 isn't that the god exists, but that if something is a god, it is a living thing than which nothing in nature is more excellent.

[70] See e.g. *St. rep.* 1052B, *Com. not.* 1075E, or Cicero, *Tusc.* 4.53–4, which argues that the Peripatetic conception of courage is incompatible with the preconception. This is often taken to be a bad kind of argument, but it isn't clear why it is bad to infer that a position that is incompatible with your knowledge is false. A more serious objection is that preconceptions don't amount to knowledge.

[71] S.E., *M.* 9.196 (*SVF* 2.337): πρὸς τούτοις εἰ ἔστι θεός. ἔστιν αἴτιον· οὗτος γὰρ ἦν ὁ τὰ ὅλα διοικῶν· ἔστι δέ γε κατὰ τὰς κοινὰς ἐννοίας τῶν ἀνθρώπων θεός· ἔστιν ἄρα αἴτιον· καίτοι κἂν μὴ θεὸς ὑπάρχῃ, ἔστιν αἴτιον· τὸ γὰρ μὴ εἶναι θεοὺς διά τινα αἰτίαν γίνεται· καὶ τῷ οὖν ὑπάρχειν θεὸν καὶ τῷ μὴ ὑπάρχειν ἐπ' ἴσης ἀκολουθεῖ τὸ εἶναί τι αἴτιον. *M.* 9. 123 (*SVF* 2.1017): σκοπῶμεν δὲ ἑξῆς καὶ τὸν τρόπον τῶν ἀκολουθούντων ἀτόπων τοῖς ἀναιροῦσι τὸ θεῖον . . . καὶ πάλιν εἰ μὴ εἰσὶ θεοί, ἀνύπαρκτός ἐστιν ἡ ὁσιότης, δικαιοσύνη τις οὖσα πρὸς θεούς· ἔστι δέ γε κατὰ τὰς κοινὰς ἐννοίας καὶ προλήψεις πάντων ἀνθρώπων ὁσιότης, καθό τι καὶ ὅσιόν ἐστιν. καὶ <τὸ> θεῖον ἄρα ἔστιν.

they did. The first option, the more difficult one in theological contexts, is found, somewhat obscurely, in Cicero's *De natura deorum* 2.4–15, where we learn that the origin of our concept of god lies in the world, i.e. in god. The second option, perhaps more promising in this case, consists in arguing that certain facts about human culture – for instance, our language, mannerisms, early poetry, records of the views of wise forebears, or widely shared, enduring and spontaneous agreement about the issue – attest to the naturalness of the relevant concept.[72]

If this is correct, we should not confuse the Stoics' appeals to e.g. *consensus omnium* or 'ordinary experience' (*consuetudo/sunētheia*) to attest the naturalness of a concept, with the theory of common conceptions such evidence is supposed to support. Nor, on the other hand, should we infer from the deployment in tandem of both the latter and the former that our sources have necessarily conflated the two kinds of Stoic argument.[73] That the alternative resources were not taken to be evident or criterial is obvious in the case of 'ordinary experience', since Chrysippus wrote two books for and against it, and saw no difficulty in either rejecting it in the *paradoxa* or using it as a source of probable views elsewhere.[74] This is also clear in the case of his use of the import of certain expressions in ordinary language, as well as of poetry, mannerisms etc., to determine the location of the governing part of the soul, reported extensively in Galen's *De placitis Hippocratis et Platonis*. For Chrysippus explicitly distinguished these procedures from evident or criterial ones, which were unavailable in this case.[75] Thus I take it that appeals to a stable *consensus omnium* such as the ones in *De natura deorum* 2.4–5 and 12 fin. are theoretically quite distinct from the deployment of the common conceptions or preconceptions they are used to support.[76]

But it is not clear how much this defence can help the Stoics in the case of ordinary people. For on this account, the elements of our concepts that derive from our preconceptions are only identified by means of a set of beliefs which are likely to be confused with – or not easily distinguished from – the beliefs that underwrite our preconceptions themselves (the

---

[72] On the functions of Stoic allegory, see Long 1992; on etymology, see James Allen's essay in this volume.

[73] *Contra* Obbink 1992: 216–31.   [74] See D.L. 7.183, e.g., and Obbink 1992: 214 n. 72.

[75] See Galen, *PHP* 3.1.15 (*SVF* 2.885.11–16): οὕτω φαίνεται διαφεύγειν ὁ τόπος ἡμᾶς. οὔτ' αἰσθήσεως ἐκφανοῦς γενομένης, ὅπερ ἐπὶ τῶν λοιπῶν συντετύχηκεν οὔτε τῶν τεκμηρίων, δι' ὧν ἄν τις συλλογίσαιτο τοῦτο· οὐδὲ γὰρ ἂν ἀντιλογία ἐπὶ τοσοῦτον προῆλθεν καὶ ἐν ἰατροῖς καὶ ἐν φιλοσόφοις. Cf. Atherton 1993: 95–7 and Tieleman 1996 Part II, esp. 160–8 on *koinē phorē*. Obbink 1992: 216–23 (esp. 221 n. 76) conflates this 'probable' technique with the common conceptions, despite noting the distinction in the case of 'common experience' – see the previous note.

[76] This is also supported by the fact that the deliverances of *koinē phorē* and *sunētheia* often amount to claims about the *communis opinio* – see Tieleman 1996: 160–8.

aphormai or their products). Even if we can distinguish between the two kinds of true belief we have concerning a particular subject – for instance, on the basis of their distinct kinds of content – it is hard to see how we are going to be able to discriminate any of these from the relevant false beliefs we have, without a preconception to serve as a criterion.[77] Nor will it be adequate here to appeal to general teleological constraints on the nature of our minds: the Stoics can't claim that we just do make these discriminations, consciously or not, since most of us clearly do not in most of the controversial cases.

These difficulties suggest three conclusions. First, some of the common conceptions are not common to all rational beings (or, at least, are not available to all of them) – indeed, the more interesting philosophical ones are likely to be extremely rare.[78] But this isn't surprising, since we know that the Stoics think that most people are perverse. Nor need it wreck the Stoics' overall project, provided that most of us retain (or, at least, retain access to) most of our common conceptions – for instance, our preconceptions of colours, cows, etc. Secondly, it may often be difficult to identify consciously the elements of the content of our concepts that derive from preconceptions. This is clear in the controversial case of gods considered above or the case of mixtures reported by Alexander. But it also points to a more general third problem, even in simple, agreed cases, where we might allow that ordinary people retain their preconceptions. For even if one has no false beliefs about a thing, it is still unclear how the content of the preconception can be perfectly isolated, within the set of beliefs that are involved in possessing a concept, as a single proposition (or *lekton*).[79] If so, it looks as though there is some tension between the Stoic views about the immediate functions of concepts in perception, thought and speech, and their application as criteria for philosophical inquiry. For if we allow the ordinary concepts applied in thought and perception to be determinate and relatively simple, it is hard to see how they could constitute the preconceptions the Stoics need for philosophical research; and if we take them to be relatively indeterminate and complex, it is difficult to understand how our preconceptions can be isolated and used as criteria.

---

[77] Perhaps this just happens, for instance when we hear a Stoic setting out the preconception of god. But the history of interpretations of the *De natura deorum* doesn't encourage this line of thought.

[78] This is the principal thesis of Obbink 1992.

[79] Frede 1999: 319–21 argues persuasively that the original set of impressions must be cataleptic. But he points out that rational mastery of a concept involves certain 'assumptions' about the thing involved in addition to the merely perceptual knowledge (the 'experience' of Aëtius 4.11) that originally generated it. I take it that even the imperfect mastery of normal concepts by an ordinary *adult* will also involve at least some further 'assumptions'.

PART 2 STOIC DEFINITION

The precise connections between ordinary language, preconceptions or common conceptions, and definitions were no doubt explained in the formal theories of definition that Chrysippus and his followers elaborated. Given their general understanding of the process of inquiry, one might hope to find some evidence that the Stoics distinguished between something like *nominal* definitions capturing ordinary linguistic usage, *preliminary* definitions capturing the knowledge contained in our preconceptions, with which we start out (ideally), and *real* definitions presenting the articulated conceptions that are the results of successful inquiries. Yet, despite the large number of definitions contained in our sources for the Stoics, this hope appears to be frustrated by the texts we have.[80] The first section in this part reviews the inadequate evidence for the Stoic theory of provisional definition or 'delineation' (*hupographē*); the second contrasts the Stoic theory of common conceptions with a theory of 'ennoematic definition' found in Galen and Porphyry; and the third section draws some tentative conclusions about the relations between ordinary language, preconceptions, and real definitions in the Stoa. The idea is to devise a plausible Stoic model that connects these items in a way that is both consistent with the results of Part 1 and conducive to the development of later models of common sense.

Section one: Stoic theories of definition

The basic evidence for the Stoic theory of definition is given by Diogenes Laertius in an appendix to his report on the grammatical part of dialectic:

According to Antipater in Book One of his *On Definitions*, a definition is a statement by analysis expressed commensurably; alternatively, as Chrysippus has it in his *On Definitions*, it is a rendering of a peculiar characteristic (*idion*). A delineation (*hupographē*) is an account introducing the things (*pragmata*) in outline, or a definition having the effect of a definition in a simpler fashion.[81] (D.L. 7.60, FDS 621, SVF 2.226)

---

[80] See Hülser *FDS* 621–31, Long and Sedley 1987: II, §32, and *SVF* 2.224–30. I have not been able to find much secondary literature. The most useful work I know of is Rieth 1933: 36–54, Long and Sedley 1987: I, 193–5 and Mansfeld 1992: 326–31.

[81] D.L. 7.60–2 (*FDS* 621; *SVF* 3.D.25, 3.A.23, 2.226): Ὅρος δέ ἐστιν, ὥς φησιν Ἀντίπατρος ἐν τῷ πρώτῳ Περὶ ὅρων, λόγος κατ᾽ ἀνάλυσιν ἀπαρτιζόντως ἐκφερόμενος. ἤ, ὡς Χρύσιππος ἐν τῷ Περὶ ὅρων, ἰδίου ἀπόδοσις. ὑπογραφὴ δέ ἐστι λόγος τυπωδῶς εἰσάγων εἰς τὰ πράγματα, ἢ ὅρος [Sedley: ὅρου] ἁπλούστερον τὴν τοῦ ὅρου δύναμιν προσενηνεγμένος. The translation follows the MSS; Sedley's emendation of the genitive (*horou*) for the MSS nominative (*horos*) in the last clause (Long and Sedley 1987: II, 194) yields 'or <a statement> having the effect of a definition in a simpler fashion than a definition'. This implies that there are two kinds of delineation, or two different ways to characterise delineations; the received text instead disambiguates two senses of the word 'delineation' – i.e. roughly, between 'introductory book' and 'provisional definition'.

The precise interpretation of the two initial definitions of *strict* definition is controversial. For the purpose of this section, it will be enough, I hope, merely to assert four points about strict definition that are relevant for the interpretation of provisional definitions or 'delineations':

(a) Chrysippus' definition *may* require only that a strict definition specify a necessary property of the definiendum that is unique to it.[82]
(b) Antipater's definition *does* require only that a strict definition specify a necessary property of the definiendum that is unique to it.[83]
(c) In the case of strict definitions of 'natural kinds', the property the Stoics sought was in fact the 'common quality' – i.e. something like the 'essence' – in virtue of which it was a kind.[84]
(d) Chrysippus probably thought that a strict definition could be analysed as an indefinite conditional, for example: 'If something is a man, that thing is a rational mortal animal.'[85]

However, since (a) is uncertain, it seems safest to assume in the light of (c) and the common example in (d) that the two definitions yield two distinct conceptions of strict definition, both of which presumably yield *real* definitions: Chrysippus' definitions capturing something like the 'essences' of the definienda, and Antipater's capturing necessary properties unique to the definienda.

[82] Chrysippus' definition is also ascribed to him in a scholion to Dionysius Thrax (*FDS* 627, *SVF* 2.226), and probably alluded to by Alexander *in Top.* 42–3 (*FDS* 628, *SVF* 2.228). Rieth 1933: 513 and Long and Sedley 1987: I, 194 take 'peculiar characteristic' (*idion*) as a Stoic term indicating the essential nature of the definiendum, rather than in its ordinary logical sense of 'property unique to x' (Aristotle mentions both senses in *Top.* 1.4). This is possible; but it seems more plausible to understand Antipater's definition as a version of Chrysippus' than a criticism of it. One reason for thinking that Chrysippus did not want to mention 'essential properties' in his definition may be that it is supposed to cover any definition, and hence definitions of things that don't have 'common' or 'peculiar qualities', like *lekta* or proofs.

[83] Antipater's definition is likewise ascribed to him in the scholion to Dionysius Thrax (*FDS* 627, *SVF* 2.226), and alluded to by Alexander, *in Top.* 42–3 (*FDS* 628, *SVF* 2.228); but it is also given with minor variants and without any ascription in [Galen] *Def. med.* (*FDS* 624, *SVF* 2.227) and twice in the *Suda* (under *horos* and *apartian*, *FDS* 625–6). Alexander spells out Antipater's definition as a statement containing 'an unfolding (*exaplōsis*) of the definiendum' (= 'by analysis') which 'neither exceeds nor falls short' (= 'commensurably'). The scholion replaces 'by analysis' with 'by necessity', and glosses the latter as 'reciprocal' (*kat' antistrophēn*) – and the second gloss is repeated in the second citation from the *Suda*. As far as I can see, none of these variants suggest that Antipater was concerned to capture the essential properties of definienda.

[84] Rieth 1933: 52 cites Diogenes of Babylon ap. D.L. 7.58 (cf. n. 8 above), and Simplicius *in Cat.* 222.30 (*SVF* 2.378), which notes that the Stoics identified common qualities by 'peculiarities' (*idiotēs*) – although this term may not be a Stoic one, given its use by Porphyry at e.g. *in Ptol. harm.* 8.7–11. The individuating functions of these qualities are explained in Sedley 1982 and Menn 1999.

[85] See S.E., *M.* 11.8, *SVF* 2.224, *FDS* 629 – cf. Cicero *Ac.* 2.21, and n. 30 above. Sextus' point seems to be that 'universals' and indefinite conditionals have the same truth conditions. But Chrysippus may have been trying to avoid the appearance of hypostasising a generic Man in his definitions – see e.g. Caston 1999: 192–9 and the alternative interpretation of Chrysippian 'conceptual objects' in Egli 1979: 266–7.

At first sight, one might think that the notion of a 'delineation' should be more straightforward. The two definitions Diogenes gives are:

(i) An account introducing (or leading to) the things (*pragmata*) in outline, or

(ii) A definition having the effect of a definition in a simpler fashion.[86]

The first seems to identify a kind of manual, i.e. a book giving 'an outline' of a subject, or an 'introduction', rather than a kind of definition, and if so, is included in order to avoid ambiguity. (Galen e.g. sometimes uses 'delineation' (*hupographē*) in this sense, though rarely in his own voice.)[87] So we can ignore (i). It is perhaps natural to think that a delineating account in the second sense is one that identifies what something is, whether as a prelude to strict definition or for the purpose of discussion or teaching, without (usually) disclosing its 'essence'.[88] After all, the metaphors in these definitions are just formalisations of the ones regularly applied in this context by Aristotle. In *De anima* 2.1 fin., for instance, he deploys all the metaphors used in the Stoic definitions in tandem:

This should be enough to define (*dihorizein*) and delineate an account (*hupographein*) of the soul in outline (*tupos*). (413a9–10)[89]

And, as Aristotle uses these metaphors, 'delineating an account' is synonymous with 'defining in outline', and both are provisional definitions. But, as this case – Aristotle's definition of the soul – shows, a provisional definition may be very close or even identical to the best formulation we find of a strict definition.[90] That is, it may be 'provisional' in the sense that we start out with it, and later confirm it, or a 'delineation' in the sense that it is a concise expression of a definition that might otherwise take pages to enunciate.

This case suggests that a more cautious approach to the second meaning of 'delineation' ((ii) above) may be required. If delineations perform the function of a strict definition 'in a simpler fashion', it seems likely that there

---

[86] These definitions are repeated in the *Suda* under *horos* (*FDS* 625), which also gives the correct Stoic definitions of strict definition. [Galen] *Def. med.* 1.6 (*FDS* 624, *SVF* 2.227) seems to offer related definitions. Other possibly Stoic definitions are discussed in section two.

[87] See Galen, *Syn. puls.* 9.431.5 or *Lib. prop.* 19.11.7, which note the use of 'Delineation', 'Outline', 'Introduction', 'Synopsis' etc. as titles for books for beginners. A Stoic example of the first title is the work *Delineation of ethical reason* found in the catalogue of Chrysippus' books at D.L. 7.199. (I am indebted to Jonathan Barnes for pointing out the correct sense of definition (i).)

[88] Cf. e.g. Long and Sedley 1987: I, 194 or Atherton 1993: 110.

[89] τύπῳ μὲν οὖν ταύτῃ διωρίσθω καὶ ὑπογεγράφθω περὶ ψυχῆς.

[90] I assume that this is Aristotle's strict definition of the soul, despite his demand for the second kind of definition he recognises – i.e. including the cause, *Pos. an.* 2.10 at 413a15, and despite the problems about such a general definition of 'soul' raised at 402b1–9 (which greatly exercised the commentators – see Eustratius, *in Ethic.* 41.12–15, Philoponus, *in Cat.* 167.12–17, *in An.* 38.11–17, Simplicius, *in An.* 13.1–21, and Themistius, *in An.* 13.16–14.11).

will be at least as many kinds of delineation as there are of strict definition. We may thus tentatively identify the following types:

(1) A concise or simplified formulation of a Chrysippian definition – i.e. something that captures the 'essence' of the definiendum.

(2) An abbreviated or simpler version of an Antipatrian definition – i.e. something that captures a necessary property of the definiendum that is unique to it. To these we may perhaps add two further possible candidates on the basis of the results of Part 1 and normal philosophical usage, respectively:

(3) A *preliminary* definition – i.e. a formulation of the content of a (Stoic) common conception, which will capture the essence of the definiendum as type (1) does, but in a way that requires further 'articulation' and research.

(4) Any short formulation that gives a characterisation of a thing – i.e. something that identifies a thing either in the way types (1)–(3) do, or through non-necessary or common properties, or by examples etc.

(The dominant technical sense of 'delineation' in later philosophical writers is something like type (2), though the same authors also use the term non-technically in the manner of type (4).)[91]

Although the evidence may be confused by interference from some of the sources, we can get some idea of the Stoics' use of delineations by looking at three examples contained in *SVF* 2–3.[92] A simple case is Stobaeus' remark about 'madness':

They also say that every bad person is mad, because he is ignorant about himself and his circumstances, which is madness. Ignorance is the vice opposed to wisdom; when it is relatively disposed, and provides unstable and fluttering impulses, it is madness. Hence they delineate madness thus: fluttering ignorance. (*Ec.* 2.68, *SVF* 3.663)[93]

---

[91] Type (2): Alexander takes delineations to be accounts specifying *per se* properties that are inseparable and peculiar (*idia*) to the definiendum at *in Met.* 176.25 (cf. *in Top.* 421.28–31); his view is followed by most of the commentators – see e.g. Ammonius *in Isag.* 54.6–7. Porphyry ap. Simplicius, *in Cat.* 30.5–15 takes delineations to capture the 'peculiarity' (*idiotēs*) of the thing but not the essence (and hence to cover items that don't have an essence (*ousia*), such as the highest genera under discussion); see further section two below. Type (4): see e.g. Aristotle *Soph. elen.* 181a 2, Alexander, *in Top.* 25.15, Porphyry, *De abst.* 2.52, *in Ptol. harm.* 52.3–4, etc. The TLG version of the *CAG* and indices such as Bonitz's on Aristotle generate more examples than one can deal with; I am indebted to Jonathan Barnes for his lucid discussion of the way the term 'delineation' is used by Porphyry and other commentators (Barnes 2003: 56–62, *ad Isag.* 2.10–14).

[92] The cases I found were of *axiōma* (2.166), *sēmeion* (2.221), *apodeixis* (2.266), *pros ti* (2.404) – all from Sextus – *kakon* (3.74, Stobaeus), *agathon* (3.75, Sextus), *aretai* (3.263, Philo), *epitēdeuma* (3.294, Stobaeus), *pathos* (3.389, Stobaeus; 462, 479, Chrysippus ap. Galen), *hosiotēs* (3.660, Stobaeus) and *mania* (3.663, Stobaeus). Many of these cases are questionable, however, because they only employ the verb 'delineate', which more often has the vaguer, non-technical sense of my type (4).

[93] Ἔτι δὲ λέγουσι πάντα φαῦλον μαίνεσθαι, ἄγνοιαν ἔχοντα αὑτοῦ καὶ τῶν καθ' αὑτόν, ὅπερ ἐστὶ μανία. Τὴν δ' ἄγνοιαν εἶναι ἐναντίαν κακίαν τῇ φρονήσει· ταύτην δὲ πρός τί πως ἔχουσαν

This delineation gives the genus and differentia of the definiendum in an admirably concise form. If you knew the Stoic definitions of ignorance and fluttering, this would allow you to understand what madness is; if you knew only what 'ignorance' and 'fluttering' mean in ordinary Greek, it would not. This case perhaps fits type (1); at any rate, the 'delineating' element is simply concision. The second case is Sextus' remark about *axiōmata* ('propositions') in the course of his discussion of the Stoics' views about what is signified:

... the signified thing or *lekton*, which can be true or false. But this isn't the case for all *lekta*, since some are incomplete, and others complete. Among the latter is what they call an *axiōma*, which they delineate as follows: an *axiōma* is what is true or false. (*M.* 8.12, *SVF* 2.166)[94]

This isn't an abbreviation of the definition of a 'proposition' found in other texts; and yet, taken with its context, it identifies all and only the relevant class (i.e. if and only if something is a complete *lekton* of the kind that is true or false, it is an *axiōma*).[95] Hence this case seems to fulfil the conditions of Antipater's definition of *strict* definition 'in a simpler fashion' – e.g. by omitting the kind of true or false thing it is – and thus is a delineation of type (2). A final example is from Stobaeus' and Chrysippus' commentaries on the 'definition' of emotion (*pathos*):

[*Definition:*] They say that an emotion is an impulse that is excessive and disobedient to the demands of reason, or a motion of the soul that is <irrational> and contrary to nature . . . (*Ec.* 2.88.8–9, *SVF* 3.378)

[*Stobaeus:*] 'Contrary to nature' is included in the delineation of emotion, because it comes about contrary to reason in its correct and natural state . . . (*Ec.* 2.89.14–16, *SVF* 3.389)

[*Chrysippus:*] Given that the impulse outruns reason and is borne off in a rush against it, it is rightly said to be 'excessive' and on this account to come about 'contrary to nature' and to be 'irrational', as we delineated <it>. (*PHP* 4.5 p. 263, *SVF* 3.479)[96]

ἀκαταστάτους καὶ πτοιώδεις παρεχομένην τὰς ὁρμὰς μανίαν εἶναι· διὸ καὶ ὑπογράφουσι τὴν μανίαν οὕτως· ἄγνοιαν πτοιώδη.

[94] τὸ σημαινόμενον πρᾶγμα, καὶ λεκτόν, ὅπερ ἀληθές τε γίνεται ἢ ψεῦδος. καὶ τοῦτο οὐ κοινῶς πᾶν, ἀλλὰ τὸ μὲν ἐλλιπὲς τὸ δὲ αὐτοτελές. καὶ τοῦ αὐτοτελοῦς τὸ καλούμενον ἀξίωμα, ὅπερ καὶ ὑπογράφοντές φασιν ἀξίωμά ἐστιν ὅ ἐστιν ἀληθὲς ἢ ψεῦδος.

[95] So Frede 1974: 40–4; Mates 1961: 27–9, though he allows that it might have been considered a definition by some Stoics, on the strength of Cicero, *Ac.* 2.95; and Bobzien 1999: 92–5, who says that this gives an essential property of *axiōmata*.

[96] Stobaeus, *Ec.* 2.88.8–9 (*SVF* 3.378): Πάθος δ᾽ εἶναί φασιν ὁρμὴν πλεονάζουσαν καὶ ἀπειθῆ τῷ αἱροῦντι λόγῳ ἢ κίνησιν ψυχῆς <ἄλογον> παρὰ φύσιν . . . Stobaeus, *Ec.* 2.89, 14–16, *SVF* 3.389: καὶ τὸ 'παρὰ φύσιν᾽ δ᾽ εἴληπται ἐν τῇ τοῦ πάθους ὑπογραφῇ, ὡς συμβαίνοντος παρὰ τὸν

This is the most interesting case in *SVF*, I think, because it describes what are often called the Stoic 'definitions' of emotion – for instance, by Chrysippus himself in *PHP* 4.2 (p. 240, *SVF* 3.462) – as 'delineations', and Stobaeus' use of that term is confirmed by a direct quotation from Chrysippus. The reason in this case seems to be that the two Zenonian 'definitions' need to be interpreted as if they were combined to produce the strict definition.[97] If so, this case is an abbreviation, and presumably a delineation of type (1). (The other cases listed in note 92 seem to me to fit either this model of simplification or the concision exemplified by 'madness' above.)

A survey of the attested Stoic *uses* of delineations thus confirms the second definition given by Diogenes ((11) above): a delineation is a statement having the effect of a definition in a simpler fashion than a definition – i.e. one that gives a concise or simplified formulation of a strict definition, usually (in the extant cases) of type (1), but sometimes of type (2). It is perhaps not very surprising that many of the 'definitions' we find in our sources are in fact delineations of type (1), since the texts we have are largely doxographical and pedagogical. Sextus reports that one of the principal purposes of defining was to aid teaching (*P.H.* 2.205–11, *FDS* 623), and one might think that this is best done by simplified or concise formulations of *real* definitions capturing the 'essence' (or at least necessary properties) of the things. This may also explain the curious fact that many of the 'definitions' we have are disjunctive or multiple; e.g. the delineation of *pathos* above, or Cicero's review of the multiple definitions of courage by both Sphaerus and Chrysippus at *Tusc.* 4.53. So much for the delineations we have.

Section two: Ennoematic definition

Part 1 section four argued that the process of inquiry ideally starts from the secure or known content of a preconception; and I suggested above that it is tempting to think that that content would be expressed in a *preliminary* definition that would amount to a delineation of type (3) – i.e. a statement of one's antecedent knowledge which captures the 'essence' of the definiendum without articulating it, and could be used as a criterion for a strict Chrysippian or real definition. The review of the evidence in section

---

ὀρθὸν καὶ κατὰ φύσιν λόγον. Galen, *PHP* 4.5 p. 263 (*SVF* 3.479): ὑπερβαίνουσα γὰρ τὸν λόγον ἡ ὁρμὴ καὶ παρὰ τοῦτον ἀθρόως φερομένη οἰκείως τ᾽ ἂν πλεονάζειν ῥηθείη καὶ κατὰ τοῦτο παρὰ φύσιν γίγνεσθαι καὶ εἶναι ἄλογος, ὡς ὑπογράφομεν.
[97] See Brennan 1998: 30–1 and n. 19, who argues persuasively that Chrysippus wanted to claim that Zeno got the definition right, but that it could be more easily understood in his own alternative formulation.

one above gave no sign that the Stoics recognised this kind of preliminary definition at all. Nevertheless, I think that there is *some* evidence for this; but since it is slight, I introduce it after looking at a false, yet potentially illuminating, trail laid by some of the fragment collectors.[98]

Von Arnim and Hülser offer bits of the following excerpt from Galen as part of the evidence for a Stoic theory of definition:

. . . some of the younger doctors . . . think that they have given a *substantial* (*ousiōdēs*) definition of the pulse. But as well as being greatly mistaken in that, they also only gave that kind of definition, without first giving one in accordance with the conception (*ennoia*), which has been shown by our arguments about these matters to be the *criterion* of a definition in accordance with substance . . . . So let us start again from *ennoematic* (*ennoēmatikos*) definitions, which we said were those that induce *nothing more than what all men know*. But it looks like no such definition has been proposed even by the Empiricists, who are the ones particularly suited to use such definitions (which the sophisticators of names don't consider to be definitions, but rather call 'delineations' (*hupographē*) and 'sketches' (*hupotupōsis*)). (*Diff. puls.* book 4, pp. 708.16–709.5 K – cf. *FDS* 306, *SVF* 2.229)[99]

Von Arnim perhaps thought that an 'ennoematic' or conceptual definition was a Stoic delineation of type (3), i.e. a statement outlining the conception of the thing designated by a word; and Hülser may have thought that the

---

[98] A second false trail is from Galen, *Def. med.* 1.6 (*FDS* 624, LS 32D = S.E., *P.H.* 2.212): 'a definition is a statement leading us, by a short reminder, to a conception of the things underlying the words'. ἢ ὅρος ἐστὶ διὰ βραχείας ὑπομνήσεως εἰς ἔννοιαν ἡμᾶς ἄγων τῶν ὑποτεταγμένων ταῖς φωναῖς πραγμάτων. As Long and Sedley point out (II.194), the only reason to think that this may be another Stoic definition of 'delineation' (misclassified by Sextus and [Galen] as one of strict definition) is that it comes after Antipater's version of strict definition in [Galen]. But Galen elsewhere suggests that it isn't, by ascribing a very similar definition to Heracleides while explaining his delineation of 'pulse': 'We know, of course, that the Empiricists aren't at all eager to define things, but rather use "sketches" (*hupotupōsis*) and "delineations" (*hupographē*) – for that's what they call statements that induce, in a short compass, a conception of the thing whose name we utter.' Ὁ μὲν Ταραντῖνος Ἡρακλείδης ἐμπειρικῷ πρέπουσαν ὑπογραφὴν ποιούμενος τὸν σφυγμὸν εἶναί φησι κίνησιν ἀρτηριῶν καὶ καρδίας. ἴσμεν δ' ὅτι τὴν ἀρχὴν οὐδ' ὁρίζεσθαι σπουδάζουσιν οἱ ἀπὸ τῆς ἐμπειρικῆς αἱρέσεως, ἀλλ' ὑποτυπώσεσί τε καὶ ὑπογραφαῖς χρῶνται. καλοῦσι δ' οὕτως αὐτοὶ τοὺς λόγους, ὅσοι διὰ βραχέων ἑρμηνεύουσι τὴν ἔννοιαν τοῦ πράγματος, οὗ τὴν προσηγορίαν φθεγγόμεθα (*Diff. puls.* Book 4, p. 720.5–9 K = Deichgräber frr. 172). Given the Empiricists' use of 'hypomnestic signs' (Deichgräber frr. 80–1), it seems very likely that the two formulations are variants of a single Empiricist definition.

[99] Galen, *Diff. puls.* 708.9–9.5 (*SVF* 2.229+, *FDS* 306+): πρόσκειται δὲ τῷ λόγῳ τὸ ἀκριβῶς, ὅτι τῶν κατὰ τὴν οὐσίαν ἄλλος ἄλλο προσθέντες ἔνιοι τῶν νεωτέρων ἰατρῶν οὐσιώδη νομίζουσιν ὅρον εἰρηκέναι τοῦ σφυγμοῦ, πρὸς τῷ κἀκεῖνο μέγιστον ἡμαρτηκέναι, τὸν μόνον εἰρηκέναι τὸ ὁριζόμενον ὑπ' αὐτῶν οὐσιώδη, μὴ προειρημένου τοῦ κατὰ τὴν ἔννοιαν, ὃς ἐν τοῖς περὶ τούτων λογισμοῖς ἡμῖν ἐπιδέδεικται κριτήριον γενόμενος τοῦ κατὰ τὴν οὐσίαν. ἀλλ' οὐδὲ τοῦτ' αὐτὸ γινώσκοντες, εἰκότως ἀποφαίνονται τὸ δόξαν ἀλόγως ἑαυτοῖς. ἀρξώμεθα οὖν αὖθις ἀπὸ τῶν ἐννοηματικῶν ὅρων. οὓς οὐδὲν ἔφαμεν ἑρμηνεύειν πλέον ὧν ἅπαντες ἄνθρωποι γινώσκουσιν. ἔοικε δ' οὐδεὶς εἰρῆσθαι τοιοῦτος οὐδ' ὑπὸ τῶν ἐμπειρικῶν, οἷς ἔπρεπε μάλιστα πάντων ὅροις χρῆσθαι τοιούτοις, οὓς οἱ δεινοὶ περὶ τὰς προσηγορίας οὐδ' ὅρους ἀξιοῦσιν, ἀλλ' ὑπογραφάς τε καὶ ὑποτυπώσεις ὀνομάζειν.

conception must be a Stoic preconception or common conception, since it is supposed to serve as a *criterion* for a real definition. Their motives for thinking that this text is evidence for a *Stoic* view were probably two: first, Galen's dismissive comment in the final bracket above, identifying ennoematic definitions with delineations, and ascribing the latter to 'the sophisticators of names'; and secondly, the general context of the work, which is largely directed at Archigenes' practice of definition and division in his work *On Pulses*. (Archigenes was a 'Pneumatic' doctor, and hence indirectly linked to the Stoa via the school's founder Athenaeus, a student of Posidonius.[100])

But if this is evidence for a Stoic view, then that view is presumably the one Galen sets out in the pages surrounding this excerpt (pp. 704–11, Kühn), which distinguish *ennoematic* from *substantial* definitions.[101] The characteristics of the former kind can be summarised in four points:

(1) Ennoematic definitions are agreed by all or all users of the same language (708.17, 704.12);
(2) they are criteria for substantial definitions (708.14, cf. 704.7–11);
(3) they amount to what Aristotle called a *logos onomatōdēs* (*APo.* 2.10) or 'nominal definition' (704.11–13); and
(4) they don't grasp the essence of the thing, but only its accidents (704.17–5.7, 705.14–18).

Galen explains 'substantial' or real definitions by direct appeal to his commentary on Aristotle's discussion in the *Posterior Analytics* (705.13–6.3), and in particular to 2.10. (Galen notes that there are two kinds of real definition at 712.9–13.)

If there was a Stoic original of this theory of definition, it presumably distinguished between giving a delineation setting out the content of our preconception or common conception of the thing and giving a strict definition of its Chrysippian *idion*. Curiously, as Rieth pointed out (1933: 38), it looks as if there is further evidence to support this hypothesis in a fragment of Porphyry (replying to a criticism by Plotinus (*Enn.* 6.1.10.1) of Aristotle's explanation of 'quality' via 'qualified things' (*Cat.* 8b25)):

---

100 See Posidonius, fr. 190 EK (Galen, *De causis contentivis* 2.1–2). The pneumatic doctors have not received much scholarly attention; see Wellman 1896, Kudlein 1968, and Wellman 1895 esp. 5–22 and 169–201 (a reconstruction of Archigenes' work on pulses). The Stoic elements of their theory appear to be entirely 'physical' and hence medical – e.g. the pneuma itself, the location of the 'mind' in the heart, the causal theories reported in Posidonius, fr. 190, etc. I have not found any evidence that Archigenes was interested in 'logic' or philosophy as such.

101 Elsewhere Galen uses 'ennoematic' technical terminology rather sparingly; see *Thrasybulus* 5. 811.9–15 K, and *De tremore* 7.607.4 and 609.17 K. It doesn't seem to have been a usual part of his own Aristotelian theory of definition; see *Ars medica* 1.306.12–15 K.

The definition of quality is ennoematic, not substantial. An *ennoematic* definition is one taken from what is known to all and agreed by all in common, for instance: [i] 'The good is that from which one can be benefited.' [ii] 'The soul is that from which being alive results.' [iii] 'Utterance is the proper object of hearing.' *Substantial* definitions, however, are those which also teach the substance of the definienda, for instance: [i+] 'Good is virtue or what participates in virtue.' [ii+] 'Soul is a self-moving substance.' [iii+] 'Utterance is beaten air.' Further, *ennoematic* definitions are the same for all because they are agreed by all in common; whereas *substantial* definitions are contradicted by their promoters' opponents because they are adduced by distinct schools. So [iii-] the ancients don't agree with those who say that utterance is air, because they define it as an incorporeal activity and blow; and [ii-] those who extend the good through all <the alleged kinds of good> disagree with those who put it in virtue and fineness alone. So the right thing to do is to use the definitions agreed by all in introductory works, since they are more familiar and more suitable for a first reading, while the other kind of definition requires first philosophy, which examines beings *qua* beings. Hence Aristotle gave the substantial definition of quality in the *Metaphysics*, and the ennoematic definition here. (Porphyry ap. Simp. *in Cat.* 213.8– 28)[102]

Porphyry contributes three improvements. First, he generalises the ennoematic/substantial distinction – that is, he removes it from the specifically Aristotelian conception of real definition, by ascribing the ennoematic half to all the philosophical schools. Secondly, he offers three examples that are clearly Stoic, and also plausible candidates for the category of Stoic common conceptions.[103] And thirdly, though not in this passage, he routinely describes ennoematic definitions as 'delineations' (e.g. at Porphyry

---

[102] πρὸς ὅ φησιν ὁ Πορφύριος, ὅτι ὁ περὶ τῆς ποιότητος λόγος ἐννοηματικός ἐστιν, ἀλλ᾽ οὐκ οὐσιώδης. ἔστιν δὲ ἐννοηματικὸς ὁ ἀπὸ τῶν γνωρίμων τοῖς πᾶσιν εἰλημμένος καὶ κοινῇ παρὰ πᾶσιν ὁμολογούμενος, οἷον ὅτι ᾽ἀγαθόν ἐστιν ἀφ᾽ οὗ συμβαίνει ὠφελεῖσθαι, ψυχή ἐστιν ἀφ᾽ ἧς ὑπάρχει τὸ ζῆν, φωνή ἐστιν τὸ ἴδιον αἰσθητὸν ἀκοῆς᾽. οὐσιώδεις δέ εἰσιν ὅροι οἱ καὶ τὴν οὐσίαν αὐτὴν τῶν ὁριζομένων διδάσκοντες, οἷον ᾽ἀγαθόν ἐστιν ἡ ἀρετὴ ἢ τὸ μετέχον ἀρετῆς, ψυχή ἐστιν οὐσία αὐτοκίνητος, φωνή ἐστιν ἀὴρ πεπληγμένος᾽. καὶ οἱ μὲν ἐννοηματικοὶ ὅροι ἅτε κοινῇ παρὰ πᾶσιν ὁμολογούμενοι οἱ αὐτοί εἰσιν, οἱ δὲ οὐσιώδεις κατὰ αἱρέσεις ἰδίας προαγόμενοι ἀντιλέγονται ὑπὸ τῶν ἑτεροδόξων· τοῖς γοῦν λέγουσιν ἀέρα τὴν φωνὴν καὶ σῶμα οὐχ ὁμογνωμονοῦσιν οἱ ἀρχαῖοι κατ᾽ ἐνέργειαν αὐτὴν ἀσώματον ἀφοριζόμενοι καὶ πληγήν, καὶ τοῖς τὸ ἀγαθὸν ἐν ἀρετῇ καὶ μόνῳ τῷ καλῷ τιθεμένοις ἀμφισβητοῦσιν οἱ διὰ πάντων αὐτὸ διατείνοντες. δέδοκται οὖν ἐν ταῖς πρώταις εἰσαγωγαῖς τοῖς παρὰ πᾶσιν ὁμολογουμένοις ὅροις κεχρῆσθαι· αὐτοὶ γάρ εἰσιν γνωριμώτεροι καὶ πρὸς τὴν πρώτην ἀκρόασιν ἐπιτηδειότεροι, οἱ δὲ ἕτεροι τῆς πρώτης δέονται φιλοσοφίας, ἥτις τὰ ὄντα ᾗ ὄντα θεωρεῖ. διόπερ τὸν μὲν οὐσιώδη λόγον τῆς ποιότητος ἐν τοῖς Μετὰ τὰ φυσικὰ ὁ Ἀριστοτέλης ἀποδέδωκεν, τὸν δὲ ἐννοηματικὸν ἐνταῦθα.

[103] (iii) and (iii+) are apparently direct borrowings from Diogenes of Babylon (D.L. 7.55, *SVF* 3.D.17). (i) and (i+) identify the Stoic preconception of the good and its primary referent (S.E., *M.* 11 25, *SVF* 3.75 – cf. 74 and 76, from D.L. 7.94 and Stobaeus, *Ec.* 2.69). (ii+) uses '*ousia*' in an unusual sense for a Stoic, but adequately captures a Stoic view (*SVF* 2.777, 780).

in Cat. 73.22). Thus one might think that this begins to look like a more or less direct borrowing from the Stoa.[104]

Sadly, it isn't: the passage from Galen doesn't refer to the Stoics directly by the phrase 'the sophisticators of names' or indirectly in the earlier attack on Archigenes in *Diff. puls.* First, the 'sophisticators of names' in this passage are pretty clearly the Empiricists themselves, rather than the Stoics. For, although the insult seems like a typical Galenic slur on the Stoa, and the terminology looks Stoic, both appear to be used only on one other occasion in the relevant senses, and neither refers to the Stoics. The insult is applied to unspecified medical writers in contrast to Hippocrates (*in Hipp. prog.* 3, p. 255 K); and the combination of *hupographē* and *hupotupōsis* reappears later in the *Diff. puls.* (book 4, p. 720.5–9 K, cited in note 98 above), where they are explained as the Empiricists' own terms for their supposedly non-dogmatic definitions – which is presumably why Galen calls them 'sophisticators of names'.[105] Perhaps more telling, however, is the indirect context: the point of Galen's long excursus on ennoematic definition is precisely to explain to all previous writers on the pulse why their substantial definitions have gone wrong: they (and hence Archigenes) *didn't* use an ennoematic definition to secure their various conflicting candidates. As for Porphyry, it seems clear that he *has* specifically chosen Stoic philosophical doctrines for his +group, but that he did so in order to be able to show how philosophical doctrines can be mistaken, unlike the ennoematic definitions *all* philosophical schools rely on.[106]

This negative result is consistent with the view of the common conceptions sketched in Part 1. For on that view, the later theory of Galen and Porphyry is incompatible with the Stoic theory in three respects: it assumes that an ennoematic definition is (1) agreed by everyone, (3) equivalent to a nominal definition, and (4) restricted to grasping accidents of the thing (see p. 193). The rough relation between these points in the later theory is fairly clear, I think: the theory assumes that concept- and hence language-acquisition depends in the first instance on normal perception, and that normal perception delivers *accidental* features of the relevant kinds, but ones

---

[104] The ennoematic/substantial distinction was picked up from Porphyry by the Aristotelian commentators in connection with explaining the difference between delineations and real definitions (loc. cit. n. 91 above, and Barnes 2003: 56–62, *ad Isag.* 2.10–14), and applied to definitions of the Aristotelian 10 genera (*ad* Porphyry *Isag.* 3.19; see e.g. Ammonius *in Isag.* 56 and 69). As a result, there is a lot of 'evidence' of this kind in the *CAG*.

[105] Galen *does* frequently call Archigenes et al. 'sophists of names' in book 2, but the terms are different (*sophistai tōn onomatōn* in book 2; *deinoi peri tas prosēgorias* in book 4).

[106] The ennoematic definitions Porphyry cites are all familiar from arguments in Plato: e.g. something like (i) is found at *Prt.* 333d; (ii) at *Phd.* 105; and (iii) at *Tht.* 185a.

generally sufficient to single out ordinary individuals falling under those kinds.[107] The fundamental difference between this and the Stoic theory is the final point (4): since Stoic preconceptions yield secure, if only partial, knowledge of what the thing is, they don't yield 'conceptual' or linguistic knowledge *as opposed to* knowledge about the substance or essence of the things.[108] Hence, for the Stoics, the content of a preconception *isn't*, or may *not* be, equivalent to ordinary linguistic meaning – the word 'god' doesn't *mean* blessed and imperishable animal that is beneficent to men, in ordinary English.[109] But this is not to suggest that the word 'god' in the sentence 'There is a god' doesn't *signify* that there is something such that it is a blessed and imperishable animal that is beneficent to men, on the Stoic view. It is rather the claim that that isn't what everyone who speaks English understands, or even the majority of people, when they speak or hear that sentence.

Section three: Ordinary language, preconception and definition in the Stoa

The theories of 'ennoematic definition' in Galen and Porphyry are clearly not identical with the Stoic theory of the common conceptions or with any Stoic theory of preliminary definition the latter may have led to. Nor are these later views *theories* of 'common sense' if a common-sense theory is one that posits a general and immediate relation between ordinary thought or concepts and the essential nature of the world – for they claim that ordinary language and thought capture only accidental features of the world (or of the parts of it relevant to philosophical inquiry). Despite the serious differences between these later views and the Stoics', however, it is still tempting to think that the two are connected, since both groups start out with a 'common conception' of some sort, and both use it as a criterion for

---

[107] The motives Galen and Porphyry have for holding the later theory differ: Galen thinks that perception is or provides a fundamental criterion of truth (see e.g. Hankinson 1994), while Porphyry needed something like a Stoic theory of empirically generated conceptual genera in order to maintain his interpretation of the *Categories* as a logical work, rather than an exercise in metaphysics (see Rieth's brilliant Excursus 8, 1933: 177–80, and e.g. Lloyd 1990: ch. 2 or Ebbesen 1990).

[108] This is my principal disagreement with Rieth (e.g. 1933: 38). On Rieth's view the Stoics started off with (i) the content of their preconception, i.e. in his view, the ordinary meaning of the word, and transformed it into a technical conception by means of four further procedures: (ii) etymology; which led to (iii) a division of the senses of a word; (iv) a division (or partition) of the relevant thing; and (v) a definition, yielding understanding. As well as disagreeing with his interpretation of (i), I think that the purpose of (ii) was to try to guarantee that (i) was in fact a preconception; and I think that (iii) is posterior to the discovery of real definitions (his (v)).

[109] I assume that the Greek word '*theos*' probably meant something more like 'superhuman being to whom ritual honours are due' – i.e. that it singles out accidental features of god in line with the later theory's prediction.

some kind of strict definition. But it would be more tempting if there were some evidence to show, first, that the Stoics actually had something like a theory of preliminary definitions (see below), and secondly, that there was a discernible process of development between the Stoic theory and these later theories in Galen and Porphyry (see Part 3).

Unfortunately, although the evidence collected in Part 1 section four shows that the Stoics needed, or at least had an obvious space for, a theory of preliminary definition, *direct* evidence is hard to find. We are explicitly informed about a direct relation between the content of a common conception and a technical definition only in one controversial passage from Sextus:

The Stoics, relying on the common conceptions, *define* (*horizein*) the good in this way: 'Good is benefit or not other than benefit.' They say that virtue and virtuous action are benefit, and the excellent man and the friend are not other than virtue . . . So every good is covered by the *definition* (*horos*), whether it happens to be benefit or not other than benefit. Hence, and as a consequence of this, they say that 'good' is said in three senses, and they go on to *delineate* (*hupographein*) each of its significations individually. In one way, they say, that by which or from which one is benefited . . . is said to be good [virtue]. In another way, that in accordance with which it results that one is benefited . . . [virtue and virtuous action]. In the third and final way, what is capable of benefiting is said to be good, and this *rendition* (*apodosis*) includes both the virtues and virtuous actions and friends and good daimons. (*M.* 11.22–7; *SVF* 3.75)[110]

On the face of it, this passage connects three distinct items – the common conceptions, a definition of the good, and delineations of three 'significations' apparently of the term 'good' – by two processes: the common conceptions yield a definition, and the definition yields three 'significations'. If we follow Sextus' directions here, the order of discovery in this case will be something like this. First, identify the *content* of the common conception of the good, which other sources suggest is 'something is good

[110] οἱ μὲν οὖν Στωϊκοὶ τῶν κοινῶν ὡς εἰπεῖν ἐννοιῶν ἐχόμενοι ὁρίζονται τἀγαθὸν τρόπῳ τῷδε 'ἀγαθόν ἐστιν ὠφέλεια ἢ οὐχ ἕτερον ὠφελείας' ὠφέλειαν μὲν λέγοντες τὴν ἀρετὴν καὶ τὴν σπουδαίαν πρᾶξιν, οὐχ ἕτερον δὲ ὠφελείας τὸν σπουδαῖον ἄνθρωπον καὶ τὸν φίλον· . . . ὥστε πᾶν ἀγαθὸν τῷ ὅρῳ ἐμπεριειλῆφθαι, ἐάν τε ἐξ εὐθείας ὠφέλεια τυγχάνῃ, ἐάν τε μὴ ᾖ ἕτερον ὠφελείας. Ἔνθεν καὶ κατ' ἀκολουθίαν τριχῶς εἰπόντες ἀγαθὸν προσαγορεύεσθαι, ἕκαστον τῶν σημαινομένων κατ' ἰδίαν πάλιν ἐπιβολὴν ὑπογράφουσιν. Λέγεται γὰρ ἀγαθόν, φασί, καθ' ἕνα μὲν τρόπον τὸ ὑφ' οὗ ἢ ἀφ' οὗ ἔστιν ὠφελεῖσθαι, ὃ δὴ ἀρχικώτατον ὑπῆρχε καὶ ἀρετή· ἀπὸ γὰρ ταύτης ὥσπερ τινὸς πηγῆς πᾶσα πέφυκε ἀνίσχειν ὠφέλεια. καθ' ἕτερον δὲ τὸ καθ' ὃ συμβαίνει ὠφελεῖσθαι· οὕτως οὐ μόνον αἱ ἀρεταὶ λεχθήσονται ἀγαθά, ἀλλὰ καὶ αἱ κατ' αὐτὰς πράξεις, εἴπερ καὶ κατὰ ταύτας συμβαίνει ὠφελεῖσθαι. κατὰ δὲ τὸν τρίτον καὶ τελευταῖον τρόπον λέγεται ἀγαθὸν τὸ οἷόν τε ὠφελεῖν, ἐμπεριλαμβανούσης τῆς ἀποδόσεως ταύτης τάς τε ἀρετὰς καὶ τὰς ἐναρέτους πράξεις καὶ τοὺς φίλους καὶ τοὺς σπουδαίους ἀνθρώπους, θεούς τε καὶ σπουδαίους δαίμονας.

if and only if it is beneficial'.[111] Next, using that and, presumably, the common conceptions of benefit and virtue (etc.), work out *what* is good: virtue, virtuous actions, virtuous people. Then, give a *real* definition of the good: 'benefit or not other than benefit'.[112] And finally work out the connections between these goods: all of them are capable of benefiting, but in different ways (i.e. the nested significations 1–3).

The final stage is controversial, partly because its semantic terminology seems to reflect a post-Chrysippian Stoic position, despite the close parallels to this passage in D.L. 7.94 and Stobaeus, 2.69 (*SVF* 3.74 and 76)[113] – but mainly because it is unclear what its precise function is here. The first and second significations of 'good' give the causes of benefit, construed narrowly and more broadly (respectively); and the third signification seems to restate the real definition in terms designed to point out why things 'not other than benefit' should also be considered good.[114] This looks to me something like a semantic version of the material distinctions between kinds of good as 'productive' or 'constitutive' or both (set out e.g. in Cicero, *Fin.* 3.55 and D.L. 7.96, *SVF* 3.107). But whatever exactly the authors of this triple distinction were doing, it seems clear that they weren't attempting to achieve a technical definition by means of lexical analysis of ordinary language or nominal definitions.[115] For there is no reason to doubt Sextus' explicit claim that this was an activity subsequent to the discovery of the real definition; and our other evidence shows that these patently Stoic and philosophical 'significations' cannot have been the content of 'the common conceptions' which Sextus says were used to make that definition.

Unfortunately, once the irrelevance of the final stage of the process is granted, Sextus reports only the final stage of real definition, merely noting that it rests on some preconceptions. His failure to elucidate the earlier stage explicitly, and his confused definitional terminology, make it impossible to take this passage as direct *evidence* that the Stoics used a preliminary

[111] This is derived from D.L. 7.94 init. (ἀγαθὸν δὲ κοινῶς μὲν τὸ τὶ ὄφελος . . . 'The good is generically something beneficial . . .') and Simplicius *in Ench.* 68.19–25 Dübner = p. 319 Hadot (αἱ κοιναὶ τῶν ἀνθρώπων περὶ τῆς τῶν πραγμάτων φύσεως ἔννοιαι, καθ' ἃς οὐ διαφερόμεθα, ἀλλ' ὁμοδοξοῦμεν ἀλλήλοις οἱ ἄνθρωποι· οἷον, ὅτι τὸ ἀγαθὸν ὠφέλιμόν ἐστιν, καὶ τὸ ὠφέλιμον ἀγαθόν . . . 'The common conceptions of men about the nature of the things are those in accordance with which we men don't differ but have the same beliefs as each other – for example, that the good is beneficial and the beneficial is good . . .'). Cf. Porphyry ap. Simp. *in Cat.* 213.8–28, cited in n. 102, and Epictetus, *Diss.* 1.22.1.
[112] *M.* 11.22–4 and D.L. 7.94 *idiōs*.
[113] See Atherton 1993: 105–6. On the relations between these three passages, see Mansfeld 1989.
[114] *M.* 11.27 and Stobaeus, 2.69.
[115] *Contra* Rieth 1933: 36–54. Sextus clearly suggests that distinguishing the significations of this term was posterior to discovering the general strict definition; see further Atherton 1993: 105–6.

definition or 'delineation' of type (3) as a 'criterion' with which to construct their real definition of the good. But it is, of course, further evidence that common conceptions were criterial for definitions in some sense. And one can reasonably claim on the basis of this passage, I think, that, if the real definition can be more or less correctly summarised in such a way that it adds only 'or not other than' to the formulation of the content of the common conception, then the common conception captures an essential property of goodness, rather than accidental features or the ordinary meaning of 'good'.

The terminological results of this Part can be summarised thus:

- the Stoics did not describe delineations or definitions as 'ennoematic' (Galen, *Diff. puls.* 4, pp. 708–9, *FDS* 306, *SVF* 2.229; Porphyry ap. Simp. *in Cat.* 213.8–28);
- they probably did not describe delineations as 'short reminders' (Galen, *Def. med.* 1.6, *FDS* 624, = S.E., *P.H.* 2.212);
- they did describe simplified or concise versions of strict definitions of 'essences' as 'delineations' (type (1) in section one, e.g. 'madness');
- they, or some of them, probably did describe accounts specifying necessary and unique properties as 'delineations' (type (2) in section one, e.g. 'proposition');
- they may have described preliminary definitions giving the content of common conceptions as 'delineations' (type (3) in section one), but the direct evidence does not confirm this.

If these conclusions are right, the hypotheses that the Stoics had an explicit theory of preliminary definition and that a theory of common sense developed from this will only be plausible if a more direct link between the Stoic and later theories can be identified.

PART 3 CICERO'S RHETORICAL THEORY OF DEFINITION

The Stoics thought that the common conceptions grasped essential features of a range of objects sufficient to generate 'wisdom' once the content of those conceptions had been 'articulated' and supplemented with empirical evidence. If they had a formal theory of preliminary definition, that theory claimed that the content of the common conceptions set out in preliminary definitions served as the criterion for the real definitions which articulated it. But preliminary definitions are not equivalent to nominal definitions specifying the ordinary linguistic 'meaning' of the definienda, since, while the common conceptions are in principle common to all rational beings *qua* rational, their content is often lost or at least obscured and distorted by ordinary people. The later ennoematic theory of definition recorded in Galen and Porphyry, by contrast, claims that ordinary competence in a natural language presupposes the possession of 'common conceptions' which identify *accidental* features of the basic natural kinds that structure the world, and can thus be used as partial criteria for the real definitions that philosophers seek.

A theory of preliminary definition claiming that ordinary concepts accessible to all competent language users yield a partial grasp of *essential* properties, would constitute a theory of 'common sense', since it would imply that we can *understand* the basic structure of the world just in virtue of concepts generated by ordinary experience. Such a theory would also provide the direct historical link between the Stoic and later ennoematic theories, if it were found in a source directly informed by the Stoa, but also diverging from it, ideally under the influence of the late Academy (see notes 4–5 above). In this part, I argue that Cicero's late rhetorical works outline a theory of preliminary definition which is intermediate between the two theories discussed in Part 2. Section one briefly reviews three passages from the *Topica* which suggest that Cicero's theory of definition was conceived in a generally Stoic framework; and section two sketches a novel connection between common sense, preconception and definition in some of Cicero's rhetorical works which modifies the Stoic view in the direction of the later theory of ennoematic definition.

Section one: Cicero's formal theory of definition

Definition appears as a theoretical subject in Cicero's rhetorical works in three contexts: as the second *stasis* in his various theories of 'invention', as a device for organising a speech or systematising an art, and as an 'intrinsic topic' or general source of arguments for orators.[116] The sources of most of these passages are extremely controversial, and the details of his evolving theory of definition (and division and partition) in the later works are quite obscure.[117] But there is no reason to doubt Cicero's repeated claims that his mature rhetorical theory is an original synthesis of the technical rhetorical material he learned in his youth, his own extensive experience of

---

[116] The principal loci, in chronological order, are: *De inventione* 2.52–6, *De oratore* 1.189 and 3.115, *Orator* 116–17, *Partitiones oratoriae* 41, 62 and 123–4, and *Topica* 8–10, 26–34 and 81–3.

[117] Source questions usually revolve around whether Cicero took a theory from Antiochus, from Philo of Larissa, or made it up himself; for an example concerning *De or.* 3.115, see Brittain 2001: ch. 5. The most useful discussions I have found on the theory of the later works are Mansfeld 1992: 326–31, Nörr 1972 and Riposati 1947. The best commentaries on this material are still the *De difinitionibus* by Marius Victorinus (ascribed to Boethius in the *PL* (vol. 64, cols. 891–910); ed. in Hadot 1971) and the *Com. in Top. Ciceronis* of Boethius. But see now T. Reinhardt (ed.) *Cicero's Topica* (Oxford) 2004.

forensic oratory, and his philosophical interests in the Stoa and late Academy (under Philo and Antiochus). For our purposes, it is sufficient, I think, merely to note that the philosophers who influenced him were themselves interested in rhetorical theory, and, at least in the case of the Stoics and Philo, taught rhetoric as part of the philosophical education they offered Roman students in the first century BC. There is thus sufficient reason to see Cicero's rhetorical theory of definition as part of the philosophical debate on the connections between language and the world, whether it is his own creation or a direct borrowing from the Stoa or an Academic adaptation of a Stoic original.

Cicero's closest approach to a formal theory of definition, and his most clearly Stoicising treatment of the subject, is set out in the *Topica*, his last rhetorical work (written in 44 BC). His definition of definition is given there in the form of a practical rule:

There are also other kinds of definition [beyond those from divisions and partitions], but they aren't relevant to the purpose of this book. All that remains is to give the method by which one makes a definition. The ancients gave the following rule: when you have got hold of the properties common to the thing you want to define and to other things, carry on until a unique property (*proprium*) is produced, i.e. one which can't be transferred onto anything else. (*Top.* 28–9)[118]

This rule for discovering a definition is compatible with Antipater's definition of strict definition, since it requires only a *proprium* of the definiendum. But the context makes it relatively clear that Cicero at least sometimes intended this to meet Chrysippus' conditions for strict definition, since he takes it to supply 'differentiations' of species of a genus – i.e. definitions by genus and differentia (see *Top.* 31, cited below).

The *Topica* thus works with a notion of strict definition that is at least compatible with the Stoic definitions we have. Despite the obscurity of Cicero's theory of definition in *Top.* 26–34, two further passages provide some reason to think that it was in fact conceived within a roughly Stoic framework.[119] The first is a notoriously perplexing distinction of definienda:

[118] *Top.* 28–9: *Sunt etiam alia genera definitionum, sed ad huius libri institutum illa nihil pertinent; tantum est dicendum qui sit definitionis modus.* [29] *Sic igitur veteres praecipiunt: cum sumpseris ea quae sint ei rei quam definire velis cum aliis communia, usque eo persequi, dum proprium efficiatur, quod nullam in aliam rem transferri possit.*

[119] One reason for the obscurity is that Cicero doesn't distinguish the topic of definition (*ex toto*, 8) from the topic of the enumeration of parts (*ex partibus*, 8) in this section of the work. Some of the problems in his three apparently inconsistent explanations of definition – distinguishing types of definienda (*Top.* 26–7), means of definition (division and partition, *Top.* 28), and the method (*Top.* 28–9) – may stem from this failure.

A definition is an account that explains what the definiendum is. There are two principal kinds of definition: one of things that exist, and the other of things that are understood (*intelleguntur*). By those that exist I mean things which can be perceived (*cerni*) or touched, like a farm or building . . . By those that don't exist I mean things which cannot be touched or pointed out, but can be perceived (*cerni*) or understood by the mind, like a property right by occupation, or guardianship or clan . . . things which no body underlies, but of which there is a delineation (*conformatio*) marked and impressed on the intellect, or what I call a 'concept'. The latter must often be explained by a definition during your argument. (*Top.* 26–7)[120]

At first sight, Cicero seems to be appealing to a Stoic distinction between existents (bodies) and non-existents (e.g. *lekta* and *ennoēmata*). But if so, he doesn't capture it very well, since his examples of the second category are Stoic relations, which are underlain and explained by bodies.[121] At a second glance, it looks like a pre-emption of the distinction between substantial and ennoematic definitions.[122] But it doesn't fit the later theory in Galen or Porphyry, since that theory depends on there being *two* kinds of definition for the *same* definiendum, and correlates ennoematic definition with perceptible properties and substantial definition with non-perceptible properties, while *Top.* 26–7 does the reverse. Furthermore, the passage doesn't fit Cicero's own theory, since it turns out that all definitions by division – which include definitions of both kinds of thing (*Top.* 29) – involve the explication of concepts. Thus it is hard not to agree with Boethius' comment that this distinction is a concession to the vain (i.e. materialist) opinions of his audience rather than something directed at the truth.[123] Still, one point in this passage seems clearly Stoic: the elucidation of a 'concept' (*notio*) as a 'delineation' (*conformatio*) marked and impressed on the intellect (*intellegentia*). For although '*conformatio*' occurs only here in this sense, it is a simple variant on '*informatio*', a term used

---

[120] *Top.* 26–7: *Definitio est oratio quae id quod definitur explicat quid sit. Definitionum autem duo genera prima: unum earum rerum quae sunt, alterum earum quae intelleguntur.* [27] *Esse ea dico quae cerni tangique possunt, ut fundum aedes, parietem stillicidium, mancipium pecudem, supellectilem penus et cetera; quo ex genere quaedam interdum vobis definienda sunt. Non esse rursus ea dico quae tangi demonstrarive non possunt, cerni tamen animo atque intellegi possunt, ut si usus capionem, si tutelam, si gentem, si agnationem definias, quarum rerum nullum subest corpus, est tamen quaedam* conformatio *insignita et impressa intellegentia [Di Maria: intellegentiae], quam notionem voco. ea saepe in argumentando definitione explicanda est.*

[121] Boethius points out that there are bodies that underlie property-rights, guardianships and clans (*in Top. Ciceronis* 1092b–1093b). Cf. Riposati 1947: 60–1, who is rightly sceptical of Wallies 1878: 30–1.

[122] So Wallies 1878: 30–1.

[123] Boethius, *in Top. Ciceronis* 1092d. Marius Victorinus also assumed that Cicero did not intend a Stoic distinction here (he gives 'virtue' as an example of something that doesn't exist on Cicero's view); his reaction is to point out that, unlike Cicero, *we* follow Aristotle's categories (*De dif.* 899a–b).

to describe Stoic and Epicurean preconceptions (*ND* 1.44 and 2.13); and, given the examples he uses, it seems unlikely that Cicero means these to be *innate* concepts of Platonic forms, as opposed to ones generated by an empirical process.[124]

If this is correct, it may help to explain the second obscure passage:

> They [the Greeks] define genus and species in this way. A genus is a concept pertaining to several differentiations; a species is a concept whose differentiation can be referred to the head or as it were source that is the genus. I call a 'concept' what the Greeks call an '*ennoia*' or a '*prolēpsis*'. It is an engrafted understanding [some eds. and Boethius read: of the form] of each thing, known by the mind, which requires explication. [Some MSS: It is an engrafted and previously grasped understanding of each thing, which requires explication.] Thus species are what a genus can be divided into without any omission, for instance, if one divides right (*ius*) into positive law, custom and equity. (*Top.* 31)[125]

The central points here are, first, that species are determinate sub-sets of genera and are characterised by the properties of the genus, and, secondly, that both genera and species are 'concepts'. The second point seems odd. Boethius tried to remedy it by making a Ciceronian concept the concept *of* a form (whether Platonic or Aristotelian); but this makes the definition of the 'forms' – i.e. of genus and species – incoherent. But the key to this passage is to recognise that Cicero systematically conflates 'concepts' with 'conceptual objects': this seems to be a metaphysical distinction he never observed, and which perhaps escaped him. Given this, we can see that his aim here is to sketch a Stoicising 'conceptualist' theory of genera (cf. D.L. 7.60–1, *SVF* 3.D.25, *FDS* 621).[126] For our purpose, however, Cicero's gloss of '*notio*' by both '*ennoia*' and '*prolēpsis*' is perhaps more significant than his elusive forays into (Stoicising) metaphysics. For while this remark is consistent with his usual practice of conflating these Greek terms (cf. *Ac.* 2.30), it seems out of place here, unless he wants to intimate that either kind of 'concept' may constitute a 'form'. If that is right, his purpose may be to claim that genera and species are ways of classifying things

---

124 They might still be Antiochian forms, however, as *Ac.* 1.30–2 shows. On Cicero's translations of these 'conceptual' terms, see Hartung 1970: 78–101.

125 *Top.* 31: *Genus et formam definiunt hoc modo: Genus est notio ad pluris differentias pertinens; forma est notio cuius differentia ad caput generis et quasi fontem referri potest. Notionem appello quod Graeci tum ἔννοιαν tum πρόληψιν. Ea est insita et ante percepta* [or: *animo praecepta*] *cuiusque* [some MSS and Boethius add: *formae*] *cognitio enodationis indigens. Formae sunt igitur eae in quas genus sine ullis praetermissione dividitur; ut si quis ius in legem, morem, aequitatem dividat.*

126 See e.g. Egli 1979: 266–7, Sedley 1985, and n. 85 above. On the lacuna at the end of D.L. 7.60–1, see Brunschwig 1994: 108–10 (*contra* Von Arnim, Long and Sedley 1987: I, 179–83 and II, 182, and Marcovich ad loc., who adopt the emendation suggested in the margin of one manuscript).

that result partly from a natural process of concept formation from perceptual experience ('preconception'), and partly from subsequent thought or
attention ('conception'). This interpretation leaves it open whether Cicero's
direct source was Academic, Antiochian or Stoic. But it does yield an additional point which is authentically Stoic: our preconceptions grasp essential
features of things, though they do so in a way that requires further 'articulation'.[127]

These passages are not, of course, conclusive evidence that Cicero was
working within a Stoic framework. But his theory of definition is relevantly
similar in three significant respects: its definition and method of definition
are compatible with the two Stoic definitions; it is fiercely (if naïvely)
'conceptualist' about genera and species; and it assumes that real definition
is a matter of the articulation of concepts.

Section two: Cicero's commonsense theory of definition

The basic evolution in Cicero's treatments of definition, and his increasing
interest in the topic, can be seen in two passages which preceded the more
formal theory of the *Topica*. The first is the most detailed discussion of the
stasis of definition in the early *De inventione* (from the 80s BC). When a
legal case turns on a disagreement about the nature of the action:

> The first task for the prosecution is a brief and obvious definition following ordinary
> thought (*ex opinione hominum*) of the word whose meaning (*vis*) is in question . . .
> Once this has been given, it should be supported by further words and arguments
> and shown to be as you have described it. (*Inv.* 2.53)[128]

This doesn't present or imply a theory of definition; it merely prescribes for
a series of wrangles about whether e.g. stealing sacred objects from a private
house is a case of 'theft' or of 'sacrilege'. The kind of definition involved here
looks entirely 'rhetorical', as Marius Victorinus noted dismissively in *De*

---

[127] Boethius thinks that the genus needs articulation into species (*in Top. Ciceronis* 1106c–1107a); but,
unlike our concept of it, a genus isn't the kind of thing that needs articulation. (It is possible that
the articulation of one's concept of a genus is what Cicero means by his strange suggestion in *Orator*
116–17 that one should start with a definition identifying the genus of the thing, and, if necessary,
thereafter specify its species or parts (cf. Montefusco 1987: 69–70). On the other hand, he may
have just been misdescribing the difference between defining something by its differentia and the
genus *it* falls under, with defining the *species* that fall under it.)

[128] *Primus ergo accusatoris locus est eius nominis cuius de vi quaeritur brevis et aperta et ex opinione*
hominum definitio . . . hoc sic breviter expositum pluribus verbis est et rationibus confirmandum et ita
esse ut descripseris ostendendum . . .

difinitionibus 893b–c. The second passage is Cicero's influential definition of definition from the *De oratore* (written in 55 BC):

A definition is a brief and outline (*circumscripte*) explanation (*explicatio*) of the properties belonging to (*propriae*) the thing which one wishes to define. (*De or.* 1.189)[129]

The context is a discussion of how to organise an art of civil law: first define the goal of the art, then classify its genera and their 'parts', and finally define each of those. This is clearly intended to introduce a rigorous system of classification and definition, but the context still gives reason to doubt that it amounted to a formal theory of *strict* definition.[130] We can infer from these passages, I think, that Cicero's discussions of definition prior to the *Topica* do not usually, and certainly do not always, involve *strict* definition.

A first approach to something like the theory of *preliminary* definition we are interested in is found in Cicero's first philosophically influenced reworking of the *stasis* of definition from *Inv.* 2.53 (cited above) into a source for arguments in the *De oratore*:

Arguments from definitions occur in four ways. When [1] one investigates what is as it were *impressed on the common mind* – for instance, in discussing whether justice is the interest of the stronger. Or [2] when one investigates what the unique property (*proprium*) of each thing is – for instance, whether elegant speech is the unique property of orators or other people can also achieve this. Or [3] when a thing is partitioned into parts – for instance, in investigating the classes of ends, e.g. asking whether they are three (goods of the body, of the soul, and of external things). Or [4] when one describes the form and as if it were natural characteristic of each thing – for instance, in investigating the type of an avaricious or seditious or vainglorious person. (*De or.* 3.115 – cf. *Part. or.* 61–2 and *Top.* 81–3)[131]

---

[129] *Est enim definitio rerum earum, quae sunt eius rei propriae, quam definire volumus, brevis et circumscripta quaedam explicatio.*

[130] One reason is the casual substitution of 'part' for 'species' in the preceding lines, which is characterised as a 'dumb' error in *Topica* 31 ('*non satis acute*'), indicative of someone who cannot properly distinguish division from partition. A second reason is the similarity between *De or.* 1.189 and the rather baffling description of definition in *Orator* 116–17 (see n. 127 above). The kind of classificatory system Crassus is suggesting for jurisprudence is exemplified by the standard rhetorical handbooks themselves; but the study of classification doesn't seem to have been regarded as a part of the content of rhetoric.

[131] *Definitionis autem sunt disceptationes aut, cum quaeritur, quid in* communi mente *quasi impressum sit, ut si disseratur, idne sit ius, quod maximae parti sit utile; aut, cum quid cuiusque sit proprium exquiritur, ut ornate dicere propriumne sit oratoris an id etiam aliquis praeterea facere possit, aut, cum res distribuitur in partis, ut si quaeratur, quot sint genera rerum expetendarum, ut sintne tria, corporis, animi externarumque rerum, aut, cum, quae forma et quasi naturalis nota cuiusque sit, describitur, ut si quaeratur avari species, seditiosi, gloriosi.*

The four kinds of 'definitional' arguments set out in this passage depend
on a theory of definition something like the one Cicero was later to offer
in the *Topica*. Arguments of kinds (2) and (3) are the products of division into species and partition, which are themselves the means by which
the definitions that generate arguments of type (1) ideally come about. In
the later theory of the *Topica*, the vaguer topic of *descriptio*, the source of
arguments of type (4), is relegated to a subsidiary role. But the parallel
passage in the earlier *Part. or.* 41 explains that *descriptio* is useful because
establishing the *propria* that lead to a definition is often controversial (cf.
Inv. 2.53 fin. above). Thus, since '*descriptio*' is glossed by the Latin commentators as *hupographikē* – 'delineation' – it seems clear that, despite the
relative sophistication of this passage in comparison with *Inv.* 2.53, the
kind of definitions Cicero is interested in in *De or.* 3.115 are still provisional
definitions.

What matters in *De or.* 3.115 for our purpose, however, is the way it
identifies the origins of the provisional definitions of type (1). In *Inv.* 2.53
the meaning of the term to be defined was gleaned from ordinary thought
(*ex opinione hominum*); here it derives from what is impressed on the common mind (*communis mens*). The significance of this change is spelled out
in the elaboration of this philosophically revised topic in the *Partitiones
oratoriae* (from 46/5 BC):

> In this topic [definition] the rules for the prosecution and defence are the same.
> For the one who penetrates further into the <u>sense</u> (*sensum*) or <u>thought</u> (*opinionem*)
> of the judge by defining or describing a word, and the one who comes closest to
> the <u>common meaning</u> (*vim*) of the word and to the *preconception* (*praeceptionem*)
> which his listeners have <u>in outline</u> (*incohatam*) in their minds, will necessarily be
> the winner. (*Part. or.* 123)[132]

The meaning of the disputed word is ultimately determined by the *preconception* the audience have of the thing it names. The competing definitions
the lawyers give are thus attempts to approximate the content of this preconception; the closer one gets to it, the more likely one is to win. Although
Cicero doesn't say explicitly that there is *one* 'preconception' shared by everyone pretty much universally, this is the obvious implication of the phrase
'*communis mens*' in *De or.* 3.115. And this is confirmed when *communis mens*

---

[132] *Communia dantur in isto genere accusatori defensorique praecepta. Uter enim definiendo describendoque
verbo magis ad sensum iudicis opinionemque penetrarit, et uter ad communem verbi vim et ad eam
praeceptionem quam incohatam habebunt in animis ei qui audient magis et propius accesserit, is vincat
necesse est.*

is replaced by *communis sensus*, the phrase Cicero uses most often to characterise 'common sense' (*Part. or.* 126).[133]

The connection between meaning and preconception posited by Cicero
here is also found in the later rhetorical tradition, where the range of the
rhetorical *thesis* – the subject under discussion in *De or.* 3.109–19 – is usually
determined to be exhausted by 'practical' theses on 'civic' or 'political'
questions, i.e. *subjects that fall under the 'common conceptions'*.[134] The point
in these later texts is the straightforward one that there are some subjects
which anyone can discuss, because everyone has some *understanding* of
e.g. moral matters, whereas other subjects require technical expertise.[135] It
doesn't follow that there is universal agreement on all such questions; if
there was, there would be no point in presenting a *thesis* on them. But
Cicero's assumption is clearly that the content of preconceptions will gain
general assent if it is correctly formulated. This assumption is also evident
in the use of appeals to 'common sense' in his own speeches, where it is
consistently tied to the 'commendation of human nature' (*Pro Cluentio* 17,
De domo suo 97, and *Pro Plancio* 31 and 34).

The rhetorical 'preconceptions' of *Part. or.* 123 are, I think, direct ana-
logues of the Stoic common conceptions, and were no doubt modelled on
Cicero's own Stoicising exposition of the natural and empirical origin of
reason in *De legibus* 1.30. We are informed there about common conceptions
that:

(1) they are 'inchoate', i.e. incomplete sketches, representing partial knowl-
    edge of the object;
(2) their content is properly subject to universal agreement, since they
    are imprinted on the mind by nature, though our agreement can be
    obscured by differing formulations; and
(3) they constitute the basis of reason, i.e. if properly formulated, their
    content amounts to a 'preliminary definition'.

133 Cf. e.g. *De or.* 1.12, 2.68, 3.195 (?). I presume the English phrase 'common sense' derives directly
from Cicero. (Philosophical Greek doesn't permit this sense of *aisthēsis*, but Plutarch uses *koinos
nous* at *Com. not.* 1077E.)
134 See Hermogenes, *Progymnasmata* p. 17 (Spengel 1853–6: vol. I), along with the parallels in Aphthonius (vol. II, p. 49), Nicholaos (vol. III, p. 493) and the disagreement of Theon (vol. II, p. 121).
Hermogenes' – or Cicero's – view is also maintained in the Latin tradition, e.g. in the full discussion
in Augustine, *Rhet.* 4 (pp. 138–9 in Halm 1863: *sunt autem civiles quaestiones quarum perspectio in
communem animi conceptionem potest cadere . . .*), and the briefer remarks of Fortunatianus, *Ars rhet.*
1.1 (p. 6 ed. Halm): *Quae sunt civiles quaestiones? quae in communem animi conceptionem possunt
cadere, id est, quas unusquisque potest intellegere, ut cum quaeritur de aequo et bono.*
135 Cf. the Stoic distinction between preconception and conception in Aëtius 4.11, *SVF* 2.83 (cited in
n. 16 above).

(Whether or not Cicero's exposition in *Leg.* 1.30–4 is in fact a direct borrowing from a Stoic source – as I think – or mediated through a late Academic lens, is controversial. But since the general features (1)–(3) are attested for the Stoics elsewhere, and since we are anyhow looking for possibly Academic influenced developments from the Stoa, this question is not important here.[136])

The rhetorical preconceptions are also inchoate, subject to initial but not fundamental disagreement, and, I have argued, when articulated, amount only to delineations or provisional definitions. But the two theories are distinct for at least two significant reasons. The first is that the rhetorical theory doesn't allow for *De legibus* 1.31–4, where we are reminded that in the philosophical theory the common conceptions are in fact subsequently thoroughly obscured by the perversions or misconceptions of human reason (cf. note 66). In this respect, the rhetorical works offer a common sense theory of preliminary definition that points towards the ennoematic definition found in Galen and Porphyry: *everyone agrees*.

The second major difference between the rhetorical view and either philosophical theory, of course, is that rhetorical definitions are *rhetorical*, i.e. *pragmatic*: a definition approved by common sense is just whatever the crowd and hence the judge will accept. It is not clear that Cicero takes them to have any scientific or philosophical value at all (cf. *De or.* 1.12 and 44). But Cicero wasn't always sceptical about common sense (see note 3), and his formal theory of definition in the *Topica* seems to *define* genera as preconceptions (see section one). So Cicero's intermittent scepticism needn't stand in the way of the hypothesis that his writings attest a development from the Stoic theory of the common conceptions to one of 'common sense'.

Section one has argued that Cicero was working within a roughly Stoic framework; and this section has argued that he identifies fundamental word-meaning with the content of preconceptions, and preconceptions with 'common sense'. Since he also thinks that provisional definitions delineate the content of preconceptions, it is perhaps not implausible to think that his theory is a modification of an original Stoic theory of preliminary definition, and one that points towards the later ennoematic view. At any rate, irrespective of its place in a more general history of 'common conceptions', Cicero's theory of definition is, I think, a fragment of a theory of common sense, since – unlike the Stoic and later ennoematic theories – it implies

---

[136] For Stoic parallels to points (1) and (3) above, see Part 1 section four and Cicero, e.g. *Ac.* 1.42; for point (2), see Part 1 section three and Cicero, e.g. *Tusc.* 4.53.

a general and immediate relation between the ordinary thought and language captured in Ciceronian preconceptions and the essential nature of the world.[137]

[137] Some indirect evidence that something like this may be present in Cicero is found in Boethius' comment on *Top.* 28 fin.: 'There are many kinds of definition which are used in speeches but aren't proper definitions. The name they are all covered by is "descriptio" [= *hupographikē*]. Some of them come about by partition, some by division in the way discussed above. Others still include *substantial differentiae, but don't add the genus; this kind is call "ennoematic" by Victorinus*, i.e. *containing*, as it were, *some common conception*. An example is: "Man is what flourishes with rational thought and is subject to mortality." In this case the genus isn't given, but only the substantial differentiae.' (*Earum vero definitionum quae in oratione consistunt, neque tamen sunt propriae, multae sunt diversitates. Quarum est omnium nomen communis* <u>descriptio</u>. *Harum aliae fiunt partitione, aliae divisione, de quibus superius, ut dictum est. Aliae vero substantiales quidem differentias sumunt, sed genus non adjiciunt, atque haec quidem a Victorino* ἐννοηματική *dicitur, quasi quamdam communem continens notionem, veluti si quis dicat: Homo est quod rationali conceptione viget mortalitatique subjectum est. Hic igitur genus positum non est, sed differentiae substantiales* (Boethius, *in Topica Ciceronis* book 3, 1099a–b).) Unlike Porphyry or Galen, Marius Victorinus and Boethius perhaps thought that an 'ennoematic definition' *could* be a preliminary definition that captured the content of a common conception *and thereby* some of the essential properties of its object. (It is possible that Boethius' text of Victorinus was corrupt, however, since the relevant lines of *De dif.* don't mention 'common conceptions', but instead read '*Secunda dicitur ennoēmatikē, quam "notionem" non proprio sed communi possumus dicere*' (902b). (Hadot 1971: 171–4 is not helpful.))

CHAPTER 7

Varro's anti-analogist

David Blank*

In the Summer of 47 BC Varro promised to dedicate a large and important work to Cicero (*Att.* 13.12.3 = 13.24.3 Kasten). In mid 45 Cicero was still waiting for the fulfilment of Varro's promise, and his irritation over this delay may have caused him not to accede immediately to Atticus' advice to dedicate a work to Varro.[1] Scholars agree that the large work Varro intended to dedicate to Cicero was the treatise *De lingua Latina*, which in its eventual twenty-five books was certainly weighty enough. It was also appropriate as a gift to Cicero, offering both theoretical discussions of the methods to be used in determining linguistic correctness and counsel on how to apply the methods deemed best in practice.

Varro organised his work according to a three-fold division of speech into the 'imposition', 'flexion', and 'combination' of words (8.1). For each of the first two of these, corresponding to the study of etymology and of analogy in inflection-derivation (or 'flexion': *declinatio*, Greek *klisis*), Varro wrote six books, the first three dealing with the discipline itself – one arguing against the existence and utility of such a discipline, one arguing for the discipline, and one expounding it – and the next three comprising applications of the discipline. Since we know, at least for the second century AD, that there were arguments for and against the existence of a discipline of syntax,[2] it is likely that the last section of the work, that on syntax, followed a similar pattern, only at twice the length. It has often been thought

---

* My thanks go to Catherine Atherton, Maria Broggiato and Andrew Dyck, who commented on earlier versions of this paper, as well as the editors of this volume. The revision is also indebted to the lively discussion held at the Symposium.
[1] See the discussion of this question in Barwick 1957b: 298–304, at 302–4 and Ax 1995: 146–77, at 146–52.
[2] See Apollonius Dyscolus, *Syntax* 1.13 = 16.6–11 and 1.60 = 51.1, with Blank 1982: 11–19, 71–5. To judge from the only substantive fragment of the syntactical books (fr. 29, from Gellius, *Noct. Att.* 16.8.6–14), Varro dealt at some length with the theory of the proposition and the combination of propositions to form arguments and other types of connected discourse, as in the Stoic 'syntax of *lekta*', on which see Frede 1978.

that the first book on flexion, book 8, which gives arguments against the existence and the advisability of analogies in flexion, was taken from Crates of Mallos, who was therefore thought to have been an anti-analogist, or indeed an 'anomalist'. In this paper, I shall argue for a different picture of *LL* 8. Its major source, I shall claim, was an empiricist attack on the analogical discipline which studies flexion. Crates appeared in this source as a grammarian who disagreed with Aristarchus over how to interpret and apply the rules of analogy; their disagreement was cited by Varro's source in an argument from 'disagreement' (*diaphōnia*): if two of analogy's major proponents did not agree on its application, then analogy has no claim on our attention. Varro, however, may not have realised that Crates was not actually a protagonist in the debate, but had been used as an example.

A major reason to clarify Crates' role in Varro's book is that one interpretation of the history of grammatical studies in antiquity has as its centre-piece a great struggle between Crates' Pergamene school of 'critics' and the Alexandrian 'philologists' under Aristarchus, the latter arguing for 'analogy' or the regularity of linguistic phenomena and the former arguing against such regularity and for 'anomaly'.[3] This view takes off from Varro's work, especially *LL* 9.1, and it can be seen already in Gellius,[4] who is wholly dependent upon Varro.[5] While some scholars have made this supposed quarrel the major fact of the development of grammar in the Hellenistic period, others have made it more a matter of emphasis: should one rather follow analogical rules or avoid them in favour of common usage? Still others, myself included, have denied that the quarrel between analogists and anomalists took place at all.[6] Since Varro is our only source for the quarrel, it will not do to interpret it in a way that goes contrary to his indications. But, while Varro's anti-analogist insists that one follow common usage or what he also calls 'anomalies' or 'dissimilarities', rather than analogical rules, he also indicates that those rules are non-existent and that any grammatical study which goes beyond what is strictly necessary for clear and brief speaking and writing – which is possible with observation of common usage alone – is a useless waste of time. This is exactly the same attitude taken to grammar by the sceptical philosopher Sextus Empiricus

---

[3] For references to this literature, see, e.g., Blank 1982: 1–5, Taylor 1986; for another view see, e.g., Ax 1991.

[4] *Noct. Att.* 2.25.1–11, especially 4: 'Two famous Greek grammarians, Aristarchus and Crates, with the highest skill used to defend analogy and anomaly respectively.'

[5] The argument for this dependence is made by Fehling 1956: 223–4.

[6] This line was taken especially by Fehling 1956–7.

in his book *Against the Grammarians*,[7] but it is not the attitude of a grammarian of any stripe at all, let alone one of Crates' stature. Thus, Varro's account of a quarrel should be interpreted in the same light as that of Sextus, as a struggle over the technicity of grammar, including the epistemological status of its rules and its usefulness for life. The analogist side was technical and rationalist, maintaining that language was a rationally ordered system which could be described and understood through precise rules allowing the solution of questions which might arise in the course of reading, writing and interpreting. The empiricist side argued that no complex expertise of grammar could exist, that the rules of technical grammar were incoherent, and that all one needed was the ability to observe common usage and model one's own linguistic practice on that. While there were clearly disagreements among grammarians over the way in which grammatical rules and criteria should be applied, the empiricists were evidently not grammarians, but rather included Epicureans, Pyrrhonian sceptics, and (probably) Academics. These philosophers used their standard techniques to undermine the utility and/or the existence of grammatical science, for which they also drew on the disagreements among grammarians. I shall argue that the source of Varro's *LL* 8 was such an empiricist book.

THE STRUCTURE OF *DE LINGUA LATINA*

Of the original twenty-five books of this work, books 5–10 are preserved in a corrupt and somewhat lacunose state in a Laurentian manuscript written in Cassino in the eleventh century. From other books we have a number of citations by grammarians, from Quintilian to Gellius and Diomedes. In these citations books 3, 7, 8, 11, 13, 22, 23 and 24 are said to be from a work dedicated to Cicero, and other citations also mention Cicero as the dedicatee, but without a book number. Subscriptions marking two transitions from one book to another (4–5, 9–10) in the Laurentian manuscript also speak of the work as dedicated to Cicero.[8]

Introducing his fifth book to its unidentified addressee, Varro says (5.1): 'I have undertaken in six books to expound the way in which words were imposed on things. Of these I wrote three books before this one, which I sent to Septumius,[9] in which I treat of the discipline which they call *etymologikē* ("etymological art") what is said against it in the first volume, what for it in the second, what concerning it in the third. In these I shall

---

[7] Hence, Mette 1952 took over much of Sextus' book, in addition to large chunks of Varro's eighth book, as 'fragments' of Crates.

[8] Cf. Barwick 1957b: 298–300.   [9] I.e. Publius Septumius, Varro's *quaestor*.

write to you from which things (*a quibus rebus*) words have been imposed in the Latin language . . .' Thus, books 2–4 were addressed to Septumius and presumably published separately. It appears that books 5–7, which contain several references to their addressee,[10] were also published separately. This addressee is commonly assumed to be Cicero, who was also the addressee of the entire work.[11] In the later books, as they have come down to us, there are no further references to sending any of the books to an addressee, although there are numerous references to a second person singular, some of them undoubtedly hypothetical ('if you do this, you will see', etc.) and thus not clearly implying a specific addressee. This state of affairs has given rise to much speculation about the publication and dedication of parts of *LL*, as well as the whole.[12] I incline to believe that the sets of books 2–4 and 5–7 were dedicated separately and published separately, but that a second edition was made once all the books were finished and this edition, dedicated to Cicero,[13] may have been published after Cicero's death on 7 December 43.[14] Further, we may have, not the second, but the first edition of books 5–7, i.e. the edition which was sent to Cicero: it continues to speak of books 2–4 as having been sent to Septumius, and it indicates that books 5–7 are being sent separately to their addressee. Our copy of books 8–10 would then belong to the final product, which would not have spoken of books being sent to their dedicatee Cicero, who would no longer have been alive.[15] The first book was presumably a general introduction, written for the complete edition.

At 7.109 Varro repeats his explanation of the contents of the books on the origins of words:

Therefore, since six books have been set up about how Latin names were imposed upon things for our use (of which I wrote three to P. Septumius who was my quaestor, three to you, of which this is the third, the former [2–4] about the

---

[10] Besides the initial reference in 5.1, see 6.97 and 7.110.

[11] For the practice of dedication and revision in the time of Cicero, see the excellent treatment in Griffin 1997, which focuses on Cicero's *Academica*, a treatise in whose genesis a dedication to Varro played a substantial role.

[12] These are well summarised by Ax 1995: 149–52.

[13] The existence of two editions would explain the fact that book 3 is once cited as being dedicated to Cicero, along with the citations which indicate that the entire work was dedicated to Cicero.

[14] Varro died in 27. That he may have finished and dedicated the entire work to Cicero after the latter's death was suggested by Müller 1833: iv–xi, followed by others; the suggestion has been revived by Ax 1995: 151, who also allows for the possibility that the final edition was undertaken by an editor after Varro's death.

[15] It is, of course, still possible to argue that books 8–10 did not receive Varro's own final polish (so Ax 1995: 176, who suggests posthumous publication by an editor). But such an argument relies on judgements of the coherence, consistency, and finish of the work, rather than on the presence or absence of an addressee.

discipline of the origin of words (*de disciplina verborum originis*), the latter [5–7] about the origins of words), in the first of the earlier books [2] is what is said as to why *etumologikē* ('the alleged etymological art') is neither an expertise (*ars*) nor useful (*utilis*), in the second [3] what the arguments are as to why it is an expertise and useful, in the third [4] what is the shape (*forma*) of etymology; in the second three books, similarly divided by genera, which I have sent to you, the first [5] is that in which are the origins of the words for places and the things which tend to be in places, the second [6] is that in which it is said by which words times are indicated and the things which happen in time, the third [7] is this one, in which those which I gave in the two books for prose are taken up by the poets.

On this description, the first set of three books on etymology, now lost, corresponded to the three preserved books on inflection. Varro also gives us brief characterisations of these books: 'About the flexions (*declinationibus*) of each kind [viz., voluntary and natural] I shall write two sets of three books, the first three [8–10] about the discipline of these flexions, the latter three [11–13] about the results of this discipline (*eius disciplinae propaginibus*). The first of the former books [8] will be this one, [which will contain] what is said against similarity (*similitudinem*) of flexions, the second [9] [what is said] against dissimilarity (*dissimilitudinem*), the third [10] [what is said] about the form of similarity';[16] 'About this thing [viz., the discipline of derivations of words] in the first book [8] I have stated what is said about why dissimilarity should be our guide, in the second [9] what is said against it, why it is rather better to prefer similarity. Since the foundations of these things have not been laid by anyone nor has their order and nature been explained as the subject matter demands, I myself shall expound [10] the form of this thing' (10.1).

ANALOGY AND ETYMOLOGY: PROPONENTS AND OPPONENTS

I begin by stressing the relationship between the two sets of books, 2–4 and 8–10. They deal with the two criteria of Hellenism which Quintilian, probably following Varro, says comprise 'reason'.[17] *Ratio*, in fact, is the overarching principle of Varro's entire approach to language, which is divided (8.1) into these two parts, imposition and flexion of names, and

---

[16] 8.24; cf. 8.25: *quod huiusce libri est dicere contra eos qui similitudinem sequuntur . . .*

[17] *Inst. Orat.* 1.6.1.1: *Sermo constat ratione uetustate auctoritate consuetudine. Rationem praestat praecipue analogia, nonnumquam etymologia.* Fehling 1956: 253 makes the case that the combination of the otherwise separate criteria *analogia* and *etymologia* under the heading of *ratio* was Varro's own way (in his *De sermone Latino*) of keeping the number of criteria at four, once he had added his own favourite, *natura*. He also (268) notes the relation between Varro's books 2–4 and 8–10, adding ironically that only the loss of books 2–4 has prevented historians of linguistics from speaking of a millennium long feud between '"Etymologisten" und – wie soll ich sagen – "Anti-Etymologisten"'.

also a third, in which one shows how words 'joined by reason express a thought' (*ratione coniuncta sententiam efferant*). Both sets of books have the same overall structure and sequence of topics, and these topics reflect the caution or keen judgement which, as Quintilian says, is demanded in the application of the criteria of Hellenism, especially analogy.[18] Unlike the criteria of antiquity, authority and usage, etymology and analogy are based on a theory of language, and their application can easily result in con-flict between the theoretically correct form and that which is commonly accepted. Quintilian's discussions of the criteria are weighted accordingly: analogy, as the one requiring the most careful judgement, is treated in paragraphs 4–27, etymology in 28–38; then the others are handled quickly: antiquity from 39–41, authority in 42, and usage in 43–45.

Early treatments of Hellenism and Latinity seem to have devoted much discussion to these criteria, focusing on their justification, the rules for their use, the order of their application, and the resolution of cases in which they give conflicting results.[19] The particular answers will surely have varied according to the purpose each writer had in mind: the rules used in deter-mining the proper reading of a passage of Homer will be different from those used to decide how to speak to crowds. The champions of analogy and etymology will have been in first instance philosophers, and then philol-ogists. The Stoics in particular developed the discussion of Hellenism – which was already a 'principle of diction' for Aristotle (*Rhetoric* 1407a19) and one of Theophrastus' 'virtues of style' – in the context of their log-ical project to allow the analysis of the *pragmata* signified by sentences, and this project was guided by the ubiquity and correctness of *logos* in the world. Students of literature then developed an 'expertise of grammar' or of 'criticism' to cover their activity as a whole. They developed the themes taken up by the Stoics in the 'expertise concerning voice' into the 'expert part' of grammatical or critical expertise, whose centerpiece was the 'exper-tise of Hellenism'.[20] Analogy was central to this expertise, which Sextus says was built around that principle (*M.* 1.176) to the extent that he even refers

---

[18] 1.6.3–4: *Omnia tamen haec exigunt acre iudicium, analogia praecipue.*
[19] Works called *On Hellenism, On Latinity*, and other comparable titles (e.g. Caesar's *De Analogia*, Varro's *De sermone Latino*, Pliny's *De dubio sermone*) are attested (evidence in Funaioli 1907: 118; Siebenborn 1976: 32–52), but none *On Anomaly* beyond Chrysippus', and Fehling (*passim*) makes the 'Introduction to the *technē peri Hēllēnismon*' (his reconstruction of these works builds on Barwick 1922: 176, 200, 227) the source used by Varro for his treatment of analogy in books 8–9. There were, however, also sections on Hellenism in more general grammars, and one of these, by Asclepiades of Myrlea, was Sextus' source. It will be apparent, however, that I think the direct sources of *LL* 8 and *M.* 1 were not these grammatical works, but empiricist treatises which used them (cf. Blank 1998: xlv–l).
[20] On the parts of grammar, see Blank 2000.

to Hellenism as 'the analogical expertise' (*M.* 1.214; cf. 179, 199). The same philosophers and philologists were also proponents of etymology,[21] which played an important role in judging many doubtful points: the meaning of obscure words (γλῶσσαι) was often determined by means of etymological analysis, as is still the case today; orthographical questions were also resolved in this way, for instance the aspiration of words which could be seen as derived from words which themselves had initial aspiration. How did the 'rational' criteria of Hellenism, analogy and etymology, become so important? After all, one might think that observation of common usage, or of the usage of good, respectable authors would be the basis of speaking and writing good Greek. It is, of course, also true in fact that usage was the basis of grammar and philology. What was at stake here was rather the understanding by philologists or grammarians that they practised an expertise or science (*technē*). This required rules, a method by which all or nearly all cases or questions could be regulated, for which observation of usage would not have been enough.[22]

The opponents of this expertise of Hellenism, then, argued that observation of usage was sufficient to allow one to express oneself clearly and correctly – or at least correctly enough for practical purposes. Further, they argued that the theoretically based considerations of the Hellenists were not well founded and would lead one into absurdities and contradictions. These opponents will not have been philologists, for it is evident that the philologist's work is found mostly in those points which are dubious and which would not be settled by observing usage.[23] While it would be important to 'explain Homer from (observation of) Homer' and his usage, this would not be enough to resolve all questions relating to the Homeric text without exception; at some points, appeals to principle, i.e. to theoretically based rules, must be made to choose between alternatives. It might have been possible to argue for a grammatical expertise based solely on

---

[21] Thus, it seems perverse of Gourinat 2000: 166 to separate the proponents of analogy and etymology, assigning the Stoics to 'those who judge Hellenism by etymology' and citing *M.* 1.241, where Sextus moves from his demolition of the analogical discipline of Hellenism to attack analogy. For there Sextus says: 'The same things must also be said against them when they want to judge Hellenism by means of etymology', whereby it is clear that those who relied on etymology and analogy were the same.

[22] See Herodian, who says (*On Uniquely Declined Words* 909.18 Lentz) that 'whether words are common or rare, they will be known by analogy which produces predictions about every Greek word and with its expertise contains (συνέχει) as if in a net the manifold utterance of human language'.

[23] This is constantly assumed by Sextus – who, of course, argues against the technicians' position; cf., e.g., *M.* 1.93: the grammarians explain what is unclearly said, judge the sound and the unsound, and sort the genuine from the spurious; 184–5; and 278 on the literary part of grammar: what is useful in poetry is what is clear and not in need of grammatical explanation.

empirical principles, such as historical research (viz. the criteria of 'antiq-uity' and 'authority'), autopsy (i.e. observation of 'usage'), and transition to the similar. This would have looked something like empirical medicine, which claimed that it lacked nothing of medical expertise, while avoid-ing 'rationalist' modes of argumentation.[24] Yet nowhere do we have any indication that this was done. The arguments over whether grammar is an expertise (*technē*) or a kind of experience (*empeiria*), for example in the commentaries on Dionysius Thrax's grammatical handbook (e.g. Sch. Vat. 165.16 ff.), do not mention the possible exclusion of rationalist criteria, but only the limitations on their application. On the contrary, everything indicates that to oppose grammatical analogy and etymology was to favour not having an expertise of grammar at all which went beyond the skills of reading and writing contained in a kind of basic art sometimes called 'grammatistic'.[25]

Thus, Apollonius Dyscolus says that 'some people who act ignorantly in these matters soothe their ignorance by saying that one need not spend time in such investigations and assume that these phenomena have been imposed by chance' (*Syntax* 1.13 = 16.6 ff.), and complains that 'Since such constructions as these are so obvious, some people will think they can observe correct syntax even if they do not grasp the reason behind it' (1.60 = 51.1 ff.). These are the typical moves of the opponent of analogical grammar: one ought not to waste one's time on grammatical investigation; grammatical phenomena are (at least in part) a matter of chance, rather than rational ordering; in any case, it is easy to observe enough to correct one's own usage by listening to one's fellow citizens.

These are also the characteristic moves of Sextus in his attack on grammar as a whole and on Hellenism or analogy in particular.[26] Sextus employs two basic strategies in this work, which he characterises in the introduction to *Against the Musicians* (*M.* 6.4–6) as Epicurean and sceptical respectively: the Epicurean arguments show that musical expertise is not useful for happiness and even harmful; the sceptical arguments aim to shake the fundamental hypotheses of the musicians and thereby destroy all of musical expertise (cf. 1.1–7).[27]

About Varro's book against the discipline of etymology we know virtually nothing besides what I have already cited from the later books, particularly

---

[24] See Frede 1987: 243–60.
[25] Sextus insists that 'grammatistic' both exists and is useful, qualities he denies to expert grammar: *M.* 1.49–53; note too the assertion at 177 of the existence of 'two kinds of Hellenism', the second of which is non-technical and legitimate.
[26] See especially *M.* 1.189, 191–2.   [27] See the discussion in Blank 1998: xxviii–xxxii.

7.109: 'in the first of the earlier books is what is said as to why *etumologikē* is neither an expertise nor useful'. Even this much, however, is enough to show that the concerns of this book will have been very much in line with what we know in general about attacks on grammar. The claim that etymology is not an expertise gives the impression that the opponent is not a philologist.[28] The claim that it is not useful makes one think immediately that the opponent may be an Epicurean.

DE LINGUA LATINA 8, A BRIEF SUMMARY

Varro begins this set of books with an explanation of flexion, including both inflection and derivation (8.1–24) which he will eventually (21) refer to as 'natural' and 'voluntary' flexion (*naturalis, voluntaria declinatio*) respectively, organising his treatment into why flexion exists, what are its products, and how it occurs. Flexion was introduced into all languages because it was useful and necessary to minimise the number of different, unrelated words one had to learn: it would be more difficult to learn Latin if what is expressed by *lego* and *legi* were expressed instead by *Priamus* and *Hecuba*, which give no idea of the unity expressed by the former pair (8.3). While only a 'historical' study can deal with imposed or primary names, for derived or declined names an expert treatment is required, in which a few rules can be made to explain innumerable word forms (5). Varro admits that there are disturbances in the system by which word forms are inflected, but he claims that they are not as serious as people think: it is less important that *scopae* (nominative plural) expresses a singular object (a broom) by a plural name than that it is just as easy to derive *scoparum* (genitive plural) from it as to derive the genitive singular from the nominative singular (8). He then defines where one will find flexion, namely in the declinable words, the names and verbs (9–12), and he goes on to speak of the kinds of derivation and inflection which will be found in these classes (13–20). Finally, under the heading of how flexion occurs, Varro introduces the distinction of inflection and derivation, in his terms natural versus voluntary flexion, and the fact that in each of them there are elements of similarity and dissimilarity among the words so formed. This mixture of the similar and dissimilar, Varro says, has induced Greeks and Romans to write many books, 'since, on the one hand, some thought it right that those words be followed in speaking which were similarly derived (*declinata*) from similar words, which they called *analogias*, while on the other hand, some thought

---

[28] See especially the charge that investigation beyond what is necessary to speak as correctly as others do would be idle (8.27).

this should be ignored (*negligendum*) and dissimilitude was rather to be followed, which is in customary usage (*consuetudine*), and which they called *anomalian* (8.23). Unfortunately, Varro gives no indication here of what these many books were or who wrote them. For his part, though, Varro thinks (23) that both principles ought to be followed, anomaly being more present in voluntary flexion, analogy in natural.

At this point (25) Varro's anti-analogist advocate says that he will speak[29] against those who follow similarity, first against analogy in general (*contra universam analogiam*), then concerning its individual parts (*de singulis partibus*). The attack begins from the nature of speech, which he says ought to be aimed at utility and thus should be clear (*aperta*) and brief (*brevis*), the former quality allowing it to be understood, and the latter allowing it to be understood quickly.[30] These two qualities are achieved by the speaker's adherence to common usage (*consuetudo*) and his self-control (*temperantia*) respectively, so that analogy is unnecessary. After all, once one has obtained one's object, it is idle to go further, and such additional investigation ought to be avoided (26–7).

The general argument against analogy continues (28–30) with a set piece to the effect that in the things of life – e.g. tools, clothing, buildings, furniture – we seek dissimilarity or variety, rather than similarity, so that dissimilarity ought not to be rejected. Even if refinement (*elegantia*) is added to utility as a natural goal in our use of things, we can see that variety is a greater source of pleasure than is similarity (31–2).

But if we must seek similarity, it will be either the similarity which is present in usage or that which is not; if the former, then we do not need expert rules (*praecepta*); if the latter, we will be called crazy for using strange 'analogical' forms (33). Further, analogy is simply not borne out in our language: it is not the case that from dissimilar forms are derived dissimilar forms, as one would expect, given that similar forms are supposed to be derived from similar forms; in fact, even from the same words dissimilars may be derived, while the same word forms may be derived from dissimilar ones (34–6). If there is analogy in speech because there is similarity in many

[29] Ax 1995: 154–5 helpfully distinguishes between Varro's different voices, the 'Autor-Ich' and the 'Rollen-Ich' of the prosecuting attorney. Their separation is far from clean. Here (25), for instance, Varro speaks about the purpose of *this book* (usually a task of the authorial voice), saying what 'I' will do in it, then he says 'I shall speak (*dicam*) against', failing to do anything to introduce another persona to us. I think that we need not find the authorial persona anywhere in this book after 24.

[30] These are two of the virtues of a *narratio* in rhetorical theory (e.g. Anaximenes, *Rhet.* 1438a21–2 'clearly, briefly, not implausibly'; [Cicero], *Rhet. ad Her.* 1.14: 'A narrative should have three things: brevity, clarity, verisimilitude'; Quintilian 4.2.32, where these virtues are attributed to Isocrates, while Aristotle is said to have ridiculed Isocrates' call for brevity; and Aphthonius, *Rhetores Graeci* 10.3.3 Walz: clarity, brevity, persuasiveness, Hellenism), as well as two of the virtues of style commended by the Stoics (D.L. 7.59: Hellenism, clarity, brevity, appropriateness, adornment; cf. Atherton 1988).

words, then since there is dissimilarity in still more words, we ought not to follow analogy (37); if there is analogy in speech, it must be in all parts of speech or in just one part, but it is not in all, and being in just one part is not sufficient, as the Ethiopian's white teeth are not enough to make him white (38).

Finally, the proponents of analogy promise that forms derived from similar words will be similar; but since they then say that words are similar only if they decline similarly, they reveal their ignorance both of where analogy should be located and of how one judges whether similarity is present. Therefore, as they are incapable of speaking about analogy, we ought not to follow them (39). About this incapability Varro gives two arguments (40–1) and (42–3), which I shall go into later.

Next (44–fin.) comes the argument against analogy in the individual parts of speech. These parts are divided into those with case, with tense, with neither, and with both, sometimes called the parts of 'naming, saying, supporting and joining'. The first to be treated will be those of naming, of which there are four kinds, each of which should have three genders, two numbers, and both nominative and oblique cases. But it is not the case that all examples of the word classes exhibit the same number of genders, numbers and cases (44–51). The common nouns (*vocabula*) are treated first (52–74). These undergo four kinds of flexion: thus, *equus* > *equile* ('horse > stable': naming), *equus* > *equum* (nominative > accusative: case), *album* > *albius* ('white > whiter': augmentation), *cista* > *cistula* ('box > little box': diminution). But the derivation of new words or nominatives does not follow analogy (53–62). Neither do nominatives decline to form their cases in a regular way, an area in which the Aristarcheans exerted their energies (63–74). Degrees of comparison also do not follow analogy (75–8), any more than the words which have diminutives and augmentives do (79). The final preserved chapters of the book begin the demolition of analogy in proper names (80–4). From the responses in book 9.95–109 to the lost arguments of book 8, we can tell that Varro did go on in this book to argue against analogy in verbs (cf. Gellius 2.25.5 ff.). His final argument was that there is no analogy because those who have written about it disagree, or else, where they agree, their precepts disagree with common usage (9.111–12).

CRATES AND THE OPPONENT(S) OF ANALOGY

A couple of things seem clear about the 'many books' Varro says (23) were written by the Greeks and Romans, in which they advocated following analogies or anomaly in speaking. First, they dealt with recommendations for the word forms one should actually use in speaking: should one use the forms which grammatical expertise deduces should be the correct forms, or the forms which are in customary usage. They did not, therefore, deal with the methods appropriate to editing Homeric texts and other philological tasks. They may have been written by grammarians intending to produce rules for speaking, by rhetorical theorists or by practical orators, like Caesar in Varro's own time, who wrote a book *De Analogia* in which he recommended the use of forms derived from *rerum natura*, as opposed to certain customary forms.[31] Second, they did not include the books Chrysippus wrote *On Anomaly*, in which Varro says (9.1) the Stoic does not write about which forms to use, but rather 'intends to show that similar things are denoted by dissimilar words and dissimilar things by similar appellatives', which, as Varro notes, is true.[32]

Because Crates is mentioned in this book twice for disagreements with Aristarchus (8.63–5, 68–9), and because he is said in the beginning of the next book to have 'worked against analogy and Aristarchus', he has frequently been taken to be the major source of the anti-analogical arguments of book 8.[33] It is true that Crates founded his own school for the study of classical literature and set up his 'critical expertise' in conscious distinction to Alexandrian 'philology', which he said covered a small and subaltern part of what the 'critic' had to know.[34] It is also true that Crates and Aristarchus often disagreed in their interpretations of Homer, and that Aristarchus and some of his pupils wrote books against Crates' interpretations. On the other hand, there is nothing to indicate that Crates held the attitudes which characterise Varro's anti-analogist in general: that usage is all one needs to speak correctly, that clarity and brevity are the only virtues of speech, that it is useless and idle to inquire further into matters of language once one

[31] On Caesar's book, see Papke 1988.
[32] Presumably, these are the books mentioned in the bibliography of Chrysippus in Diogenes Laertius 7.192: 'On the Anomaly regarding Words (*lexeis*) Against Dion (four books)', which appears in the first group of works of the logical area concerning words and the *logos* which is in accord with them.
[33] See especially Dahlmann 1932: 52–4; 1940, *passim*, especially 4–5 and 163, where an otherwise unknown book by Crates *On Anomaly*, written against Aristarchus (presumably, the existence of this book is simply inferred from *LL* 9.1, where Crates is said to have attacked analogy and Aristarchus depending on Chrysippus, who wrote *On Anomaly*), and works of unknown Roman Crateteans are made the source; Mette 1952; Siebenborn 1976: 8–9, and 107 where he adds the qualification that Varro depends on Crates indirectly, *via* Asclepiades of Myrlea (an inference from similarities between Varro and Sextus); *contra*, see De Marco 1957: 134, 146–8.
[34] Cf., e.g., S.E., *M*. 1.79, 248–9 (Crates, F 94 Broggiato) and Blank 1998: ad locc. One must not assume that this unilateral distinction, with its consequent devaluation of 'grammar', was accepted by subsequent generations of Alexandrians, as Dionysius Thrax made the judgement (*krisis*) of poems the 'finest part of the discipline' of grammar, and we are told that the 'Aristarchean grammarian' Pamphilos of Alexandria wrote a *Kritikē Technē*, along with 'many grammatical works' (*Suda* π 142).

has conformed one's usage to that of one's fellow-citizens, and that the rational criteria of analogy and etymology are to be rejected by anyone who wants to speak correctly. The fact that Crates' student Tauriscus made the 'technical' a part of his discipline of 'criticism' should argue against his teacher's having held that grammatical investigation was useless and not a *technē*.[35] One might urge against this that Tauriscus' work dealt with the criticism of literature, and therefore need not have indicated a stance on how to use the Greek language in ordinary speech and writing. But outside of Varro – and Gellius, who depends entirely on him – we have no reports about Crates' attitude to practical contemporary language usage. Nor is there any reason to suppose that one who thinks that there are grammatical rules and principles, which govern the restoration and interpretation of historical texts, should argue that there are no rules or principles to be applied in linguistic usage, beyond observation of the practice of others.

We have a number of fragments of Crates' work as a practical philologist. Except for his use of interpretation according to 'logical theorems' on such passages as the famous Cup of Nestor, which allows Crates to find there adumbrations of Stoic physics, there is little to distinguish his philological methods from those of Aristarchus. In particular, both made extensive use of etymology as a criterion for establishing the correct meaning and orthography of Homeric glosses. For example, the two grammarians gave opposing explanations of Apollo's epithet ἤιε (Sch. A on *Iliad* 15.365a (= Herodian 2.95.26 Lentz)), Aristarchus arguing that the word came from ἵημι ('hurl') and hence aspirating it, while Crates (F 23 Broggiato) wanted to derive it from ἰάομαι ('heal') and pronounce it unaspirated. In this case, our source, Herodian, who developed the canons of analogy to their greatest degree, argued that Crates' aspiration was correct, but that he should have proved it with reference to the rule that *ēta* is never aspirated before a vowel. Crates, however, was interested in solving a problem of interpretation: was Apollo, in the *Iliad*, capable of healing.[36] In the A scholium at *Iliad* 21.323b1 we learn that the word ΤΥΜΒΟΧΟΗΣ was interpreted by Crates (F 31 Broggiato) as a genitive singular (i.e., 'of a tumulus'), like οἰνοχόης ('of a pitcher'), and accented accordingly, but by Aristarchus as an elided aorist infinitive ('to make a tumulus') and accented τυμβοχοῆσ'.[37] At *Sch.* A *Il.* 24.253b where Crates (F 35 Broggiato) wrote the masculine plural adjective

---

[35] On Tauriscus' system, see the sources in the preceding note, with Blank 2000.

[36] That Crates had recourse to etymology primarily in order to solve interpretive problems is emphasised by Broggiato 2001: lx–lxiii; her commentary should be consulted regarding all the fragments mentioned here.

[37] Helck 1905: 65, conjectures that the analogical reasoning here attributed to Crates is actually Herodian's own reconstruction of the process by which Crates arrived at his interpretation of the word as a genitive (cf. Broggiato 2001: 195).

κατηφέες ('lowering the eyes, ashamed'), Aristarchus is said to have thought that the feminine noun κατηφόνες ('worthy of death, shameful') was appropriately used of Priam's sons as an insult. In *Odyssey* 19.229 Crates (F 66 Broggiato = *Sch. Od.* ad loc.) said that the participle λάων ('holding onto') represented the verb from which ἀλαός ('blind') was derived by the addition of the privative and thus meant 'seeing', while Aristarchus interpreted it as meaning the same as ἀπολαύων ('using, enjoying').

In the remainder of this paper I shall analyse the passages in which Varro's anti-analogist indicates that Crates and Aristarchus disagreed. These points are: whether one ought to allow oblique case forms of the names of the letters of the Greek alphabet, and if not, then why not; and whether the names *Philomēdēs*, *Heraclidēs*, *Melicertēs* are 'similar' or not, i.e. whether they ought to be placed under the same inflectional canon.

NARRATIVE CONFUSION AROUND THE CITATIONS OF CRATES

The section of book 8 in which Crates is cited is a departure from what has gone before, a departure marked both explicitly and narratologically, and the narratological peculiarities of this passage and its relation to the rest of the book call for a digression. At 24 Varro says, using the authorial 'I', that this book will give 'what is said against similarity of inflexions' and the next 'what (is said) against dissimilarity', distancing himself from these opposing partisan arguments. Then at 25 the author adopts an anti-analogist persona to put these arguments; for a first-person singular voice says that 'since it belongs to this book to speak against those who follow similarity . . . I shall speak first against analogy on the whole, then about its individual parts. I shall begin from the nature of speech'.[38] This first part (26–38) of the polemic uses the first-person plural (27, 28, 33) and singular (36), appropriately equating the advocate's own practice with that of people in general. What we should say is given impersonally; the analogist arguments are cited, if at all, impersonally and hypothetically: 'if analogy must be followed by us' (33, also 34). This part is divided into two sections, one on whether similarity or dissimilarity is to be sought in various spheres of life (27–32), and the second (33–8) giving well-known arguments[39] against regularity in speech in general. Presumably, the arguments in neither part

---

[38] For the analysis which follows, compare Ax 1995: 154–5.

[39] The argument about following either the regularity present in ordinary speech or that which is not present there, together with the example in which it is claimed that one would be crazy to use 'Iuppitri' and 'Marspitrem' (33), is closely paralleled in S.E., *M.* 1.177–9; with the argument (34) that similar words decline dissimilarly, see S.E. 1.237; Dahlmann 1940: 109 gives parallels for the use of different ethnics to name the citizens of similarly named cities (35); on the question (37–8) of how much of speech has to be covered by analogy, see S.E. 224–5.

are directed against actual claims of analogical grammarians, so that the analogists are not really cited and the anti-analogists do not really make an appearance either: everything is couched in terms of what is or should or should not be done by us.

From 39–43 the argument is directed against the analogists' general claims about flexion, and the mode of presentation shifts markedly.[40] From the outset, the analogists appear in the third-person plural: 'since those who say that there are analogies promise' (39; also later in 39, twice in 41, and 43). The first-person singular advocate, absent since 25, makes his reappearance in this section: 'I ask' (40; also 42, twice in 43).[41] As before, the first-person plurals in 39 ('we must not follow them') and 40 are meant to show the relevance of the points made to language users in general, not to refer to the advocate specifically.

Next, the anti-analogist advocate announces (44 *dicam*) his promised treatment of analogy in the individual parts of speech and continues to refer to himself in the first-person singular in 8.51,[42] 53, 55, 59, 61. The first-person plural recurs here for the first time since 40 ('we shall say'; twice in 56, once in 57, thrice in 59), referring to common usage, and its reappearance may be conditioned by the introduction of a second-person singular addressee in 47 ('examine the individual parts, so that you may see more easily that nowhere are there analogies which we should follow') and 53 (cf. the jussive in 50).[43]

The analogists make an initial appearance in this section in the third-person plural, as they had done in the previous section (39–43): 'these they call (the parts) of calling, saying, etc.' (44). After that, they disappear until the 'separate' discussion of the derivation of compound words in 61–2:

Since there is a class of words which they call (*appellant*) compound and they deny (*negant*) that it should be compared with the simple words about which I have thus far spoken, I shall speak separately about compounds. Since *tibicines* ('pipers') are so called from *tibiae* ('pipes') and *canere* ('to play', 'sing'), they ask (*qu<a>erunt*), if it is right to follow analogies, why do we not, from *cithara* ('harp') and *psalterium* ('psaltery') and *pandura* ('Pan's strings'), say *citharicen* and in the same way other words?

---

[40] Ax 1995: 154 does not correlate the narratological change here with a difference in subject-matter.

[41] Ax 1995: 154 assigns the last comment to the 'Autor-Ich', but I do not see why one should follow him in this.

[42] 'I have treated this class rather sparingly, since I think that the scribes will do these quite thorny things less than diligently' (51) could be viewed as an exceptional intervention of the authorial voice, but it could also show the assimilation of the advocate to the author, worried about the likely inaccuracy of copies of his work.

[43] Previously in this book the second-person singular occurred only in the introductory section, where Varro speaks as author, as a stylistic variant for the impersonal: 'the reasoning by which you learn to decline one word you can use in an infinite number of words' (6, cf. 10).

Until now the anti-analogical arguments have always appeared in the first-person singular, the analogist opponents in the third-person plural. In 61–2, however, and then in 63–74, which are marked off as a special section on analogy in case forms, the third-person plural begins to be used for the anti-analogists. Thus, the third-person plural is used of the analogists in the sentence introducing the section on compounds, where the anti-analogist advocate speaks in the first-person singular. In the very next sentence, which begins the actual argument that compounds do not follow analogy, the third-person plural refers without warning to the anti-analogists, who ask why certain analogical formations are not used. The new usage opens the section on case: 63 'First, if there were analogy in these, they say . . .'; but in the second argument (64) Crates is said to have asked (*cur*) the first question; then Varro's advocate says he would ask further (*qu<a>eram, cur*), while the third-person plural (65) refers to Greek analogists (*sin quod scribunt dicent*). The anti-analogists are again the third-person plural in the third argument (*quae si esset, negant . . . debuisse* 66), and they must be understood as those arguing in 67. The next argument (68–9) is given in personal terms as between Crates and Aristarchus, and this is followed by one introduced with 'he says' (*inquit, cur* 70). 'They', i.e. the anti-analogists, ask a final question (*item qu<a>erunt, si sit analogia, cur appellant omnes . . .* 71), but the analogists reappear in the third person in 72 (*item secundum illorum rationem debemus . . .*) and in 73 where they are said to disregard analogy in the declension of *pater familias* and told that they ought to follow the orator Sisenna in saying *patres familiarum* in the genitive plural. The narrative point of view, then, in this entire section is thoroughly confused,[44] and this must be somehow related to the way in which authorities are cited here.

CRATES' ROLE IN THE CONTROVERSIES OVER ANALOGY

The appearance of Crates in 63 is the first time any particular authority is named, since the mention of Aristotle in the author's general introduction (11). The passages, argument and counter-argument, relevant to the first of the two controversies for which Crates is cited are these:

8.63–5 (F 102 Broggiato): relinquitur de casibus, in quo Aristarchei suos contendunt nervos. primum si in his esse[n]t analogia, dicunt debuisse omnis nominat[i]u[o]s et articulos habere totidem casus: nunc alios habere unum solum, ut litteras singulas omnes, alios tris, ut praedium praedii praedio, alios quattuor, ut mel mellis melli

---

[44] Ax 1995 takes it as evidence that Varro at some point wrote this book in dialogue form and it was revised carelessly. Fehling 1957: 82 n. 2 thinks that Varro wrote the various paragraphs of his book each on its own, then put them together later.

melle, alios quinque, ut quintus quinti quinto quintum quinte, alios sex, ut unus unius uni unum une uno: non esse ergo in casibus analogias. (64) secundo quod Crates, cur quae singulos habent casus, ut litterae graecae, non dicantur alpha alphati alphatos, si idem mihi respondebitur quod Crateti, non esse vocabula nostra, sed penitus barbara, qu<a>eram, cur idem nostra nomina et Persarum et ceterorum quos vocant barbaros cum casibus dica<n>t. (65) quare si essent in analogia, aut, ut Poenicum et <A>egyptiorum vocabula singulis casibus dicerent, aut pluribus, ut Gallorum ac ceterorum: nam dicunt alacco alaucus et sic alia. sin quod scribunt dicent, quod Poenicum si<n>t, singulis casibus ideo eas litteras graecas nominari: sic Graeci nostra senis casibus non quinis dicere debebant; quod cum non faciunt, non est analogia.

The question concerning the cases, to which the Aristarcheans bent their efforts, remains. First, if there were analogy in these, they say that all names and articles should have the same number of cases; but as it is some have only one, like all the individual letters, others three, like *praedium praedii praedio* ('farm'), others four, like *mel mellis melli melle* ('honey'), others five, like *quintus quinti quinto quintum quinte* ('fifth'), others six, like *unus unius uni unum une uno* ('one'); therefore there are no analogies in cases. (64) Second, regarding what Crates said, namely why those words which have only one case, like the Greek letters, are not said *alpha alphati alphatos*, if I receive the same answer as Crates, that they are not our own words, but quite barbarous, I shall ask why these same people use the cases of our names and those of the Persians and of other peoples whom they call barbarians. (65) Thus, if they were in analogy, either they would say these names in only one case, like Phoenician and Egyptian words, or in several, like those of Gauls and others: for they say *alacco alaucus* (nom. and gen. of 'lark') and others similarly. But if they say what they write, that the Greek letters are named with only one case because they belong to the Phoenicians, then Greeks ought to say our words in six cases, not five; since they do not do so, there is no analogy.

9.51: dicunt, quod vocabula litterarum latinarum non declinentur in casus, non esse analogias. hi ea quae natura declinari non possunt, eorum declinatus requirunt, proinde ut non eo<rum> dicatur esse analogia quae ab similibus verbis similiter esse<nt> declinata. quare non solum in vocabulis litterarum haec non requirenda analogia, sed <ne> in syllaba quidem ulla, quod dicimus hoc BA, huius BA, sic alia.

They say that, since the words for the Latin letters are not declined in cases, there are no analogies. They are demanding declension of those words which by nature cannot be declined, as if analogy were not said to belong to those words which were declined in a similar manner from similar words. Thus, it is not only in the names of letters that this analogy is not to be demanded, but not in any syllable either, since we say 'BA' in the nominative and genitive, etc.

In the first argument, then, the anti-analogists say that all naming-words and articles should have the same number of cases, but this is not what happens, since some, like the names of the individual letters, have only one, others three, like *praedium praedii praedio*, etc. Therefore, there are no analogies in the cases. Their second argument (64) relates to the fact that Crates asked why those names with one form, since they are Greek letters, are not said in different cases: Varro says (in the voice of the anti-analogist) that, if the analogists answer him as they did Crates, saying that the letters are barbarian, he would ask why the Greeks decline Latin and Persian names. In 65 the argument continues, based on this query: if these names were in analogy, the Greeks would say them in as many cases as are used in the source languages. If, as in their books, the analogists claim that the letters are Phoenician and therefore said in one case each, then the Greeks ought to have said Latin names in six cases, not five. Since they do not, there is no analogy.

The second argument picks up the single-case words from the first (*cur quae singulos habent casus*), but whereas the first gave only Latin examples and must represent an argument given by (notional or real) Roman anti-analogists, the second abandons all the other (Latin) examples of naming-words with an unusual number of case forms to concentrate specifically on letter-names, which it assumes are Greek (*ut litterae Graecae*). Note too that Crates' query is couched impersonally: 'why are they not said'. The next argument is added in the first person; it assumes again that we are talking about Latin letters and cites the Greeks, whose speaking practice is under discussion, in the third person; the analogists, presumably the followers of Aristarchus who responded to Crates, are also cited in the third person. This third argument, like the first, must represent the Roman anti-analogists whose arguments Varro presents in this book.

The Roman anti-analogists are envisioned as using the lack of different case forms for the Latin letters as evidence for the non-existence of analogy. Was Crates doing the same thing when he 'asked' about the Greek letters? The separation of his query from the argument and further query put by the Romans and by Varro's anti-analogist suggest that he was not. Nor is he actually represented as doing so by Varro. For Varro seems to divide this entire section into only two arguments against analogy: first, the one based on the existence of various naming-words with an unusual number of case forms; second, the one which inverts it by claiming that the analogists would have to advocate using all foreign words in the number of cases used in their language of origin.[45] The second argument takes off from the analogists' response to Crates, but perhaps Crates was doing something

---

[45] Note that in the response in 9.51 the opponent is 'they', i.e. the Roman anti-analogists.

else: 'why are those which have only one case, as Greek letters, not said
in cases, like *alpha alphati alphatos*' can be interpreted as a suggestion that
one *ought* to decline the Greek letter-names. Such a suggestion is by no
means unheard of, as Democritus is said (DK68 B20 = Sch. Dion. Thr.
184.3 Hilgard) to have recommended it. In this case, Crates would be saying
that the letter-names ought to be taken as similar to other Greek words,
and analogy ought to be applied to them. Aristarchus and his followers, on
the other hand, denied that the letters were similar to other Greek words
and therefore also that such treatment would not in fact be analogical in
this instance.

The second controversy between Crates and Aristarchus, over the need
for similar common nouns to have similar vocatives as well as similar nominatives, first appears (8.42) – without either man's name – as part of a
longer argument about the notion of likeness (8.39–43), which forms the
last argument against analogy in general. The anti-analogist here argues that
those who assert that similar words will inflect similarly thereby reveal their
ignorance both of the locus of likeness – whether it should be sought in the
word's sound, *significatum*, or both – and also of how to recognise whether
likeness is present or absent. He telegraphs the conclusion of this argument
at the beginning (39): due to their ignorance, the analogists cannot speak
about analogy and we ought not to follow them.

The first point is made by indicating that: (i) if similarity must be found
in spoken words *qua* sounds, then it makes no difference whether these
words denote quite different things in the world, e.g. male or female, or
whether they are common or proper nouns, which the analogists say is
important;[46] while (ii) if words are thought to be similar because what
they signify is similar, then Dion and Theon, two men with similar names,
may not be similar, if one is old and the other young, one white and

---

[46] On the conditions which must be met, if two words are to be considered 'similar' and thus eligible
to be used in an analogy with one another, see Siebenborn 1976, 72–83. One list of criteria indicates
that words are judged 'similar' if they have the same: gender, type (i.e. proper noun or appellative),
schema (i.e. simplex or compound), number, accent, case, ending in the nominative singular, type
and quantity of the penultimate syllable, number of syllables, type of consonant before the ending
(cf. Siebenborn 1976: 73, mostly from Herodian 2.634.5 ff. Lentz). On the basis of all these criteria,
all of Herodian's canons (rules defining declensional classes) can be formulated. Varro himself speaks
of these conditions in 10.9 ff., dividing them into *similitudines* in *verborum materia* and in *materiae
figura*. He also speaks of *perfecta similitudo* and *perfecta analogia* (10.12, 63–9), in which both *res*
and *vox* are similar; at 10.77 similarity is required by Varro in form, meaning and declension: *simile
verbum verbo tum quom et re quam significat et voce qua significat et in figura e transitu declinationis
parile* (cf. Siebenborn 1976: 78–80). There are also a number of instances in which Aristarchus
compared words which are similar not only in form, but also in meaning, e.g. *thameiai – pukinai –
tarpheiai*, all of which mean 'densely packed' and which are compared in order to establish the
end-accent on the first of them in a scholium (bT ex Hrd.) on *Iliad* 1.52.

the other black, etc.; and (iii) if similar words must be similar in both sound and meaning, there should not be pairs wanting in one of these respects, such as Perpenna and Alfena, where two similar word forms name a man and a woman, respectively. Therefore, because they are unable to demonstrate where the similarity ought to be, those who say that analogies exist are shameless (40–1).[47] This argument resembles one found in Sextus (*M.* 1.155–8), to the effect that the grammarians must specify whether by the sentence they mean the segment of voice or what it signifies: actually it can be neither, and 'if neither the voice nor the incorporeal sayable signified by the voice is a sentence, and it is not possible to conceive anything besides these two things, then the sentence is nothing'.

The second point is made more briefly (42–3): saying that nouns in the nominative are only similar when their vocatives are also similar is like saying that one cannot decide whether the Menaechmus twins are alike, without first seeing their children too. Nothing, Varro, says, ought to be brought in from outside (*extrinsecus*) to help judge the similarity of two items. Again, he concludes that since the analogists 'are ignorant of how similarity should be supposed, they cannot speak about analogy'.

This series of arguments was introduced with these words (39):

Since those who say that analogies exist promise [a] that similar words will come from similar words when they are declined, and since they then say [b] that one word is similar to another if it can be shown that beginning from the same gender and form it moves from case to case in a similar way, those who say this [c] are ignorant of both things, both where similarity should be and how it is usually observed whether or not there is similarity. Given that they are ignorant of these things, it follows that, since they are incapable of speaking about analogy, we ought not to follow them [*or:* it].[48]

However, it is hardly clear from what is attributed to the analogists (a and b) that they will be found ignorant in the ways indicated in (c). Instead, the initial presentation of the matter in (a) and (b) seems designed to set up a different argument: the proponents of analogy beg the question by promising that similar words will decline similarly while stipulating that words are only similar if they decline similarly.

This is exactly the argument which we find closing the second use of this point, in 8.68–9: 'thus, they say, Aristarchus did not answer the question, since he could use any difference in their oblique cases as a reason

---

[47] The conclusion in 41 reads: *quare quoniam ubi similitudo esse debeat nequeunt ostendere, impudentes sunt qui dicunt esse analogias.* Varro's response to this first argument is found at 9.40–2.

[48] 39, concluding: *quae cum ignorant, sequitur ut, cum analogiam dicere non possint, sequi <non> debeamus.*

to claim that they were not relevantly similar; but the question is whether the two nominatives are similar, and nothing should be brought in from outside to answer this'. Varro has cited the same point in two different arguments, recycling what must have been limited material for use at different stages in the argumentative scheme he has chosen. The second, more detailed, appearance of this point is likely to have been the one Varro found in his Latin source, or, if he had none, it was probably the version he wrote first, as it corresponds to the way in which the argument is introduced; the first is more likely to be Varro's own adaptation of the point to the 'general' argument against analogy. Similarly, points which were made only in the particular argumentation against regularity in nominals have been briefly used by Varro in an introductory section of the defence of analogy in general, including a short mention of the problem of the names of letters of the alphabet, which do not decline (9.38, cf. 8.64). That Varro is not overly concerned with the specificity of these points is shown by the fact that, although he recalls the argument about similarity in the nominatives and vocatives (again without the names of Crates or Aristarchus) by saying that the anti-analogists (third plural) had claimed that Aristarchus had given this answer 'shamelessly' (*impudenter* 9.43), Varro had actually said that 'those who assert that analogies exist are shameless' (*impudentes*) at the conclusion of the previous point (8.41), that the analogists do not know whether likeness is found in a word's sound or denotation.

Now I turn to the second appearance of the point about nominatives and vocatives, whose conclusion I have just mentioned:

8.67–9 (F 103 Broggiato): item cum, si sit analogia, debeant ab similibus verbis similiter declinatis similia fieri et id non fieri ostendi possit, despiciendam eam esse rationem. atqui ostenditur: nam qui potest similius esse quam gens, mens, dens? cum horum casus patricus et accusativus in multitudine sint disparilis: nam a primo fit gentium et gentis, utrubique ut sit <I>, ab secundo mentium et mentes, ut in priore solo sit I, ab tertio dentum et dentes, ut in neutro sit. (68) sic item quoniam simile est recto casu surus lupus lepus, rogant, quor non dicatur proportione[m] item suro lupo lepo. sin respondeatur similia non esse, quod ea vocemus dissimiliter sure lupe lepus (sic enim respondere voluit Aristarc<h>us Crateti: nam cum scripsisset similia esse Philomedes Heraclides Melicertes, dixit non esse similia: in vocando enim cum <E> brevi dici Philomede<s>, cum E longo Heraclide, cum <A> brevi Melicerta), in hoc dicunt Aristarc<h>um non intellexisse quod qu<a>eretur se non solvere[t]. (69) sic enim, ut quicque in obliquis casibus discrepavit, dicere potuit propter eam rem rectos casus non esse similis; quom qu<a>eratur duo inter se similia sint necne, non debere extrinsecus adsum<i> cur similia sunt.

In the same way [they say that], if there is analogy, similar forms should arise from similar words declined in a similar way and it can be demonstrated that this does not happen, then this 'rationality' is to be rejected; but it is demonstrated. For how can anything be more similar than *gens* ('clan'), *mens* ('mind'), *dens* ('tooth')? Yet their genitive and accusative case are dissimilar in the plural, since from the first come *gentium* and *gentis*, both with *-i-*, from the second *mentium* and *mentes*, with *-i-* only in the former, from the third *dentum* and *dentes*, with *-i-* in neither form. (68) So in the same way, they ask, since *surus* ('stake') *lupus* ('wolf') *lepus* ('hare') are similar in the nominative, why does one not say *suro lupo lepo* [dative or ablative] in the same way? If one answers that they are not similar, because we will call upon them dissimilarly: *sure lupe lepus* (indeed, that was how Aristarchus wanted to answer Crates: for when he had written that *Philomedes Heraclides Melicertes* were not alike, because when he is called [i.e., in the vocative] 'Philomedes' is said with a short *-e-*, 'Heraclidē' with a long *-e-* and 'Melicerta' with a short *-a-*), they say that in this [answer] Aristarchus failed to understand that he had not answered what was asked. (69) For in this way, whenever there was any difference in the oblique cases, he could say that for that very reason the nominative cases were not similar: since the question is whether two nominatives are similar or not, nothing should be brought in from outside [to show] why they are alike or different.

9.91: <reprehendunt>[49] Aristarchum, quod haec nomina Melicertes et Philomedes similia neget esse, quod vocandi casus habet alter Melicerta, alter Philomede<s>, sic qui dicat lepus et lupus non esse simile, quod alterius vocandi casus sit lupe, alterius lepus, sic socer, macer, quod in transitu fiat ab altero trisyllabum soceri, ab altero bisyllabum macri.

[They scold] Aristarchus because he denied that the names 'Melicertes' and 'Philomedes' were similar, since one has the vocative 'Melicerta' and the other 'Philomedes', [and the same for] one who says that *lepus* ('hare') and *lupus* ('wolf') are not similar, since the vocative of the latter is *lupe* and of the former *lepus*, and the same [holds for] *socer* ('father-in-law') and *macer* ('lean'), since from the former in case-change comes the trisyllabic *soceri* [in the genitive] but from the latter the bisyllabic *macri*.

In 8.67–9 the argument is given entirely to the Roman anti-analogists. They point to a series of words with similar forms in the nominative singular and plural, but not in the genitive and accusative plural; then they ask why we do not say *suro lupo lepo* analogically in the dative or ablative, given that *surus lupus lepus* are alike in the nominative. Crates is brought up in a particular point, as the author of a claim to which Aristarchus wished to respond. This claim was simply that the Greek names *Philomēdēs, Hērakleidēs, Melikertēs* were '*similia*'. Aristarchus is said to have responded that they were not alike, due to the difference in their vocative case forms.

---

[49] This is added (or it carries over) from the beginning of 90.

The Roman anti-analogists are then said to have responded to Aristarchus' claim by saying that he was not answering what was being asked, since the question was whether two nominatives were similar, and nothing else should be brought in to help answer that question.

Now, it is possible that Varro means to say that Crates actually asked a question, perhaps: 'since these nominatives are similar, why don't they decline similarly'? Such a question could be taken to imply either 'they ought to decline similarly, and since they do not, there are no analogies in names', or 'since these nominatives are similar, is there anything to prevent us from using similar forms in all their cases?' On the other hand, the 'asking' is said by Varro to regard 'whether *two* nominatives are similar' (69), while Crates had been talking about three such words. This difference suggests that Crates did not actually ask this question at all. The same conclusion is suggested by the fact that in book 9's reply, in which Aristarchus is named, while his opponent is referred to as 'they' and are, one assumes, the Roman anti-analogists, only two names are at issue, *Melicertes* and *Philomedes*.[50] In that case, Crates cannot be saddled with the actual anti-analogical argument. Rather, he merely said that the three names were 'similar' (*nam cum scripsisset similia esse Philomedes Heraclides Melicertes*), and he presumably also suggested that analogy therefore be applied to their oblique case forms.

Thus, both citations of Crates can be interpreted in the same way: Crates said that certain words were similar and should be analogous with one another in their case forms. Aristarchus responded by denying that the words were similar and that analogy should be applied among them. This duplicates the situation we have in the Homeric scholia: whenever Crates and Aristarchus are cited in disagreement, Aristarchus is fully aware of Crates' argument and responds to it; Crates is not shown responding to Aristarchus.[51] This by itself would also argue against the view that the

---

[50] The Roman anti-analogists add another example, that of *socer* and *macer*, and this too causes trouble. These two words do not belong to the same class, on most accounts of the criteria of similarity, so that one would not have to adduce their vocatives at all in order to find a dissimilarity between them. When Sextus deals with these sorts of examples (*M.* 236–9), he treats proper names (with the atheteses proposed in Blank 1998: 253–4), then verbs, participles, then names homonymic with participles, getting to the latter *via* ἄρχων, a participle which has come to be used as common noun.

[51] This was seen by Schmidt 1976: 189; it is now sustained by Broggiato in her edition of the fragments of Crates, who (2001: 153) also gives the single possible exception to this rule: Crates states (Sch. A ad *Il.* 9.169a (Ariston.)) that ἔπειτα in that line is used in the sense of δή, that is, to emphasise the point of αὐτάρ ('besides'). This interpretation tacitly contradicts that of Aristarchus, who understood ἔπειτα as 'afterward', in order to split the embassy passage into two parts and thereby get around the problem posed by the infamous duals of lines 182–98. But Broggiato reminds us that Aristarchus' solution could have been around before and Crates could thus oppose its use without having read Aristarchus.

responses given by Varro's anti-analogist to Aristarchus and Aristarcheans stemmed from Crates. With these, however, go the claims that analogy does not exist or ought not to be followed.

Why does Varro's anti-analogical source suddenly begin to mention Aristarchus (or Aristarcheans) and Crates in 8.63–4? The discussion in Varro's source was conducted for the most part on a rather general level in both the general and particular sections. In the part about cases, however, matters change, and we have the citations of grammarians. Both citations deal with the same sort of point, however: a disagreement between two top grammarians over whether certain words are 'similar'.[52] These facts, I think, lead directly to the conclusion that Crates and Aristarchus were cited in an argument from disagreement (*diaphōnia*). And we do indeed have evidence of such an argument in Varro.

At 9.111–12 Varro responds to 'the last' point in the previous book:

de eo quod in priore libro extremum est, ideo non es<se> analogia<m>, quod qui de ea scripserint aut inter se non conveniant aut in quibus conveniant ea cum consuetudinis discrepent verbis, utrumque <est leve>: sic enim omnis repudiandum erit artis, quod et in medicina et in musica et in aliis multis discrepant scriptores; item in quibus conveniunt in scriptis, si etiam repudiat natura: quod ita ut dicitur, non sit ars, sed artifex reprehendendus, qui <dici> debet in scribendo non vidisse verum, non ideo non posse scribi verum. (112) qui dicit hoc monti et hoc fonti, cum alii dicant hoc monte et hoc fonte, sic alia quae duobus modis dicuntur, cum alterum sit verum, alterum falsum, non uter peccat tollit analogias, sed uter recte dicit confirmat; et quemadmodum is qui [cum] peccat in his verbis, ubi duobus modis dicuntur, non tollit rationem cum sequitur falsum, sic etiam in his <quae> non [in] duobus dicuntur, si quis aliter putat dici oportere atque oportet, non scientiam tollit orationis, sed suam inscientiam denudat.

About the last argument in the preceding book, that there is no analogy because either those who have written about it do not agree with one another or the things on which they agree differ from the words in common usage, both points <are negligible>. For in this way all the kinds of expertise will have to be rejected, since in medicine, music and many other arts writers are in disagreement; the same holds for what they agree on in their writings, if nature rejects it, since, as one says, it is not the expertise which should be blamed, but the expert, who should be said not to have seen the truth when he wrote, but [it should] not for that reason

---

[52] The close relation between these two arguments of the Roman anti-analogists is also shown by the fact that Varro's answer to the criticism of Aristarchus for saying that 'Melicertes' and 'Philomedes' were not alike is said (9.92) to have been given by him already in 9.39's reflections on different types of wool, which can only be seen to be dissimilar if one takes their *effectus* ('performance, effect': Apulian wool lasts longer than Gallic) into account (at 9.92–3 one example is of two apples which look but do not taste the same); 9.39 does not mention Melicertes and Philomedes, but it follows a mention of the demand that case forms be inflected from A and B (9.38) and it precedes a treatment of whether the sound or meaning is the locus of similarity in words (9.40). The nominative-vocative problem comes up at 43, but without mention of the different kinds of wool.

[be said] that the truth cannot be written down. (112) As for one who says *monti* and *fonti* [in the ablative], while others say *monte* and *fonte*, and similarly other words which are said in two ways, if one is true and the other false, it is not the case that the one who errs destroys analogies, while the one who speaks correctly confirms them. And just as he who errs in these words where they are said in two ways does not destroy rationality when he follows what is false, so too in those [which] are not said in two ways, if someone thinks they should be said differently than they ought, he does not destroy the science of speech, but exposes his own lack of scientific knowledge.

The final argument answered in this passage fell into two parts, the first of which is quite clear, while the second is more obscure. The first part was a straightforward argument from disagreement, such as one finds frequently in Sextus Empiricus.[53] Of course, Varro does not state here what the disagreement was about or who the parties to it were, but we are, I think, safe in assuming that its meat was our two problems about determining whether names were similar, and the disagreeing parties were Crates and Aristarchus. Because these grammarians disagreed about the assignment of similarity to words, analogy does not exist. The second part argues that even where analogists agree with one another they disagree with common usage. This is perhaps a further argument from disagreement, not among the experts this time, but between the experts and everyone else. Perhaps it was an argument 'from the results': all the analogists agree to speak thus, but as that is different from common usage, all they will reap from their science is ridicule.[54] The response is that neither argument is valid: writers about all fields of expertise disagree with one another, but that does not mean that they all have no basis; in the same way, if such writers agree with one another, but nature rejects their conclusions, that does not mean that the expertise is wrong; rather, it is the particular writer or *artifex* who is at fault: he made a mistake, but the expertise itself could eventually find the correct answer. The uses of *consuetudo* and *natura* here are noteworthy. It is not clear why it should count as an argument against the analogists that they agree in recommending word forms which are at

---

[53] 'Disagreement' was the first of the 'five modes' leading to the suspension of judgement offered by Agrippa (D.L. 9.88; S.E., *P.H.* 1.164–5). It involves a problem disagreement about which causes irresoluble dissension of philosophers with one another or with laymen (e.g. *P.H.* 1.90). Such dissension should cause the sceptic to suspend judgement on the point at issue, although Sextus may use it as evidence of the non-existence of a science or of its futility.

[54] Sextus divides his proof of the futility of orthographical science into an argument from 'disagreement' and one 'from the results' (*M.* 1.170, 173). In the former, it 'seems vain because of disagreement, since the experts quarrel and will go on quarrelling with one another forever, thinking the same word should be spelled in this way or that way'. In the latter, the fact that the same word is understood whether it is spelled ζμιλίον or σμιλίον ('scalpel') shows that orthography is a useless expertise.

odds with common usage, since *ex hypothesi* this possibility has always been present in their practice: presumably something like exposure to general ridicule is at issue, as in S.E. *M.* 1.178 and 195, and Varro himself discusses who can use analogical word forms safely and under what circumstances (9.4–6). While it is *consuetudo* which the anti-analogist had said was at variance with the analogists' prescriptions, the analogist says that *natura* rejects the false conclusions of experts in the various sciences, and this reflects his own standpoint: expertise should be based on and agree with the nature of things.[55] The response that even if grammarians are wrong, that fact does not destroy analogy is pretty poor: it requires us to take the ability of the expertise to get things right eventually on faith, although the principles of the expertise might be entirely wrong, and it would never improve, or the subject-matter might be unsuitable to an expertise.

The point made in 112 is linked to this last observation only by the idea that the individual, not the expertise, is at fault: one who chooses the false one of two word forms does not destroy analogy, but one who chooses the correct one strengthens analogy; thus, one who does not use the only form which is in use but employs a different one does not destroy the expertise, but merely shows his own ignorance. The errant speaker in each case uses the wrong word form out of sheer ignorance, which says nothing against the rule-governed nature of language, while the correct speaker reinforces analogy by adding to its base of correct usage.[56] This is related to arguments in 8.66 and 9.90. In the former, the anti-analogists observe that if there is analogy there ought not to exist alternative case forms of the same word, such as *montes fontes* and *montis fontis*. The latter answers the criticism that names with two forms, such as *Alcmaeus* and *Alcmaeo*, may be declined now starting from one form, now from the other: this is not a problem with analogy itself, but with careless speakers who mix their declensions and do not follow one set of analogies. At 112 Varro has taken examples of a general point made by the anti-analogists, that phenomena exist which ought not to exist, if there is analogy, and combined them to make a final argument which does not address the final argument of the opponent, but rather the general tenor of his argumentation. Each of the related passages (8.66, 9.90) directly precedes a discussion of the disagreements between Crates

---

[55] This corrects Blank 1998: xxxix. Note the opposition of usage and nature in 9.57, 58 and 62.

[56] It is possible that Varro means rather that one errs as a result of a calculation of analogy, incorrectly plumping for the wrong one of two forms in the first case and inappropriately correcting usage in the second. The fact that one man is said to 'think' that words found in only one form in general usage 'should be said differently than they ought' seems to indicate a principled choice; but the parallel passages point in the opposite direction.

and Aristarchus (8.67 and 9.91), thus confirming that these disagreements were indeed the basis of the argument from disagreement which was at the heart of the final argument of book 8.

Once again, if this is so, then the conclusion is inescapable that Crates and Aristarchus were both cited by Varro and his source as representatives of analogy. This is what we should expect from Sextus Empiricus' treatment of the kinds of grammar (*M.* 1.44): 'Used in the particular sense it is the complete grammar worked out by the followers of Crates of Mallos and of Aristophanes and Aristarchus.'

What, then, of the opening of book 9?:

9.1 (F 104 Broggiato): < . . . insignis eorum est error qui malunt quae>[57] nesciunt docere quam discere quae ignorant: in quo fuit Crates, nobilis grammaticus, qui fretus Chrysippo, homine acutissimo qui reliquit *peri anōmalias* III libros,[58] contra analogian atque Aristarchum est nixus, sed ita, ut scripta indicant eius, ut neutrius videatur pervidisse voluntatem, quod et Chrysippus de inaequabilitate cum scribit sermonis, propositum habet ostendere similes res dissimilibus verbis et dissimiles similibus esse vocabulis notatas, id quod est ver[b]um, et [cum] Aristarchus, de aequabilitate cum scribit ei<us>de<m>, verborum similitudinem qua[ru]ndam <in> inclinatione[s] sequi iubet, quoad patiatur consuetudo.

< . . . they commit a great error who prefer> to teach what they do not know than to learn that of which they are ignorant. In this error was Crates, a noble grammarian who, relying on Chrysippus, a razor-sharp man who left three books *On Anomaly*, opposed analogy and Aristarchus, but in such a way, as his writings indicate, as not to appear to have fully understood what either man wanted. For when Chrysippus writes about the inconsistency of speech, he intends to show that similar things are denoted by dissimilar words and dissimilar things by similar words, which is true; and when Aristarchus writes about its consistency, he bids us follow a certain similarity of words in flexion, as far as common usage allows.

Varro treats Chrysippus as an advocate of analogy, as he was also an advocate of etymology: in 5.9, Varro says that he has studied at the lamp not only of Aristophanes, but also of Cleanthes; in 6.2, Chrysippus and Antipater are mentioned along with Aristophanes and Apollodorus; in 10.59, Chrysippus is cited as a witness in favour of the evidently analogist procedure of correcting corrupt forms of nouns from other forms, singulars from plurals, or nominatives from oblique cases. Aristarchus is certainly treated as an analogist. Our passage, however, leaves it quite unclear what Crates' position was. He is said not to have understood Chrysippus' position on anomaly, which I doubt, or Aristarchus' on analogy, which also seems rather

---

[57] The initial lacuna was not very long; its end is here filled *exempli gratia* after Boot 1894.
[58] Spengel: *lei libri* MS; but the book listed in D.L. 7.192 had four books.

improbable. I have argued that Crates may have advocated the application of analogy in places where Aristarchus did not, even if it seems that it was Aristarchus who criticised Crates, rather than vice-versa. This might have led to Varro's interpretation that Crates did not understand that Aristarchus wanted to follow analogy only as far as common usage allowed, i.e. that he was against Chrysippus' version of analogy, and this is perhaps what lies behind 'opposed analogy and Aristarchus'. The beginning of this passage is lost, but the state of the manuscript gives reason to believe that not very much is missing, as the page contains twenty-three lines instead of the usual thirty-nine and traces of the title used to be visible on it. Given the final argument of book 8, which I have just discussed, perhaps the defence in book 9 opened with a warning that Crates cannot be used as a counter-example to Aristarchus, since he understood neither him nor Chrysippus.

Finally, we come to the question of the nature of Varro's anti-analogical arguments. As I noted earlier, these are unlikely to come from a grammatical source, since they say that grammatical investigation which goes beyond noticing how one's neighbours speak is a waste of time (8.27). This, however, is exactly the view of Sextus Empiricus (*M.* 1.50, 176, 191–3), as it is of the Epicureans who serve as the source of many of his arguments in *M.* 1–6. The emphasis on getting the utility out of correct speech and on not doing anything which works against that, however, when examined with an eye on Sextus' distinction between his own sceptical approach and that of the Epicureans – who argue, as Varro says he will do in book 8, that the analogical expertise is neither an expertise nor useful – indicates that Varro's anti-analogist may have been an Epicurean.[59] The Epicureans, of course, taught that there was no *ars dicendi* or art of speaking (Cicero, *Academica Posteriora* 1.5, a passage put into the mouth of Varro). Philodemus states that there is no expertise of Hellenism such as the orators claim to have, and he cites various definitions of Hellenism in what appears to be an argument from disagreement to prove his point (*Rhetoric* 4, *PHerc.* 1423 cols. 11.4–12.13). The same conclusion is also urged by the anti-analogist's confinement of the virtues of speech to clarity and brevity (8.26). Epicurus is said to have made clarity the sole virtue of style (D.L. 10.13 = fr. 54 Usener), and we are told that a goal in the refinement of languages was that indications should become less ambiguous among themselves and should be signified more briefly (D.L. 10.75). This also agrees in the main with what Sextus says, perhaps from his Epicurean source (*M.* 1.194): 'Hence,

---

[59] For Epicurean elements in Varro, see Dam 1930: 49–52.

if Hellenism too has won acceptance for two main reasons, the clarity (*saphēneia*) and the ease (*prosēneia*) of what it designates (for following upon these, speaking metaphorically, emphatically, and according to the rest of the tropes have been added from outside), then we shall investigate from which those qualities are more likely to arise, whether from common usage or from analogy, so that we can side with it.'[60]

Thus, Varro's source was an empiricist work, possibly that of an Epicurean. I think it is clear that Crates' role in that work was parallel to that of Aristarchus, as one of two great grammarians whose disagreement on the application of analogy in flexion was used to discredit the entire analogical enterprise. As to the way in which the two disagreed, there are two possibilities. Aristarchus, Varro says, thought that analogical word forms should be used, to the extent that common usage permits. Perhaps, then, Crates thought that analogical formations, while they have their use, ought to be substituted for the forms of common usage in even fewer situations than did Aristarchus. I have argued for a stronger alternative: Crates thought that analogical forms ought to be substituted for forms in common use. Whichever of these is true, Crates was an advocate of grammatical science and thus miles away from the anti-analogist advocate of *LL* 8.

---

[60] 'Ease' seems to refer to the acceptability of an utterance, its failure to occasion offence or ridicule: see Atherton 1996: 252–3, Blank: 1998: 222–3. At other points Sextus says language should be: clear and accurate (176) or correct (192).

CHAPTER 8

The Stoics on fallacies of equivocation

Susanne Bobzien

The Stoics extensively discussed logical paradoxes and fallacies, both of which they would call sophisms (σοφίσματα). They wrote numerous books on the paradoxes of the Liar and the Sorites, which today – again – are the subject of extensive research; they investigated a number of paradoxes and fallacies that are based on puzzles connected with demonstratives, identity, presuppositions and ambiguities, and there are still many questions unanswered about their treatment of each of these. In this paper I take up the Stoic treatment of sophisms or fallacies which contain ambiguities, more precisely which contain an ambiguous word which is responsible for there being a fallacy. In modern terms, these are lexical, as opposed to grammatical or structural, ambiguities, and this kind of fallacy is often called 'fallacy of equivocation',[1] although we cannot assume that the Stoic understanding of such ambiguities fully coincides with any modern ones. The Peripatetics called such fallacies fallacies of homonymy, and the Stoics are likely to have called them fallacies of homonymy in single words.[2] The Stoic discussion of this type of fallacies has been written upon with fruitful results by several scholars, but the precise nature of the Stoic view is still a matter of debate. In this paper, I try to sort out the difficulties for an interpretation of the Stoic treatment of such fallacies based on lexical ambiguities, compare it with Aristotle's treatment of this type of sophisms, and explore what we can learn from it about Stoic theory of logic and language.

I THE EVIDENCE

The central text for the Stoic treatment of fallacies of homonymy is a passage from Simplicius' *Commentary on Aristotle's Categories*. As there are

[1] Contrasted with 'fallacy of amphiboly' as a name for fallacies of syntactic ambiguity. Hence the title of this paper. The modern names ultimately go back to Aristotle's distinction in the *Sophistical Refutations* between παραλογισμὸς παρὰ τὴν ὁμωνυμίαν and παραλογισμὸς παρὰ τὴν ἀμφιβολίαν.
[2] Cf. Simpl. *Cat.* 24.5–6; Galen, *De Soph.* 13.4–6 (ἐν τοῖς ἁπλοῖς), see also Arist. *SE* ch. 19.

several ways of translating the text which correspond to several different interpretations, and since to find the best interpretation of the text is one of the goals of this paper, I will refrain from giving a translation here, but rather present the Greek text together with an English paraphrase which leaves open most of the interpretative problems. As the ambiguous word on which the fallacy turns (ἀνδρεῖος) has no ambiguous equivalent in English,[3] in order to preserve the ambiguity, I will list its two meanings thus: {for men/manly}. The reader is then asked to imagine that this is *one* word which has those two meanings.

(1) διὸ καὶ ἐν τοῖς παρ' ὁμωνυμίαν συλλογισμοῖς ἡσυχάζειν οἱ διαλεκτικοὶ παρακελεύονται, (2) ἕως ἂν ἐπ' ἄλλο σημαινόμενον ὁ ἐρωτῶν μεταγάγῃ τὸ ὄνομα. (3) οἷον, εἴ τις ἐρωτᾷ εἰ ὁ χιτὼν ἀνδρεῖος, εἰ τύχοι ἀνδρεῖος ὤν, συγχωρησόμεθα. (4) κἂν ἐρωτήσῃ εἰ ὁ ἀνδρεῖος εὔψυχος, καὶ τοῦτο συγχωρησόμεθα, ἀληθὲς γάρ. (5) εἰ δὲ συναγάγῃ ὅτι ὁ χιτὼν ἄρα εὔψυχος, (6) ἐνταῦθα τὴν ὁμωνυμίαν τοῦ ἀνδρείου διαστείλασθαι (7) καὶ δεῖξαι [τὴν ἀνδρείαν ἤγουν τὴν εὐψυχίαν] ὅτι ἄλλως μὲν ἐπὶ τοῦ χιτῶνος, ἄλλως δὲ ἐπὶ τοῦ τὴν ἀνδρείαν ἔχοντος λέγεται. (Simpl. *Cat.* 24.9–21)

(1) This is why the logicians advise <us> to be silent in the case of syllogisms based on a homonymy. (2) In such syllogisms, at some point the questioner transfers the ambiguous word to another signification. (3) For example, if someone asks whether the garment is {manly/for men}, if it happens to be {manly/for men}, we will concede this. (4) And if he asks whether being {manly/for men} is being courageous, we will concede this, too, for it is true. (5) But if he infers that the garment is therefore courageous, (6) <they advise us> to separate the homonymy of the word '{manly/for men}' (7) and show [manliness, that is courage] that it is said or intended in one way in the case of the garment, in another in the case of the one who has manliness.

This passage has given rise not only to a number of different interpretations, but also to some puzzlement. In order to be able to produce a fully satisfactory interpretation and dissolve the difficulties, I start with a brief set of comments on the text, before looking at the philosophical issues it involves. The context of the passage is Simplicius' commentary on Aristotle's definition of homonymy at *Categories* 1a1–2. The problem Simplicius discusses is why, if the topic of the *Categories* is meaningful speech, not things, Aristotle talks about things which share a name (*homonyms*) rather

---

[3] Common devices to get around this difficulty are substituting the Greek example by a suitable English ambiguous word with a different meaning, or choosing for each occurrence the meaning that is (most likely to be) intended by speaker or listener. Either practice prevents us from an adequate analysis of the text, hence I introduce my – admittedly – awkward nomenclature. (Atherton 1993: 420–1, leaves the word ἀνδρεῖος untranslated; Long and Sedley 1987: 1, 228–9, translate ἀνδρεῖος by 'manly' throughout, presumably in the hope that it is close enough to its second meaning 'for men'.)

than, as one would expect, expressions with a multiplicity of significations (*homonymies*). The 'logicians' are somehow invoked to testify that it is primarily things, and not words, that generate homonymies.[4] Of course we have no reason to assume that this was the original purpose of the Stoic argumentation reported by Simplicius.[5]

(1) ἐν τοῖς παρ' ὁμωνυμίαν συλλογισμοῖς ἡσυχάζειν οἱ διαλεκτικοὶ παρακελεύονται:

- οἱ διαλεκτικοὶ: 'the logicians', 'the dialecticians': Simplicius simply calls the philosophers at issue logicians (or dialecticians). However, there can be little doubt that these logicians were Stoics.[6] The terminology is Stoic, the method suggested for dealing with the fallacy seems to be Stoic, and most importantly, the example of a simple homonymy we get, that ἀνδρεῖος can be said of a shirt and of a man in different meanings, is exactly the one we obtain in Galen's list of Stoic ambiguities.

- ὁμωνυμία: 'homonymy': homonymies are the second and third types of ambiguities in Galen's list of Stoic types of ambiguities (Gal. *De Soph.* 13.4–7 Gabler, 22 Ebbesen). At issue in our passage is 'homonymy in single words',[7] a class in which fall terms that are homonymous in isolation.

- συλλογισμοί: 'syllogisms': it is odd that Simplicius (or his source) calls these fallacies syllogisms. For syllogisms are, for Aristotle and the Peripatetics as well as for the Stoics, *valid* arguments, whereas validity should at least be doubtful in the case of fallacies. There is of course the possibility that the Stoics considered fallacies of equivocation as valid but unsound syllogisms.[8] More likely, συλλογισμοί is not part of the excerpt from the Stoics, but Simplicius' doing. Perhaps this is just carelessness on the part of Simplicius, writing 'syllogism' instead of 'sophism'.[9]

---

[4] Simplicius may here confound, to his advantage, the common Stoic use of πράγματα for things signified (roughly meanings) with the Aristotelian and early Peripatetic use of πράγματα for things.

[5] As rightly pointed out by Atherton 1993: 420 n.14.

[6] So also shown by Atherton 1993: 421–2.

[7] For the Stoic distinction between homonymy in single words (or 'in simples', ὁμωνυμία ἐν τοῖς ἁπλοῖς) and homonymy in compounds (ὁμωνυμία ἐν τοῖς συνθέτοις) see Galen, *De Soph.* 13.4–6 and Atherton 1993: 273–7.

[8] There is a Stoic classification that allows for fallacies that are in fact valid (D.L. 7.44, cf. also S.E. *P.H.* 2.229); but I doubt that the one at issue here belongs in that class.

[9] It is possible that – when disregarding the possibility of ambiguity – the Peripatetics considered the *linguistic* form of the fallacy as a valid form of syllogistic (in a wider sense). Alternatively, 'syllogism' could have been used in the sense of apparent syllogism by Simplicius. For Aristotle writes, at *SE* 171b18–19: ὥστε ὅ τε περὶ τῶνδε φαινόμενος συλλογισμὸς ἐριστικός λόγος.

- παρακελεύονται: 'they recommend', 'they prescribe', 'they advise': this choice of term, that the logicians recommend a particular strategy, shows that we are in the context of dialectical discourse. Advice is given how to 'play' the dialectical 'game'. So, strictly, this passage does not tell us how the Stoics produce a solution (λύσις) in the case of fallacies of homonymy, although from their recommendation we will be able to venture a good guess what such a solution would have looked like.

- ἡσυχάζειν: 'keep quiet', 'fall silent': what exactly is meant by this expression in this sentence and what its scope is, are matters of controversy. I discuss these questions below in section 7.

(2) ἕως ἂν ἐπ' ἄλλο σημαινόμενον ὁ ἐρωτῶν μεταγάγῃ τὸ ὄνομα

- ἕως: There are three ways of reading this conjunctive expression, and they each lead to different kinds of interpretation of the text: we can either read it as meaning 'until', or as 'while' / 'at the point when', or as 'as long as'. More is said on this in section 7.

- σημαινόμενον: 'that which is signified', 'signification', 'meaning': this could be Stoic terminology, in which case it refers to what they called 'sayables' (λεκτά), in this case a predicate, which is an incomplete sayable (D.L. 7.63). Alternatively, σημαινόμενον simply refers to 'that which is signified', in a philosophically neutral sense, as used by logicians in the second century AD and later, including Peripatetics. (There is an ongoing debate in particular regarding Aristotelian philosophy, whether words like σημαινόμενον may ever be translated as meaning. Since it is natural in the context of ambiguity of expressions to talk about the several meanings of a term, and since the Stoic sayables can in a wide sense be considered as meanings, I will talk about the two meanings of an expression, etc. No particular technical slant should be attached to my use of the word 'meaning', though.)

- ὁ ἐρωτῶν: 'the questioner': this expression again shows that a dialectical discourse is at issue. It involves a questioner and an answerer; the former tries to make the latter contradict himself, or get him into logical trouble otherwise.[10]

- μεταγάγῃ: 'transfers': some manuscripts have μετάγῃ instead of μεταγάγῃ. Which reading is preferable depends on the overall interpretation of the passage one chooses. (See below section 7.) Kv has ἐπαγάγῃ, which makes less sense.

---

[10] See e.g. Smith 1997, the introduction, for a good discussion of dialectical discourse and dialectical games.

- The exact meaning of the whole clause (2) can only be given later. But a translation such as 'the questioner transfers the word to a different meaning' will prove adequate. In any event, we can infer from (2) that the Stoics held that one word can have more than one signification or meaning, and that users of the word can – somehow – transfer such a word from one of its meanings to another.

(3) οἷον, εἴ τις ἐρωτᾷ εἰ ὁ χιτὼν ἀνδρεῖος, εἰ τύχοι ἀνδρεῖος ὤν, συγχωρησόμεθα

- οἷον: 'for example': this phrase introduces an example of a fallacy of homonymy, and how the Stoics advise us to deal with it.
- εἴ τις ἐρωτᾷ: 'if someone asks': again, this shows the dialectical context.
- ὁ χιτὼν ἀνδρεῖος: this is the first premiss of the fallacy, if in question form, though there is in this case in fact no difference in the Greek. We also obtain the first meaning of the ambiguous word ἀνδρεῖος, namely 'for men', 'of a man', as used e.g. of clothes.
- συγχωρησόμεθα: 'we will agree', 'we will assent', 'we will concede': the person questioned is asked to 'concede' the premiss. συγχωρεῖν is commonly used to describe public, verbal, explicit, assent to a premiss or conclusion, in a dialectical discourse, and more generally.[11] I believe that is the meaning it has in this passage.

(4) κἂν ἐρωτήσῃ εἰ ὁ ἀνδρεῖος εὔψυχος, καὶ τοῦτο συγχωρησόμεθα, ἀληθὲς γάρ.

- κἂν: 'and if': this conjunction introduces the 'asking' of the second premiss.
- ἐρωτήσῃ: 'he asks': again, the terminology is that of the dialectical game.
- ὁ ἀνδρεῖος εὔψυχος: this is the second premiss of the fallacy, and also brings in the second meaning of the ambiguous word ἀνδρεῖος, viz. 'manly', as in 'brave'.

(5) εἰ δὲ συναγάγῃ ὅτι ὁ χιτὼν ἄρα εὔψυχος

- εἰ δὲ: 'but if': this phrase introduces the conclusion, and its being drawn by the questioner.
- συναγάγῃ: 'he infers': συνάγειν is a common Stoic term for drawing the conclusion of an argument,[12] but is also used quite generally in ancient logic.[13]

---

[11] For passages see below note 62.   [12] E.g. S.E. *P.H.* 2.228, 229; D.L. 7.78.
[13] Alex. *AnPr.* 2.1, 19.8, 21.28, 22.6, etc.; cf. Arist. *Rhet.* 1357a8, 1395b25, *Met.* 1042a3.

- ὁ χιτὼν ἄρα εὔψυχος: This is the conclusion of the fallacy, ἄρα being the particle used by the Stoics, and again by ancient philosophers generally, to indicate that a sentence or a proposition is the conclusion of an argument.

(6) ἐνταῦθα τὴν ὁμωνυμίαν τοῦ ἀνδρείου διαστείλασθαι

- ἐνταῦθα: we can assume either a temporal meaning here, 'at the very time', 'at this point', 'then', indicating the time at which the fallacious character and elements of the – apparent – argument are meant to be uncovered; or something like 'at this point in the argument'.

- τὴν ὁμωνυμίαν τοῦ ἀνδρείου διαστείλασθαι: 'one must separate the homonymy of "{manly/for men}"' (i.e. distinguish the two meanings of the word): διαστείλασθαι is used elsewhere to indicate the revealing of the ambiguity of a term.[14]

(7) καὶ δεῖξαι [τὴν ἀνδρείαν ἤγουν τὴν εὐψυχίαν] ὅτι ἄλλως μὲν ἐπὶ τοῦ χιτῶνος, ἄλλως δὲ ἐπὶ τοῦ τὴν ἀνδρείαν ἔχοντος λέγεται.

- καὶ δεῖξαι: I assume this here simply means show (as opposed to prove in a strict sense); the respondent is meant to show up the double meaning at this point.

- [τὴν ἀνδρείαν ἤγουν τὴν εὐψυχίαν]: '[manliness, that is, courage]': this has been excised by some editors, and indeed it seems somewhat superfluous and out of place; it could have been a marginal note that found its way into the text. Possibly the author of the phrase thought he had better point out that manliness is the same as (or implies) courage, in case this wasn't clear from the fact that being manly implies being courageous.

- ὅτι ἄλλως μὲν ἐπὶ τοῦ χιτῶνος, ἄλλως δὲ ἐπὶ τοῦ τὴν ἀνδρείαν ἔχοντος λέγεται: 'that it is said/intended in one way in the case of the garment, in another in the case of the one who has manliness': this clause can be taken in two ways, at two levels of generality; see below, section 4.

2 THE FALLACY

The – or some – Stoics defined ambiguity (ἀμφιβολία) as 'an expression that signifies two or more things in its common linguistic use and in its proper senses and in the same linguistic idiom, so that the several things are

---

[14] Cf. S.E. *P.H.* 2.256–57 ἐπὶ τῆς διαστολῆς τῶν ἀμφιβολιῶν; διαστελλουμένους ἀμφιβολίας; ἡ διαστολή . . . Note also that διαστέλλω was used for the separation of words by punctuation. Such separation is essential for solving structural ambiguities, such as those the Stoics called homonymy of compounds.

understood simultaneously in this expression'.[15] Homonymy (ὁμωνυμία) is a species of ambiguity, and homonymy in single words (ἐν τοῖς ἁπλοῖς) is one of two kinds of homonymy.[16] Ideally, the ambiguous expression on which the fallacious character of a fallacy of equivocation is grounded should satisfy the Stoic definition of ambiguity. In our fallacy, the Greek word ἀνδρεῖος, with its two meanings 'for men' and 'manly' appears to do so at least when it is considered in isolation. The word has both meanings in its common linguistic use, i.e. neither is a technical or otherwise unusual expression; in its proper senses, i.e. not metaphorically; and in the same linguistic idiom; and it has the meanings at the same time. Moreover, Galen presents it as paradigm for Stoics ambiguities in single words.[17]

The Simplicius text allows us to reconstruct the fallacy with some certainty:

(1) ὁ χιτὼν ἀνδρεῖος.
    ὁ δ' ἀνδρεῖος, εὔψυχος.
    ὁ χιτὼν ἄρα εὔψυχος.

This fallacy (as the majority of Greek fallacies) cannot be straightforwardly translated into English without losing its sophistic character. In order to retain it, instead of translating the ambiguous expressions, I will list their two meanings, as indicated in section 1, thus: {for men/manly}, and invite the reader to imagine that this is one word which has those two meanings.

The garment is {for men/manly}.
But {what/who} is {for men/manly} is courageous.
Therefore, the garment is courageous.

This triplet of sentences is indeed a fallacy, since what seem to be the premisses appear to be true and to entail the conclusion, which in turn is clearly false. The fallacy does not have the form of a Stoic syllogism. I here speak of the linguistic form of the fallacy, i.e. the three grammatical sentences, and disregard any ambiguities in expressions.[18] We would get a fallacy with a linguistic form the Stoics may have accepted as that of a valid argument by making slight changes:[19]

---

[15] D.L. 7.62, λέξις δύο ἢ καὶ πλείονα πράγματα σημαίνουσα λεκτικῶς καὶ κυρίως καὶ κατὰ τὸ αὐτὸ ἔθος, ὥσθ' ἅμα τὰ πλείονα ἐκδέξασθαι κατὰ ταύτην τὴν λέξιν. For an in-depth discussion of this definition see Atherton 1993: 135–72. My understanding of the definition owes much to Atherton.

[16] Galen, *De Soph.* 13.4–7, see above, note 7.   [17] Gal. *De Soph.* 13.4–5 Gabler, 22 Ebbesen.

[18] Although in the Stoic view syllogisms are not linguistic items (see section 3), we recognise their form in the way they are expressed in language; for this to be possible, the Stoics introduced various kinds of language regulations.

[19] See Atherton 1993: 420, n.15 for a different suggestion.

(2a) ὁ χιτὼν ἀνδρεῖος.   or   (2b) ὁ χιτὼν ἀνδρεῖος.
εἴ τί ἀνδρεῖον, ἐκεῖνο εὔψυχον.   εἴ τίς ἀνδρεῖος, ἐκεῖνος εὔψυχος.
ὁ χιτὼν ἄρα εὔψυχος.   ὁ χιτὼν ἄρα εὔψυχος.

The garment is {for men/manly}.   The garment is {for men/manly}.
If some*thing* is {for men/manly}, it is   If some*one* is {for men/manly},
  courageous.   that one is courageous.
Therefore, the garment is courageous.   Therefore, the garment is courageous.

Or, with the more common order of the sentences that express the premisses:[20]

εἴ τί ἀνδρεῖον, ἐκεῖνο εὔψυχον.   or   εἴ τίς ἀνδρεῖος, ἐκεῖνος εὔψυχος.
ὁ δὲ χιτὼν ἀνδρεῖος.   ὁ δὲ χιτὼν ἀνδρεῖος.
ὁ χιτὼν ἄρα εὔψυχος.   ὁ χιτὼν ἄρα εὔψυχος.

If some*thing* is {for men/manly},   If some*one* is {for men/manly},
  it is courageous.   that one is courageous.
The garment is {for men/manly}.   The garment is {for men/manly}.
Therefore, the garment is courageous.   Therefore, the garment is courageous.

This still does not have the exact form of a Stoic indemonstrable argument,[21] but there is some evidence that arguments of this form (not fallacies, of course) were accepted by the Stoics as valid.[22] The fallacy can be seen as an abbreviating reformulation of this argument which would retain the validity.[23] We can see why the fallacy was presented as (1) rather than any of the versions of (2). For in the case of (2), a decision has to be made whether to use (2a) 'something' (τί), etc., or (2b) 'someone' (τίς), etc. But (2b) would be understood by a Greek speaker as being clearly about persons, and thus the lack of connection with the first (simple) premiss would be too obvious;

[20] For the Stoics, the order of the premisses did not matter for whether something is a syllogism, and presumably a valid argument, see Bobzien 1996: 181 (premiss permutation) together with 136 and 152. Nonetheless, customarily the simple premiss would not be placed first in a syllogism.

[21] For the Stoic indemonstrables see D.L. 7.79–81, S.E. *P.H.* 2.157–8, and Bobzien 1996: 134–41.

[22] Cf. Augustine *Dial.* III.84–6 (Pinborg) for an example; see also Cic. *Fat.* 11–15. For Stoic indefinite conditionals see S.E. *M.* 11.8, 10, 11; D.L. 7.75 and Bobzien 1999: 155–6.

[23] See Alex. *Top.* 8.20–2 for a Stoic example formulated as '{What/who} is F, is G' (ὁ ἀναπνέων ζῇ). With manipulation in one direction, the fallacy thus takes on the form of a Stoic valid argument; with slight modification in another direction, it takes on a form considered valid by the Peripatetics:

This garment is {for men/manly}.   This garment is {for men/manly}.
What is {for men/manly} is courageous.   All things {for men/manly} are courageous.
Therefore, this garment is courageous.   Therefore, this garment is courageous.

This fact is significant insofar as it shows that the fallacy could have been used and been of interest to both philosophical schools, see also section 6 below. (Interestingly, Alexander in the *Topics* passage just quoted distinguishes between ὁ ἀναπνέων ζῇ and the Peripatetic πᾶς ὁ ἀναπνέων ζῇ.)

whereas in the case (2a), the sentence would sound somewhat funny, since εὔψυχος and ἀνδρεῖος, which would then have the neuter form εὔψυχον and ἀνδρεῖον (in the required meaning of 'manly'), really make sense only for persons.

By contrast, the formulation in the text, i.e. (1), '{What/who} is {for men/manly} is courageous' (ὁ ἀνδρεῖος, εὔψυχος) is on the one hand a generally accepted 'synonymous' linguistic variant of the sense-making 'If someone is {for men/manly}, that one is courageous' (εἴ τίς ἀνδρεῖος, ἐκεῖνος εὔψυχος); and on the other, on superficial reading, seems to pick up the ὁ ('the') from ὁ χιτών ('the garment') in the first premiss, so that there is at least an apparent connection between the premisses. It becomes clear here that it is essential for the fallacy to work smoothly that the word for a garment chosen is masculine. In this way the whole argument goes through with the masculine forms, and its deceptive nature is harder to pin down. Of course, the main element which makes the argument fallacious is the ambiguous word '{for men/manly}'. But as most good fallacies, this one, too, employs more than one device to trick the listener. Sometimes they are cooperative in producing the illusion of soundness or validity, as in this case; sometimes they seem to be introduced into the sophism to distract us from the main fallacious element; and the function of some elements of deception can be interpreted either way.

3 WHAT SORT OF THING THE STOICS THOUGHT A FALLACY OF HOMONYMY IS

For the Stoics, an argument is a compound of premisses and conclusion. Premisses and conclusion are assertibles or propositions (ἀξιώματα), and as such incorporeal entities.[24] They are things signified (or significations, σημαινόμενα). Premisses and conclusion are expressed in meaningful sentences. Thus, we may assume that the three sentences

'If it is day, it is light', 'It is day' and 'It is light'

express the three assertibles or propositions

IF IT IS DAY, IT IS LIGHT, IT IS DAY and IT IS LIGHT.

When such sentences are meant to express an argument (a compound of premisses and conclusion) the Stoics usually indicate this further by particles as follows

---

[24] They have, however, in principle the ability to change their truth-value and modal properties over time. See Bobzien 1999: 93–6, 117.

'If it is day, it is light', 'But it is day', 'Therefore, it is light.'

These sentences, taken together, express a Stoic first indemonstrable syllogism. What then is the relation between arguments and fallacies, and what *is* a fallacy in the Stoic view? The Stoics classify the discussion of fallacies under logic, i.e. that part of dialectics (διαλεκτική) that deals with the things signified. On the other hand, ambiguities are discussed in that part of dialectics that is concerned with language, utterances or speech (φωνή). From this fact alone, we can surmise that the Stoic treatment of fallacies of ambiguity draws on both these parts of dialectics.

As Atherton rightly emphasises,[25] a fallacy of homonymy cannot be (just) an argument, as an argument on its own cannot be fallacious for reasons of ambiguity. For arguments, being at the level of sayables and assertibles, cannot contain ambiguities, whereas the fallacies we are interested in here are fallacies based on ambiguity. So the fallacy must comprise both elements from the level of meanings or things signified and linguistic elements. It arises as a result of incongruities between the two, which are made use of in a cunning way by the designer or proponent of the fallacy.

Our fallacy, for instance, comprises at least the assertibles that THE GARMENT IS FOR MEN, that WHAT[26] IS MANLY IS COURAGEOUS, that THE GARMENT IS MANLY, that THE GARMENT IS COURAGEOUS, and the argument THE GARMENT IS MANLY, BUT WHAT IS MANLY IS COURAGEOUS, THEREFORE THE GARMENT IS COURAGEOUS. It comprises the sentences 'the garment is {for men/manly}', '<but> {who/what} is {for men/manly} is courageous', and '<therefore> the garment is courageous', and it comprises them in that order, so that they have the appearance of expressing an argument. This *complex* of meaning items and linguistic items is a fallacy, because it gives, at least at superficial perusal, the impression of being a bit of language expressing a valid and sound argument, but in fact is not. (Naturally, one can discuss sayables and arguments only when they are clad in language; there is no other option. Hence, in principle, ambiguities are always a possibility, and consequently, so are fallacies.)

From a Stoic perspective, fallacies of homonymy thus straddle the realm of meaning and the realm of linguistic expression; however, they also involve the realm of pragmatics. They are the result of an interplay between the first two, based on contingent facts about language (ambiguities), and the intentional use[27] of linguistic items to express meaning items in such a way

---

[25] Atherton 1993: 413.   [26] Or 'who', see previous section.
[27] Possibly, initially the use is unintentional.

that they appear to represent validity and soundness, but in fact do not.[28] Hence they also essentially involve a pragmatic component: a fallacy will only exist if someone has actually formulated and entertained it. (Unlike Stoic propositions, which, at least in the prevalent interpretation, are there even when not in use,[29] for the Stoics, linguistic items only exist when they are actually used by speakers or writers or thinkers.) Moreover, without the potential to deceive, they are not fallacies (σοφίσματα).[30] But being (able to be) deceived is a psychological disposition that can be reduced neither to language nor to 'meaning'.

It does not follow that, for the Stoics, fallacies are 'tokens', fleeting occurrences in time, temporary complexes of significations (meanings) and linguistic items. For, the Stoics talk about many fallacies as 'the so-and-so argument'.[31] Thus, as in the case of arguments, there are tokens of them, performances of them, if you want, but the fallacies themselves are not just such tokens, and are not reducible to such tokens or performances. We can identify the fallacy with its type. But note that this type is an abstraction, in the same way in which concepts (ἐννοήματα), for instance, are abstractions for the Stoics, and are not something that has the status of a subsisting entity, as Stoic sayables and assertibles, but are only quasi-somethings.[32]

4 THE STOIC ADVICE AND CONTEXTUAL DISAMBIGUATION

Simplicius' Stoics advise that the answerer concede both premisses, and each time they give a reason why and when they should be conceded. The justifications why we should concede the premisses are most interesting. In the case of the first premiss, we are told to consent to the proposition expressed

---

[28] The Stoics seem also to have allowed for sophisms that are valid, but do not appear to be, cf. S.E. *P.H.* 2.229, but our fallacy does not belong to this special group.

[29] The mode of being there of Stoic propositions (assertibles) is that they subsist (ὑφίστασθαι); they resemble Frege's thoughts or Carnap's propositions in that respect. For the prevalent interpretation see e.g. Frede 1994a, Schubert 1994: ch. 1, Barnes 1999: 211, Bobzien 1998: 21–6.

[30] I use 'fallacy' as translation of the Greek σόφισμα; the meaning of the latter does not entirely coincide with the meaning of 'fallacy' as used in contemporary English.

[31] Thus the Stoics talk about the Idle argument (ἀργὸς λόγος, Origen *Cels.* 342.62–3), the Master argument (κυριεύων λόγος, Epict. *Diss.* 2.19.1), the Liar arguments (ψευδόμενοι λόγοι, D.L. 7.196), the Little-by-little argument (ὁ παρὰ μικρὸν λόγος, D.L. 7.197) or Sorites, all of which they consider sophisms, and they talk generally about intractable arguments (ἄποροι λόγοι, D.L. 7.82). There is a problem here, as strictly speaking, for the Stoics even λόγος, i.e. argument, would be an incorrect description, as a fallacy is not occurring at the level of arguments, but at the level of the relation between linguistic expressions and propositions. Still, they may have called the fallacies so-and-so arguments because they were known under those names before the Stoics tried their hands at them; or alternatively, 'argument' is used in the loose sense of 'apparent argument'.

[32] Cf. Stob. 1.136.21–137.6.

in the sentence 'the garment is {manly/for men}', if the garment happens to be {manly/for men}. From this we learn the following: the expression 'the garment' is used demonstratively in the argument; the assumption is that the premiss is true if 'the garment' (together with an act of pointing) is used to 'demonstrate', or refer to, a garment that is {manly/for men}. At first sight, this is just an application of the Stoic truth-criterion for definite propositions as we find it in Sextus Empiricus.[33] But there is more to it. The assumption that the premiss is true if the garment is {manly/for men} allows us to infer that the Stoics understand the meaning of the expression '{manly/for men}' *in this premiss* to be FOR MEN. (For the proposition that THE GARMENT IS MANLY would never be true, and at the level of truth, which is the level of sayables and propositions, there is no room for ambiguity.)[34] Thus there is, at the time when the first premiss is requested, only *one* proposition expressed by the sentence 'the garment is {manly/for men}', and that is that THE GARMENT WHICH IS DEMONSTRATED IS FOR MEN.[35] Possibly, the Stoics also thought that only this one proposition was intended by speaker and listener; however, this is a different point. Which proposition or propositions are expressed by a sentence appears to be in principle independent of speaker and listener intention.

The case of the second premiss is even more straightforward. We are advised to concede the second premiss 'because it is true'. Now the sentence '{who/what} is {manly/for men} is courageous' can be used to express a truth only if the expression '{manly/for men}' has the meaning MANLY. Thus the Stoics assume – at least for the purpose of treating the fallacy – that the sentence, when asked, is not ambiguous,[36] and hence that the word '{manly/for men}' *qua being used in the sentence* is not ambiguous.[37] We can take it that the premiss would count as a true Stoic conditional,[38] and thus that – unlike in the case of the first premiss – its truth-value is not context- or time-dependent. Again, speaker and listener intention were

---

[33] S.E. *M.* 8.100, on ὡρισμένα ἀξιώματα.   [34] See previous section.

[35] This is worth noting on its own, but also because Aristotle's position on this point is different, see below section 6.

[36] I am not sure whether the Stoics would call a whole sentence 'ambiguous' (ἀμφίβολος), if it contains an ambiguous expression that is not disambiguated by its linguistic context (for examples see section 8 below), or whether they would reserve the term 'ambiguity' for the largest phrase in such a sentence that can be taken in more than one way. If the latter, a more careful formulation, such as 'the sentence, when and as being asked, does not contain an ambiguity', may be preferable.

[37] The word '{manly/for men}' as used in the sentence is not such that 'several things are understood simultaneously in this' word, and thus does not satisfy the Stoic definition of ambiguity preserved at D.L. 7.62, for which see section 2 above.

[38] It would be what the Stoics called an indefinite conditional, see above note 22. For their truth-conditions see Bobzien 1999: 112–13.

likely to be taken to coincide, this time in their both intending the meaning
MANLY; again, it does not follow that for the Stoics it depends on the
speaker or listener intention what proposition is expressed by the premiss
sentence.

This treatment of the two premisses by the Stoics suggests that they
endorsed an interesting theory of ambiguity. One way of describing it would
be that they assume that context disambiguates. In order not to misinterpret
the Stoics here, it is useful to make the following distinction. When I say
'the context disambiguates' I mean by this an entirely non-psychological,
non-mental fact: whereas an expression or phrase considered on its own, out
of context or without a context, linguistic or otherwise, may be ambiguous
in the Stoic understanding, when it is used in a certain kind of context
(e.g. a context in which one of two meanings clearly produces a truth, the
other clearly a falsehood, and the context ensures that a true statement
is intended), it is no longer ambiguous in that sense. It is no longer the
case that 'several things are understood simultaneously in this' expression
or phrase. From this 'disambiguation by context' I wish to distinguish 'the
mental process of disambiguation by speaker and/or listener'. Such a process
involves that the person at issue runs in their mind (whether they are fully
aware of it or not) through two or more meanings of an expression or clause,
and, e.g. as a result of assessing the context, discards all but one of them;
eliminates all the irrelevant meanings and retains only the relevant one.
These two notions of disambiguation, although they each tend to involve
context, are very different things.

It seems to me borne out by our text that the abstract observation that
context disambiguates was part of the Stoic theory. Thus in Stoic philosophy of language a distinction is required between (i) an ambiguous
expression, which is considered *on its own* to always have simultaneous
semantic multiplicity, and (ii) a sentence uttered at a time *t* which contains
an ambiguous expression, but which at *t* may express only one proposition,
and thus involve only one meaning of the expression – despite the fact
that even at *t* the expression considered on its own has its two meanings. I
assume that the Stoics took most such sentences to express at most times
only one proposition (the same one each time).[39] In fact, Augustine, in his
work *On Dialectic*, provides a distinction similar to this one, which may
well go back to the Stoics:[40]

---

[39] Neither (i) nor (ii) require reference to speaker's intentions.
[40] Cf. Ebbesen 1981: 1, 32, Atherton 1993: 289–90; Catherine Atherton has confirmed in conversation
that on page 290, lines 8–10, in the sentence 'the second <argument> could also be Stoic' she refers
to the argument I quote.

(1) For when it is said that every word is ambiguous, this is said about single (separate, individual) words. . . . (2) And yet, while every word is ambiguous, nobody explains the ambiguity of the words with anything but words which once combined are not ambiguous. (3) For just as, if I were to say 'every soldier is two-footed', it wouldn't follow from this that a cohort of two-footed soldiers was therefore two-footed, so when I say that every word is ambiguous, I don't say that the sentence or the discourse <is ambiguous>, despite the fact that they are compounded from those very words.[41] (*Dial.* ch. 9)

As context for the argument in sentences (2) and (3) we have to imagine an opponent of the Stoic view that every word is ambiguous arguing somewhat as follows: if every word is ambiguous, then you can never disambiguate; for you disambiguate with words; but they are by assumption all ambiguous. The explicitly stated defence of the Stoic view in sentence (2) is that disambiguation of a word w is done not by providing a single word for each meaning of w, but by using a plurality of words compounded into a phrase or sentence. Underlying this response is the assumption that whole phrases or sentences, although consisting of nothing but – ambiguous – words, are themselves not ambiguous, or at least need not be. Sentence (3) uses the soldier analogy to make the logical point that from the fact that something is truly predicated of each of a group of individuals it does not follow that one can truly predicate it of the group as a whole.[42] Thus, if one can truly predicate of each word in a phrase or sentence that it is ambiguous, it does not follow that the group of words as a whole (the phrase or sentence or discourse) is ambiguous. Pertinent to my argument is the underlying assumption in this passage that from the fact that an individual word is ambiguous (has more than one meaning) it does not follow that a whole sentence or phrase which contains this word is ambiguous (has more than one meaning). This is similar to what the Simplicius passage implies about sentences which contain ambiguous words.

However, it follows neither from the Simplicius nor from the Augustine passage that whenever an ambiguous word or phrase is embedded in a sentence, it is thereby disambiguated by context. Some linguistic contexts retain the ambiguity (see also section 8 below). Moreover, presumably for most sentences a non-linguistic context could be imagined in which the

---

[41] *Quod enim dictum est omne verbum esse ambiguum de verbis singulis dictum est.* . . . (2) *Et tamen cum omne verbum ambiguum sit, nemo verborum ambiguitatem nisi sed iam coniunctis quae ambigua non erunt explicabit.* (3) *Ut enim, si dicerem 'omnis miles bipes est', non ex eo sequeretur ut cohors ex militibus utique bipedibus ita constaret, ita, cum dico ambiguum esse omne verbum, non dico sententiam, non disputationem, quamvis verba ista texantur.*

[42] For the Stoics on the special status of things that are groups of individuals, including armies, cf. Simpl. *Cat.* 214–15, S.E. *M.* 9.78, 7.102.

disambiguation by linguistic context is countered or undone, as it were. In such cases a mental process of disambiguation would be likely to occur in the listener. However, I am doubtful whether the Stoics thought that there occurred in cases like our fallacy mental processes in which an elimination of the irrelevant meanings of the expression at issue takes place. Our evidence is certainly compatible with the assumption that the Stoics took it that, as long as there is no strong contextual pressure to the contrary, no such elimination process takes place, and thus no process of disambiguation, simply because no more than one meaning ever presents itself to (or is called up by) the mind. They may have thought that when someone utters the sentence 'the garment is {manly/for men}', in any *ordinary* circumstances it just means that the garment is for men, and hence nothing else is considered by either speaker or listener. Of course this does not rule out that in the course of an analysis of the sentence out of context, or at some later time, the other meaning is called up in the mind, and a mental disambiguation process does occur.

Let us finally look at the Stoic advice concerning the concluding sentence of the fallacy. At the point when the questioner draws the conclusion and tries to get the respondent to concede it, too, the respondent is to jib:

(5) But if he infers that the garment is therefore courageous, (6) <they advise us> to separate the homonymy of the word '{manly/for men}' (7) and show that it is said/intended in one way in the case of the garment, in another in the case of the one who has manliness.

It is not expressly stated, but we can take it for granted that the Stoics do not want the respondent to concede the conclusion. Rather, at this point, the respondent is to state that the word '{manly/for men}' is used differently in each premiss.

The that-clause (ὅτι clause) in (7) can be taken in two ways, at two levels of generality; a point which may be of philosophical interest. Either, this clause is short for: (i) 'that "{manly/for men}" had been taken in one way in the first premiss, and in another in the second premiss' – and that hence the conclusion does not follow. Or, it could be taken more generally: (ii) 'that "{manly/for men}", when said of a garment, generally means one thing (i.e. for men), and when said of someone who has courage or manliness, generally means another thing (i.e. manly)'. In that case, (i) is taken to be implied by this, and thus again, the conclusion has been shown not to follow. The way the truth of the premisses is meant to be taken for granted (see above) suggests to me that the second reading is more likely. It tallies with a theory of ambiguity in which context disambiguates, but in which no mental process of disambiguation occurs in ordinary circumstances if the linguistic context suggests clearly only one meaning.

5 HOW THE STOICS WOULD HAVE SOLVED THE FALLACY

We still need to integrate into our interpretation phrase (2) from the Simplicius passage: 'the questioner transfers the word to another meaning'. Here we are clearly dealing with mental phenomena. The transfer at issue is a mental process. In order for it to be possible that such a transfer occurs, there needs first to be a connection the speaker holds between the word and one of its meanings, then such a connection between the word and its other meaning. This connection could be thought of as speaker intention, in which case what is expressed here is a change of speaker intention.

There are two possibilities as to when this transfer may be thought to take place. The first is: at the time of the drawing of the conclusion,[43] the second: at the time of the asking of the second premiss.[44] I opt for the first. The main disadvantage of the second possibility seems to me that interpreted thus, the phrase does not really contribute anything germane to the way the Stoics want the fallacy to be dealt with. (For a full discussion of this point see below section 7.) If we assume that the transfer of the word to another meaning happens at the point when the questioner draws the conclusion, we can now make sense of it easily, even though this way of looking at things is decidedly different from modern philosophy of language. There are in fact two – parallel – possibilities here:[45]

(i) At the point when he draws the conclusion, the questioner transfers the word '{manly/for men}' *in the first premiss* from the meaning or predicate FOR MEN to the meaning or predicate MANLY. Why would he do that? Because in this way, there comes to be a valid argument (not formally, but still valid, see above section 2). And a conclusion can only be *drawn*, if the argument is valid.

We need to distinguish here between the linguistic expression consisting of the three sentences, and the argument expressed, or the three propositions expressed. The linguistic expression *appears* valid (or more precisely, appears to express a valid argument) all the time – as long as we look at it

---

[43] Adopted by Ebbesen 1981: 1, 31 ('keep calm until'); Long and Sedley 1987: 1, 37S (' "become quiescent" until'); *FDS* IV, frg. 1257 ('in dem Moment zu schweigen . . . in dem'). But note that Ebbesen and Long and Sedley on the one hand, and Hülser on the other, differ in their interpretation of the meaning of ἡσυχάζειν, see below, section 7.
[44] Adopted by Atherton 1993: 419–20.
[45] This fact is not mentioned by Ebbesen and Atherton, perhaps because it is of no great relevance.

without considering the possibility of ambiguity of any of its expressions. However, for the Stoics the bearers of validity are the arguments, not the linguistic expressions thereof, and this point becomes relevant precisely when there is an ambiguity in the linguistic expression. At the point when the conclusion is drawn, the first premiss has become a different proposition (a fourth one), since the word '{manly/for men}' has been transferred to a different predicate. We now have the new – and false – proposition that THE GARMENT IS MANLY.

(ii) Alternatively, at the point when he draws the conclusion, the questioner transfers the word '{manly/for men}' *in the second premiss* from the meaning MANLY to the meaning FOR MEN. Again, there comes to be a valid argument. Again, for the Stoics, it is not the linguistic expression, but what it expresses, that is valid. This argument, evidently, is a different one than in case (i). For now the second premiss has been replaced by a different proposition (a fifth one).[46] This is the – false – proposition that WHAT IS FOR MEN IS COURAGEOUS.[47]

We cannot say which of the premisses the Stoics assumed the questioner would change. Perhaps they left it open, as it is in the end irrelevant for the solution of the fallacy. Psychologically, it is more likely to be the first. For it is further away, temporally, from the drawing of the conclusion, and hence will be less clear in the listener's mind.[48] Whether (i) or (ii) was what the Stoics had in mind, or whether they thought it did not matter which, in any event, *at the very moment* when the word is transferred to the other meaning, the respective premiss of the fallacy becomes a false one. Hence, the conclusion cannot be detached from the premisses, although the argument under consideration has at that point become a valid one. The questioner's hope is of course that the respondent will not be able to figure this out.

Thus the Stoic theory fits well with the – reasonable – assumption that in cases of fallacies, while one concentrates on the premisses, the focus is on the truth of the premisses, while when one draws the conclusion, the focus switches to the validity of the argument.[49] More importantly for the Stoics, rightly, fallacies based on ambiguity consist not just in the artful choice and manipulation of *words* or *linguistic expressions*. Such fallacies work at

---

[46] The individuation of arguments occurs at the level of propositions (ἀξιώματα); and on that level there is no ambiguity.

[47] Or that WHOEVER IS FOR MEN IS COURAGEOUS.

[48] Of course, we could switch the premiss sentences round. But as it stands, the fallacy is more likely to confuse the listener (see above, section 2), hence this order of the premiss sentences is presumably not a matter of chance.

[49] See Tappenden 1993.

the level of interaction of meaning and expressions. As long as one looks at the words only, one cannot solve them. As long as one considers solely the level of meaning, they cannot even occur.[50]

We now have all the information we need to see how the Stoics would – presumably – have solved the fallacy. We know that for the Stoics it would not be sufficient, if the respondent just pointed out that the word '{manly/for men}' in the fallacy is ambiguous; for they, or at least Chrysippus, held that all words are ambiguous.[51] The explanation that would serve as solution (λύσις) needs to comprise more than that. Catherine Atherton has given the following account of it:[52]

Suppose that a homonym figures in both of the sentences used to signify the premisses of an argument and the contents of the remainders of each sentence ensure that each of the signified propositions will be true if and only if the homonym has a different sense in each, that appropriate to its context. . . . The signified argument can be declared false either on the grounds that at least one premiss of this argument is false, although the argument is concludent, or else on the grounds that the premisses of this argument are both true, but, thanks to linguistic expression, (only) appear to have something in common. In the jargon of Stoic logic, this argument is invalid because it is incoherent: the premisses have nothing to do with one another . . . But in each case it is a different argument which is being assessed.

This description of what is going on in fallacies of homonymy of the kind the Stoics discussed, including our example in Simplicius, seems to me basically accurate. However, it is what I will call a 'static' analysis of the fallacy, an analysis that looks at the fallacy without considering the factor of time. In order to capture fully what the Stoics think is going on when the fallacy is used in a dialectical context, I believe, a 'dynamic' analysis is more helpful. (I will explicate this presently.) For that, we need to expand the above picture.

In some sense at least, Atherton is clearly correct with her claim that there are two different arguments underlying the sophism.[53] In the sense that from the various propositions entertained at one time or other by one

---

[50] If no distinction is made between premisses and sentences that express premisses; between a level of language at which there is ambiguity, and a level that concerns meaning (whether also linguistic, as Aristotle does, or incorporeal, as the Stoics think), then it becomes difficult to solve the fallacy, i.e. to give a satisfactory explanation of what goes wrong in it. It is possible that the Stoics used this fallacy for more than teaching students to recognise such faulty ways of arguing; they could have used it to show the necessity to distinguish between such levels.

[51] Gellius *Noct. Att.* 11.12.1 (LS 37N); also pointed out by Ebbesen 1981: 1, 31.

[52] Atherton 1993: 414.

[53] Or rather, three, depending on which premiss is taken to be false (see above); but the two arguments with a false premiss would function logically in the same way.

or the other of the interlocutors two such arguments can be constructed. However, in the Simplicius passage, the argument is developed over a period of time, in an interplay between questioner and answerer, and it repays our effort to investigate when and by whom each argument is entertained. Let me explain:

- At time t_1, when the first premiss sentence is proposed and accepted, nothing more than the true proposition THE GARMENT IS FOR MEN is part of the dialectical game. This is the proposition both questioner and answerer appear to intend.
- At time t_2, when the second premiss sentence is proposed and accepted, either only the true proposition WHOEVER IS MANLY IS COURAGEOUS is at issue, and seems intended by both questioner and answerer, or this one together with the proposition proposed at t_1, i.e. the pair of propositions.
- Sometime between t_2 and t_3, when the conclusion THEREFORE THE GARMENT IS COURAGEOUS is drawn and offered up for approval, the word '{manly/for men}' is transferred by the questioner to a different meaning, i.e. the questioner moves from the proposition THE GARMENT IS FOR MEN to the proposition THE GARMENT IS MANLY.[54] As a result, at time t_3 this new proposition is in the game, as only in this way the conclusion can be drawn. And, as the meaning has been transferred, we can assume the old proposition is now no longer entertained by the questioner. As one can only draw a conclusion if one has its premisses present (in some sense), at this point, I assume, the questioner entertains a whole argument, an argument that is valid, but has one false premiss, viz. THE GARMENT IS MANLY.
- What is going on on the side of the respondent between t_2 and t_3 and at t_3? If he is taken in, which is unlikely in the case of so simple a fallacy as ours, he also moves to the other meaning, but without being aware of it. If he is not taken in, we can assume him to resist the move; and in line with the Stoics' advice to point out that '{manly/for men}' is used in two different meanings in the two propositions that make up the premisses. This suggests that the answerer would not follow the questioner in his transference of meaning, but would insist on taking the premisses to be those propositions that have been agreed upon. And in the two propositions that have been agreed upon, the word '{manly/for men}' has different meanings. Thus, for the answerer, the argument assumed to be under discussion is: THE GARMENT IS FOR MEN. BUT

---

[54] Or the questioner does the same with the second premiss, see above.

WHOEVER IS MANLY IS COURAGEOUS. THEREFORE THE GAR-
MENT IS COURAGEOUS. This is an argument with two true premisses
and a false conclusion which is invalid for reasons of disconnectedness or
incoherence (διάρτησις, cf. S.E. *M.* 8.430) of the premisses.

Thus the following picture arises: the questioner, when drawing the conclusion, switches one of the premisses for another which has the same linguistic
form, and entertains a valid argument with one false premiss. At the same
time his hope must be that the respondent does not notice the transference, sticks to his belief that the premisses are both true, as they certainly
were when he agreed to them, and, being befuddled by the appearance of
validity of the fallacy, which it has when the possibility of ambiguity is dis-
regarded, feels he has to agree to the conclusion, and thus has lost the game,
having had to agree to an obvious falsehood. An answerer trained in Stoic
logic, however, will not have been taken in. He knows that linguistically
identical sentences can express different propositions. He will not follow
the questioner in transferring the meaning of one of the premisses halfway
through the argument. He will stick to the propositions he actually agreed
to and will reveal that the argument presented is in fact invalid owing to
disconnectedness of the premisses. Thus the valid but unsound argument
comes in only as a result of the questioner's illicit procedure of transferring meaning within the course of argumentation. The argument that is
in fact part of the game, in the sense that its premisses have in fact been
agreed upon by both parties, has true premisses and a false conclusion and
is invalid.

6 COMPARISON BETWEEN ARISTOTLE'S AND THE STOICS' TREATMENT OF FALLACIES OF HOMONYMY

Aristotle, too, discussed fallacies of equivocation or homonymy, and a comparison between his and the Stoic view is instructive. For Aristotle, truth-
bearers, at least those relevant to sophistic discourse, are linguistic items
(Arist. *Int.* 16a9–11, 16b33–17a3). Thus, declarative sentences, and in particular affirmations and negations, are the entities that are either true or false.
In the context of dialectics, these declarative sentences are the answers to
dialectical questions. For example, if the question is 'Is animal the genus
of human?', the possible answers are the affirmative statement 'Animal is
the genus of human' and the negative statement 'Animal is not the genus
of human'. 'Yes' and 'no' are abbreviations for the affirmative and negative answer respectively.[55] Aristotle also sometimes says that what is said

---

[55] Cf. e.g. Whittaker 1996: 101.

in a dialectical question is 'true' or 'false'.[56] We can assume that what is (in this sense) said in a question could be expressed by the corresponding affirmative statement.

In his *Sophistical Refutations*, in chapter 17, Aristotle has this to say about fallacies of homonymy:

> If nobody ever made two questions into one question, the fallacy based on homonymy and ambiguity would not have come about, but either a refutation or no refutation. For how does asking whether Callias and Themistocles are musical differ from <what one might ask> if both, though being different people, shared a single name? *For if the name signified more than one thing, <the questioner> had asked more than one question.* Now, if it is not right to ask to be given without qualification one answer to two questions, it is clear that it is not proper to answer without qualification any homonymous <questions>. (Arist. *SE* 175b39–176a5, my italics)

Thus, according to Aristotle, if, as in the case of fallacies of homonymy, we have as a premiss or as conclusion a question sentence that contains an ambiguous term, the questioner has asked more than one question: two questions if the term has two significations, three questions if the term has three significations, etc.[57] In Aristotle's *De Interpretatione*, chapter 8, we find a parallel passage, in which the focus is on statements rather than on questions:

> But if one name is given to two things which do not make up one thing, there is not a single affirmation. Suppose, for example, that one gave the name cloak to horse and to human being; then 'a cloak is white' would not be a single affirmation. For to say this is no different from saying a horse and a human being is white, and this is no different from saying a horse is white and a human being is white. *So if these last signify more than one thing and are more than one <affirmation>, clearly the first also signifies either more than one thing* or else nothing (for there is nothing like a horse-human-being). (Arist. *Int.* 18a18–26, my italics)

As C. W. A. Whittaker has shown nicely, in the *De Interpretatione* Aristotle discusses affirmations and negations insofar as they are relevant for dialectics.[58] In the passage quoted, Aristotle discusses cases (which in the *Sophistical Refutations* he would classify as cases) of homonymy as they would occur in dialectics, i.e. in fallacies of homonymy.[59] This time, as throughout in *De Interpretatione*, Aristotle focuses on statements rather than on questions, but his point is basically the same: in dialectics, in the

---

[56] E.g. Arist. *Top.* 160a25.
[57] There can be absolutely no doubt that in this passage Aristotle has homonyms in mind – he mentions them three times – the third time at the end of the section, at 176a15.
[58] Whittaker 1996 *passim.*   [59] See the passage from *SE* just quoted.

case of declarative sentences that contain what he classifies as homonymies in the *Sophistical Refutations* there will be more than one affirmation in the sentence.[60] (This, if the relevant sentence is in the affirmative, otherwise more than one negation.) Thus for Aristotle, in dialectics, (i) someone using a homonymous expression in a question sentence asks two questions, (ii) there are two things said with that question,[61] and (iii) someone using an expression that signifies two things in a declarative sentence makes two statements (two affirmations or two negations).[62]

Returning to our fallacy in Simplicius, in Aristotle's view, the declarative sentence 'the garment is {manly/for men}' would hence be more than one affirmation. The two affirmations can be separated in English as (i) 'the garment is for men' and (ii) 'the garment is manly'. The sentence would signify more than one thing (perhaps manliness and for-men-ness; or a garment that is manly and a garment that is for men).[63] The same holds for questions: the question sentence 'is the garment {manly/for men}?' would be more than one question; they could be separated in English as 'is the garment for men?' and 'is the garment manly?'

Thus, for Aristotle, one declarative sentence is more than one affirmation, one question sentence more than one question. How can this be? Sentences as well as affirmations and questions are linguistic items, but evidently they must be of different kinds, as they are individuated differently. We could say that *by* uttering one question sentence the speaker asks two questions; and *by* uttering one declarative sentence the speaker makes two affirmations or affirms two things. (We can think of the sentences as grammatical items, the affirmations and negations as statements, the questions as questions asked.) So we can expect that whenever the questioner offers

---

[60] Whittaker, following Ackrill, believes that the passage quoted does not cover homonyms. But in the light of (i) the close parallel to the passage quoted from *SE* (175b39–176a5), which explicitly deals with homonyms, and (ii) the fact that *Int.* deals with dialectics, I have no doubts that in *Int.* 8 Aristotle intended to cover what in *SE* he regards to be homonyms as they occur in dialectics. (I argue this point in more detail elsewhere.) For readers who are wedded to Ackrill's view, I mention that for my argument it is sufficient to rely on the passages from *SE* and *Top.*

[61] Cf. also *Top.* 160a23–9, quoted below.

[62] We can imagine a fallacy put in declarative sentences rather than questions for instance when someone tries to solve it by himself, at his leisure, without being subjected to questions. Aristotle mentions this possibility e.g. at *SE* 175a20–2.

[63] Unlike Shields 1999: 80–1, n. 8, I take it that in *Int.* 8 Aristotle uses the verb 'to signify' (18a24, 25) as follows: that which signifies are affirmations (αὗται allows only κατάφασις as antecedent), and that which is signified by the affirmations are the things referred to by the subject expression in the affirmation – a horse and a human being, or perhaps a white horse and a white human being. The sentence 'a cloak is white' is then said to either both signify horse and signify human being or to signify a horse-human-being, which is nothing; and in the first case the sentence contains two affirmations, in the second no affirmation.

up for consent the premiss-questions of a fallacy of homonymy which have the same ambiguous expression in either premiss, each time he asks two questions; and if he stated the argument in non-question form, he would each time make two affirmations.

Aristotle discusses ways of responding to fallacies of homonymy in his *Sophistical Refutations*, chapters 17 and 19. In chapter 19 he begins with some general remarks about such fallacies:

(1) Now, of the refutations that depend upon homonymy and ambiguity some have one of the premiss-questions with more than one signified thing . . . e.g. . . . in the <argument> that the one who knows does not understand <what he knows> one of the premiss-questions is ambiguous. (2) And that which is said/meant in two ways is in one case <true> and in the other isn't; and that which is said/meant in two ways signifies something that is and something that is not . . . (Arist. *SE* 177a9–15)

I take it from (1) that for Aristotle a premiss-question is ambiguous if it is or contains an expression that signifies more than one thing. In (2), Aristotle seems to pick up on what he said at *SE* 175b39–176a18 (quoted above), i.e. that the questioner asks two questions in one, and that the ambiguous expression has two 'signified things' at the same time.[64] If we apply Aristotle's point to the Simplicius fallacy, the piece of speech 'the garment is {manly/for men}' would be said in two ways, even though one way is rather non-sensical. It would be true in one case ('the garment is for men'), but not true in the other ('the garment is manly'). It would signify something that is (perhaps a garment that is for men) and something that is not (perhaps a garment that is manly).[65]

Here are then some passages from chapters 17 and 19 of the *Sophistical Refutations* and from *Topics* 8.7, in which Aristotle gives advice on how to deal with fallacies of homonymy. They also further corroborate the point

---

[64] The first clause of (2) makes sense only if we assume that with the phrase 'is in one case <true> and in the other isn't' (ὁτὲ μὲν . . . ὁτὲ δ'. . .) Aristotle intends the two ways in which the thing is said, more precisely, these two ways as they are both signified *when* the premiss-question is uttered. For only then is it reasonable to say that one is (true), the other isn't. If Aristotle had meant to use ὁτὲ μὲν . . . ὁτὲ δ'. . . temporally, to be translated as 'at one time . . . at another time . . .' or similarly, then we would have expected him to say that both are <true>: i.e. at one time, in one context, one of the two things said in the question sentence is (true), at another time, in another context, the other is (true); that is, that Aristotle would have alerted us to the fact that ambiguous expressions have different meanings in different contexts. But Aristotle does not say that. Thus ὁτὲ μὲν . . . ὁτὲ δ'. . . must here be used non-temporally to pick out the two things said by the two questions; only then does what Aristotle says make sense, fit the context, and is true. (Aristotle makes a similar point at *Top.* 160a26, using ἐπὶ τὶ μὲν . . . ἐπὶ τὶ δ'. . . ; cf. also Arist. *SE* 177a21–2; both passages are quoted below.)

[65] Or alternatively, maybe, the garment's being for men and the garment's being manly?

that he believes that the questioner asks two questions at the same time, and that with the question sentence two things are said at the same time:

... since if someone does not distinguish the <different meanings in the> ambiguity, it is unclear whether he has been refuted or has not been refuted, and since, in the context of arguments, it is granted that he may draw distinctions, it is evident that if he grants the question without drawing distinctions and without qualification, this is a mistake. (Arist. *SE* 175b28–31)

Now, if it is not right to ask to be given without qualification one answer to two questions, it is clear that it is not proper to answer without qualification any homonymous <questions>. (Arist. *SE* 176a3–5)

Now, if one should not give a single answer to two questions, it is evident that in the case of homonyms one should not say 'yes' or 'no' either; for the one who says <that> has not given an answer, he just spoke. (Arist. *SE* 176a14–16)

[*continuing the quotation from chapter 19 above*] ... (3) Whenever <that which is said in several ways> lies in the premiss-questions, it is not necessary to begin by denying that which is said/meant in two ways; for argument is not for the sake of this, but through this. (4) At the beginning one should reply concerning that which is said in two ways, whether it is a word or a phrase, in this way, that in one sense it is so, and in another not so, (5) for example that speaking of the silent is possible in one sense but not in another; and that in one sense one should do what must be done, but not in another; for what must be done is said/meant in several ways. (Arist. *SE* 177a18–24)

If <the answerer> understands the question, but it is said in several ways,[66] then ... if what is said/meant *is in one case false and in the other true*, he should indicate that it is said in several ways, and that in one it is false, in the other true. For if he makes the distinction only later, it is unclear whether he saw the ambiguity at the beginning. (Arist. *Top.* 160a23–9, my emphasis)

These quotes taken together give us some idea about Aristotle's view of how one should respond to fallacies based on homonymy. At least one of the question sentences (premiss-questions and conclusions-question) contains an ambiguous expression, and is hence two questions. Answering those two questions with one word ('yes'/'no') or one statement (the affirmative/ negative corresponding to the question) without any qualification and without drawing any distinctions is a mistake (*SE* 175b28–31), is not proper (*SE* 176a3–5), is no answer at all (*SE* 176a14–16), leaves it unclear whether the answerer noticed the ambiguity (*Top.* 160a23–9), and leaves it indeterminate which of the two questions the answerer intends to answer. Aristotle reports that according to the rules of dialectics, in addition to saying 'yes' and 'no',

[66] I.e. has several meanings or significations.

the answerer is allowed to point out ambiguities or to ask for clarification (*Top.* ch. 8.7 and *SE* 175b30). Hence the answerer should disambiguate, i.e. should (i) distinguish the two things said in the two questions, and (ii) state which one is true, and which one is false. It is implied, I presume, that (iii) the answerer accepts the true statement and does not accept the false one (cf. e.g. *Top.* 160a24–8).[67]

Aristotle seems to advise the respondent to expose the ambiguity of a term or phrase immediately when the premiss containing it is 'asked' (see sentence (4) and *Top.* 160a23–9).[68] We can understand this as a preemptive move. The answerer explicitly disambiguates the expression, i.e. points out the two – or more – things signified by the question, *including those that would be unusual readings of the sentence and false.*[69] (Naturally, this presupposes a mental process of disambiguation.) Aristotle assumes that *in the premiss question asked* the ambiguous expression has both meanings, even if the respondent intends only one meaning, and even if one meaning makes the premiss false or absurd. For this reason, Aristotle wishes the ambiguity to be made *explicit* as soon as it occurs. As a result, when the questioner attempts to draw the conclusion, the answerer can fall back on the disambiguation he proffered earlier and refuse to accept the conclusion e.g. by accusing the questioner of a Fallacy of Homonymy or perhaps of a Fallacy of Many Questions.[70]

---

[67] Can the facts (i) that at *SE* 166a4–5 Aristotle uses ὁτὲ μέν . . . ὁτὲ δ' . . . to explain double meaning, and (ii) that at *SE* 166a20–1 he uses ἢ . . . ἢ . . . when saying that an expression signifies two things, be used to rebut my claim that for Aristotle in dialectical contexts question sentences and declarative sentences containing ambiguous expressions have two significations at the same time? I believe not. In note 64 I have shown that Aristotle uses ὁτὲ μέν . . . ὁτὲ δ' . . . non-temporally for double meaning. At 166a4–5 he may do just the same. And as in English the two sentences ' "bank" means both "verge of river" and "financial institution" ' and ' "bank" means either "verge of river" or "financial institution" ' do not usually allow any inference as to whether the speaker assumes that the word has both meanings at the same time, so for Greek sentences with ἢ . . . ἢ . . . (Cf. also in the *same* passage on ambiguity the use of καί . . . καί . . . at 166a8 and of καί at 166a14 in sentences stating double meaning.) Alternatively, one has to assume that what Aristotle says about homonymy in chapter 4 of *SE* does not tally with what he says in chapters 17 and 19.

[68] If the answerer didn't spot the ambiguity immediately, all is not lost. He can still disambiguate at the end. Cf. 'However, if <that which is said in two ways> escapes one, one must correct it at the end adding something to the question: "Is speaking of the silent possible?" "No, but it is possible to speak of this person who is being silent".' (Arist. *SE* 177a24–6) and 'But if he doesn't foresee the ambiguity, but concedes the question having in view the one signification of the words, then, if the questioner takes it with the other signification, he should say: "that was not what I had in view when I conceded it, but rather the other signification"' (Arist. *Top.* 160a.29–32).

[69] Cf. e.g. Arist. *SE* 166a12–14: 'speaking of the silent' has as one of its meanings that the one who is speaking is silent; and 166a18–21: 'knowing letters' has as one of its meanings that the letters have knowledge.

[70] In *SE* chapter 17 Aristotle classifies the fallacy of homonymy as a kind of the fallacy of double question; in chapter 19 he discusses fallacies of homonymy and amphiboly on their own.

If we compare Aristotle and the Stoics, we see that they differ both in their philosophico-linguistic analysis of fallacies of homonymy and – consequently – in the strategies they recommend how to tackle them. Aristotle assumes that in the fallacy the question sentences that contain the homonymous expression, when uttered, have two significations, say two things, and have two statements corresponding to them. Usually, but not necessarily, one will be true, the other false. The two significations appear to be independent of speaker intention: for Aristotle considers the case that one can try to solve a fallacy at one's leisure without anybody actually asking the questions (*SE* 177a6–8), and thus without any questioner having any intentions. The Stoics, on the other hand, assume that the premiss questions of the fallacy, when uttered, have only one signification: the one which rational speakers and listeners in ordinary circumstances would assume them to have, i.e. usually the meaning that makes them true.

Concerning strategy, in line with his assumption of a double question, Aristotle recommends that the respondent expressly disambiguate the question sentence as soon as it is asked, and to state which question says something true, which not, and presumably which one he accepts. This presupposes a process of mental disambiguation on the side of the respondent. The Stoics, by contrast, do not require an explicit disambiguation, since they assume that at the time of utterance there is in fact nothing to disambiguate. Accordingly, no process of mental disambiguation is required either. The exception would be special situations such as those in which one is trying to list ambiguous sentences, or intends to 'play on' the ambiguity (but not to deceive). For the Stoics, fallacies do not provide such special situations.

7 THE QUESTION OF BEING SILENT (ἡσυχάζειν)

We now have a viable interpretation of what the Stoics of the Simplicius passage considered the nature of the fallacy to be, what philosophical and linguistic assumptions underlie their understanding of the fallacy, and how they recommended the answerer to escape being caught in it. What remains is to give an interpretation of what those Stoics mean when they say the answerer should fall silent or keep quiet (ἡσυχάζειν).

In her masterful book *The Stoics on Ambiguity*, Catherine Atherton has suggested the following interpretation: She translates: '(1') And that is why, in syllogisms due to homonymy, the dialecticians recommend keeping quiet [ἡσυχάζειν], (2') so long as the questioner transfers the word to another signification.'[71] She comments: 'the transfer to another meaning must occur when the second premiss is posed, not at the conclusion, whereas we "keep quiet" (see the main text) until then, that is, so long as the questioner continues to change his meaning. This is not possible reading "μεταγάγῃ" at 24.14 (i.e., with an aorist subjunctive). I thus read "μετάγῃ" with two of the MSS.'[72]

After having mentioned the Sorites, Atherton writes further: 'According to Simplicius, respondents are explicitly told to assent to the premisses *The tunic is male attire* and *The brave is courageous*. What he failed to note is that they will not make their assent public, and that they will make no contribution to the proceedings, either openly agreeing or openly objecting, until the fraudulent attempt to draw a conclusion. "Keeping quiet" covers, and must cover, silent assent even in the case of the Soritic arguments, since it would be absurd and wrong to withhold assent from the obvious truths leading up to the unclear premisses. As with Soritic arguments, a further assumption is at work: that questioning by the interlocutor will continue until an explicit response, positive or negative, is won.'[73] This view leads her to the following assessment of S.E. *P.H.* 2.253: 'Sextus' interpretation of "falling silent" as Skeptical ἐποχή, *P.H.* II.253, is malicious and polemical.'[74]

There are some drawbacks to this interpretation:

(i) The occurrence of conceding (συγχωρεῖν) in either premiss has to be understood as *silent* assent (συγκατάθεσις).[75] This seems to me a very unlikely meaning. The term 'to concede' is standardly used for the public action of admitting a premiss or sentence as true, and I believe this is what it means in our passage, too.[76]

(ii) The transfer of the ambiguous word to another meaning is taken to occur when the second premiss is posed. This, too, strikes me as unlikely. First, in this way what Simplicius says seems not to be very relevant to the rest of the passage. He could just as well have said: 'the dialecticians recommend keeping quiet until the conclusion has been drawn'. Moreover, in Atherton's view, the transference is completed after the second premiss has been asked; but, according to her, the silence is only to be broken after the conclusion has been asked.

---

[71] Atherton 1993: 419–20. [72] Atherton 1993: 420, n. 14. [73] Atherton 1993: 422.
[74] Atherton 1993: 422 n. 19. [75] Atherton 1993: 422.
[76] See e.g. S.E. *P.H.* 2.232; *M.* 8.303; Alex. *Apr* 17.3, 17.23 (of conclusion); 18.26–7 in a dialectical syllogism, i.e. within dialectical discourse.

(iii) The assumption is that the questioning by the interlocutor continues
even when the respondent remains silent.[77] There is no evidence that
this is how the dialectical discourse went; it seems much more likely
that as soon as the respondent refuses to respond 'yes' or 'no' and
chooses to keep silent, the 'game' (as conducted on the object level) is
over.[78]

(iv) Simplicius has to be interpreted as having left out some essential information (i.e. that keeping quiet covers the case of someone withholding
public assent but giving silent assent). Every interpretation that has to
state that the author of the passage left out something or got something
wrong is weak in that respect, if there are alternative interpretations that
do not require this, so that without that requirement the text makes
sense and has an equally or more natural reading of the expressions
used.

(v) Similarly, an interpretation that does not have to disregard a passage
as polemical or malicious is preferable to one that does, if there are no
specific requirements to assume that polemics or malice are at work.
The cases I have in mind are those where the only reasons for claiming
that an author is distorting Stoic doctrine where he *reports* it (besides
the fact that he is a polemical author) is that it vindicates a particular
modern interpretation of a bit of Stoic theory, and where there are
viable alternative interpretations available for that bit of theory that
do not require such a claim of distortion. This is, in my view, the case
for Sextus' use of 'to stop and hold back' (ἵστασθαι καὶ ἐπέχειν) in
the context of the Sorites at *P.H.* 2.253.[79]

---

[77] Long and Sedley's translation of and comments on the Simplicius passage imply the same assumption
(Long and Sedley 1987: 1, 228–9; 11, 232).

[78] Carneades' response to the Stoic strategy for Sorites arguments at Cic. *Acad.Pr.* 93 is a case in point
that the questioning did not just continue. He suggests that when the Stoic falls silent at the question
'are n many' someone may come and ask 'and when I add one to the number at which you fell silent,
is the result then many?' Hence the assumption is not that the questioning simply continues; rather,
Carneades' fictitious questioner switches to a different type of question. The Stoic would of course
simply be silent again, and therewith this type of questioning would have come to an end, too. In
the case of Sorites series asked with conditionals or negated conjunctions (as in D.L. 7.82) there is
another reason why in the Sorites the questioning would not have continued: even if only one of
the complex premisses has not been assented to, no conclusion can be drawn.

[79] I am in no way denying that Sextus is frequently polemical and malicious in his *interpretation* or
explication of Stoic doctrine. At the same time he is often a very reliable source where he *reports* or
presents Stoic theory – he is one of our best sources for Stoic logic. Wilful misinterpretation is then
one thing, wilful misreporting another. In *P.H.* 2.253, in the sceptical context in which the report
of Chrysippus' view is embedded, Sextus uses 'to hold back' (ἐπέχειν) twice; each time the context
requires that by holding back is intended not answering 'yes' or 'no' to a dialectical question. Nothing
is implied about internal suspension of belief, although I believe it likely that explicit and internal
holding back were taken to go hand in hand. Thus the most natural reading of 'holding back' in

Atherton accepts these drawbacks in her interpretation,[80] because she believes that her interpretation is required in order to overcome the following interpretational difficulties:

(1) There is first her assumption 'That in the Sorites "keeping quiet" covers and must cover, silent assent since it would be absurd and wrong to withhold assent from the obvious truths leading up to the unclear premisses.' This difficulty can be solved however. As I have shown elsewhere,[81] in the Sorites 'keeping quiet' can (and should) be interpreted as openly and publicly ceasing to respond to the questioner's question, with the additional assumption that the answerer does not silently assent either, but is also inwardly quiet. This allows us to interpret Sextus at *P.H.* 2.253 as not being malicious, but using 'to stop and hold back' (ἵστασθαι καὶ ἐπέχειν) for falling silent outwardly and simultaneously withholding assent inwardly.[82]

(2) Second, there is Atherton's assumption that, if the Sorites required silent assent, this silent assent was taken to be the required response in all cases in which being silent (ἡσυχάζειν) was recommended. But for example in Gellius (*Noct. Att.* 16.2) we find cases of fallacious questions in which falling silent is recommended but internal assent as response is clearly neither required nor desired.

(1) They say that in the art of dialectics there is the following rule: if there is an inquiry and discussion about some thing, and in that context you are asked to answer a question, then you should say nothing more than solely this which is asked, either affirming it or denying it. And those who do not follow this rule and answer either more or something different from what they were asked are regarded as being uneducated and as not observing the customary practice and principle of <dialectical> discourse. (2) In fact, what they say without doubt ought to happen in most debates. . . . (4) But there seem to be some cases in which you are caught <in a fallacy>, if you answer what you have been asked briefly and to the point. . . . [*there follow examples of fallacies in which one would have to say more than 'yes' or 'no' if one wanted not to be caught in them*] . . . (12) But such an answer <in which more is said than was asked> is not given in accordance with the above-mentioned rule; for more than what has been asked is answered. (13) For this reason the following

the clause that purports to report Chrysippus is that by it, too, is intended not answering 'yes' or 'no' to a dialectical question. For this clause is used to justify the sceptics' not answering dialectical questions. Internal suspension of belief is secondary for the entire passage *P.H.* 2.253. Thus there is no need for Sextus to misreport Chrysippus' view here. Note also that Plutarch, at *Adv. Colotem* 1124A, appears to use holding back (ἐπέχειν) and falling silent (ἡσυχάζειν) to describe the same strategy.

[80] I don't wish to imply that Catherine Atherton considered all of (i)–(v) as drawbacks.
[81] Bobzien 2002: sections 4–6.
[82] It would also bring Sextus in line with Plutarch *Adv. Colotem* 1124A.

addition is usually also made to that rule, that one need not answer fallacious questions.[83] (Gell. *Noct. Att.* 16.2)[84]

The fact that silent assent would be the wrong reaction in the cases of the Gellius passage seems to me to confirm that it was never part of the strategy of falling silent.

(3) Third, there is Atherton's assumption that in the Simplicius passage 'being silent' is used in the same semi-technical way as in the passages we have about the Sorites (and in my view in Gellius).[85] This assumption is reasonable, but not certain, as ἡσυχάζειν is a very common word that is used in Greek in ordinary discourse without any technical overtones.

I will now present two interpretations of the Simplicius passage that do not share the drawbacks Atherton accepts in her interpretation, but at the same time also do not raise the problems she assumes other interpretations will automatically face. Both interpretations assume that the transfer of the word to a different meaning happens when the questioner draws the conclusion (see above section 5).

In the *first interpretation* ἕως is taken to mean 'until'. ἡσυχάζειν is understood as 'keeping quiet' in the sense that when the premisses are asked, the respondent openly accepts them, taking them to be true as the text indicates, and keeps quiet *about the ambiguity of the term* ἀνδρεῖος in them, and the difficulties this could lead to. The emphasis on ἡσυχάζειν can here be understood as meant to alert one to the contrast with Aristotle, who, as we have seen, asks the answerer to point out any ambiguities immediately when the premisses are asked.[86] It could have been either the Stoics themselves, or Simplicius, who used the phrasing 'to be silent' to delimit the Stoic position from Aristotle's.

[83] (1) *Legem esse aiunt disciplinae dialecticae, si de quapiam re quaeratur disputeturque atque ibi quid rogere, ut respondeas, tum ne amplius quid dicas, quam id solum, quod es rogatus, aut aias aut neges; eamque legem qui non servent et aut plus aut aliter, quam sunt rogati respondeant, existumantur indoctique esse disputandique morem atque rationem non tenere.* (2) *Hoc quidem, quod dicunt, in plerisque disputationibus procul dubio fieri oportet . . .* (4) *Sed enim esse quaedam videntur, in quibus, si breviter et ad id, quod rogatus fueris, respondeas, capiare . . .* (12) *Sed huiuscemodi respondisio non fit ea lege, quam diximus; plus enim, quam quod rogatus est, respondet.* (13) *Et propterea id quoque ad eam legem addi solet non esse captiosis interrogationibus respondendum.*
[84] The respondent is meant to fall silent when confronted with the Horn Fallacy: 'If you haven't lost something, you have it. But you haven't lost horns. Therefore you have horns.' I discuss the details of this case in another paper.
[85] The meaning of ἡσυχάζειν is not technical in the passages on the Sorites, it just means what it usually means: being silent. The use as a – third – legitimate response in dialectical discourse could perhaps be regarded as technical.
[86] This interpretation, I believe, squares with the reading of the text given by Ebbesen 1981: 1, 31–2; however, Ebbesen does not note that the reason why Simplicius' Stoics (or Simplicius), put the advice the way they do may have been that they wished to distinguish their (the Stoic) position from Aristotle's.

A translation-cum-explication of the passage would then go like this:

In the case of syllogisms based on a homonymy the logicians advise us to be silent <with respect to pointing out the possibility of fallaciousness> until the questioner transfers the <ambiguous> word to another meaning; e.g. if someone asked whether the garment is {manly/for men}, if it happens to be for men, we will concede this. <And we are silent about the fact that '{manly/for men}' is ambiguous, and can also mean *manly*.> And if he asks whether that which is {manly/for men} is courageous, we will concede this, too, for it is true. <Again, we are silent about the fact that '{manly/for men}' is ambiguous, and can also mean *for men*.> But when he infers that the garment is therefore courageous, <they advise us> <to cease to be silent about the ambiguity and> to separate the homonymy of the word '{manly/for men}' and show that it is said/intended in one way in the case of the garment, in another in the case of the one who has manliness.

In this interpretation ἡσυχάζειν is regarded as being used in an entirely non-technical way. It does not mean what it means in the case of the Sorites (and in the above cited passages in Sextus, Plutarch and Gellius), i.e. not answering the questioner, and thus ending the game on the object level, in order to climb onto a meta-level to explain the fallacy. Rather it is intended to mean keeping quiet with respect to the homonymy, in contrast with Aristotle's advice to mention ambiguities as soon as they occur. ἡσυχάζειν is a common enough Greek word for this to be possible;[87] and there are many cases in which the Stoics use one and the same word sometimes in a technical or semi-technical way, sometimes in its ordinary, common usage.[88]

My *second interpretation* takes ἡσυχάζειν to mean literally 'be silent' and to refer to the respondent's not answering the questioner when he asks approval for the conclusion, and thus at that point stepping out of the game.[89] The contrast is not with Aristotle, but with playing the dialectical yes/no game, as it is exemplified in the Gellius passage quoted above. The strategy is the same that Gellius describes as one to be used in the case of fallacious questions. Thus ἡσυχάζειν is used in the same way it is used in the Gellius, Sextus and Plutarch passages mentioned.[90] In order to make

---

[87] The Stoics use ἡσυχάζειν in a different way than for the Sorites strategy for instance also at *SVF* 2.500 (Simpl. *Cat*).

[88] Examples are e.g. πρᾶγμα, λόγος, δυνατόν, δύνασθαι, ἀνάγκη, ἀναγκαῖος, ἀρχή, τέλος, αὐτοτελής, φύσις, λέγειν, μάχεσθαι, μάχη, πρᾶξις, τρόπος, ἀόριστος, δείκνυμι.

[89] As I said above, I do not think the dialectical game continued once the respondent fell silent instead of answering 'yes' or 'no' to a question.

[90] If ἡσυχάζειν was to be understood in this way, it is clear that the being silent was meant to happen at the point of the conclusion. For in the Stoic view the premises asked are not fallacious, but true; cf. section 4.

sense of the passage, one has to read μετάγη instead of μεταγάγη, and ἕως needs to be translated as 'while'.[91]

In this case, a translation-cum-explication of the passage would rather be as follows:

In the case of syllogisms based on a homonymy the logicians advise us to be silent <i.e. not answer the questioner any more> while the questioner transfers the word onto another meaning; e.g. if someone asks whether the garment is {manly/for men}, if it happens to be manly, we will concede this <and thus not be silent>. And if he asks whether that which is {manly/for men} is courageous, we will concede this, too, for it is true <and again will thus not be silent>. But if he infers that the garment is therefore courageous, <they advise us> <to be silent, i.e. not answer anymore, and instead expressly> to separate the homonymy of the word '{manly/for men}' and show that it is said/intended in one way in the case of the garment, in another in the case of the one who has manliness.

Can we decide between these two interpretations? I believe not. The first may be seen as having the disadvantage of requiring ἡσυχάζειν to be used in a different way than in the Sorites. But then it is entirely plausible that the Stoics used it in that way in our particular context.[92] Moreover, it provides a good contrast to Aristotle. So, someone who favours this interpretation may be more inclined to think that Simplicius presents the view of some later Stoics, Stoics who are acquainted with Aristotle's logic (like those mentioned in Simplicius' *Categories* who discussed Aristotle's sea-battle example).[93] The second interpretation will make us more inclined to consider this passage as in line with early Stoic or Chrysippean logic, as it works in parallel with what we know about the Stoic treatment of the Sorites. It has the advantage of uniformity of use of ἡσυχάζειν; and it would confirm that the Stoics followed one method in dealing with fallacies which have in common that answering 'yes' or 'no' would get the respondent into trouble.

What are the difficulties the respondent would get into in the case of the fallacy of homonymy? Well, having simply agreed to the premises when they were propounded, if the answerer responded with 'yes' when the conclusion is asked, he would concede something clearly false and thus would have lost the game. On the other hand, if the respondent were to reply 'no' when the conclusion is asked, the questioner would probably

---

[91] Alternatively, for this interpretation, one might want to emend ἕως to ὡς, to be rendered as 'when' or 'as soon as'. Hülser's translation of ἕως as 'in dem Moment . . . in dem' (Hülser 1987–8: IV, frg. 1257) fits this emendation to ὡς.

[92] Or, of course, it may have been Simplicius who used that particular word for describing the Stoic method.

[93] Simpl. *Cat.* 406.34–407.5.

point out to him that the argument is valid (see section 2 above) and that, having conceded the premisses, the answerer is hence forced to concede the conclusion.[94] At this point the respondent would need to be able to say: 'yes, the conclusion follows, *if* you assume that the meaning of "{manly/for men}" was the same in both premisses, but in fact this is *not* what we agreed upon earlier'. By responding neither 'yes' nor 'no', but being silent, and then separating the homonymy expressly, the respondent does not agree to an obvious falsehood and provides reasons that will prevent the questioner from scoring points by adducing the – apparent – validity of the argument at this point.

As I cannot give decisive reasons for choosing one interpretation over the other, I leave you with both, for you to select one at your convenience.

8 THE SCOPE OF THE STOIC METHOD FOR FALLACIES OF HOMONYMY

Aristotle gives two-fold advice to the respondents as to how to proceed in cases of fallacies of homonymy. If they are aware of an ambiguity in a premiss, they are meant to lay it bare as soon as the premiss has been asked. However, in case the ambiguity escapes them and only occurs to them when the conclusion is drawn, they are meant to uncover the ambiguity then.

The Stoic advice is not two-fold; it does not need to be. Their method works with all fallacies of homonymy in single words, as can be shown. First we can state a general requirement for fallacies of homonymy in single words: for such a fallacy to work, it is necessary that in each premiss there is only one reading of the relevant ambiguous word that makes the premiss true, and in at least one premiss the meaning must be different than in the other or others. This can be shown by elimination of all the other possible cases.

If in one of the two sentences proposed as expressing a premiss both meanings of the word led to true propositions,[95] then no fallacy would ensue. Take an argument with the Greek ambiguous word κύων, i.e. '{dog/seadog}' in my nomenclature:

If something is a {dog/seadog}, it is an animal.
This is a {dog/seadog} (pointing at the German shepherd Fido).
Therefore this is an animal (again pointing at the German shepherd Fido).

---

94 This could again be done in the form of questions.
95 If we imagine fallacies with more than two premisses, we have to say 'in all but one premiss'.

Here the first sentence expresses a true premiss with either reading of {dog/seadog}.[96] The respondent hence cannot go wrong by agreeing, even though it is not quite clear what he would be agreeing to, if he says just 'yes'.[97] More importantly, he would go wrong if he said 'no'. The conclusion of the 'argument' is true, harmless, unobjectionable; hence we should not assume the respondent to want to deny it. Can we imagine the respondent (following the Stoic method) to balk at the drawing of the conclusion and to say 'no, the conclusion does not follow – the premisses are unconnected'? If we generalise the Stoic approach slightly, then the answer is 'no'. (Of course there is no evidence that the Stoics considered arguments like the one under discussion.) All we have to do is to take as context of {dog/seadog} not just each premiss individually, but the two premisses together. Thus by agreeing to the first question, the interlocutor knows he has not made a mistake, whichever way he might take it. At the point when the second premiss is introduced, the context would almost automatically be regarded to be the two premisses taken together, and at that point a mental process of disambiguating in favour of 'dog' takes place, as this is the only reading that is promising for a proper (valid and sound) argument.[98] Thus the assumption here is no longer only that obvious truth serves as guidance, but also that obvious connectedness of the premisses serves equally as a guide. (We can again imagine some sort of theory of implicature at work here; e.g. something like: 'if you are asked questions, base your answer on the assumption that the argument is valid'.) If this is so, the answerer cannot reasonably deny the conclusion.

What if the two possible readings are true in both sentences that purport to express a premiss?[99]

If {dogs/seadogs} are animals, then {dogs/seadogs} are living beings.
But {dogs/seadogs} are animals.
Therefore {dogs/seadogs} are living beings.

Here we have no context that allows disambiguation, but again the sentence that expresses what is concluded is harmless, and there is no reason for the interlocutor to hold back consent at any time.[100]

---

[96] κύων has actually a third and a fourth meaning in Greek, the dogstar (*if* that is a separate meaning), and the fetlock-joint of a horse, both of which I will ignore here for reasons of simplification of the examples.

[97] How many questions would the Stoics think the questioner asks? To how many questions would they think the answerer responds? Would this depend on the intention of speaker or listener? Would they say this is so in the case of utterances, tokens of (what looks like) a question? What if intention of speaker and listener differ? A host of problems opens up here, not surprisingly.

[98] A further question suggests itself here: can one *temporarily* leave open which meaning is intended?

[99] Or all, if we consider fallacies with more than two premisses.

[100] All the questions of note 78 recur here and remain unanswered.

What, finally, if there are no readings which make all premisses true?

If something is a {dog/seadog}, then it is a plant.
This is a {dog/seadog} (pointing at Fido or at some seadog).
Therefore, this is a plant (again pointing at Fido or at some seadog).

In this case the answerer is not going to agree to the sentence purported to express the first premiss (no matter what reading). Hence the complex of sentences purported to express an 'argument', whether fallacious or not, does not get off the ground to start with.

Thus the above-mentioned requirement holds: a fallacy of homonymy proper presupposes that in either premiss sentence there is exactly one reading of the ambiguous word that makes the sentence express a true proposition; and that these are two different readings.[101] And as this kind of fallacy is covered by the Stoic method or advice, it follows, that the Stoic method or advice that Simplicius reports works in all cases.[102]

---

[101] The same holds *mutatis mutandis* for multiple premiss 'arguments'.
[102] I wish to thank Myles Burnyeat and Catherine Atherton for most helpful comments on a draft of the paper and the editors for their patience and generosity.

CHAPTER 9

What is a disjunction?

Jonathan Barnes

Stoic logicians attended to words rather than to things: so claimed Galen, a dozen times or more; and so claimed Alexander of Aphrodisias. Galen and Alexander meant the claim as an accusation and a criticism: it was because they thought not of things but of words, that the Stoics made fundamental errors in their logic.

Nineteenth-century historians of logic echoed the ancient claim, and they too thought that Stoic logic was ruined by its passion for words. Twentieth-century historians of logic also echoed the ancient claim. But for them it was not a criticism. On the contrary, it was a sign that the Stoic logicians were 'formalists' – and it is good thing for a logician to be a formalist.

But whether it is bad or good to attend to words rather than to things can scarcely be decided until we know what it means to attend to words rather than to things. In the following pages I shall discuss one or two aspects of the ancient claim and one or two of the texts pertinent to it. The texts concern complex propositions – conditionals, conjunctions, disjunctions. Such items form the foundations of Stoic logic. According to Galen and Alexander, the Stoics made fundamental errors about these fundamental items: they did so because they attended to words rather than to things, because their misdirected gaze encouraged them to misclassify compound propositions.

A contemporary logician, asked to explain what – say – a disjunction is, might begin his answer by invoking an artificial language; and he might end by saying something like this: a sentence expresses a disjunction if and only if it is synonymous with an expression of the form 'P v Q'. Such a logician might be said to 'pay attention to words' in classifying compound propositions. But that fashion of attending to words was not Stoic – if only because neither they nor any other ancient logician ever considered inventing an artifical language for the use of logic.

Another contemporary logician, asked to explain what a disjunction is, might appeal to canonical expressions rather than to artificial languages. Taking, for example, 'Entweder P oder Q' as the canonical form of a disjunctive sentence, specifying the sense of the connector 'Entweder . . . oder . . .', and indicating what expressions may replace 'P' and 'Q', he will suggest that a sentence expresses a disjunction if and only if it is synonymous with such a canonically disjunctive sentence. Such a logician might also be said to 'attend to words'. Perhaps the Stoics attended to words in that way?

In his account of Stoic logic, Diogenes Laertius gives an illustrated list of compound statables or ἀξιώματα. Of disjunctions he says this:

A disjoined statable is one which is disjoined by the disjunctive connector 'ἤτοι'; for example,
ἤτοι ἡμέρα ἐστὶν ἢ νύξ ἐστιν.
This connector announces that one of the statables is false. (7.72)[1]

The account certainly 'attends to words' inasmuch as it explains or defines disjunctions in terms of a connector – or, almost, in terms of a canonical expression: 'ἤτοι X ἢ Y'.

And the account appears to have some weak points. For example, it explains disjunctions by means of a connector which is – or was taken to be – ambiguous. Again, it suggests that a disjunctive statable contains exactly two disjuncts; but the Greek connector is polyadic, capable of linking an indefinite number of disjuncts. Again – and more evidently – the connector 'ἤτοι' is a Greek particle, so that the account implies that all disjunctions are Greek, or expressed in Greek. (Moreover, Greek itself has other connectors – most obviously, the simple 'ἢ' – which appear to be capable of producing disjunctions.) Again, Stoic statables are not linguistic entities but items expressed by such entities: they are a sort of λεκτόν, not a sort of λέξις. How can a connector, which is a linguistic entity, disjoin, or otherwise attach itself to, items which are not themselves linguistic? And again, why refer specifically to disjunctive statables? There are other types of complete λεκτά – questions, for example, or commands – which can be compounded. But Diogenes' account leaves no room for them.

Diogenes is offering his readers a summary based on an epitome. His account of disjunction – like his accounts of most other things – is best construed as what the ancients called an ὑπογραφή, as a sketch or delineation

[1] διεζευγμένον δέ ἐστιν ὁ ὑπὸ τοῦ ἤτοι διαζευκτικοῦ συνδέσμου διέζευκται, οἷον ἤτοι ἡμέρα ἐστὶν ἢ νύξ ἐστιν. ἐπαγγέλλεται δ' ὁ σύνδεσμος οὗτος τὸ ἕτερον τῶν ἀξιωμάτων ψεῦδος εἶναι.

rather than as a formal definition. Then what did the Stoics say when they were asked to go beyond an introductory sketch of the matter?

They might have started from the last clause of Diogenes' description, a clause which I have thus far neglected: 'This connector announces that one of the statables is false.' Something similar, and less cryptic, may be found in the following passages, the first from Sextus and the second from Apollonius Dyscolus:

A sound disjoined item announces that one of the items in it is sound and the other or others false (together with conflict). (*P.H.* 2.191)[2]

That . . . it is disjoined by what is indicated by the connector will become clear from 'Either it is day or it is night.' For only one of the objects thought of can be accepted at any one time: the announcement of disjunctives announces the holding of one and the removal of the remaining one or ones. (*Conj.* 216.11–16)[3]

There are significant differences between the two passages; and in truth, neither Sextus nor Apollonius says that he is rehearsing a Stoic thesis – the Sextan passage is part of an argument addressed generally to 'the dogmatists' (2.185), and Apollonius is explaining, *in propria persona*, how it is that a connecting particle may disjoin the items it allies. Nonetheless, the passages have an important thesis in common, namely the thesis that 'a disjunction is true provided that exactly one of its disjuncts is true'.[4] And it is reasonable to take this thesis to be Stoic – even if it was not peculiarly Stoic.

The thesis implicitly addresses some of the criticisms which Diogenes' sketch of disjunction aroused. Thus there is no invocation of an ambiguous connector – indeed, Sextus' version invokes no connector at all. Nor is there any restrictive reference to Greek, or to any other language. Again, disjunctions are expressly allowed to contain more than two disjuncts. Again, Apollonius, who is speaking of disjunctive sentences, does not mingle linguistic entities with λεκτά. It might perhaps be said that there is an implicit confusion in Sextus, who is speaking of statables (ἀξιώματα: 2.189). For it is linguistic items, and not λεκτά, which 'announce' things, so that Sextus improperly says of the disjunctive λεκτόν what Apollonius (and Diogenes) properly say of the disjunctive connector. But that is cavilling.

---

[2] τὸ γὰρ ὑγιὲς διεζευγμένον ἐπαγγέλλεται ἓν τῶν ἐν αὐτῷ ὑγιὲς εἶναι, τὸ δὲ λοιπὸν ἢ τὰ λοιπὰ ψεῦδος ἢ ψευδῆ μετὰ μάχης. It is tempting to delete the first 'ὑγιὲς', which is logically offensive; but no doubt it is the author rather than his copyist who is at fault.

[3] ὡς δὲ . . . διαζεύγνυται . . . ὑπὸ τοῦ δηλουμένου τοῦ ἀπὸ τοῦ συνδέσμου, σαφὲς γενήσεται ἐκ τοῦ ἡμέρα ἐστὶν ἢ νύξ ἐστι. μόνον γὰρ ἓν ἔστι τῶν νοουμένων πραγμάτων κατὰ τὸ αὐτὸ παραλαμβάνεσθαι. ἡ ἐπαγγελία τῶν διαζευκτικῶν ἑνὸς ὕπαρξιν ἐπαγγέλλεται, τοῦ δ' ὑπολειπομένου ἢ τῶν ὑπολειπομένων ἀναίρεσιν. (The text depends on scholarly surmise at several points; but the general sense is not in doubt.)

[4] Disjunction is thus taken 'exclusively' rather than 'inclusively': so it was, almost invariably, in ancient logic, and so it will be throughout these pages.

Finally, does the thesis limit disjunctions to statables? Sextus, at least, is expressly considering statables and not compound complete λεκτά in general. And it might be thought that this is not insignificant: did not the Stoics, when they distinguished among types of compound complete λεκτά, in fact limit their remarks to statables? After all, so it is throughout the pertinent passage in Diogenes (7.68–76); and so too, for example, in S.E., *M.* 8.95. Yet Apollonius at least has excellent reasons for exceeding the limit. And in fact it is easily exceeded.

For example, start with the notion of a canonically disjunctive sentence, defined thus: 'S is a canonically disjunctive sentence if and only if S has the form $D(S_1{}^*, S_2{}^*, \ldots, S_n{}^*)$' – where D is a polyadic disjunctive sentential connector and each $S_i{}^*$ is a sentence. Next, define the connector: 'A polyadic connector D is disjunctive if and only if a sentence of the form $D(S_1+, S_2+, \ldots, S_n+)$ expresses a truth if and only if exactly one of its component S_i+s expresses a truth.'

Note that the S_i+s must be, roughly speaking, indicative sentences – sentences which express, or can express, something true or false; but that the $S_i{}^*s$ may be sentences of any type – interrogatives, say. Thus 'Is he in heaven or is he in hell, that d****d elusive Pimpernel?' is (perhaps) a canonically disjunctive sentence.

To be sure, the disjunctive connector is here defined in terms of truth. But it does not follow that it can only be used to conjoin sentences which are either true or false. You might define the word 'dagger' by saying: ' "dagger" is true of an item if and only if that item is a dagger'; and the definition, given in terms of truth-conditions, will give the sense of the word 'dagger' in such sentences as: 'Is that a dagger which I see before me?' The fact that the Stoics define disjunctives in terms of 'holding' or of truth does not show that disjunction is defined only for statables.

But the account of disjunction is not yet complete. Next, then, introduce the general notion of a disjunctive sentence: 'S is a disjunctive sentence if and only if there is a canonically disjunctive sentence synonymous with S.' It follows trivially that every canonically disjunctive sentence is a disjunctive sentence. A disjunction is a sort of λεκτόν, not a sentence; so, finally, explain disjunctions in terms of disjunctive sentences:

An item is a disjunction if and only if in saying it you can say something disjunctively. You say something disjunctively if and only if you can say it in uttering a disjunctive sentence.

That such an account works modestly well for disjunctive statables is plain. That it also works for other types of complete λεκτά may be seen by way of the schema:

X.

In uttering S, you say that
– where the demonstrative pronoun 'that' refers to X. Consider a particular instance of the schema:
Is he in heaven or is he in hell, that d****d elusive Pimpernel?
In uttering 'Is he in heaven or is he in hell, that d****d elusive Pimpernel?'
I said that.

What is said in the first line – in the replacement for 'X' in the schema – is a disjunction; it is an interrogative disjunction.[5]

An account of disjunction along these lines is readily adapted to other complete compound λεκτά. It requires philosophical refinement; and it has certain consequences which might be judged unwelcome. In addition, it seems to be defective as a version of what ancient logicians intended by disjunction; for it contains nothing which corresponds to the last clause in the passage from *P.H.* 2.191: 'together with conflict'.

The essay of Apollonius Dyscolus *On Connectors* – or *On Conjunctions*, to give it its normal and misleading English title – survives in a single manuscript. Time has been unkind to the book; Apollonius' Greek is unfriendly; his argument is usually contorted: the essay presents the most abominable difficulties. A substantial part of it is devoted to disjunctions – and primarily, for such is Apollonius' design, to Greek disjunctive connectors.

At one stage in his argument Apollonius makes this remark:

Let us not omit what the Stoics say: they make a distinction within naturally disjoined items between what conflicts and what contradicts. Something conflicts if it cannot be accepted at the same time . . . :
Either it is day or it is night
Either I am speaking or I am silent
and the like. Something contradicts if it exceeds by a negation (and so is in effect conflicting):
Either I am speaking or I am not speaking
Either it is day or it is not day
For the second sentence exceeds by a negation. (*Conj.* 218.20–27)[6]

---

[5] A decent account of interrogative disjunctions would need to distinguish among at least: (a) the questioning of a disjunction – 'Is it the case that (P or Q)?', which invites the answer 'Yes' or 'No'; and (b) the disjoining of questions – 'Is it the case that P or is it the case that Q ?', which invites the answer 'P' or 'Q'. And there are other neighbouring phenomena. ('Stands the church clock at half past three, and is there honey still for tea?' : a conjunction of questions, or the questioning of a conjunction ?)

[6] μηδὲ τὸ πρὸς τῶν Στωϊκῶν λεγόμενον παραλείπωμεν, παρ' οἷς ἐστί τις διαφορὰ ἐν τοῖς κατὰ φύσιν διεζευγμένοις μαχομένου καὶ ἀντικειμένου. καὶ ἦν μαχόμενον τὸ μὴ δυνάμενον κατὰ τὸ αὐτὸ παραληφϑῆναι . . .
ἢ ἡμέρα ἐστὶν ἢ νύξ ἐστιν

The distinction between conflict and contradiction is found in a few other texts (S.E., *P.H.* 1.190, 198; Ammonius, *in Int.* 91.9–10). Apollonius explicitly ascribes it to the Stoics. He may be suspected of imprecision – for he is talking of sentences whereas any Stoic distinction was presumably between λεκτά. But although the ascription is unique, there is no reason to regard it as factitious.

That Apollonius was familiar with Stoic logical and linguistic theories is certain; and it is equally certain that he sometimes adopted some parts of those theories. How Stoic he is in the piece on connectors is a nice question. Near the beginning of the essay he criticises certain of his predecessors – according to the standard edition of the text – in the following words:

Some, actually using words alien to those which contribute to the science of grammar, introduce Stoic doctrines, the tradition of which is not particularly useful for the technique which contributes to the science of grammar. (*Conj.* 213.7–10)[7]

This reads like an outright rejection of Stoic doctrine. But the word 'Στωϊκάς' does not appear in the manuscript (nor is there a blank space on the page): it was added by Bekker. He was presumably relying on Apollonius' next remark:

The observation of language [φωνή] is a long and arduous business. By it all dialects and all formations which contribute to the tradition of readings in Greek are corrected – a subject on which the work of the Stoics on language [φωνή] does not touch at all. (*Conj.* 213.11–15)[8]

But here Apollonius is not complaining of the insinuation of Stoic doctrine into grammatical theory – on the contrary, he grumbles that the Stoics do not touch on the particular issue in hand. Thus the passage does not support Bekker's supplement. It is not clear that any supplement is needed; and if an adjective is to be introduced, why 'Στωϊκάς' rather than a dozen others?

However that may be, a few lines later Apollonius observes that in composing his essay he will take over various items from his predecessors,

---

ἢ φθέγγομαι ἢ σιγῶ
καὶ ἔτι τὰ τούτοις ὅμοια. ἀντικείμενον δὲ τὸ πλεονάζον ἀποφάσει, ὅπερ δυνάμει πάλιν μαχόμενον
ἢ φθέγγομαι ἢ οὐ φθέγγομαι,
ἢ ἡμέρα ἐστὶν ἢ οὐκ ἐστιν ἡμέρα.
ὁ γὰρ ἕτερος λόγος ἐπλεόνασε τῇ ἀποφάσει.
(The text is doubtful in more places than one; but nothing will hang on any of the doubtful parts.)

[7] οἱ δὲ καὶ ὀνόμασιν ἀλλοτρίοις προσχρησάμενοι ἥπερ τοῖς εἰς γραμματικὴν συντείνουσι, Στωϊκὰς παρεισφέρουσι δόξας, ὧν ἡ παράδοσις οὐκ ἄγαν χρειώδης πρὸς τὴν εἰς γραμματικὴν συντείνουσαν τεχνολογίαν.

[8] ἔστιν οὖν πολλή τις καὶ δυσπερίληπτος ἡ περὶ τὰς φωνὰς τήρησις δι' ἧς κατορθοῦται πᾶσα διάλεκτος, πᾶς σχηματισμὸς συντείνων εἰς Ἑλληνικὴν παράδοσιν ἀναγνωσμάτων, ἧς οὐδὲ κατ' ὀλίγον ἐπιψαύει ὁ παρὰ τοῖς Στωϊκοῖς περὶ φωνῆς λόγος.

and, having in addition thought some things up for ourselves, we shall set matters
out with the necessary clarity, not going wholly outside the doctrine of the Stoics.
Posidonius, in his *On Connectors*, says . . . (*Conj.* 214.1–5)[9]

Apollonius will not depart completely from Stoic doctrine – and he at once
proceeds to cite the Stoic Posidonius. (No one, I think, any longer takes
seriously the suggestion that 'Posidonius' here designates someone other
than the celebrated Stoic philosopher.) Some have taken the passage in a
strong sense: they gloss 'not going wholly outside' as 'not departing a whit
from' – so that Apollonius declares himself a thorough Stoic for the course
of the essay. But the Greek can hardly carry this meaning; and in any event,
the obvious sense – 'not being wholly unStoic' – is surely right.

I return to 218.20–7. Apollonius says that the Stoics make a distinction
among 'natural' disjuncts. The distinction is as clear as the notion of conflict
is clear. It is plainly a necessary, but not a sufficient, condition for a conflict
to hold between two items that it be impossible for both of them to hold
at the same time – more generally, if the members of a group of items are
in mutual conflict, then it is impossible that more than one of them be
the case. It seems, too, that contradiction is a special sort of conflict, as
Apollonius stumblingly states. There is a contradiction between two items
if and only if one 'exceeds the other by a negation', i.e. by a negative particle.
Contradiction holds between pairs of items and not among larger groups.
The expression 'exceed by a negation' needs a careful gloss (see S.E., *M.*
8.89–90); but it is plain that if two items contradict one another they are
in conflict, but not *vice versa*. Contradiction is a special case of two-party
conflict.

All natural disjuncts, then, involve conflict. This ties Apollonius' text to
the clause in the Sextan passage: disjunctions are 'together with conflict'.
This might be glossed as follows: 'A disjunction is true if and only if one of
its disjuncts is true and it is impossible for more than one to be true.' But
it seems likely that the right gloss is rather this: 'A disjunction is true if and
only if, necessarily, exactly one of its disjuncts is true.' To see the difference
between these two theses, consider, say: 'Either it's Monday or it's Tuesday.'

However that may be, Apollonius offers a touch which is missing in
Sextus: he speaks of natural disjuncts. What are they? Apollonius introduces
them in 216.16–218.19, a text of stunning difficulty. I take it in spasms.[10]

---

[9] πρὸς οἷς καὶ αὐτοί τι ἐπινοήσαντες μετὰ τῆς δεούσης σαφηνείας παραδώσομεν, οὐκ
ἐκτὸς γινόμενοι κατὰ τὸ παντελὲς τῆς τῶν Στωϊκῶν δόξης. Ποσειδώνιος ἐν τῷ περὶ
συνδέσμων . . . φησὶν . . .
[10] For the Greek see Appendix A.

Again, some of them [i.e. some disjoined items] have received their disjoining naturally and others have not accepted their disjoining naturally.

'Naturally' (κατὰ φύσιν), at both occurrences, has been supplied by editors: the manuscript is blank. Some have preferred 'true' as a supplement, a word which occurs in the next sentence. The length of the blank favours 'naturally'; but those who prefer 'true' probably understand it in the sense of 'genuine', and between 'genuine' and 'natural' there is no pertinent difference.

For the remark
> Either it is day or it is night

stands in a true disjoined item; for these circumstances will never occur at the same time. But the remark
> Either Apollonius will be present or Tryphon will

announces the disjoining as relative to an occasion.[11] Thus the first example, even if it does not take the disjunctive connector, will still be in a disjoining:
> It is day. It is night.

The one is true – if we were to say thus, it being day:
> It is day.

'The one is true' means 'One and only one is true' – so too a few lines later on. Apollonius asserts that items naturally disjoined are 'in a disjoining' whether or not they take a disjunctive connector: this feature is a mark of natural disjunction – but it is, for the moment, the murkiest of marks. And the last clause, 'if we were to say . . .', is hardly pellucid.

But in the other, things are certainly not so:
> Tryphon will be present. Apollonius will be present.

For such items are not disjoined if they do not take the disjunctive connector.

'τὸ . . . ἕτερον' here contrasts not with the preceding 'τὸ ἕτερον' but rather with 'τὸ . . . πρότερον' in line 11/12; and 'οὐ πάντως' here means 'certainly not', whereas later it will mean 'not certainly'. Not clear, nor elegant – but that is Apollonius. And what is the function of the double example?

In these cases you can also set down the connectors which conflict with the disjunctive ones –
> Both Apollonius will be present and Tryphon will be present.
> If Tryphon will be present, Apollonius too will be present.

But in the case of items naturally disjoined you cannot; for 'Both it is day and it is night' will not cohere; nor will 'If it is day, it is night.'

---

[11] For 'relative to an occasion' (πρὸς καιρόν) in contrast to 'naturally' see S.E., *P.H.* 2.97–9; *M.* 8.145–50: the phrase is not found elsewhere in Apollonius.

This is a second mark of natural disjunction: naturally disjoined items cannot be linked by connectors which conflict with disjunctive connectors. Presumably 'Both . . . and . . .' conflicts with 'Either . . . or . . .' inasmuch as any sentence of the form 'Both P and Q' conflicts with its counterpart of the form 'Either P or Q'; that is to say, the two cannot be true at the same time – though in some cases, where the disjunction is not natural, they will each be true at different times. But why think that 'Either . . . or . . .' conflicts with 'If . . . then . . .'? Why is it only in natural cases that you cannot set down the conflicting connectors? And what does Apollonius mean when he says that certain sentences 'will not cohere' (οὐ . . . συστήσεται)'?

So there are some sentences disjoined or conjoined by the connectors, and also some so colligated; and there are some which do not perforce announce the colligation by way of connectors but actually indicate it in themselves – or again, some which are disjoined do not indicate the disjoining by the disjunctives but in themselves.

'Colligation' is 'τὸ συναφές' – connected with the verb 'συνάπτειν', whence 'συνημμένον', the standard Stoic term for conditional λεκτά. So a colligation is a link of conditionality. Just as there are naturally disjoined items, so there are naturally colligated items. Apollonius does not say that there are also naturally conjoined items; and I suppose that there are not.

In these cases, exchanges will not take place. Let us set out some examples. Someone who says 'It is day' has indicated that it is also light. In this case the following will not be possible:
  Either it is day or it is light.
  If I am alive, I am breathing
– for 'Either I am alive or I am breathing' will not be possible. For the colligating of breathing in being alive does not admit the disjunctive, as we have already said. And because its being day and its being night are disjoined, the one is true. In this case the colligative will not cohere since at the same time as you say
  It is day
it has been indicated that it is not night, and what stands in a colligation must also stand in a sequence.

The two marks of natural connections are here put together: if certain items indicate a connection in themselves, without the need of connectors, then 'exchanges will not take place'; that is to say, as the examples make plain, you will not be able to replace one connector by another conflicting connector: if 'If P, then Q' is true, then 'Either P or Q' is never true, cannot be true. Such items 'do not admit' certain connectors; certain compound sentences 'will not be possible' or 'will not cohere'. The latter mark is taken as a consequence of the former.

And the former mark becomes a little less dark. An earlier phrase seemed to suggest that if you utter the two sentences, 'It's day.' 'It's night' just like that, without linking them by any connector, you have thereby said something disjunctively. But the suggestion was misleading; for we now learn that Apollonius is thinking of someone who utters just: 'It's day.' That was the point behind the obscure expression 'if one were to say thus . . .'; and that indicates the way to take the double examples – they are, precisely, a pair of examples (and not a single disjunctive or conjunctive example).

Someone who utters just: 'It's day' thereby indicates that it is not night. In the same way, if you say 'It's day,' it is thereby indicated that it is also light. The colligation is implicit in the sentence 'It is day' – there is no need to construct a colligation by way of a colligative connector.

It is not that the utterance of 'It's day' is the saying of a disjunction or of a colligation. 'It is day' is not short or elliptical for 'If it is day, it is light', in the way in which some thought 'γράφω' to be elliptical for 'ἐγὼ γράφω'.[12] After all, there is a world of difference between saying 'It's day' and saying 'Either it's day or it's night,' or 'If it's day, it's light.' And neither Apollonius nor any logician can have missed that evident fact. Rather, 'It's day' indicates the disjunction and the colligation in itself.

In general, 'Q' is naturally colligated to 'P' if and only if, in uttering affirmatively 'P', you thereby indicate that Q. And 'P', 'Q', 'R', . . . are naturally disjoined if and only if, in uttering affirmatively one of them, you thereby indicate that none of the others holds.

Why or how do you indicate such things? You indicate them – or they are indicated – by the very sentence you utter. That is to say, the sense of 'It is day' is such that, necessarily, if it is day it is not night and if it is day it is light.

And so certain sentences are impossible, do not cohere. The text continues.

The remaining sentences – I mean those which do not fall into this class – undergo disjoining and colligating by the connectors themselves. As when you say:
Either pillage or divide all in two.
Both pillage and divide all in two.

At the beginning the ink has been washed off the manuscript, and the traces are baffling. But the general sense of the lines is clear: one who says 'Pillage' does not thereby say 'Don't divide all in two.' Hence any disjoining or conjoining must be fabricated by the use of the appropriate connectors.

---

[12] See Apollonius, *Synt.* 2.51 [165.4] – Apollonius rejects the thesis.

And just as it is not possible to assign an article to every declinable word, but only to one which can take it on, in the same way it is not possible to link every connector to every sentence. I mean a sentence which in itself announces a colligating – for where the disjunctive connector applies, the colligative does not; and where the colligative applies, the disjunctive does not.

Articles, in Greek, do not attach to every declinable expression: 'ἀλλήλους', for example, does not take the article (*Synt.* 2.70 [59.12–60.12]); nor does 'ἀμφότεροι' (ibid. 2.71 [60.13–61.23]).[13] Thus, in English, I say 'It's hard to lose either when you have both.' I do not say 'It's hard to lose either when you have the both.' This latter sentence is not possible, it does not cohere.

Elsewhere, Apollonius produces other examples of impossibilities and incoherences. Thus it is not possible to apply 'οὗτος' to a feminine or to a plural noun – not even at night (*Synt.* 3.9 [274.7–12]). Thus 'We talked to us' does not cohere (ibid. 3.5 [271.2–4]); nor does 'Dio is a philosopher converses' – unless you put an 'and' in front of the last word (ibid. 1.107 [90.7–10]). And in just the same way 'Both it is day and it is night' and 'If it is day, it is night' are not possible, do not cohere.

The cases do not seem to be parallel. 'The both' or 'We talked to us' are impossible inasmuch as they are ill-formed, ungrammatical. But 'If it is day, it is night' is grammatically impeccable and beautifully formed. Moreover, such sentences have their uses – for example, as conclusions to *reductio ad absurdum* arguments.

But it need not be supposed that Apollonius means to brand 'If it is day, it is night' as ungrammatical. (Indeed, he does not operate with anything like the notion of grammaticality.) Rather, that expression, like 'The both' or 'We talked to us', does not cohere insofar as it offends against the rules of language, insofar as its very linguistic form rules it out of court. The expressions are all – as we or Wittgenstein might put it – nonsense.

This category of nonsense, you might object, is too general – and perhaps too indeterminate – to be of any logical utility. At any rate, a logician must distinguish among different types or different causes of nonsense. But it is easy enough to do so. 'If it is day, it is night' is nonsense inasmuch as, given the meaning of its constituent terms, it cannot ever express a truth. And this is so inasmuch as 'It is day' and 'It is night' are naturally disjoined. On the other hand, although 'Either Apollonius will be here or Tryphon will be here' may well be true, 'Apollonius will be here' and 'Tryphon will be here' are not naturally disjoined, so that both 'Both Apollonius will be here

---

[13] Similarly, nouns in the vocative take no article, the definite article having no vocative: see the long discussion at *Synt.* 1.73–9 [62.6–67.8]. For other related phenomena see e.g. *Synt.* 1.135 [111.4–9]; *Adv.* 182.27–183.4.

and Tryphon will be here' and also 'If Apollonius will be here, Trypho will be here' cohere and are not impossible – the two sentences are sometimes true.

If that is Apollonius' conception of a natural disjunction, is it also a Stoic conception? Did the Stoic logicians distinguish, as Apollonius does, between natural and occasional disjunctions? Apollonius does not say so. He says only that the Stoics made a distinction, between conflict and contradiction, which applies within the class of natural disjunctions. On the other hand, he surely gives his readers the impression that the Stoics spoke of natural disjunctions.

No other text attributes the conception to the Stoics. To be sure, at *Conj.* 214.8–10, Apollonius says that Posidonius set out 'the natural connectors'. But it is not clear that the expression 'natural connector' comes from Posidonius; and in any case, a theory of natural connectors has nothing to do with a theory of naturally connected sentences. Perhaps, then, the theory came from some other philosophical party? Boethius, for example, distinguishes between two sorts of conditional proposition, 'the one so by accident, the other being such as to have a certain consequence by nature' (*Hyp. syll.* 1.3.6). The distinction is presumably Peripatetic: it perhaps goes back to Theophrastus and Eudemus, and it surely was developed before Apollonius' day. True – but it is not the same distinction as the one in Apollonius, and there is no reason to torture it into a spurious conformity. Perhaps, then, the theory comes from the grammarians rather than from the philosophers? After all, Apollonius himself is always concerned to distinguish what is natural in language from what is not. True – but he never elsewhere distinguishes the natural from the occasional.

In short, there is some gentle reason to ascribe the theory to the Stoics; and no reason to attribute it to others. In any event, it is tempting to imagine that the disjunctions which interested the Stoics are Apollonius' natural disjunctions: after all, Sextus insists that disjunctions come 'together with conflict', and in natural disjunctions the component disjuncts are in conflict with one another. But all natural disjunctions are true. Hence if Stoic disjunctions are natural disjunctions, then all Stoic disjunctions are true. And that is absurd.

Then perhaps a Stoic disjunction is true if and only if it is natural? All natural disjunctions are true, and perhaps all true disjunctions are natural.[14] False disjunctions abound. They fall into two discrete classes. A false disjunction may disjoin items which are not disjoined at all – for example

[14] So at *Conj.* 217.2 (and perhaps at 216.16 and 217.1) perhaps after all 'true' means 'true' rather than 'genuine'?

'Either Geneva is in Switzerland or Hamburg is in Germany.' And there are false disjunctions in which the items are disjoined, but not naturally – for example 'Either Apollonius will be here or Trypho will be here.' For there is no conflict between these disjuncts.

This may seem absurd: surely the first of the two sentences I have just adduced is true, and surely the second may have been true? Well, anyone who holds that a disjunction is true if and only if it is natural has a choice here: either those two sentences are not true or else they do not express disjunctions. If you choose the latter option, then you will presumably have an account of disjunctions which does not pay attention to expressions rather than to things. If you choose the former option, you will need to explain why those sentences are so easily taken for true.

There is a further feature of Apollonius' discussion which may be considered. He holds that, when 'P' and 'Q' are naturally disjoined, then both 'Both P and Q' and also 'If P then Q' are impossible. The former contention is unremarkable. Not so the latter. Sentences such as 'If it is odd, it is even' have their uses. One sort of case is particularly striking. Presumably, for any 'P', 'P' and 'not-P' are naturally disjoined: whatever 'P' may be, 'P' and 'not-P' are contradictory and therefore in conflict. But sentences of the form 'If not-P, then P,' far from being universally impossible, are used and used as truths in a number of ancient arguments.

According to Sextus, the Dogmatic philosophers produce an argument for the existence of signs which runs thus:

If there are signs, then there are signs.
If there are no signs, then there are signs.
Either there are signs or there are no signs.
Therefore: there are signs.

(See *P.H.* 2.131.) A parallel argument, with the word 'proof' substituted throughout for 'sign', supposedly established the existence of proofs (*P.H.* 2.186). The Dogmatists who offered these arguments, and who are frequently taken to be Stoics, cannot consistently suppose that if 'P' and 'Q' are naturally disjoined then 'If P, then Q' is impossible.

At *P.H.* 2.132 Sextus criticises the Dogmatic argument by producing a parallel to it:

If there are no signs, then there are no signs.
If there are signs, then there are no signs.
Either there are no signs or there are signs.
Therefore: there are no signs.

This argument, he claims, is as good as the Dogmatic argument – and so the Dogmatic argument cannot establish the existence of signs. At *P.H.* 2.189 he makes a different attack: the Dogmatic argument cannot be advanced by the Dogmatists; for 'it is impossible, according to them, for a conditional composed of conflicting statables to be sound'. The Dogmatists' own principles prove that their argument is unacceptable.

It has been claimed that Sextus is foisting a principle on the Dogmatists. When he says that the principle holds 'according to them', then he means not that they have enunciated the principle but rather that they are committed to it. And it has been claimed, further, that Sextus is mistaken: the commitment which he purports to discern does not exist. In other words, the principle is no principle of the Dogmatists. And all the better – for the principle is false.

But Apollonius provides a parallel to Sextus, proving that the principle had some life outside Sextus' inventive brain. Moreover, if Apollonius is reporting or paraphrasing Stoic doctrine, then we must agree with those Sextan exegetes who have construed the passage as a straightforward and truthful document in the history of Stoic logic.

Moreover, Apollonius offers an argument in favour of the principle. Sextus says that the Dogmatists must accept the principle, since

a conditional announces that if its antecedent is the case, then so too is its consequent, whereas conflicting items announce the contrary – that if either one of them is the case, it is impossible for the other to hold. (*P.H.* 2.189)

It is hard to see why that should have been thought a reason in favour of the principle. Apollonius has something different:

In this case the colligative will not cohere since at the same time as you say
    It is day
it has been indicated that it is not night, and what stands in a colligation must also stand in a sequence.

What is in colligation must also be in sequence: natural disjuncts are not in sequence – hence they cannot be colligated.

What does Apollonius mean by 'sequence' (ἀκολουθία)? The answer comes in the last lines of the text which we are examining:

And it is clear from the case before us that the announcement of the colligatives and also of the conjunctives conflicts with that of the disjunctives, although in one way the conjunctives do not differ. For the disjunctives are not in sequence, and neither are the conjunctives. For if we assert thus
    Either it is day or it is night,
or again by inversion
    Either it is night or it is day,

288   J. BARNES

it makes no difference. So too:
  Both Apollonius will be present and Trypho will be present
  Both Trypho will be present and Apollonius will be.

Conjunctions and disjunctions are not in sequence: that is to say, the order of their elements is indifferent, they are commutative – 'Both P and Q' means the same as (or at least is equivalent to) 'Both Q and P', and 'Either P or Q' as 'Either Q or P'. Conditionals, on the other hand, are not commutative: 'If P, then Q' is not equivalent to 'If Q, then P'.

Grant all that to be true – what follows? Apollonius infers that if 'Either P or Q' is true, then 'If P, then Q' is not true. The inference is patently fallacious.

Galen's *Institutio logica*, like Apollonius' *On Connectors*, survives in a single manuscript; and the single manuscript is in a miserable state. On the other hand, Galen's Greek is not Apollonian, and his argumentation is usually semi-transparent. There are two pertinent and parallel texts, one in chapter iv, where Galen discusses conflict, and the other in chapter xiv, where he turns to the use of hypothetical syllogisms in proofs.[15] It will be best to follow the latter text.

The development of the argument in xiv 3–8 is at first sight perplexing. §3 opens with the following assertion:

That not a single syllogism by way of a negated conjunction is useful for proof . . . has been demonstrated elsewhere.

Galen has his sights on the 'third indemonstrable' of Stoic logic:
  Not both P and Q; P: so not-Q
For §4 begins thus:

Therefore a third indemonstrable which the Chrysippeans think to conclude from a negated conjunction and one of its elements to the opposite of the other element . . .

'is of no use at all', we expect Galen to say. Not a bit of it; the sentence continues as follows:

. . . we have shown to be useful for numerous proofs in ordinary life, even in the law-courts.

Thus Galen first denies that syllogisms based on negated conjunctions are useful, adding that this is not the place to discuss useless or superfluous parts of logical theory. And then, paradoxically, he indulges in a lengthy

[15] Greek texts in Appendix B.

discussion of these allegedly useless syllogisms, claiming to have shown that they are, after all, useful for proofs. In §9 he apologises for the protracted nature of the discussion.

The text of §4 is risibly corrupt; but no emendation will do away with the paradox, and the summary which I have just given answers, *grosso modo*, to what Galen intended to say. The way out of the paradox is this. First, the word 'οὖν' at the start of §4, which I translated as 'therefore', must be given a resumptive rather than an inferential force: 'I shall not discuss useless syllogisms. Well then, to get back to business . . .'. Secondly, when Galen says that 'the Chrysippeans think' that a third indemonstrable starts from a negated conjunction, he means just that: they think so – but, as we shall see, they are wrong to think so. So §4 introduces a form of hypothetical syllogism which, Galen claims, the Stoics had misclassified.

Then what is the syllogism in question? Galen offered an illustrative example: 'as in the following sort of case'. The manuscript offers us the sentence: 'Dio is both in Athens and at the Isthmus.' Evidently, this will not do. Equally evidently, the example which Galen had in mind was the following:

It is not the case both that Dio is in Athens and that Dio is at the Isthmus.
Dio is in Athens.
So: Dio is not at the Isthmus

Whether the whole syllogism should be inserted into the text may be doubted;[16] but that this was Galen's syllogism is undeniable. And its legal potential is also plain. His client charged with armed robbery at the Isthmus, the defending counsel puts forward Galen's syllogism: 'My case rests, M'Lud.'

Yet if any syllogism uses a negated conjunction, surely this syllogism does? For who could deny that 'It is not the case both that Dio is in Athens and that he is at the Isthmus' is a negated conjunction? It carries its form on its face. But Galen claims that, *pace* Chrysippus, his syllogism does not start from a negated conjunction.

He explains himself in §5, which recalls and elaborates the account of conflict given in chapter iv. There are perfect and complete conflicts, when two items cannot both obtain and cannot both fail to obtain; and there are defective or half conflicts, when two items cannot both

---

[16] There are numerous cases in Galen's writings where a single proposition, or a pair of propositions, stand in for a whole syllogism; and it is not clear that all these cases need to be emended out of existence.

obtain but may both fail to obtain.[17] Now in iv 4 Galen had stated that

in the case of defective conflict, the Greeks customarily speak like this:
    It is not the case that Dio is both in Athens and at the Isthmus
And you will take this expression [φωνή] to be indicative of defective conflict.

That is to say, 'not both . . . and . . .', in cases of this sort, signifies, according to Greek usage, a defective conflict. And so, in xiv 6, Galen announces, of defective conflicts, that

in the case of items of this sort, the syllogism we described is useful. It uses the same expression as Chrysippus, but it is constructed not on a conjunction but on conflicting elements.

Galen is at any rate half right: given that Athens and the Isthmus are two separate places, then there is a defective conflict between Dio's being in Athens and his being in the Isthmus. He might be in neither place; but if he is in one, he cannot be in the other. But surely Galen is also half wrong; for even though its components are in conflict, 'It is not the case both that Dio is in Athens and that he is at the Isthmus' is surely a negated conjunction.

Galen demurs. After all, 'many disputes come about in connection with conjoined statables'.[18] And his reason emerges in §7. Again, the text is difficult; but there is no doubt about what Galen intended to say:

There are three differences among items: one, a difference in respect of conflict, applying to items which never obtain together; a second, in respect of sequence, applying to items which always obtain together; and those items which possess neither a necessary sequence nor a conflict constitute conjunctive statables.

In Galen, 'sequence' has its normal logical sense of 'implication', and not Apollonius' sense. So Galen means that a pair of items, X and Y, may be such that
    (A) X conflicts with Y
    (B) X implies or is implied by Y
    (C) X does not conflict with Y and neither implies nor is implied by Y.
There are obscurities here. But it is plain, first, that the three classes are intended to be jointly exhaustive: any pair, X and Y, must fall into one or other of the classes. This is guaranteed by the definition of class (C).

---

[17] Conflict need not be bilateral; but it is easier – and undeceptive – to conduct the discussion in terms of the simplest case.

[18] Text and interpretation of this sentence are uncertain. My version supposes that the word 'διαφορά' is used in different senses in successive lines. This is unwelcome – but other interpretations seem to me to have even greater disadvantages.

Secondly, and for the same reason, no pair can be in (A) and also in (C), nor in (B) and also in (C). Galen does not say that no pair can belong both to (A) and to (B); but it is a safe bet that he thought so.

The distinction between (A) and (B) is an ancient commonplace. Items exclude one another or embrace one another, they conflict or they imply, they disjoin or they colligate: conflict and implication, μαχή and ἀκολουθία, are the two logical relations *par excellence*. Every schoolboy, and every orator, knew that. And it is easy enough to think that the two relations are mutually exclusive: how on earth could one item both exclude another and also imply it?

Galen tacitly supports the principle which Sextus ascribes to the Dogmatists and which Apollonius affirms on his own behalf. It is reasonable to infer that the principle was not a special theorem of Stoic logic, supported by some subtlety which we no longer know. Rather, it was taken to be an obvious corollary of a logical commonplace: in logic we are interested in conflict and implication, in incompatibilities and entailments – two relations which are quite different and (or so anyone will unreflectingly suppose) mutually exclusive. *Odi et amo* may do for poetry, but it will not wash in logic.

Let me return to the text of Galen. Of class (C) he says that

those items which possess neither a necessary sequence nor a conflict constitute conjunctive statables.

That is to say, as Galen had put it in iv 4,

If the expression [sc. 'Not both . . .and . . .'] is said of other cases, which possess neither mutual sequence nor conflict, we shall call such a statable a negative conjunction, as in the case of
   Dio is walking
and
   Theo is talking.
For these possess neither conflict nor sequence and are expressed by way of conjunction.

Conjunctions unite items which belong to class (C).

And in xiv 7–8 Galen discusses syllogisms based on what are indeed negated conjunctions. Among items in class (C), he says, are the following:

   Dio is walking
and
   Theo is talking.
Clearly, the negation of this will be:
   It is not the case both that Dio is walking and that Theo is talking.

There are two additional premisses:
But Dio is walking
and again,
But Theo is talking.
The conclusion for the one additional premiss is
Therefore Theo is not talking
and for the other
Therefore Dio is not walking.
This sort of material has been shown to be utterly useless for proofs.

Galen does not repeat here his proof that such arguments are useless for
proofs; and I shall refrain from speculation – for there is no proof to be
found. However that may be, Galen is evidently right on one point: the
two illustrative arguments are based on negated conjunctions. On the other
hand, Galen holds that 'It is not the case both that Dio is in Athens and
Dio is at the Isthmus' is not a negated conjunction. For 'Both Dio is in
Athens and Dio is at the Isthmus' is not a conjunction. For a proposition
is a conjunction if and only if it has the form 'D(X$_1$, X$_2$, . . . , X$_n$)', where
the X$_i$s all belong pairwise to class (C), and D is a conjunctive connector.
And a connector D is conjunctive if and only if 'D(X$_1$, X$_2$, . . . , X$_n$)' is true
if and only if every X$_i$ is true.

Perhaps that is an idiosyncratic account of conjunction (though Galen
does not think so). But it appears to be a coherent account. Nor should
we be worried by the question: If 'Both Dio is in Athens and Dio is at the
Isthmus' is not a conjunction, then what on earth is it? It is *sui generis*.

Galen's remarks about conjunction presumably hold, *mutatis mutandis*,
for disjunction and for colligation: just as class (C) produces conjunctions,
so classes (A) and (B) produce disjunctions and colligations. Galen does
not explicitly say that class (B) grounds colligation; but at xiv 5 he does
state that 'items in complete conflict I have decided to call by the name
of disjunction.' Apollonius associated natural disjunction with class (A)
in general. Galen divides class (A) in two: items in class (Ai), complete
conflict, support disjunction; items in (Aii), deficient conflict, support a
different type of compound statable. Perhaps Galen's verb 'I have decided'
(ἠξίωκα) records a departure from standard usage.

Whither all this? Here is a simplified version of Galen's general position:

Compound statables are to be classified according to the type of connector which
governs them and the class of items which the connector connects. Suppose that
we have an implicative connector DI, a disjunctive connector DD, a connector of
partial conflict, DP, and a conjunctive connector DC. Then:

(1) A statable is an implication if and only if it has the form 'DI(X,Y)' and X and Y are in class (B).
(2) A statable is a disjunction if and only if it has the form 'DD(X,Y)' and X and Y are in class (Ai).
(3) A statable is a partial conflict if and only if it has the form 'DP(X,Y)' and X and Y are in class (Aii).
(4) A statable is a conjunction if and only if it has the form 'DC(X,Y)' and X and Y are in class (C).

No doubt this has a certain charm and coherence. But it does not take much reflection to show that it provides a curious basis for logical theory. Galen is in a mess.

Rather than expose the mess, I end by asking why Galen got into it. The answer is to be found in iv 6:

But here too the Chrysippeans give their attention to expressions rather than to objects, and they call a conjunction anything which is constructed by way of the so-called conjunctive connectors, even if it is constructed from conflicting items or from sequential items.

The Stoics identify disjunctions by way of certain Greek connectors; they hold that a λεκτόν is disjunctive if and only if it is expressible by way of a sentence of the form 'ἤτοι ... ἤ ...' But this is absurd: it is not the vocables 'ἤτοι ... ἤ ...' which make something a disjunction – it is the objects themselves.

The negative part of Galen's complaint is correct: the presence of 'ἤτοι ... ἤ ...' is neither a necessary nor a sufficient condition for a sentence's expressing a disjunction. (It is another question whether any Stoic logician ever thought that it was.) The positive part of the criticism is less easy to fathom: 'Look at the objects, the πράγματα' – what objects?

Galen does not urge us to consider how things lie in the world, to look for the facts of the matter. The πράγματα in question are, to put it crudely, the meanings of the sentences. In other words, Galen's exhortation is this: 'If you want to determine what sort of compound λεκτόν is expressed by a given sentence, do not look only at the vocables which connect its parts – look also at what its parts mean.'

Suppose you have a sentence with the structure 'D(X,Y)', and you are wondering whether the thing expresses a disjunction. What must you do? It is not enough, according to Galen, to note that 'D' here is 'ἤτοι...ἤ...'. True – but will it not be enough to determine what 'D' means? After all, if 'D' is a disjunctive connector, then surely it follows that the sentence is a disjunction? I suppose – or hope – that Galen would have agreed.

But he would also have added a further point. In order to determine what 'D' means, you must look at it in its context ; and its context is given, in part, by the senses of the items which it conjoins. That is to say, the sense of 'X' and 'Y' will fix the sense which 'D' takes in the sentence. This is the message of iv 4: in order to determine whether a sentence of the form

οὐχὶ καὶ Χ καὶ Υ

is a negated conjunction, you must determine the sense, in this context, of the connectors; and you will not determine that sense unless you attend to X and Y.

And this, I confess, seems to me to be eminently sane.[19]

---

[19] I thank the members of the Hamburg Symposium, whose questions and comments helped me to avoid several crass errors. I am also grateful to Tad Brennan, for a sheaf of written remarks; to Mauro Nasti, who made me see the pertinence of the Apollonian passage to the dispute over *P.H.* 2.189; and to Suzanne Bobzien, who scrutinized a penultimate version and suggested several substantial ameliorations.

Appendix A: Apollonius, Conj. 216.16–218.19

καὶ ἔστι πάλιν αὐτῶν ἃ μὲν <u>κατὰ φύσιν τὴν</u> διάζευξιν ἀναδεδεγμένα, ἃ
δὲ οὐκέτι κατὰ φύσιν τὴν διάζευξιν παρειληφότα. τὸ γὰρ λεγό<u>μενον</u>
<u>ἢ</u> ἡμέρα ἐστὶν ἢ νύξ ἐστιν
ἐν ἀληθεῖ καθέστηκε <u>διε</u>ζευγμένῳ· ταῦτα γὰρ τὰ καταστήματα
5 <u>οὐδέποτε</u> κατὰ ταὐτὸ γενήσεται. τὸ δὲ λεγόμενον
ἢ Ἀπολλώνιος παρέσται ἢ Τρύφων
ὡς πρὸς καιρὸν τὴν διάζευξιν ἐπαγγέλλεται. τὸ γοῦν πρότερον
ὑπόδειγμα, κἂν μὴ <u>λάβῃ</u> τὸν διαζευκτικὸν σύνδεσμον, πάλιν ἐν
διαζεύξει ἔσται
10 ἡμέρα ἐστί, νύξ ἐστι.
τὸ ἕτερον ἀληθές· εἰ φαίημεν <u>οὕτως</u>, ἡμέρας οὔσης,
ἡμέρα ἐστί.
τὸ δὲ ἕτερον οὐ πάντως
Τρύφων παρέσται, Ἀπολλώνιος παρέσται·

Underlined letters are supplements where the MS is blank. All supplements are due to Bekker unless otherwise indicated. ‖ 2 suppl Lehrs; κ ἀληθῆ suppl Bekker ‖ 14 Ἀπολλώνιος + οὐ cod, del Brennan

οὐ διαζεύγνυται γὰρ τὰ τοιαῦτα, ἐὰν μὴ λάβῃ τὸν διαζευκτικὸν σύνδεσμον. ἐφ᾽ ὧν ἔστι καὶ τοὺς μαχομένους τοῖς διαζευκτικοῖς συνδέσμους παραθέσθαι
καὶ Ἀπολλώνιος παρέσται καὶ Τρύφων παρέσται·
5 εἰ Τρύφων παρέσται, καὶ Ἀπολλώνιος παρέσται.
ἐπὶ μέντοι τῶν κατὰ φύσιν διεζευγμένων οὐκέτι· οὐ γὰρ συστήσεται τὸ καὶ ἡμέρα ἐστὶ καὶ νύξ ἐστιν, οὐδὲ τὸ εἰ ἡμέρα ἐστί, νύξ ἐστιν.
ὡς εἰσί τινες λόγοι ὑπὸ τῶν συνδέσμων διαζευγνύμενοι ἢ συμπλεκόμενοι, τινὲς δὲ συναπτόμενοι, τινές τε οὐ πάντως ὑπὸ τῶν
10 συνδέσμων τὸ συναφὲς ἐπαγγελλόμενοι ἀλλὰ καὶ δι᾽ αὐτῶν δηλοῦντες· ἢ καὶ διαζευγνύμενοι πάλιν οὐχ ὑπὸ τῶν διαζευκτικῶν ἀλλ᾽ ἐξ αὐτῶν τὴν διάζευξιν δηλοῦντες, ἐφ᾽ ὧν οὐκ ἐναλλαγαὶ γενήσονται. ἐκκείσθω δὲ ὑποδείγματα· ὁ λέγων τὸ ἡμέρα ἐστί δεδήλωκεν ὅτι καὶ φῶς ἐστίν. ἐπὶ τούτου οὐκέτι τοῦτο ἐγχωρήσει
15 ἤτοι ἡμέρα ἐστὶν ἢ φῶς ἐστι.
εἰ ζῶ ἀναπνέω.
οὐ γὰρ ἔτι ἐγχωρήσει τὸ ἤτοι ζῶ ἢ ἀναπνέω. ἡ συνάφεια γὰρ ἐν τῷ ζῆν τοῦ ἀναπνεῖν ἀπαράδεκτός ἐστι τοῦ διαζευκτικοῦ, καθὼς προείπομεν. διὰ δὲ τὸ διεζεῦχθαι ἡμέραν εἶναι καὶ νύκτα εἶναι, τὸ ἕτερον ἀληθεύει.
20 ἐπὶ τοῦ τοιούτου τὸ συναπτικὸν οὐ συστήσεται, ἐπεὶ ἅμα τῷ λέγειν ἡμέρα ἐστίν
δεδήλωται ὅτι οὐ νύξ, τὸ δ᾽ ἐν συναφείᾳ δεῖ καὶ ἐν ἀκολουθίᾳ καθίστασθαι. τὰ μέντοι ὑπολειπόμενα ταῦτα τῶν λόγων, λέγω τὰ μὴ ὑποπίπτοντα ὑπὸ τὸ τοιοῦτον εἶδος, ὑπ᾽ αὐτῶν τῶν συνδέσμων
25 πείσεται τὸ διεζεῦχθαι ἢ συνῆφθαι. ὡς εἴ τις λέγοι
ἠὲ διαπραθέειν ἢ ἄνδιχα πάντα δάσασθαι
καὶ διαπραθέειν καὶ ἄνδιχα πάντα δάσασθαι
καὶ ὃν τρόπον οὐχ οἷόν τε παντὶ πτωτικῷ ἄρθρον προσνέμειν, τῷ δὲ δυναμένῳ ἐπιδέξασθαι, τὸν αὐτὸν τρόπον οὐχ οἷόν τέ ἐστι παντὶ
30 λόγῳ πάντα σύνδεσμον συντάττειν. λέγω δὲ λόγον τὸν δι᾽ ἑαυτοῦ ἐπαγγελλόμενον συνάφειαν. ἐφ᾽ οὗ γὰρ ὁ διαζευκτικός, ἐκεῖ οὐχ ὁ συναπτικός· καὶ ὅπου ὁ συναπτικός, ἐκεῖ οὐκέτι ὁ διαζευκτικός. καὶ

---

3 συνδέσμους (Bekker)] συνδέσμοις cod. ‖ 8 ἢ add Bekker ‖ 12 suppl Schneider + Dalimier ‖ 14 suppl Dalimier ‖ 16 supplevi; καὶ ζῶ καὶ suppl Bekker ‖ 18 suppl Dalimier ‖ 20 suppl Schneider ‖ 21 suppl Schneider ‖ 22 suppl Schneider ‖ 23 suppl Schneider + Barnes ‖ 24 suppl Schneider

296 J. BARNES

σαφὲς ἐκ τοῦ προκειμένου ὡς μάχεται ἥ τε τῶν συναπτικῶν ἐπαγγελία
καὶ ἔτι τῶν συμπλεκτικῶν πρὸς τὴν τῶν διαζευκτικῶν, καθ' ἕνα τρόπον
τῶν συμπλεκτικῶν ἀδιαφορούντων. ὡς γὰρ οἱ διαζευκτικοὶ οὐκ ἐν
ἀκολουθίᾳ, οὐδ' οἱ συμπλεκτικοί. εἰ γὰρ ὧδ' ἀποφαινοίμεθα
5   ἤτοι ἡμέρα ἐστὶν ἢ νύξ ἐστιν,
ἢ καὶ κατὰ ἀναστροφήν
ἤτοι νύξ ἐστιν ἢ ἡμέρα ἐστίν
ἀδιαφορεῖ, ὡς εἰ
καὶ Ἀπολλώνιος παρέσται καὶ Τρύφων παρέσται,
10 καὶ Τρύφων παρέσται καὶ Ἀπολλώνιος.

Appendix B: Galen, Inst. log.

(1) iv 4–6

[4] ἐπὶ μὲν οὖν τῆς ἐλλειπούσης μάχης ἐν ἔθει τοῖς Ἕλλησίν ἐστιν οὕτω
λέγειν
οὐκ ἔστιν Ἀθήνησί τε καὶ Ἰσθμοῖ Δίων.
ἐνδεικτικὴν δὲ ἕξεις τὴν τοιαύτην φωνὴν τῆς ἐλλιποῦς μάχης· εἰ δὲ ἐφ'
5   ἑτέρων λέγοιτο ἡ φωνὴ ἃ μήτε ἀκολουθίαν ἔχει πρὸς ἄλληλα μήτε
μάχην, ἀποφατικὸν συμπεπλεγμένον καλέσομεν τὸ τοιοῦτον ἀξίωμα,
καθάπερ ἐπὶ τοῦ
Δίων περιπατεῖ
καὶ
10 Θέων διαλέγεται·
ταυτὶ γὰρ οὔτε μάχην οὔτε ἀκολουθίαν ἔχοντα κατὰ συμπλοκὴν
ἑρμηνεύεται. [5] διὸ κἀπειδὰν ἀποφάσκωμεν αὐτά, τὸν λόγον ἐκεῖνον
ἤτοι γε ἀποφατικὴν συμπλοκὴν ἢ ἀποφατικὸν εἶναι συμπεπλεγμένον
φήσομεν. (οὐδὲν γὰρ πρὸς τὸ παρὸν διαφέρει συμπεπλεγμένον λέγειν
15 ἀποφατικὸν ἢ συμπλοκὴν ἀποφατικήν, ἔχοντός γέ σου σκοπὸν
ἐν ἁπάσῃ λέξει τὸ δηλῶσαι σαφῶς τοῖς πέλας ὅτιπερ ἂν αὐτὸς
ἐννοῇς.)
[6] ἀλλ' οἱ περὶ Χρύσιππον κἀνταῦθα τῇ λέξει μᾶλλον ἢ τοῖς
πράγμασι προσέχοντες τὸν νοῦν ἅπαντα τὰ διὰ τῶν συμπλεκτικῶν

4 ἕξεις (Irvine)] ἕξει cod ‖ φωνήν] + ὅσοις cod ‖ 5 ἡ φωνὴ (von Arnim)] φωνὴν cod ‖ ἃ add
Kalbfleisch ‖ 6 ἀποφατικὸν] -ὴν cod, del Kalbfleisch ‖ 12 ἑρμηνεύεται (Kalbflesich)] ἑρμηνεύει cod
προσέχοντες (Kalbfleisch)] προσέχουσι cod

καλουμένων συνδέσμων συνιστάμενα, κἂν ἐκ μαχομένων ἢ ἀκολούθων
ᾖ, συμπεπλεγμένα καλοῦσιν, . . .

(2) xiv 3–8:

[3] ὅτι δὲ δι᾽ ἀποφατικοῦ συμπεπλεγμένου συλλογισμὸς εἰς ἀπόδειξιν
χρήσιμος οὐδὲ εἷς ἐστι, καθάπερ γε καὶ εἰ τομῇ γ᾽ ἕκτος ἐστιν
5 ἢ ἕβδομος ἢ ὄγδοος ἢ ἔνατος ἤ τις ἄλλος ὡς ἐκεῖνοι λέγουσι
συλλογισμός, ἀποδέδεικται δι᾽ ἑτέρων· ἀλλὰ νῦν πρόκειται τὰ χρήσιμα
μόνον διέρχεσθαι, παραλιπόντας τοὺς ἐλέγχους τῶν περιττῶς
προστιθεμένων. [4] τρίτον οὖν ἀναπόδεικτον τῶν περὶ τὸν Χρύσιππον
ἡγουμένων ἐξ ἀποφατικοῦ συμπεπλεγμένου καὶ θατέρου τῶν ἐν αὐτῷ
10 τὸ ἀντικείμενον τοῦ λοιποῦ περαίνοντα, ὡς ἐπὶ τῶν τοιούτων
οὐχὶ καὶ Ἀθήνησίν ἐστι καὶ Ἰσθμοῖ Δίων,
καὶ τόνδ᾽ ἐπεδείξαμεν εἰς πολλὰς τῶν κατὰ τὸν βίον ἀποδείξεις εἶναι
χρήσιμον ἄχρι καὶ τῶν δικαστηρίων. [5] ἐπεὶ δὲ τῶν μαχομένων
ἀλλήλοις πραγμάτων τε καὶ λόγων ἔνια μὲν ὁλόκληρόν τε καὶ τελείαν
15 ἔχει τὴν μάχην μήθ᾽ ὑπάρχειν ἅμα μήτ᾽ οὐχ ὑπάρχειν δυνάμενα,
τινὰ δὲ ἐξ ἡμίσεος ὑπάρχειν μὲν ἅμα μὴ δυνάμενα, μὴ ὑπάρχειν δὲ
ἅμα δυνάμενα, διὰ τοῦτο τὰ μὲν κατὰ τὴν τελείαν μάχην τὴν τοῦ
διεζευγμένου προσηγορίαν καλεῖν ἠξίωκα, τὰ δὲ κατὰ τὴν ἐλλιπῆ
τὴν τῆς μάχης ἁπλῶς ἢ καὶ μετὰ προσθήκης. [6] ἐν τούτοις οὖν τοῖς
20 πράγμασιν ὁ εἰρημένος συλλογισμὸς χρήσιμός ἐστι, τῇ μὲν αὐτῇ λέξει
χρώμενος ᾗ Χρύσιπος, οὐ μὴν ἐπὶ συμπεπλεγμένῳ συνιστάμενος
ἀλλ᾽ ἐπὶ τοῖς μαχομένοις· ᾧ καὶ διαφοραὶ πάμπολλαι κατὰ τὸ
συμπεπλεγμένον ἀξίωμα συνίστανται.
[7] τριῶν γὰρ οὐσῶν διαφορῶν ἐν τοῖς πράγμασι, μιᾶς μὲν τῆς
25 κατὰ τὴν μάχην ἐπὶ τῶν μηδέποτε συνυπαρχόντων, ἑτέρας δὲ τῆς
κατὰ τὴν ἀκολουθίαν ἐπὶ τῶν ἀεὶ συνυπαρχόντων, ὅσα μήτε τὴν
ἀκολουθίαν ἀναγκαῖαν ἔχει μήτε τὴν μάχην, τὸ συμπεπλεγμένον
ἀξίωμα συνίστησιν, ὁποῖα τὰ τοιαῦτά ἐστι
Δίων περιπατεῖ
30 καὶ
Θέων διαλέγεται.

2 ᾖ addidi ‖ 3 ὅτι (Mynas)] ὅτε cod ‖ συλλογισμός (Kalbfleisch)] -μοῦ cod ‖ 4 εἰ τομῇ γ᾽ (Irvine)]
τὸ μὴ ὁ cod; ὅτι μὴ Kalbfleisch ‖ ἕκτος] + τ᾽ cod; + τίς Kalbfleisch ‖ 7 μόνον] + αὐτὰ cod ‖
11 οὐχὶ] ἔχει cod; ἔχει· οὐχί Kalbfleisch ‖ 12 τόνδ᾽ ἐπεδείξαμεν (cj Kalbfleisch)] τοῦδε παιδίον μὲν
cod ‖ κατὰ] καθόλου cod ‖ 13 ἐπεὶ (Kalbfleisch)] ἐπὶ cod ‖ 15 μήθ᾽ (Kalbfleisch)] ἅμα θ᾽ cod ‖
19 προσθήκης] + ἐλλιποῦς μάχης cod. ‖ 26 ἀεὶ] + μὴ cod

298   J. BARNES

δῆλον δὲ καὶ τὸ ἀποφατικὸν αὐτοῦ τοιοῦτον ἐσόμενον·
οὐχὶ καὶ Δίων περιπατεῖ καὶ Θέων διαλέγεται.
αἱ δὲ προσλήψεις δύο·
   ἀλλὰ μὴν Δίων περιπατεῖ,
5 [8] ἔτι δὲ
   ἀλλὰ μὴν Θέων διαλέγεται·
συμπέρασμα δὲ κατὰ μὲν τὴν ἑτέραν πρόσληψιν
   οὐκ ἄρα Θέων διαλέγεται,
κατὰ δὲ τὴν ἑτέραν
10   οὐκ ἄρα Δίων περιπατεῖ·
πρὸς ἀπόδειξιν δὲ ἡ τοιαύτη τῶν ὑλῶν δέδεικται καὶ παντάπασιν
ἄχρηστος οὖσα.

2/3 καὶ Θέων . . . δνό] addidi post Kalbfleisch

CHAPTER 10

Theories of language in the Hellenistic age and in the twelfth and thirteenth centuries

Sten Ebbesen

In Western Europe during the twelfth and thirteenth centuries, interesting theories concerning various aspects of language were prolific. In intellectual energy, these centuries could compete with those of Plato, Aristotle, Theophrastus, Epicurus and Chrysippus.[1] One might add the first half of the fourteenth century, but I shall leave it out of account, mainly because the new developments in semantics (due to Burley, Ockham, Buridan and others) were accompanied by an astonishing loss of interest in grammar.

In trying to compare and connect some pieces of scholastic theory with Hellenistic theory I use a totally conventional limitation of the Hellenistic age to the years between 323 BC and 31 BC. I take it for granted, though, that linguistic doctrine attested in Quintilian and/or Sextus Empiricus is almost invariably of Hellenistic origin.

At the beginning of the twenty-first century we do not possess a single major work on linguistic issues from the time between Aristotle and Apollonius Dyscolus. Our scholastic predecessors in academe had even less access to the theories of that age than we have. *Inter alia*, most of the Greek texts from which we collect our fragments of the theories of the various schools had not been translated into Latin, and nobody read Greek. Besides, some of our Latin 'classics' were virtually unknown. Quintilian, for instance, was not a household name to medieval scholars.

For all that, the influence of Hellenistic theorising on developments more than a thousand years later cannot be doubted. Only, the story is

---

[1] For a general survey of medieval theories of language, see Ebbesen 1998 and 1995, where further bibliography may be found. Since the 1980s Irène Rosier (also publishing under the name Rosier-Catach) has been one of the most productive and innovative scholars in the field, with articles and books on a great number of different problems. Much original scholarship has been published in the acts of the European Symposia on Medieval Logic and Semantics (9 volumes, with varying publishers, since 1976). Particularly important journals are *CIMAGL = Cahiers de l' Institut du Moyen Age Grec et Latin* (Copenhagen, mainly text editions), *Histoire Épistémologie Langage* (Paris, discussion articles, not limited to the Middle Ages), *Vivarium* (Leiden, both discussion articles and text editions).

not one of a continuous survival of whole bodies of theory, but rather one of the survival of certain seminal ideas (λόγοι σπερματικοί) that were in due time to produce a new harvest. Certain inherited conceptual tools continued to be used, and to develop. Certain intellectual attitudes survived or were resurrected. Often, it must be admitted, it is impossible to tell whether a piece of medieval lore was directly inspired by a similar piece of Hellenistic lore, or whether we are presented with similar answers to the same theoretical demands in two philosophical cultures that shared many presuppositions; a notoriously difficult case is that of the Stoic λεκτόν and the very similar twelfth-century *dictum* or *enuntiabile*.

One important tool in medieval linguistic speculation was the notion of *imposition*, the assignment of a certain meaning to a certain sound. The medievals knew nothing of *Cratylus*, and their dear Aristotle said nothing about imposition or impositors of names though he did hold that words are significative by convention. But they had Boethius, and in particular his account of two impositions in his commentary on Aristotle's *Categories*. A first imposition creates a language to speak about the physical world, and a second imposition creates words with which to speak about the first set of words.[2]

Boethius owed the theory to Porphyry[3] – whether directly, as I prefer to believe, or indirectly, as some think. For Porphyry the two impositions served two purposes. First to structure the *Organon:* in *Categories* we study words that signify items of the physical world and *qua* significative, in *Perihermeneias* we move up a level where we study linguistic entities *qua* parts of linguistic structures. Second, by taking *Categories* to be a book about words concerned with the physical world Porphyry made it harmless in a Neoplatonic context: it did not present a rival account to Platonic metaphysics.

So, Porphyry could have invented the double imposition. But doing so would be a most uncharacteristic procedure on his part. He usually adapted existing pieces of theory instead of starting from scratch. We know that the notion of imposition was an important one in Hellenistic times. Varro is sufficient proof of that.[4] To my mind, a Hellenistic, and more specifically a Stoic, origin of the notion of the double imposition remains a plausible hypothesis. On the Stoic theory the first imposition will have created the πρωτότυπα of words for real things (ὄντα = σώματα), whereas it took a separate step to introduce words for quasi-things

[2] Boethius, *Cat. PL* 64: 1159A–C.   [3] Porphyry, *Cat.*, *CAG* IV.1: 57–8.
[4] See especially *De lingua latina* book 8.

('sayable', for instance) and generally to introduce a vocabulary of dialectic.[5]

Every medieval thinker assigned great importance to imposition. To most, 'imposition day' was a once-in-a-lifetime affair for each word: it was the day when a given combination of speech-sounds had its capacity to signify fixed for ever, though in rare cases the same sound-complex might be reused at another imposition, the result being equivocation. Equivocation actually requires that the decisions taken on imposition day remain in force. Otherwise you can never tell if a word is equivocal or not.[6]

It might be objected that equivocation does not require a repeated imposition of the same sound since every word is equivocal in that it can signify its significate or its own type (autonymous use). As Chrysippus famously observed: every word is ambiguous.[7] Most scholastics, however, preferred to refer this ambiguity to the theory of supposition which deals with different *uses* (*diversa acceptio*) of a word with just one *signification*. So, in 'horses run fast' the term 'horses' has personal supposition and refers to horses; in 'horses is plural' the same term has material supposition and refers to the word form 'horses' (how exactly this works will depend on the particular author's theory of universals). Augustine's *De dialectica* – and thus indirectly some Hellenistic source (Varro?, Stoics?) – may have given some inspiration to medieval research into material supposition, but the work was not very influential, and in the main the medieval work in this field was independent of ancient sources.[8]

The Porphyrian, and perhaps Stoic, double imposition introduced an extremely important idea: that of levels of language and different types of vocabulary. And that idea was to be fertile in the hands of twelfth-century

[5] I do not know who first proposed a Stoic origin, but it was the standard assumption in Copenhagen when I learned my Stoicism in the late 1960s. Cf. Pinborg 1962. The idea seems to have been forgotten in the meantime, not because it has been discredited but because there has been little or no interest in searching for the origin of the theory of two impositions.
[6] The most comprehensive discussion of imposition bound equivocation is found in Marmo 1994.
[7] Gellius, *Noctes Atticae* 11.12.1: '*Chrysippus ait omne verbum ambiguum natura esse, quoniam ex eodem duo vel plura accipi possunt.*' It is not certain that Chrysippus was thinking of mention/use ambiguity, but the possibility is suggested by a comparison with Augustine, *De dialectica* ch. 9, p. 106 Pinborg = 15 Crecelius. The two texts = fragments 636 and 637 in *FDS* I.
[8] On Augustine and the Stoics see the contributions by J. Allen and A. A. Long in this volume. The doctrine of supposition was a late twelfth-century product. The best-known versions of the theory are those of Peter of Spain, William of Ockham and John Buridan, but there are many variants from the period 1200–1500, and even a few from the sixteenth and seventeenth centuries. For an introduction, see Pinborg 1972. Until the fourteenth century, counting ambiguous supposition as a sort of equivocation was a distinctly English tradition; see, e.g. Roger Bacon, *De signis* 3.2.48 in Fredborg et al. 1978. Bacon and his contemporary Henry of Ghent are among the few scholastics to have made extensive use of Augustine's *De dialectica*. For Henry's use of the text see Rosier 1995.

thinkers. To exemplify second imposition words Porphyry and Boethius had
only given grammatical terms. Dexippus included logical terms – quite in
accordance with Porphyry's intentions, I believe – but this was unknown
to the West, and so there was a tendency to reserve the second imposition
for grammatical terms – 'noun', 'verb' and so on.[9] Nevertheless, twelfth-
century commentators on the *Categories* got the right idea, and started to
sift the vocabulary so as to separate *praedicamentalia* relating to the primary
constituents of created reality from *extrapraedicamentalia*.[10] This sifting was
one, at least, of the historical roots of the notion of transcendentals.

One particular school, that of Gilbert of Poitiers († 1154), the *Porretani*,
went one step further, combining the idea of a primary and a secondary
language with the Stoic division of science into natural, moral and rational
and, finally, with the doctrine that religious language is based on *translatio*,
the loan of words from a different sphere.[11] The medieval notion of *translatio* (also sometimes called *transumptio*) was directly descended from the
Hellenistic doctrine of tropes, transmitted by several sources, one of them
the popular Donatus who defined a trope as 'an expression transferred from
its proper signification to a non-proper similar signification for the sake of
stylistic embellishment, or out of necessity'.[12]

The Porretanean idea is beautifully simple. With our first language we
acquire the word 'high', which is applicable to mountains and the like. This

[9] Porphyry, *Cat.* 57.32–3; Boethius, *Cat.* 159B–C; Dexippus, *Cat.* 13–16, 26–7 (in fact, Dexippus seems
to take just any non-categorial word to be one of the second imposition, so that 'being', 'whole' and
'part', e.g., are included in the group as well as 'name' and 'species'). Cf. Ebbesen 1981: I, 155.
[10] See the commentary by Anonymus D'Orvillensis (1190s?) edited in Ebbesen 1999: 273.
[11] For the Porretan theory, see also Ebbesen, 2004. The best source for the non-theological part is
the anonymous *Compendium logicae Porretanum* edited by Ebbesen et al. 1983. On *translatio* in
twelfth-century theology, see Valente 1997, 1999.
[12] Donatus, *Ars grammatica* 3.6, Holtz 1981: 667. '*Tropos est dictio translata a propria significa-
tione ad non propriam similitudinem ornatus necessitatisue causa.*' Donatus' definition is paraphrased in the widely used *Grecismus* of Eberhardus Bethuniensis, I, 94–7, p. 8 Wrobel: '*Ast
proprie tropus modus esto siue figura, | Cum translatatur oratio dictio siue | Improprie causa metri
uel commoditatis | Siue necessarii.*' Other important sources for the medieval notion of transla-
tion were (1) Boethius, *In Categorias, Patrologia Latina* 64: 166D–167A (derived from Porphyry)
[less important: Boethius, *In Topica Ciceronis* III *versus finem, Patrologia Latina* 64: 1108A–B];
(2) Augustine, *De trinitate* 5.8.9 ('*Situs vero et habitus et loca et tempora non proprie sed translate
ac per similitudinem dicuntur in deo*'); *De dialectica* ch. 10, p. 116 Pinborg = 19 Crecelius. Cf.
Valente 1997: II, 5 and III, 4. Aristotle's remarks about metaphor in *Topics, Rhetoric* and *Poetics* were
of marginal or no importance, since the *Topics* only became common reading in the first half of
the thirteenth century, and the two other works were not even available in Latin till the second
half of that century. Quintilian was unknown, but *Institutio oratoria* 8.6.1–2 and 5–6 can be used
to show that Donatus' definition of trope and Boethius' Porphyrian understanding of metaphor go
back a long time. *Rhetorica ad Herennium* was a well-known text, but its treatment of tropes left few
traces in the philosophical and theological debates of the twelfth and thirteenth centuries (though
see Rosier-Catach 1997a).

is the language of *naturalis facultas*. Secondarily we create vocabulary for the products of culture, including evaluation, by transferring words from the first language, and thus we call prices 'high'. This is the language of *moralis facultas*. In the same way we create the language of grammar and logic (*rationalis facultas*), in which we may say that one genus is 'higher' than another. And similarly the language of theology is the result of *translatio*: God is 'highest'. Now, the important point is this: in the basic language, that of nature, certain syntactical and inferential rules apply, and the preservation of those rules is a precondition for the intelligibility of statements in which some or all of the terms are used in a transferred sense, losing their original meaning. You can't both change the meaning of words and the logical syntax if you want your new language to be intelligible.

The original impetus for the Porretanean theory was the wish to account for the possibility of speaking about the unknowable God, and the Porretans famously claimed that *Deus est deitas* ('God is godhood') is false while *Deus est deus deitate* ('God is god by virtue of godhood') is true, on the ground that in the language of nature an abstract noun is never predicated truly of the corresponding concrete noun, whereas for any true statement of the form 'X is Y', if 'Y' is a concrete noun, 'X is Y by virtue of Y-hood' is also true, 'Y-hood' being the corresponding abstract noun. *Via* the problem of *translatio in divinis* the Porretans were led to some serious reflection about the general role of *translatio* in human language.[13]

The Porretanean theory leaves one wondering whether the Stoics must not, in at least one respect, have reached the same conclusions. I am thinking of the vocabulary of *rationalis facultas*. Stoics knew perfectly well that the vocabulary of dialectic was for the most part a recent creation, in fact, to a considerable extent their own creation, and it is hard to see how they could possibly deny that it had been created by *translatio*. 'Lying downside up' obviously was first imposed to characterise plain physical entities, not predicates. Yet they called certain predicates ὕπτια.

* * *

Sextus Empiricus – never one to be concise – dedicates several pages of his *Against the Grammarians* to a refutation of normative grammar, the type of grammar that takes ἀναλογία for its criterion of rectitude. I will not here take up the old discussion whether some ancient city housed a school of stiff-necked analogists while another was peopled only by pervert

---

[13] The Porretan theses about *deus* and *deitas* are discussed on the basis of Gilbert's own writings in Nielsen 1982: 158–63, but the clearest account of the issue is that of Gilbert's pupil Everard of Ypres in Haring 1953.

anomalists.[14] The point is that if you want to produce a grammar with claims to scientific status, it must be an analogist one in the sense that it says what must inevitably be the correct solution given certain conditions. As Sextus says: 'Grammarians wish to lay down certain universal considerations (καθολικὰ θεωρήματα) and then use them to judge all the particular names as to whether they are Greek or not.'[15]

A *katholikon* (καθολικόν) is not just a universal proposition, it is a *true* universal.[16] In its morphology part the grammar for a specific language must contain rules of the type 'If a noun in case A ends in *x*, its case B form will end in *y*.' All sorts of restrictions are in principle admissible, even semantic ones, such as 'presupposing that it does not signify a tool'. And the same applies on the syntactic level, where probably it will be a good idea to operate solely with a system of grammatical categories that are not essentially linked to morphological features, so that you can say 'If you have got a noun of nominative case and singular number, and add a verb of the indicative mood, third person and singular number, you have got it right, you have got a construction' – as, indeed, grammarians did say for centuries.

Every grammarian faces a practical problem in the morphology: in all or most inflecting languages, even tightly regulated literary languages, and certainly in literary Greek, the variety of inflection is such that it is very hard to make a fool-proof algorithm for deducing an unknown word form from a known one. The list of conditions that must be known before the unknown form can be deduced risks becoming so long that the grammar becomes useless for didactic purposes: the pupils might as well learn the inflection of every single word by itself.

Sextus has no difficulties in producing any number of similar nominative singular forms whose corresponding genitives are dissimilar. *Arēs, Charēs, chartēs* ("Αρης, Χάρης, χάρτης) and *Memnōn, Theōn, leōn* (Μέμνων, Θέων,

[14] On this issue see the article by David Blank in this volume.
[15] S.E., *Adv. gram.* 221 Θέλουσι μὲν γὰρ καθολικά τινα θεωρήματα συστησάμενοι ἀπὸ τούτων πάντα τὰ κατὰ μέρος κρίνειν ὀνόματα εἴτε ἑλληνικά ἐστιν εἴτε καὶ μή. Blank 1998: 44–5 translates 'They have put together some universal theorems, and they want to judge from these theorems whether every particular word is good Greek or not.' Blank thus leaves συστησάμενοι outside the scope of the initial Θέλουσι and makes the passage a statement about what grammarians are doing (they have some rules, they try to use them) rather than a general claim about any grammarian's ideal. I think the sandwiching of καθολικά τινα θεωρήματα συστησάμενοι between Θέλουσι and κρίνειν favours my interpretation.
[16] S.E., *Adv. gram.* 225, τὸ μὲν καθολικὸν οὐδέποτε ἡμᾶς διαψεύδεται, τὸ δὲ ὡς τὸ πολὺ κατὰ τὸ σπάνιον 'the universal never fails to come out true, whereas "for the most part" does so, though rarely'. Sextus' text would seem to echo a technical discussion of καθολικά in which they were required to possess omnitemporal universal truth. Cf. Aristotle's explanation of κατὰ παντός in *APo.* 1.4.28–9.

λέων*)* would seem to form two morphological groups, but six different types of genitive come out: *Areōs, Charētos, chartou, Memnonos, Theōnos, leontos* (Ἄρεως, Χάρητος, χάρτου, Μέμνονος, Θέωνος, λέοντος) – unless, that is, you take θέων to be a participle, in which case its genitive will be *theontos* (θέοντος) like *leontos* (λέοντος). Similarly with verbs. The future form of *pherō* (φέρω) is not related to the present the way the future of *thelō* (θέλω) is. We have *thelō–thelēsō* (θέλω – θελήσω), but not *pherō–pherēsō* (φέρω – φερήσω).[17]

And if we leave the established literary language, we will find forms that ought not to be there according to rules of grammar. In Alexandria they say *apelēluthan* (ἀπελήλυθαν) instead of the *apelēluthasin* (ἀπεληλύθασιν) prescribed by grammarians.[18] So what, they do not speak correct Greek. Problem is, their wrong form creates no problem for understanding, so if the ultimate test of correct language is intelligibility, grammar must be wrong in blaming those who say *apelēluthan* (ἀπελήλυθαν). As Sextus would say, it does not harm us that anyone speaks that way: οὐδὲν βλαπτόμεθα.[19]

Sextus would also have us believe that intelligibility is not impaired if somebody points at a woman and says 'He'.[20] Here he is on slippery ground. I have a Finnish colleague who habitually uses 'he' as a deictic of females, and unless he is literally or metaphorically pointing with both indices, this does create problems. Similarly when politically correct speakers refer to dead male philosophers as 'she'. But it must be admitted that on some occasions we do understand the speaker even if he uses the wrong gender of a deictic.

The problem with the deictic pronoun is also touched on by Quintilian, according to whom 'Some also think that the same flaw [solecism in one word] is involved if what is pointed at by means of the word is different from what is pointed at by a nod or by the hand,'[21] and by Donatus, who says that 'Many mistakenly think that solecism may also occur in one part

---

[17] The nouns used as examples are taken from Sextus Empiricus, *Adv. gram.* 237–9, the verbs from 195. Several of Sextus' objections are very similar to objections mentioned by Quintilian, so a Hellenistic origin is assured. There are textual problems in Sextus Empiricus, loc. cit., and Blank 1998: 253 wants to excise the examples χάρτης and λέων. His reasons can scarcely be called cogent, and I find it hard to believe in the 'eager reader' to whom he attributes a systematic augmentation of the number of examples from two to three. Anyhow, for my present purpose the exact constitution of the text is inconsequential.

[18] S.E., *Adv. gram.* 213. By Sextus' days -ασι(ν) seems to have disappeared from ordinary spoken language. See, e.g., Mandilaras 1973: 212–13.

[19] S.E., *Adv. gram.* 173 (talking about insignificant orthographical aberrations).

[20] S.E., *Adv. gram.* 212. Discussion of the passage in Blank 1998: 234–6, with a useful reference to Apollonius Dyscolus, *Synt.* 3.8–10, *Grammatici Graeci* II.2.273–6.

[21] Quintilian, *Inst.* 1.5.36: '*Illud eruditius quaeritur, an in singulis quoque verbis possit fieri soloecismus . . . In gestu etiam nonnulli putant idem vitium inesse, cum aliud voce, aliud nutu vel manu demonstratur.*'

of speech, if, [e.g.,] we point at a man and say 'she', or at a woman and say 'he'.[22]

Some Stoic(s) criticised by Alexander of Aphrodisias had taken *houtos peripatei* (οὗτος περιπατεῖ) ('This one (masculine) is walking') to be equivalent to 'There is someone male at whom I am pointing, and that one is walking.' As a result, there is no grammatical error in pointing at a woman, but in that case the proposition would be false, as would also the corresponding negative *houtos ou peripatei* (οὗτος οὐ περιπατεῖ).[23] The two Latin writers take another road, deciding that the nod or pointing plays the role of an extra word, so that we have a sort of syntactical mismatch, something like *hic mulier* or *est mulier; hic . . .* – and the same road was to be taken by Robert Kilwardby in his thirteenth-century commentary on Donatus' *Barbarismus* (= *Ars grammatica* 3).[24]

This leads us to problems on the syntactical level. 'The police are investigating the case' is correct English. But isn't 'police' singular and 'are' plural? We might find a way to declare 'police' a plural noun, but what about 'The department are in favour of the proposal'? This is incorrect, but the likelihood of a misunderstanding is nil. An expression of that sort used on purpose would be a *figura* to the ancients and to the medievals. *Turba ruunt*, or more fully: *Turba ruunt in me luxuriosa proci*[25] was a standard example to the medievals; another one was *Iactamus iampridem omnis te Roma beatum.*[26] Quintilian offers *gladio pugnacissima gens Romani.*[27]

Sextus adduces the following example of an incorrect construction: *polla peripatēsas kopiâi mou ta skelē* (πολλὰ περιπατήσας κοπιᾶι μου τὰ σκέλη): 'I having walked much my legs are tired.'[28] The absolute nominative is impermissible, but the whole sentence perfectly understandable. In the thirteenth century the same problem was illustrated by the Biblical example *In convertendo dominus captivitatem Sion facti sumus sicut consolati.*[29]

---

[22] Donatus, *Ars Maior* 3.1.2, Holtz 1981: 655: '*multi errant, qui putant etiam in una parte orationis fieri soloecismum, si aut demonstrantes uirum hanc dicamus, aut feminam hunc.*'

[23] Alexander, *APr.*, *CAG* 11.1: 402 = *FDS* fr. 901.

[24] Quintilian, *Inst.* 1.5.37: '*Huic opinioni neque omnino accedo neque plane dissentio; nam id fateor accidere voce una, non tamen aliter quam si sit aliquid quod vim alterius vocis optineat ad quod vox illa referatur: ut soloecismus ex complexu fiat eorum quibus res significantur {significatur malim} et voluntas ostenditur.*' Donatus, *Ars Maior* 3.1.2, Holtz 1981: 655 '*cum utique praecedens demonstratio . . . uim contextae orationis obtineat.*' Kilwardby 1984: 40–1.

[25] A quote from Ovid, *Heroides* 1.88. For the example in medieval texts, see Rosier 1991: 229.

[26] A quote from Horace, *Epistulae* 1.16.18. For its use in medieval texts, see Rosier 1991: 224.

[27] Quintilian, *Inst.* 9.3.8.   [28] S.E., *Adv. gram.* 214.

[29] *Psalms.* 125 (126).1. For medieval texts that use the example, see Rosier 1991: 223. The grammatical difficulty is peculiar to the Latin *Vulgate*; it does not exist in the *Septuagint* nor has it left any trace in the English Bible of King James.

Sextus has a very good point. Standard grammar is too weak to let you predict the result in every case if you know the initial conditions. If you make it strong enough, it may become pedagogically worthless. And in either case you may expect people to say something that the rules do not foresee because nobody had thought of saying it when the rules were formulated. And yet that rule-breaking utterance may be perfectly understandable.

Medieval Western Europe inherited the Hellenistic ideal of a scientific grammar. Their main source for ancient theory was Priscian, who depended very heavily on Apollonius Dyscolus. He in turn, as everybody agrees, owed a lot to the Stoa, though the details of the story are very unclear. In the late thirteenth century, when the university of Paris was at its peak, some scholars there did some of the finest work in grammar ever done. Using Priscian's *Institutiones grammaticae* as a textbook, and Aristotle's *Posterior Analytics* as a guide to scientific method they produced the so-called modistic theory of grammar, which took very seriously the notion of *katholika theōrēmata* (καθολικὰ θεωρήματα), or as they would say, *principia* of the discipline.[30]

The greatest of the modists was Boethius of Dacia, a Dane who was active at the university of Paris in the years round 1270. In the main, my description of modistic theory will be based on his works, but most of the points I shall touch on were not controversial among the modists.[31] Boethius' most important methodological principle was this:

No expert in any discipline can bring about, concede or deny anything except on the basis of the principles of his science.[32]

Each science, that is, is fundamentally an autonomous theory. Now, to the modists language was essentially significative and only secondarily vocal. Signs need not be vocal, but (it was assumed) vocal sound is the only medium flexible enough to meet the needs of human communication, and so the consideration of vocal sound does belong to grammar, but only insofar as that vocal sound functions as a sign.[33] In modern terms

---

[30] For literature on modism consult Rosier-Catach 1999 and Marmo 1994. The classic study is Pinborg 1967.

[31] To the few and chosen who read Danish a comprehensive account of Boethius' philosophy is available in Ebbesen 2002. His theory of science is presented in Ebbesen 2000.

[32] '*Nullus artifex potest aliquid causare, concedere vel negare nisi ex principiis suae scientiae.*' Here quoted from Boethius, *De aeternitate mundi*, CPhD VI.2: 347–8.

[33] Boethius, *Modi Significandi*, CPhD IV: 27–8: '*si esset aliquid aliud quam vox ipsa quod ita conveniens rei signum posset esse vel subiectum modorum significandi, non magis consideraret grammaticus vocem quam illud aliud; . . . quia tamen nihil est huiusmodi . . . ergo* etc.' = 'if there were some other thing than vocal sound that was equally capable of functioning as a sign or as the bearer of modes of signifying, the grammarian would not privilege the study of vocal sound over [the study of]

this means that pure phonetics is not really the grammarian's business, whereas phonematics is within his province. Also, in case there were some not-conventional connection between certain sounds and certain types of meaning, that might be a matter for the grammarian to study.

The way the sign-function of words is stressed cannot but remind one of the Stoics, and there surely is a historical connection. Of course, Aristotle does use σημεῖον and σημαίνειν in the *Perihermeneias*, but it was the Stoics who put the duo of sign and signified at the centre of linguistic theory, and through numerous channels that piece of Stoic thought reached the medievals and became the mould in which much of their own thinking about language was formed.[34]

On the other hand, the modists could not set out to study natural relationships between sounds and meanings the way a Stoic could, for to the modists it was an important truth that the linking of a particular meaning with a particular sound is a matter of pure convention.

For the same reason, modists had little to say about morphology. The choice of phonetic means to carry lexical meaning and grammatical categories is, they held, beyond scientific description, since it is a matter of convention. Of course, one may assume that the impositors, those wise men who invented the basic vocabulary of each particular language, did exercise some wisdom also in the choice of sounds to carry particular meanings, and so it seems probable that we Latins say *lapidem* because the impositor thought of the fact that a stone *laedit pedem*, and that he chose to make it a masculine noun exactly because he thought of the stone as an active nuisance. Similarly the same or some other impositor decided on *petra* as an alternative word for the same thing because he thought of another characteristic of a stone, namely that my foot subjects it to wear, it gets *pede trita*, and when thought of in that passive role it is appropriate that it should be designated by a feminine noun.[35]

---

that other thing; [. . .] since, however, there is no such thing, therefore etc. [i.e., therefore vocal sound pertains in a non-accidental way to the grammarian's field of study]'. The same sentiment, though with a slightly different twist in Martinus, *Modus Significandi* ii.10, *CPhD* ii:7: '*sciendum quod vox per accidens consideratur a grammatico. Quia omne quod potest esse signum rei significatae etiam potest esse de consideratione grammatici. Sed quia vox est habilius signum quam aliquid aliud, utpote nutus corporeus et conniventia oculorum et huiusmodi, ideo plus consideratur a grammatico, et intelligendum quod hoc est per accidens.*' = 'Vocal sound is only accidentally studied by grammarians, because anything that may function as a sign of a signified thing may equally well be studied by grammarians; since, however, vocal sound is a more subtle sort of sign than any other – say, nodding or winking – vocal sound is more closely studied by grammarians, but one should understand that this is a matter of accident.'

34 Cf. Ebbesen, forthcoming.

35 This standard example is used by Martinus, *Modi significandi*, *CPhD* ii: 35–7.

We here hear echoes of ancient, and particularly Stoic, speculation about the origin of names and a certain naturalness in the choice of sounds and of grammatical categories, even in cases where they might seem semantically irrelevant. This, however, was not in any way important to the modistic theory. In fact, such speculation was a historical left-over of which they found it difficult to rid themselves completely, but strictly speaking, to their mind, it did not belong to grammar at all. The choice of expression is basically *ad placitum* and inaccessible to scientific description.

What is not *ad placitum* is the way humans conceptualise reality. Reality has a certain structure, and it is not only structured in natural kinds – humans, cows, daisies, granite, black, red, blue etc. The fundamental units are not universals but Avicennian common natures, neither being nor not being, neither universal nor particular etc. These common natures are not accessible to direct intellection, only when combined with a modal structure, so that they manifest themselves as existing and particular, for instance, or as universal, as static or as dynamic and in many other ways. We can grasp the common nature in any one of its appearances, with any one of its modes of being (*modi essendi*), but only thus.[36]

Now, since signification is so important to language, couldn't the science of language be concerned with what words signify, their *significata*? No! That would mean incorporating all other sciences into linguistics. The linguist presupposes the existence of an extralinguistic reality for language to be about, but he cannot generate it from linguistic principles: 'in fact, a noun which signifies no sort of thing ("nothing", e.g.), is no less a noun than one that does signify some sort of thing ("man", e.g.)'.[37]

The linguist must presuppose the existence of things with modes of being and also our concepts are derived from extramental reality, and that just as a common nature is attended by a number of modes of being, all of which cannot be actualised simultaneously, so a concept consists of an indeterminate nucleus and a number of modes of understanding. An actual thought of some sort of thing is always of the thing modified in some particular way. We have to choose between thinking of it universally or particularly, as potentially or as actually existing. The linguist will finally assume that whatever we can coherently think we can express in language. Words, then, must be endowed with (a) significata corresponding to the conceptual

---

[36] Admittedly, there was some confusion concerning the intelligibility of nude common natures. See Ebbesen 1988.

[37] Boethius Dacus, *Modi Significandi* qu. 11, *CPhD* iv: 45.86–8: '*Illud enim ita bene est nomen quod nullam rem specialem significat, sicut illud quod significat. Nam sicut hoc quod est "nihil" est nomen, sic hoc nomen "homo".*'

nuclei and (b) modes of signifying corresponding to the attendant modes of understanding.

The significata are none of the linguist's business. The modes of signifying are. Boethius describes the chain from realities and their modes to signs, significata and modes of signifying in the following words:

The modes of signifying have been derived from modes of understanding, and the same degree of diversity that occurs among modes of signifying occurs among the modes of understanding from which they are derived; and further, the same degree of diversity that occurs among those modes of understanding must necessarily occur among the modes of being from which they are derived.[38]

The chain from language to reality is unbroken: 'The modes of understanding have been derived from the proper modes of being of realities, or else they would be figments of the mind.'[39] They would be chimeras, that is. But of course, one should remember that what is preserved in language is only the structure, the modes of reality; which things there are around cannot be revealed through an inspection of language.

How the same common nature can be expressed in different ways is illustrated by means of the example PAIN: *dolor* ('pain', noun), *doleo* ('I am in pain', verb), *dolens* ('being in pain', participle), *dolenter* ('painfully', adverb), *heu* ('ouch', interjection).[40]

The structure of reality determines how humans can think about it, and this in turn determines the structure of language whose purpose is to allow us to express whatever we have in mind, no matter which department of reality we are thinking of. The subject-matter of grammar is accordingly defined as 'the way to express the intended concept of the mind through congruous discourse in every field'.[41] Since humans are not born with a language, this means people must have reflected on their own thoughts to

---

[38] Boethius Dacus, *Modi Significandi*, CPhD IV: 6–7: '*Modi enim significandi . . . a modis intelligendi accepti sunt, et quanta est differentia inter modos significandi tanta est differentia inter modos intelligendi a quibus accepti sunt . . . Et quanta est differentia inter istos modos intelligendi, tanta necessario debet esse inter modos essendi rerum a quibus accepti sunt.*'

[39] Op. cit., loc. cit. (continuation of preceding quotation): '*Modi autem intelligendi accepti sunt a propriis modis essendi rerum. Aliter enim essent figmenta intellectus.*'

[40] Boethius Dacus, *Modi Significandi*, qu. 14, CPhD IV: 55.61–56.7: '*idem conceptus mentis potest esse significatum cuiuslibet partis orationis. Quicquid enim a mente concipi potest, hoc potest per quamlibet partem orationis significari, dummodo modus significandi specificus partium illi non repugnet; et ille mentis conceptus cadens sub modo significandi specifico nominis facit significatum nominis, et cadens sub modo specifico verbi facit significatum verbi et sic de aliis ut patet dicendo sic: "dolor, doleo, dolens, dolenter, et heu", quae omnia idem significant. Et idem potest significare pronomen cum eis; quicquid enim pronomen potest demonstrare vel referre, hoc potest significare.*'

[41] Boethius Dacus, *Modi Significandi* qu. 7, CPhD IV: 32.106–8: '*Docet ergo grammatica modum exprimendi conceptum mentis intentum per sermonem congruum in omni materia.*'

find how to map the structure of thought onto sound. This has been done independently, it seems, by different peoples. The medium itself, sound, has a structure of its own, but nothing compels the creator of a language, the *impositor* as he is called, to choose one realisable sound to mean 'man' rather than another, nor is he compelled to choose endings rather than prothetic words (articles) to be the carriers of such modes of signifying as case or number. It is interesting to see which solutions have been preferred in particular languages, but the differences are superficial; the fundamental structure, the grammar, is the same everywhere.

Since the natures of realities are alike among all people, the modes of being and understanding are alike among all the speakers of the various languages, and as a consequence the modes of signifying are alike, and as a further consequence the modes of construing or speaking are alike, and so the whole grammar of one language is like that of any other language. [. . .] For it necessarily is just one specifically, only differentiated in respect of phonetic shape, and phonetic shape is accidental to grammar. The parts of speech are essentially the same in different languages, and differentiated only in accidental ways, as are the words used by Greeks compared to those used by Latins – the Greeks, e.g., use the noun 'anthropos' and the Latins the noun 'homo' . . . As for the fact that they [i.e. the Greeks] have an article and we do not have one, that is totally a matter of accident.[42]

All human languages sharing the same structure also guarantees total translatability.

The task of the grammarian is to make an exhaustive inventory of the modes of signifying needed to express any possible thought; and to state the rules for licit combinations of modes of signifying: 'Grammar is complete when there cannot occur a concept in the mind whose corresponding mode of expression is not taught in grammar.'[43]

When applied to the analysis of a particular language modistic grammar amounts to this. You look at a word and extract the encoded information,

---

[42] Boethius Dacus, *Modi Significandi* qu. 2, *CPhD* IV: 12: '*quia naturae rerum sunt similes apud omnes, ideo et modi essendi et modi intelligendi sunt similes apud omnes illos, apud quos sunt illa diversa idiomata, et per consequens similes modi significandi, et ergo per consequens similes modi construendi vel loquendi. Et sic tota grammatica quae est in uno idiomate est similis illi quae est in alio idiomate . . . Ipsa enim una est necessario in specie, solum diversificata secundum diversas figurationes vocum, quae sunt accidentales grammaticae . . . partes orationis in diversis idiomatibus sunt eaedem essentialiter et diversificatae accidentaliter, ut voces apud graecos et apud latinos, ut hoc nomen "antropos" apud graecos et hoc nomen "homo" apud latinos; . . . Quod autem ipsi habent articulum, nos autem non, hoc totum accidit.*'

[43] Boethius Dacus, *Modi Significandi* qu. 14, *CPhD* IV: 56.79–82: '*tunc complete habetur grammatica, quando nullus conceptus potest ex re in mente fieri, quin sibi respondeat aliquis modus exprimendi similis sibi traditus in grammatica.*'

you list its modes of signifying: 'this is a verb, that is, it signifies in a processual way, it signifies in the third-person way, singularly, transitively' – and so on. Then you apply your rule of construction, saying, 'This implies that a correct construction will occur if it is combined with a word endowed with the modes of signifying of a noun in the nominative singular, and also if another word endowed with the modes of signifying of a noun in the accusative singular or plural is added.'

The one sin the grammarian must not commit is to make *ad hoc* solutions by appealing to something not included in the principles of his science. Boethius castigates Priscian for treating the verb *fulminat* 'thunders' differently from such ordinary verbs as *currit* 'runs'.[44] It is bad grammar to allow one to be a complete sentence but not the other on the ground that there is only one possible agent of thundering, namely Jove, but several possible subjects of running. Priscian applies his knowledge about the core significates of the words 'thunder' and 'runs', but those are facts of the world that do not pertain to the grammarian. Similarly Boethius castigates Priscian for claiming that nouns signify substance and for basing the order of the parts of speech on the different sorts of things they signify: Priscian 'committed the mistake of transgressing the boundaries of his science by introducing categorial things, for they are outside the boundaries of grammar'.[45]

Modistic theory is a genuinely scientific theory of language, a genuine *grammatica speculativa*. We are offered a finite number of primitive terms – the modes of signifying – and a finite number of rules of combination permitting us to construct correct sentences and to check sentences for correctness. We are offered a system of sufficiently high abstraction that it can be applied to all languages.

Let us turn to logic. Our main source for Boethius' doctrine concerning the objects of logic are his questions on Aristotle's *Topics*, and that means we primarily have his treatment of the logical entities dealt with there, but the main outline of a general theory of logical entities is discernible. The *Topics*-related issues fall in two main classes: common ways of viewing (*communes intentiones*) and topical relationships (*habitudines locales*). Genus, species, whole and part, cause and effect are common ways of viewing, or intentions for short, while the relationship between a genus and its species, between a whole and its part, or between a cause and an effect, are topical relationships. Since, for Boethius, the topical relationships are derivative from the common intentions, we can concentrate on the latter.

[44] Boethius Dacus, *Modi Significandi*, qu. 11, *CPhD* IV: 47.
[45] Boethius Dacus, *Modi Significandi*, qu. 31, *CPhD* IV: 97.63–98.65: '*Peccabat etiam in hoc, quod excedebat metas suae scientiae, cum inducit res praedicamentales, quae sunt extra metas grammaticae.*'

To Boethius, grammar and logic were very similar, parallel, yet distinct disciplines. We have heard him say that we have developed a complete grammar when for any concept that may occur in our mind, the grammar has registered a corresponding way of expressing it. But he goes on and says: 'And the same holds for dialectic.'[46]

Just as the ways of being of things are the foundation of the ways of understanding them, which in turn are the foundation of the ways of signifying them, so the ways of being of things are the foundation of the common intentions. Ways of understanding and signifying are common, so that once you have got them you need no longer think about those definite things which in your own history or in that of humanity gave rise to them. In the same way the intentions are free of ties to some definite things. Further, ways of signifying and intentions are also common in the sense that they do not only concern a certain section of the total reality. Everything has properties that must be signified in one way or another, and everything has properties in virtue of which it enters into logical relationships.[47]

The thing signified by the word 'animal' has a way of being that makes it divisible by means of specific differences, and that is why the intention 'genus' belongs to it. It is characteristic of intentions, and consequently of their underlying modes of being, that they are relative. A genus is only a genus in relation to other things which are its species.

Boethius also calls the intentions 'ways of knowing' (*modi sciendi*),[48] and he seems to waver slightly over whether they belong ontologically in the thing or in the intellect. But at least they clearly are not in a strong sense real: the notion of intention only has a function in connection with an intellect.

Using the intentions as primitive notions we can formulate topical relationships and maxims that spell out the conceptual content. We thus have the topical relationship between a genus and its species, that between one and the other of two opposites, and axioms such as 'every genus is predicated of each of its species', 'affirming one opposite implies denying the other opposite'. The latter maxim may be used to support the inference 'This is hot, consequently it is not cold', but if you do so you leave pure logic, for 'hot' and 'cold' are not logical notions, they belong in natural science.[49]

[46] Boethius, *Modi Significandi* qu. 14, *CPhD* IV.56: '*tunc complete habetur grammatica, quando nullus conceptus potest ex re in mente fieri, quin sibi respondeat aliquis modus exprimendi similis sibi traditus in grammatica, et similiter dico de dialectica.*'
[47] Boethius, *Qu. Top.* 1.2, *CPhD* VI.1: 14–15.   [48] Boethius, *Qu. Top.* prooemium, *CPhD* VI.1: 6.65.
[49] Boethius Dacus, *Modi Significandi* qu. 18, *CPhD* IV: 68f.; cf. qu. 8, p. 34.

The intentions of logic are abstract mappings of real relationships, they are, as Boethius says, signs of such relationships, not their causes. If Socrates is a man, it follows that he is an animal, but the cause of this *consequentia* is not to be sought in the relationship between genus and species, but in the nature of things. To find out about this matter you will have to leave logic and learn what a man is and what an animal is.[50] It is important for Boethius to stress that things ground the logical relationships, not the other way round; he does not want to make relative notions into real causes.

Thus Boethius' logic is formal, in a modern sense of this word. It is like a language with its own terms and a syntax. However, unlike in ordinary language, all logical expressions are uninterpreted, no logical expression signifies an identifiable thing. We can say much that is true about genus, species, predication and negation without saying anything whatsoever about some identifiable thing. If we start to talk about men and animals we have left logic and moved into the field of the real sciences.

In this Boethius' logic agrees perfectly with his grammar. It is good grammar to talk about the rules of concord concerning number and person that will permit a congruent construction of a noun with a verb. But if you start to talk about the lexical meaning of some definite noun, you have left the sphere of grammar.

For this reason Boethius happily accepts 'I shall run yesterday' as a well-formed sentence.[51] From a grammatical point of view what matters is only that 'shall run' is a verb and 'yesterday' an adverb. Incompatibility of their lexical meanings is none of the grammarian's concern.

We have moved a long way away from Hellenistic theories of language. But a little scrutiny will show that Boethius owes a considerable debt to Hellenism. One of the foundations of the theory is the view that grammaticality is decided on a different level than surface language: insensible grammatical features, his *modi significandi*, determine grammaticality because they will only combine according to certain laws. The oldest source Boethius knew for this idea was Priscian (though he did not talk of *modi significandi*, of course). Priscian derived his conception of grammatical features as intelligible entities from Apollonius. But it looks as though the Stoics were the first to realise that logical and grammatical analysis requires a level at which one can operate with formal quasi-things rather than with words or their referents. One might cite Plato's ὄνομα – ῥῆμα analysis of the proposition as a precursor (*Sophist* 261–2), and one might say that *de facto* Aristotle in his logic created a world of logical quasi-things, such as universal negative

[50] Boethius Dacus, *Qu. Top.* 1.4–5, *CPhD* vi.l: 17–24.
[51] Boethius Dacus, *Modi significandi* qu. 85, *CPhD* iv: 203.35–6.

propositions, but the Stoics seem to have realised the implications, at least to some extent, as evidenced by their special vocabulary in which formal entities are marked by the ending -μα as opposed to real entities in -σις and by their explicit attribution of a special ontological status to sayables and the like.[52]

In some ways, I think, we may see Boethius' highly developed conception of a formal logic and a formal grammar as a mature version of a Stoic idea. He had inherited their dialectic in a much changed version in which, among other violence, it had suffered being cleaved into two. But he brought the two halves very close together with his theory of grammatical and logical objects and their common derivation from reality.

* * *

Modist grammar raises a number of interesting questions. For instance: how is the set of modes of signifying related to the morphological devices of a language? The basic, naïve, assumption was that Latin inflection is a true guide to the number of modes of signifying. But Greek, it was thought, used articles to indicate case, not endings. This suggests that there may be any number of ways to express a given mode of signifying, and so counting the categories used in Latin inflection may be of little use. Some logical intentions appear to have no grammatical counterparts. But why don't we have a *modus significandi per modum universalis* with an appropriate morphological device to express it? The sad fact was that the modists could not *a priori* deduce the set of modes of signifying, nor that of logical *intentiones*.

If the modists had known Quintilian, they might have taken comfort in the fact that the same type of problem had plagued men in the Hellenistic age. Quintilian wonders whether there is a grammatical function shared by Greek and Latin but without independent morphological manifestation in either. There would seem to be some *vis*, he says, that in Latin borrows the form of the ablative and in Greek that of the dative.[53] We have a name for that *vis:* it is *casus instrumentalis*, but then, of course, we are acquainted

---

[52] Notice, I am not claiming that there was a Stoic syntactic analysis just like that of later times. It remains possible that the 'subject' and the predicate were treated differently, so that the basic analysis was '(*a*) noun/pronoun signifying (*A*) some existing thing(s) + (*b*) expression including a verb, which signifies (*B*) an activity (πρᾶγμα, κατηγόρημα) caused by *A*'. If this was the analysis, *A* and *B* were not of the same ontological type, and it would only be the *B* type of significate that inspired later generations. For discussion of Stoic syntax, see especially Frede 1977, id. 1978, and Luhtala 2000. Also notice that whatever the genuine Stoic view, Augustine assigns a λεκτόν to every (categorematic) word. '*Quicquid autem ex verbo non aures sed animus sentit et ipso animo tenetur inclusum, dicibile vocatur*', he says in *De dialectica* c.5, p. 88 Pinborg = 8 Crecelius.

[53] Quintilian, *Inst.* 1.4.25: '*Quaerat etiam < sc. an intelligent teacher > sitne apud Graecos vis quaedam sexti casus et apud nos quoque septimi. Nam cum dico "hasta percussi" non utor ablativi natura, nec si idem graece dicam, dativi.*'

with languages that actually have an independent instrumental in their morphology.

Beautiful as Boethius' theory of grammar and logic is, he had not managed to get rid of the inherent weakness of all formal grammar, namely that in order to get a manageable system it must disregard pragmatics and condemn unusual, yet intelligible, utterances.[54] Sextus' objections remain, and the medievals were painfully aware of the fact. The discussion of *figurae* was a traditional part of grammatical investigation, and by definition there is no way a figure consisting in a mismatch of modes of signifying can be declared acceptable by modist grammar. In one way or another one will have to introduce a human ability to understand a speaker's intentions even when they are transmitted in a basically unintelligible linguistic form. For most medievals the result was a sort of split personality: when dealing with grammar in general they would be formalists, when looking at figurative speech they would in one way or another introduce a *bonitas intelligentis* allowing the receiver of a flawed message to take extralinguistic facts into account in such a way that he can (a) reconstruct the canonical form of the message, and (b) register the reasons that pushed the producer of the message to prefer a non-canonical form (the *ratio qua potuit fieri* and the *ratio qua debuit fieri*). With a formula of Hellenistic origin a figure was often described as a *vitium ratione excusatum*.[55] Nobody managed to incorporate the excusing reasons into the principal theory of syntax, and so people had to live with the paradoxical notion of an excusable, and hence correct, flawed expression.

Just as we have seen the medievals in their formalist mood use tools originally forged in the Hellenistic era, we see them using a Hellenistic tool to challenge their own formalism. I take it that the medieval notion of *figura* was of Stoic origin. However, even if that is not the case, it certainly has its roots in Hellenistic times.

There is, perhaps, one way out of the formalist's dilemma. Suppose you basically give up the notion of a set of linguistic laws that describe a given language, and concentrate instead on the notion of transmission of information. Any transfer of information in which linguistic tools are used will count as correct if the transfer succeeds. It is still necessary to

[54] The following part about non-formal trends in the Middle Ages is heavily indebted to studies by Rosier-Catach. See her 1999 article, where references to older studies may be found.
[55] Cf. Quintilian, *Inst.* 1.5.5 '*Prima barbarismi ac soloecismi foeditas absit. Sed quia interim excusantur haec vitia aut consuetudine aut auctoritate aut vetustate aut denique vicinitate virtutum (nam saepe a figuris ea separare difficile est). . . .*'. For an example of a medieval (thirteenth-century) discussion of vices and figures see Kilwardby 1984.

operate with certain norms, but only as a background situation: the receiver of a message has certain expectations as regards its linguistic form, but there are many other factors at work in the transmission of information, and so, if the form of the message does not deviate too much from the listener's expectations he may catch it and he may also modify his linguistic assumptions. This allows a speaker to innovate at any time. The linguistic system becomes dynamic rather than static.

This was the line of thought adopted by Roger Bacon, an older contemporary of Boethius of Dacia. Bacon had some extraordinary ideas about linguistic communication.[56] He saw that as just one of the many ways information or power could be transmitted – to him the two were basically identical. Words do not work in isolation, but factors such as the speaker's intention are also important for the efficacy of linguistic acts. Magic and persuasion may have a common explanation: words pronounced in the right situation by someone who wills something definite may change reality. Bacon's notion of information (*species*) owes little if anything to Hellenistic speculation; on the other hand, he would scarcely have arrived at his theory if the notion of a *vis verborum* had not been traditional, and the notion of a *vis* or δύναμις possessed by linguistic expressions had only become important in Hellenistic times.[57] But perhaps the striking example of Bacon's innovative use of Hellenistic conceptual tools is his use of the notion of *imposition* coupled with *translatio*, another Hellenistic notion.

Bacon simply claims that we are performing new impositions all the time. You have got a name for some living person, John. He is run over by a cart and you say 'Carry John away so that he can be washed and buried.' Everybody understands you, but actually you have performed a new imposition, adding, by *translatio*, a new meaning to 'John', so that it can now also designate a dead body. By this new imposition you have rendered the word equivocal. But things may get much worse. The following example is of my own making, but it illustrates modes of imposition discussed by Bacon:[58]

Let us assume that some hundred years ago the word 'dodo' was instituted as a sign of an actually existing universal instantiated in several individuals. The word did not cease to be significant by falling into disuse, so all the

---

[56] The best accounts of Bacon's thoughts about language are Rosier 1994 and Rosier-Catach 1997b, where references to important older literature will be found.

[57] Plato, *Cratylus* 394b suggests that each name has a δύναμις just as each medical drug has a peculiar δύναμις, but only later was the word developed into a full-blown technical term of linguistics.

[58] The following paragraph is for the most part a literal quotation of Ebbesen 1983: 76. Further on Bacon, imposition and translation in Rosier 1994, ch. 4, where source references may be found (principal sources: Bacon's *De signis* and his *Compendium studii theologiae*).

S. EBBESEN

time from its imposition to the death of the last dodo the word signified
a certain universal. However, people also used the word to signify other
things, an individual dodo, for instance. But the first to call an individual
bird a dodo, thereby gave the word a new signification: he performed a new
imposition and now it was equivocal. If he noticed the fact, he may have
said 'dodo is equivocal', thus using the word in a third sense, and actually
performing a new imposition, making 'dodo' signify the word 'dodo'. Let
us now suppose that he kills the dodo, and that it was the last of its species.
If he then looks at the dead bird and says 'The dodo is beautiful,' he
performs a fourth imposition, transferring the word to become a sign of
bones, flesh, feathers etc. that once belonged to a dodo. And if he continues
with a remark about the species, saying 'Indeed, the dodo is the funniest
of all birds,' he is unknowingly performing a fifth imposition, because
he uses the word as a sign of an imagined universal, not of an actual
one, as he himself destroyed the actuality of the species by killing the last
specimen.

According to Chrysippus every word is ambiguous. According to Bacon
every normal word is multiply ambiguous, but for the most part this just
does not matter. Speakers generally manage to get the intended message
across in spite of constant violations of previously established linguistic
practice.

Of course, *translationes* tend to follow a pattern, so that the receiver of a
message will often be able to decode it by looking at a small set of standard
types of *translatio*, such as the ones illustrated in the dodo example, and
decide which one is most likely to be the relevant one in the situation.
Bacon does not give up on listing types of supposition and *translatio*. But
his deeper point seems to be that rules can always be overruled by the needs
of the moment, and that the wonderful thing about language is that you
can work creatively with it so that you can actually say new things and
make people understand them.

Boethius and Bacon may have met each other. They were both in Paris
in the late 1260s, so far as we can figure out. Both were very intelligent, and
both very sure of themselves. What a discussion they could have had! In an
important sense, they represented the conflict between an analogist view of
language and an anomalist one. Boethius with his analogist attitude could
make a beautiful static description of the language with great predictive
value as to what would be correct and what not. Bacon with his anomalist
attitude offered a picture, in many ways convincing, of a dynamic language,
but he would not be able to offer much guidance on what would be an
acceptable utterance and what not.

Somehow, it seems necessary to ride the fence and be both an anomalist and an analogist – as, in fact, Quintilian had realised, though perhaps without a deeper understanding of the psychology of the real scientist who so desperately wants there to be a system that one may spell out in a finite number of propositions.

* * *

Postscript The sixteenth-century humanistic attempt on the life of real science culminated in the work of Petrus Ramus who espoused the Stoic definition of *ars* as a system of normative propositions (*praecepta*), produced a set of primitive terms in the shape of elementary topical notions (*argumenta*), with no other warrant for its sufficiency than Cicero's authority, and with no clear operational rules attached to them – and otherwise let good *usus* (Sextus' συνήθεια, Quintilian's *consuetudo*) decide not only what was beautiful but also what was truth-preserving, perhaps even what was truth-making. I am convinced that Chrysippus would have considered Ramus a caricature of himself – after all, the man never bothered to work out the fine details of any theory, since that would reveal a petty scholastic mind with no understanding of the dynamic universe. But still, the caricature raises questions about the model. One would like to know how conscious Chrysippus was of the tension between his vision of a dynamic universe – be it one with an unalterable, finite programme – and his scientific urge to produce closed, complete theories. And also to which degree he was aware of – and elaborated – the formalism of his διαλεκτική.

References

Ackrill, J. (1963) *Aristotle's Categories and De Interpretatione*. Oxford.

Adrados, F. Rodríguez (1999) *History of the Graeco-Latin Fable: Introduction and From the Origins to the Hellenistic Age*. Vol. 1. tr. by L. A. Ray; rev. and upd. by the author and G.-J. van Dijk. Mnemosyne Suppl. 201. Leiden–Boston–Cologne.

Algra, K. (1997) 'Lucretius and the Epicurean other', in *Lucretius and His Intellectual Background*, eds. K. A. Algra et al. Amsterdam, etc.: 141–50.

Algra, K., J. Barnes, J. Mansfeld, and M. Schofield (eds.) (1999) *The Cambridge History of Hellenistic Philosophy*. Cambridge.

Allen, J. (1998) 'Epicurean inferences: the evidence of Philodemus' *De Signis'*, in *Method in Ancient Philosophy*, ed. J. Gentzler. Oxford: 306–49.

(2001) *Inference from Signs. Ancient Debates about the Nature of Evidence*. Oxford.

Annas, J. (1993) 'Epicurus on agency', in *Passions & Perceptions. Studies in the Hellenistic Philosophy of Mind* (Proceedings of the Fifth Symposium Hellenisticum), eds. J. Brunschwig and M. Nussbaum. Cambridge and Paris: 53–71.

Apelt, O. (tr.) (1955) Diogenes Laertius: *Leben und Meinungen berühmter Philosophen*. Berlin (originally published in 1921).

Arrighetti, G. (ed.) (1973) *Epicuro: Opere*. 2nd ed., Biblioteca di cultura filosofica 41. Turin. 1st ed. 1960.

Asmis, E. (1984) *Epicurus' Scientific Method*. Ithaca–London.

Atherton, C. (1988) 'Hand over fist: the failure of Stoic rhetoric', *CQ* 38: 392–427.

(1993) *The Stoics on Ambiguity*. Cambridge.

(1996) 'What every grammarian knows?', *CQ* 46: 236–90.

(forthcoming) *Lucretius on the Origins of Language*.

Augustine (1975) *De dialectica*, ed. J. Pinborg. Dordrecht and Boston.

Avramides, A. (1989) *Meaning and Mind*. Cambridge, Mass.–London.

(1997) 'Intention and convention', in *A Companion to the Philosophy of Language*, eds. B. Hale, C. Wright. Oxford: 60–86.

Ax, W. (1978) 'ψόφος, φωνή und διάλεκτος als Grundbegriffe der aristotelischen Theorie', *Glotta* 56: 245–71, reprinted in Ax (2000) 19–39.

(1991) 'Sprache als Gegenstand der alexandrinischen und pergamenischen Philologie', in *Sprachtheorien der abendländischen Antike*, ed. P. Schmitter. Tübingen: 275–301.

(1995) 'Disputare in utramque partem. Zum literarischen Plan und zur dialektischen Methode Varros in de lingua Latina 8–10', *RhM* 138: 146–77.

(2000) *Lexis und Logos: Studien zur antiken Grammatik und Rhetorik*. Stuttgart.

Babcock, B. A. (1978) *The Reversible World: Symbolic Inversion in Art and Society*. Ithaca.

Bacon, Roger (1988) *Compendium of the Study of Theology*, ed. and tr. Th. S. Maloney, Studien und Texte zur Geistesgeschichte des Mittelalters 20. Leiden.

Bacon, Roger: *De Signis*. See Fredborg et al. 1978.

Bailey, C. (ed.) (1926) *Epicurus: The Extant Remains*. Oxford.

(1928) *Greek Atomists and Epicurus*. Oxford.

(ed.) (1947) *T. Lucreti Cari De Rerum Natura Libri Sex* (3 vols.). Oxford. Corr. ed. 1963.

Barnes, J. (1993) 'Meaning, saying and thinking', in *Dialektiker und Stoiker. Zur Logik der Stoa und ihrer Vorläufer*, eds. K. Döring and T. Ebert. Stuttgart: 47–61.

(1999) 'Linguistics: meaning' = 'Language 1.2', in Algra et al. (1999) 193–213.

(2003) *Porphyry: Introduction*, Clarendon Later Ancient Philosophy, Oxford.

Barney, R. (2001) *Names and Nature in Plato's Cratylus*. New York.

Barwick, K. (1922) *Remmius Palaemon und die römische ars grammatica. Philologus Suppl.* 15, 1922.

(1957a) 'Probleme der stoischen Sprachlehre und Rhetorik', *Abh. der sächsischen Akademie der Wissenschaften zu Leipzig*, Phil.-hist. Kl. Band 49 Heft 3. Berlin.

(1957b) 'Widmung und Entstehungsgeschichte von Varros De Lingua Latina', *Philologus* 101: 298–304.

Bertoli, E. (1980) *Tempora rerum. Modalità del progresso humano in Lucrezio*. Verona.

Bett, R. (1997) *Sextus Empiricus. Against the Ethicists*. Oxford.

Blank, D. L. (1982) *Ancient Grammar and Philosophy. The Syntax of Apollonius Dyscolus*. Chico, Calif.

(1995) 'Philodemus on the technicity of rhetoric', in Obbink (1995) 178–88.

(1998) *Sextus Empiricus: Against the Grammarians*. Oxford.

(2000) 'The organization of grammar in Ancient Greece', in *History of the Language Sciences*, eds. S. Auroux et al. Berlin–New York: 1 400–17.

Bobzien, S. (1996) 'Stoic syllogistic', *OSAP* 14: 133–92.

(1998) *Determinism and Freedom in Stoic Philosophy*. Oxford.

(1999) 'Logic: Megarics, Stoics', in Algra et al. (1999) 83–157.

(2002) 'Chrysippus and the epistemic theory of vagueness', *Proceedings of the Aristotelian Society* vol. 102: 217–38.

Boegehold, A. L. (1999) *When a Gesture was Expected. A Selection of Examples from Archaic and Classical Greek Literature*. Princeton.

Boethius Dacus (1969) *Modi significandi sive Quaestiones super Priscianum maiorem*, eds. J. Pinborg and H. Roos, Corpus Philosophorum Danicorum Medii Aevi IV. Copenhagen.

(1976a) *Quaestiones super librum Topicorum*, eds. N. J. Green-Pedersen and J. Pinborg, Corpus Philosophorum Danicorum Medii Aevi VI.1. Copenhagen.

(1976b) *De aeternitate mundi*, ed. N. J. Green-Pedersen, Corpus Philosophorum Danicorum Medii Aevi VI.2. Copenhagen.

Boethius, Manlius Severinus (1847) *In Categorias Aristotelis commentaria*, in *Patrologia Latina*, ed. J.-P. Migne, LXIV: 159A–294C. Paris.

Bollack, J., M. Bollack, and H. Wismann (eds.) (1971) *La lettre d' Epicure [à Hérodote]*. Paris.

Bollack, M. (1978) *La raison de Lucrèce*. Paris.

Boot, J. C. G. (1894) *Mnemosyne* 22, 409–12.

Bouffartigue, J. and M. Patillon (eds.) (1977) *Porphyre: De l'abstinence I*. Paris.

Boyancé, P. (1963) *Lucrèce et l'Épicurisme*. Paris.

Boys-Stones, G. R. (2001) *Post-Hellenistic Philosophy: A Study in its Development from the Stoics to Origen*. Oxford.

Brancacci, A. (1990) *Oikeios Logos: la filosofia del linguaggio di Antistene*. Naples.

Brandt, S. (ed.) (1890) *L. Caeli Firmiani Lactanti opera omnia*. Pars I. Prague etc.
(1891) 'Lactantius und Lucretius', *Neue Jahrbücher für Philologie und Pädagogik* 61 (= *Jahrbücher für classische Philologie* 37): 225–59.

Branham, R. B. (1989) *Unruly Eloquence. Lucian and the Comedy of Traditions*. Cambridge, Mass.: ch.1, 11–63 (= the Rhetoric of Laughter).
(1996) 'Defacing the currency. Diogenes' rhetoric and the invention of cynicism', in Branham and Goulet-Cazé (1996) 81–104 (= (1993) Goulet-Cazé and Goulet: 445–73).

Branham, R. B. and Marie-Odile Goulet-Cazé (1996) *The Cynics. The Cynic Movement in Antiquity and Its Legacy*. Berkeley.

Bremmer, J. and H. Roodenburg (1991) *A Cultural History of Gesture. From Antiquity to the Present Day*. Cambridge.

Brennan, T. (1998) 'The old Stoic theory of emotions', in *The Emotions in Hellenistic Philosophy*, eds. J. Sihvola and T. Engberg-Pedersen. Dordrecht: 21–70.

Brittain, C. (2001) *Philo of Larissa*. Oxford.
(2002) 'Non-rational perception in the Stoics and Augustine', *OSAP* 22.1: 253–308.

Broggiato, M. (2001) *Cratete di Mallo. I frammenti*. La Spezia.

Broich, U. (1985) 'Formen der Markierung von Intertextualität', in *Intertextualität. Formen, Funktionen, anglistische Fallstudien*, eds. U. Broich and M. Pfister. Tübingen: 31–47.

Browning Cole, E. (1992) 'Theophrastus and Aristotle on animal intelligence', in *Theophrastus. His Psychological, Doxographical, and Scientific Writings*, eds. W. W. Fortenbaugh and D. Gutas. New Brunswick–London (Rutgers University Studies in Classical Humanities 5) 45–62.

Brunschwig, J. (1994) *Papers in Hellenistic Philosophy*. Cambridge.
(1995) *Études sur les philosophies hellénistiques*. Paris.

Brunschwig, J. and G. E. R. Lloyd (eds.) (1996) *Le Savoir Grec*. Paris.

Buchholz, E. (1884) *Die homerischen Realien* III 2. Leipzig.

Burnyeat, M. (1977) 'Wittgenstein and Augustine *DE MAGISTRO*', *Proceedings of the Aristotelian Society* suppl. 61:1–24.

Casanova, A. (ed.) (1984) *I Frammenti di Diogene d'Oenoande.* Studi e testi 6. Florence.

Caston, V. (1999) 'Something and nothing: the Stoics on concepts and universals', *OSAP* 17: 145–213.

Chandler, C. (1996) 'References to "Common Parlance" in Philodemus' *Rhetorica* Book III', in *Epicureismo Greco e Romano*, vol. II, eds. G. Giannantoni and M. Gigante. Naples: 587–610.

Chauve, A. (1993) 'Le cynisme des cyniques', in *Scepticisme et Exégèse: hommage à Camille Pernot*, ed. B. Besnier. Fontenay-aux-Roses: 77–84.

Cherniss, H. (1977) *Selected Papers.* Leiden.

(1986) *Plutarch's Moralia, XIII Part II*, Cambridge, Mass.

Cherry, C. (1978) *On Human Communication. A Review, a Survey and a Criticism*, 3rd ed. 1st ed. 1957; 2nd ed. 1966. Cambridge, Mass.

Chilton, C. W. (1962) 'The Epicurean theory of the origin of language. A study of Diogenes of Oenoanda, fragments X and XI (W.)', *AJP* 83: 159–67.

(ed.) (1967) *Diogenes Oenoandensis.* Leipzig.

(tr.) (1971) *Diogenes of Oenoanda. The Fragments.* London–New York–Toronto.

Cole, T. (1990) *Democritus and the Sources of Greek Anthropology*, 2nd ed. Atlanta.

Conche, M. (ed.) (1987) *Épicure: Lettres et maximes*, 2nd ed. Paris.

Costa, C. D. N. (ed.) (1984) *Lucretius. De rerum natura* v, with introduction and commentary. Oxford.

Csapo, E. and W. J. Slater (1995) *The Context of Ancient Drama.* Ann Arbor.

Dahlmann, J. H. (1928) *De philosophorum Graecorum sententiis ad loquellae originem pertinentibus capita duo.* Diss. Leipzig.

(1932) *Varro und die hellenistische Sprachtheorie.* Berlin–Zürich, reprinted 1964.

(1940) *Varro, De lingua latina, Buch VIII.* Berlin, reprinted 1966.

Dam, R. J. (1930) *De Analogia observationes in Varronem grammaticamque Romanorum.* Diss. Amsterdam.

Decleva Caizzi, F. (1966) *Antisthenis Fragmenta.* Milan.

Deichgräber, K. (1965²) *Die Griechische Empirikerschule.* Berlin.

De Lacy, P. (1939) 'The Epicurean analysis of language', *AJPh* 60: 85–92.

(1957) 'Limit and variation in the Epicurean philosophy', *Phoenix* 23: 104–12.

(1980–1) *Galen. On the Doctrines of Hippocrates and Plato*, Corpus Medicorum Graecorum v 4, 1.2 (2 vols.). Berlin.

De Lacy, E. and P. (eds.) (1941) *Philodemus: On Methods of Inference.* Philadelphia.

(1978) *Philodemus: On Methods of Inference*, rev. ed. La scuola di Epicuro 1. Naples.

De Marco, V. (1957) 'La contesa *analogia-anomalia* I. Sesto Empirico', *Rendiconti dell'Accademia di Archeologia, Lettere e Belle Arti di Napoli* 32: 129–48.

Dexippus (1888) *In Aristotelis Categorias Commentarium*, ed. A. Busse, Commentaria in Aristotelem Graeca IV.2. Berlin.

Diller, H. (1934) *Wanderarzt und Aitiologie. Studien zur hippokratischen Schrift* περὶ ἀέρων ὑδάτων τόπων. Philologus Supplementband 26, vol. III. Leipzig.

Dodds, E. R. (1973) *The Ancient Concept of Progress and Other Essays.* Oxford.

Döring, K. (1993) ' "Spielereien, mit verdecktem Ernst vermischt". Unterhaltsame Formen literarischer Wissenschaftsvermittlung bei Diogenes von Sinope und den frühen Kynikern', in *Vermittlung und Tradierung von Wissen in der griechischen Kultur*, eds. W. Kullmann and J. Althoff. Tübingen: 337–52.

Doty, R. (1976) '*Ennoēmata. Prolēpsis* and common notions', *Southwestern Journal of Philosophy* 7.3: 143–8.

Downing, F. G. (1993) 'Cynics and Christians, Oedipus and Thyestes', *JEH* 44: 1–10.

Dudley, D. R. (1967) *History of Cynicism. From Diogenes to the 6th cent. AD.* Hildesheim.

Dyson, H. (2003) *Prolepsis and Common Conception in the Early Stoa.* Diss. Emory University.

Ebbesen, S. (1981) *Commentators and Commentaries on Aristotle's Sophistici Elenchi. A Study of Post-Aristotelian Ancient and Medieval Writings on Fallacies*, vols. I–III = Corpus Latinum Commentariorum in Aristotelem Graecorum VII.1–3. Brill: Leiden. [Part of vol. I reprinted as Ebbesen (1990).]

(1983) 'The Odyssey of semantics from the Stoa to Buridan', in Eschbach and Trabant (1983) 67–85, Italian translation in Fedriga and Puggioni (1993) 165–83.

(1988) 'Concrete accidental terms: late thirteenth-century debates about problems relating to such terms as "album" ', in *Meaning and Inference in Medieval Philosophy*, ed. N. Kretzmann. Dordrecht: 107–74.

(1990) 'Porphyry's legacy to logic: a reconstruction', in *Aristotle Transformed. The Ancient Commentators and their Influence*, ed. R. Sorabji. Ithaca: 141–71.

(ed.) (1995) *Sprachtheorien in Spätantike und Mittelalter*, = P. Schmitter (ed.) *Geschichte der Sprachtheorie* III, Tübingen.

(1998) 'Medieval theories of language', in *Routledge Encyclopedia of Philosophy.* London–New York, V 389–414.

(1999) 'Anonymus D'Orvillensis' commentary on Aristotle's *Categories*', *CIMAGL* 70: 229–423.

(2000) 'Boethius of Dacia: Science is a serious game', *Theoria* 66: 145–58.

(2002) *Den danske filosofis historie i middelalderen, ca. 1170–1536.* Copenhagen.

(2004) 'Where were the Stoics in the Middle Ages?', in *Stoicism: Traditions and Transformations*, eds. J. Zupko and S. Strange. Cambridge: 108–31.

Ebbesen, S., K. M. Fredborg, and L. O. Nielsen (eds.) (1983) 'Compendium logicae Porretanum ex codice Oxoniensi Collegii Corporis Christi 250: A manual of Porretan doctrine by a pupil of Gilbert's', *CIMAGL* 46: iii–xviii + 1–113.

Ebbesen, S. and R. L. Friedmann (eds.) (1999) *Medieval Analyses in Language and Cognition. Acts of the Symposium 'The Copenhagen School of Medieval Philosophy, January 10–13, 1996'*, Det Kongelige Danske Videnskabernes Selskab, Historisk-filosofiske Meddelelser LXXVII. Copenhagen.

Eberhardus Bethuniensis (1887) *Graecismus*, ed. J. Wrobel. Bratislava, reprinted Hildesheim 1987.

Edelstein, L. and I. Kidd (eds.) (1972) *Posidonius: Vol. 1, The Fragments*, Cambridge.

Egli, U. (1979) 'The Stoic concept of anaphora', in *Semantics from Different Points of View*, eds. R. Bäuerle, U. Egli, and A. von Stechow. Berlin: 266–83.

Ekman, P. and W. V. Friesen (1969) 'The repertoire of nonverbal behavior: categories, origins, usage and coding', *Semiotica* 1: 49–98.

Erler, M. (1994) '1.Epikur', in *Grundriss der Geschichte der Philosophie. Die Philosophie der Antike*: IV: *Die hellenistische Philosophie*, ed. H. Flashar. Basle: 29–202.

Ernout, A. (ed.) (1955) *Lucrèce. De la nature. Texte établi et traduit* (2 vols.), 9th ed. 1st ed. 1920. Paris.

Ernout, A. and L. Robin (eds.) (1962) (cited as Robin (1962)) *Lucrèce. De Rerum Natura. Commentaire exégétique et critique*, 2nd ed. 1st ed. 1925–8 (3 vols.). Paris.

Eschbach, A. and J. Trabant (eds.) (1983) *History of Semiotics*, Foundations of Semiotics VII. Amsterdam: 67–85.

Everson, S. (ed.) (1994) *Language: Cambridge Companions to Ancient Thought 3*. Cambridge.

Fedriga, R. and S. Puggioni (eds.) (1993) *Logica e linguaggio nel medioevo*. Milano.

Fehling, D. (1956–7) 'Varro und die grammatische Lehre von der Analogie und der Flexion', *Glotta* 35: 214–70; 36: 48–100.

(1965) 'Zwei Untersuchungen zur griechischen Sprachphilosophie', *RhM* 108: 212–29.

Fortenbaugh, W. W. (1984) *Quellen zur Ethik Theophrasts*. Studien zur antiken Philosophie 12. Amsterdam.

Fredborg, K. M., L. O. Nielsen, and J. Pinborg (1978) 'An unedited part of Roger Bacon's 'Opus Maius': 'De Signis', *Traditio* 34: 75–136.

Frede, M. (1974) *Die stoische Logik*, Göttingen.

(1977) 'The origins of traditional grammar', in *Historical and Philosophical Dimensions of Logic. Methodology and Philosophy of Science*, eds. R. E. Butts and J. Hintikka. Dordrecht: 51–79, reprinted in Frede (1987) 338–59.

(1978) 'Principles of Stoic grammar', in *The Stoics*, ed. J. M. Rist. Berkeley: 27–75, reprinted in Frede (1987) 301–37.

(1987) *Essays in Ancient Philosophy*. Oxford and New York.

(1989) 'Chaeremon der Stoiker', *ANRW* II.36.3. Berlin: 2066–2103.

(1990) 'An empiricist view of knowledge: memorism', in *Cambridge Companions to Ancient Thought 1. Epistemology*, ed. S. Everson. Cambridge: 225–50.

(1994a) 'The Stoic notion of a *lekton*', in Everson (1994) 109–28.

(1994b) 'The Stoic conception of reason', in *Hellenistic Philosophy* vol. II, ed. K. Boudouris. Athens: 50–63.

(1994c) 'The Stoic notion of a grammatical case', *BICS* 39: 13–24.

(1999) 'Stoic epistemology', in Algra et al. (1999) 295–322.

Fredouille, J. C. (1972) 'Lucrèce et le "double progrès contrastant"', *Pallas* 19: 11–27.

Friedländer, P. (1941) 'Pattern of sound and atomistic theory in Lucretius', *AJP* 62: 13–24; repr. in his *Studien zur antiken Literatur und Kunst* (Berlin 1969): 337–53.

(1964) *Platon* 1, 3rd ed. Berlin.

Funaioli, G. (1907) *Grammaticae Romanae fragmenta*. Leipzig.

Garbo, G. (1936) 'Società e stato nella concezione di Epicuro', *Atene e Roma* ser. 3.4: 243 ff.

Gardiner, A. H. (1932) *The Theory of Speech and Language*. Oxford.

Gates Jr., H. L. (1988) *The Signifying Monkey: A Theory of Afro-American Literary Criticism*. New York.

Geertz, C. (1973) *The Interpretation of Cultures. Selected Essays*. New York.

Giannantoni, G. (1990) *Socratis et Socraticorum Reliquiae*, vol. IV. Elenchos 18, Naples: 413–41.

Giannantoni, G. and M. Gigante (eds.) (1996) *Atti del Congresso Internazionale 'l' Epicureismo greco e romano*. Naples.

Giussani, C. (ed.) (1892–6¹) *T. Lucreti Cari Libri sex, revisione del testo, commento e studi introduttivi*. Torino.

Glidden, D. (1994) 'Parrots, Pyrrhonists, and native speakers', in Everson (1994) 129–48.

Goetz, G. and G. Gundermann (eds.) (1888) *Corpus glossariorum Latinorum*, vol. II: *Glossae Latinograecae et Graecolatinae*. Leipzig.

Goffman, E. (1959) *The Presentation of Self in Everyday Life*. Garden City N.Y.
(1970) *Strategic Interaction*. Oxford.

Goldschmidt, V. (1978) 'Remarques sur l'origine Épicurienne de la "prénotion"', in *Les stoïciens et leur logique*, ed. J. Brunschwig. Paris: 155–69.

Gould, J. (1970) *The Philosophy of Chrysippus*. Albany.

Goulet-Cazé, M.-O. (1992) 'Le livre VI de Diogène Laërce: Analyse de sa structure et réflexions méthodologiques', *ANRW* II.36.6: 3880–4048.

Goulet-Cazé, M. and R. Goulet (1993) *Le Cynisme ancien et ses prolongements; actes du Colloque international du CNRS. Paris, 22–25 juillet, 1991*. Paris.

Gourinat, J.-B. (2000) *La dialectique des Stoiciens (Histoire des doctrines de l'antiquité classique* xxii). Paris.

Greenblatt, S. (1980) *Renaissance Self-Fashioning. From More to Shakespeare*. Chicago.
(1997) 'The touch of the real', *Representations* 59: 14–29.

Grice, P. (1989a) *Studies in the Way of Words*. Cambridge, Mass.–London. Contains (1989b) 'Meaning' 213–23, (1989c) 'Meaning revisited' 283–303, (1989d) 'Utterer's meaning and intentions' 86–116, (1989e) 'Utterer's meaning, sentence-meaning, and word-meaning' 117–37.

Griffin, M. (1993) 'Le mouvement cynique et les Romains', in Goulet-Cazé and Goulet (1993) 241–58.
(1997) 'The composition of the Academica: motives and versions', in *Assent and Argument: Studies in Cicero's Academic Books*: Proceedings of the 7th Symposium Hellenisticum, eds. B. Inwood and J. Mansfeld. Leiden: 1–35.

Gutas, D. (1993) 'Sayings of Diogenes preserved in Arabic', in Goulet-Cazé and Goulet (1993) 475–518.

Hackett, J. (ed.) (1997) *Roger Bacon and the Sciences*, Studien und Texte zur Geistesgeschichte des Mittelalters LVII. Leiden– N.Y.–Cologne.

Hadot, P. (1971) *Marius Victorinus. Recherches sur sa vie et ses oeuvres*, Paris.

Hall, E. T. (1959) *The Silent Language*. Garden City N.Y.

(1966) *The Hidden Dimension*. Garden City N.Y.

Haller, R. (1962) 'Untersuchungen zum Bedeutungsproblem in der antiken und mittelalterlichen Philosophie', *Archiv für Begriffsgeschichte* 7: 57–119.

Halliwell, S. (1991) 'Comic satire and freedom of speech in classical Athens', *JHS* 111: 48–70.

Halm, C. (ed.) (1863) *Rhetores Latini Minores*, Leipzig.

Hammerstaedt, J. (1996) 'Il ruolo della πρόληψις epicurea nell' interpretazione di Epicuro, *Epistula ad Herodotum* 37f', in Giannantoni and Gigante (1996) 221–37.

Hankinson, R. J. (1994) 'Usage and abusage: Galen on language', in Everson (1994) 166–87.

Haring, N. M. (1953) 'A Latin dialogue on the doctrine of Gilbert of Poitiers', *Mediaeval Studies* 15: 243–89.

Hartung, H.-J. (1970) *Ciceros Methode bei der Übersetzung griechischer philosophischer Termini*. Diss. Hamburg.

Hauser, M. D. (1996) *The Evolution of Communication*. Cambridge, Mass.– London.

Hays, R. S. (1983) *Lucius Annaeus Cornutus' Epidrome: Introduction, Translation and Notes*. Diss. University of Texas at Austin.

Heck, E. (1966) *Die Bezeugung von Ciceros Schrift De republica*, Spudasmata 4. Hildesheim.

Heinimann, F. (1965) *Nomos und Physis. Herkunft und Bedeutung einer Antithese im griechischen Denken des 5. Jahrhunderts*. Basle.

Heintz, W. (1972²) *Studien zu Sextus Empiricus*, Hildesheim.

Helck, J. (1905) *De Cratetis Mallotae studiis criticis quae ad Iliadem spectant*. Leipzig.

Hicks, R. D. (ed.) (1925) *Diogenes Laertius: Lives of Eminent Philosophers*. Loeb Classical Library. London–Cambridge, Mass.

Hock, R. F. (1997) 'Cynics and Rhetoric', in *Handbook of Classical Rhetoric in the Hellenistic Period. 330 BC–AD 400*, ed. S. E. Porter. Leiden: 755–73.

Hofmann, J. B. and A. Szantyr (1965) *Lateinische Syntax und Stilistik*. Munich.

Höistad, R. (1948) *Cynic Hero and Cynic King. Studies in the Cynic Conception of Man*. Lund.

Holtz, L. (1981) *Donat et la tradition de l'enseignement grammatical*. Paris.

Hossenfelder, M. (1996) 'Epikureer', in *Geschichte der Sprachtheorie: 2. Sprachtheorien der abendlandischen Antike*, ed. P. Schmitter. 2nd ed. Tübingen: 217–37.

Hülser, K.-H. (ed.) (1987–8) *Die Fragmente zur Dialektik der Stoiker* (4 vols). Stuttgart–Bad Cannstatt.

Indelli, G. (ed.) (1978) *Polistrato: Sul disprezzo irrazionale delle opinioni popolari*, La scuola di Epicuro 2. Naples.

Jackson, B. D. and J. Pinborg (eds. and trans.) (1975) *Augustine: De dialectica*. Dordrecht.

Janson, T. (1979) 'Lucretius on the origin of language', *Historiographia Linguistica* 6: 149–57.

Kenney, E. J. (1977) *Lucretius*. Greece and Rome New Surveys in the Classics 11. Oxford.

Kidd, I. (1989) '*Orthos Logos* as a criterion of truth in the Stoa', in *The Criterion of Truth*, eds. P. Huby and G. Neal. Liverpool: 137–50.

Kilwardby, R. (1984) *Donati Artem maiorem III*, ed. Laurentius Schmuecker. Brixen-Weger.

Kindstrand, J. F. (1986) 'Diogenes Laertius and the *Chreia* tradition', *Elenchos* 7: 217–43.

Kleve, K. (1963) *Gnosis Theon: Die Lehre von der natürlichen Gotteserkenntnis in der epikureischen Theologie*, Symbolae Osloenses Suppl. 19. Oslo.

    (1978) 'The philosophical polemics in Lucretius', in *Lucrèce* (Entretiens Hardt 24). Vandoeuvres–Geneva: 39–71.

Konstan, D. (1973) *Some Aspects of Epicurean Psychology*, Philosophia antiqua 25. Leiden.

Kretzmann, N. (1970) 'Medieval logicians on the meaning of the *propositio*', *Journal of Philosophy* 67: 767–87.

    (1971) 'Plato on the correctness of names', *American Philosophical Quarterly* 8: 126–38.

Kretzmann, N., A. Kenny, and J. Pinborg (eds.) (1982) *The Cambridge History of Later Medieval Philosophy*. Cambridge.

Krueger, D. (1996) 'The Bawdy and society. The shamelessness of Diogenes in Roman Imperial culture', in Branham and Goulet-Cazé (1996) 222–39.

Kudlien, F. (1968) 'Pneumatische Ärtze', *RE* Supp. z: 1097–1108, Stuttgart.

Kühner R. and Gerth, B. (1898/1904) *Ausführliche Grammatik der griechischen Sprache*. 11. *Satzlehre* (2 vols.). Hannover–Leipzig.

Lammert, F. (1920–1) 'Eine neue Quelle für die Philosophie der mittleren Stoa 11', *Wiener Studien* 42: 34–46.

Lateiner, D. (1987) 'Nonverbal communication in the histories of Herodotus', *Arethusa* 20: 83–119; 143–5.

    (1995) *Sardonic Smile: Nonverbal Behavior in Homeric Epic*. Ann Arbor (Mich.).

Laursen, S. (1987) 'Epicurus, *On nature* xxv', *Cronache Ercolanesi* 17: 77–8.

    (1995) 'The early part of Epicurus, *On nature* xxv', *Cronache Ercolanesi* 25: 5–110.

    (1997) 'The later part of Epicurus, *On nature* xxv', *Cronache Ercolanesi* 27: 5–82.

Leopoldi, H. (1892) *De Agatharchide Cnidio*. Diss. Rostock.

Liverpool–Manchester seminar (ed.) (1989) 'Claudius Ptolemaeus, *On the Kriterion and Hegemonikon*, edited by Liverpool–Manchester seminar on ancient Greek philosophy', in *The Criterion of Truth: Essays in Honour of G. Kerferd*, eds. P. Huby and G. Neal. Liverpool: 179–230.

Lloyd, A. C. (1990) *The Anatomy of Neoplatonism*, Oxford.

Long, A. A. (ed.) (1971a) *Problems in Stoicism*. London (repr. 1996).

    (1971b) '*Aisthēsis, prolēpsis* and linguistic theory in Epicurus', *BICS* 18: 114–33.

    (1988) 'Ptolemy *On the Criterion*: An epistemology for the practicing scientist', in *The Question of 'Eclecticism': Studies in Later Greek Philosophy*, eds. J. M. Dillon and A. A. Long. Berkeley–Los Angeles: 176–207.

(1992) 'Stoic readings of Homer', in *Homer's Ancient Readers. The Hermeneutics of Greek Epic's Earliest Exegetes*, eds. R. Lamberton and J. Keaney. Princeton: 41–66.

(1996a) 'The Socratic tradition: Diogenes, Crates and Hellenistic ethics', in Branham and Goulet-Cazé (1996) 28–46.

(1996b) *Stoic Studies*. Cambridge.

(1996c) 'Stoic psychology and the elucidation of language', in Manetti (1996) 109–31.

(1999) 'The Socratic legacy', in Algra et al. (1999) 617–41.

(2002) 'Stoic reactions to Plato's Cratylus', in *Le Style de la pensée: Recueil de textes en hommage à Jacques Brunschwig*, eds. M. Canto-Sperber and P. Pellegrin. Paris: 395–411.

Long, A. A. and D. N. Sedley (eds.) (1987) *The Hellenistic Philosophers*, with trans. and comm. (2 vols.). Cambridge.

Longo Auricchio, F. (ed.) (1977) 'Φιλοδήμου περὶ ῥητορικῆς, libri primus et secundus', in *Ricerche sui papiri ercolanesi*, ed. F. Sbordone. Naples.

(1988) *Ermarco: Frammenti*, La scuola di Epicuro 6. Naples.

Luhtala, A. (2000) *On the Origin of Syntactical Description in Stoic Logic*. Münster.

Lyons, J. (1977) *Semantics* (2 vols.). Cambridge.

Malherbe, A. J. (1977) *The Cynic Epistles. A Study Edition*. Missoula (Mont.).

(1982) 'Self-definition among Epicureans and Cynics', in *Jewish and Christian Self-Definition*, vol. III: *Self-Definition in the Greco-Roman World*, eds. B. F. Meyer and E. P. Sanders. London.

Mandilaras, B. G. (1973) *The Verb in the Greek Non-Literary Papyri*. Athens.

Manetti, G. (ed.) (1996) *Knowledge Through Signs. Ancient Semiotic Theories and Practices*. Brussels.

Mansfeld, J. (1986) 'Diogenes Laertius on Stoic philosophy', *Elenchos* 7: 295–382.

(1989) 'Stoic definitions of the good (Diog. Laert. VII 94)', *Mnemosyne* 42: 487–91.

(1992) *Heresiography in Context*. Leiden.

(2000) 'Diogenes Laertius 7.83', *Mnemosyne* 53: 592–7.

Manuli, P. (1981) 'Claudio Tolomeo: Il criterio e il principio', *Rivista critica di storia della filosofia* 36: 64–88.

Manuwald, A. (1972) *Die Prolepsislehre Epikurs*. Bonn.

Manuwald, B. (1980) *Der Aufbau der lukrezischen Kulturentstehungslehre*, AAWM, Geistes- und sozialwiss. Klasse 1980.3. Mainz–Wiesbaden.

(1996) 'Platon oder Protagoras? Zur grossen Rede des Protagoras (Plat. *Prot.* 320c8–328d2)', in ΛΗΝΑΙΚΑ: *Festschrift für C. W. Müller*, eds. Chr. Mueller-Goldingen and K. Sier. Stuttgart-Leipzig: 102–31.

Marcovich, M. (1999) *Diogenis Laertii Vitae Philosophorum*, vol. I. Stuttgart.

Marmo, C. (1994) *Semiotica e linguaggio nella scolastica: Parigi, Bologna, Erfurt 1270–1330*. Rome.

Martinus Dacus (1961) *Modi Significandi* in: *Opera*, ed. H. Roos, Corpus Philosophorum Danicorum Medii Aevi II. Copenhagen.

Mates, B. (1961) *Stoic Logic*. Berkeley.

Menn, S. (1999) 'The Stoic theory of categories', *OSAP* 27: 215–47.

Mette, H. J. (1952) *Parateresis. Untersuchungen zur Sprachtheorie des Krates von Pergamon.* Halle.

Milanese, G. (1996) 'Aspetti del rapporto tra denominazione e referenzialità in Epicuro e nella tradizione epicurea', in Giannantoni and Gigante (1996) 269–86.

Moles, J. (2000) 'The Cynics', in *The Cambridge History of Greek and Roman Political Thought*, eds. C. Rowe and M. Schofield. Cambridge: 415–34.

Montefusco, L. (1987) 'La funzione della "partitio" nel discorso oratorio', in *Studi di retorica oggi in Italia*, ed. A. Pennacini. Bologna: 69–85.

Morford, M. (2002) *The Roman Philosophers from Cato Censor to Marcus Aurelius.* London.

Morgan, T. (1998) *Literate Education in the Hellenistic and Roman Worlds.* Cambridge.

Morris, C. (1946) *Signs, Language, and Behaviour.* Englewood Cliffs, N.J., repr. in his *Writings on the General Theory of Signs.* The Hague 1971.

Most, G. W. (1989) 'Cornutus and Stoic allegoresis: a preliminary report', *ANRW* II.36.3: 2014–65.

Müller, C. W. (1967) 'Protagoras über die Götter', in Müller (1999) 253–77.

(1999) *Kleine Schriften zur antiken Literatur und Geistesgeschichte.* Stuttgart–Leipzig.

Müller, G. (1975) 'Die fehlende Theologie im Lukreztext,' in *Monumentum Chiloniense. Kieler Festschrift für E. Burck*, ed. E. Lefèvre. Amsterdam: 277–95.

Müller, K. O. (1833) *M. T. Varronis de lingua Latina.* Leipzig.

Müller, R. (1970) 'Sur le concept de *physis* dans la philosophie épicurienne de la droit', in *Actes du VIIIe congrès Guillaume Budé.* Paris: 305–18.

(1972) *Die epikureische Gesellschaftstheorie*, 2nd ed. Berlin.

Navia, L. E. (1998) *Diogenes of Sinope. The Man in the Tub.* Westport.

Neubecker, A. J. (ed.) (1986) *Philodem: Über die Musik. IV. Buch. Text, Übersetzung und Kommentar*, La scuola di Epicuro 4. Naples.

Nichols, J. H. Jr. (1976) *Epicurean Political Philosophy. The De rerum natura of Lucretius.* Ithaca–London.

Niehues-Pröbsting, H. (1979) *Der Kynismus des Diogenes und der Begriff des Zynismus.* Munich.

Nielsen, L. O. (1982) *Theology and Philosophy in the Twelfth Century*, Acta Theologica Danica xv. Leiden.

Nörr, D. (1972) *Divisio und Partitio. Bemerkungen zur römischen Rechtsquellenlehre und zur antiken Wissenschaftstheorie.* Berlin.

Obbink, D. (1992) 'What all men believe – must be true: Common conceptions and consensio omnium in Aristotle and Hellenistic philosophy', *OSAP* 10: 193–231.

(ed.) (1995) *Philodemus and Poetry.* Oxford.

(ed.) (1996) *Philodemus: On Piety*, Part I: Critical text with commentary. Oxford.

O'Daly, G. (1987) *Augustine's Philosophy of Mind.* London.

Offermann, H. (1972) 'Lukrez v, 1028–1090', *RhM* 115: 150–6.

Owen, G. (1961) 'Tithenai ta phainomena', in *Aristote et les problèmes de la méthode*, ed. S. Mansion. Louvain: 83–103.

Papke, Roland (1988) *Caesars De analogia*. Diss. Eichstätt.

Péllicer, A. (1966) *Natura. Étude sémantique et historique du mot latin*. Paris.

Pépin, J. (1976) *Saint Augustin et la Dialectique*. Wetteren, Belgium.

Pfligersdorffer, G. (1988) 'Zur Sprachentstehung nach Lukrez', in *Antike Rechts- und Sozialphilosophie*, eds. O. Gigon and M. W. Fischer. Frankfurt a. M.: 138–46.

Pfister, M. (1985) 'Konzepte der Intertextualität', in *Intertextualität. Formen, Funktionen, anglistische Fallstudien*, eds. U. Broich and M. Pfister. Tübingen: 1–30.

Philippson, R. (1929) Rev. of Dahlmann (1928), *Philologische Wochenschrift* 49: 666–76.

Pigeaud, J.-M. (1984) 'Épicure et Lucrèce et l'origine du langage', *REL* 61: 122–4.

Pinborg, J. (1962) 'Das Sprachdenken der Stoa und Augustins Dialektik', *Classica et Mediaevalia* 23: 148–77.

(1967) *Die Entwicklung der Sprachtheorie im Mittelalter*, Beiträge zur Geschichte der Philosophie und Theologie des Mittelalters XLII.2. Münster.

(1972) *Logik und Semantik im Mittelalter. Ein Überblick*. Stuttgart–Bad Cannstatt.

Pohlenz, M. (1940) *Grundfragen der Stoischen Philosophie*, Gesellschaft der Wissenschaften zu Göttingen, Abhandlungen Philol.-Hist. Klasse Folge 3 N.26:1–122. Göttingen.

(1970⁴) *Die Stoa. Geschichte einer geistigen Bewegung*, Göttingen.

Porphyrius (1887) *Isagoge et in Aristotelis Categorias commentarium*, ed. A. Busse. Commentaria in Aristotelem Graeca IV.1. Berlin.

Provine, R. (1983) 'Yawning as a stereotyped action pattern and releasing stimulus', *Ethology* 72: 109–22.

(1989) 'Contagious yawning and infant imitation' *Bulletin of the Psychonomic Society* 27: 125–6.

Puglia, E. (ed.) (1988) *Demetrio Lacone: Aporie testuali ed esegetiche in Epicuro*. Ed., trad. e comm. La scuola di Epicuro 8. Naples.

Purinton, J. S. (1996) 'Epicurus on the degrees of responsibility of "things begotten" for their actions: a new reading of *On Nature* XXV', in Giannantoni and Gigante (1996) 155–68.

Radermacher, L. (1953) 'πορδή', *RE* XXII, 1: 235–40.

Rau, P. (1967) *Paratragödia. Untersuchung einer komischen Form des Aristophanes*. Munich.

Reid, J. (1885) *M. Tulli Ciceronis Academica*, London.

Reinhardt, K. (1912) 'Hekataios von Abdera und Demokrit', *Hermes* 47: 492–513, reprinted in Reinhardt (1960) 114–32.

(1960) *Vermächtnis der Antike: Gesammelte Essays zur Philosophie und Geschichtsschreibung*. Göttingen.

Rieth, O. (1933) *Grundbegriffe der stoischen Ethik*, Berlin.

Riposati, B. (1947) *Studi sui Topica di Cicerone*, Milan.

Rosen, R. M. (1988) 'Old comedy and the Iambographic tradition', *American Classical Studies* 19. Atlanta.

Rosen, R. M. and D. R. Marks (1999) 'Comedies of transgression in Gangsta Rap and ancient classical poetry', *New Literary History* 30. 4: 897–928.

Rosier, I. (1991) 'Les sophismes grammaticaux au xiiiᵉ siècle', *Medioevo* 17: 175–230.

(1994) *La parole comme acte. Sur la grammaire et la sémantique au xiiiᵉ siècle.* Paris.

(1995) 'Henri de Gand, le *De Dialectica* d'Augustin, et l'institution des noms divins', *Documenti et studi sulla tradizione filosofica medievale* 6: 145–253.

Rosier-Catach, I. (1997a) 'Prata rident', in *Langages et philosophie. Hommage à Jean Jolivet*, eds. A. de Libera et al. Études de philosophie médiévale lxxiv. Paris: 156–76.

(1997b) 'Roger Bacon and grammar', in Hackett (1997) 67–102.

(1999) 'Modisme, pré-modisme, proto-modisme: vers une définition modulaire', in Ebbesen and Friedman (1999) 45–81.

Ruef, H. (1981) *Augustin über Semiotik und Sprache. Sprachtheoretische Analysen zu Augustins Schrift 'De Dialectica' mit einer deutschen Übersetzung.* Bern.

Ruesch, J. and K. Weldon (1972) *Nonverbal Communication. Notes on the Visual Perception of Human Relations.* Berkeley.

Salem, J. (1990) *La mort n'est rien pour nous. Lucrèce et l'éthique.* Paris.

Sallmann, K. (1962) 'Studien zum philosophischen Naturbegriff der Römer mit besonderer Berücksichtigung des Lukrez', *Archiv für Begriffsgeschichte* 7: 140–284.

Sandbach, F. (1996²) 'Ennoia and prolepsis', in *Problems in Stoicism*, ed. A. Long. London: 22–37.

Schian, R. (1993) *Untersuchungen über das 'argumentum e consensu omnium'*, Spudasmata 28. Hildesheim–New York.

Schiesaro, A. (1990) *Simulacrum et imago. Gli argomenti analogici nel De rerum natura.* Pisa.

Schiffer, S. (1972) *Meaning.* Oxford.

(1981) 'Intention-based semantics', *Notre Dame Journal of Formal Logic* 43: 119–56.

Schmidt, M. (1976) *Die Erklärungen zum Weltbild Homers und zur Kultur der Heroenzeit in den bT-Scholien zur Ilias.* Munich.

Schmidt, R. (1839) *Stoicorum Grammatica.* Halle (repr. Amsterdam 1967).

Schofield, M. (1972) 'A displacement in the text of the *Cratylus*', *CQ* 22: 246–53.

(1980) 'Preconception, argument, and God', in *Doubt and Dogmatism*, eds. M. Schofield, M. Burnyeat and J. Barnes. Oxford: 283–308.

(1982) 'The dénouement of the Cratylus', in *Language and Logos: Studies in Ancient Greek Philosophy presented to G. E. L. Owen*, eds. M. Schofield and M. Nussbaum. Cambridge: 61–81.

Schreiber, Scott G. (2002) *Aristotle on False Reasoning.* Albany, N.Y.

Schrijvers, P. H. (1974) 'La pensée de Lucrèce sur l'origine du langage (*DRN*. v, 1019–1090)', *Mnemosyne* iv. 27: 337–63, reprinted in Schrijvers (1999).

(1999) *Lucrèce et les sciences de la vie*, Mnemosyne Suppl. 186. Leiden–Boston–Köln.

Schubert, A. (1994) *Untersuchungen zur stoischen Bedeutungslehre.* Göttingen.

Scott, D. (1988) 'Innatism and the Stoa', *PCPS* 214: 123–53.

Sedley, D. N. (1973) 'Epicurus, *On nature*, Book xxviii', *CErc* 3: 5–83.
 (1982) 'The Stoic criterion of identity', *Phronesis* 27: 255–75.
 (1984) 'The character of Epicurus' *On Nature*', in *Atti del XVII Congresso Internazionale di papirologia*. Naples: 381–7.
 (1985) 'The Stoic theory of universals', *Southern Journal of Philosophy* supp. 23: 87–92.
 (1988) 'Epicurean anti-reductionism', in *Matter and Metaphysics*, eds. J. Barnes and M. Mignucci. Naples: 297–327.
 (1996) 'Aristotle's *De Interpretatione* and ancient semiotics', in Manetti (1996) 87–108.
 (1998a) *Lucretius and the Transformation of Greek Wisdom*. Cambridge.
 (1998b) 'The etymologies in Plato's Cratylus', *JHS* 118: 140–54.
 (2003) *Plato's Cratylus*. Cambridge.
Shields, C. (1999) *Order in Multiplicity*. Oxford.
Siebenborn, E. (1976) *Die Lehre von der Sprachrichtigkeit und ihren Kriterien. Studien zur antiken normativen Grammatik* (*Studien zur antiken Philosophie* 5), Amsterdam.
Silverman, A. (1992) 'Plato's *Cratylus*: the naming of nature and the nature of naming', *OSAP* 10: 25–72.
Sluiter, I. (1990) *Ancient Grammar in Context*. Amsterdam.
 (2000) *Taaltheorie en vrijheid van meningsuiting* [*The Linguistics of Freedom of Speech*]. Inaugural Address Leiden Univ.
Sluiter, I. and R. M. Rosen (2003) 'General Introduction', in *ANDREIA. Studies in Manliness and Courage in Classical Antiquity*, eds. R. M. Rosen and I. Sluiter. Leiden.
Smith, M. F. (ed.) (1993) *Diogenes of Oenoanda: The Epicurean Inscription*. La scuola di Epicuro. Suppl. 1. Naples.
Smith, R. (1997) *Aristotle's Topics Books I and VIII*. Oxford.
Solmsen, F. (1961) 'Αἴσθησις in Aristotelian and Epicurean thought', *Mededelingen der koninklijke Nederlandse Akademie van Wetenschappen. afd. Letterkunde* N.S. 24 no. 8.
Sommerstein, A. H. (forthcoming) 'Harassing the satirist: the alleged attempts to prosecute Aristophanes', in *Free Speech in Classical Antiquity*, eds. I. Sluiter and R. M. Rosen. Leiden.
Sorabji, R. (ed.) (1990) *Aristotle Transformed*. London.
 (1993) *Animal Minds and Human Morals. The Origins of the Western Debate*. London.
Spade, P. (1982) 'The semantics of terms', in Kretzmann et al. (1982) 188–96.
Spengel, L. (1853–6) *Rhetores Graeci*, vols. i–iii, Leipzig.
Spoerri, W. (1959) *Späthellenistische Berichte über Welt, Kultur und Götter: Untersuchungen zu Diodor von Sizilien*, Schweizerische Beiträge zur Altertumswissenschaft 9. Basle.
Stallybrass, P. and A. White (1986) *The Politics and Poetics of Transgression*. Ithaca.
Stevens, E. B. (1941) 'Topics of pity in poetry of the Roman Republic', *AJP* 62: 426–46.
Stevenson, C. L. (1944) *Ethics and Language*. New Haven.

Stock, B. (1996) *Augustine the Reader*. Cambridge, Mass.

Striker, G. (1996) '*Kriterion tēs alētheias*', in her *Essays on Hellenistic Epistemology and Ethics*, Cambridge: 22–76.

Sudhaus, S. (ed.) (1892–6) *Philodemi volumina rhetorica* (2 vols.). Leipzig.

Tappenden, J. (1993) 'The Liar and Sorites paradoxes: Toward a unified treatment', *Journal of Philosophy* 90: 551–77.

Taylor, C. C. W. (1980) 'All perceptions are true', in *Doubt and Dogmatism: Studies in Hellenistic Epistemology*, eds. M. Schofield, M. Burnyeat, and J. Barnes. Oxford: 105–24.

Taylor, D. J. (1986) 'Rethinking the history of language science in classical antiquity', *Historiographia Linguistica* 13: 175–90.

Taylor, M. (1947) 'Progress and primitivism in Lucretius', *AJP* 68: 180–94.

Tieleman, T. (1996) *Galen and Chrysippus on the Soul*, Leiden.

Todd, R. (1973) 'The Stoic common notions: A re-examination and reinterpretation', *Symbolae Osloenses* 48: 46–75.

Usener, H. (ed.) (1887) *Epicurea*. Leipzig.

   (1977) *Glossarium Epicureum*, eds. M. Gigante and W. Schmid. Rome.

Valente, L. (1997) *Phantasia contrarietatis. Contraddizzioni scritturali, discorso teologico e arti del linguaggio nel* De tropis loquendi *di Pietro Cantore (†1197)*, Corpus Philosophorum Medii Aevi, Testi e studi XIII. Florence.

   (1999) *Doctrines linguistiques et théologie dans les écoles de la seconde emoitié du XIIIe siècle*, unpublished thèse de doctorat, Université Paris 7 – Denis Diderot, UFR Linguistique. [A revised version is due to be published soon]

Verlinsky, A. (1994/5) 'οὐ συνορώμενα πράγματα (Epicurus, *Ep. Hdt.* 76)', *Hyperboreus* 1.2: 46–86 (in Russian with English summary).

   (1996) 'Do animals have freewill? (Epicurus, *On Nature*, 20J and 20B Long–Sedley),' *Hyperboreus* 2.1: 125–38.

   (1998) 'The Epicureans against the first inventors', *Hyperboreus* 4: 302–39 (in Russian with English summary).

   (2003) 'Socrates' method of etymology in the *Cratylus*', *Hyperboreus* 9.1: 56–78.

Vlastos, G. (1946) 'On the prehistory in Diodorus', *AJPh* 67: 51–9.

   (1965) 'Minimal parts in Epicurean atomism' *Isis* 56: 121–47; repr. in his *Studies in Greek Philosophy II. Socrates, Plato and their tradition*, ed. D. W. Graham, Princeton 1995: 285–314.

Von der Mühll, P. (ed.) (1922) *Epicuri epistulae tres et ratae sententiae a Laertio Diogene servatae.* Leipzig.

Wallace, R. W. (1994) 'The Athenian laws against slander', in *Symposion 1993. Vorträge zur griechischen und hellenistischen Rechtsgeschichte (Graz-Andritz, 12.–16. September 1993)*, ed. G. Thür. Cologne: 109–24.

Wallies, M. (1878) *De Fontibus Topicorum Ciceronis*, Halle.

Wardy, R. B. B. (1988) 'Lucretius on what atoms are not', *CPh* 83: 112–28.

Wellmann, M. (1895) *Die Pneumatische Schule bis auf Archigenes in ihrer Entwicklung dargestellt*, Philologische Untersuchungen 14, Berlin.

   (1896) 'Archigenes', *RE* II: 484–6. Stuttgart.

Westphalen, K. (1957) *Die Kulturentstehungslehre des Lukrez*. Diss. Munich.

Whitney, W. D. (1875) *La vie du langage*. Paris.
Whittaker, C. W. A. (1996) *Aristotle's* De Interpretatione – *Contradiction and Dialectic*. Oxford.
Widmann, H. (1935) *Beiträge zur Syntax Epikurs*. Stuttgart.
Wigodsky, M. (1995) 'The alleged impossibility of philosophical poetry', in Obbink (1995) 58–68.
Williams, B. (1982) 'Cratylus' theory of names and its refutation', in *Language and Logos: Studies in Ancient Greek Philosophy Presented to G. E. L. Owen*, eds. M. Schofield and M. Nussbaum. Cambridge: 83–93.

Index nominum et rerum

abstraction 82, 249
Academics 165, 201, 212
accidental properties 81
Aëtius 170, 171
affirmation 259–60
Agatharchides 87–90
akolouthia (sequence, consequence) 173, 287, 290
Alexander of Aphrodisias 165, 169, 175, 187, 246, 274, 306
Alexandrian school 211, 221
ambiguity 66, 74, 239, 242, 244, 250, 251–2, 318
Ammonius 28
analogist vs anomalist 211, 223, 318
analogy 210, 214–18, 222, 228–34, 237, 238, 303
  analogical extension 135; *see also* resemblance
animal sounds 59, 68, 69, 70
anomaly 211, 219
anthropology 26, 38, 39, 103
Antiochus 201
Antipater 180, 201, 236
Antisthenes 140, 153
aphormai (starting point) 179, 185
Apollodorus 236
Apollonius Dyscolus 217, 276–88, 292, 299, 307, 314
apophthegms 154
arbitrariness of assignment 43, 71
Archigenes 193, 195
argument 247, 248, 249, 254–5, 256, 258
  indemonstrable 246, 248, 288
Aristarchus 211, 221–3, 227, 228, 229–34, 236–7
Aristophanes 154, 156, 158, 236
Aristotle 19, 24–5, 37, 47, 59, 70, 150, 164, 165, 193–4, 215, 225, 239, 240, 241, 258–64, 268–9, 270, 271, 299, 300, 307, 308, 312, 314
article 284 (definite)
articulation 59, 61, 67–9, 102, 111, 114, 136, 204
  (of concepts)

artificial 136
  likeness 123
  language 274
assent 265, 272
ataraxia 63
Athenaeus 193
atomic compound/complex 104
Atticus 210
Augustine 16–17, 28, 33–4, 35, 37, 49–55, 180, 219–20, 301
Avicennian common natures 309, 310
awareness 107, 123
axiōma (statable, assertible) 247, 275, 276, 292

Bacon, Roger 301, 317–18
behaviourism 117, 127, 129
belief, *see* opinion
birds 70, 137
body, bodily processes 139, 144, 145, 163
Boethius 202, 203, 209, 285, 300, 302
Boethius of Dacia 307, 310–18
Buridan 299, 301

Caesar 221
Carnap 249
Carneades 266
cats, feline mating 54, 117–18
causal mechanism 106, 111, 112
chance 124, 217
choice 116, 137, 309
chreia 140, 148, 149–51, 153, 160
Chrysippus 14, 18, 25, 33, 36, 46, 168, 170, 176, 178–9, 184, 186, 201, 221, 236–7, 256, 266, 289, 301, 318, 319
Cicero 38, 40, 41, 164, 165, 174, 184, 199–209, 210, 212–13, 319
civilisation and culture 90, 97, 105, 178, 184, origin of 56, 60, 65, development of 63, 65
Cleanthes 236

Index locorum